THE KEY TO A POSTAL CAREER IS IN YOUR HANDS...

What you need to succeed...

The secret to your success is an age-old formula that never fails:

TRAINING + COMMITMENT = SUCCESS.

Pathfinder provides the guaranteed training program. You provide the commitment. By definition, training consists of instruction and practice. Pathfinder furnishes detailed instruction on exam content and test taking strategies plus six complete practice tests. On Postal exams, knowledge is of little value without sufficient practice to develop the required speed and skills.

With Pathfinder's help, your success is guaranteed – **literally!**

PATHFINDER

How hard can the test really be?

Why do I need all this help?

Postal authorities advise that over 70% of all applicants fail their exams. What's more, the average score of those who manage to pass is only a 76. Experts advise that a score in the high 90's is needed to be called in for employment within a reasonable period of time. Those who succeed on their exams and get the jobs are usually the ones who use the best test preparation tools. This exam may be the most important test you ever take. Therefore, choosing the right study guide may be one of the most important decisions you ever make.

Choose carefully...choose the best... **choose Pathfinder!**

FREE Live Support

Answers & advice from a real person as you prepare for your exam!

This guide prepares you for 8 career positions...

• City Carrier • Clerk • Mail Handler • Mail Processor • Mark-Up Clerk •
• Distribution Clerk, Machine • Flat Sorting Machine Operator • Rural Carrier •

JUST LISTEN TO WHAT OTHERS HAVE TO SAY ABOUT PATHFINDER...

"People that do not know what to expect on the exam often experience a great deal of difficulty. Those who prepare always do better. I know first hand the difficulty most people encounter with the Address Memory Section. Pathfinder took this difficult section and made it easy for everyone. After working through their guide, you will be prepared."

– L.C., retired U.S. Postal Exam Specialist

"If everyone knew what this guide has to offer, everyone taking the exam would buy a copy."

– S.T., New York

"Thank you for such an outstanding training package. I wish I had known about your course before I wasted my money on three other books."

– J.V., Florida

"Thank you for the study course and for your support as I was preparing for the exam. I was amazed at the results. I received a score of 100."

– C. S., Ohio

PATHFINDER

POSTAL EXAM TRAINING GUIDE

General Entrance Test Battery 470 & Rural Carrier Exam 460

To my family ...

After the sacrifices you endured over the months I labored on my new series of Postal exam training guides and test taking tools, a note of appreciation and love is in order.

First and foremost, to my wife, Rebecca, thanks for the incredible patience (spelled "L-O-V-E") you displayed during this project. The long hours, the distraction, and my temperament surely left a great deal to be desired. Plus, your research contributions and your occasional editing advice were excellent – even though I usually resented the editing. Rebecca, you're still my lovely young bride and will be no matter how many anniversaries we celebrate. Thanks a zillion!

Next, to my children – Sarah, Sam, and Savannah. They too have entrusted Dad with unconditional love and have endured the project heroically. Plus, they each have their own unique gifts ...

Sarah, my teenager, keeps me on my toes with her quick intellect. Thanks, Sarah, for your keen and probing insights. By prompting me to view challenges from a different perspective, you frequently lead me to better solutions.

Sam, my middle child, has an astonishing vocabulary and an ability to work magic with words. Thanks, Sam, for your suggestions as I composed this book. I am in awe of your talent, and I readily welcome your recommendations.

Savannah, my youngest, can teach the world volumes about love with a single word or gesture. Thanks, Savannah, for reminding me that this book should be more than a collection of technical information. It is foremost about caring, sharing, and motivation.

Thanks, family, for your love and support. I love you too. Without you, I would be lost.

This, dear reader, is the meaning of life ...

Fifth Edition

Copyright © 1993, 1995, 1996, 1997, 2000 by T. W. Parnell

Published by Pathfinder Distributing Company, P.O. Box 1368, Pinehurst, TX 77362-1368

ISBN 0-94-018211-4

Manufactured in the United States of America

A Note of Appreciation ...

My new series of publications would not have been possible without the support of various individuals and groups. I would like to thank a few to whom I owe a giant debt of gratitude ...

Thanks to the U.S. Postal Service for invaluable facts and information received from individuals and departments at all levels – all the way from the Selection, Evaluation & Recognition Section in Washington, DC ... to the National Test Administration Center in Merrifield, VA ... to the many Postal Exam Specialists across the country who shared bits of knowledge gleaned from years of experience.

Thanks to the Postal labor union whose members have so consistently used my publications, and thanks to the union leadership for sanctioning my books for use by members based upon continued successes.

Thanks to libraries nationwide for inventorying my books and study programs as public resources and for inviting me to make presentations to their patrons and staff.

Thanks to the thousands of Postal exam applicants nationwide who have used my test preparation tools over the years. Notes of appreciation from regular everyday folks who have succeeded on their exams after using my tools make it all worthwhile.

And finally, many thanks to my new customers – to you. It is humbling to be entrusted with your confidence as you prepare for the most important test of your life. As I express my appreciation, I express confidence as well that you will find this guide to meet and even to exceed your expectations. It is to this end that I have devoted my life's work. It would mean much for me to hear your comments on how well this book worked for you.

Good luck on your exam. And, more importantly, good luck on your new Postal career.

Sincerely,

T. W. Parnell

Mr. Parnell welcomes feedback from his customers and is available, schedule permitting, for occasional public presentations. Mr. Parnell can be reached via E-mail at info@pathfinderdc.com or via mail c/o Pathfinder Distributing Company, P.O. Box 1368, Pinehurst, TX 77362-1368.

A message from the author ...

Dear Postal Exam Applicant,

The U.S. Postal Service, the nation's largest civilian employer, offers **career opportunities with great wages, full benefits, and unbeatable job security** without demanding specialized education or work experience. As of January 1, 2000, beginning wages for entry-level career positions were $13.50 to15.08 per hour.

But, **there is a catch – first you have to get past an employment exam** ... an exam that most people find impossible to pass ... an exam whose complex application procedures seem to defy comprehension.

What can you do to overcome the odds? The answer is in a formula frequently quoted as the secret to success in athletics. This formula is your secret to success as well ...

TRAINING + COMMITMENT = SUCCESS

Training is defined as preparation for a test of skill by means of instruction and practice. A Postal exam is indeed a test of skill, but the skills being tested are ones that you've never even dreamed of, much less mastered. The required instruction is provided in this training guide – instruction on exam content and on performance proven test-taking strategies. The required practice tools are provided as well – authentic practice tests and exercises.

What about the commitment? Commitment is the only element we cannot provide – it must come from within. Success calls for dedication and hard work. We provide the tools, but you must provide the effort.

The good news is that, with a little initiative, **this training guide is your key to success.** *After completing this book, you will walk into your test armed with the knowledge, with the strategies, with the skills, with the speed, and with the confidence you need to <u>achieve your highest possible score – guaranteed</u>!*

Taking a Postal employment exam offers what may be a once in a lifetime opportunity. Success lies within your grasp. The tools necessary to achieve success are now in your hands. Please do not let this golden opportunity pass you by.

Sincerely,

T. W. Parnell

TABLE OF CONTENTS

FOREWORD

Many people from all walks of life are searching for a solid career opportunity. The U.S. Postal Service, the nation's largest civilian employer, offers such **opportunities without demanding specialized education or work experience**. A high school diploma is not even required. The only real requirements are that you must be a U.S. citizen or permanent resident and you must be between the ages of 18 and 65. Of course, there will be the usual background check and drug screening. Inquire with the nearest Human Resources Office of the U.S. Postal Service for details.

But, like most things that sound too good to be true, **there is a catch --- first you have to get past an employment exam.** Many people find the complex application procedures to be frustrating and the exam itself virtually impossible to pass. A very real problem for many exam applicants is test anxiety – performing poorly due to fear of failure, apprehension about the unknown content of the exam, and a lack of confidence due to insufficient preparation. Postal authorities advise that over 70% of all applicants fail completely and that the average score of those who manage to pass is only a 76. The highest possible score (without veterans preference points) is 100, and 70 is passing. Experts agree that a score in the high 90's is needed to be called in for employment within a reasonable period of time.

After hearing all these discouraging statistics, what can you do to overcome the odds? If everyone else performs so poorly, what can you do to assure success? The answer is in a formula frequently quoted by professionals as the secret to success in athletics. This is your secret to success as well … **training + commitment = success**.

This formula was more fully explained in my introductory message. Simply put, this guide provides your training needs – instruction and practice tools. You must provide the commitment – the dedication and the effort. **If you commit yourself to a regular study and practice schedule as instructed in this book, success will follow.**

For the most effective use of this guide, **just follow the step-by-step and page-by-page instructions.** You will first learn about the circumstances surrounding the exam and about exam content. Then you will learn about critically needed test taking strategies. Finally you will find a quantity of practice tests with instructions for their use.

You have purchased the best Postal exam training tools available. The key now is commitment – your commitment. You have everything to gain and nothing to lose. The end results are in your hands. Show the initiative. Muster the effort. Go forth and conquer!

GENERAL ENTRANCE TEST BATTERY 470

The 470 exam is a phenomenally popular test. It is used to fill all entry level processing, distribution, and delivery career positions – the majority of all career positions available with the Postal Service. However, it is usually offered only once every few years in any given area. As you might expect, many thousands of people apply on the rare occasions that it is offered. A Postal Exam Specialist in Chicago advised that over 169,000 people took the 470 exam when it was last given there. What this means to you is (1) that the competition is fierce, (2) that you probably aren't going to get another chance for several years, and (3) that you absolutely must make the highest score possible on this one rare chance you do have! If you are truly serious about seeking Postal employment, and therefore about preparing for your exam, you must be willing to invest time and effort.

Application Process and Test Date

Postal exams are given by individual Postal districts on an as-needed basis. There are some 85 Postal districts across the U.S., and they all do their hiring and testing independently. They may be testing New York this week, Miami next week, and Dallas next month. In fact, they are almost always testing somewhere or another - but once they test an area, it may be several years before they test there again. **The bad news is that, historically, the 470 exam has been offered to the general public only about once every four years in any given area. The good news is that there is talk that they may begin giving it more frequently – perhaps once or twice a year.**

When you take a test in a particular district, you are in essence applying for a job in that district and in that district only. One district rarely knows anything about what another district is doing. There is no central clearinghouse for testing information nationwide. So, if you want to learn about testing opportunities in several districts, you must contact each one individually and regularly. **For your assistance, a list of district offices and other key Postal offices with their respective "Hiring and Testing Hotline" phone numbers is provided in the back of your book.**

When a district decides to give the 470, **first they announce an application period**, which is simply a designated period of time during which interested individuals must apply to take the test. With the Postal Service, you usually don't apply for a job – you apply for a test. Historically, the application period has usually been a five consecutive weekday (Monday through Friday) period. But, this can vary widely. In some cases applications are accepted over a period of several weeks or even months.

During the application period, **where and how do you apply? Historically, we have had to fill out application cards.** Sometimes application cards were available at any Postal facility within the district. Other times, they were available at only one or two specified locations. Traditionally, PS Form 2479-B, a yellow application card, has been used. Recently, PS Form 2479-C, a newer white card, has been used by many districts.

However, we have been advised that **they are in the process of converting to a national application-by-phone system** that will be administered by Postal headquarters. This automated system will expedite the application process for them and make applying much more convenient for us. They hope to have this new system functional by early 2001.

The big mystery is **how, when, and where to find out about the application period** and application instructions. First, remember that this happens only once every few years, so you cannot afford to miss the announcement. Other than military veterans that meet certain qualifications, those who do not apply as directed during the scheduled application period simply do not take the test. The rules are absolutely rigid – there is no such thing, no matter what the reason, as applying later because you missed the application window. If you miss the application period, you will not be able to take the exam until it is eventually offered again. To make matters worse, details about the application period seem to be kept confidential by the Postal Service as long as possible, and announcements frequently seem to be made at the very last moment. Described below are some of the ways you might, and might not, find out about application periods:

- In every case, Postal policy requires that a **notice be placed in the lobbies** of all Postal facilities in the area to be tested.

- Some districts place **announcements in local newspapers** – but don't count on it. Frequently the Postal Service is deluged with applicants even without promotional efforts, so it seems as though the last thing they want to do is advertise for more.

- In larger metropolitan areas, the Postal Service has a **"Hiring and Testing Hotline"**. This is a phone number that rings into a recorded announcement. You can call 24 hours a day and seven days a week to check for announcements. The recording is updated periodically to advise the public of testing opportunities. You must call very regularly. Occasionally, the recording will announce an application period several weeks in advance. But more frequently, the recording is updated at the very last moment. It is not uncommon for the recording to be updated on a Monday morning to announce that applications will be accepted that very same week. Thus, if you skipped a few weeks, you may miss out altogether. Such a phone number for your local area may not be listed in the phone book, but asking about it at your local Post Office may pay off. **For your assistance, a list of district offices and other key Postal offices with their respective "Hiring and Testing Hotline" numbers is provided in the back of your book.**

- However, **asking at your local Post Office about the application period will probably not pay off**. Other than the actual Postal Exam Specialists responsible for scheduling the application period and for actually giving the exam, most Postal employees are just as much in the dark as we are.

- Inquiries to the nearest **District Human Resources Office** for the Postal Service may pay off, but this office may not be easily accessible to the public. And for good reasons, they may not readily welcome such calls. They have many demanding responsibilities that will not get accomplished if they must handle hundreds or even thousands of continuing inquiries about testing and application opportunities. Callers are frequently referred to the "Hiring and Testing Hotline" number for information.

What about the application itself? As previously mentioned, the application has historically been a card, not much bigger than a post card, that asks for basic information - name, address, phone number, birth date, social security number, military status, etc. It is not your typical long and detailed employment application – you don't get to fill one of those out unless you score high enough on the test.

Recently, some districts have experimented with applications submitted via touch-tone phone. And, again as previously mentioned, they are now supposedly converting to an application-by-phone system for use nationwide.

The **rules governing how the traditional application cards are distributed** vary widely. It appears that the local districts have the authority to set and enforce their own rules. Given below are some the scenarios that have been experienced when applying:

- It is possible that you will be able to get **one application only.** And, you may not be allowed to leave with it – you may be required to fill it out right there and then. In some cases, it is permissible to take the card with you and return it (or mail it back) when completed, but in every case it must be returned by the end of the application period.

- In other cases you may be able to get **a number of applications**. If allowed to leave with them, you can take them home to relatives, friends, etc. who may not be able to get to the application site during scheduled hours. On the other hand, you may be able to get a number of cards, but you may not be allowed to leave with them. To help your friends in this case, you must have the proper information with you in order to fill out cards for them. The card typically used does not call for a signature, so the applicant does not have to personally fill it out.

In every case, however, **only one application card per person per test should be filled out.** If duplicate cards are submitted for the same person and for the same test, one of two actions will be taken: (1) The better alternative is that the duplicate card(s) may simply be thrown out. (2) However, some Postal Exam Specialists advise that applicants for whom duplicate cards are submitted will be disqualified. It is permissible to fill out applications to take exams in multiple areas to be tested. In fact, you are encouraged to do so in order to multiply your chances of employment. But, do not submit multiple applications for the same test and/or area.

What about being assigned a **test date**? Usually, a few weeks after you apply, a notice is received via mail assigning you a specific test date, time, and location. Occasionally, a test date is assigned immediately as you apply. Typically, the test date is four to six weeks after you apply. However, there have been cases where the test was given as early as one week after the application period and as late as nine months after.

An occasionally asked question deals with the possibility of **rescheduling your test date**. Some districts seem to be more flexible than others on this subject, but generally test dates can be rescheduled subject to the following parameters. The choices for rescheduled dates or times are very limited. You see, the many thousands of exam applicants will be tested in scheduled shifts over a series of days. Depending on the size of the facility used, anywhere from 100 to over 1,000 will be tested per shift – perhaps one shift on a Monday morning; then a shift on Monday afternoon; in some cases there may be a Monday evening test shift; and then the cycle starts over again on Tuesday morning. It will take a number of days and many testing shifts to test all the applicants. If your test date is rescheduled, it can only be rescheduled to another date or time during the several days that the test was already being given in this manner anyway. It will not be possible to reschedule for a date or time outside of this range. To inquire about rescheduling, contact the Postal Service at the address or phone number that appears on your scheduling notice.

Choice of Locations, Employee Transfers, and Transferring Scores

When you take your test, you usually able to choose the Postal installations where you prefer to work. If so, **you can designate up to three locations,** and you will be considered for employment only at the locations you mark. You are encouraged to mark the maximum of three locations. Doing so will give you more chances of employment (assuming you score high enough) than if you picked only one. However, **some districts do not allow a choice of locations**. In these districts you are instructed that, when you take the test, you are in essence applying for any location within the district where an opening happens to occur.

Regardless, the objective for most applicants is landing the job, not getting a particular installation. If you end up at a less desirable location, **employee transfers can be granted**. Transfers cannot be guaranteed, but they do happen all the time. It is not unusual for individuals who miss the test in their own district to take it in another area with the sole objective of eventually getting transferred back home. There are a number of known cases where this very plan has worked successfully.

On the subject of locations, a frequently asked question has to do with **transferring your exam score to another Postal district.** Is this possible? Yes, but only under particular circumstances. Specifically, you can transfer your exam score to another district only when the other district is in the process of giving their own exam in order to create a new hiring register. You then have the choice of either taking the test again in the other district or transferring your existing score to the other district. But, if you transfer your score to the other district, it will be removed from the first district's register, which effectively kills any chance of employment in the first district. A better idea, if feasible, may be just to go take the test again in the other district.

Choice of Positions and Job Descriptions

Also when you take your test, you are usually given the opportunity to apply for specific positions. **There are seven entry-level career positions filled from the 470, and you can choose up to all seven of them**. Again, you are encouraged to check the maximum of all seven unless there are some that you simply will not or cannot do. Checking all seven will greatly multiply your chances of employment. As with the choice of installations, even if you do not get the job of your choice, transfers from one craft to another do happen. However, again as with the choice of installations, some districts may not allow you a choice.

Not every installation has all seven positions available. Smaller installations may serve fewer functions, and may therefore have no need for some of the seven positions. These smaller installations will accordingly post openings only for the few particular positions for which they have a need. Consequently, your choice of installations may affect the number of employment options available to you. If this is true, you are generally so notified in advance.

Recently, there have been more and more cases where the 470 is given strictly to fill City Carrier positions. In such cases, applicants are not permitted to apply for other positions – the exam is given to fill only City Carrier positions. We have been told that, due to higher turnover and/or shorter hiring registers for this position, it sometimes becomes necessary to recruit and test City Carrier applicants more frequently than for the other entry level positions filled by the 470 exam.

**Following are titles and job descriptions for the
seven entry-level career positions hired from the 470 exam:**

City Carriers deliver and collect mail. They walk and/or drive trucks. Carriers must be outdoors in all kinds of weather. Almost all carriers have to carry mailbags on their shoulders that can weigh up to 35 pounds. Carriers have to load and unload sacks of mail weighing as much as 70 pounds. City Carrier applicants must have a current valid state driver's license and are required to have a safe driving record. In some offices, City Carriers are required to work on weekends.

Clerks work indoors. Clerks have to handle parcels, bundles, and sacks of mail weighing as much as 70 pounds. They sort mail by zip code or by a memorized plan. Some clerks work at public windows doing such jobs as selling stamps and weighing parcels, and are personally responsible for all money and stamps. Clerks may have to be on their feet all day. They also have to stretch, reach, and bend frequently when distributing mail. In some offices, clerks are required to work at night and on weekends.

Distribution Clerks, Machine (DCM's) operate a letter-sorting machine to distribute letters by a memorized plan or by reading the zip code. They enter distribution codes on a special purpose keyboard at a rate of up to 60 per minute. Applicants must be able to demonstrate the operation of this machine at an accuracy rate of 98%. They must have the ability to maintain close visual attention for long periods of time. DCM's must also load and/or unload machines. DCM's are usually required to work at night and on weekends.

Flat Sorting Machine Operators operate a machine to distribute large, flat pieces of mail by a memorized plan or by reading the zip code. They enter distribution codes on a special purpose keyboard at a rate of up to 45 per minute. Applicants must be able to demonstrate the operation of this machine at an accuracy rate of 98%. They must have the ability to maintain close visual attention for long periods of time. Operators must also load and/or unload machines. Flat Sorting Machine Operators are usually required to work at night and on weekends.

Mail Handlers load, unload, and move bulk mail and sacks. They may have to be on their feet all day in an industrial environment. They also have to repeatedly lift up to 70 pounds. Applicants must be able to demonstrate their ability to lift by passing a test of strength and stamina. In some offices, Mail Handlers are required to work at night and on weekends.

Mail Processors are required to stand for long periods of time loading and unloading mail from a variety of automated mail processing equipment. Their work is performed in large mail processing facilities in an industrial environment. Mail Processors are normally required to work nights and weekends.

Mark-Up Clerks enter change of address data into a computer base, process mail, and perform other clerical functions. Mark-Up Clerks operate a keyboard in order to process changes. Applicants for Mark-Up Clerk must have good data entry skills and are required to pass a typing test. They may be required to work at night and on weekends.

Preparation before the Exam

On this type of exam, **knowledge is of absolutely no use without sufficient practice** to develop the skills, strategies, and speed necessary to succeed. This calls for consistent study and practice over a period of time before the test. <u>Cramming the night before will not work!</u> Many armchair quarterbacks know a lot about football, but how well will they really perform if thrown into the game without consistent practice like the pros get? Following are several tips for your advance preparation:

- **Study all of the material and take all of the practice exams before your test date.** Use the last two days before your exam as a review. Do not wait until the day before the exam to start studying! On the other hand, do not complete all your practice work six weeks before the exam date either. Natural memory loss will cause you to lose some of the skills and speed you worked so hard to master. Depending on your individual ability, it may take 20 – 40 hours of work to complete this book. Working one or two hours per day during the last few weeks before your test date is advised. There have been individuals with a great amount of free time that, by dedicating themselves to it full-time, have completed their preparation in only a few days. And, even if you do not get your hands on this book until a few days before the test, some preparation is better than none at all. Experience has proven, though, that faithfully following a regular daily study program over a period of weeks is the best form of preparation.

- It is very important that you **take the practice exams under conditions as similar as possible to the real exam.** Find a quiet setting where you will not be disturbed while taking the practice tests. Timing yourself cannot be stressed enough during the practice tests. It is impossible to master the extreme rate of speed required without being precisely timed and experiencing the immense pressure of time. The best tool for conveniently and precisely timing yourself is our Timed Practice Test CD described on the order from in the back of the book. Use the correct answers given in the book to score each practice exercise as you complete it. This will enable you to identify any areas of weakness and concentrate more on them.

- **If you skip a question, be sure to also skip a spot on the answer sheet.** If not, and if you get out of order, from that point forward your answers will be wrong. Practice on the exercises in this book to assure that you don't make this kind of mistake on the real test.

- Due to the scoring formulas, **you should not guess on the Address Checking section. Educated guesses, but not blind guesses, are acceptable on the Address Memory section. However, even blind guesses are acceptable on the Number Series and the Following Oral Instructions sections** due to their particular scoring formulas. But, as discussed later, knowing where to guess on the Following Oral Instructions section is a problem in itself. If you make a guess, go with your first choice - don't sit and debate between two or three possible answers. Psychological tests have shown that your first choice is usually correct. Obviously, however, guessing in any form should be a last resort.

- A psychological term called the **"practice effect"** applies to all sections of the exam. The practice effect occurs when a person repeatedly takes an exam a number of times during a brief period of time. For most people, exam scores will be higher the more often you take the test because of increasing familiarity with the material. This trend should become evident as you score your practice exams. Your score on the second exam should be higher than on the first, the third should be even higher, and so on.

- As you learn to **pace yourself for speed and accuracy**, your scores should increase. For example, let's say that at first you were only able to finish half the questions on a practice exam during the time allowed. This may be discouraging, but at least you answered most of them correctly – you only missed two. You should be proud of this score, right? No, wrong --- *very wrong!* You are putting way too much emphasis on accuracy and not nearly enough on speed. To solve this, you must push yourself and practice to develop more speed. Or, let's say you finish an entire practice exam within the required time period, but half of your answers are wrong. It should be obvious that you are placing too much emphasis on speed and not enough attention on accuracy. To solve this, simply slow down and check the addresses more carefully. The key is to find a happy medium between speed and accuracy.

- This book gives you **simple short-cut strategies** that should greatly enhance your test taking ability and your score. It is critically important that you understand and master these strategies so that you can make the highest possible score.

Test Day

Once your scheduled test date arrives, here are a few pointers that will help out:

- **Get a good night's rest, and have a nutritious meal**.

- **Do not drink too many liquids before the test**. Do visit the restroom before starting your test. This may sound trivial, but it may literally make the difference between success and failure. The test will last two to three hours, and we have received reports of Postal Exam Administrators who supposedly will not allow applicants to leave the room during the test for any reason whatsoever. You surely will not perform well if forced to take the exam under uncomfortable and distracting conditions.

- **Leave home early, and plan to arrive at the test site early**. Allow time for any conceivable delays (auto problems, traffic congestion, etc.) that you can possibly imagine. If your notice says that the test is scheduled for 8:00 AM, the doors will be literally locked at precisely 8:00 AM. It doesn't matter whether you are 30 seconds or 30 minutes late – you are late period, and you will not be admitted. The rules are absolutely rigid on this matter.

- Another reason to arrive early is to have a chance to **familiarize yourself with the examination room**. Applicants who have acquainted themselves with their surroundings are more comfortable and tend to perform better.

- Yet another reason to arrive early is so that you can **choose the best seating arrangement to fit your needs.** Those with hearing or sight problems should obvious try to sit near the front. Left-handed individuals should choose a seat where a neighboring right-handed person will not interfere with their work. (This will help the right-handed person as well.) Try to choose a seat away from possible sources of distractions, that has good lighting, that is not crowded, and that has a comfortable working surface – it is terribly difficult to perform well on a tiny desk top or at an overly crowded table. Unfortunately, for the most efficient use of the available facilities regardless of the consequences, in some cases seats are assigned upon arrival. Occasionally in these cases, Exam Specialists may try to accommodate special requests, but many times they refuse except in the case of physically disabled individuals.

- **Bring the scheduling package that you received by mail and a picture I.D.** You will be checked at the door for these items, and you will not be admitted into the test site or allowed to take the test if you do not have them.

The scheduling package, by the way, is a 12 page booklet. In addition to the date, time, and location of your test, it contains general information about the testing process and a few sample questions for each section of the exam. These sample questions are provided simply to make unprepared applicants aware of exam content. Altogether, these few sample questions do not represent even 10% of a complete practice test, and they provide no real practice value.

Note, however, that the format of these few sample questions confirms that the exam format in this book is accurate and up-to-date. Do not be confused by conflicting formats that may be presented in other books.

Note also that the booklet repeatedly states "You will not be expected to be able to answer all the questsions in the time allowed." This is certainly true of the general public, most of who completely fail their exams. After completing this book, you, however, will be prepared to excel on the exam. You will have mastered the skills and speed necessary to succeed.

Finally, note that the sample Address Memory questions confirm the accuracy of the repeating elements and of the Second Digit Strategy to be discussed later.

Be wary, though, of two points. To save paper, the sample Address Memory questions in the booklet are presented on a single page. However, on the actual exam, and likewise in this book, each segment of the Address Memory Section is spread across two facing pages. Also, the booklet may confuse you by mentioning that you will have "three practice exercises" in the Address Memory Section. This is indeed true. But, for some reason, they do not mention that you will have an introductory exercise and two study periods as well before the final segment. Be assured that the Address Memory Section on the real exam actually consists of seven individual segments, exactly as presented in this book.

- **Bring pencils** as instructed in your test-scheduling packet and as discussed later in this book. Usually there are plenty of extra pencils made available at the test site, but don't automatically assume that such will be true. If you don't bring your own pencils, and if they don't provide any for you, how can you take the test?

- **Work diligently on each section of the test until you are instructed to stop.** Every second counts! But, do not ever open your test booklets or pick up your pencil until your are instructed to do so. Likewise, immediately stop working, close your test booklets, and put down your pencil upon being instructed to do so. Failure to comply may look like an attempt to cheat and may cause you to be disqualified. It would be heartbreaking to be disqualified because you innocently doodled with your pencil or because you absentmindedly opened your test booklet when you were not supposed to. An excellent training tool to help avoid such catastrophes is our Timed Practice Test CD described on the order form at the back of the book. In addition to precisely timing you as you take your practice tests, this CD reviews the instructions for you section by section and emphatically directs you exactly when to open or close your booklet and when to pick up or put down your pencil.

- **Mark the answer sheet clearly.** If you erase, do it completely. The machine scoring your answer sheet is not able to distinguish between intentional marks and accidental marks or changes.

- **Pace yourself.** Find a happy medium between speed and accuracy. Do not spend too much time on any one question.

- **Try not to let other people or noises distract you** – and there will be distractions and noises no matter how hard the Test Administrators try to avoid it.

- If you finish before time is called, **go back to check your answers in that section**.

Sections of the Exam

In late 1993, the Postal Service rewrote its entire testing program. The newly created 470 exam replaced and superceded several former exams that were retired as the 470 was introduced. The 470 consists of the below four sections, each of which was excerpted from one or more of the retired exams. However, as these sections were brought forward to the new 470 exam, they were revised from their original state – revised radically in some cases as with the Address Memory Section's new repeating format to be discussed later.

The **Address Checking Section** has 95 questions, each of which consists of a pair of addresses. You will be given only six minutes to compare the address pairs in all 95 questions and to answer if they are exactly alike in every way or if they are different in any way at all. To score this section, subtract the number of wrong answers from the number of correct answers. The result is your score. (Important Note: See the below insert on unanswered questions.)

The **Address Memory Section** requires you to memorize 25 addresses found in five boxes. You will have several three to five minute timed segments during which you are to memorize the locations of these addresses and/or to complete related practice exercises. During the final segment, you are given only five minutes to answer 88 questions from memory about the locations of these addresses. This is by far the hardest part of the exam. To score, subtract ¼ of the number of wrong answers from the number of correct answers. The result is your score. (Important Note: See the below insert on unanswered questions.)

The **Number Series Section** gives you 20 minutes to answer 24 mathematical questions. Each question consists of a series of numbers whose elements follow one or more sequences. You are to figure out the sequences involved and calculate what two numbers would accordingly follow in the series. To score this section, simply count the number of correct answers. (Important Note: See the below insert on unanswered questions.)

The **Following Oral Instructions Section** has about 31 questions and lasts as long as it takes for the test administrator to read the questions aloud to the group of test takers. The administrator reads a set of instructions for each question, you mark your test booklet page appropriately, and then on the answer sheet you darken the answer created by following the instructions read to you. To score this section, simply count the number correct answers. (Important Note: See the below insert on unanswered questions.)

How Unanswered Questions Affect Your Score

As you may have noticed, unanswered questions are not mentioned in the scoring formulas for the above sections. But, do not mistakenly assume that this means unanswered questions are acceptable. Just the opposite, unanswered questions severely hurt your exam score. Consider this … There are 238 questions on the exam. Therefore, if you answered every question correctly, you would accumulate 238 points. To make a high score, you need to capture as many of these points as possible. Every point you fail to capture, whether by leaving a question unanswered or by answering it incorrectly, reduces your final score. Obviously, it is to your advantage to correctly answer as many questions as possible and to leave the fewest possible questions unanswered or blank.

Your answers for the four sections of the exam will be marked on an **Answer Sheet**. The answer sheet is broken into four titled sections. You mark answers in the section appropriately titled in each case. To see a sample of an answer sheet, turn to the answer sheets in the back of your book.

In 1996, the Postal Service began experimenting with a **Personality Inventory Section** as a possible addition to the 460 and 470 exams. This section was included on actual exams at select locations during an extended experimental period. Accordingly, in the 1996 and 1997 editions of my study guide, I provided details on this experiment, information on the content of this section, and strategies for use when taking it. However, in December of 1999 – just as this 2000 edition of my study guide was going into print – the Postal Service advised that a decision had been reached to <u>not</u> include the Personality Inventory Section as a permanent addition after all. Therefore, you should not expect to see this section on your exam, and these comments are included only as a historical note. For the record, the Personality Inventory Section, as included at chosen experimental sites, gave you 45 minutes to answer 206 True/False questions, each of which had to do with your personality. There were no right or wrong answers – you simply answered whether or not a statement reflected your own personality, likes, dislikes, etc. The purpose seemed to be for the Postal Service to obtain a profile of your personality, temperament, work ethics, etc. in order to better gauge what type of employee you might make. The Personality Inventory Section was not scored and therefore did not influence your exam score.

Overall Scores

The Postal Service will not release the formulas for calculating final overall exam scores for fear of compromising the integrity of their testing process. We know how they score the individual sections, but not how they mix those individual scores together to come up with a final score.

To confuse matters more, **most applicants receive two or more different scores** for the same test. The Postal Service creates two or more different hiring registers, or lists of names ranked in order by score, from a single test. As noted earlier in this book, there are seven entry-level career positions filled from the 470 exam. The Postal Service seems to create two or more hiring registers, each of which relates to a select few of these seven positions. They apparently have multiple, but similar, scoring formulas that are applied to your test results – one for each of these registers. Therefore, depending on how many and on which of these positions you marked, you may receive multiple scores. The multiple scores are different but usually fairly close to each other.

From experience, **we do know a few things about the final exam score**. We know that the highest possible score (without veterans' preference points) is 100, and that 70 is passing. We know that there are 238 questions on the exam. Therefore, if you answered every question correctly, you would accumulate 238 points. We know also that you do not have to answer every question correctly in order to score a perfect 100. We have learned that you can still score a perfect 100 even after losing ten to twelve points out of the possible 238 points by answering several questions incorrectly or by leaving them unanswered. However, every point you miss after the first ten or twelve, whether by answering incorrectly or by leaving the question unanswered, hurts your final score.

Hiring Procedures

Once the testing process is completed, **the scores will be used to create hiring registers**. Again, hiring registers are simply lists of names ranked in order by score. The names of those who pass the test (score 70 or higher) will be placed on one or more registers depending on which positions they marked. Those who fail (score below 70) will not be included. To fill immediate positions as well as those that become available in the future, the highest scores on the list will be called in for an interview. These registers will be used to fill jobs for several years until the test is finally given again. At that point, new registers will be created from the results of the new test, and the old registers will be discarded. If you have not been called in by that point, and if you still want to be considered, you must take the test again.

Your goal is to be as close to the top of the register as possible. As previously pointed out, there will be thousands of applicants and competition will be fierce. In addition, the number of available positions will not be tremendous. Most experts agree that your chances of being called in for employment within a reasonable period of time are limited if you do not score in the high 90's. And, most applicants are more interested in getting a job now than in waiting for a few years.

An extremely critical term involved in the hiring process that you need to understand is **Part Time Flexible** or PTF. When you are offered an entry-level career position, they usually hire you as a PTF. This is a probationary position in which you will remain for a period of 90 days. Afterwards, you will graduate to official full-time career status. A PTF's work schedule and compensation is usually similar to that of a full-time employee. One assumption is that they start new-hires out in this probationary position so that it will be easier to discharge any that do not meet Postal standards. We have all heard stories about how difficult it supposedly is to fire a career federal employee. Without realizing that they were actually turning down the career positions for which they had worked so hard, many unfortunate applicants have refused their PTF offers thinking that it was only a part time job.

On a related subject, questions are frequently asked about the feasibility of **turning down an offer but keeping your name on the register**. This can indeed be done. If they offer a job that you are not prepared to accept at that time, but you want to keep your name on the hiring register, you must specifically request such in writing. For details, inquire at the time of the offer or of the interview.

Employment Interview

The most important element of the hiring process is your score. Without a high enough score, nothing else matters. But, there is another important step – the employment interview. As with any other potential employer, you must go through the interviewing process, and **the interview can make or break you**. There are many publications available about how to present yourself in an interview. It is advisable to review one in preparation for your interview. Below are points to consider and/or to be prepared for:

- Arrive early. <u>Do not be late!</u>
- Remember - first impressions are lasting.
- Your personal appearance, grooming, attitude, and behavior are being examined.
- Establish eye contact with the interviewer. Failure to do so leaves a poor impression.
- Be attentive and interested. Ask relevant questions.
- Try to relax. Speak clearly and in a normal tone of voice.
- Don't respond too quickly. Pause to think before answering.
- Be prepared to answer honestly about past work experiences and work relationships.
- Do not make excuses for past mistakes. Show that you have learned from them.
- Be prepared to discuss why you want a Postal career and what you can contribute.
- Thank the interviewer for his/her time. Make his/her last impression of you favorable.

Military Veterans

Military veterans may be eligible for extra testing, scoring, and hiring benefits. Depending on service and medical history, veterans may be eligible for five or ten preference points. If eligible, these extra points will be added to the veteran's raw exam score. Eligible veterans are the only applicants that can make a score of over 100. Postal Exam Specialists advise that qualified veterans may be placed on a special hiring register that must be depleted before non-veteran applicants can be hired. In addition, veterans have the right to apply for a Postal exam within 120 days before or after their discharge date. Ten point veterans may have the right to apply at any time regardless of discharge date. But, supposedly they can only exercise this right once per district. Either way, qualified veterans may not have to wait a few years for the next scheduled public test. Instead, they will be given the test within a reasonable period of time, and their scores will be added to the existing registers. There may be additional benefits as well. For details or to determine their eligibility status, veterans should contact their local Veterans Administration facility or check with the nearest Human Resources Office of the Postal Service.

RURAL CARRIER EXAM 460

The Rural Carrier Exam 460 is totally and completely identical to the 470 exam in every way. Therefore, most of the topics discussed for the 470 will be equally applicable to the 460. The 460 exam has a different title and is offered on different occasions because different types of people with different employment objectives take the 460 as opposed to the 470.

The 460 exam is used to fill **Rural Carrier Associate** (RCA) positions. This is a **part time relief position** designed to fulfill the duties of a full time career Rural Carrier when he/she is not available due to days off, vacation time, illness, etc. Beginning wages for an RCA were $11.96 per hour as of January 1, 2000. Rural Carrier responsibilities are similar to those of a City Carrier as described on page 12, but in a rural environment. Plus, he/she has additional duties such as selling postage stamps to rural patrons.

An RCA will usually work only a few days each week – perhaps some scheduled days and other days on a call-in basis. The RCA must be very flexible and willing to respond affirmatively almost every time they are called in unexpectedly. Excessive refusals may result in termination.

An RCA should have a reliable vehicle. At some Post Offices, RCA's are required to use their own vehicles to deliver mail. If so, the RCA receives reimbursement for use of his/her personal vehicle.

It is possible for an RCA to work his/her way into a full time career Rural Carrier position. Typically, an RCA will work part time for several years before a full time position becomes available. It is possible, but rare, to be hired directly into a full time Rural Carrier position if there are no available RCA's to fill it.

Since RCA positions are less popular and more difficult to fill, **applications to take the 460 exam are accepted frequently** – in many districts they are accepted continuously year round. Likewise, depending on the number of applications received or upon a fixed schedule, **the test itself is given frequently** – perhaps two or more times per year.

Even if you are not seriously interested in an RCA position, taking the 460 exam for the practice value as you prepare for the 470 exam is an excellent idea. Since the 460 is given much more frequently than the 470, it is quite possible that you will be able to apply for the 460 and actually take it before being scheduled for the 470. There is tremendous value in experiencing a real exam. Of the various benefits such an experience offers, one of the greatest is the confidence you will feel when you later take the actual 470. This psychological boost can contribute significantly to your performance on the 470. Most individuals taking the 470 enter the test site full of apprehension, which is certainly detrimental to their performance. This, of course, is one of the reasons you are preparing for your exam. Adding the experience of taking an actual Postal exam to your preparation efforts will contribute greatly to your chances of success.

EXAM CONTENT AND TEST TAKING STRATEGIES
Overview

There are four elements essential to successful Postal exam preparation – knowledge of exam content, test taking strategies, practice tests, and commitment. Remember your formula for success: *training* + *commitment* = *success*. This book provides the information on exam content, effective strategies, and authentic practice tests. The only element we cannot provide is commitment. Hard work and a great deal of practice are required. The faint hearted may fall by the way side. Thorough and complete test preparation demands dedication and a drive to succeed.

Following are important points of which you should be aware as you begin your preparation:

- When you take the real exam, and likewise when you take the practice tests in your book, in every case **you will be working with two 8-1/2" X 11" booklets** or pages - the very size of this book. One will be the test booklet containing the questions. The other will be the answer sheet booklet where you mark your answers.

- **The questions are all multiple choice, and the answers are always in the form of a letter – A, B, C, D, or E.** The way you mark answers on the answer sheet is to darken the circle (or more accurately, the oval shape) containing the correct answer.

- On the Address Checking and Address Memory sections of the exam, you are absolutely <u>not</u> allowed to make any **marks in the question booklet** – doing so may result in disqualification. However, on the Number Series section, it is necessary to perform calculations in the question booklet (in the margins, etc.) in order to find the answer. And, on the Following Oral Instructions section, you are specifically instructed to make certain marks in the question booklet in order to determine the correct answer.

If you finish all the questions in one section before time is called, can you go back to other sections to finish questions there you did not have time complete? No, absolutely not. You will be specifically instructed to open your test booklet only to the section you are taking at that moment, and then to close it immediately when time is called. Opening your booklet to another section is grounds for disqualification.

Success is virtually impossible without effective test taking strategies. First, we will consider strategies that apply to the test as a whole. Then, we will learn about strategies designed for each individual section of the exam.

Exam Strategy #1 | You may have heard of the military strategy: **"Divide and Conquer"**. This will be our approach. If you divide the exam into its individual sections and master each section individually, you cannot help but succeed on the exam as a whole.

Exam Strategy #2 | **Check frequently to assure that the number of the question you are answering matches the number of the answer sheet item you are marking.** Let's say you are looking at question number 78 in the test booklet but suddenly discover that you marking its answer on item number 79 of the answer sheet. Why? Because you've already marked an answer to some other question at item number 78 on the answer sheet – probably the answer to question number 77. Obviously, at some point you got out of sync on the answer sheet – but where? It is entirely possible that you got out of order back on question number 3 and that you have been marking answers in the wrong spot for each question since. If this happens to you, which means you have likely blown the last 75 questions, you might as well give up and go home. There is no recovery after losing 75 points.

Exam Strategy #3 To increase your speed and to avoid getting out of sync as described above, **the test booklet and answer sheet should be placed as close together as possible** at all times. If both booklets are fully opened, you are working on at least 11" X 34" of paper spread out on top of your table or desk, as pictured in the below illustration. The questions and answer spots are so far apart that errors are likely to happen.

Your first strategy to avoid this problem is to **fold the booklets in half at the stapled seams and place the folded booklets next to each other**. This one step cuts the distance between questions and answers by half. Flip the folded booklets over as needed and as you progress through the exam. Then, depending on the positions of the questions and answers, **you can usually even lay one booklet partially on top the other**, as pictured in the below illustration. Now the questions and answers may be only a few inches apart. These strategies can bring the questions and answer spots very close together indeed for greater speed and accuracy.

Note: Over the years, we have heard of a few rare occasions where an exam administrator would not allow applicants to manipulate their booklets as outlined above. You will almost surely be able to do so on your exam, but be aware there is a slight chance that you will not.

Exam Strategy #4 Another strategy to avoid getting out of sync is to **use one of your spare pencils, the side of your hand, or your finger(s) to guide your eyes** back and forth between the test booklet and the answer sheet. In essence, you are using one of these items to mark your spot and track your progress as you race through the test so that you don't accidentally skip a question and get out of sync. But, do not use any thing else (like a ruler or a piece of paper) for a guide as you practice at home. It may be easier, but you will not have access to anything like that on the actual test. During the exam, the only items you are allowed to have with you are the ones you were instructed to bring – which include only yourself (complete with all parts of your body) and your pencils. Becoming dependent on a tool that will not be available at the real exam can have disastrous results.

Exam Strategy #5 **If you somehow get out of sync despite efforts to the contrary, all may not be lost**. The best plan to salvage such a predicament is to skip to the next question and continue - being cautious to mark answers in the correct spot. Then, when you finish and if sufficient time remains, you can try to find where you got off track and attempt corrections.

Exam Strategy #6 **Each strategy presented offers value in terms of points earned** on the test. Some strategies enable you to capture many points, and others only a few. The sum total is what is important to you. To achieve your highest possible score, you should master all these strategies through practice - do not ignore the ones that may seem less valuable. Any tool that can add any points at all to your score is incredibly valuable.

Exam Strategy #7   All sections of the exam are rigidly timed. In each section you are asked to complete more questions in a limited period of time than a most people could ever hope to accomplish without some kind of help. This book is your help. Your goals are to [1] learn about the contents of the exam; [2] study the strategies given; and [3] use the sample tests to practice (and practice and practice and practice) in order to develop the skills, strategies, and speed necessary to master the exam. **Practice cannot be stressed enough, and you cannot practice too much!** As previously mentioned, our Timed Practice Test CD described on the order form in the back of the book is a convenient tool for practicing realistically and for timing yourself precisely in order to master the needed speed.

Exam Strategy #8   **Once you master the necessary level of speed, you will notice that you develop a certain pace** – not unlike a runner competing in a race. What happens to a runner who stumbles or stops in the middle of a race? Not only does the runner lose time while he/she is stopped, the runner also loses time as he/she strives to regain the original pace – the runner is not moving as rapidly until his/her maximum pace is again achieved. The runner would have performed much better if he/she had not stopped. The same holds true on the Address Checking and Address Memory sections of this exam where speed is the most critical element. As you race through these sections marking answers at maximum speed, **do not stop to make a correction if you suddenly realize that you have answered a question incorrectly**. Like the runner, you would be giving yourself a double whammy – you lose time while you're stopped, plus you work more slowly (answer fewer questions) as you rebuild your pace. Think of the seconds lost as you accomplish the following steps to make a correction:

1.   Stop writing.
2.   Raise your pencil away from the paper.
3.   Reverse the position of your pencil so that the eraser is facing the paper.
4.   Erase the wrong answer.
5.   Raise your pencil away from the paper again.
6.   Reverse the position of your pencil again so that the lead is facing the paper.
7.   Brush away the bits of rubber that were ground off your eraser as you used it.
8.   Invariably, you see that part of the mark remains, so you decide to erase again.
9.   So, you raise your pencil away from the paper again.
10. Reverse your pencil again so that the eraser is facing the paper.
11. Erase the remaining marks.
12. Raise your pencil away from the paper again.
13. Reverse the position of your pencil again so that the lead is facing the paper.
14. Brush away the bits of rubber again.
15. Look closely to assure that you really did erase all of the mark this time.
16. Mark the correct answer.
17. Attempt to rebuild you original pace as you answer the next several questions.

Most people go through these 17 counterproductive and time consuming steps every time they stop to make a correction. A better idea would be to pause just long enough to make a tiny dot next to the incorrect answer. Then, when you finish all the questions in that section (and you should be able to finish all of them all after mastering what this book has to offer), go back to correct the answers where your made the tiny dots. This strategy enables you to make the best use of the limited time available.

Exam Strategy #9   As you are beginning to see, and will shortly see even more, this exam is not like any other test you've ever taken before. In many cases, the information and strategies presented will be understood better and will be appreciated more after actually experiencing the exam. Accordingly, you are encouraged to **review all the instructions and strategies again after completing each of your practice tests.**

Address Checking Section

As noted earlier, on this section you will be given 95 questions, each consisting of a pair of addresses, that must be answered in only 6 minutes. Your job is to determine whether the two addresses in each question are exactly alike in every way or if they or different in any way. If they are alike, you mark the answer "A" for Alike. If they are different, you mark the answer "D" for Different. On this section, you have only two answer choices – A or D. On all other sections, you have five choices – A, B, C, D, or E. For a clearer picture, review the two samples below:

Sample 1.　　5432 Lassiter Rd　　5432 Lassiter Rd　　　　Ⓐ Ⓓ

The two addresses in this sample are exactly alike, so you would darken the oval with the letter "A".

Sample 2.　　Susquehanna, PA　　Susquehana, PA　　　　Ⓐ Ⓓ

These two addresses are different. The letter "n" appears twice in the city name to the left, but only once in the spelling on the right. So, you would darken the oval with the letter "D".

This section is truly a speed test. **Comparing addresses is not terribly difficult, but doing so accurately at the pace demanded is next to impossible without the right strategies and a great deal of practice.** This section is important for several reasons, not the least of which is the fact that it offers the most potential points – it has more questions, meaning more points you can capture, than any other section. Following are the strategies needed to master this section:

Address Checking Strategy #1　**Push yourself for speed.** Force yourself to practice at pace beyond your level of comfort. When you become comfortable at that faster speed, push yourself yet again to an even faster pace beyond your newly acquired level of comfort. Then repeat the cycle over and over as you continually increase your ability and tolerance for speed. Virtually all of us learned in school to place most of our emphasis on accuracy and little, if any, emphasis on speed. When taking a math or geography test, it was not unusual for the teacher to give us extra time to assure completion. You can be sure that the teacher will not give you extra time on this test! The result is that most of us have a speed/accuracy imbalance – at least in terms of this exam. The challenge is, over time and via consistent practice, to learn to place more a little more emphasis on speed and a little less emphasis on accuracy. This may sound counterproductive, but consider this: "How good a score should you expect if every question you answered was correct, but you were only fast enough to answer half the questions in the time allowed?" You will score far better if you answer all the questions within the time allowed, even if you answer a few incorrectly because you were working so fast! Your specific goals as you practice are (1) to develop the speed necessary to answer all 95 questions in six minutes or less, and (2) once you have reached the required level of speed, to develop the skills/strategies necessary to answer the questions more correctly at that pace.

Address Checking Strategy #2　There are two terms used to describe practice – **Mass Practice and Distributive Practice**. Mass Practice is what we normally call cramming the night before the test, and it will not work on any section of this exam – especially not for the Address Checking section. Distributive Practice is what athletes do. It is consistent practice over a period of time. This is precisely what we need to do in preparation for our test. When considering the extreme speed, the subtle muscle control, and the level of eye/hand coordination demanded, this section is really quite similar to an athletic event. Approach your practice as though you were training for the Postal Olympics rather than a Postal exam.

You should do an Address Checking practice exercise every day or two initially. During the last few weeks before your scheduled test date, you should begin doing at least two or three practice exercises per day. This means that you will eventually repeat each Address Checking exercise in you book several times – there are sufficient extra Address Checking answer sheets to accommodate this. Plus, ten extra Address Checking practice exercises are included in your book in addition to those provided as part of the six complete practice tests.

However, each time you repeat an exercise, it should seem like a new one. You should not remember the exercise from the first time around. By the time you do all the exercises before repeating the first one again, you will have dealt with over 3,000 individual addresses. In the midst of this confusing muddle of addresses, there is almost no way you could remember any of the addresses from the first time around – it should indeed seem like a brand new exercise.

If you don't yet know the actual date of your exam, how will you know when to start your final few weeks of aggressive practicing? As stated before, on the average, your test date will fall about 4 to 6 weeks after you apply. Although this can vary, it makes a handy standard for predicting your probable test date. Also, applicants generally receive their scheduling notice 2 to 3 weeks before their actual test dates. This can make an even handier planning tool. Although this is generally true, be aware that it is not true 100% of the time. We have heard of cases where the scheduling packet was received only a few days before a scheduled test date. Unfortunately, there is no sure-fire way to predict your actual test date until the scheduling package is received.

Address Checking Strategy #3 On every section of the test, the exam administrator will briefly explain the instructions, advise you to open your booklets, direct you to pick up your pencil, and finally tell you to begin. The vast majority of exam applicants do not know what to expect, but **your preparation will give you a distinct advantage** at this point. Unlike the others who are hanging on the administrator's every word and therefore have a delayed reaction time, you (1) should have your finger on the edge of your booklet before the administrator says the first word; (2) immediately flip it open as the administrator begins to utter the words "Open your test booklet"; (3) as the administrator gives further instructions, answer the first few questions in your mind; and (4) when the administrator says to pick up your pencil, immediately mark those first few answers that you did in your mind. You did not cheat, but you did pick up an advantage of a few points on everybody else by using your foreknowledge and common sense.

Address Checking Strategy #4 Train yourself to **glance over the shorter or easier address pairs only once, and the longer or more difficult address pairs only twice.** *NEVER MAKE A THIRD PASS!* There is simply not enough time. With practice, this can be accomplished.

Address Checking Strategy #5 **What if you find that, near the end of the six minutes allowed for this section, you do not have time to complete the final few questions at your present pace?** In such a case, speed through the final questions allowing only one glance-over per question no matter how difficult the addresses look. The odds are in your favor that you will get more right than wrong. The resulting score should be better than if you had not answered the final few questions at all.

Address Checking Strategy #6 **As you move your eyes back and forth from the test booklet to the answer sheet and back again, use this back and forth motion to do your one or two glance-over's.** For a right-handed test taker who has just marked an answer on the answer sheet located on his/her far right, it would be a waste of critical milliseconds to not begin the next glance-over until after having moved his/her eyes all the way back to the question on the far side of the test booklet located on his/her left. Picture a circle of movement where half of the motion is wasted. Why not make productive use of all the motion in both directions? To do so, after marking an answer, glance over the next address pair from right to left (rather than the normal left to right) as your eyes return from the answer sheet, and begin another glance-over (this time from left to right) as your eyes begin moving back toward the answer sheet. Left-handed individuals may need to reverse these directions.

Address Checking Strategy #7 If you finish before the six minute period expires, you should obviously **check you answers**. But - should you check all of them? Should you check only the ones marked "A" for alike? Or, should you check only the ones marked "D" for different? You do not have time to check all the answers, so the best approach is to check only the ones marked "A" for alike. Our studies indicate that most of the answers you marked "D" for different are probably correct – you marked them as being different because you really saw a difference between the two addresses. Most mistakes occur when you miss a subtle difference between two addresses because you are working so fast, and you mark the answer "A" for alike rather than "D" for different. Therefore, most incorrect answers will be found among the answers marked "A" for alike.

Address Checking Strategy #8 Once you find a difference between the two addresses in a question, immediately mark the answer D for different, and move on to the next question. **Do not continue to look for additional possible differences.** Finding additional differences will not matter at all. One difference makes the two addresses just as different as ten would. There is no need to look for additional differences. Looking for additional differences would only serve to waste what precious little time you have.

Address Checking Strategy #9 **Do not guess blindly on the Address Checking section.** Due to the scoring formula, wrong answers count against you. On this section, there is more risk of harm than good when guessing blindly.

Address Checking Strategy #10 **Practice cannot be stressed enough, and you cannot practice too much.** As noted earlier, this section calls for the most practice, so extra practice tools are included. Address Checking Strategy #2 goes into detail about how and when to practice. The extra practice materials included enable you to follow through as instructed. And, also as noted earlier, using our Timed Practice Test CD described on the order form in the back of the book is the most convenient and realistic way to practice.

Can you make notes or marks during the Address Checking Section?
No, absolutely not. You are not allowed to write or make any marks of any kind in the test booklet during this section. The only marks you are allowed to make are the answers you darken on the answer sheet.

Address Memory Section

The Address Memory section is important due to the number of potential points available – second only to the Address Checking section. The scored portion of the Address Memory section has 88 questions to be answered in five minutes. Turn to the Address Memory section in one of your practice tests of this book to see how the section is structured and what the questions look like.

This is by far the hardest part of the exam for almost everyone. Without the right strategies, the speed required is as formidable as in the Address Checking section, and the memorization is virtually impossible. This one section is the single biggest reason why so many fail their exams. The Address Memory strategies suggested in some books frequently seem so complicated and technical that they do more harm than good. **Of the many benefits provided by this book, perhaps the greatest is the simple yet phenomenally successful Address Memory strategies you are about to learn.**

On this section, you are to memorize 25 addresses in five boxes as displayed in the sample below.

A	B	C	D	E
4700-5599 Camp Ishee 5600-6499 Sarah Kaytham 4400-4699 Lang	6800-6999 Camp Hunter 6500-6799 Sarah Island 5600-6499 Lang	5600-6499 Camp Dearman 6800-6999 Sarah Carlton 6500-6799 Lang	6500-6799 Camp Norwalk 4400-4699 Sarah Nultey 4700-5599 Lang	4400-4699 Camp Plank 4700-5599 Sarah Airline 6800-6999 Lang

The five boxes are labeled as A, B, C, D, and E. **Your goal is to remember in which box each address is located.** Each question in the Address Memory section is an address from one of the boxes. To answer, you darken the letter of the box from which it came – A, B, C, D, or E.

Notice that, in each box of our sample, at the top is an address with a number, the next one down is a word address without numbers, in the middle spot another number address, then another word address, and finally at the bottom a number address again. **This is the exact format you will see on the actual exam.**

The format that the addresses follow as we examine the boxes proves to be very repetitive. These repeating addresses make memorization much more difficult. Looking at all five boxes horizontally, we notice that the top number addresses all contain the same street name "Camp". Viewed horizontally again, the middle number address in each box contains the street name "Sarah", and the bottom number addresses all contain the street name "Lang". Each street name is repeated five times horizontally. Looking at the top address in Box A, we see the number 4700-5599. In this particular sample, the number 4700-5599 repeats at the bottom of Box D and in the middle of Box E. A close examination shows that most the numbers seem to repeat two or three times at various locations in the different boxes. Again, **you will see these very types of repeating formats on the actual exam.**

This section is broken into seven timed segments, as described below in the proper order, the format of which adds even more confusion to an already bewildering task:

1. A simple three minute exercise consisting of only a few questions with the boxes shown. The purpose of this segment is simply to demonstrate how to answer the questions. The boxes and addresses shown in this segment are the same ones that will be used throughout all seven segments.

2. A three minute segment during which you are to study and memorize the locations of the 25 addresses. There are no questions in this segment. You are provided only with the five boxes to be studied and memorized.

3. A three minute exercise during which you are asked to answer 88 questions from memory if possible, but the boxes are available if you need to refer to them. This is a practice exercise. It is not scored and will not affect your exam score.

4. A three minute exercise during which you are asked to answer 88 questions from memory. You are not given the boxes to use – you must work from memory. Thankfully, this is another practice exercise that is not scored and will not affect your exam score.

5. Another study period like Segment 2 above with the same boxes and addresses, but five minutes long instead of three.

6. An 88 question exercise similar to Segment 3 above, but five minutes long instead of three. You are asked to answer from memory if possible, but the boxes are shown for your use if needed.

7. **This final segment is the one and only part of the Address Memory section that is scored**. Your score on this segment is your score for the Address Memory section, and it does affect your overall exam score. Presumably, the prior segments of the Address Memory section were there to help you remember the addresses for this final scored segment. Most people, however, find the strange format and broken periods of concentration to be more confusing that helpful. On this final segment, you are given 88 questions to answer in only five minutes, and you must work from memory – the boxes are not displayed.

Following are the strategies needed to master the Address Memory section. These strategies should enable you to vastly reduce the volume of material to be memorized, to more easily memorize the remaining material, and to answer the 88 questions within the five minutes allowed.

Address Memory Strategy #1 **Memorize the addresses horizontally across the page**, not vertically down the page. Most people find horizontal memorization to be more natural and manageable.

Address Memory Strategy #2 **Memorize only the first four boxes – Boxes A, B, C, and D.** Ignore Box E – the fifth box. As you take the test, mark the addresses appropriately that you recognize as having come from Boxes A, B, C, or D. By the process of elimination, where did any address come from that you don't recognize? Necessarily, from Box E – the one you did not memorize. So, mark every address you don't recognize with the answer "E". Using this strategy, you can correctly answer every question dealing with Box E even though you intentionally did not memorize any of the addresses in Box E. This one simple common sense strategy alone reduces the material to be memorized by 20%!

30

Address Memory Strategy #3   **Use imagery and/or association to horizontally memorize the word addresses** in Boxes A, B, C, and D. Simply put, tie the words together to form an image, mental picture, phrase, or concept to which you can relate and that you can therefore remember more easily. It helps to form an image or association where the words are imagined to interact with each other in some way. The more realistic, lifelike, and/or graphic your image or association – the better you can remember it. Each person will see a different image or association in the word addresses based upon his/her individual personality, experiences, likes, dislikes, etc. It may take a little thought, but you should eventually be able to find an image or association in almost any series of words. It becomes easier with practice. A vivid imagination contributes to your effort. The words must be tied together and memorized in the same order as they appear from left to right.

Using the five boxes given earlier as samples, let's try out this strategy. The word addresses in these sample boxes, by the way, are actual addresses from real exams I have taken.

- The first horizontal row of word addresses from the Boxes A, B, C, and D read as follows. Remember, we are only concentrating on the first four boxes. We will ignore Box E.

Ishee Hunter Dearman Norwalk

As an outdoor sports enthusiast, I immediately saw something to which I could relate when looking at these words. I used parts of the words to create the sentence:

"I hunt deer now."

Notice the highlighted parts of the words:

Ishee **Hunt**er **Dear**man **Norw**alk

I took liberty with the word "dear" out of "Dearman" and used it to refer to animal "deer". Also, I played with the sequence of the letters in the word "Norwalk" to come up with the word "now". Being a hunter, I can very easily remember this sentence. Let's say I formerly hunted ducks but wanted to try something different – so… "I hunt deer now".

How does this association help? If I see any of the words Ishee, Hunter, Dearman, or Norwalk in a question as I take the test, I silently recite to myself the memorized association/sentence "I hunt deer now." If the word in the question is Ishee, which relates to "I" (the first element of my memorized sentence), the answer is A. Why? Because (1) we memorized the words in horizontal order from left to right; (2) therefore, the first word in my memorized sentence necessarily came from the first box – Box A; and (3) the word in the question relates to the first word in my sentence which relates to the first box – Box A. If the word in the question is Hunter, the answer will be Box B – second word in my memorized sentence…second box…Box B. If the word in the question is Dearman, the answer is Box C – third word…third box…Box C. And of course, the word Norwalk will relate to my fourth word "now" so the answer would be Box D – the fourth box. In each case, I silently recite my sentence which immediately tells me the answer by the position of the word in my sentence – first/A, second/B, third/C, or fourth/C.

- Now let's look at the other horizontal row of word addresses from Boxes A, B, C, and D:

  Kaytham Island Carlton Nultey

  When taking a real exam, I again immediately saw something in the words that related to me. You see, my wife has a friend named Kay who is a real car nut. She always seems to be trading in her current car for a new one, only to do it again just a few months later. Here's what I saw:

  "Kay is (a) car nut."

  Notice the highlighted parts of these words:

  Kaytham **Is**land **Car**lton **Nul**t**e**y

  As in the previous example, I used parts of words and did a little rearranging of the letters in the word "Nultey". In this case, as I silently recite my sentence, I sort of mumble and play down the "a" in my sentence to emphasize that it is not a key word. It is only an aid to help me make sense of the key words that relate to Boxes A, B, C, and D. Just like before, when I see one of the words Kaytham, Island, Carlton, or Nultey in a question – I silently recite my sentence, and the position of the word in my sentence tells me what box the address came from. First word…first box…Box A; second word…second box…Box B; etc.

- The situation I am about to suggest has not actually happened to me, but it is a possibility, so we must be prepared. The two word address examples we have just discussed came from different exams. But, what if they had been on the same test? Here's the problem – you have two "i" words: "Ishee" in the first sample from Box A and "Island" in the second one from Box B. As a matter of fact, they are both "is" words. This probably would have caused confusion in such a case if I had used the sentences as they are. Instead, this is what I would have done upon discovering such duplication, and you should change your image or association similarly if caught in such a circumstance. I would have gone back to the first sentence and used "She" from "Ishee" instead of "I" to make the sentence "She hunts deer now". No problem – my wife occasionally hunts with me. So, "she hunts deer now" rather than ducks.

- Occasionally I am asked: "What if I recite the wrong phrase/sentence? What if I recite the one that is supposed to go with the other horizontal row of word addresses?" No problem! The word address in the question should prompt you to recite the proper phrase/sentence. But even if you recite the wrong one, don't worry. There's only two of them. If the first one doesn't fit, recite the other one – it probably will fit. What if the word address in the question doesn't fit either of your memorized sentences? That's OK too. Some of them are not supposed to – the ones from Box E, which you purposely did not memorize. As reiterated below, you will be able to correctly answer all Box E questions by the process of elimination even though you intentionally did not memorize any of the addresses in Box E.

- As we take the test in this manner, how do we answer questions with words we don't recognize because they came from Box E – the one we didn't memorize? We simply mark the answer E. This is part of our plan. By the process of elimination, any word address we don't recognize necessarily came from Box E. So, we mark all unrecognized word addresses as "E" and get every one of them right without even trying to really memorize them!

Can you make notes or marks during the Address Memory Section?
No, absolutely not. You are not allowed to write or make any marks of any kind in the test booklet during this section. The only marks you are allowed to make are the answers you darken on the answer sheet. For many people, it would be easier to memorize if they could write the addresses down, but this is expressly forbidden.

| Address Memory Strategy #4 | **Use the "Second Digit Strategy" to memorize the number addresses.** Here's how it works:

Look at the top row of number addresses across the sample boxes horizontally from left to right as shown below. We see at least 65 characters that we must memorize:

Box A	Box B	Box C	Box D	Box E
4700-5599 Camp	6800-6999 Camp	5600-6499 Camp	6500-6799 Camp	4400-4699 Camp

By ignoring Box E as previously discussed, we can reduce the number to something over 50, but that's still a lot. What if we could identify a single key character from each box and memorize only that one item. This would cut the material to be memorized by over 90%. But with all the repetition from box to box, is there a key non-repeating element in each case on which we can concentrate? Let's analyze the addresses to see if anything does not repeat…

We can rule out the street names – in our sample boxes the street names Camp, Sarah, and Lang that accompany the number addresses repeat horizontally across all five boxes. What about the numbers themselves? Let's look at the top numbers from all five boxes:

Box A	Box B	Box C	Box D	Box E
4700-5599	**6**800-6999	**5**600-6499	**6**500-6799	**4**400-4699

Look at the first digits from each address in order horizontally as highlighted above. The character in the first digit location of Box A is the number "4", in Box B it is a "6", in Box C it is a "5", in Box D a "6", and in Box E a "4". The first digits won't help us because of the repetition. The first digit in both Boxes A and E is a "4". Also, the number "6" repeats as the first digit location of both Boxes B and D.

What about the other digits? The third digit in each box is a 0. Same for the fourth digit. In the fifth digit location, the number 6 repeats three times – in Boxes B, C, and D. The number 9 appears in both the seventh and eighth digit locations of all five boxes. As you see, the numbers repeat all across the board. This is true for all the number addresses in all the boxes.

But, what about the second digit numbers? We didn't try them. Let's try our sample and see:

Box A	Box B	Box C	Box D	Box E
4**7**00-5599	6**8**00-6999	5**6**00-6499	6**5**00-6799	4**4**00-4699

The second digit characters in order horizontally, as highlighted above, are the numbers 7, 8, 6, 5, and 4. *They don't repeat!* Here is our key non-repeating element. But, how do we use it? First, remember we only memorize the first four boxes – A, B, C, and D. Using our Second Digit Strategy, the only elements we will memorize are the second digit numbers from each address followed by the street name, which means all we want to memorize from this sample is "7 8 6 5 Camp" – or in a condensed form "7865 Camp" – which sounds and looks like a single address itself. This is something you can remember easily … "7865 Camp". Close the book for a moment and silently recite it. See, you've already got it memorized! This is tremendously easier than trying to memorize over 65 characters spread across the top row of five boxes.

So, we've memorized "7865 Camp". What do we do now? As you take the test, any time you see a question with the street name Camp, look at the number in the second digit location of the question. Look only at the second digit - ignore all the other numbers. Let's say that the address in the question is "4700-5599 Camp". We look at the second digit in the question and see that it is a "7". Now, we silently recite what we memorized - "7865 Camp". The second digit in the question (the number 7) matches the first number in the series we memorized. So the answer is "A" - the question relates to the first number we memorized which relates to the first box - Box A. If the second digit of the question matched the fourth number in the series we memorized, the answer would be "D" - the question relates to the fourth number in our series which relates to the fourth box - Box D. And so on.

Using the Second Digit Strategy on the other horizontal rows of number addresses in our sample boxes, we would memorize "6584 Sarah" and "4657 Lang". When taking the test, if you find a question with the address "6500-6799 Sarah", the answer is automatically "B". The second digit in the question matches the second number in the series we memorized for Sarah, which relates to the second box – Box B. If the question is "6500-6799 Lang", we silently recite "4657 Lang" and quickly discover that the answer is "C". The second digit in the question is the number "5", which is the third number in the series we memorized for Lang. So, the answer is "C" – the question relates to the third number in our series which relates to the third box – Box C. With practice, this strategy becomes second nature and allows you to phenomenally increase your Address Memory speed and accuracy.

Some people, by the way, find it easier to remember the numbers to be memorized if they associate the numbers with (or picture the numbers in their minds as) sports scores, test scores, temperatures, dates, years, etc. Try this strategy to see if it works for you.

What if the second digit in the question doesn't match any of the numbers we memorized? No problem – it means that the address in the question necessarily came from Box E. Remember, we intentionally did not memorize any of the addresses from Box E. So, we mark the answer "E" for any address we don't recognize and thereby correctly answer all Box E questions by the process of elimination.

The only location we did not consider was the sixth digit location, which, like the second digit, also does not repeat. If necessary, you can use the sixth digit in the same fashion, but the second digit is in a more convenient location with which to work.

The pattern just discussed has appeared on every exam of which we have knowledge since the Postal Service created the 470 exam and rewrote the 460 exam in late 1993. This pattern and likewise this strategy have held true in every case without a single exception. The National Test Administration Center for the Postal Service has indicated by phone that no revisions are planned in the foreseeable future. However, in the highly improbable (almost impossible) case that you find the second and/or sixth digits to repeat on your exam, simply look for a another digit that does not repeat and use the same strategy for that particular digit.

The first four strategies alone have transformed the Address Memory section into a manageable task. We have reduced the memorization into the below brief items.

7865 Camp
She hunts deer now.
6584 Sarah
Kay is (a) car nut.
4657 Lang

And, there are even more helpful Address Memory strategies yet to come …

Address Memory Strategy #5 Refer back to explanation of the seven timed segments from the Address Memory section. Notice that segment 1 and 3 each give you three minutes to do practice exercises with the boxes shown for your use. Segment 6 is a similar five-minute exercise with the boxes shown. In all three of these segments, you are asked to mark answers, but these segments are not scored. Since they are not scored, it doesn't matter what answers you mark. Wouldn't it be great if you could use these three segments for **extra minutes of study and memorization time** instead of marking answers? Well, you can – but with care. When given instructions during the exam, you are expected to follow them, but there is a way around it in this case. Here's how…

- In segment 1, you are given the five boxes and asked to answer several sample questions in three minutes, but again this exercise will not be scored. The purpose of this exercise is simply to acquaint test takers with the format of the Address Memory section – but you already know all about the format. So, take a few seconds to mark random answers (it doesn't matter what answers you mark because they will not be scored), and then spend the rest of the allotted time memorizing.

- Likewise, in segment 3 you are given three minutes to do an 88 question exercise with the boxes shown – but again, it will not be scored, and you are certainly not expected to answer all 88 questions. From past experience, they know you will only be able to answer a small portion of that number, and with very little accuracy at that. So, take a few seconds to make a handful of random marks on the answer sheet, and then spend the rest of the time memorizing.

- The same is true for segment 6, but you are allowed five minutes. Again, the boxes are shown. And again, you make a handful of random marks and spend the time memorizing. Since this exercise will not be scored, there is no reason to make a sincere attempt.

You just picked up an extra eleven minutes for memorization! You now have five study periods, three at 3 minutes each and two at 5 minutes each, for a total of 19 minutes to memorize.

Referring back to the Second Digit Strategy, let's say you want to memorize 7865 Camp, 6584 Sarah, and 4657 Lang. Some people prefer to memorize in pairs rather than all four numbers at once. To do so, spend the first three 3 minute study periods (a total of 9 minutes) memorizing the first two numbers for each - **78** Camp, **65** Sarah, and **46** Lang. Then, spend the final two study periods (a total of 10 minutes) memorizing the last two numbers for each to complete the job - 78**65** Camp, 65**84** Sarah, and 46**57** Lang. Smaller, manageable tasks can be easier.

Address Memory Strategy #6 **Answer the 88 questions in order.** Do not attempt to go through the test twice - answering only the word address questions the first time and then the number address questions the second time, or vice versa. Some people find one or the other type of question to be more manageable and are tempted to first answer the ones they find to be easier. Unfortunately, *you simply do not have enough time to take the test twice!* And that is in effect exactly what you would be doing. Answering 88 questions in five minutes is challenging enough. To attempt going though the test twice, in essence going though 176 questions, in five minutes is an absolute impossibility.

Address Memory Strategy #7 Speed is just as important as memorization. If you memorize all the addresses perfectly but can only answer half the questions in the time allowed, you have gained nothing at all. As with the Address Checking section, practice is absolutely essential to develop the skills and the speed required. **Practice cannot be stressed enough, and you cannot practice too much.** And, as mentioned previously, our Timed Practice Test CD is the most convenient way to practice realistically and time yourself precisely. Plus, the CD repeats the instructions for you section by section. This really helps on the Address Memory section with its confusing format of seven segments.

Address Memory Strategy #8 **Complete and stop the Address Memory practice work about two days before your scheduled test date for the real exam.** Do not continue doing Address Memory practice exercises all the way up to the night before. If you do, you may confuse the addresses from this book with those on the real exam - the addresses from the practice work may still be lingering in your mind as you attempt to take the actual exam. Do not let this happen to you. The end result could be sure failure.

Number Series Section

In the Number Series section you will be given 20 minutes to answer 24 mathematical questions – just under one minute per question. Each question consists of a series of numbers followed by two blanks. Turn to the Number Series section in one of your practice tests to see what the questions look like. Within each series of numbers are one or more sequences. **Your job is to identify the sequences and to calculate, based upon the sequences you identified, what two numbers would logically follow in the series.** Again, these are multiple choice questions. You will have five possible answers from which to choose – A, B, C, D, and E. Each possible answer consists of a pair of numbers, but only one contains the correct pair of numbers in the proper order. You will encounter several types of sequences. Each will be discussed in detail as we examine Strategy #1 – Circles and Squares. The strategies needed to master the Number Series section follow:

Number Series Strategy #1   First let's review the types of sequences found in these mathematical questions. Then we will discuss the **Circles and Squares Strategy** used to solve the more difficult types of sequences. Simple mathematical principles rather than a particular strategy are used to solve the first two types of sequences.

- NUMBER SERIES – ADDITION: Below are examples of series where the relationship between the numbers is one of simple addition. This is the simplest type of series. It can usually be identified and solved with a quick examination.

  Sample 1:   21   25   29   33   37   41   45   ____   ____

  A quick examination shows this is an addition sequence increasing by 4. (21 + 4 = 25; 25 + 4 = 29; 29 + 4 = 33; and so on.) We can now go to the last shown number of 45 and calculate that the correct answers are 49 and 53. (45 + 4 = 49; 49 + 4 = 53)

  Sample 2:   21   42   63   84   105   126   147   ____   ____

  This one may appear a little more difficult, but upon examination it proves to be another fairly simple addition sequence increasing by 21. (21 + 21 = 42; 42 + 21 = 63; 63 + 21 = 84; and so on.) We can now go to the last shown number of 147 and calculate that the answers are 168 and 189. (147 + 21 = 168; 168 + 21 = 189)

- NUMBER SERIES – SUBTRACTION: This is a similar type of sequence, but the relationship between the numbers involved is one of simple subtraction. Examples follow.

  Sample 1:   23   20   17   14   11   8   ____   ____

  A glance at this sample shows that it is a subtraction series decreasing by 3. (23 – 3 = 20; 20 – 3 = 17; 17 – 3 = 14; and so on.) By applying the subtraction sequence to the last shown number of 8, we find that the answers are 5 and 2. (8 – 3 = 5; 5 – 3 = 2).

  Sample 2:   60   53   46   39   32   25   ____   ____

  Again, this is quickly recognized as a subtraction series decreasing by 7. (60 – 7 = 53; 53 – 7 = 46; 46 – 7 = 39; and so on.) We apply this sequence to the last shown number and find the answers to be 18 and 11. (25 – 7 = 18; 18 – 7 = 11)

- NUMBER SERIES – ALTERNATING ADDITION: Now we find the series becoming more difficult. There will be two separate addition sequences in a single series. Here is where we learn the benefits of a simple yet effective strategy called Circles and Squares. Examples follow:

Sample 1:   2   1   4   2   6   3   8   ____   ____

This appears to be a confusing series indeed. To solve the series, we must identify and separate the sequences involved using the Circles and Squares strategy. Here's how it works… First, draw a circle around any numbers you see that seem obviously related. In this case, I see the sequence 2, 4, 6, and 8; so I put circles around these numbers like so:

Next, I draw squares around any remaining numbers that don't appear to be related to the circled sequence – yielding a series that looks like this:

Now we need to determine where the blanks fit into our sequences by following the pattern of circles and squares. It is easy to see that we are alternating a circle, then a square, then another circle, and another square. Following this pattern, the first blank will obviously be a square, and the second blank will be a circle. Now our series with completed circle and square patterns looks like this:

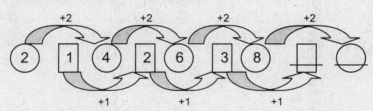

Finally, we find our answers by following the numbers in the two separate patterns. Following the circles, we quickly see an addition sequence increasing by 2. By adding 2 to the last shown number in the circle pattern, which is an 8, we find that the answer to the second blank with a circle around it will be a 10. Following the square pattern, we see an addition sequence increasing by 1. We add 1 to the last shown square pattern number, which is a 3, and find that the answer to the first blank with a square around it will be a 4. We have our answers --- 4 and 10.

Sample 2:   22   7   9   23   11   13   24   ____   ____

This is another case of two separate addition sequences within one series. Again, let's look for some numbers that obviously go together. Right away, I notice that the 22, 23, and 24 follow a pattern, so I'll put circles around them. Then, I'll put squares around any remaining numbers. The result should look like this:

We've identified the two patterns/sequences, but what pattern will the blanks fit into? Looking at our circles and squares, we see a pattern of one circle and then two squares, one circle and then two squares, and so on. Applying this pattern to our blanks, we see that they will both be squares and will look like this:

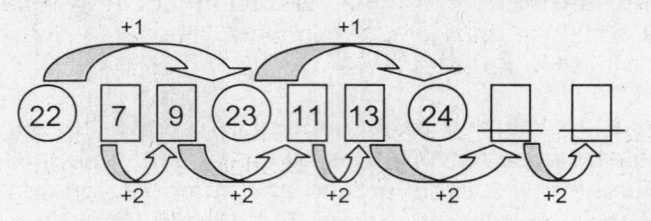

We have learned that the circle pattern can be ignored because both answers fit into the square pattern only. If we solve the square pattern, we will have found our answers. The square pattern is obviously an addition sequence increasing by 2. (7 + 2 = 9; 9 + 2 = 11; 11 + 2 = 13) Now, we can apply this sequence to the last shown square pattern number of 13 to find that our answers are 15 and 17. (13 + 2 = 15; 15 + 2 = 17)

- NUMBER SERIES – ALTERNATING SUBTRACTION: These problems are similar to those above, but the two sequences involved deal with subtraction. Examples follow:

Sample 1.   42   41   40   21   20   39   38   ____   ____

Right away, I see some related numbers – 42, 41, 40, 39, and 38. I will put circles around those numbers and squares around anything remaining as displayed below:

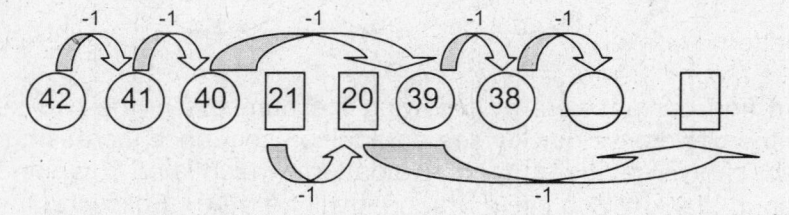

Now, following the patterns of three circles, two squares, and so on; we see that the first blank will be a circle and that the second blank will be a square – like this:

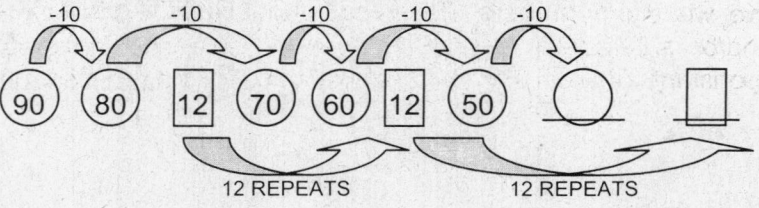

The circle pattern is decreasing by one. So, we apply this pattern to the last shown circle number of 38 and find that the first blank will be a 37. The square pattern is also decreasing by one. We likewise apply this pattern to the last shown square number of 20 and find that the second blank will be a 19. We have the answers – 37 and 19.

Sample 2.   90   80   12   70   60   12   50   ____   ____

Again, at least one pattern is readily visible – 90, 80, 70, 60, and 50 – so we circle these numbers and put a square around any remaining numbers.

Now by following the pattern of two circles, one square, two circles, one square, and so on; we can see that the first blank will be a circle and that the second blank will be a square. Let's solve the circles first – they are decreasing by 10 each time. We apply this pattern to the last shown circle and find that the first blank will be a 40. The square pattern is simply the number 12 repeating over and over - so the second blank will be a 12. We have the answers – 40 and 12.

- NUMBER SERIES – ALTERNATING ADDITION AND SUBTRACTION: One of the sequences within the series this time will be addition, and the other will be subtraction. Examples follow:

Sample 1.   13   12   3   5   11   10   7   ____   ____

The first related numbers I see are 13, 12, 11, and 10 – so I put a circle around them and a square around any remaining numbers – like this:

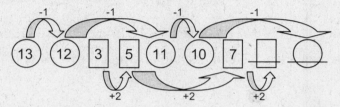

Following the pattern of two circles, two squares, and so on; we see that the first blank will be a square and that the second blank will be a circle. Looking at the circle pattern, which is decreasing by 1 each time, we find that the second blank will be a 9. Looking at the square pattern, which is increasing by 2 each time, we find that the first blank will be a 9 also. We have the answers – 9 and 9.

Sample 2.   50   26   24   55   22   20   60   ____   ____

The first pattern I see is the 50, 55, and 60. So, I will put circles around these numbers and squares around any remaining numbers – like this:

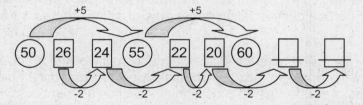

Following the pattern of one circle, two squares, and so on; we see that both blanks will be squares. We can ignore the circle pattern and find our answers by solving the square pattern only. The square pattern is decreasing by 2 each time. By applying this to the last shown square number of 20, we find that our answers will be 18 and 16.

- NUMBER SERIES – GRADUATING ADDITION AND/OR SUBTRACTION: The final type of series we will examine have graduating sequences. In this type of sequence, the addition and/or subtraction factors increase or decrease systematically rather than remaining constant. Review the following examples for a more clear understanding.

Sample 1.　2　3　5　8　12　17　_____　_____

This is a graduating addition series where the addition factor begins as a "1" but then increases by "1" each time it is used as displayed below:

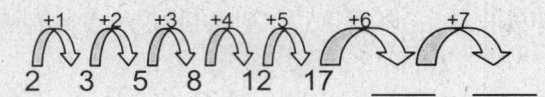

Following this graduating sequence, we can see that the answers will be 23 and 30. (17 + 6 = 23; 23 + 7 = 30)

Sample 2.　1　2　4　8　16　32　_____　_____

In this graduating addition sequence, each number in the series is added to itself to create the next number as displayed in the following diagram:

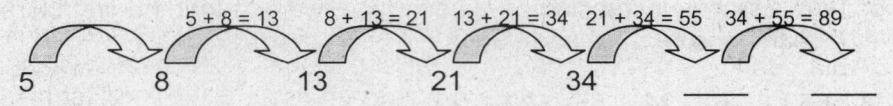

By following the sequence, we see that the answers will be 64 and 128. (32 + 32 = 64; 64 + 64 = 128)

Sample 3.　5　8　13　21　34　_____　_____

In this graduating addition sequence, each number is added to the number before it in order to create the next number in the series. Note the following diagram:

```
             5 + 8 = 13   8 + 13 = 21   13 + 21 = 34   21 + 34 = 55   34 + 55 = 89
   5      8      13      21      34      ____    ____
```

By following the sequence, we see that the answers will be 55 and 89.

The above three examples are all of Graduating Addition Series. Graduating Subtraction Series would obviously be similar, but the relationship between the elements in the series would be one of subtraction rather than of addition. You will likely see both types on your exam.

You will also likely find alternating series questions involving graduating addition and/or subtraction sequences. In fact, you should expect to experience questions where all the different types of sequences discussed in this section of your book are mixed together in various fashions. Likewise, the Number Series practice tests in your book contain questions with all types of intermingled sequences. Remember to use the Circles and Squares Strategy to solve any type of alternating series where two or more sequences are mixed together.

| Number Series Strategy #2 | Fairly simple examples were intentionally used above. The intent is to more easily demonstrate the strategies given. The use of more challenging sequences would only serve to confuse you and divert your attention away from the strategies being presented. There will be some simpler and easier problems on your actual exam. But, there will certainly be some difficult ones as well. This also holds true for the practice tests in this book. **With practice, you will learn to knock out the easier ones quickly so that you will have more time to solve the difficult one by applying your strategies.**

Number Series Strategy #3   **On this section, you should attempt to answer the easier looking questions first and then go back to work on the harder looking ones**. They are all worth exactly one point, no more and no less, whether they are easy or difficult. Look at it this way… What if you used up the final remaining few minutes of the test trying to work on a very difficult question - say number 21. As you close your test booklet, you glance over questions 22, 23, and 24 (that you never even got to try because you were still working on number 21) and see that they look incredibly easy. You mentally kick yourself and think "If I would have just skipped number 21 and gone on to 22, 23, and 24; I would have picked up those three points easily. Instead, I lost all four points by wasting the last few minutes on number 21." You have an average of just under one minute per question. If you quickly answer the easy ones first, you will have more than one minute each left for the harder ones.

Number Series Strategy #4   **They will make ingenious attempts to confuse you.** There may be two, three, or maybe even four different sequences within a single series. There will be unrelated numbers mixed in just to throw you off. There will cases where the same number repeats over and over within the series. (See NUMBER SERIES – ALTERNATING SUBTRACTION sample number 2). The secret is to remain calm and to use your strategies to Divide and Conquer. Don't get flustered. Remember, there are two basic rules for solving all number series problems: [1] find the pattern or patterns, and [2] apply the pattern or patterns to determine what two numbers would logically follow in the series.

Number Series Strategy #5   **Do not leave any questions blank – blind guesses are acceptable.** This section is scored by simply counting the number of correct answers. So, if time is about to be called and you have not finished the last few questions, guess blindly. It cannot hurt you, and you just may get one or two right – which means one or two extra points.

Number Series Strategy #6   **If you can solve one pattern but not the other, choose the answer by the process of elimination.** You will have five choices, each consisting of a pair of numbers, for possible answers. If you are sure that the answer in the first blank should be the number 67 but cannot figure out what number should be in the second blank, look over the answer choices. If only one of the choices has the number 67 in the first blank location, you have found the correct answer no matter what the other number is. If more than one answer choice shows the number 67 in the first blank location, make your best educated guess.

Number Series Strategy #7   **Solutions for all the Number Series problems are given in the back of the book.** For a better understanding of the problems that you missed, closely review their solutions. This should enable you to correctly answer such questions the next time you encounter them. **Number lines, like those used to diagram these solutions, can be used as another tool to solve problems on the test.** Most people find the Circles and Squares Strategy to be quicker and easier. However, if number lines are easier for you – especially on more difficult problems – you should certainly use them.

Number Series Strategy #8   **Practice cannot be stressed enough, and you cannot practice too much.** Practice is the key to mastering your strategies and to recognizing sequences. And again, our Timed Practice Test CD is the best tool for practicing realistically.

Can you make notes or marks during the Number Series Section?
Yes. In order to answer the questions, you must do your calculations somewhere. You will be instructed to do your calculations in the spaces between the questions, in the margins, and in other blank spaces found in the Number Series Section of the test booklet.

Following Oral Instructions Section

In this section, an Exam Administrator reads a number questions aloud to the group of test takers. By following the instructions given to you verbally for each question, you will create the correct answer, which you will then mark on your answer sheet. This section is very difficult for many until they fully understand it. One Postal Exam Specialist advised that over 60% of all test takers fail this section entirely. This is because **many people never really comprehend how to answer the questions correctly**. But, once it is understood, the Oral Instructions section becomes the easiest for many test takers.

When taking this part of the test, you have no questions to read. Instead, you will be looking at a page in the test booklet containing circles, squares, lines, words, numbers, letters, etc. The instructions, which will be read to the group of test takers by the Exam Administrator, will direct you to select or mark certain items on the page. The selections/marks you make, coupled with the instructions you hear, will lead you to the correct answer. Note the below examples:

Sample 1.   _____ A   _____ B   _____ C   _____ D   _____ E

For a question like this on the actual exam, you may be told to write the number "67" on the line beside the third letter from the left, and then to mark on your answer sheet the number-letter combination you just created. Accordingly, you would write the number "67" beside the letter "C", which is the third letter from the left. Then you would darken item "67-C" on your answer sheet.

Sample 2.   [___ 45]   [___ 14]   [___ 73]   [___ 57]   [___ 38]

On this question, you may be instructed to write the letter "D" on the line inside the box with the largest number, and then to mark the number-letter combination you just made on your answer sheet. So, you would write the letter "D" on the line inside the box containing the number "73", which is the largest number. The number-letter combination you created by writing the letter "D" beside the number "73" is "73-D". Accordingly, you should darken item "73-D" on your answer sheet.

If you are a normal and at least partially sane human being, the above samples probably only confused you even more. The following strategies should give you a better understanding of the Following Oral Instructions section and provide the test taking tips needed to master this section:

| Following Oral Instructions Strategy #1 | **Number-Letter Combination.** A clear understanding of this term is essential for answering correctly. Most of the verbal questions/instructions will cause you to create a number-letter combination, which is simply a number and a letter paired together. For instance, a particular question may instruct you to write the letter B beside the number 18 and then to mark the resulting number-letter combination on your answer sheet. The number letter combination you have just created is 18-B. The answer to this question is 18-B. To mark the answer, go to number 18 on the answer sheet and darken letter B.

The problem is that you may be answering question number 3, yet you are marking an answer at item number 18 on the answer sheet. This goes against everything we have ever learned about taking a test. Up until this very point in our lives, we have always marked the answer to question 3 at item number 3 on the answer sheet, and marked the answer to question 18 at answer sheet item 18, and so on. Herein lies the problem. For this section of the exam, we must unlearn our orderly approach toward test taking.

On the Following Oral Instructions section, the number of the question will have nothing whatsoever to do with where you mark your answer. The one and only thing that dictates where you mark your answer is the number-letter combination. If the number-letter combination for question 13 is 77-D, you mark the letter D at item number 77 on the answer sheet. The fact that this is question number 13 does not matter at all. If the number-letter combination for question number 25 is 4-C, you mark the letter C at item number 4 on the answer sheet.

Occasionally, you will be instructed to simply darken a certain letter at a particular item number on the answer sheet without having first created a number-letter combination. For instance, for question number 23 you may simply be told to darken the letter A at item number 6 on the answer sheet. There was no number-letter combination involved. But, for the most part, a number-letter combination will be involved and will dictate where you mark your answer.

Following Oral Instructions Strategy #2 **Multiple Answers.** There will be instructions that cause you to create several number-letter combinations for a single question. This causes incredible confusion for most individuals when they are told to mark their answers. Being orderly test takers, we expect only one answer for each question and only want to mark one answer for each question. Again, we must unlearn our orderly approach. Be aware that there will indeed be several questions that have multiple answers and that you are indeed expected to mark all of them.

Following Oral instructions Strategy #3 **Timing.** The questions/instructions will be read to you at a rather slow and deliberate rate of approximately 75 words per minute. The reader will pause for about five seconds between each question for you to mark your answers. Do so rapidly and be ready to listen to the next question. If the question has multiple answers, mark them quickly so that you will be ready for the next question. The reader will start again in about five seconds whether you are ready or not. And, how can you possibly answer the next question correctly if you do not hear the complete question?

Following Oral Instructions Strategy #4 **If you become confused on a particular question**, should you [1] continue worrying with it and trying to salvage it while the Exam Administrator moves on and begins reading the next question or [2] **skip it and be ready to listen to the next question**? If you didn't get it, then you didn't get it. Let it go. Why miss the next question (maybe even the next two or three questions) worrying over the one you already lost. It makes much more sense to let it go and be prepared to capture the next point(s).

Following Oral Instructions Strategy #5 **You _can_ mark in the question booklet during this section** of the exam. As a matter of fact, you are specifically directed to do so in the instructions you hear. But remember, you are only allowed to mark in the question booklet on this section and on the Number Series section. You are absolutely not allowed to do so on the Address Checking and the Address Memory sections.

Following Oral Instructions Strategy #6 **Guessing, where possible, on this section is acceptable**. Like the Number series section, this one is scored by simply counting your correct answers. So, why not guess? You may pick up a few extra points. But, there are two problems with guessing in this case. First, where do you guess? Since the number of the question has nothing to do with where you mark you answer, how do you know where to mark your guess? You cannot guess unless you understood at least enough of the question to know where to make a guess. Secondly, there are only about 31 questions, but there are 88 answer spots on the answer sheet. Again, where do you guess? Same answer. You can only guess if you understood the question well enough to know where to make a guess (A, B, C, D, or E) on the answer sheet.

Following Oral Instructions Strategy #7 The key to success is to **listen closely to the instructions and then to follow them explicitly.** The questions will intentionally sound confusing. You cannot allow you mind to wander or to try to make some type of rational sense out of what you are hearing. Simply listen, and do everything you are told to do exactly as you are told to do it.

Following Oral Instructions Strategy #8 **The majority rules!** Several questions will instruct you to mark a certain answer if a particular item of information read to you as part of the question is true/accurate. The Exam Administrator will then follow up by instructing you to mark a different answer if that particular item of information is not true/accurate. For instance, a question might read: "If 82 is greater than 55 and 14 is less than 18, mark the number-letter combination 77-B on your answer sheet. If not, mark the number-letter combination 25-D." In this case, the information read to you is accurate, so you would mark 77-B. Bear in mind however, that most such questions will more challenging than this rather simple example.

It can be beneficial to pay attention to the other test takers (there will be hundreds of them) around you when answering such questions. Let's assume, for instance, that you are taking your exam, and the Administrator is in the middle of reading such a question. Let's assume further that you feel that the first item of information given is not true/accurate, so you choose not to mark the first answer offered by the Administrator. Instead, you plan to mark the second answer choice that the Administrator is about to offer. But, during the pause as you wait to be given the second answer choice, you hear a great deal of scribbling noises from throughout the room as the majority of your neighbors mark the first answer choice on their answer sheets. What's more, with your peripheral vision, you notice a great deal of frantic movement as your neighbors mark the first answer.

Stop and think… Is it more likely that you are the only one who properly understood the question and that all your neighbors are complete idiots? Or, is it perhaps more probable that the majority of your neighbors understood the question better than you did and that you are about to answer incorrectly? I propose that the majority understood better than you did and that you will be ahead of the game to follow their lead. _The majority rules!_

Just the opposite, if you begin marking the first answer choice offered but notice that no one around you seems to be marking anything on their answer sheets, again I suggest that you stop and think. It would likely be best to choose the second answer choice as the majority of your neighbors seem to have done.

In the introduction to this section, it was mentioned that many applicants completely fail this section of the exam. However, just because most of your neighbors do not understand how and where to correctly mark their answers (number-letter combinations), this does not necessarily mean that they do not know what the correct answers are. It is most unlikely that they are all morons who are ignorant of the basic principles of math, social studies, etc. For the most part, they are probably intelligent individuals who simply failed to grasp the strange instructions for this illogical and irrational part of the exam.

Following Oral Instructions Strategy #9 **Make notes.** When you looked at one of the Following Oral Instructions practice tests in the back of your book, you probably noticed that the sample test booklet page contains a number of questions consisting of rows of items – shapes (circles, squares, rectangles, boxes), numbers, letters, lines, etc. Frequently, the instructions read to you will provide identifying information about the items in the row. Such a question may sound and look something like the following sample:

> "Look at the five boxes in question number 8. Starting from the left side, the first box has mail for Jackson and Canton. The second box has mail for Greenville and Glendale. The third box has mail for Kingsville and San Marcos. The fourth box has mail for Houston and Dallas. The fifth box has mail for Lawerenceburg and Auburn. Write the letter "D" as in dog on the blank line beside the number in the box that has mail for Greenville and Glendale. Write the letter "A" as in apple on the line beside the number in the box that has mail for Houston and Dallas. Now, mark the number-letter combinations you have made on your answer sheet."

8. [_____ 49]   [_____ 18]   [_____ 62]   [_____ 14]   [_____ 87]

By the time you have listened to this long and confusing question in its entirety, how in the world are you supposed to recall which box is which in order to mark the correct answer? The solution is for you to make brief notes as you hear the question. Remember, you <u>can</u> mark in your test booklet on this section of the exam. So, as the Administrator gives you identifying information about particular items, make notes accordingly. In this case, you should have written the respective city names (probably in an abbreviated form) beside each box for later recognition.

Following Oral Instructions Strategy #10 **Converting time of day into numbers.** Several questions will instruct you to convert a time of day into a number. You may be told to find the first two numbers of the time 5:30 PM on the answer sheet and then to darken the letter B. The first two numbers in the time of 5:30 PM are a 5 and a 3. Put together, they make the number 53. So, we would find number 53 on the answer sheet and darken the letter B. Or, you may be told to find the last two numbers of this time and to darken the letter A. So, you would find the number 30 and darken the letter A. If you were told to find the first number, it would be the number 5. As previously discussed, simply do as you are instructed. Don't waste time trying to make sense of it.

Following Oral Instructions Strategy #11   To **practice realistically**, you must either [1] have a friend or relative read all the practice tests to you or [2] listen to the practice tests on the Oral Instructions Practice Tests compact disc from Pathfinder Distributing Co. _Do not read the questions yourself as you take the practice tests!_ ' This would be cheating yourself because you most certainly will not be able to read the questions yourself when taking the real exam. On the real exam, you must answer exclusively based upon what you hear. If you want to succeed on the actual test, you absolutely must practice the same way – by having the questions read to you.

Unfortunately, we do not all have a friend or relative conveniently at hand to read the questions to us at a moment's notice and at any hour of the day or night. In response to recurring requests, Pathfinder Distributing Co. has produced an **Oral Directions Practice Tests CD** containing the complete Following Oral Instructions sections from all six practice tests in your book. Recorded by the author, Mr. T. W. Parnell, this CD presents the questions professionally and realistically at the proper pace and with proper diction. This CD makes practicing the Following Oral Directions section convenient anytime and anywhere you choose – you are no longer dependent on someone else's schedule or whims. For more details on the Oral Instructions Practice Tests CD and ordering information, see the order form at the back of your book.

Following Oral Instructions Strategy #12   **Practice cannot be stressed enough, and you cannot practice too much.** Practice is the key to mastering your strategies, to developing the talent of listening attentively, and to train yourself to simply follow instructions without attempting to rationalize what you hear.

Can you make notes or marks during the Following Oral Instructions Section?
Yes. The questions you hear will specifically instruct you to make certain marks and to write certain number or letters in the test booklet. It will be impossible to find the correct answers without doing so.

Speed Marking
A Revolutionary Breakthrough in Test Taking Technology

Pathfinder has brought together science and common sense to create a breakthrough in test taking technology. We are proud to announce the release of our new "Postal Exam Speed Marking System." Research indicates that this system, which combines unique strategies with a specially designed test taking pencil, can more than double your marking speed.

As you should have discovered by now, speed means everything on the Postal exam. You have been encouraged to sacrifice a measure of accuracy in favor of speed. It has been proven to you that knowledge is of no value without sufficient speed to answer all the questions within the allotted time period. You have been instructed to practice zealously to develop the level of speed required. Most of the strategies suggested serve a single purpose – to increase your speed.

What if you were offered a magic tool that would more than double your speed at marking answers? Imagine the extra time you would have to answer more questions --- to make more points --- to achieve the highest possible score! Sure, we're only talking about saving a second or two per question. But, those seconds add up to minutes, which add up to points, which add up to exam scores, which make or break Postal careers. That's what this book is all about – adding points to your exam score to increase your chance of success. To quote a point made earlier in the book: "Any tool that adds points to your score is incredibly valuable." So, how does this magic system work? Like this …

Speed Marking Strategy #1 **Use the ergonomically designed "Speed Pencil"** A few years ago, I discovered a phenomenal new pencil ideal for taking standardized tests. Since this uncommon new pencil, which we have nicknamed the "Speed Pencil," is not readily available at traditional retail outlets, Pathfinder Distributing Company has obtained a distributorship and has made it available to Postal exam applicants as part of a Speed Marking System. See the order form at the back of the book for details. Features of this revolutionary new test-taking tool include:

- *An oversize tripod grip with ergonomically designed contact points.* Benefits include relaxed hand posture, efficient muscle action, more comfort, enhanced control, and less fatigue. The Speed Pencil seems to become an extension of your hand rather than a burdensome writing implement.

- *A larger diameter number 2 graphite lead nearly double the size of regular pencils.* The broader marking surface enables you to darken answers more than twice as fast.

- *Triangular longitudinal design to avoid roll-away's.* Nothing is more frustrating than chasing roll-away pencils under tables and across floors when you are supposed to be answering questions on a rigidly timed test. Normal pencils with their more rounded construction seem to roll away at every chance. This benefit may sound trivial at first, but it can literally make the difference between success and failure. I'm embarrassed to admit that this roll-away disaster has happened to me. Once, before discovering the Speed Pencil, I was taking the exam with standard pencils. As insurance, I had four pencils with me. In the middle of the exam, I accidentally dropped the pencil I was using. Not only did this pencil roll off the table, in the process it bumped into my spare pencils, and they rolled off as well. So, off I go literally chasing pencils under tables and across floors while everyone else was marking answers. Fortunately, I was taking the exam, as I typically do, to stay abreast of any new developments. Had I been serious about the exam and about pursuing a Postal career, such an incident would have resulted in certain failure. Since discovering the Speed Pencil, the roll-away disaster has not happened to me again – nor do I expect it to.

Speed Marking Strategy #2 **Use a dulled pencil.** The scheduling packet sent to you will instruct you to bring two number 2 lead pencils. What condition will you want these pencils to be in? Sharp, of course! Frequently, they have extra pencils available at the test site for applicants who forget their own pencils or for applicants who break the lead on their own pencils. What condition will these extra pencils be in? Sharp, of course! We have always been taught to use a freshly sharpened pencil, and we prefer to use a freshly sharpened pencil. So, we will naturally bring sharp pencils with us to the test. If offered extras at the test site from a box of loose pencils, which will we choose? The sharpest ones we can find, of course.

This is exactly and precisely the opposite of what we should do. Picture in your mind a fine point ink pen and a broad tipped marker. If you wanted to darken a large circle in a hurry, which would you use? Which would enable you to darken a given area faster? The broad tipped marker, of course, because of its larger marking surface. It would take forever to darken a large circle with a fine point pen. The same principle holds true for pencils. Picture a freshly sharpened pencil and one with a dulled and blunted lead. Which one has a broader marking surface? Which one will darken a circle quicker? Which one will mark answers faster on your exam? The one with the dulled and blunted lead, of course. This is your second Speed Marking Strategy --- **make sure your pencil, preferably your "Speed Pencil", has a dulled and blunted point.** If offered extras, choose dulled ones. If only sharpened pencils are available, immediately dull them. A sharp pencil is you worst enemy.

Speed Marking Strategy #3 **Use an enhanced pencil position and grasp.** The following two techniques can significantly increase your speed. Most people find these techniques to be lifesavers. Practicing these techniques will improve your success with them and will make them become second nature for you.

- **The first strategy is to hold the pencil in a more horizontal than vertical position so that you can use the larger and broader side of the pencil lead, rather than the point, as your marking surface** as displayed in the below illustration. Experiment with different angles of contact to find which works best for you. Using the side of the pencil lead, rather than the point, as your contact surface dramatically increases your speed at marking answers.

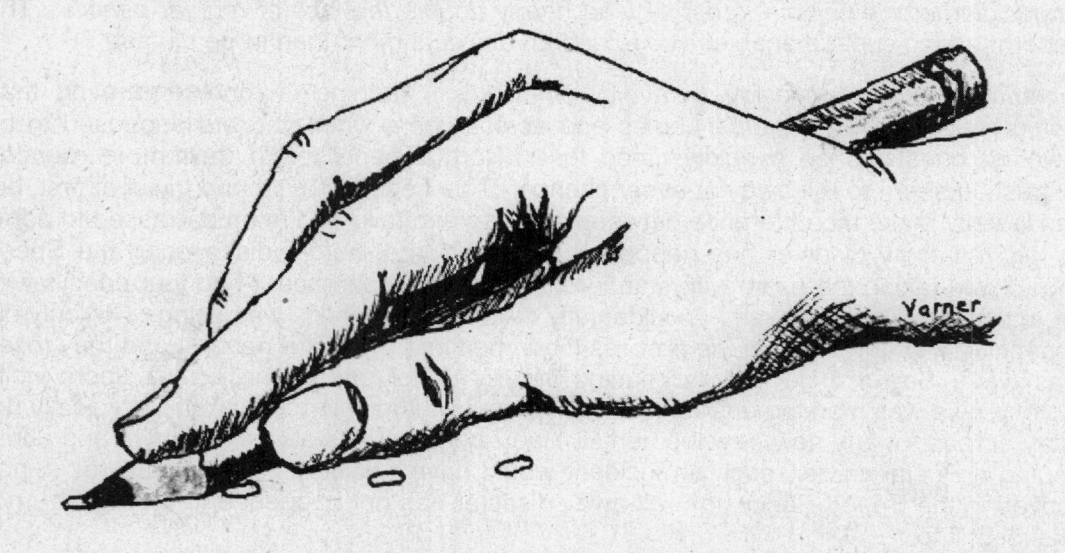

- **The second strategy is to grasp the pencil each time you pick it up so that your thumb (or forefinger) is always touching the side with the printing on it** – usually the manufacturer's name and/or logo. Pick it up and hold it the very same way each time so that you consistently use the same broad and flattened edge as your contact surface. When laying the pencil down, always place it with the printed side facing up so that you can more easily grasp it properly when picking it up again. Most people tend to rotate the pencil within their grasp as they write with it, which in turn tends preserve the lead's conical point. In a normal writing situation, this is logical. However, there is nothing normal or logical about this test. By consistently holding the pencil in the same position all the time as suggested, you maintain the integrity of the dulled and flattened contact point, and you even improve and broaden the contact surface by constant contact with the paper at the same point.

Speed Marking Strategy #4   **Use only two to three revolutions of your pencil to darken each answer.** With the speed pencil, you may be able to do so in only one or two revolutions. With practice and by using the above strategies, this is indeed possible. What's more – it is necessary in order to answer all the questions within the time allowed. You do not have time to endlessly scribble around and around inside the circle to assure that you have darkened every nook and cranny. Your goal is to darken 80% to 90% of the circle. The scanner that scores your test will register an answer that is 80% to 90% darkened. The extra time and effort to try for 100% is not necessary. But, an answer darkened only 50% to 60% may not register. Your goal should be 80% to 90%.

As you have learned, speed is particularly critical on the Address Checking and Address Memory sections. You will want to use your speed marking strategies on those sections for sure. Speed is important, but not quite as imperative, on the Number Series and the Following Oral Instructions sections. As a matter of fact, the marking you do on the latter two sections is closer to normal writing than it is on the first two. Accordingly, on the Number Series and the Following Oral Instructions sections, it will not hurt to hold your pencil in a more normal fashion or to choose a sharper pencil with which to work.

Test Preparation Support

The instructions, strategies, and concepts discussed in this guide are presented in the simplest of fashions to assure full understanding. If a particular subject seems confusing, reviewing that subject and/or reading over that section again will usually clear up any confusion. You may want to review the subject more than once – perhaps after each practice test. Experiencing a particular subject on a practice test is frequently the best way to grasp it. If, after attempting these measures, you are still experiencing difficulty, visit our web site at www.postalexam.com. A wealth of information on Postal exams and answers to frequently asked questions are presented on our site. For assistance with particularly urgent matters that can't be resolved by the above steps, contact us by E-mail at support@pathfinderdc.com or call 281-259-2302 Monday through Friday (except holidays) from 8:00 AM to 5:00 PM in the Central Time Zone. To receive such assistance, you must confirm your status as, and register as, a Pathfinder customer by providing the code number from your individual book. This code number can be found at the bottom of page 3, the title page. When contacting us by E-mail, please include your code number in the message. When contacting us by phone, please have your book in hand in order to provide the code number.

COMPLETE PRACTICE TEST #1

This practice test contains samples of all four sections of the actual exam. The instructions given are similar to those on the actual exam. The format of this practice test is identical to that of the actual exam. Where pertinent, hints are given about your test taking strategies. Of course, these hints will not appear on the actual exam.

It is imperative that you take this practice test in as realistic a fashion as possible. **Your practice will have no value unless it is done realistically.** Therefore, you must precisely time yourself on the Address Checking, Address Memory, and Number Series sections. Our Timed Practice Test CD is a convenient way to practice realistically and time yourself precisely. Also, you must either listen to the Following Oral Instructions questions on our Oral Instructions Practice Tests CD or have someone read them to you – *do not read the questions yourself!* The Following Oral Instructions questions can be found in the back of your book if someone will be reading them to you.

To take this practice test, first turn to the back of your book and carefully tear out one of the **Complete Practice Test Answer Sheets.** Mark the answers to the scored segments of the practice test on this answer sheet. (Remember, of the seven segments on the Address Memory Section, only the final one is scored. Accordingly, you should mark answers for only the final Address Memory segment on your Complete Practice Test Answer Sheet. The other segments of the Address Memory Section that call for answers have accompanying sample answer sheets where you should mark answers.)

The correct answers are provided in the back of your book. Immediately upon completing this practice test, **it is imperative that you score each section** using the formulas given under the Sections of the Exam heading in your book. Scoring is necessary in order to gauge your progress and to identify your individual areas of weakness that may need extra attention.

After completing and scoring each practice test, move on to the next. **After finishing all six complete practice tests and the extra Address Checking practice tests as instructed, you should be prepared for the actual exam.** If you feel the need to practice more, repeat as many of the practice tests as you like. After that much practice, the questions will likely have become a confusing blur in your mind. It is highly unlikely that you will be able to remember many of the individual questions or answers. Therefore, you should be able to gain practice value from the exercises even though you have already taken them once.

Do not look over the practice test questions until you are ready to start – usually meaning until you have set a timer for the allotted period of time. Similarly, after completing one section of the practice test, do not look over the next one until your are ready to start it. Likewise, stop working and put down your pencil immediately when the allotted period of time has expired. As has been emphasized before but cannot be emphasized enough, your practice is of absolutely no value unless it is done realistically. Also, you must train yourself (1) to not open your test booklet or pick up your pencil until instructed to do so and (2) to close your booklet and put down your pencil immediately upon being so instructed. The Postal Service has a zero tolerance policy on these matters. Any variance may be viewed as cheating and may result in your disqualification.

Good luck on your practice test, and even better luck on your actual exam!

52

COMPLETE PRACTICE TEST #1
Part A – Address Checking

Directions

In this part of the test, you will have to decide whether two addresses are alike or different. You will have 6 minutes to answer 95 questions. Each question consists of a pair of addresses. If the two addresses in the pair are exactly alike in every way, darken the oval with the letter "A" for _Alike_. If the two addresses are different in any way, darken the oval with the letter "D" for _Different_. Mark your answers on the Complete Practice Test Answer Sheet in the section entitled Address Checking.

Turn the page and begin when you are prepared to time yourself for precisely 6 minutes.

Note: You will notice that this section of your practice test is spread across two pages. This is the exact same format that you will actually experience on the Address Checking section of the real exam. For economy and convenience, other study guides frequently condense the two pages of this section down to only one. You will also notice that the Address Checking questions are presented in a font, or type of print, that is different from the rest of the book. This font matches what is actually used on the real exam, and, as you will see, it makes this section even more challenging. However, it is imperative that you practice realistically and that you become acquainted with and comfortable with the actual format of the exam. We have accordingly formatted this practice test realistically for your benefit.

Hint: Remember your strategies:
- _Pace yourself for speed and accuracy – <u>emphasis on speed</u>!_
- _Use one glance-over for easier/shorter addresses._
- _Use two glance-over's for harder/longer addresses._
- _Never make a third pass or glance-over!_
- _Overlap the answer sheet & the questions to keep them as close together as possible._
- _Use your extra pencil, your hand, or your fingers to mark/keep your place._
- _Use your Speed Pencil and your Speed Marking strategies for much greater speed._

COMPLETE PRACTICE TEST #1
Part A – Address Checking

1.	5643 52nd St.	5643 53rd St.

1. 5643 52nd St. | 5643 53rd St.
2. 1111 Liegh Dr. | 1111 Liegh Dr.
3. Oak Ridge, Mn. 44777 | Oak Ridge, Mn. 44477
4. 832 Rich Ave. NW | 832 Rich Ave. NW
5. 232 Sunset Blvd. | 323 Sunset Blvd.
6. 7463 Washington Cir. | 7464 Washington Cir.
7. Pearl, Ms. | Pearl, Ms.
8. 4532 Pecan Village Apt. | 4532 Pecan Village Apt.
9. 9356 Main Drive West | 9356 Main Drive East
10. 601 W Oklahoma | 601 W Oklahoma
11. Lake Falls, Nev. 98007 | Lake Falls, Nev. 98007
12. Newton, W. Va. | Newton, W. Va.
13. 8729 East Randall St. | 8792 East Randall St.
14. 877 39th Ave. | 877 39th Ave.
15. 218 Pinelawn NW | 218 Pinlawn NW
16. 1940 Dewey Cir. | 1940 Dewey Cir.
17. Rolling Fork, S.D. 44532 | Rolling Fork, S.D. 44532
18. 3022 Thomas Jefferson St. | 3202 Thomas Jefferson St.
19. 10013 Tower Bridge Rd. | 10013 Tower Bridge Rd.
20. 7113 Raggio Lane | 7113 Raggio Lane
21. 1009 Lynn Ave. | 1009 Lyne Ave.
22. 768 Vandanburg NW | 768 Vandanburg NW
23. Marshal, Tex. 70043 | Marshal, Tex. 70034
24. 204-A Fechet Dr. | 204-A Fechet Dr.
25. 324 Harmon Circle | 323 Harmin Circle
26. Twin Oaks, Ark. 70054 | Twin Oaks, Ark. 70054
27. 305 Parkview Dr. | 305 Parkview Dr.
28. 205-B Bay Springs Lane | 205-B Bay Sprins Lane
29. Porter, Pa. 22087 | Porter, Pa. 22087
30. 1335 Lafayette Dr. | 1335 Lafayette Dr.
31. 6212 North St. | 6212 North St.
32. 211 Brynmawr Av. | 211 Brymnawr Av.
33. 5908 Gulf Stream | 5980 Gulf Stream
34. Anderson, Ala. 46477 | Anderson, Alk. 46477
35. 787 St. George Square | 787 St. George Square
36. Beauvoir Manor Apt. SW | Beauvoir Manor Apt. SE
37. Lee, Ind. 77889 | Lee, Ind. 77889
38. 100 Van Buren Ave. | 100 Van Buren Ave.
39. 2234 Bilmarsan Dr. | 2234 Bilmaran Dr.
40. 212 Mocking Bird Rd. | 212 Mocking Bird Rd.
41. 1343 West 9th Ave. | 1434 West 9th Ave.
42. 209 Jeff Davis Ave. | 209 Jeff Savis Ave.
43. 4934 Running Brook Farms | 4934 Running Brook Farms
44. New Haven, Conn. 06515 | New Haven, Conn. 06515
45. 7449 53rd St. NW | 7449 53rd St. SW
46. Normal, Ala. 35762 | Normal, Ala. 34567
47. 4408 W. Railroad St. | 4408 W. Railroad St.
48. 97883 North 15th St. | 97883 North 15th St.

49.	3323 Court House Rd.	3232 Court House Rd.
50.	Mt. St. Helen NE	Mt. St. Helen NW
51.	454 Maple Grove Blvd.	454 Maple Grove Blvd.
52.	Shakopee, Minn. 47484	Shakopee, Minn. 47494
53.	#1 Shell Square	#1 Shell Squares
54.	8583 Northridge	3583 Northridge
55.	101 McGoey SE	101 McGoey SE
56.	Rolling Hills, Wyo. 23785	Rolling Hills, Wyo. 32785
57.	2004 West Brooklyn Ave.	2804 West Brooklyn Ave.
58.	672 Beatline	673 Beatline
59.	5944 Millroad St.	5944 Millroad SW
60.	212 Klondyke Rd.	212 Klondyke Dr.
61.	4767 Rushing Wave	4767 Rushing Wave
62.	66672 Wekls	66627 Wekls
63.	Rainbow Inn South	Rainbow End South
64.	3424 Cook Drive	3424 Cook Drive
65.	8823 Railway	8823 Railway
66.	Milkwaukee, Wis.	Milkwaukee, Wis.
67.	1422 North Gate S	1422 North Gate N
68.	2345 97th Ave.	2435 97th Ave.
69.	8456 Alabama St.	8436 Alabama St.
70.	Sunnydale, MO	Sunnydale, MI
71.	0672 Rich Lane	672 Rich Mane
72.	1234 Rosewood	1234 Rosewood
73.	98 Dogg Cove	889 Dogg Cove
74.	Pearl Center SSW	Pearl Center SWS
75.	7455 Galloway	7455 Galloway
76.	433 Old Pass Rd.	433 Old Pass Rd.
77.	1111Gardendale	11111 Gardendale
78.	3573 St. Charles Ave.	3573 Charles Ave.
79.	San Cosa del Ray	San Coas del Ray
80.	6340 Alexander Rd.	6340 Alexander Rd.
81.	411 Porche SW	411 Porche SW
82.	Bloomington NW	Bloomington N
83.	3332 Wishing Dr.	3332 Wishing Dr.
84.	Waveland, OR 96643	Waveland, OR 96643
85.	6632 Taylor	3212 Taylor
86.	5598 Longview Rd.	5598 Lonview Rd.
87.	213 Bilmarsan Dr.	213 Bilmarsan Dr.
88.	6244 Yorkshire Lane	6422 Yorkshire Lande
89.	225 Acacia Av	225 Acacia Av
90.	Rustwood, Mass. 24665	Rustwood, Mass. 24665
91.	739 Nixon Rd.	739 Mixon Rd.
92.	8654 Lakelawn Blvd	8654 Lakelawn Blvd
93.	11000 Tucker rd	1100 Tucker rd
94.	1686 Bilglade	1686 Bilglade
95.	14 Back Bay	14 Black Bay

COMPLETE PRACTICE TEST #1
Part B – Address Memory

Directions

In this part of the test, you will have to memorize the locations of 25 addresses in five boxes. During this section, you will have several study periods and practice exercises to help you memorize the location of the addresses shown in the five boxes. Answer the questions by darkening the oval containing the letter (A, B, C, D, or E) of the box in which the address is located – Box A, Box B, Box C, Box D, or Box E. At the end of each segment, you will be given instructions on how and where to continue. After completing six preliminary segments, the actual test will be given as segment #7.

Turn the page to begin Segment #1.

Note: You will notice on your practice test that the various segments of the Address Memory section are spread across two pages. Where applicable, the five boxes, the 88 questions, and/or the sample answer sheets are spread across two pages. This is the same format that you will experience on most segments of the Address Memory section on the actual exam. For economy and convenience, other study guides frequently condense the two pages down to only one. However, it is imperative that you practice realistically and that you become acquainted with and comfortable with the actual format of the exam. We have accordingly formatted this practice test realistically for your benefit.

Hint: Remember your strategies:
- *Memorize horizontally.*
- *Memorize only Boxes A, B, C, and D.*
- *You can correctly answer all Box E questions by the process of elimination.*
- *Use the Second Digit Strategy to memorize the number addresses.*
- *Use imagery/association to memorize the word addresses.*
- *Overlap the answer sheet & the questions to keep them as close together as possible.*
- *Use your extra pencil, your hand, or your fingers to mark/keep your place.*
- *Use your Speed Pencil and your Speed Marking strategies for much greater speed.*

COMPLETE PRACTICE TEST #1
Part B – Address Memory – Segment #1

Directions

Five sample boxes, each containing five addresses, and five sample questions about these boxes are given on the following two pages. The purpose of this small exercise is simply to acquaint you with the format of this section and with how the questions should be answered. The first two sample questions are answered for you. You are to spend three minutes becoming acquainted with the format and answering sample questions 3, 4, and 5. After completing Segment #1, turn to Segment #2 for further instructions.

Turn the page and begin when you are prepared to time yourself for precisely three minutes.

Hint: Remember your strategies! This segment is not scored, so do not take the sample questions seriously. Instead, mark random answers and use the three minutes to study and memorize the addresses. The sample boxes and addresses in this segment are the very same ones that will be repeated throughout this section of the exam.

A	B	C
4700-5599 Camp	6800-6999 Camp	5600-6499 Camp
Oak	Broad	State
5600-6499 Sarah	6500-6799 Sarah	6800-6999 Sarah
Magnolia	Dearman	Cox
4400-4699 Lang	5600-6499 Lang	6500-6799 Lang

1. 4400-4699 Sarah   Ⓐ Ⓑ Ⓒ ⬤ Ⓔ
This address came from Box D, so we sill darken the oval with the letter D.

2. Dearman   Ⓐ ⬤ Ⓒ Ⓓ Ⓔ
This address came from Box B, so we will darken the oval with the letter B.

3. Oak   Ⓐ Ⓑ Ⓒ Ⓓ Ⓔ
Now that you know how to answer, you do questions 3, 4, and 5.

4. 6500-6799 Camp   Ⓐ Ⓑ Ⓒ Ⓓ Ⓔ

5. 5600-6499 Camp   Ⓐ Ⓑ Ⓒ Ⓓ Ⓔ

The correct answers are D, B, A, D, and C.

D	E
6500-6799 Camp Orchid	4400-4699 Camp Forest
4400-4699 Sarah Ocean	4700-5599 Sarah Pittman
4700-5599 Lang	6800-6999 Lang

62

COMPLETE PRACTICE TEST #1
Part B – Address Memory – Segment #2

Directions

In this segment, you are given three minutes to study and memorize the addresses. There are no questions to answer in this segment – it is a study period only. However, on the actual exam, the boxes are not reprinted for your use. Instead, you are instructed to turn back to Address Memory Segment #1 on the preceding pages of the exam and to spend three minutes studying the boxes displayed there. So, we will do the very same on this practice test. After studying for three minutes, turn to Segment #3 for directions on how to continue the Address Memory Section of the exam.

Begin studying when you are prepared to time yourself for precisely three minutes.

COMPLETE PRACTICE TEST #1
Part B – Address Memory – Segment #3

Directions

In this segment you have three minutes to attempt answering 88 questions. You are to try to answer from memory, but the boxes are shown if you need to refer to them. Your answers are to be marked on the sample answer sheet at the bottom of the pages of Segment #3 – do not use the Compete Practice Test Answer Sheet for this segment. After completing this segment, turn to Segment #4 for further instructions.

Turn the page and begin when you are prepared to time yourself for precisely three minutes.

Hint: Remember your strategies! This segment is not scored, so do not take the questions seriously. Instead, mark a handful of random answers and use the three minutes to study and memorize the addresses.

A	B	C
4700-5599 Camp	6800-6999 Camp	5600-6499 Camp
Oak	Broad	State
5600-6499 Sarah	6500-6799 Sarah	6800-6999 Sarah
Magnolia	Dearman	Cox
4400-4699 Lang	5600-6499 Lang	6500-6799 Lang

1. 5600-6499 Lang
2. Forest
3. State
4. 4400-4699 Sarah
5. 4700-5599 Lang
6. Magnolia
7. Broad
8. 4400-4699 Lang

9. 4400-4699 Camp
10. 4700-5599 Camp
11. Pittman
12. 6800-6999 Lang
13. 6500-6799 Camp
14. Ocean
15. Cox
16. 4700-5599 Sarah

17. Oak
18. 5600-6499 Camp
19. 5600-6499 Sarah
20. Orchid
21. 6800-6999 Camp
22. 4400-4699 Sarah
23. 6500-6799 Sarah
24. 5600-6499 Lang

25. Oak
26. Forest
27. 5600-6499 Camp
28. Broad
29. 5600-6499 Sarah
30. Dearman
31. 6500-6799 Lang
32. Pittman

33. 4700-5599 Sarah
34. 5600-6499 Lang
35. Magnolia
36. Cox
37. 6800-6999 Lang
38. 6500-6799 Camp
39. 4400-4699 Camp
40. 6800-6999 Sarah

41. 4700-5599 Camp
42. Forest
43. Cox
44. Dearman
45. 5600-6499 Camp
46. State
47. 4400-4699 Lang
48. Magnolia

1 Ⓐ Ⓑ Ⓒ Ⓓ Ⓔ
2 Ⓐ Ⓑ Ⓒ Ⓓ Ⓔ
3 Ⓐ Ⓑ Ⓒ Ⓓ Ⓔ
4 Ⓐ Ⓑ Ⓒ Ⓓ Ⓔ
5 Ⓐ Ⓑ Ⓒ Ⓓ Ⓔ
6 Ⓐ Ⓑ Ⓒ Ⓓ Ⓔ
7 Ⓐ Ⓑ Ⓒ Ⓓ Ⓔ
8 Ⓐ Ⓑ Ⓒ Ⓓ Ⓔ
9 Ⓐ Ⓑ Ⓒ Ⓓ Ⓔ
10 Ⓐ Ⓑ Ⓒ Ⓓ Ⓔ
11 Ⓐ Ⓑ Ⓒ Ⓓ Ⓔ
12 Ⓐ Ⓑ Ⓒ Ⓓ Ⓔ
13 Ⓐ Ⓑ Ⓒ Ⓓ Ⓔ
14 Ⓐ Ⓑ Ⓒ Ⓓ Ⓔ
15 Ⓐ Ⓑ Ⓒ Ⓓ Ⓔ
16 Ⓐ Ⓑ Ⓒ Ⓓ Ⓔ

17 Ⓐ Ⓑ Ⓒ Ⓓ Ⓔ
18 Ⓐ Ⓑ Ⓒ Ⓓ Ⓔ
19 Ⓐ Ⓑ Ⓒ Ⓓ Ⓔ
20 Ⓐ Ⓑ Ⓒ Ⓓ Ⓔ
21 Ⓐ Ⓑ Ⓒ Ⓓ Ⓔ
22 Ⓐ Ⓑ Ⓒ Ⓓ Ⓔ
23 Ⓐ Ⓑ Ⓒ Ⓓ Ⓔ
24 Ⓐ Ⓑ Ⓒ Ⓓ Ⓔ
25 Ⓐ Ⓑ Ⓒ Ⓓ Ⓔ
26 Ⓐ Ⓑ Ⓒ Ⓓ Ⓔ
27 Ⓐ Ⓑ Ⓒ Ⓓ Ⓔ
28 Ⓐ Ⓑ Ⓒ Ⓓ Ⓔ
29 Ⓐ Ⓑ Ⓒ Ⓓ Ⓔ
30 Ⓐ Ⓑ Ⓒ Ⓓ Ⓔ
31 Ⓐ Ⓑ Ⓒ Ⓓ Ⓔ
32 Ⓐ Ⓑ Ⓒ Ⓓ Ⓔ

33 Ⓐ Ⓑ Ⓒ Ⓓ Ⓔ
34 Ⓐ Ⓑ Ⓒ Ⓓ Ⓔ
35 Ⓐ Ⓑ Ⓒ Ⓓ Ⓔ
36 Ⓐ Ⓑ Ⓒ Ⓓ Ⓔ
37 Ⓐ Ⓑ Ⓒ Ⓓ Ⓔ
38 Ⓐ Ⓑ Ⓒ Ⓓ Ⓔ
39 Ⓐ Ⓑ Ⓒ Ⓓ Ⓔ
40 Ⓐ Ⓑ Ⓒ Ⓓ Ⓔ
41 Ⓐ Ⓑ Ⓒ Ⓓ Ⓔ
42 Ⓐ Ⓑ Ⓒ Ⓓ Ⓔ
43 Ⓐ Ⓑ Ⓒ Ⓓ Ⓔ
44 Ⓐ Ⓑ Ⓒ Ⓓ Ⓔ
45 Ⓐ Ⓑ Ⓒ Ⓓ Ⓔ
46 Ⓐ Ⓑ Ⓒ Ⓓ Ⓔ
47 Ⓐ Ⓑ Ⓒ Ⓓ Ⓔ
48 Ⓐ Ⓑ Ⓒ Ⓓ Ⓔ

D	E
6500-6799 Camp	4400-4699 Camp
Orchid	Forest
4400-4699 Sarah	4700-5599 Sarah
Ocean	Pittman
4700-5599 Lang	6800-6999 Lang

49. Ocean
50. 6500-6799 Lang
51. 4400-4699 Sarah
52. 6800-6999 Camp
53. 4400-4699 Camp
54. Broad
55. Orchid
56. 5600-6499 Lang

57. 4700-5599 Sarah
58. Pittman
59. 5600-6499 Sarah
60. 6800-6999 Sarah
61. Forest
62. Cox
63. 6500-6799 Camp
64. 5600-6499 Camp

65. 4400-4699 Sarah
66. Pittman
67. Cox
68. 6800-6999 Camp
69. 4700-5599 Camp
70. Forest
71. 4400-4699 Sarah
72. State

73. 6500-6799 Sarah
74. 5600-6499 Lang
75. 5600-6499 Camp
76. Broad
77. Magnolia
78. Oak
79. Pittman
80. 5600-6499 Sarah

81. 4400-4699 Camp
82. 4700-5599 Sarah
83. Ocean
84. State
85. 4400-4699 Lang
86. 6500-6799 Lang
87. Dearman
88. Orchid

49. Ⓐ Ⓑ Ⓒ Ⓓ Ⓔ
50. Ⓐ Ⓑ Ⓒ Ⓓ Ⓔ
51. Ⓐ Ⓑ Ⓒ Ⓓ Ⓔ
52. Ⓐ Ⓑ Ⓒ Ⓓ Ⓔ
53. Ⓐ Ⓑ Ⓒ Ⓓ Ⓔ
54. Ⓐ Ⓑ Ⓒ Ⓓ Ⓔ
55. Ⓐ Ⓑ Ⓒ Ⓓ Ⓔ
56. Ⓐ Ⓑ Ⓒ Ⓓ Ⓔ

57. Ⓐ Ⓑ Ⓒ Ⓓ Ⓔ
58. Ⓐ Ⓑ Ⓒ Ⓓ Ⓔ
59. Ⓐ Ⓑ Ⓒ Ⓓ Ⓔ
60. Ⓐ Ⓑ Ⓒ Ⓓ Ⓔ
61. Ⓐ Ⓑ Ⓒ Ⓓ Ⓔ
62. Ⓐ Ⓑ Ⓒ Ⓓ Ⓔ
63. Ⓐ Ⓑ Ⓒ Ⓓ Ⓔ
64. Ⓐ Ⓑ Ⓒ Ⓓ Ⓔ

65. Ⓐ Ⓑ Ⓒ Ⓓ Ⓔ
66. Ⓐ Ⓑ Ⓒ Ⓓ Ⓔ
67. Ⓐ Ⓑ Ⓒ Ⓓ Ⓔ
68. Ⓐ Ⓑ Ⓒ Ⓓ Ⓔ
69. Ⓐ Ⓑ Ⓒ Ⓓ Ⓔ
70. Ⓐ Ⓑ Ⓒ Ⓓ Ⓔ
71. Ⓐ Ⓑ Ⓒ Ⓓ Ⓔ
72. Ⓐ Ⓑ Ⓒ Ⓓ Ⓔ

73. Ⓐ Ⓑ Ⓒ Ⓓ Ⓔ
74. Ⓐ Ⓑ Ⓒ Ⓓ Ⓔ
75. Ⓐ Ⓑ Ⓒ Ⓓ Ⓔ
76. Ⓐ Ⓑ Ⓒ Ⓓ Ⓔ
77. Ⓐ Ⓑ Ⓒ Ⓓ Ⓔ
78. Ⓐ Ⓑ Ⓒ Ⓓ Ⓔ
79. Ⓐ Ⓑ Ⓒ Ⓓ Ⓔ
80. Ⓐ Ⓑ Ⓒ Ⓓ Ⓔ

81. Ⓐ Ⓑ Ⓒ Ⓓ Ⓔ
82. Ⓐ Ⓑ Ⓒ Ⓓ Ⓔ
83. Ⓐ Ⓑ Ⓒ Ⓓ Ⓔ
84. Ⓐ Ⓑ Ⓒ Ⓓ Ⓔ
85. Ⓐ Ⓑ Ⓒ Ⓓ Ⓔ
86. Ⓐ Ⓑ Ⓒ Ⓓ Ⓔ
87. Ⓐ Ⓑ Ⓒ Ⓓ Ⓔ
88. Ⓐ Ⓑ Ⓒ Ⓓ Ⓔ

COMPLETE PRACTICE TEST #1
Part B – Address Memory – Segment #4

Directions

In this segment you have three minutes to attempt answering 88 questions. You must answer from memory. The boxes are not shown. Your answers are to be marked on the sample answer sheet at the bottom of the pages of Segment #4 – do not use the Compete Practice Test Answer Sheet for this segment. After completing this segment, turn to Segment #5 for further instructions.

Turn the page and begin when you are prepared to time yourself for precisely three minutes.

Hint: Remember, this segment is not scored, so you should not worry about your inability to answer all 88 questions, or your inability to answer all of them accurately, in only three minutes. Neither task is really possible in only three minutes. However, this is an ideal opportunity for you to test how well you have mastered your strategies and memorization so far. By sincerely trying to answer the questions, you can identify the areas where you are weaker and where you need to apply more effort.

1. 4400-4699 Sarah
2. Orchid
3. Oak
4. 6500-6799 Camp
5. 5600-6499 Camp
6. Ocean
7. 6800-6999 Lang
8. Dearman

9. 6500-6799 Lang
10. 4400-4699 Lang
11. State
12. Ocean
13. 4400-4699 Sarah
14. 4400-4699 Camp
15. 5600-6499 Sarah
16. Pittman

17. Oak
18. Magnolia
19. Broad
20. 5600-6499 Camp
21. 5600-6499 Lang
22. 6500-6799 Sarah
23. Forest
24. 4700-5599 Camp

25. 6800-6999 Camp
26. Cox
27. Pittman
28. 4400-4699 Sarah
29. 5600-6499 Camp
30. 6500-6799 Camp
31. Cox
32. Forest

33. 6800-6999 Sarah
34. 5600-6499 Sarah
35. Pittman
36. 4700-5599 Sarah
37. 6500-6799 Lang
38. Orchid
39. Broad
40. 4400-4699 Camp

41. 6800-6999 Camp
42. 4400-4699 Sarah
43. 4700-5599 Camp
44. Ocean
45. Magnolia
46. 4400-4699 Lang
47. State
48. 5600-6499 Camp

1 Ⓐ Ⓑ Ⓒ Ⓓ Ⓔ
2 Ⓐ Ⓑ Ⓒ Ⓓ Ⓔ
3 Ⓐ Ⓑ Ⓒ Ⓓ Ⓔ
4 Ⓐ Ⓑ Ⓒ Ⓓ Ⓔ
5 Ⓐ Ⓑ Ⓒ Ⓓ Ⓔ
6 Ⓐ Ⓑ Ⓒ Ⓓ Ⓔ
7 Ⓐ Ⓑ Ⓒ Ⓓ Ⓔ
8 Ⓐ Ⓑ Ⓒ Ⓓ Ⓔ

9 Ⓐ Ⓑ Ⓒ Ⓓ Ⓔ
10 Ⓐ Ⓑ Ⓒ Ⓓ Ⓔ
11 Ⓐ Ⓑ Ⓒ Ⓓ Ⓔ
12 Ⓐ Ⓑ Ⓒ Ⓓ Ⓔ
13 Ⓐ Ⓑ Ⓒ Ⓓ Ⓔ
14 Ⓐ Ⓑ Ⓒ Ⓓ Ⓔ
15 Ⓐ Ⓑ Ⓒ Ⓓ Ⓔ
16 Ⓐ Ⓑ Ⓒ Ⓓ Ⓔ

17 Ⓐ Ⓑ Ⓒ Ⓓ Ⓔ
18 Ⓐ Ⓑ Ⓒ Ⓓ Ⓔ
19 Ⓐ Ⓑ Ⓒ Ⓓ Ⓔ
20 Ⓐ Ⓑ Ⓒ Ⓓ Ⓔ
21 Ⓐ Ⓑ Ⓒ Ⓓ Ⓔ
22 Ⓐ Ⓑ Ⓒ Ⓓ Ⓔ
23 Ⓐ Ⓑ Ⓒ Ⓓ Ⓔ
24 Ⓐ Ⓑ Ⓒ Ⓓ Ⓔ

25 Ⓐ Ⓑ Ⓒ Ⓓ Ⓔ
26 Ⓐ Ⓑ Ⓒ Ⓓ Ⓔ
27 Ⓐ Ⓑ Ⓒ Ⓓ Ⓔ
28 Ⓐ Ⓑ Ⓒ Ⓓ Ⓔ
29 Ⓐ Ⓑ Ⓒ Ⓓ Ⓔ
30 Ⓐ Ⓑ Ⓒ Ⓓ Ⓔ
31 Ⓐ Ⓑ Ⓒ Ⓓ Ⓔ
32 Ⓐ Ⓑ Ⓒ Ⓓ Ⓔ

33 Ⓐ Ⓑ Ⓒ Ⓓ Ⓔ
34 Ⓐ Ⓑ Ⓒ Ⓓ Ⓔ
35 Ⓐ Ⓑ Ⓒ Ⓓ Ⓔ
36 Ⓐ Ⓑ Ⓒ Ⓓ Ⓔ
37 Ⓐ Ⓑ Ⓒ Ⓓ Ⓔ
38 Ⓐ Ⓑ Ⓒ Ⓓ Ⓔ
39 Ⓐ Ⓑ Ⓒ Ⓓ Ⓔ
40 Ⓐ Ⓑ Ⓒ Ⓓ Ⓔ

41 Ⓐ Ⓑ Ⓒ Ⓓ Ⓔ
42 Ⓐ Ⓑ Ⓒ Ⓓ Ⓔ
43 Ⓐ Ⓑ Ⓒ Ⓓ Ⓔ
44 Ⓐ Ⓑ Ⓒ Ⓓ Ⓔ
45 Ⓐ Ⓑ Ⓒ Ⓓ Ⓔ
46 Ⓐ Ⓑ Ⓒ Ⓓ Ⓔ
47 Ⓐ Ⓑ Ⓒ Ⓓ Ⓔ
48 Ⓐ Ⓑ Ⓒ Ⓓ Ⓔ

49. Dearman
50. Cox
51. Forest
52. 4700-5599 Camp
53. 6800-6999 Sarah
54. 4400-4699 Camp
55. 6500-6799 Camp
56. 6800-6999 Lang

57. Cox
58. Magnolia
59. 5600-6499 Lang
60. 4700-5599 Sarah
61. Pittman
62. 6500-6799 Lang
63. Dearman
64. 5600-6499 Sarah

65. Broad
66. 5600-6499 Camp
67. Forest
68. Oak
69. 5600-6499 Lang
70. 6500-6799 Sarah
71. 4400-4699 Sarah
72. 6800-6999 Camp

73. Orchid
74. 5600-6499 Sarah
75. Forest
76. State
77. 4400-4699 Sarah
78. 4700-5599 Lang
79. Magnolia
80. Broad

81. 4400-4699 Lang
82. 4400-4699 Camp
83. 4700-5599 Camp
84. Pittman
85. 6800-6999 Lang
86. 6500-6799 Camp
87. Ocean
88. Cox

49 Ⓐ Ⓑ Ⓒ Ⓓ Ⓔ
50 Ⓐ Ⓑ Ⓒ Ⓓ Ⓔ
51 Ⓐ Ⓑ Ⓒ Ⓓ Ⓔ
52 Ⓐ Ⓑ Ⓒ Ⓓ Ⓔ
53 Ⓐ Ⓑ Ⓒ Ⓓ Ⓔ
54 Ⓐ Ⓑ Ⓒ Ⓓ Ⓔ
55 Ⓐ Ⓑ Ⓒ Ⓓ Ⓔ
56 Ⓐ Ⓑ Ⓒ Ⓓ Ⓔ

57 Ⓐ Ⓑ Ⓒ Ⓓ Ⓔ
58 Ⓐ Ⓑ Ⓒ Ⓓ Ⓔ
59 Ⓐ Ⓑ Ⓒ Ⓓ Ⓔ
60 Ⓐ Ⓑ Ⓒ Ⓓ Ⓔ
61 Ⓐ Ⓑ Ⓒ Ⓓ Ⓔ
62 Ⓐ Ⓑ Ⓒ Ⓓ Ⓔ
63 Ⓐ Ⓑ Ⓒ Ⓓ Ⓔ
64 Ⓐ Ⓑ Ⓒ Ⓓ Ⓔ

65 Ⓐ Ⓑ Ⓒ Ⓓ Ⓔ
66 Ⓐ Ⓑ Ⓒ Ⓓ Ⓔ
67 Ⓐ Ⓑ Ⓒ Ⓓ Ⓔ
68 Ⓐ Ⓑ Ⓒ Ⓓ Ⓔ
69 Ⓐ Ⓑ Ⓒ Ⓓ Ⓔ
70 Ⓐ Ⓑ Ⓒ Ⓓ Ⓔ
71 Ⓐ Ⓑ Ⓒ Ⓓ Ⓔ
72 Ⓐ Ⓑ Ⓒ Ⓓ Ⓔ

73 Ⓐ Ⓑ Ⓒ Ⓓ Ⓔ
74 Ⓐ Ⓑ Ⓒ Ⓓ Ⓔ
75 Ⓐ Ⓑ Ⓒ Ⓓ Ⓔ
76 Ⓐ Ⓑ Ⓒ Ⓓ Ⓔ
77 Ⓐ Ⓑ Ⓒ Ⓓ Ⓔ
78 Ⓐ Ⓑ Ⓒ Ⓓ Ⓔ
79 Ⓐ Ⓑ Ⓒ Ⓓ Ⓔ
80 Ⓐ Ⓑ Ⓒ Ⓓ Ⓔ

81 Ⓐ Ⓑ Ⓒ Ⓓ Ⓔ
82 Ⓐ Ⓑ Ⓒ Ⓓ Ⓔ
83 Ⓐ Ⓑ Ⓒ Ⓓ Ⓔ
84 Ⓐ Ⓑ Ⓒ Ⓓ Ⓔ
85 Ⓐ Ⓑ Ⓒ Ⓓ Ⓔ
86 Ⓐ Ⓑ Ⓒ Ⓓ Ⓔ
87 Ⓐ Ⓑ Ⓒ Ⓓ Ⓔ
88 Ⓐ Ⓑ Ⓒ Ⓓ Ⓔ

COMPLETE PRACTICE TEST #1
Part B – Address Memory – Segment #5

Directions

In this segment, you are given five minutes to study the addresses. There are no questions to answer in this segment – it is a study period only. As before, the boxes are not reprinted here for your use. Instead, you are instructed to turn back to Address Memory Segment #1 and to spend five minutes studying the boxes displayed there. After studying for five minutes, turn to Segment #6 for directions on how to continue.

Begin studying when you are prepared to time yourself for precisely five minutes.

COMPLETE PRACTICE TEST #1
Part B – Address Memory – Segment #6

Directions

In this segment, you have five minutes to attempt answering 88 questions. You are to try to answer from memory, but the boxes are shown if you need to refer to them. Your answers are to be marked on the sample answer sheet at the bottom of the pages of Segment #6 – do not use the Compete Practice Test Answer Sheet for this segment. After completing this segment, turn to Segment #7 for further instructions.

Turn the page and begin when you are prepared to time yourself for precisely five minutes.

Hint: Remember your strategies! This segment is not scored, so do not take the questions seriously. Instead, mark a handful of random answers and use the five minutes to study and memorize the addresses.

COMPLETE PRACTICE TEST #1
Part B – Address Memory – Segment #6

A	B	C
4700-5599 Camp	6800-6999 Camp	5600-6499 Camp
Oak	Broad	State
5600-6499 Sarah	6500-6799 Sarah	6800-6999 Sarah
Magnolia	Dearman	Cox
4400-4699 Lang	5600-6499 Lang	6500-6799 Lang

1. 5600-6499 Lang
2. Forest
3. State
4. 4400-4699 Sarah
5. 4700-5599 Lang
6. Magnolia
7. Broad
8. 4400-4699 Lang

9. 4400-4699 Camp
10. 4700-5599 Camp
11. Pittman
12. 6800-6999 Lang
13. 6500-6799 Camp
14. Ocean
15. Cox
16. 4700-5599 Sarah

17. Oak
18. 5600-6499 Camp
19. 5600-6499 Sarah
20. Orchid
21. 6800-6999 Camp
22. 4400-4699 Sarah
23. 6500-6799 Sarah
24. 5600-6499 Lang

25. Oak
26. Forest
27. 5600-6499 Camp
28. Broad
29. 5600-6499 Sarah
30. Dearman
31. 6500-6799 Lang
32. Pittman

33. 4700-5599 Sarah
34. 5600-6499 Lang
35. Magnolia
36. Cox
37. 6800-6999 Lang
38. 6500-6799 Camp
39. 4400-4699 Camp
40. 6800-6999 Sarah

41. 4700-5599 Camp
42. Forest
43. Cox
44. Dearman
45. 5600-6499 Camp
46. State
47. 4400-4699 Lang
48. Magnolia

1 Ⓐ Ⓑ Ⓒ Ⓓ Ⓔ
2 Ⓐ Ⓑ Ⓒ Ⓓ Ⓔ
3 Ⓐ Ⓑ Ⓒ Ⓓ Ⓔ
4 Ⓐ Ⓑ Ⓒ Ⓓ Ⓔ
5 Ⓐ Ⓑ Ⓒ Ⓓ Ⓔ
6 Ⓐ Ⓑ Ⓒ Ⓓ Ⓔ
7 Ⓐ Ⓑ Ⓒ Ⓓ Ⓔ
8 Ⓐ Ⓑ Ⓒ Ⓓ Ⓔ

9 Ⓐ Ⓑ Ⓒ Ⓓ Ⓔ
10 Ⓐ Ⓑ Ⓒ Ⓓ Ⓔ
11 Ⓐ Ⓑ Ⓒ Ⓓ Ⓔ
12 Ⓐ Ⓑ Ⓒ Ⓓ Ⓔ
13 Ⓐ Ⓑ Ⓒ Ⓓ Ⓔ
14 Ⓐ Ⓑ Ⓒ Ⓓ Ⓔ
15 Ⓐ Ⓑ Ⓒ Ⓓ Ⓔ
16 Ⓐ Ⓑ Ⓒ Ⓓ Ⓔ

17 Ⓐ Ⓑ Ⓒ Ⓓ Ⓔ
18 Ⓐ Ⓑ Ⓒ Ⓓ Ⓔ
19 Ⓐ Ⓑ Ⓒ Ⓓ Ⓔ
20 Ⓐ Ⓑ Ⓒ Ⓓ Ⓔ
21 Ⓐ Ⓑ Ⓒ Ⓓ Ⓔ
22 Ⓐ Ⓑ Ⓒ Ⓓ Ⓔ
23 Ⓐ Ⓑ Ⓒ Ⓓ Ⓔ
24 Ⓐ Ⓑ Ⓒ Ⓓ Ⓔ

25 Ⓐ Ⓑ Ⓒ Ⓓ Ⓔ
26 Ⓐ Ⓑ Ⓒ Ⓓ Ⓔ
27 Ⓐ Ⓑ Ⓒ Ⓓ Ⓔ
28 Ⓐ Ⓑ Ⓒ Ⓓ Ⓔ
29 Ⓐ Ⓑ Ⓒ Ⓓ Ⓔ
30 Ⓐ Ⓑ Ⓒ Ⓓ Ⓔ
31 Ⓐ Ⓑ Ⓒ Ⓓ Ⓔ
32 Ⓐ Ⓑ Ⓒ Ⓓ Ⓔ

33 Ⓐ Ⓑ Ⓒ Ⓓ Ⓔ
34 Ⓐ Ⓑ Ⓒ Ⓓ Ⓔ
35 Ⓐ Ⓑ Ⓒ Ⓓ Ⓔ
36 Ⓐ Ⓑ Ⓒ Ⓓ Ⓔ
37 Ⓐ Ⓑ Ⓒ Ⓓ Ⓔ
38 Ⓐ Ⓑ Ⓒ Ⓓ Ⓔ
39 Ⓐ Ⓑ Ⓒ Ⓓ Ⓔ
40 Ⓐ Ⓑ Ⓒ Ⓓ Ⓔ

41 Ⓐ Ⓑ Ⓒ Ⓓ Ⓔ
42 Ⓐ Ⓑ Ⓒ Ⓓ Ⓔ
43 Ⓐ Ⓑ Ⓒ Ⓓ Ⓔ
44 Ⓐ Ⓑ Ⓒ Ⓓ Ⓔ
45 Ⓐ Ⓑ Ⓒ Ⓓ Ⓔ
46 Ⓐ Ⓑ Ⓒ Ⓓ Ⓔ
47 Ⓐ Ⓑ Ⓒ Ⓓ Ⓔ
48 Ⓐ Ⓑ Ⓒ Ⓓ Ⓔ

D	**E**
6500-6799 Camp	4400-4699 Camp
Orchid	Forest
4400-4699 Sarah	4700-5599 Sarah
Ocean	Pittman
4700-5599 Lang	6800-6999 Lang

49. Ocean
50. 6500-6799 Lang
51. 4400-4699 Sarah
52. 6800-6999 Camp
53. 4400-4699 Camp
54. Broad
55. Orchid
56. 5600-6499 Lang

57. 4700-5599 Sarah
58. Pittman
59. 5600-6499 Sarah
60. 6800-6999 Sarah
61. Forest
62. Cox
63. 6500-6799 Camp
64. 5600-6499 Camp

65. 4400-4699 Sarah
66. Pittman
67. Cox
68. 6800-6999 Camp
69. 4700-5599 Camp
70. Forest
71. 4400-4699 Sarah
72. State

73. 6500-6799 Sarah
74. 5600-6499 Lang
75. 5600-6499 Camp
76. Broad
77. Magnolia
78. Oak
79. Pittman
80. 5600-6499 Sarah

81. 4400-4699 Camp
82. 4700-5599 Sarah
83. Ocean
84. State
85. 4400-4699 Lang
86. 6500-6799 Lang
87. Dearman
88. Orchid

49 Ⓐ Ⓑ Ⓒ Ⓓ Ⓔ
50 Ⓐ Ⓑ Ⓒ Ⓓ Ⓔ
51 Ⓐ Ⓑ Ⓒ Ⓓ Ⓔ
52 Ⓐ Ⓑ Ⓒ Ⓓ Ⓔ
53 Ⓐ Ⓑ Ⓒ Ⓓ Ⓔ
54 Ⓐ Ⓑ Ⓒ Ⓓ Ⓔ
55 Ⓐ Ⓑ Ⓒ Ⓓ Ⓔ
56 Ⓐ Ⓑ Ⓒ Ⓓ Ⓔ

57 Ⓐ Ⓑ Ⓒ Ⓓ Ⓔ
58 Ⓐ Ⓑ Ⓒ Ⓓ Ⓔ
59 Ⓐ Ⓑ Ⓒ Ⓓ Ⓔ
60 Ⓐ Ⓑ Ⓒ Ⓓ Ⓔ
61 Ⓐ Ⓑ Ⓒ Ⓓ Ⓔ
62 Ⓐ Ⓑ Ⓒ Ⓓ Ⓔ
63 Ⓐ Ⓑ Ⓒ Ⓓ Ⓔ
64 Ⓐ Ⓑ Ⓒ Ⓓ Ⓔ

65 Ⓐ Ⓑ Ⓒ Ⓓ Ⓔ
66 Ⓐ Ⓑ Ⓒ Ⓓ Ⓔ
67 Ⓐ Ⓑ Ⓒ Ⓓ Ⓔ
68 Ⓐ Ⓑ Ⓒ Ⓓ Ⓔ
69 Ⓐ Ⓑ Ⓒ Ⓓ Ⓔ
70 Ⓐ Ⓑ Ⓒ Ⓓ Ⓔ
71 Ⓐ Ⓑ Ⓒ Ⓓ Ⓔ
72 Ⓐ Ⓑ Ⓒ Ⓓ Ⓔ

73 Ⓐ Ⓑ Ⓒ Ⓓ Ⓔ
74 Ⓐ Ⓑ Ⓒ Ⓓ Ⓔ
75 Ⓐ Ⓑ Ⓒ Ⓓ Ⓔ
76 Ⓐ Ⓑ Ⓒ Ⓓ Ⓔ
77 Ⓐ Ⓑ Ⓒ Ⓓ Ⓔ
78 Ⓐ Ⓑ Ⓒ Ⓓ Ⓔ
79 Ⓐ Ⓑ Ⓒ Ⓓ Ⓔ
80 Ⓐ Ⓑ Ⓒ Ⓓ Ⓔ

81 Ⓐ Ⓑ Ⓒ Ⓓ Ⓔ
82 Ⓐ Ⓑ Ⓒ Ⓓ Ⓔ
83 Ⓐ Ⓑ Ⓒ Ⓓ Ⓔ
84 Ⓐ Ⓑ Ⓒ Ⓓ Ⓔ
85 Ⓐ Ⓑ Ⓒ Ⓓ Ⓔ
86 Ⓐ Ⓑ Ⓒ Ⓓ Ⓔ
87 Ⓐ Ⓑ Ⓒ Ⓓ Ⓔ
88 Ⓐ Ⓑ Ⓒ Ⓓ Ⓔ

COMPLETE PRACTICE TEST #1
Part B – Address Memory – Segment #7

Directions

This is the final segment of the Address Memory section. You have five minutes to answer 88 questions. You must answer from memory. The boxes are not shown. On this segment, there is not a sample answer sheet at the bottom of the page. Instead, mark your answers on the Complete Practice Test Answer Sheet that your tore out of the book. After completing this segment, you have finished the full Address Memory section. Turn to the Number Series section of the practice test for instructions on how to continue.

Turn the page and begin when you are prepared to time yourself for precisely five minutes.

1. 4400-4699 Sarah
2. Orchid
3. Oak
4. 6500-6799 Camp
5. 5600-6499 Camp
6. Ocean
7. 6800-6999 Lang
8. Dearman

9. 6500-6799 Lang
10. 4400-4699 Lang
11. State
12. Ocean
13. 4400-4699 Sarah
14. 4400-4699 Camp
15. 5600-6499 Sarah
16. Pittman

17. Oak
18. Magnolia
19. Broad
20. 5600-6499 Camp
21. 5600-6499 Lang
22. 6500-6799 Sarah
23. Forest
24. 4700-5599 Camp

25. 6800-6999 Camp
26. Cox
27. Pittman
28. 4400-4699 Sarah
29. 5600-6499 Camp
30. 6500-6799 Camp
31. Cox
32. Forest

33. 6800-6999 Sarah
34. 5600-6499 Sarah
35. Pittman
36. 4700-5599 Sarah
37. 6500-6799 Lang
38. Orchid
39. Broad
40. 4400-4699 Camp

41. 6800-6999 Camp
42. 4400-4699 Sarah
43. 4700-5599 Camp
44. Ocean
45. Magnolia
46. 4400-4699 Lang
47. State
48. 5600-6499 Camp

49. Dearman
50. Cox
51. Forest
52. 4700-5599 Camp
53. 6800-6999 Sarah
54. 4400-4699 Camp
55. 6500-6799 Camp
56. 6800-6999 Lang

57. Cox
58. Magnolia
59. 5600-6499 Lang
60. 4700-5599 Sarah
61. Pittman
62. 6500-6799 Lang
63. Dearman
64. 5600-6499 Sarah

65. Broad
66. 5600-6499 Camp
67. Forest
68. Oak
69. 5600-6499 Lang
70. 6500-6799 Sarah
71. 4400-4699 Sarah
72. 6800-6999 Camp

73. Orchid
74. 5600-6499 Sarah
75. Forest
76. State
77. 4400-4699 Sarah
78. 4700-5599 Lang
79. Magnolia
80. Broad

81. 4400-4699 Lang
82. 4400-4699 Camp
83. 4700-5599 Camp
84. Pittman
85. 6800-6999 Lang
86. 6500-6799 Camp
87. Ocean
88. Cox

COMPLETE PRACTICE TEST #1
Part C – Number Series

Directions

On this section, you have 20 minutes to answer 24 mathematical questions. Each question consists of a series of numbers followed by two blanks. You are to calculate what two numbers would logically follow in the series and that would therefore fit into the two blanks. Choose the answer – A, B, C, D, or E – that contains the correct two numbers, in the proper order, that should follow in the series. Mark your answers on the Complete Practice Test Answer Sheet in the section entitled Number Series. After completing this section, turn to the Following Oral Instructions section for directions on how to continue.

The solutions to all the Number Series questions in all six of the practice tests are given in the back of your book. After scoring each Number Series practice test, find and review the solutions for the questions you missed. This should better prepare you to answer similar questions on the other practice tests as well as on your actual exam.

Turn the page and begin when you are prepared to time yourself for precisely 20 minutes.

Hint: Remember to use the Circles and Squares Strategy to identify, separate, and solve the multiple sequences found in many questions.

COMPLETE PRACTICE TEST #1
Part C – Number Series

1. 31 32 33 34 35 36 ___ ___   A) 38,37 B) 37,38 C) 38,40 D) 35,34 E) 39,41

2. 5 5 5 10 5 5 5 10 5 5 ___ ___   A) 5,10 B) 10,5 C) 5,5 D) 5,0 E) 0,5

3. 22 10 22 9 22 8 22 7 ___ ___   A) 6,22 B) 20,22 C) 6,8 D) 8,6 E) 22,6

4. 1 2 4 5 7 8 10 ___ ___   A) 11,13 B) 10,9 C) 8,7 D) 12,14 E) 13,29

5. 1 2 0 3 4 0 5 6 0 7 ___ ___   A) 8,0 B) 0,8 C) 9,0 D) 12,13 E) 7,0

6. 2 5 9 12 16 19 23 ___ ___   A) 25,29 B) 27,31 C) 26,30 D) 30,34 E) 32,36

7. 2 4 6 10 16 26 ___ ___   A) 42,68 B) 28,64 C) 68,84 D) 42,86 E) 44,48

8. 89 88 87 86 85 ___ ___   A) 82,81 B) 85,86 C) 84,83 D) 84,81 E) 85,83

9. 2 4 8 16 ___ ___   A) 32,64 B) 34,64 C) 30,64 D) 42,74 E) 52,84

10. 2 17 32 47 ___ ___   A) 60,75 B) 32,47 C) 85,97 D) 62,77 E) 68,79

11. 16 16 33 33 16 16 33 ___ ___   A) 31,17 B) 30,20 C) 33,16 D) 29,21 E) 28,27

12. 65 20 55 30 45 40 35 ___ ___   A) 60,35 B) 40,15 C) 30,45 D) 40,25 E) 50,25

13. 18 18 15 15 12 12 9 ___ ___   A) 9,9 B) 6,6 C) 9,7 D) 12,9 E) 9,6

14. 1 14 27 40 ___ ___   A) 51,64 B) 53,66 C) 50,63 D) 63,76 E) 50,65

15. 8 29 11 26 14 23 17 20 20 ___ ___   A) 21,21 B) 17,23 C) 23,15 D) 18,21 E) 18,24

16. 2 4 8 10 14 16 20 ___ ___   A) 22,24 B) 20,26 C) 22,26 D) 26,28 E) 21,23

17. 3 6 9 15 18 21 27 30 ___ ___   A) 33,36 B) 33,39 C) 36,39 D) 40,43 E) 41,44

18. 80 50 70 60 60 70 50 ___ ___   A) 70,30 B) 50,60 C) 80,40 D) 20,40 E) 90,50

19. 13 83 23 63 33 43 ___ ___   A) 13,44 B) 32,67 C) 45,46 D) 43,23 E) 28,59

20. 31 3 31 4 31 5 31 ___ ___   A) 4,28 B) 3,21 C) 6,31 D) 8,32 E) 10,37

21. 8 16 24 32 40 ___ ___   A) 45,50 B) 46,52 C) 47,54 D) 48,56 E) 49,58

22. 1 5 25 15 49 25 ___ ___   A) 45,93 B) 43,35 C) 73,35 D) 76,65 E) 53,65

23. 21 18 10 8 15 12 6 ___ ___   A) 8,10 B) 4,9 C) 5,8 D) 3,7 E) 2,6

24. 10 6 12 5 14 4 16 ___ ___   A) 2,15 B) 3,18 C) 4,20 D) 5,17 E) 5,21

98

COMPLETE PRACTICE TEST #1
Part D – Following Oral Instructions

Directions

On this section of the test, the Exam Administrator will read questions/instructions aloud to the group of test takers. These oral instructions will direct you to write/mark certain items in your test booklet, which in turn will lead you to the correct answer(s). Finally, you will be verbally instructed to mark the correct answer(s) on your answer sheet. You must answer exclusively based upon what you hear – there are no questions for you to read.

The following pages of this practice test are samples of the test booklet pages on which you will write/mark as verbally instructed. Mark your answers on the Complete Practice Test Answer Sheet in the Following Oral Instructions section.

To practice realistically, you must either listen to the questions on the author's recording or have someone read them aloud to you. Do not look over the questions before taking the practice test. Once you have completed the practice test, you should then review the questions you missed in order to determine what caused you to miss them. This review should enable you to be more successful on similar questions next time.

The author's recording of all six Following Oral Directions practice tests is an ideal and convenient way to practice. The recorded questions are presented in the proper format, at the proper pace, and with proper diction. These recordings allow you to practice anytime and anywhere you wish. With these recordings, your practice – and in turn your success – will not be dependent upon someone else's schedule and whims. For details and ordering information, see the order form at the back of your book.

If someone will be reading the questions to you, he/she will find the questions for each practice test in the back of your book in the section entitled Following Oral Instructions – Practice Test Questions. The reader should carefully tear the questions out of your book in order to use them. The questions should be read at a rather slow and steady pace of approximately 75 words per minute and with proper diction. The reader should also pause between instructions/questions as directed in the wording of each question.

Once you complete the Following Oral Instructions section, you have finished this practice test, and you should then begin the next practice test in your book. Once you have completed all six practice tests plus the Extra Address Checking Practice Exercises as instructed, you should be fully prepared to excel on the actual exam.

Turn the page and begin when you are prepared to listen to the questions from the author's recording or from someone who will read the questions to you in the proper fashion.

Hint: Remember your strategies:
- *You will answer by marking number-letter combinations.*
- *Where you mark an answer on the answer sheet will not match the question number.*
- *Listen closely and attentively.*
- *Simply follow the instructions you hear – do not try to figure them out.*
- *Some questions will have multiple answers, and you must mark all of them.*
- *Mark your answers quickly and be ready to listen to the next question.*
- *Make identifying notes for later recall.*

COMPLETE PRACTICE TEST #1
Part D – Following Oral Instructions

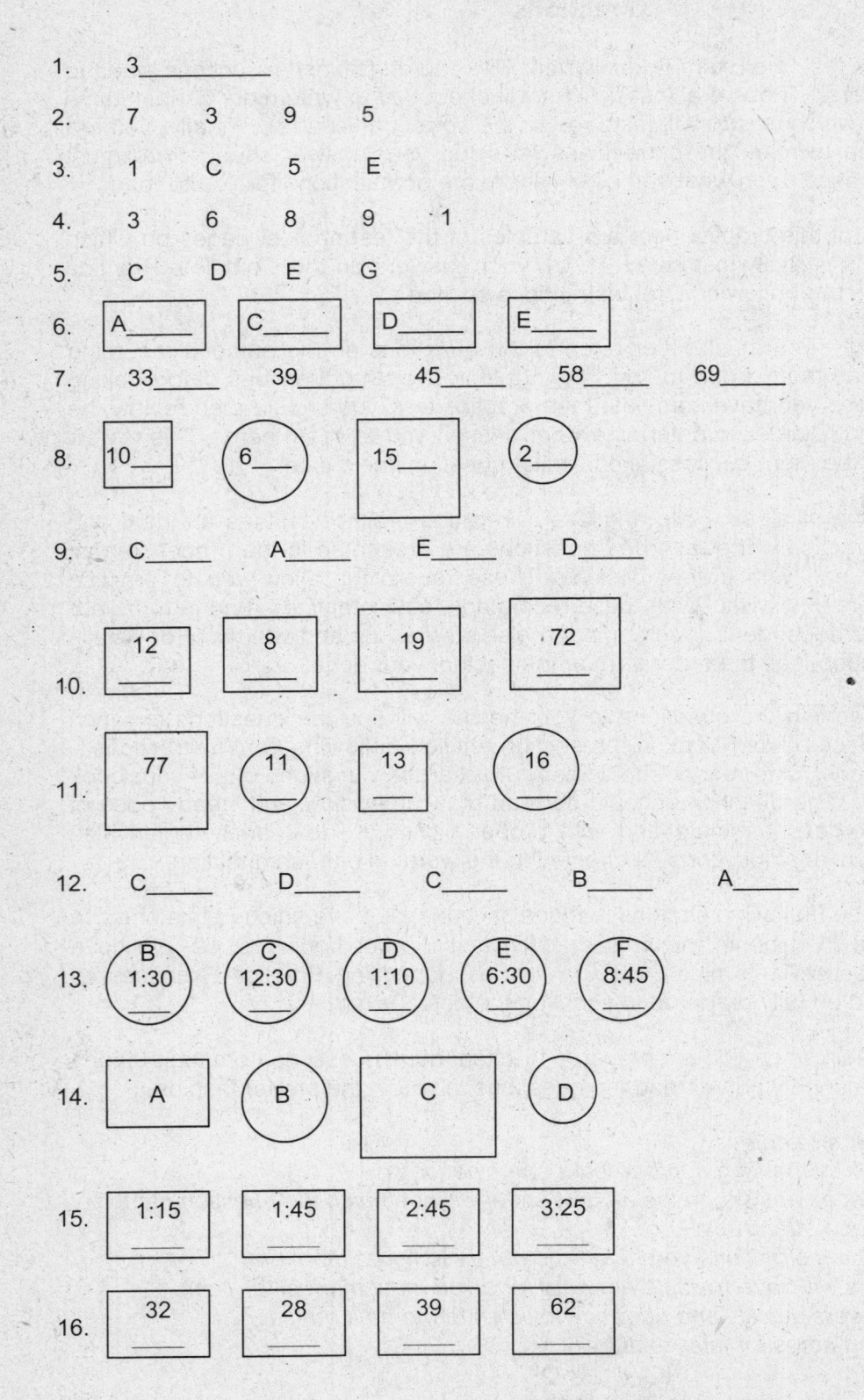

1. 3_____

2. 7   3   9   5

3. 1   C   5   E

4. 3   6   8   9   1

5. C   D   E   G

6. | A____ | | C____ | | D____ | | E____ |

7. 33____   39____   45____   58____   69____

8. | 10__ | (6__) | 15__ | (2__)

9. C____   A____   E____   D____

10. | 12 | | 8 | | 19 | | 72 |
     ___   ___   ___   ___

11. | 77 | (11) | 13 | (16)
     ___   ___   ___   ___

12. C____   D____   C____   B____   A____

13. (B 1:30) (C 12:30) (D 1:10) (E 6:30) (F 8:45)

14. | A | (B) | C | (D)

15. | 1:15 | | 1:45 | | 2:45 | | 3:25 |
     ____   ____   ____   ____

16. | 32 | | 28 | | 39 | | 62 |
     ___   ___   ___   ___

88

17.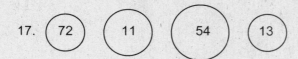

18.   _____

19. | 1:30 | | 3:30 | | 1:45 | | 4:45 |

20.   47   32   28   33

21. | DENVER | | CLEVELAND | | CHICAGO | | DALLAS |

22.   16F

23.   13   22   31   15

24. | 81___ | | 17___ | | 6___ |

25.   ___E   ___D   ___C   ___A   ___B

26.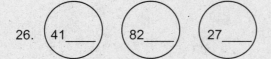

27. | Town 27 ___ Pop. 837 | | Town 82 ___ Pop. 3,781 | | Town 16 ___ Pop. 631 |

COMPLETE PRACTICE TEST #2

This practice test contains samples of all four sections of the actual exam. The instructions given are similar to those on the actual exam. The format of this practice test is identical to that of the actual exam. Where pertinent, hints are given about your test taking strategies. Of course, these hints will not appear on the actual exam.

It is imperative that you take this practice test in as realistic a fashion as possible. **Your practice will have no value unless it is done realistically.** Therefore, you must precisely time yourself on the Address Checking, Address Memory, and Number Series sections. Our Timed Practice Test CD is a convenient way to practice realistically and time yourself precisely. Also, you must either listen to the Following Oral Instructions questions on our Oral Instructions Practice Tests CD or have someone read them to you – *do not read the questions yourself!* The Following Oral Instructions questions can be found in the back of your book if someone will be reading them to you.

To take this practice test, first turn to the back of your book and carefully tear out one of the **Complete Practice Test Answer Sheets.** Mark the answers to the scored segments of the practice test on this answer sheet. (Remember, of the seven segments on the Address Memory Section, only the final one is scored. Accordingly, you should mark answers for only the final Address Memory segment on your Complete Practice Test Answer Sheet. The other segments of the Address Memory Section that call for answers have accompanying sample answer sheets where you should mark answers.)

The correct answers are provided in the back of your book. Immediately upon completing the practice test, **it is imperative that you score each section** using the formulas given under the Sections of the Exam heading in your book. Scoring is necessary in order to gauge your progress and to identify your individual areas of weakness that may need extra attention.

After completing and scoring each practice test, move on to the next. **After completing all six complete practice tests and the extra Address Checking exercises as instructed, you should be prepared for the actual exam.** If you feel the need to practice more, repeat as many of the practice tests as you like. After that much practice, the questions will likely have become a confusing blur in your mind. It is highly unlikely that you will be able to remember many of the individual questions or answers. Therefore, you should be able to gain practice value from the exercises even though you have already taken them once.

Do not look over the practice test questions until you are ready to start – meaning until you have set a timer for the allotted period of time. Similarly, after completing one section of the practice test, do not look over the next one until your are ready to start it. Likewise, stop working and put down your pencil immediately when the allotted period of time has expired. As has been emphasized before but cannot be emphasized enough, your practice is of absolutely no value unless it is done realistically. Also, you must train yourself (1) to not open your test booklet or pick up your pencil until instructed to do so and (2) to close your booklet and put down your pencil immediately upon being so instructed. The Postal Service has a zero tolerance policy on these matters. Any variance may be viewed as cheating and may result in your disqualification.

Good luck on your practice test, and even better luck on your actual exam!

COMPLETE PRACTICE TEST #2
Part A – Address Checking

Directions

In this part of the test, you will have to decide whether two addresses are alike or different. You will have 6 minutes to answer 95 questions. Each question consists of a pair of addresses. If the two addresses in the pair are exactly alike in every way, darken the oval with the letter "A" for _Alike_. If the two addresses are different in any way, darken the oval with the letter "D" for _Different_. Mark your answers on the Complete Practice Test Answer Sheet in the section entitled Address Checking.

Turn the page and begin when you are prepared to time yourself for precisely 6 minutes.

Note: You will notice that this section of your practice test is spread across two pages. This is the exact same format that you will actually experience on the Address Checking section of the real exam. For economy and convenience, other study guides frequently condense the two pages of this section down to only one. You will also notice that the Address Checking questions are presented in a font, or type of print, that is different from the rest of the book. This font matches what is actually used on the real exam, and, as you will see, it makes this section even more challenging. However, it is imperative that you practice realistically and that you become acquainted with and comfortable with the actual format of the exam. We have accordingly formatted this practice test realistically for your benefit.

Hint: Remember your strategies:
- _Pace yourself for speed and accuracy – emphasis on speed!_
- _Use one glance-over for easier/shorter addresses._
- _Use two glance-over's for harder/longer addresses._
- _Never make a third pass or glance-over!_
- _Overlap the answer sheet & the questions to keep them as close together as possible._
- _Use your extra pencil, your hand, or your fingers to mark/keep your place._
- _Use your Speed Pencil and your Speed Marking strategies for much greater speed._

COMPLETE PRACTICE TEST #2
Part A – Address Checking

1.	8757 Lee Blvd.	8757 Lee Blvd.
2.	Roundfield, Mass. 78645	Roundfield, Mass. 78654
3.	109 Boggs Circle SW	109 Boggs Circle SW
4.	315 E. Fourth St.	315 E. Fourth St.
5.	Lurch, Az. 22344	Lurch, Az. 23344
6.	555 Van Buren Ave.	55 Van Buren Ave.
7.	2343 Camron Mills	2343 Canron Mills
8.	Rolling Fork, Ms. 39255	Rolling Fork, Ms. 39255
9.	Hinds, N.H.	Hinds, N.H.
10.	456 Cuevas Dr.	456 Cuevas Dr.
11.	9834 Wellings NW	9834 Willings NW
12.	982 Brymnawr Ave.	982 Brynmawr Ave.
13.	Kinston, S.C. 77896	Kingston, S.C. 77896
14.	212 Columbia Rd.	212 Columbia R.
15.	2000 Sylva Mannor Dr.	2000 Sylva Mannor Dr.
16.	305 Park Row	305 Park Row
17.	1335 Main Road East	1334 Main Road East
18.	999 Jefferson Davis Cir.	999 Jefferson Davis Cir.
19.	Mt. Olive, N.S. 35074	Mt. Olive, N.S. 35047
20.	878 St. George Sq.	878 St. George Sq.
21.	215 Beaumont Dr. West	215 Beaumont Dr. East
22.	Summit, Wash. 94590	Summit, Wash. 94590
23.	220 West Beach	220 West Beach
24.	6242 Lynnwood Cir. East	6244 Lynnwood Cir. East
25.	Portland, Org. 95580	Portland, Org. 95580
26.	905 Morse Code Rd.	905 Morse Code Rd.
27.	1221 North Street East	1221 East Street North
28.	5544 Mockingbird Lane	4455 Mockingbird Land
29.	104-A N. Island View	104-A N. Island View
30.	106 Carroll Ave. South	106 Carrol Ave. South
31.	1001 Mitchell Blvd. NW	1001 Mitchell Blvd. NE
32.	Eaton Village, Okla.	Eaton Village, Okla.
33.	255 Ann St. South	255 Ane St. South
34.	605 Camp Ave.	605 Camp Ave.
35.	3007 Memory Lane	3007 Mimory Lane
36.	Miller, W. Va. 55665	Miller, W.Va. 56655
37.	905 Coutel blvd. North	905 Coutel blvd. North
38.	101 Westwood Pl.	101 Westwood Pl.
39.	102 Trautman Ave.	102 Trautman Dr.
40.	209 Jeff Davis SE	209 Jeff Davis SE
41.	956 Powers Pl.	956 Powers Pl.
42.	St. Bay Louis, Mich. 78655	St. Bay Louis, Mich. 78556
43.	1952 Bilmar Dr.	1952 Bilmar Dr.
44.	504 Gulf View N	405 Gulf View N
45.	303 Mesa Villa Rd.	303 Mesa Vila Rd.
46.	4004 Oak Place	4004 Oak Place
47.	217 Leigh St. NW	217 Lee St. NW
48.	5064 E Mission Lane	5064 E Mission Lane

49.	Great Andes, Calif. 99033	Great Ander, Calif. 99033
50.	Beach Oak Apts. NW	Beach Oak Apts. NE
51.	4234 Newton Park	4324 Newton Park
52.	205-B Ranch Road East	205-B Ranch Road East
53.	Houston, Texas 77055	Houston, Texas 77050
54.	0489 East Old Pass Road	0489 East Old Pass Rd.
55.	515 W. Nicholson Ave.	515 W. Nicholson Ave.
56.	Orange Grove, Fla. 40097	Orange Grove, Fla. 40097
57.	909 Sinwell Market St.	909 Sinwell Market Ave.
58.	4763 Oak Pl. Apt 6-B	4763 Oak Ct. Apt, 6-B
59.	6749 Beach Ct.	6794 Beach Ct.
60.	00601 Area Blvd.	06001 Area Blvd.
61.	321-B Menarney St.	321-B Menarney St.
62.	1724 Maple Ct.	1742 Maple Ct.
63.	303-D Sweeney Dr.	303-B Sweeney Dr.
64.	Vandenburg, VA 67495	Vandenburg, VA 67945
65.	09572 Waycross Dr.	09572 Waycross Dr.
66.	07523 Bienville Dr.	07253 Bienville Dr.
67.	Holly Hills, KY 38572	Holly Hills, KY 38572
68.	399 Santa Maria Cr.	339 Santa Maria Cr.
69.	3097 Rodenburg Ave.	3097 Rodenburg Ave.
70.	0132 Regency Blvd.	0123 Regency Blvd.
71.	Merigold, Mass. 68975	Meriglod, Miss. 68975
72.	212 South Shore St.	212 South Shore Ct.
73.	Kensington, LA 57391	Kensington, LA 57931
74.	696 Camp Wilkes	696 Camp Willie
75.	1658 Cherry Circle	1658 Cherry Circle
76.	Sycamore, NY 76983	Sycamore, NY 76983
77.	0060 DeMountluzin Ave.	00600 De Montluzin Ave.
78.	44-B Daisy Vestry Rd.	44-B Daisy View Rd.
79.	717 Acacia Apt. A	717 Acacia Apt. A
80.	397 N Paradise Pt.	379 N Paradise Pt.
81.	112 Felicity View W	122 Felicity View W
82.	0435 Ballentine N	0453 Ballentine W
83.	17 S Crawford Court	17 S Crawford Circle
84.	Lameuse, Texas 48275	Lameuse, Texas 48725
85.	47-C Rolling Hills Ave.	47-C Rolling Hills Ave.
86.	Everbreeze, S.D. 29402	Evergreen, S.D. 29042
87.	Grand Island, Nebraska 00	Grand Isle, Nebraska 07001
88.	Rock Chester, NJ 79538	Rock Chester, NM 97358
89.	07864 Knollwood Dr.	07684 Knollwood Dr.
90.	001 E. Rustwood St.	001 E. Rustwood St.
91.	W. Vandenburg Heights #68	W. Vandenburg Heights #86
92.	Muskego, Ohio 35426	Muskego, Ohio 35246
93.	Yorkshire N Apt. 66	Yorkshire N Apt. 66
94.	6226 Heibenhein Ct.	6262 Heibenhein Ct.
95.	Shasta Place #242 W	Shasta Place #424 W

COMPLETE PRACTICE TEST #2
Part B – Address Memory

Directions

In this part of the test, you will have to memorize the locations of 25 addresses in five boxes. During this section, you will have several study periods and practice exercises to help you memorize the location of the addresses shown in the five boxes. Answer the questions by darkening the oval containing the letter (A, B, C, D, or E) of the box in which the address is located – Box A, Box B, Box C, Box D, or Box E. At the end of each segment, you will be given instructions on how and where to continue. After completing six preliminary segments, the actual test will be given as segment #7.

Turn the page to begin Segment #1.

Note: You will notice on your practice test that the various segments of the Address Memory section are spread across two pages. Where applicable, the five boxes, the 88 questions, and/or the sample answer sheets are spread across two pages. This is the same format that you will experience on most segments of the Address Memory section on the actual exam. For economy and convenience, other study guides frequently condense the two pages down to only one. However, it is imperative that you practice realistically and that you become acquainted with and comfortable with the actual format of the exam. We have accordingly formatted this practice test realistically for your benefit.

Hint: Remember your strategies:
- *Memorize horizontally.*
- *Memorize only Boxes A, B, C, and D.*
- *You can correctly answer all Box E questions by the process of elimination.*
- *Use the Second Digit Strategy to memorize the number addresses.*
- *Use imagery/association to memorize the word addresses.*
- *Overlap the answer sheet & the questions to keep them as close together as possible.*
- *Use your extra pencil, your hand, or your fingers to mark/keep your place.*
- *Use your Speed Pencil and your Speed Marking strategies for much greater speed.*

COMPLETE PRACTICE TEST #2
Part B – Address Memory – Segment #1

Directions

Five sample boxes, each containing five addresses, and five sample questions about these boxes are given on the following two pages. The purpose of this small exercise is simply to acquaint you with the format of this section and with how the questions should be answered. The first two sample questions are answered for you. You are to spend three minutes becoming acquainted with the format and answering sample questions 3, 4, and 5. After completing Segment #1, turn to Segment #2 for further instructions.

Turn the page and begin when you are prepared to time yourself for precisely three minutes.

Hint: Remember your strategies! This segment is not scored, so do not take the sample questions seriously. Instead, mark random answers and use the three minutes to study and memorize the addresses. The sample boxes and addresses in this segment are the very same ones that will be repeated throughout this section of the exam.

A	B	C
6800-7599 Beach	8900-8999 Beach	7700-8499 Beach
Island View	Galloway	Alexander
7700-8499 West	8600-8799 West	8900-8999 West
Carroll	Runnels	Driftwood
6500-6699 Samuel	7700-8499 Samuel	8600-8799 Samuel

1. Clifford   Ⓐ Ⓑ Ⓒ Ⓓ ⬤E
   This address came from Box E, so we sill darken the oval with the letter E.

2. 6500-6699 Samuel   ⬤A Ⓑ Ⓒ Ⓓ Ⓔ
   This address came from Box A, so we will darken the oval with the letter A.

3. 8900-8999 West   Ⓐ Ⓑ Ⓒ Ⓓ Ⓔ
   Now that you know how to answer, you do questions 3, 4, and 5.

4. 7700-8499 Samuel   Ⓐ Ⓑ Ⓒ Ⓓ Ⓔ

5. Alexander   Ⓐ Ⓑ Ⓒ Ⓓ Ⓔ

The correct answers are E, A, C, B, and C.

D	E
8600-8799 Beach	6500-6699 Beach
Mathison	Clifford
6500-6699 West	6800-7599 West
Pirate	Lynwood
6800-7599 Samuel	8900-8999 Samuel

COMPLETE PRACTICE TEST #2
Part B – Address Memory – Segment #2

Directions

In this segment, you are given three minutes to study and memorize the addresses. There are no questions to answer in this segment – it is a study period only. However, on the actual exam, the boxes are not reprinted for your use. Instead, you are instructed to turn back to Address Memory Segment #1 on the preceding pages of the exam and to spend three minutes studying the boxes displayed there. So, we will do the very same on this practice test. After studying for three minutes, turn to Segment #3 for directions on how to continue the Address Memory Section of the exam.

Begin studying when you are prepared to time yourself for precisely three minutes.

COMPLETE PRACTICE TEST #2
Part B – Address Memory – Segment #3

Directions

In this segment you have three minutes to attempt answering 88 questions. You are to try to answer from memory, but the boxes are shown if you need to refer to them. Your answers are to be marked on the sample answer sheet at the bottom of the pages of Segment #3 – do not use the Compete Practice Test Answer Sheet for this segment. After completing this segment, turn to Segment #4 for further instructions.

Turn the page and begin when you are prepared to time yourself for precisely three minutes.

Hint: Remember your strategies! This segment is not scored, so do not take the questions seriously. Instead, mark a handful of random answers and use the three minutes to study and memorize the addresses.

A	B	C
6800-7599 Beach	8900-8999 Beach	7700-8499 Beach
Island View	Galloway	Alexander
7700-8499 West	8600-8799 West	8900-8999 West
Carroll	Runnels	Driftwood
6500-6699 Samuel	7700-8499 Samuel	8600-8799 Samuel

1. 8600-8799 West
2. Alexander
3. 6500-6699 West
4. Mathison
5. 6800-7599 Beach
6. 8900-8999 Samuel
7. Carroll
8. 7700-8499

9. Lynwood
10. Island View
11. 6500-6699 Samuel
12. 8900-8999 Beach
13. Pirate
14. 7700-8499 West
15. Clifford
16. 6500-6699 Beach

17. 8900-8999 West
18. 7700-8499 Samuel
19. Driftwood
20. 6800-7599 Samuel
21. Galloway
22. Mathison
23. 8600-8799 Samuel
24. 6800-7599 Beach

25. 6500-6699 Beach
26. Runnels
27. 7700-8499 West
28. 6800-7599 West
29. 7700-8499 Beach
30. Pirate
31. 6500-6699 West
32. Lynwood

33. Alexander
34. 8900-8999 West
35. 7700-8499 Samuel
36. 6500-6699 Beach
37. 6500-6699 Samuel
38. 8900-8999 Beach
39. 8600-8799 West
40. 6800-7599 Samuel

41. Island View
42. Carroll
43. 7700-8499 West
44. Driftwood
45. Galloway
46. 6800-7599 Beach
47. 8900-8999 Samuel
48. Mathison

1. Ⓐ Ⓑ Ⓒ Ⓓ Ⓔ
2. Ⓐ Ⓑ Ⓒ Ⓓ Ⓔ
3. Ⓐ Ⓑ Ⓒ Ⓓ Ⓔ
4. Ⓐ Ⓑ Ⓒ Ⓓ Ⓔ
5. Ⓐ Ⓑ Ⓒ Ⓓ Ⓔ
6. Ⓐ Ⓑ Ⓒ Ⓓ Ⓔ
7. Ⓐ Ⓑ Ⓒ Ⓓ Ⓔ
8. Ⓐ Ⓑ Ⓒ Ⓓ Ⓔ
9. Ⓐ Ⓑ Ⓒ Ⓓ Ⓔ
10. Ⓐ Ⓑ Ⓒ Ⓓ Ⓔ
11. Ⓐ Ⓑ Ⓒ Ⓓ Ⓔ
12. Ⓐ Ⓑ Ⓒ Ⓓ Ⓔ
13. Ⓐ Ⓑ Ⓒ Ⓓ Ⓔ
14. Ⓐ Ⓑ Ⓒ Ⓓ Ⓔ
15. Ⓐ Ⓑ Ⓒ Ⓓ Ⓔ
16. Ⓐ Ⓑ Ⓒ Ⓓ Ⓔ

17. Ⓐ Ⓑ Ⓒ Ⓓ Ⓔ
18. Ⓐ Ⓑ Ⓒ Ⓓ Ⓔ
19. Ⓐ Ⓑ Ⓒ Ⓓ Ⓔ
20. Ⓐ Ⓑ Ⓒ Ⓓ Ⓔ
21. Ⓐ Ⓑ Ⓒ Ⓓ Ⓔ
22. Ⓐ Ⓑ Ⓒ Ⓓ Ⓔ
23. Ⓐ Ⓑ Ⓒ Ⓓ Ⓔ
24. Ⓐ Ⓑ Ⓒ Ⓓ Ⓔ
25. Ⓐ Ⓑ Ⓒ Ⓓ Ⓔ
26. Ⓐ Ⓑ Ⓒ Ⓓ Ⓔ
27. Ⓐ Ⓑ Ⓒ Ⓓ Ⓔ
28. Ⓐ Ⓑ Ⓒ Ⓓ Ⓔ
29. Ⓐ Ⓑ Ⓒ Ⓓ Ⓔ
30. Ⓐ Ⓑ Ⓒ Ⓓ Ⓔ
31. Ⓐ Ⓑ Ⓒ Ⓓ Ⓔ
32. Ⓐ Ⓑ Ⓒ Ⓓ Ⓔ

33. Ⓐ Ⓑ Ⓒ Ⓓ Ⓔ
34. Ⓐ Ⓑ Ⓒ Ⓓ Ⓔ
35. Ⓐ Ⓑ Ⓒ Ⓓ Ⓔ
36. Ⓐ Ⓑ Ⓒ Ⓓ Ⓔ
37. Ⓐ Ⓑ Ⓒ Ⓓ Ⓔ
38. Ⓐ Ⓑ Ⓒ Ⓓ Ⓔ
39. Ⓐ Ⓑ Ⓒ Ⓓ Ⓔ
40. Ⓐ Ⓑ Ⓒ Ⓓ Ⓔ
41. Ⓐ Ⓑ Ⓒ Ⓓ Ⓔ
42. Ⓐ Ⓑ Ⓒ Ⓓ Ⓔ
43. Ⓐ Ⓑ Ⓒ Ⓓ Ⓔ
44. Ⓐ Ⓑ Ⓒ Ⓓ Ⓔ
45. Ⓐ Ⓑ Ⓒ Ⓓ Ⓔ
46. Ⓐ Ⓑ Ⓒ Ⓓ Ⓔ
47. Ⓐ Ⓑ Ⓒ Ⓓ Ⓔ
48. Ⓐ Ⓑ Ⓒ Ⓓ Ⓔ

Part B – Address Memory – Segment #3
Continued

D	E
8600-8799 Beach	6500-6699 Beach
Mathison	Clifford
6500-6699 West	6800-7599 West
Pirate	Lynwood
6800-7599 Samuel	8900-8999 Samuel

49. Clifford
50. 6800-7599 West
51. 6500-6699 Samuel
52. 8600-8799 Samuel
53. Island View
54. 7700-8499 Beach
55. Runnels
56. Lynwood

57. 8600-8799 West
58. 6500-6699 West
59. Pirate
60. 6500-6699 Beach
61. Galloway
62. 8900-8999 Beach
63. 7700-8499 West
64. Clifford

65. 8600-8799 Beach
66. 6800-7599 Samuel
67. Alexander
68. 8900-8999 West
69. Driftwood
70. Carroll
71. 6800-7599 Beach
72. 8900-8999 Samuel

73. 7700-8499 Beach
74. Galloway
75. Clifford
76. 8600-8799 Samuel
77. 8900-8999 Beach
78. 6800-7599 Beach
79. Lynwood
80. 8600-8799 West

81. Mathison
82. 7700-8499 Beach
83. 6500-6699 Samuel
84. 7700-8499 Samuel
85. 6500-6699 West
86. Driftwood
87. Island View
88. 6800-7599 West

49 Ⓐ Ⓑ Ⓒ Ⓓ Ⓔ
50 Ⓐ Ⓑ Ⓒ Ⓓ Ⓔ
51 Ⓐ Ⓑ Ⓒ Ⓓ Ⓔ
52 Ⓐ Ⓑ Ⓒ Ⓓ Ⓔ
53 Ⓐ Ⓑ Ⓒ Ⓓ Ⓔ
54 Ⓐ Ⓑ Ⓒ Ⓓ Ⓔ
55 Ⓐ Ⓑ Ⓒ Ⓓ Ⓔ
56 Ⓐ Ⓑ Ⓒ Ⓓ Ⓔ

57 Ⓐ Ⓑ Ⓒ Ⓓ Ⓔ
58 Ⓐ Ⓑ Ⓒ Ⓓ Ⓔ
59 Ⓐ Ⓑ Ⓒ Ⓓ Ⓔ
60 Ⓐ Ⓑ Ⓒ Ⓓ Ⓔ
61 Ⓐ Ⓑ Ⓒ Ⓓ Ⓔ
62 Ⓐ Ⓑ Ⓒ Ⓓ Ⓔ
63 Ⓐ Ⓑ Ⓒ Ⓓ Ⓔ
64 Ⓐ Ⓑ Ⓒ Ⓓ Ⓔ

65 Ⓐ Ⓑ Ⓒ Ⓓ Ⓔ
66 Ⓐ Ⓑ Ⓒ Ⓓ Ⓔ
67 Ⓐ Ⓑ Ⓒ Ⓓ Ⓔ
68 Ⓐ Ⓑ Ⓒ Ⓓ Ⓔ
69 Ⓐ Ⓑ Ⓒ Ⓓ Ⓔ
70 Ⓐ Ⓑ Ⓒ Ⓓ Ⓔ
71 Ⓐ Ⓑ Ⓒ Ⓓ Ⓔ
72 Ⓐ Ⓑ Ⓒ Ⓓ Ⓔ

73 Ⓐ Ⓑ Ⓒ Ⓓ Ⓔ
74 Ⓐ Ⓑ Ⓒ Ⓓ Ⓔ
75 Ⓐ Ⓑ Ⓒ Ⓓ Ⓔ
76 Ⓐ Ⓑ Ⓒ Ⓓ Ⓔ
77 Ⓐ Ⓑ Ⓒ Ⓓ Ⓔ
78 Ⓐ Ⓑ Ⓒ Ⓓ Ⓔ
79 Ⓐ Ⓑ Ⓒ Ⓓ Ⓔ
80 Ⓐ Ⓑ Ⓒ Ⓓ Ⓔ

81 Ⓐ Ⓑ Ⓒ Ⓓ Ⓔ
82 Ⓐ Ⓑ Ⓒ Ⓓ Ⓔ
83 Ⓐ Ⓑ Ⓒ Ⓓ Ⓔ
84 Ⓐ Ⓑ Ⓒ Ⓓ Ⓔ
85 Ⓐ Ⓑ Ⓒ Ⓓ Ⓔ
86 Ⓐ Ⓑ Ⓒ Ⓓ Ⓔ
87 Ⓐ Ⓑ Ⓒ Ⓓ Ⓔ
88 Ⓐ Ⓑ Ⓒ Ⓓ Ⓔ

COMPLETE PRACTICE TEST #2
Part B – Address Memory – Segment #4

Directions

In this segment you have three minutes to attempt answering 88 questions. You must answer from memory. The boxes are not shown. Your answers are to be marked on the sample answer sheet at the bottom of the pages of Segment #4 – do not use the Compete Practice Test Answer Sheet for this segment. After completing this segment, turn to Segment #5 for further instructions.

Turn the page and begin when you are prepared to time yourself for precisely three minutes.

Hint: Remember, this segment is not scored, so you should not worry about your inability to answer all 88 questions, or your inability to answer all of them accurately, in only three minutes. Neither task is really possible in only three minutes. However, this is an ideal opportunity for you to test how well you have mastered your strategies and memorization so far. By sincerely trying to answer the questions, you can identify the areas where you are weaker and where you need to apply more effort.

1. Clifford	17. 7700-8499 Beach	33. Mathison
2. 8900-8999 Samuel	18. Pirate	34. Clifford
3. 8900-8999 West	19. Carroll	35. 8900-8999 Beach
4. 7700-8499 Samuel	20. Clifford	36. 6800-7599 Samuel
5. Alexander	21. 6800-7599 Samuel	37. 7700-8499 Beach
6. 6500-6699 Beach	22. 8900-8999 West	38. Island View
7. 6800-7599 West	23. 8600-8799 Beach	39. 6500-6699 West
8. 8600-8799 Samuel	24. 6800-7599 Beach	40. 6500-6699 Beach
9. Driftwood	25. Galloway	41. Carroll
10. Island View	26. 6800-7599 West	42. 6500-6699 Samuel
11. 8600-8799 West	27. 8600-8799 West	43. 8600-8799 Beach
12. 7700-8499 West	28. 8900-8999 Samuel	44. Alexander
13. 8900-8999 Samuel	29. Driftwood	45. 8900-8999 Beach
14. Runnels	30. 7700-8499 West	46. 8600-8799 Samuel
15. 8900-8999 Beach	31. 6800-7599 Beach	47. Runnels
16. 6500-6699 West	32. Lynwood	48. Pirate

1 Ⓐ Ⓑ Ⓒ Ⓓ Ⓔ   17 Ⓐ Ⓑ Ⓒ Ⓓ Ⓔ   33 Ⓐ Ⓑ Ⓒ Ⓓ Ⓔ
2 Ⓐ Ⓑ Ⓒ Ⓓ Ⓔ   18 Ⓐ Ⓑ Ⓒ Ⓓ Ⓔ   34 Ⓐ Ⓑ Ⓒ Ⓓ Ⓔ
3 Ⓐ Ⓑ Ⓒ Ⓓ Ⓔ   19 Ⓐ Ⓑ Ⓒ Ⓓ Ⓔ   35 Ⓐ Ⓑ Ⓒ Ⓓ Ⓔ
4 Ⓐ Ⓑ Ⓒ Ⓓ Ⓔ   20 Ⓐ Ⓑ Ⓒ Ⓓ Ⓔ   36 Ⓐ Ⓑ Ⓒ Ⓓ Ⓔ
5 Ⓐ Ⓑ Ⓒ Ⓓ Ⓔ   21 Ⓐ Ⓑ Ⓒ Ⓓ Ⓔ   37 Ⓐ Ⓑ Ⓒ Ⓓ Ⓔ
6 Ⓐ Ⓑ Ⓒ Ⓓ Ⓔ   22 Ⓐ Ⓑ Ⓒ Ⓓ Ⓔ   38 Ⓐ Ⓑ Ⓒ Ⓓ Ⓔ
7 Ⓐ Ⓑ Ⓒ Ⓓ Ⓔ   23 Ⓐ Ⓑ Ⓒ Ⓓ Ⓔ   39 Ⓐ Ⓑ Ⓒ Ⓓ Ⓔ
8 Ⓐ Ⓑ Ⓒ Ⓓ Ⓔ   24 Ⓐ Ⓑ Ⓒ Ⓓ Ⓔ   40 Ⓐ Ⓑ Ⓒ Ⓓ Ⓔ

9 Ⓐ Ⓑ Ⓒ Ⓓ Ⓔ   25 Ⓐ Ⓑ Ⓒ Ⓓ Ⓔ   41 Ⓐ Ⓑ Ⓒ Ⓓ Ⓔ
10 Ⓐ Ⓑ Ⓒ Ⓓ Ⓔ   26 Ⓐ Ⓑ Ⓒ Ⓓ Ⓔ   42 Ⓐ Ⓑ Ⓒ Ⓓ Ⓔ
11 Ⓐ Ⓑ Ⓒ Ⓓ Ⓔ   27 Ⓐ Ⓑ Ⓒ Ⓓ Ⓔ   43 Ⓐ Ⓑ Ⓒ Ⓓ Ⓔ
12 Ⓐ Ⓑ Ⓒ Ⓓ Ⓔ   28 Ⓐ Ⓑ Ⓒ Ⓓ Ⓔ   44 Ⓐ Ⓑ Ⓒ Ⓓ Ⓔ
13 Ⓐ Ⓑ Ⓒ Ⓓ Ⓔ   29 Ⓐ Ⓑ Ⓒ Ⓓ Ⓔ   45 Ⓐ Ⓑ Ⓒ Ⓓ Ⓔ
14 Ⓐ Ⓑ Ⓒ Ⓓ Ⓔ   30 Ⓐ Ⓑ Ⓒ Ⓓ Ⓔ   46 Ⓐ Ⓑ Ⓒ Ⓓ Ⓔ
15 Ⓐ Ⓑ Ⓒ Ⓓ Ⓔ   31 Ⓐ Ⓑ Ⓒ Ⓓ Ⓔ   47 Ⓐ Ⓑ Ⓒ Ⓓ Ⓔ
16 Ⓐ Ⓑ Ⓒ Ⓓ Ⓔ   32 Ⓐ Ⓑ Ⓒ Ⓓ Ⓔ   48 Ⓐ Ⓑ Ⓒ Ⓓ Ⓔ

49. 8600-8799 Beach	65. 6800-7599 West	81. Lynwood
50. Clifford	66. 8900-8999 West	82. 8600-8799 Beach
51. 7700-8499 West	67. Island View	83. Runnels
52. 6800-7599 Samuel	68. 8900-8999 Samuel	84. 6800-7599 Beach
53. Galloway	69. 7700-8499 Samuel	85. 6500-6699 Samuel
54. 6500-6699 Samuel	70. Mathison	86. 6800-7599 West
55. 6500-6699 Beach	71. Pirate	87. 6500-6699 Samuel
56. 8600-8799 West	72. 6500-6699 West	88. 8900-8999 Beach
57. 8900-8999 West	73. 8900-8999 Beach	
58. 6800-7599 Samuel	74. 6500-6699 West	
59. Clifford	75. Alexander	
60. Lynwood	76. Driftwood	
61. 6500-6699 Beach	77. Galloway	
62. 8600-8799 West	78. 7700-8499 Samuel	
63. Carroll	79. 6800-7599 Beach	
64. 8600-8799 Samuel	80. 8900-8999 Samuel	

49 Ⓐ Ⓑ Ⓒ Ⓓ Ⓔ
50 Ⓐ Ⓑ Ⓒ Ⓓ Ⓔ
51 Ⓐ Ⓑ Ⓒ Ⓓ Ⓔ
52 Ⓐ Ⓑ Ⓒ Ⓓ Ⓔ
53 Ⓐ Ⓑ Ⓒ Ⓓ Ⓔ
54 Ⓐ Ⓑ Ⓒ Ⓓ Ⓔ
55 Ⓐ Ⓑ Ⓒ Ⓓ Ⓔ
56 Ⓐ Ⓑ Ⓒ Ⓓ Ⓔ

57 Ⓐ Ⓑ Ⓒ Ⓓ Ⓔ
58 Ⓐ Ⓑ Ⓒ Ⓓ Ⓔ
59 Ⓐ Ⓑ Ⓒ Ⓓ Ⓔ
60 Ⓐ Ⓑ Ⓒ Ⓓ Ⓔ
61 Ⓐ Ⓑ Ⓒ Ⓓ Ⓔ
62 Ⓐ Ⓑ Ⓒ Ⓓ Ⓔ
63 Ⓐ Ⓑ Ⓒ Ⓓ Ⓔ
64 Ⓐ Ⓑ Ⓒ Ⓓ Ⓔ

65 Ⓐ Ⓑ Ⓒ Ⓓ Ⓔ
66 Ⓐ Ⓑ Ⓒ Ⓓ Ⓔ
67 Ⓐ Ⓑ Ⓒ Ⓓ Ⓔ
68 Ⓐ Ⓑ Ⓒ Ⓓ Ⓔ
69 Ⓐ Ⓑ Ⓒ Ⓓ Ⓔ
70 Ⓐ Ⓑ Ⓒ Ⓓ Ⓔ
71 Ⓐ Ⓑ Ⓒ Ⓓ Ⓔ
72 Ⓐ Ⓑ Ⓒ Ⓓ Ⓔ

73 Ⓐ Ⓑ Ⓒ Ⓓ Ⓔ
74 Ⓐ Ⓑ Ⓒ Ⓓ Ⓔ
75 Ⓐ Ⓑ Ⓒ Ⓓ Ⓔ
76 Ⓐ Ⓑ Ⓒ Ⓓ Ⓔ
77 Ⓐ Ⓑ Ⓒ Ⓓ Ⓔ
78 Ⓐ Ⓑ Ⓒ Ⓓ Ⓔ
79 Ⓐ Ⓑ Ⓒ Ⓓ Ⓔ
80 Ⓐ Ⓑ Ⓒ Ⓓ Ⓔ

81 Ⓐ Ⓑ Ⓒ Ⓓ Ⓔ
82 Ⓐ Ⓑ Ⓒ Ⓓ Ⓔ
83 Ⓐ Ⓑ Ⓒ Ⓓ Ⓔ
84 Ⓐ Ⓑ Ⓒ Ⓓ Ⓔ
85 Ⓐ Ⓑ Ⓒ Ⓓ Ⓔ
86 Ⓐ Ⓑ Ⓒ Ⓓ Ⓔ
87 Ⓐ Ⓑ Ⓒ Ⓓ Ⓔ
88 Ⓐ Ⓑ Ⓒ Ⓓ Ⓔ

COMPLETE PRACTICE TEST #2
Part B – Address Memory – Segment #5

Directions

In this segment, you are given five minutes to study the addresses. There are no questions to answer in this segment – it is a study period only. As before, the boxes are not reprinted here for your use. Instead, you are instructed to turn back to Address Memory Segment #1 and to spend five minutes studying the boxes displayed there. After studying for five minutes, turn to Segment #6 for directions on how to continue.

Begin studying when you are prepared to time yourself for precisely five minutes.

114

COMPLETE PRACTICE TEST #2
Part B – Address Memory – Segment #6

Directions

In this segment, you have five minutes to attempt answering 88 questions. You are to try to answer from memory, but the boxes are shown if you need to refer to them. Your answers are to be marked on the sample answer sheet at the bottom of the pages of Segment #6 – do not use the Compete Practice Test Answer Sheet for this segment. After completing this segment, turn to Segment #7 for further instructions.

Turn the page and begin when you are prepared to time yourself for precisely five minutes.

Hint: Remember your strategies! This segment is not scored, so do not take the questions seriously. Instead, mark a handful of random answers and use the five minutes to study and memorize the addresses.

A	B	C
6800-7599 Beach	8900-8999 Beach	7700-8499 Beach
Island View	Galloway	Alexander
7700-8499 West	8600-8799 West	8900-8999 West
Carroll	Runnels	Driftwood
6500-6699 Samuel	7700-8499 Samuel	8600-8799 Samuel

1. 8600-8799 West
2. Alexander
3. 6500-6699 West
4. Mathison
5. 6800-7599 Beach
6. 8900-8999 Samuel
7. Carroll
8. 7700-8499 Beach

9. Lynwood
10. Island View
11. 6500-6699 Samuel
12. 8900-8999 Beach
13. Pirate
14. 7700-8499 West
15. Clifford
16. 6500-6699 Beach

17. 8900-8999 West
18. 7700-8499 Samuel
19. Driftwood
20. 6800-7599 Samuel
21. Galloway
22. Mathison
23. 8600-8799 Samuel
24. 6800-7599 Beach

25. 6500-6699 Beach
26. Runnels
27. 7700-8499 West
28. 6800-7599 West
29. 7700-8499 Beach
30. Pirate
31. 6500-6699 West
32. Lynwood

33. Alexander
34. 8900-8999 West
35. 7700-8499 Samuel
36. 6500-6699 Beach
37. 6500-6699 Samuel
38. 8900-8999 Beach
39. 8600-8799 West
40. 6800-7599 Samuel

41. Island View
42. Carroll
43. 7700-8499 West
44. Driftwood
45. Galloway
46. 6800-7599 Beach
47. 8900-8999 Samuel
48. Mathison

1 Ⓐ Ⓑ Ⓒ Ⓓ Ⓔ
2 Ⓐ Ⓑ Ⓒ Ⓓ Ⓔ
3 Ⓐ Ⓑ Ⓒ Ⓓ Ⓔ
4 Ⓐ Ⓑ Ⓒ Ⓓ Ⓔ
5 Ⓐ Ⓑ Ⓒ Ⓓ Ⓔ
6 Ⓐ Ⓑ Ⓒ Ⓓ Ⓔ
7 Ⓐ Ⓑ Ⓒ Ⓓ Ⓔ
8 Ⓐ Ⓑ Ⓒ Ⓓ Ⓔ
9 Ⓐ Ⓑ Ⓒ Ⓓ Ⓔ
10 Ⓐ Ⓑ Ⓒ Ⓓ Ⓔ
11 Ⓐ Ⓑ Ⓒ Ⓓ Ⓔ
12 Ⓐ Ⓑ Ⓒ Ⓓ Ⓔ
13 Ⓐ Ⓑ Ⓒ Ⓓ Ⓔ
14 Ⓐ Ⓑ Ⓒ Ⓓ Ⓔ
15 Ⓐ Ⓑ Ⓒ Ⓓ Ⓔ
16 Ⓐ Ⓑ Ⓒ Ⓓ Ⓔ

17 Ⓐ Ⓑ Ⓒ Ⓓ Ⓔ
18 Ⓐ Ⓑ Ⓒ Ⓓ Ⓔ
19 Ⓐ Ⓑ Ⓒ Ⓓ Ⓔ
20 Ⓐ Ⓑ Ⓒ Ⓓ Ⓔ
21 Ⓐ Ⓑ Ⓒ Ⓓ Ⓔ
22 Ⓐ Ⓑ Ⓒ Ⓓ Ⓔ
23 Ⓐ Ⓑ Ⓒ Ⓓ Ⓔ
24 Ⓐ Ⓑ Ⓒ Ⓓ Ⓔ
25 Ⓐ Ⓑ Ⓒ Ⓓ Ⓔ
26 Ⓐ Ⓑ Ⓒ Ⓓ Ⓔ
27 Ⓐ Ⓑ Ⓒ Ⓓ Ⓔ
28 Ⓐ Ⓑ Ⓒ Ⓓ Ⓔ
29 Ⓐ Ⓑ Ⓒ Ⓓ Ⓔ
30 Ⓐ Ⓑ Ⓒ Ⓓ Ⓔ
31 Ⓐ Ⓑ Ⓒ Ⓓ Ⓔ
32 Ⓐ Ⓑ Ⓒ Ⓓ Ⓔ

33 Ⓐ Ⓑ Ⓒ Ⓓ Ⓔ
34 Ⓐ Ⓑ Ⓒ Ⓓ Ⓔ
35 Ⓐ Ⓑ Ⓒ Ⓓ Ⓔ
36 Ⓐ Ⓑ Ⓒ Ⓓ Ⓔ
37 Ⓐ Ⓑ Ⓒ Ⓓ Ⓔ
38 Ⓐ Ⓑ Ⓒ Ⓓ Ⓔ
39 Ⓐ Ⓑ Ⓒ Ⓓ Ⓔ
40 Ⓐ Ⓑ Ⓒ Ⓓ Ⓔ
41 Ⓐ Ⓑ Ⓒ Ⓓ Ⓔ
42 Ⓐ Ⓑ Ⓒ Ⓓ Ⓔ
43 Ⓐ Ⓑ Ⓒ Ⓓ Ⓔ
44 Ⓐ Ⓑ Ⓒ Ⓓ Ⓔ
45 Ⓐ Ⓑ Ⓒ Ⓓ Ⓔ
46 Ⓐ Ⓑ Ⓒ Ⓓ Ⓔ
47 Ⓐ Ⓑ Ⓒ Ⓓ Ⓔ
48 Ⓐ Ⓑ Ⓒ Ⓓ Ⓔ

D	E
8600-8799 Beach	6500-6699 Beach
Mathison	Clifford
6500-6699 West	6800-7599 West
Pirate	Lynwood
6800-7599 Samuel	8900-8999 Samuel

49. Clifford
50. 6800-7599 West
51. 6500-6699 Samuel
52. 8600-8799 Samuel
53. Island View
54. 7700-8499 Beach
55. Runnels
56. Lynwood

57. 8600-8799 West
58. 6500-6699 West
59. Pirate
60. 6500-6699 Beach
61. Galloway
62. 8900-8999 Beach
63. 7700-8499 West
64. Clifford

65. 8600-8799 Beach
66. 6800-7599 Samuel
67. Alexander
68. 8900-8999 West
69. Driftwood
70. Carroll
71. 6800-7599 Beach
72. 8900-8999 Samuel

73. 7700-8499 Beach
74. Galloway
75. Clifford
76. 8600-8799 Samuel
77. 8900-8999 Beach
78. 6800-7599 Beach
79. Lynwood
80. 8600-8799 West

81. Mathison
82. 7700-8499 Beach
83. 6500-6699 Samuel
84. 7700-8499 Samuel
85. 6500-6699 West
86. Driftwood
87. Island View
88. 6800-7599 West

49 Ⓐ Ⓑ Ⓒ Ⓓ Ⓔ
50 Ⓐ Ⓑ Ⓒ Ⓓ Ⓔ
51 Ⓐ Ⓑ Ⓒ Ⓓ Ⓔ
52 Ⓐ Ⓑ Ⓒ Ⓓ Ⓔ
53 Ⓐ Ⓑ Ⓒ Ⓓ Ⓔ
54 Ⓐ Ⓑ Ⓒ Ⓓ Ⓔ
55 Ⓐ Ⓑ Ⓒ Ⓓ Ⓔ
56 Ⓐ Ⓑ Ⓒ Ⓓ Ⓔ

57 Ⓐ Ⓑ Ⓒ Ⓓ Ⓔ
58 Ⓐ Ⓑ Ⓒ Ⓓ Ⓔ
59 Ⓐ Ⓑ Ⓒ Ⓓ Ⓔ
60 Ⓐ Ⓑ Ⓒ Ⓓ Ⓔ
61 Ⓐ Ⓑ Ⓒ Ⓓ Ⓔ
62 Ⓐ Ⓑ Ⓒ Ⓓ Ⓔ
63 Ⓐ Ⓑ Ⓒ Ⓓ Ⓔ
64 Ⓐ Ⓑ Ⓒ Ⓓ Ⓔ

65 Ⓐ Ⓑ Ⓒ Ⓓ Ⓔ
66 Ⓐ Ⓑ Ⓒ Ⓓ Ⓔ
67 Ⓐ Ⓑ Ⓒ Ⓓ Ⓔ
68 Ⓐ Ⓑ Ⓒ Ⓓ Ⓔ
69 Ⓐ Ⓑ Ⓒ Ⓓ Ⓔ
70 Ⓐ Ⓑ Ⓒ Ⓓ Ⓔ
71 Ⓐ Ⓑ Ⓒ Ⓓ Ⓔ
72 Ⓐ Ⓑ Ⓒ Ⓓ Ⓔ

73 Ⓐ Ⓑ Ⓒ Ⓓ Ⓔ
74 Ⓐ Ⓑ Ⓒ Ⓓ Ⓔ
75 Ⓐ Ⓑ Ⓒ Ⓓ Ⓔ
76 Ⓐ Ⓑ Ⓒ Ⓓ Ⓔ
77 Ⓐ Ⓑ Ⓒ Ⓓ Ⓔ
78 Ⓐ Ⓑ Ⓒ Ⓓ Ⓔ
79 Ⓐ Ⓑ Ⓒ Ⓓ Ⓔ
80 Ⓐ Ⓑ Ⓒ Ⓓ Ⓔ

81 Ⓐ Ⓑ Ⓒ Ⓓ Ⓔ
82 Ⓐ Ⓑ Ⓒ Ⓓ Ⓔ
83 Ⓐ Ⓑ Ⓒ Ⓓ Ⓔ
84 Ⓐ Ⓑ Ⓒ Ⓓ Ⓔ
85 Ⓐ Ⓑ Ⓒ Ⓓ Ⓔ
86 Ⓐ Ⓑ Ⓒ Ⓓ Ⓔ
87 Ⓐ Ⓑ Ⓒ Ⓓ Ⓔ
88 Ⓐ Ⓑ Ⓒ Ⓓ Ⓔ

COMPLETE PRACTICE TEST #2
Part B – Address Memory – Segment #7

Directions

This is the final segment of the Address Memory section. You have five minutes to answer 88 questions. You must answer from memory. The boxes are not shown. On this segment, there is not a sample answer sheet at the bottom of the page. Instead, mark your answers on the Complete Practice Test Answer Sheet that your tore out of the book. After completing this segment, you have finished the full Address Memory section. Turn to the Number Series section of the practice test for instructions on how to continue.

Turn the page and begin when you are prepared to time yourself for precisely five minutes.

1. Clifford
2. 8900-8999 Samuel
3. 8900-8999 West
4. 7700-8499 Samuel
5. Alexander
6. 6500-6699 Beach
7. 6800-7599 West
8. 8600-8799 Samuel

9. Driftwood
10. Island View
11. 8600-8799 West
12. 7700-8499 West
13. 8900-8999 Samuel
14. Runnels
15. 8900-8999 Beach
16. 6500-6699 West

17. 7700-8499 Beach
18. Pirate
19. Carroll
20. Clifford
21. 6800-7599 Samuel
22. 8900-8999 West
23. 8600-8799 Beach
24. 6800-7599 Beach

25. Galloway
26. 6800-7599 West
27. 8600-8799 West
28. 8900-8999 Samuel
29. Driftwood
30. 7700-8499 West
31. 6800-7599 Beach
32. Lynwood

33. Mathison
34. Clifford
35. 8900-8999 Beach
36. 6800-7599 Samuel
37. 7700-8499 Beach
38. Island View
39. 6500-6699 West
40. 6500-6699 Beach

41. Carroll
42. 6500-6699 Samuel
43. 8600-8799 Beach
44. Alexander
45. 8900-8999 Beach
46. 8600-8799 Samuel
47. Runnels
48. Pirate

49. 8600-8799 Beach
50. Clifford
51. 7700-8499 West
52. 6800-7599 Samuel
53. Galloway
54. 6500-6699 Samuel
55. 6500-6699 Beach
56. 8600-8799 West

57. 8900-8999 West
58. 6800-7599 Samuel
59. Clifford
60. Lynwood
61. 6500-6699 Beach
62. 8600-8799 West
63. Carroll
64. 8600-8799 Samuel

65. 6800-7599 West
66. 8900-8999 West
67. Island View
68. 8900-8999 Samuel
69. 7700-8499 Samuel
70. Mathison
71. Pirate
72. 6500-6699 West

73. 8900-8999 Beach
74. 6500-6699 West
75. Alexander
76. Driftwood
77. Galloway
78. 7700-8499 Samuel
79. 6800-7599 Beach
80. 8900-8999 Samuel

81. Lynwood
82. 8600-8799 Beach
83. Runnels
84. 6800-7599 Beach
85. 6500-6699 Samuel
86. 6800-7599 West
87. 6500-6699 Samuel
88. 8900-8999 Beach

COMPLETE PRACTICE TEST #2
Part C – Number Series

Directions

On this section, you have 20 minutes to answer 24 mathematical questions. Each question consists of a series of numbers followed by two blanks. You are to calculate what two numbers would logically follow in the series and that would therefore fit into the two blanks. Choose the answer – A, B, C, D, or E – that contains the correct two numbers, in the proper order, that should follow in the series. Mark your answers on the Complete Practice Test Answer Sheet in the section entitled Number Series. After completing this section, turn to the Following Oral Instructions section for directions on how to continue.

The solutions to all the Number Series questions in all six of the practice tests are given in the back of your book. After scoring each Number Series practice test, find and review the solutions for the questions you missed. This should better prepare you to answer similar questions on the other practice tests as well as on your actual exam.

Turn the page and begin when you are prepared to time yourself for precisely 20 minutes.

Hint: Remember to use the Circles and Squares Strategy to identify, separate, and solve the multiple sequences found in many questions.

COMPLETE PRACTICE TEST #2
Part C – Number Series

1. 12 11 10 9 8 7 6 ___ ___   A) 4,5 B) 5,4 C) 2,7 D) 5,5 E) 10,10

2. 14 16 18 20 22 24 ___ ___   A) 26,28 B) 29,30 C) 28,26 D) 26,24 E) 14,16

3. 4 9 14 19 24 ___ ___   A) 4,9, B) 25,29 C) 29,35 D) 29,34 E) 8,34

4. 2 5 3 11 4 17 ___ ___   A) 7,11 B) 5,23 C) 23,5 D) 5,9 E) 23,25

5. 3 8 11 13 19 18 ___ ___   A) 27,23 B) 23,28 C) 28,41 D) 33,48 E) 48,51

6. 28 25 10 12 22 19 14 ___ ___   A) 14,15 B) 12,16 C) 16,16 D) 25,30 E) 33,16

7. 33 66 44 55 55 44 ___ ___   A) 65,32 B) 68,90 C) 66,77 D) 66,33 E) 33,22

8. 21 87 24 85 27 83 ___ ___   A) 30,90 B)28,40 C) 81,96 D) 30,81 E) 40,40

9. 10 30 15 20 35 25 30 ___ ___   A) 40,35 B) 35,20 C) 20,35 D) 40,25 E) 36,15

10. 75 8 75 15 75 22 ___ ___   A) 29,15 B) 75,8 C)15,22 D) 29,8 E) 75,29

11. 1 9 8 1 9 8 ___ ___   A) 1,9 B) 8,1 C) 9,8 D) 9,9 E) 1,5

12. 13 15 90 35 37 87 ___ ___   A) 57,37 B) 89,59 C) 90,37 D) 57,59 E) 59,90

13. 1 2 4 5 7 8 10 ___ ___   A) 13,8 B) 11,4 C)13,7 D) 11,7 E) 11,13

14. 41 36 63 68 31 26 73 ___ ___   A) 78,68 B) 78,21 C)21,41 D) 78,31 E) 21,73

15. 7 12 37 17 22 40 27 ___ ___   A) 32,43 B) 43,37 C) 22,43 D) 32,17 E) 27,27

16. 14 14 14 26 17 17 17 40 20 ___ ___   A) 20,40 B) 17,17 C) 20,20 D) 14,26 E) 20,17

17. 24 22 21 34 20 19 44 ___ ___   A) 43,42 B) 17,18 C) 18,17 D)23,43 E) 43, 23

18. 1 3 4 7 11 18 ___ ___   A) 11,47 B) 18,4 C) 29,47 D) 29,32 E) 7,4

19. 2 7 12 17 ___ ___   A) 27,27 B) 22,12 C) 20,11 D)17,7 E) 22,27

20. 13 14 44 42 40 15 16 38 ___ ___   A) 36,34 B) 44,40 C)34,14 D) 15,36 E) 15,38

21. 9 10 30 28 11 12 ___ ___   A) 30,26 B) 26,24 C)28,12 D) 11,20 E) 24,30

22. 33 32 31 31 29 30 27 ___ ___   A) 28,26 B) 29,29 C) 29,25 D) 25,23 E) 31,29

23. 10 30 29 28 9 27 26 25 8 ___ ___   A) 23,22 B) 25,30 C) 29,24 D) 24,23 E) 32,21

24. 8 45 40 28 35 30 48 ___ ___   A) 24,19 B) 21,26 C) 32,40 D) 22,34 E) 25,20

COMPLETE PRACTICE TEST #2
Part D – Following Oral Instructions

Directions

On this section of the test, the Exam Administrator will read questions/instructions aloud to the group of test takers. These oral instructions will direct you to write/mark certain items in your test booklet, which in turn will lead you to the correct answer(s). Finally, you will be verbally instructed to mark the correct answer(s) on your answer sheet. You must answer exclusively based upon what you hear – there are no questions for you to read.

The following pages of this practice test are samples of the test booklet pages on which you will write/mark as verbally instructed. Mark your answers on the Complete Practice Test Answer Sheet in the Following Oral Instructions section.

To practice realistically, you must either listen to the questions on the author's recording or have someone read them aloud to you. Do not look over the questions before taking the practice test. Once you have completed the practice test, you should then review the questions you missed in order to determine what caused you to miss them. This review should enable you to be more successful on similar questions next time.

The author's recording of all six Following Oral Directions practice tests is an ideal and convenient way to practice. The recorded questions are presented in the proper format, at the proper pace, and with proper diction. These recordings allow you to practice anytime and anywhere you wish. With these recordings, your practice – and in turn your success – will not be dependent upon someone else's schedule and whims. For details and ordering information, see the order form at the back of your book.

If someone will be reading the questions to you, he/she will find the questions for each practice test in the back of your book in the section entitled Following Oral Instructions – Practice Test Questions. The reader should carefully tear the questions out of your book in order to use them. The questions should be read at a rather slow and steady pace of approximately 75 words per minute and with proper diction. The reader should also pause between instructions/questions as directed in the wording of each question.

Once you complete the Following Oral Instructions section, you have finished this practice test, and you should then begin the next practice test in your book. Once you have completed all six practice tests plus the Extra Address Checking Practice Exercises as instructed, you should be fully prepared to excel on the actual exam.

Turn the page and begin when you are prepared to listen to the questions from the author's recording or from someone who will read the questions to you in the proper fashion.

Hint: Remember your strategies:
- *You will answer by marking number-letter combinations.*
- *Where you mark an answer on the answer sheet will not match the question number.*
- *Listen closely and attentively.*
- *Simply follow the instructions you hear – do not try to figure them out.*
- *Some questions will have multiple answers, and you must mark all of them.*
- *Mark your answers quickly and be ready to listen to the next question.*
- *Make identifying notes for later recall.*

COMPLETE PRACTICE TEST #2
Part D – Following Oral Instructions

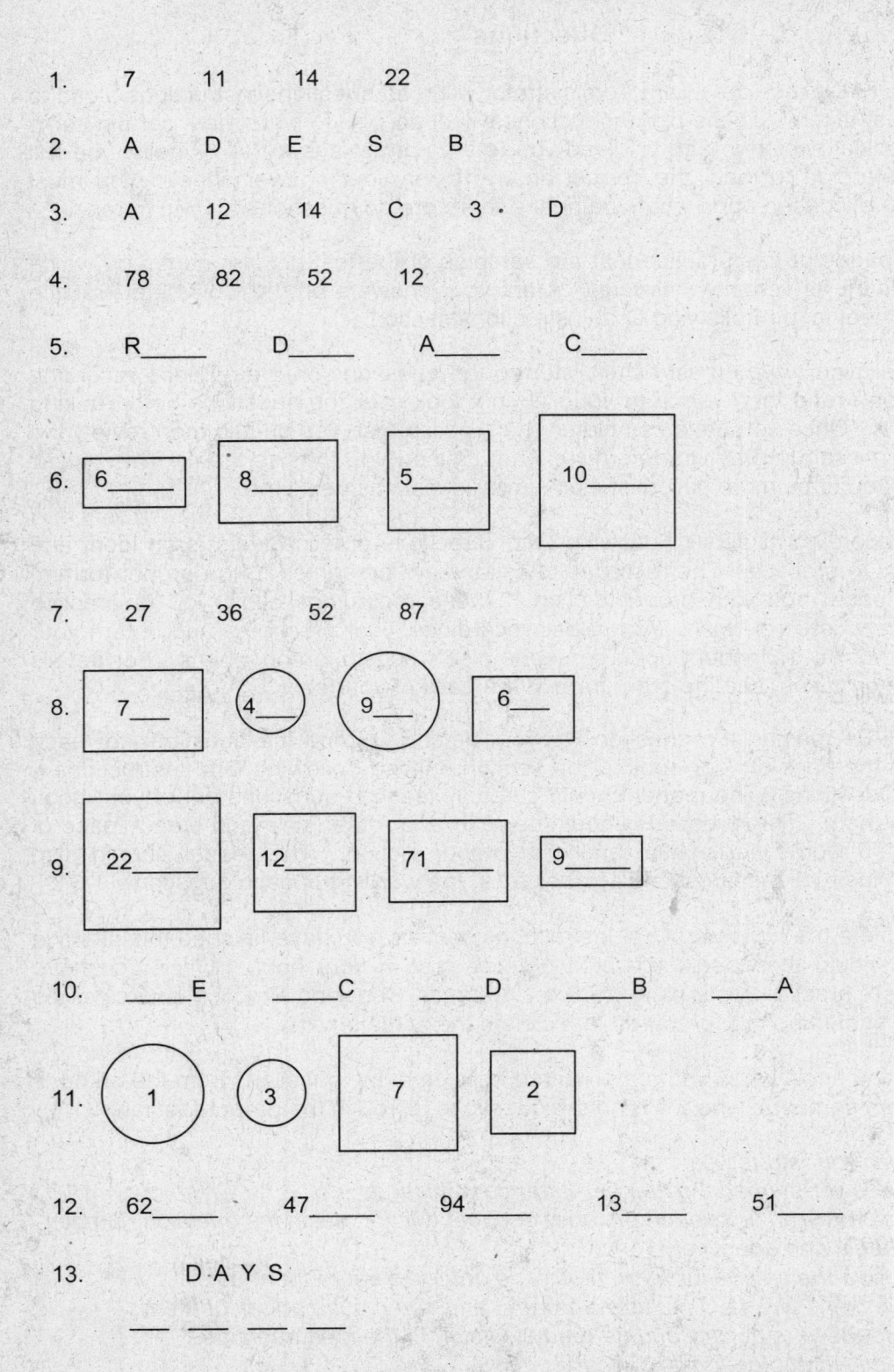

1.   7   11   14   22

2.   A   D   E   S   B

3.   A   12   14   C   3 · D

4.   78   82   52   12

5.   R____   D____   A____   C____

6. | 6____ | | 8____ | | 5____ | | 10____ |

7.   27   36   52   87

8.   7___   4___   9___   6___

9.   22____   12____   71____   9____

10.   ___E   ___C   ___D   ___B   ___A

11.   1   3   7   2

12.   62____   47____   94____   13____   51____

13.   D A Y S

    __ __ __ __

128

14. | 2:20 PM ____ | 12:05 AM ____ | 6:10 PM ____ | 9:45 AM ____ | 1:15 PM ____ |

15. _____

16. | 9___ | 32___ | 57___ | 64___ |

17. | Chicago 91 | Dallas 52 | Denver 12 | Akron 72 |

18. | 12:00 AM | 3:00 PM | 6:00 AM |

19. R   S   H   W   E

20. | 32___ | 14___ | 79___ | 51___ |

21. | 11___ | 49___ | 1___ | 17___ | 29___ |

22. _____

23. A_____   B_____   C_____   D_____   E_____

24. | Gulfport 81_____ | Gainsville 71_____ |

25. 87   21   58   88   68

26. MATH PROBLEM

130

COMPLETE PRACTICE TEST #3

This practice test contains samples of all four sections of the actual exam. The instructions given are similar to those on the actual exam. The format of this practice test is identical to that of the actual exam. Where pertinent, hints are given about your test taking strategies. Of course, these hints will not appear on the actual exam.

It is imperative that you take this practice test in as realistic a fashion as possible. **Your practice will have no value unless it is done realistically.** Therefore, you must precisely time yourself on the Address Checking, Address Memory, and Number Series sections. Our Timed Practice Test CD is a convenient way to practice realistically and time yourself precisely. Also, you must either listen to the Following Oral Instructions questions on our Oral Instructions Practice Tests CD or have someone read them to you – *do not read the questions yourself!* The Following Oral Instructions questions can be found in the back of your book if someone will be reading them to you.

To take this practice test, first turn to the back of your book and carefully tear out one of the **Complete Practice Test Answer Sheets.** Mark the answers to the scored segments of the practice test on this answer sheet. (Remember, of the seven segments on the Address Memory Section, only the final one is scored. Accordingly, you should mark answers for only the final Address Memory segment on your Complete Practice Test Answer Sheet. The other segments of the Address Memory Section that call for answers have accompanying sample answer sheets where you should mark answers.)

The correct answers are provided in the back of your book. Immediately upon completing the practice test, **it is imperative that you score each section** using the formulas given under the Sections of the Exam heading in your book. Scoring is necessary in order to gauge your progress and to identify your individual areas of weakness that may need extra attention.

After completing and scoring each practice test, move on to the next. **After completing all six practice tests and the Extra Address Checking Practice Exercises as instructed, you should be prepared for the actual exam.** If you feel the need to practice more, repeat as many of the practice tests as you like. After that much practice, the questions will likely have become a confusing blur in your mind. It is highly unlikely that you will be able to remember many of the individual questions or answers. Therefore, you should be able to gain practice value from the exercises even though you have already taken them once.

Do not look over the practice test questions until you are ready to start – meaning until you have set a timer for the allotted period of time. Similarly, after completing one section of the practice test, do not look over the next one until your are ready to start it. Likewise, stop working and put down your pencil immediately when the allotted period of time has expired. As has been emphasized before but cannot be emphasized enough, your practice is of absolutely no value unless it is done realistically. Also, you must train yourself (1) to not open your test booklet or pick up your pencil until instructed to do so and (2) to close your booklet and put down your pencil immediately upon being so instructed. The Postal Service has a zero tolerance policy on these matters. Any variance may be viewed as cheating and may result in your disqualification.

Good luck on your practice test, and even better luck on your actual exam!

COMPLETE PRACTICE TEST #3
Part A – Address Checking

Directions

In this part of the test, you will have to decide whether two addresses are alike or different. You will have 6 minutes to answer 95 questions. Each question consists of a pair of addresses. If the two addresses in the pair are exactly alike in every way, darken the oval with the letter "A" for *Alike*. If the two addresses are different in any way, darken the oval with the letter "D" for *Different*. Mark your answers on the Complete Practice Test Answer Sheet in the section entitled Address Checking.

Turn the page and begin when you are prepared to time yourself for precisely 6 minutes.

Note: You will notice that this section of your practice test is spread across two pages. This is the exact same format that you will actually experience on the Address Checking section of the real exam. For economy and convenience, other study guides frequently condense the two pages of this section down to only one. You will also notice that the Address Checking questions are presented in a font, or type of print, that is different from the rest of the book. This font matches what is actually used on the real exam, and, as you will see, it makes this section even more challenging. However, it is imperative that you practice realistically and that you become acquainted with and comfortable with the actual format of the exam. We have accordingly formatted this practice test realistically for your benefit.

Hint: Remember your strategies:
- *Pace yourself for speed and accuracy – emphasis on speed!*
- *Use one glance-over for easier/shorter addresses.*
- *Use two glance-over's for harder/longer addresses.*
- *Never make a third pass or glance-over!*
- *Overlap the answer sheet & the questions to keep them as close together as possible.*
- *Use your extra pencil, your hand, or your fingers to mark/keep your place.*
- *Use your Speed Pencil and your Speed Marking strategies for much greater speed.*

COMPLETE PRACTICE TEST #3
Part A – Address Checking

1.	3539 North Causeway	3593 North Causeway
2.	Plainsville, Ill. 36962	Plainvill, Ill. 36962
3.	352 N. 5th Ave.	352 N. 5th Ave.
4.	Saunemin, Md. 20584	Saumenin, Md. 20584
5.	#255 Apt. D-45	#255 Apt. B-45
6.	Zalma, Mo.	Zalma, Mo.
7.	1558 Cuevas Estates	1558 Cuevas Estates
8.	312 Jackson Square Notting	313 Jackson Square Notting
9.	Morris Landing, Wyo. 80399	Morris Landing, Wyo. 80399
10.	82499 West Plum Rd.	82499 East Plum Rd.
11.	104 Runnels Ave. South	104 Runnels Ave. South
12.	Collinsville, N.D. 34569	Collinsville, N.H. 93658
13.	#790 Royal Oak Roadway	#790 Royal Oak Roadway
14.	7778 Tower Hill	7778 Tower Hill
15.	Tiffany Gardens Apt. #101	Tiffany Gardens Apt. #101
16.	Metamorassa, Fla. 78232	Metmorassa, Fla. 78232
17.	975 Misson Sothe N.W.	975 Misson Sothe N.W.
18.	del Amos Hwy. 57 South	del Amos Hwy. 57 South
19.	5275 West Water Way	5725 West Water Way
20.	North Ridge, Ga. 43189	North Ridge, Ga. 43189
21.	545 Hewes Ave. S.W.	454 Hewes Ave. S.W.
22.	1106 East Old Pass Rd.	1106 East Old Pass Rd.
23.	3992 Leigh High Blvd.	3992 Leigh High Blvd.
24.	45 Townhall Express Way	45 Townhall Express Way
25.	Lake Byron, Minn. 40025	Lake Pyron, Maine 00425
26.	1212 Rual del Haban	1212 Rual del Haban
27.	Reno, Nev. 70900	Reno, Nev. 70909
28.	10004 St. Charles	1004 St. Charles
29.	67439 Ethel Avenue	67349 Ethel Avenue
30.	St. John, Maine 67948	St. John, Maine 67948
31.	2745 Cookie Ct.	2745 Cookie Ct.
32.	Juneville, N.C. 57684	Juneville, N.D. 57864
33.	147 Flower St.	1470 Flower St.
34.	Coronet, N.Y. 95847	Coronet, N.H. 95487
35.	1647 Clearview St. Apt. 6	1647 Clearview St. Apt. 6
36.	Wheatsdale, Ohio 45264	Wheatsville, Ohio 45624
37.	1684 Mushroom Blvd. N.W.	1684 Mushroom Blvd. N.
38.	88B Cinnamon Cirlce	888 Cinnamon Circle
39.	Flagg, Minn. 74925	Flagg, Minn. 74925
40.	Rustway Blvd. 69 N.E.	Rustway Blvd. 96 N.E.
41.	168500 Independence Blvd.	165860 Independence Blvd.
42.	Congress, Wash. D.C. 26734	Congress, Wash. D.C. 26374
43.	Rockchester, N.Y. 73593	Rockchester, N.Y. 73593
44.	1786 Empire St. N.E.	1789 Empire St. N.E.
45.	1475 North Shore Parkway	1475 North Shore Roadway
46.	1976 Colonial Road	1796 Colonial Road
47.	Alden Manor, West Virginia	Alden Manor, West Virginia
48.	14 Fair Lawn & Paramus N.	14 Fair Lawn & Pampas N.

49.	Staten Island, N.Y. 95874	Staten Island, N.Y. 95784
50.	369 New Haven Avenue E.	396 New Haven Avenue E.
51.	46-D Bridgeport St.	46-D Bridgeport St.
52.	7345 East Overhead Drive	7354 East Overhead Drive
53.	Billings, Mont.	Billings, Mont.
54.	303 Marice Drive NW	303 Marice Drive NW
55.	3906 Castille Dr.	3906 Castille Dr.
56.	4503 46th Ave. South	4503 46th Ave. North
57.	Parkwood, Del. 20643	Parkwood, Del. 20643
58.	3712 Reynosa Road	3712 Reynosa Road
59.	Bel-Aire Moble Home Pk.	Bel-Aire Mobil Home Pk.
60.	1700 John Quincy Adams W	1700 John Quincy Adams E
61.	#44 Racquet Club	#44 Racquet Club
62.	Crest View, Wash. 80025	Crest View, Wash. 80225
63.	1415 Avolone-Topango Rd.	1415 Avolone-Topango Rd.
64.	01800 E. Beach Blvd.	01800 E. Beach Blvd.
65.	Daemions, N.C. 75498	Deamions, N.C. 75498
66.	813 Allendale St.	813 Allendale St.
67.	1412 Genevieve Race	1413 Genevieve Race
68.	#3 Carondelet Apt.	#3 Carondlet Apt.
69.	Sherwood Village, Id. 69008	Sherwood Village, Wah. 99670
70.	Maison D'Orleans Apt. 72	Maison D'Orleans Apt. 72
71.	537 Delauney Cir. North	537 Delauney Cir. North
72.	6809 Mescalero	6809 Mesclaro
73.	Santa Maria Del Mar SW	Del Maria Mar SW
74.	875 Gorenflo Ave.	875 Gorenflo Ave.
75.	14220 Lemoyne Blvd.	14220 Lemoyne Blvd.
76.	Redding, W.V. 73996	Redding, Va. 79936
77.	8714-B 29th St. South	8714-A 29th St. South
78.	16485 Lorraine Cir.	16485 Lorraine Cir.
79.	101 Beauvoir Manor Apts.	101 Beauvoir Manor Apts.
80.	Howard, Fla. 74469	Howard, Fla. 74469
81.	517 Jefferson Davis Ave.	715 Jefferson Davis Ave.
82.	4686 Virginia Blvd. NE	4684 Virginia Blvd. NE
83.	602 West Pass	602 West Pass
84.	3432 Washington Square	3234 Washington Square
85.	1910 Switzer Dr.	1910 Switzer Dr.
86.	97 West 58th Ave. NW	97 West 58th St. NW
87.	Bullis, La. 22856	Bullis, La. 22856
88.	2423 Middlecoffe Dr.	2423 Middlecoffe Dr.
89.	1011-B Ladd Cir.	1101-B Ladd Cir.
90.	Opal, Ohio 55334	Opal, Ohio 55334
91.	14334 Jo Ellen End	1434 Jo Ellen End
92.	#56 Alexander Rd.	#56 Alexander Rd.
93.	503 Cypress Cove	503 Cypress Cove
94.	130 Richards Ave.	130 Richard Ave.
95.	137 Beach Park Place	137 Beach Park Place

COMPLETE PRACTICE TEST #3
Part B – Address Memory

Directions

In this part of the test, you will have to memorize the locations of 25 addresses in five boxes. During this section, you will have several study periods and practice exercises to help you memorize the location of the addresses shown in the five boxes. Answer the questions by darkening the oval containing the letter (A, B, C, D, or E) of the box in which the address is located – Box A, Box B, Box C, Box D, or Box E. At the end of each segment, you will be given instructions on how and where to continue. After completing six preliminary segments, the actual test will be given as segment #7.

Turn the page to begin Segment #1.

Note: You will notice on your practice test that the various segments of the Address Memory section are spread across two pages. Where applicable, the five boxes, the 88 questions, and/or the sample answer sheets are spread across two pages. This is the same format that you will experience on most segments of the Address Memory section on the actual exam. For economy and convenience, other study guides frequently condense the two pages down to only one. However, it is imperative that you practice realistically and that you become acquainted with and comfortable with the actual format of the exam. We have accordingly formatted this practice test realistically for your benefit.

Hint: Remember your strategies:
- *Memorize horizontally.*
- *Memorize only Boxes A, B, C, and D.*
- *You can correctly answer all Box E questions by the process of elimination.*
- *Use the Second Digit Strategy to memorize the number addresses.*
- *Use imagery/association to memorize the word addresses.*
- *Overlap the answer sheet & the questions to keep them as close together as possible.*
- *Use your extra pencil, your hand, or your fingers to mark/keep your place.*
- *Use your Speed Pencil and your Speed Marking strategies for much greater speed.*

COMPLETE PRACTICE TEST #3
Part B – Address Memory – Segment #1

Directions

Five sample boxes, each containing five addresses, and five sample questions about these boxes are given on the following two pages. The purpose of this small exercise is simply to acquaint you with the format of this section and with how the questions should be answered. The first two sample questions are answered for you. You are to spend three minutes becoming acquainted with the format and answering sample questions 3, 4, and 5. After completing Segment #1, turn to Segment #2 for further instructions.

Turn the page and begin when you are prepared to time yourself for precisely three minutes.

Hint: Remember your strategies! This segment is not scored, so do not take the sample questions seriously. Instead, mark random answers and use the three minutes to study and memorize the addresses. The sample boxes and addresses in this segment are the very same ones that will be repeated throughout this section of the exam.

A	**B**	**C**
1500-2399 Savannah Grafton 2400-3299 Candy Cleveland 1200-1499 Latil	3600-3999 Savannah Dambrino 3300-3599 Candy Ridge 2400-3299 Latil	2400-3299 Savannah Casper 3600-3999 Candy Mills 3300-3599 Latil

1. Maxey   Ⓐ Ⓑ Ⓒ Ⓓ **Ⓔ**
   This address came from Box E, so we sill darken the oval with the letter E.

2. Mills   Ⓐ Ⓑ **Ⓒ** Ⓓ Ⓔ
   This address came from Box C, so we will darken the oval with the letter C.

3. Ridge   Ⓐ Ⓑ Ⓒ Ⓓ Ⓔ
   Now that you know how to answer, you do questions 3, 4, and 5.

4. 1500-2399 Candy   Ⓐ Ⓑ Ⓒ Ⓓ Ⓔ

5. Lewis   Ⓐ Ⓑ Ⓒ Ⓓ Ⓔ

The correct answers are E, C, B, E, and D.

D	E
3300-3599 Savannah	1200-1499 Savannah
Richardson	Maxey
1200-1499 Candy	1500-2399 Candy
Lewis	Boggs
1500-2399 Latil	3600-3999 Latil

COMPLETE PRACTICE TEST #3
Part B – Address Memory – Segment #2

Directions

In this segment, you are given three minutes to study and memorize the addresses. There are no questions to answer in this segment – it is a study period only. However, on the actual exam, the boxes are not reprinted for your use. Instead, you are instructed to turn back to Address Memory Segment #1 on the preceding pages of the exam and to spend three minutes studying the boxes displayed there. So, we will do the very same on this practice test. After studying for three minutes, turn to Segment #3 for directions on how to continue the Address Memory Section of the exam.

Begin studying when you are prepared to time yourself for precisely three minutes.

COMPLETE PRACTICE TEST #3
Part B – Address Memory – Segment #3

Directions

In this segment you have three minutes to attempt answering 88 questions. You are to try to answer from memory, but the boxes are shown if you need to refer to them. Your answers are to be marked on the sample answer sheet at the bottom of the pages of Segment #3 – do not use the Compete Practice Test Answer Sheet for this segment. After completing this segment, turn to Segment #4 for further instructions.

Turn the page and begin when you are prepared to time yourself for precisely three minutes.

Hint: Remember your strategies! This segment is not scored, so do not take the questions seriously. Instead, mark a handful of random answers and use the three minutes to study and memorize the addresses.

A	B	C
1500-2399 Savannah Grafton 2400-3299 Candy Cleveland 1200-1499 Latil	3600-3999 Savannah Dambrino 3300-3599 Candy Ridge 2400-3299 Latil	2400-3299 Savannah Casper 3600-3999 Candy Mills 3300-3599 Latil

1. Ridge
2. 3600-3999 Savannah
3. 1200-1499 Latil
4. Lewis
5. 2400-3299 Latil
6. 1200-1499 Savannah
7. Dambrino
8. 3600-3999 Latil

9. 3300-3599 Candy
10. 2400-3299 Savannah
11. 1200-1499 Candy
12. Maxey
13. Grafton
14. Casper
15. 1500-2399 Latil
16. Cleveland

17. 2400-3299 Candy
18. 1500-2399 Candy
19. 3300-3599 Savannah
20. 2400-3299 Latil
21. Boggs
22. Mills
23. 1500-2399 Savannah
24. 1200-1499 Latil

25. 3300-3599 Latil
26. Maxey
27. Dambrino
28. 1500-2399 Latil
29. 3600-3999 Savannah
30. Grafton
31. Lewis
32. 2400-3299 Candy

33. 1200-1499 Savannah
34. 1200-1499 Latil
35. Mills
36. 3300-3599 Latil
37. 2400-3299 Savannah
38. 1200-1499 Candy
39. 3600-3999 Latil
40. 2400-3299 Latil

41. 3300-3599 Savannah
42. Dambrino
43. 3300-3599 Candy
44. Cleveland
45. Ridge
46. Richardson
47. 1500-2399 Savannah
48. Casper

1 Ⓐ Ⓑ Ⓒ Ⓓ Ⓔ
2 Ⓐ Ⓑ Ⓒ Ⓓ Ⓔ
3 Ⓐ Ⓑ Ⓒ Ⓓ Ⓔ
4 Ⓐ Ⓑ Ⓒ Ⓓ Ⓔ
5 Ⓐ Ⓑ Ⓒ Ⓓ Ⓔ
6 Ⓐ Ⓑ Ⓒ Ⓓ Ⓔ
7 Ⓐ Ⓑ Ⓒ Ⓓ Ⓔ
8 Ⓐ Ⓑ Ⓒ Ⓓ Ⓔ

9 Ⓐ Ⓑ Ⓒ Ⓓ Ⓔ
10 Ⓐ Ⓑ Ⓒ Ⓓ Ⓔ
11 Ⓐ Ⓑ Ⓒ Ⓓ Ⓔ
12 Ⓐ Ⓑ Ⓒ Ⓓ Ⓔ
13 Ⓐ Ⓑ Ⓒ Ⓓ Ⓔ
14 Ⓐ Ⓑ Ⓒ Ⓓ Ⓔ
15 Ⓐ Ⓑ Ⓒ Ⓓ Ⓔ
16 Ⓐ Ⓑ Ⓒ Ⓓ Ⓔ

17 Ⓐ Ⓑ Ⓒ Ⓓ Ⓔ
18 Ⓐ Ⓑ Ⓒ Ⓓ Ⓔ
19 Ⓐ Ⓑ Ⓒ Ⓓ Ⓔ
20 Ⓐ Ⓑ Ⓒ Ⓓ Ⓔ
21 Ⓐ Ⓑ Ⓒ Ⓓ Ⓔ
22 Ⓐ Ⓑ Ⓒ Ⓓ Ⓔ
23 Ⓐ Ⓑ Ⓒ Ⓓ Ⓔ
24 Ⓐ Ⓑ Ⓒ Ⓓ Ⓔ

25 Ⓐ Ⓑ Ⓒ Ⓓ Ⓔ
26 Ⓐ Ⓑ Ⓒ Ⓓ Ⓔ
27 Ⓐ Ⓑ Ⓒ Ⓓ Ⓔ
28 Ⓐ Ⓑ Ⓒ Ⓓ Ⓔ
29 Ⓐ Ⓑ Ⓒ Ⓓ Ⓔ
30 Ⓐ Ⓑ Ⓒ Ⓓ Ⓔ
31 Ⓐ Ⓑ Ⓒ Ⓓ Ⓔ
32 Ⓐ Ⓑ Ⓒ Ⓓ Ⓔ

33 Ⓐ Ⓑ Ⓒ Ⓓ Ⓔ
34 Ⓐ Ⓑ Ⓒ Ⓓ Ⓔ
35 Ⓐ Ⓑ Ⓒ Ⓓ Ⓔ
36 Ⓐ Ⓑ Ⓒ Ⓓ Ⓔ
37 Ⓐ Ⓑ Ⓒ Ⓓ Ⓔ
38 Ⓐ Ⓑ Ⓒ Ⓓ Ⓔ
39 Ⓐ Ⓑ Ⓒ Ⓓ Ⓔ
40 Ⓐ Ⓑ Ⓒ Ⓓ Ⓔ

41 Ⓐ Ⓑ Ⓒ Ⓓ Ⓔ
42 Ⓐ Ⓑ Ⓒ Ⓓ Ⓔ
43 Ⓐ Ⓑ Ⓒ Ⓓ Ⓔ
44 Ⓐ Ⓑ Ⓒ Ⓓ Ⓔ
45 Ⓐ Ⓑ Ⓒ Ⓓ Ⓔ
46 Ⓐ Ⓑ Ⓒ Ⓓ Ⓔ
47 Ⓐ Ⓑ Ⓒ Ⓓ Ⓔ
48 Ⓐ Ⓑ Ⓒ Ⓓ Ⓔ

D

3300-3599 Savannah
Richardson
1200-1499 Candy
Lewis
1500-2399 Latil

E

1200-1499 Savannah
Maxey
1500-2399 Candy
Boggs
3600-3999 Latil

49. 3600-3999 Candy
50. Boggs
51. 1200-1499 Candy
52. 1200-1499 Savannah
53. 2400-3299 Latil
54. Grafton
55. 2400-3299 Candy
56. 3600-3999 Latil

57. Ridge
58. 2400-3299 Savannah
59. Lewis
60. 3300-3599 Latil
61. 1500-2399 Latil
62. 1500-2399 Candy
63. Maxey
64. 3600-3999 Savannah

65. 1200-1499 Latil
66. 1500-2399 Savannah
67. 3300-3599 Savannah
68. 1200-1499 Savannah
69. Mills
70. Richardson
71. 3300-3599 Candy
72. Dambrino

73. 2400-3299 Candy
74. 1500-2399 Latil
75. 1200-1499 Candy
76. Grafton
77. Cleveland
78. Casper
79. 3600-3999 Latil
80. 2400-3299 Latil

81. 3300-3599 Latil
82. 2400-3299 Candy
83. 2400-3299 Savannah
84. Lewis
85. 1500-2399 Candy
86. Ridge
87. Mills
88. Maxey

49 Ⓐ Ⓑ Ⓒ Ⓓ Ⓔ
50 Ⓐ Ⓑ Ⓒ Ⓓ Ⓔ
51 Ⓐ Ⓑ Ⓒ Ⓓ Ⓔ
52 Ⓐ Ⓑ Ⓒ Ⓓ Ⓔ
53 Ⓐ Ⓑ Ⓒ Ⓓ Ⓔ
54 Ⓐ Ⓑ Ⓒ Ⓓ Ⓔ
55 Ⓐ Ⓑ Ⓒ Ⓓ Ⓔ
56 Ⓐ Ⓑ Ⓒ Ⓓ Ⓔ

57 Ⓐ Ⓑ Ⓒ Ⓓ Ⓔ
58 Ⓐ Ⓑ Ⓒ Ⓓ Ⓔ
59 Ⓐ Ⓑ Ⓒ Ⓓ Ⓔ
60 Ⓐ Ⓑ Ⓒ Ⓓ Ⓔ
61 Ⓐ Ⓑ Ⓒ Ⓓ Ⓔ
62 Ⓐ Ⓑ Ⓒ Ⓓ Ⓔ
63 Ⓐ Ⓑ Ⓒ Ⓓ Ⓔ
64 Ⓐ Ⓑ Ⓒ Ⓓ Ⓔ

65 Ⓐ Ⓑ Ⓒ Ⓓ Ⓔ
66 Ⓐ Ⓑ Ⓒ Ⓓ Ⓔ
67 Ⓐ Ⓑ Ⓒ Ⓓ Ⓔ
68 Ⓐ Ⓑ Ⓒ Ⓓ Ⓔ
69 Ⓐ Ⓑ Ⓒ Ⓓ Ⓔ
70 Ⓐ Ⓑ Ⓒ Ⓓ Ⓔ
71 Ⓐ Ⓑ Ⓒ Ⓓ Ⓔ
72 Ⓐ Ⓑ Ⓒ Ⓓ Ⓔ

73 Ⓐ Ⓑ Ⓒ Ⓓ Ⓔ
74 Ⓐ Ⓑ Ⓒ Ⓓ Ⓔ
75 Ⓐ Ⓑ Ⓒ Ⓓ Ⓔ
76 Ⓐ Ⓑ Ⓒ Ⓓ Ⓔ
77 Ⓐ Ⓑ Ⓒ Ⓓ Ⓔ
78 Ⓐ Ⓑ Ⓒ Ⓓ Ⓔ
79 Ⓐ Ⓑ Ⓒ Ⓓ Ⓔ
80 Ⓐ Ⓑ Ⓒ Ⓓ Ⓔ

81 Ⓐ Ⓑ Ⓒ Ⓓ Ⓔ
82 Ⓐ Ⓑ Ⓒ Ⓓ Ⓔ
83 Ⓐ Ⓑ Ⓒ Ⓓ Ⓔ
84 Ⓐ Ⓑ Ⓒ Ⓓ Ⓔ
85 Ⓐ Ⓑ Ⓒ Ⓓ Ⓔ
86 Ⓐ Ⓑ Ⓒ Ⓓ Ⓔ
87 Ⓐ Ⓑ Ⓒ Ⓓ Ⓔ
88 Ⓐ Ⓑ Ⓒ Ⓓ Ⓔ

COMPLETE PRACTICE TEST #3
Part B – Address Memory – Segment #4

Directions

In this segment you have three minutes to attempt answering 88 questions. You must answer from memory. The boxes are not shown. Your answers are to be marked on the sample answer sheet at the bottom of the pages of Segment #4 – do not use the Compete Practice Test Answer Sheet for this segment. After completing this segment, turn to Segment #5 for further instructions.

Turn the page and begin when you are prepared to time yourself for precisely three minutes.

Hint: Remember, this segment is not scored, so you should not worry about your inability to answer all 88 questions, or your inability to answer all of them accurately, in only three minutes. Neither task is really possible in only three minutes. However, this is an ideal opportunity for you to test how well you have mastered your strategies and memorization so far. By sincerely trying to answer the questions, you can identify the areas where you are weaker and where you need to apply more effort.

COMPLETE PRACTICE TEST #3
Part B – Address Memory – Segment #4

1. Maxey
2. Mills
3. Ridge
4. 1500-2399 Candy
5. Lewis
6. 2400-3299 Savannah
7. 2400-3299 Candy
8. 3300-3599 Latil

9. 2400-3299 Latil
10. 3600-3999 Latil
11. Casper
12. Cleveland
13. Grafton
14. 1200-1499 Candy
15. Dambrino
16. 3300-3599 Candy

17. Richardson
18. Mills
19. 1200-1499 Savannah
20. 3300-3599 Savannah
21. 1500-2399 Savannah
22. 1200-1499 Latil
23. 3600-3999 Savannah
24. Maxey

25. 1500-2399 Candy
26. 1500-2399 Latil
27. 3300-3599 Latil
28. Lewis
29. 2400-3299 Savannah
30. Ridge
31. 3600-3999 Latil
32. 2400-3299 Candy

33. Grafton
34. 2400-3299 Latil
35. 1200-1499 Savannah
36. 1200-1499 Candy
37. Boggs
38. 3600-3999 Candy
39. Casper
40. 1500-2399 Savannah

41. Richardson
42. Ridge
43. Cleveland
44. 3300-3599 Candy
45. Dambrino
46. 3300-3599 Savannah
47. 2400-3299 Latil
48. 3600-3999 Latil

1 Ⓐ Ⓑ Ⓒ Ⓓ Ⓔ
2 Ⓐ Ⓑ Ⓒ Ⓓ Ⓔ
3 Ⓐ Ⓑ Ⓒ Ⓓ Ⓔ
4 Ⓐ Ⓑ Ⓒ Ⓓ Ⓔ
5 Ⓐ Ⓑ Ⓒ Ⓓ Ⓔ
6 Ⓐ Ⓑ Ⓒ Ⓓ Ⓔ
7 Ⓐ Ⓑ Ⓒ Ⓓ Ⓔ
8 Ⓐ Ⓑ Ⓒ Ⓓ Ⓔ

9 Ⓐ Ⓑ Ⓒ Ⓓ Ⓔ
10 Ⓐ Ⓑ Ⓒ Ⓓ Ⓔ
11 Ⓐ Ⓑ Ⓒ Ⓓ Ⓔ
12 Ⓐ Ⓑ Ⓒ Ⓓ Ⓔ
13 Ⓐ Ⓑ Ⓒ Ⓓ Ⓔ
14 Ⓐ Ⓑ Ⓒ Ⓓ Ⓔ
15 Ⓐ Ⓑ Ⓒ Ⓓ Ⓔ
16 Ⓐ Ⓑ Ⓒ Ⓓ Ⓔ

17 Ⓐ Ⓑ Ⓒ Ⓓ Ⓔ
18 Ⓐ Ⓑ Ⓒ Ⓓ Ⓔ
19 Ⓐ Ⓑ Ⓒ Ⓓ Ⓔ
20 Ⓐ Ⓑ Ⓒ Ⓓ Ⓔ
21 Ⓐ Ⓑ Ⓒ Ⓓ Ⓔ
22 Ⓐ Ⓑ Ⓒ Ⓓ Ⓔ
23 Ⓐ Ⓑ Ⓒ Ⓓ Ⓔ
24 Ⓐ Ⓑ Ⓒ Ⓓ Ⓔ

25 Ⓐ Ⓑ Ⓒ Ⓓ Ⓔ
26 Ⓐ Ⓑ Ⓒ Ⓓ Ⓔ
27 Ⓐ Ⓑ Ⓒ Ⓓ Ⓔ
28 Ⓐ Ⓑ Ⓒ Ⓓ Ⓔ
29 Ⓐ Ⓑ Ⓒ Ⓓ Ⓔ
30 Ⓐ Ⓑ Ⓒ Ⓓ Ⓔ
31 Ⓐ Ⓑ Ⓒ Ⓓ Ⓔ
32 Ⓐ Ⓑ Ⓒ Ⓓ Ⓔ

33 Ⓐ Ⓑ Ⓒ Ⓓ Ⓔ
34 Ⓐ Ⓑ Ⓒ Ⓓ Ⓔ
35 Ⓐ Ⓑ Ⓒ Ⓓ Ⓔ
36 Ⓐ Ⓑ Ⓒ Ⓓ Ⓔ
37 Ⓐ Ⓑ Ⓒ Ⓓ Ⓔ
38 Ⓐ Ⓑ Ⓒ Ⓓ Ⓔ
39 Ⓐ Ⓑ Ⓒ Ⓓ Ⓔ
40 Ⓐ Ⓑ Ⓒ Ⓓ Ⓔ

41 Ⓐ Ⓑ Ⓒ Ⓓ Ⓔ
42 Ⓐ Ⓑ Ⓒ Ⓓ Ⓔ
43 Ⓐ Ⓑ Ⓒ Ⓓ Ⓔ
44 Ⓐ Ⓑ Ⓒ Ⓓ Ⓔ
45 Ⓐ Ⓑ Ⓒ Ⓓ Ⓔ
46 Ⓐ Ⓑ Ⓒ Ⓓ Ⓔ
47 Ⓐ Ⓑ Ⓒ Ⓓ Ⓔ
48 Ⓐ Ⓑ Ⓒ Ⓓ Ⓔ

49. 1200-1499 Candy
50. 2400-3299 Savannah
51. 3300-3599 Latil
52. Mills
53. 1200-1499 Latil
54. 1200-1499 Savannah
55. 2400-3299 Candy
56. Lewis

57. Grafton
58. 3600-3999 Savannah
59. 1500-2399 Latil
60. Dambrino
61. Maxey
62. 3300-3599 Latil
63. 1200-1499 Latil
64. 1500-2399 Savannah

65. Mills
66. Boggs
67. 2400-3299 Latil
68. 3300-3599 Savannah
69. 1500-2399 Candy
70. 2400-3299 Candy
71. Cleveland
72. 1500-2399 Latil

73. Casper
74. Grafton
75. Maxey
76. 1200-1499 Candy
77. 2400-3299 Savannah
78. 3300-3599 Candy
79. 3600-3999 Latil
80. Dambrino

81. 1200-1499 Savannah
82. 2400-3299 Latil
83. Lewis
84. 1200-1499 Latil
85. 3600-3999 Savannah
86. Ridge
87. Boggs
88. 1500-2399 Candy

49. Ⓐ Ⓑ Ⓒ Ⓓ Ⓔ
50. Ⓐ Ⓑ Ⓒ Ⓓ Ⓔ
51. Ⓐ Ⓑ Ⓒ Ⓓ Ⓔ
52. Ⓐ Ⓑ Ⓒ Ⓓ Ⓔ
53. Ⓐ Ⓑ Ⓒ Ⓓ Ⓔ
54. Ⓐ Ⓑ Ⓒ Ⓓ Ⓔ
55. Ⓐ Ⓑ Ⓒ Ⓓ Ⓔ
56. Ⓐ Ⓑ Ⓒ Ⓓ Ⓔ

57. Ⓐ Ⓑ Ⓒ Ⓓ Ⓔ
58. Ⓐ Ⓑ Ⓒ Ⓓ Ⓔ
59. Ⓐ Ⓑ Ⓒ Ⓓ Ⓔ
60. Ⓐ Ⓑ Ⓒ Ⓓ Ⓔ
61. Ⓐ Ⓑ Ⓒ Ⓓ Ⓔ
62. Ⓐ Ⓑ Ⓒ Ⓓ Ⓔ
63. Ⓐ Ⓑ Ⓒ Ⓓ Ⓔ
64. Ⓐ Ⓑ Ⓒ Ⓓ Ⓔ

65. Ⓐ Ⓑ Ⓒ Ⓓ Ⓔ
66. Ⓐ Ⓑ Ⓒ Ⓓ Ⓔ
67. Ⓐ Ⓑ Ⓒ Ⓓ Ⓔ
68. Ⓐ Ⓑ Ⓒ Ⓓ Ⓔ
69. Ⓐ Ⓑ Ⓒ Ⓓ Ⓔ
70. Ⓐ Ⓑ Ⓒ Ⓓ Ⓔ
71. Ⓐ Ⓑ Ⓒ Ⓓ Ⓔ
72. Ⓐ Ⓑ Ⓒ Ⓓ Ⓔ

73. Ⓐ Ⓑ Ⓒ Ⓓ Ⓔ
74. Ⓐ Ⓑ Ⓒ Ⓓ Ⓔ
75. Ⓐ Ⓑ Ⓒ Ⓓ Ⓔ
76. Ⓐ Ⓑ Ⓒ Ⓓ Ⓔ
77. Ⓐ Ⓑ Ⓒ Ⓓ Ⓔ
78. Ⓐ Ⓑ Ⓒ Ⓓ Ⓔ
79. Ⓐ Ⓑ Ⓒ Ⓓ Ⓔ
80. Ⓐ Ⓑ Ⓒ Ⓓ Ⓔ

81. Ⓐ Ⓑ Ⓒ Ⓓ Ⓔ
82. Ⓐ Ⓑ Ⓒ Ⓓ Ⓔ
83. Ⓐ Ⓑ Ⓒ Ⓓ Ⓔ
84. Ⓐ Ⓑ Ⓒ Ⓓ Ⓔ
85. Ⓐ Ⓑ Ⓒ Ⓓ Ⓔ
86. Ⓐ Ⓑ Ⓒ Ⓓ Ⓔ
87. Ⓐ Ⓑ Ⓒ Ⓓ Ⓔ
88. Ⓐ Ⓑ Ⓒ Ⓓ Ⓔ

COMPLETE PRACTICE TEST #3
Part B – Address Memory – Segment #5

Directions

In this segment, you are given five minutes to study the addresses. There are no questions to answer in this segment – it is a study period only. As before, the boxes are not reprinted here for your use. Instead, you are instructed to turn back to Address Memory Segment #1 and to spend five minutes studying the boxes displayed there. After studying for five minutes, turn to Segment #6 for directions on how to continue.

Begin studying when you are prepared to time yourself for precisely five minutes.

COMPLETE PRACTICE TEST #3
Part B – Address Memory – Segment #6

Directions

In this segment, you have five minutes to attempt answering 88 questions. You are to try to answer from memory, but the boxes are shown if you need to refer to them. Your answers are to be marked on the sample answer sheet at the bottom of the pages of Segment #6 – do not use the Compete Practice Test Answer Sheet for this segment. After completing this segment, turn to Segment #7 for further instructions.

Turn the page and begin when you are prepared to time yourself for precisely five minutes.

Hint: Remember your strategies! This segment is not scored, so do not take the questions seriously. Instead, mark a handful of random answers and use the five minutes to study and memorize the addresses.

A	B	C
1500-2399 Savannah	3600-3999 Savannah	2400-3299 Savannah
Grafton	Dambrino	Casper
2400-3299 Candy	3300-3599 Candy	3600-3999 Candy
Cleveland	Ridge	Mills
1200-1499 Latil	2400-3299 Latil	3300-3599 Latil

1. Ridge
2. 3600-3999 Savannah
3. 1200-1499 Latil
4. Lewis
5. 2400-3299 Latil
6. 1200-1499 Savannah
7. Dambrino
8. 3600-3999 Latil

9. 3300-3599 Candy
10. 2400-3299 Savannah
11. 1200-1499 Candy
12. Maxey
13. Grafton
14. Casper
15. 1500-2399 Latil
16. Cleveland

17. 2400-3299 Candy
18. 1500-2399 Candy
19. 3300-3599 Savannah
20. 2400-3299 Latil
21. Boggs
22. Mills
23. 1500-2399 Savannah
24. 1200-1499 Latil

25. 3300-3599 Latil
26. Maxey
27. Dambrino
28. 1500-2399 Latil
29. 3600-3999 Savannah
30. Grafton
31. Lewis
32. 2400-3299 Candy

33. 1200-1499 Savannah
34. 1200-1499 Latil
35. Mills
36. 3300-3599 Latil
37. 2400-3299 Savannah
38. 1200-1499 Candy
39. 3600-3999 Latil
40. 2400-3299 Latil

41. 3300-3599 Savannah
42. Dambrino
43. 3300-3599 Candy
44. Cleveland
45. Ridge
46. Richardson
47. 1500-2399 Savannah
48. Casper

1 Ⓐ Ⓑ Ⓒ Ⓓ Ⓔ
2 Ⓐ Ⓑ Ⓒ Ⓓ Ⓔ
3 Ⓐ Ⓑ Ⓒ Ⓓ Ⓔ
4 Ⓐ Ⓑ Ⓒ Ⓓ Ⓔ
5 Ⓐ Ⓑ Ⓒ Ⓓ Ⓔ
6 Ⓐ Ⓑ Ⓒ Ⓓ Ⓔ
7 Ⓐ Ⓑ Ⓒ Ⓓ Ⓔ
8 Ⓐ Ⓑ Ⓒ Ⓓ Ⓔ

9 Ⓐ Ⓑ Ⓒ Ⓓ Ⓔ
10 Ⓐ Ⓑ Ⓒ Ⓓ Ⓔ
11 Ⓐ Ⓑ Ⓒ Ⓓ Ⓔ
12 Ⓐ Ⓑ Ⓒ Ⓓ Ⓔ
13 Ⓐ Ⓑ Ⓒ Ⓓ Ⓔ
14 Ⓐ Ⓑ Ⓒ Ⓓ Ⓔ
15 Ⓐ Ⓑ Ⓒ Ⓓ Ⓔ
16 Ⓐ Ⓑ Ⓒ Ⓓ Ⓔ

17 Ⓐ Ⓑ Ⓒ Ⓓ Ⓔ
18 Ⓐ Ⓑ Ⓒ Ⓓ Ⓔ
19 Ⓐ Ⓑ Ⓒ Ⓓ Ⓔ
20 Ⓐ Ⓑ Ⓒ Ⓓ Ⓔ
21 Ⓐ Ⓑ Ⓒ Ⓓ Ⓔ
22 Ⓐ Ⓑ Ⓒ Ⓓ Ⓔ
23 Ⓐ Ⓑ Ⓒ Ⓓ Ⓔ
24 Ⓐ Ⓑ Ⓒ Ⓓ Ⓔ

25 Ⓐ Ⓑ Ⓒ Ⓓ Ⓔ
26 Ⓐ Ⓑ Ⓒ Ⓓ Ⓔ
27 Ⓐ Ⓑ Ⓒ Ⓓ Ⓔ
28 Ⓐ Ⓑ Ⓒ Ⓓ Ⓔ
29 Ⓐ Ⓑ Ⓒ Ⓓ Ⓔ
30 Ⓐ Ⓑ Ⓒ Ⓓ Ⓔ
31 Ⓐ Ⓑ Ⓒ Ⓓ Ⓔ
32 Ⓐ Ⓑ Ⓒ Ⓓ Ⓔ

33 Ⓐ Ⓑ Ⓒ Ⓓ Ⓔ
34 Ⓐ Ⓑ Ⓒ Ⓓ Ⓔ
35 Ⓐ Ⓑ Ⓒ Ⓓ Ⓔ
36 Ⓐ Ⓑ Ⓒ Ⓓ Ⓔ
37 Ⓐ Ⓑ Ⓒ Ⓓ Ⓔ
38 Ⓐ Ⓑ Ⓒ Ⓓ Ⓔ
39 Ⓐ Ⓑ Ⓒ Ⓓ Ⓔ
40 Ⓐ Ⓑ Ⓒ Ⓓ Ⓔ

41 Ⓐ Ⓑ Ⓒ Ⓓ Ⓔ
42 Ⓐ Ⓑ Ⓒ Ⓓ Ⓔ
43 Ⓐ Ⓑ Ⓒ Ⓓ Ⓔ
44 Ⓐ Ⓑ Ⓒ Ⓓ Ⓔ
45 Ⓐ Ⓑ Ⓒ Ⓓ Ⓔ
46 Ⓐ Ⓑ Ⓒ Ⓓ Ⓔ
47 Ⓐ Ⓑ Ⓒ Ⓓ Ⓔ
48 Ⓐ Ⓑ Ⓒ Ⓓ Ⓔ

D	**E**
3300-3599 Savannah	1200-1499 Savannah
Richardson	Maxey
1200-1499 Candy	1500-2399 Candy
Lewis	Boggs
1500-2399 Latil	3600-3999 Latil

49. 3600-3999 Candy
50. Boggs
51. 1200-1499 Candy
52. 1200-1499 Savannah
53. 2400-3299 Latil
54. Grafton
55. 2400-3299 Candy
56. 3600-3999 Latil

57. Ridge
58. 2400-3299 Savannah
59. Lewis
60. 3300-3599 Latil
61. 1500-2399 Latil
62. 1500-2399 Candy
63. Maxey
64. 3600-3999 Savannah

65. 1200-1499 Latil
66. 1500-2399 Savannah
67. 3300-3599 Savannah
68. 1200-1499 Savannah
69. Mills
70. Richardson
71. 3300-3599 Candy
72. Dambrino

73. 2400-3299 Candy
74. 1500-2399 Latil
75. 1200-1499 Candy
76. Grafton
77. Cleveland
78. Casper
79. 3600-3999 Latil
80. 2400-3299 Latil

81. 3300-3599 Latil
82. 2400-3299 Candy
83. 2400-3299 Savannah
84. Lewis
85. 1500-2399 Candy
86. Ridge
87. Mills
88. Maxey

49 (A) (B) (C) (D) (E)
50 (A) (B) (C) (D) (E)
51 (A) (B) (C) (D) (E)
52 (A) (B) (C) (D) (E)
53 (A) (B) (C) (D) (E)
54 (A) (B) (C) (D) (E)
55 (A) (B) (C) (D) (E)
56 (A) (B) (C) (D) (E)

57 (A) (B) (C) (D) (E)
58 (A) (B) (C) (D) (E)
59 (A) (B) (C) (D) (E)
60 (A) (B) (C) (D) (E)
61 (A) (B) (C) (D) (E)
62 (A) (B) (C) (D) (E)
63 (A) (B) (C) (D) (E)
64 (A) (B) (C) (D) (E)

65 (A) (B) (C) (D) (E)
66 (A) (B) (C) (D) (E)
67 (A) (B) (C) (D) (E)
68 (A) (B) (C) (D) (E)
69 (A) (B) (C) (D) (E)
70 (A) (B) (C) (D) (E)
71 (A) (B) (C) (D) (E)
72 (A) (B) (C) (D) (E)

73 (A) (B) (C) (D) (E)
74 (A) (B) (C) (D) (E)
75 (A) (B) (C) (D) (E)
76 (A) (B) (C) (D) (E)
77 (A) (B) (C) (D) (E)
78 (A) (B) (C) (D) (E)
79 (A) (B) (C) (D) (E)
80 (A) (B) (C) (D) (E)

81 (A) (B) (C) (D) (E)
82 (A) (B) (C) (D) (E)
83 (A) (B) (C) (D) (E)
84 (A) (B) (C) (D) (E)
85 (A) (B) (C) (D) (E)
86 (A) (B) (C) (D) (E)
87 (A) (B) (C) (D) (E)
88 (A) (B) (C) (D) (E)

COMPLETE PRACTICE TEST #3
Part B – Address Memory – Segment #7

Directions

This is the final segment of the Address Memory section. You have five minutes to answer 88 questions. You must answer from memory. The boxes are not shown. On this segment, there is not a sample answer sheet at the bottom of the page. Instead, mark your answers on the Complete Practice Test Answer Sheet that your tore out of the book. After completing this segment, you have finished the full Address Memory section. Turn to the Number Series section of the practice test for instructions on how to continue.

Turn the page and begin when you are prepared to time yourself for precisely five minutes.

1. Maxey
2. Mills
3. Ridge
4. 1500-2399 Candy
5. Lewis
6. 2400-3299 Savannah
7. 2400-3299 Candy
8. 3300-3599 Latil

9. 2400-3299 Latil
10. 3600-3999 Latil
11. Casper
12. Cleveland
13. Grafton
14. 1200-1499 Candy
15. Dambrino
16. 3300-3599 Candy

17. Richardson
18. Mills
19. 1200-1499 Savannah
20. 3300-3599 Savannah
21. 1500-2399 Savannah
22. 1200-1499 Latil
23. 3600-3999 Savannah
24. Maxey

25. 1500-2399 Candy
26. 1500-2399 Latil
27. 3300-3599 Latil
28. Lewis
29. 2400-3299 Savannah
30. Ridge
31. 3600-3999 Latil
32. 2400-3299 Candy

33. Grafton
34. 2400-3299 Latil
35. 1200-1499 Savannah
36. 1200-1499 Candy
37. Boggs
38. 3600-3999 Candy
39. Casper
40. 1500-2399 Savannah

41. Richardson
42. Ridge
43. Cleveland
44. 3300-3599 Candy
45. Dambrino
46. 3300-3599 Savannah
47. 2400-3299 Latil
48. 3600-3999 Latil

49. 1200-1499 Candy
50. 2400-3299 Savannah
51. 3300-3599 Latil
52. Mills
53. 1200-1499 Latil
54. 1200-1499 Savannah
55. 2400-3299 Candy
56. Lewis

57. Grafton
58. 3600-3999 Savannah
59. 1500-2399 Latil
60. Dambrino
61. Maxey
62. 3300-3599 Latil
63. 1200-1499 Latil
64. 1500-2399 Savannah

65. Mills
66. Boggs
67. 2400-3299 Latil
68. 3300-3599 Savannah
69. 1500-2399 Candy
70. 2400-3299 Candy
71. Cleveland
72. 1500-2399 Latil

73. Casper
74. Grafton
75. Maxey
76. 1200-1499 Candy
77. 2400-3299 Savannah
78. 3300-3599 Candy
79. 3600-3999 Latil
80. Dambrino

81. 1200-1499 Savannah
82. 2400-3299 Latil
83. Lewis
84. 1200-1499 Latil
85. 3600-3999 Savannah
86. Ridge
87. Boggs
88. 1500-2399 Candy

COMPLETE PRACTICE TEST #3
Part C – Number Series

Directions

On this section, you have 20 minutes to answer 24 mathematical questions. Each question consists of a series of numbers followed by two blanks. You are to calculate what two numbers would logically follow in the series and that would therefore fit into the two blanks. Choose the answer – A, B, C, D, or E – that contains the correct two numbers, in the proper order, that should follow in the series. Mark your answers on the Complete Practice Test Answer Sheet in the section entitled Number Series. After completing this section, turn to the Following Oral Instructions section for directions on how to continue.

The solutions to all the Number Series questions in all six of the practice tests are given in the back of your book. After scoring each Number Series practice test, find and review the solutions for the questions you missed. This should better prepare you to answer similar questions on the other practice tests as well as on your actual exam.

Turn the page and begin when you are prepared to time yourself for precisely 20 minutes.

Hint: Remember to use the Circles and Squares Strategy to identify, separate, and solve the multiple sequences found in many questions.

COMPLETE PRACTICE TEST #3
Part C – Number Series

1. 3 5 7 9 11 13 15 ___ ___   A) 18,21 B) 19,23 C) 17,19 D) 16,17 E) 39,41

2. 1 7 13 19 25 31 37 ___ ___   A) 38,45 B) 43,50 C) 38,46 D) 47,57 E) 43,49

3. 12 15 18 21 24 27 30 ___ ___   A) 33,36 B) 34,37 C) 33,38 D) 40,50 E) 30,36

4. 21 28 35 42 49 56 63 ___ ___   A) 72,79 B) 70,77 C) 70,80 D) 70,78 E) 73,83

5. 62 60 58 56 54 52 50 ___ ___   A) 48,44 B) 52,54 C) 46,44 D) 48,46 E) 42,40

6. 82 71 60 49 38 27 ___ ___   A) 16,5 B) 15,4 C) 17,6 D) 18,8 E) 19,9

7. 16 20 24 28 32 36 40 ___ ___   A) 42,44 B) 43,47 C) 45,49 D) 50,54 E) 44,48

8. 58 55 52 49 46 43 40 ___ ___   A) 36,33 B) 38,35 C) 37,34 D) 40,37 E) 42,39

9. 4 5 8 6 7 11 8 ___ ___   A) 8,13 B) 9,14 C) 10,15 D) 16,18 E) 12,17

10. 19 21 50 23 25 47 27 ___ ___   A) 30,45 B) 28,43 C) 27,42 D) 29,44 E) 25,45

11. 3 9 15 21 27 33 39 ___ ___   A) 45,51 B) 35,41 C) 55,61 D) 56,66 E) 56,63

12. 12 11 10 37 9 8 7 36 ___ ___   A) 9,2 B) 9,3 C) 8,4 D) 7,5 E) 6,5

13. 42 37 64 69 32 27 74 ___ ___   A) 79,20 B) 80,21 C) 82,17 D) 76,20 E) 79,22

14. 71 76 31 29 81 86 27 ___ ___   A) 24,90 B) 26,92 C) 25,91 D) 26,91 E) 26,93

15. 1 13 7 19 13 25 19 ___ ___   A) 30,24 B) 31,25 C) 32,26 D) 34,28 E) 30,20

16. 21 21 14 18 18 52 15 ___ ___   A) 15,92 B) 16,40 C) 14,52 D) 15,90 E) 45,90

17. 36 7 5 39 39 3 1 ___ ___   A) 47,47 B) 42,42 C) 42,1 D) 3,42 E) 0,48

18. 27 37 61 21 85 109 15 ___ ___   A) 133,157 B) 133,1589 C) 132,159 D) 159,165 E) 131,150

19. 11 17 7 7 7 23 3 3 ___ ___   A) 3,28 B) 3,3 C) 27,3 D) 29,28 E) 3,29

20. 80 14 32 69 65 17 35 54 50 20 ___ ___   A) 37,38 B) 18,39 C) 38,39 D) 36,38 E) 32,40

21. 15 22 25 32 35 42 45 ___ ___   A) 52,55 B) 53,54 C) 54,60 D) 52,59 E) 55,60

22. 96 96 11 75 75 14 54 ___ ___   A) 17,54 B) 54,54 C) 14,54 D) 54,17 E) 75,17

23. 27 42 57 72 87 ___ ___   A) 92,107 B) 103,116 C) 102,117 D) 103,118 E) 101,126

24. 6 7 21 10 11 26 15 ___ ___   A) 16,30 B) 17,25 C) 18,33 D) 31,17 E) 16,31

COMPLETE PRACTICE TEST #3
Part D – Following Oral Instructions

Directions

On this section of the test, the Exam Administrator will read questions/instructions aloud to the group of test takers. These oral instructions will direct you to write/mark certain items in your test booklet, which in turn will lead you to the correct answer(s). Finally, you will be verbally instructed to mark the correct answer(s) on your answer sheet. You must answer exclusively based upon what you hear – there are no questions for you to read.

The following pages of this practice test are samples of the test booklet pages on which you will write/mark as verbally instructed. Mark your answers on the Complete Practice Test Answer Sheet in the Following Oral Instructions section.

To practice realistically, you must either listen to the questions on the author's recording or have someone read them aloud to you. Do not look over the questions before taking the practice test. Once you have completed the practice test, you should then review the questions you missed in order to determine what caused you to miss them. This review should enable you to be more successful on similar questions next time.

The author's recording of all six Following Oral Directions practice tests is an ideal and convenient way to practice. The recorded questions are presented in the proper format, at the proper pace, and with proper diction. These recordings allow you to practice anytime and anywhere you wish. With these recordings, your practice – and in turn your success – will not be dependent upon someone else's schedule and whims. For details and ordering information, see the order form at the back of your book.

If someone will be reading the questions to you, he/she will find the questions for each practice test in the back of your book in the section entitled Following Oral Instructions – Practice Test Questions. The reader should carefully tear the questions out of your book in order to use them. The questions should be read at a rather slow and steady pace of approximately 75 words per minute and with proper diction. The reader should also pause between instructions/questions as directed in the wording of each question.

Once you complete the Following Oral Instructions section, you have finished this practice test, and you should then begin the next practice test in your book. Once you have completed all six practice tests plus the Extra Address Checking Practice Exercises as instructed, you should be fully prepared to excel on the actual exam.

Turn the page and begin when you are prepared to listen to the questions from the author's recording or from someone who will read the questions to you in the proper fashion.

Hint: Remember your strategies:
- *You will answer by marking number-letter combinations.*
- *Where you mark an answer on the answer sheet will not match the question number.*
- *Listen closely and attentively.*
- *Simply follow the instructions you hear – do not try to figure them out.*
- *Some questions will have multiple answers, and you must mark all of them.*
- *Mark your answers quickly and be ready to listen to the next question.*
- *Make identifying notes for later recall.*

COMPLETE PRACTICE TEST #3
Part D – Following Oral Instructions

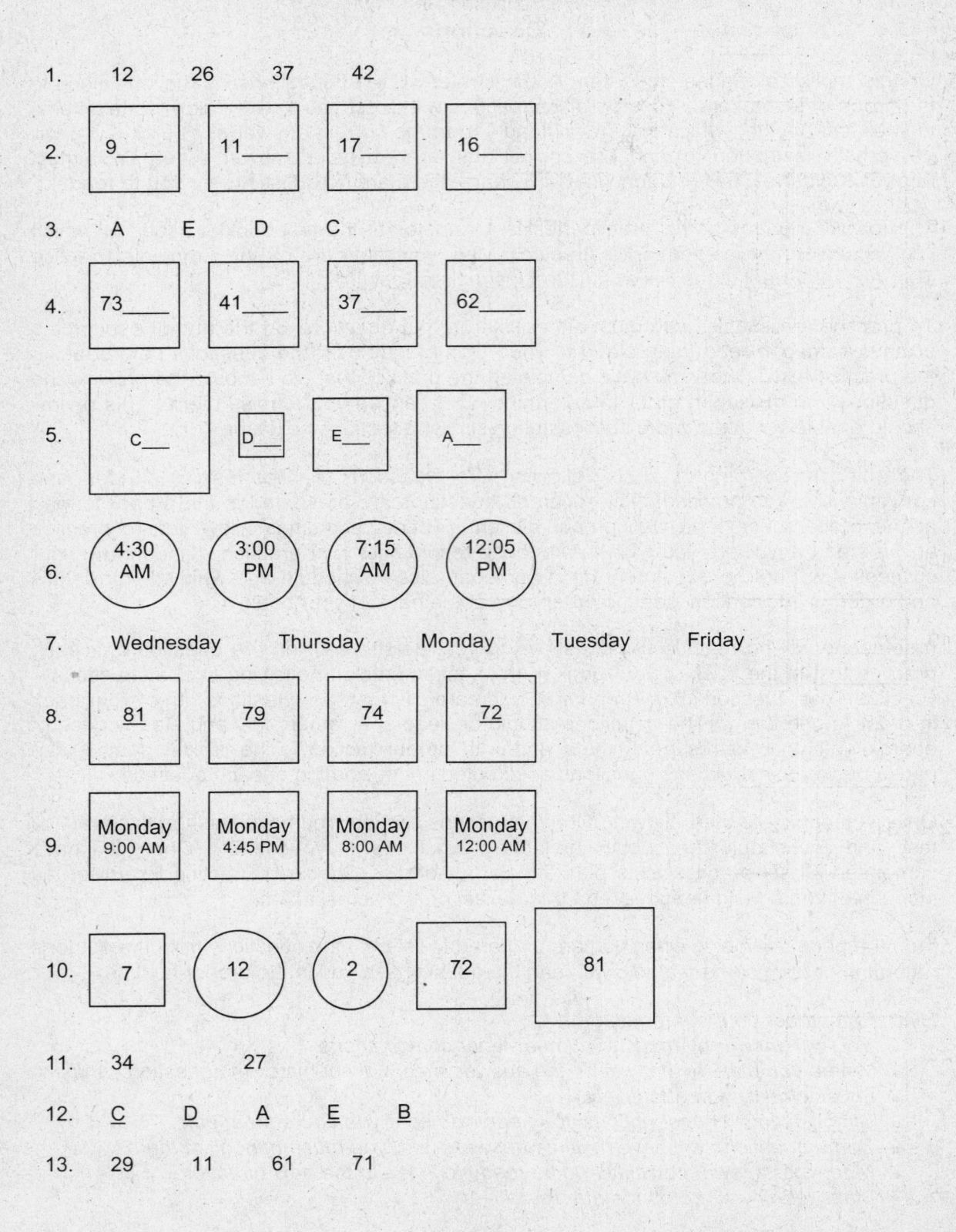

1. 12   26   37   42

2. [9___] [11___] [17___] [16___]

3. A   E   D   C

4. [73___] [41___] [37___] [62___]

5. [C___] [D___] [E___] [A___]

6. (4:30 AM) (3:00 PM) (7:15 AM) (12:05 PM)

7. Wednesday   Thursday   Monday   Tuesday   Friday

8. [81] [79] [74] [72]

9. [Monday 9:00 AM] [Monday 4:45 PM] [Monday 8:00 AM] [Monday 12:00 AM]

10. [7] (12) (2) [72] [81]

11. 34   27

12. C   D   A   E   B

13. 29   11   61   71

14. ☐ (___) ☐ (___) ___ ___

15.
| New Orleans 3:27 PM ___ | Los Angles 7:35 AM ___ | Tampa 4:15 PM ___ | New York 5:30 AM ___ |

16. ◯ 1:15 AM ___   ◯ 3:20 PM ___   ◯ 12:05 PM ___

17. ◯ 2:45 AM ___D   ◯ 5:00 AM ___C   ◯ 4:27 AM ___A   ◯ 11:15 PM ___E   ◯ 1:17 AM ___B

18.   E   C   R   S   T

19. ☐ 27___   ☐ 32___   ☐ 20___   ☐ 82___

20.   28 ___   47 ___   56 ___   19 ___

21. ☐ 81   ☐ 41   ☐ 12

22. ◯ ___C   ◯ ___B   ◯ ___D

23. ☐ 38___   ☐ 5___   ☐ 42___

24. ◯ 67___   ◯ 81___   ◯ 17___   ◯ 6___

COMPLETE PRACTICE TEST #4

This practice test contains samples of all four sections of the actual exam. The instructions given are similar to those on the actual exam. The format of this practice test is identical to that of the actual exam. Where pertinent, hints are given about your test taking strategies. Of course, these hints will not appear on the actual exam.

It is imperative that you take this practice test in as realistic a fashion as possible. **Your practice will have no value unless it is done realistically.** Therefore, you must precisely time yourself on the Address Checking, Address Memory, and Number Series sections. Our Timed Practice Test CD is a convenient way to practice realistically and time yourself precisely. Also, you must either listen to the Following Oral Instructions questions on our Oral Instructions Practice Tests CD or have someone read them to you – *do not read the questions yourself!* The Following Oral Instructions questions can be found in the back of your book if someone will be reading them to you.

To take this practice test, first turn to the back of your book and carefully tear out one of the **Complete Practice Test Answer Sheets.** Mark the answers to the scored segments of the practice test on this answer sheet. (Remember, of the seven segments on the Address Memory Section, only the final one is scored. Accordingly, you should mark answers for only the final Address Memory segment on your Complete Practice Test Answer Sheet. The other segments of the Address Memory Section that call for answers have accompanying sample answer sheets where you should mark answers.)

The correct answers are provided in the back of your book. Immediately upon completing the practice test, **it is imperative that you score each section** using the formulas given under the Sections of the Exam heading in your book. Scoring is necessary in order to gauge your progress and to identify your individual areas of weakness that may need extra attention.

After completing and scoring each practice test, move on to the next. **After completing all six practice tests and the Extra Address Checking Practice exercises as instructed, you should be prepared for the actual exam.** If you feel the need to practice more, repeat as many of the practice tests as you like. After that much practice, the questions will likely have become a confusing blur in your mind. It is highly unlikely that you will be able to remember many of the individual questions or answers. Therefore, you should be able to gain practice value from the exercises even though you have already taken them once.

Do not look over the practice test questions until you are ready to start – meaning until you have set a timer for the allotted period of time. Similarly, after completing one section of the practice test, do not look over the next one until your are ready to start it. Likewise, stop working and put down your pencil immediately when the allotted period of time has expired. As has been emphasized before but cannot be emphasized enough, your practice is of absolutely no value unless it is done realistically. Also, you must train yourself (1) to not open your test booklet or pick up your pencil until instructed to do so and (2) to close your booklet and put down your pencil immediately upon being so instructed. The Postal Service has a zero tolerance policy on these matters. Any variance may be viewed as cheating and may result in your disqualification.

Good luck on your practice test, and even better luck on your actual exam!

COMPLETE PRACTICE TEST #4
Part A – Address Checking

Directions

In this part of the test, you will have to decide whether two addresses are alike or different. You will have 6 minutes to answer 95 questions. Each question consists of a pair of addresses. If the two addresses in the pair are exactly alike in every way, darken the oval with the letter "A" for *Alike*. If the two addresses are different in any way, darken the oval with the letter "D" for *Different*. Mark your answers on the Complete Practice Test Answer Sheet in the section entitled Address Checking.

Turn the page and begin when you are prepared to time yourself for precisely 6 minutes.

Note: You will notice that this section of your practice test is spread across two pages. This is the exact same format that you will actually experience on the Address Checking section of the real exam. For economy and convenience, other study guides frequently condense the two pages of this section down to only one. You will also notice that the Address Checking questions are presented in a font, or type of print, that is different from the rest of the book. This font matches what is actually used on the real exam, and, as you will see, it makes this section even more challenging. However, it is imperative that you practice realistically and that you become acquainted with and comfortable with the actual format of the exam. We have accordingly formatted this practice test realistically for your benefit.

Hint: Remember your strategies:
- *Pace yourself for speed and accuracy – <u>emphasis on speed</u>!*
- *Use one glance-over for easier/shorter addresses.*
- *Use two glance-over's for harder/longer addresses.*
- *Never make a third pass or glance-over!*
- *Overlap the answer sheet & the questions to keep them as close together as possible.*
- *Use your extra pencil, your hand, or your fingers to mark/keep your place.*
- *Use your Speed Pencil and your Speed Marking strategies for much greater speed.*

COMPLETE PRACTICE TEST #4
Part A – Address Checking

1.	Racine WI 10697	Racine WI 10697
2.	4717 W 31st Ave	4717 W 31st Ave
3.	3908 N Robinson Ln	3908 N Robinson Ln
4.	8079 Woodstook Cir	8079 Woodstork Cir
5.	3179 Simonaux Dr	3179 Simonaux Dr
6.	Odgen UT 96781	Ogden UT 96781
7.	426 Heidenheim Ct	426 Heidenheim Ct
8.	9458 Darlene Dr	9584 Darlene Dr.
9.	1681 Irish Hill Dr	1681 Irish Hill Dr
10.	New Orleans LA 40995	New London LA 40995
11.	6450 S Balboa Cir	6450 S Ballbe Cir
12.	8721 Shawna Park	8721 Shawna Park
13.	2000 Liverpool Ave	2000 Liverpoole Ave
14.	Corpus Christi TX 93598	Corpus Christi TX 93598
15.	5154 Cooperslade Pt	5145 Cooperslade Pt
16.	4144 Marshall Ln	4144 Marshall Ln
17.	1514 Kensington Pl	1514 Kensington Pl
18.	San Francisco CA 91191	San Francisco CA 91911
19.	9003 Tennyson Cir	9003 Tennyson Cir
20.	8698 Rossmann Ln	8698 Rossmann Rd
21.	6628 W Sandypoint Tr	6628 W Sandypoint Terr
22.	Schenectady NY 67845	Schenectady NY 67845
23.	2315 Saratoga Dr	2315 Saratoga Dr
24.	6671 Barkwood Cir	6671 Bartworth Cir
25.	2583 Robertsdale Pl	2583 Robertsdale Pt
26.	2303 N Cleveland Ave	2303 N Cleveland Ave
27.	Minneapolis MN 49575	Minneapolaris MN 49575
28.	6967 W 85th St	6967 W 85th Star
29.	1411 Woolmarket Jct	1411 Woolmarket Jct
30.	Titusville Fl 32217	Titusville Fl 32217
31.	4252 Community Ave	4252 Community Ave
32.	2630 Rushing Waters Way	2630 Rusing Waters Bay
33.	2207 Shadowood Ct	2207 Shadowood Ct
34.	Kalamazoo MI 10240	Kalamazoo MS 10240
35.	8647 Grasslawn Plaza	8647 Grasslawn Plaza
36.	Chattanooga Tn 90108	Chattanooga Tn 90108
37.	7327 Horace Rd	7327 Horrace Rd
38.	3020 General Sherman St	3020 General Sherman St
39.	4100 McNamee Bridge	4100 McNamee Bridge
40.	1137 Quailridge Rd	1173 Quailridge Rd
41.	Melbourne Fl 21907	Melbourne Fl 21907
42.	2686 51st Ave	2686 51st Ave
43.	2117 E Princeton Dr	2117 W Princeton Dr
44.	1607 Mary Ellen Dr	1609 Mary Ellen Dr
45.	2882 Flounder Pt	2882 Flounder Pt
46.	Fayetteville NC 71673	Fayettetown NC 71673
47.	4984 W Ruffin Ln	4984 W Ruffin Ln
48.	8777 Partridge Pl	8777 Partridge Pl

49.	3043 Sampson Ct	3043 Sapsonite Ct
50.	1024 Greenbriar Rd	1024 Greenbriar Rd
51.	Bethlehem PA 84297	Bethleham PA 84297
52.	6051 Riverview Ln	6051 Riverview Ln
53.	1769 English Village Dr	1769 English Village Dr
54.	4217 St Augustine Pl	4772 St Augustine Pl
55.	2280 E 2nd St	2280 E 2nd St
56.	Atlantic City NJ 63636	Atlantic City NJ 63636
57.	8633 Satchfield Jct	8633 Satchfore Jct
58.	1357 Cloverdale Rd	1357 W Cloverdale Rd
59.	7877 Whorton Blvd	7877 Whorton Bd
60.	2142 Hollyheath Pt	2142 Hollyheath Pt
61.	Colorado Springs CO 16560	Colorado Springs CO 15606
62.	2481 W Stanfield Rd	2481 W Stanfold Rd
63.	6718 Bamboo Cir	6718 Bamboo Cir
64.	745 Schindler Cove	745 Schindler Cape
65.	Hot Springs AR 89651	Hot Springs AR 89651
66.	9827 Schumacker Ln	9827 Schumaker Ln
67.	5621 Annelore Pl	5621 Annelore Pl
68.	4177 Tantaloon Rd	4177 Telephone Rd
69.	6010 Railroad St	6010 Railroad St
70.	Saskatoon MN 11257	Sascatoon MN 11257
71.	Biloxi MS 39806	Buloxi Ms 39806
72.	3674 22nd St	3674 22nd St
73.	9558 W Jackson Ln	9558 E Jackson Ln
74.	2555 Ransom Way	2555 Ranson Way
75.	Jacksonville Fl 32790	Jacksonville MS 32790
76.	3910 Stephanie Bridge	3910 Stephanie Bridge
77.	8210 Tyrone Blvd	8210 Tyrone Blvd
78.	7411 W 84th St	7477 W 84th St
79.	Fort Lauderdale Fl 76708	Fort Lauderdale Fl 76708
80.	2004 Barracuda Pt	2004 Barracuda Pt
81.	3271 E Clarence	3271 E Clarence
82.	1186 Jefferson Ave	1186 S Jefferson Ave
83.	Millinocket NH 13270	Millinocket NH 13270
84.	6665 N Nottingham Cir	6665 S Nottingham Cir
85.	3330 Meadowlark Jct	3330 Meadowlark Jct
86.	1579 Rosebud Trail	1659 Rosebud Trail
87.	Winnemucca NV 56707	Winnemucca NV 56701
88.	8814 Hampstead Way	8814 Hampstead Way
89.	4969 87th Ave	4969 87th Ave
90.	6957 Homestead Ln	6957 Homestead Ln
91.	2121 Campbell Blvd	2121 Campbell Blvd
92.	Alamogorda NM 66712	Alamogordy NM 66712
93.	5111 Orchard Park	5111 Orchard Bark
94.	8814 W 15th St	8814 W 15th St
95.	Devils Lake ND 77216	Devils Lake ND 77216

COMPLETE PRACTICE TEST #4
Part B – Address Memory

Directions

In this part of the test, you will have to memorize the locations of 25 addresses in five boxes. During this section, you will have several study periods and practice exercises to help you memorize the location of the addresses shown in the five boxes. Answer the questions by darkening the oval containing the letter (A, B, C, D, or E) of the box in which the address is located – Box A, Box B, Box C, Box D, or Box E. At the end of each segment, you will be given instructions on how and where to continue. After completing six preliminary segments, the actual test will be given as segment #7.

Turn the page to begin Segment #1.

Note: You will notice on your practice test that the various segments of the Address Memory section are spread across two pages. Where applicable, the five boxes, the 88 questions, and/or the sample answer sheets are spread across two pages. This is the same format that you will experience on most segments of the Address Memory section on the actual exam. For economy and convenience, other study guides frequently condense the two pages down to only one. However, it is imperative that you practice realistically and that you become acquainted with and comfortable with the actual format of the exam. We have accordingly formatted this practice test realistically for your benefit.

Hint: Remember your strategies:
- *Memorize horizontally.*
- *Memorize only Boxes A, B, C, and D.*
- *You can correctly answer all Box E questions by the process of elimination.*
- *Use the Second Digit Strategy to memorize the number addresses.*
- *Use imagery/association to memorize the word addresses.*
- *Overlap the answer sheet & the questions to keep them as close together as possible.*
- *Use your extra pencil, your hand, or your fingers to mark/keep your place.*
- *Use your Speed Pencil and your Speed Marking strategies for much greater speed.*

COMPLETE PRACTICE TEST #4
Part B – Address Memory – Segment #1

Directions

Five sample boxes, each containing five addresses, and five sample questions about these boxes are given on the following two pages. The purpose of this small exercise is simply to acquaint you with the format of this section and with how the questions should be answered. The first two sample questions are answered for you. You are to spend three minutes becoming acquainted with the format and answering sample questions 3, 4, and 5. After completing Segment #1, turn to Segment #2 for further instructions.

Turn the page and begin when you are prepared to time yourself for precisely three minutes.

Hint: Remember your strategies! This segment is not scored, so do not take the sample questions seriously. Instead, mark random answers and use the three minutes to study and memorize the addresses. The sample boxes and addresses in this segment are the very same ones that will be repeated throughout this section of the exam.

COMPLETE PRACTICE TEST #4
Part B – Address Memory – Segment #1

A	**B**	**C**
5100-5299 Owen	8700-8899 Owen	3300-3499 Owen
Adolph	Walda	Odessa
3300-3499 Grove	8200-8399 Grove	5800-5999 Grove
Brodie	Eddy	Halter
5800-5999 Tuck	3300-3499 Tuck	8200-8399 Tuck

1. 5100-5299 Owen   Ⓐ Ⓑ Ⓒ Ⓓ Ⓔ
This address came from Box A, so we sill darken the oval with the letter A.

2. 5800-5999 Grove   Ⓐ Ⓑ Ⓒ Ⓓ Ⓔ
This address came from Box C, so we will darken the oval with the letter C.

3. 8200-8399 Owen   Ⓐ Ⓑ Ⓒ Ⓓ Ⓔ
Now that you know how to answer, you do questions 3, 4, and 5.

4. Walda   Ⓐ Ⓑ Ⓒ Ⓓ Ⓔ

5. Bayou   Ⓐ Ⓑ Ⓒ Ⓓ Ⓔ

The correct answers are A, C, E, B, and E.

180

D	E
5800-5999 Owen	8200-8399 Owen
Sonja	Bayou
5100-5299 Grove	8700-8899 Grove
Benoit	Trehern
8700-8899 Tuck	5100-5299 Tuck

COMPLETE PRACTICE TEST #4
Part B – Address Memory – Segment #2

Directions

In this segment, you are given three minutes to study and memorize the addresses. There are no questions to answer in this segment – it is a study period only. However, on the actual exam, the boxes are not reprinted for your use. Instead, you are instructed to turn back to Address Memory Segment #1 on the preceding pages of the exam and to spend three minutes studying the boxes displayed there. So, we will do the very same on this practice test. After studying for three minutes, turn to Segment #3 for directions on how to continue the Address Memory Section of the exam.

Begin studying when you are prepared to time yourself for precisely three minutes.

COMPLETE PRACTICE TEST #4
Part B – Address Memory – Segment #3

Directions

In this segment you have three minutes to attempt answering 88 questions. You are to try to answer from memory, but the boxes are shown if you need to refer to them. Your answers are to be marked on the sample answer sheet at the bottom of the pages of Segment #3 – do not use the Compete Practice Test Answer Sheet for this segment. After completing this segment, turn to Segment #4 for further instructions.

Turn the page and begin when you are prepared to time yourself for precisely three minutes.

Hint: Remember your strategies! This segment is not scored, so do not take the questions seriously. Instead, mark a handful of random answers and use the three minutes to study and memorize the addresses.

A

5100-5299 Owen

Adolph

3300-3499 Grove

Brodie

5800-5999 Tuck

B

8700-8899 Owen

Walda

8200-8399 Grove

Eddy

3300-3499 Tuck

C

3300-3499 Owen

Odessa

5800-5999 Grove

Halter

8200-8399 Tuck

1. 8700-8899 Grove
2. Halter
3. Trehern
4. 5100-5299 Grove
5. 5800-5999 Tuck
6. 8200-8399 Tuck
7. 5800-5999 Owen
8. Walda

9. 5100-5299 Owen
10. Benoit
11. 3300-3499 Tuck
12. Bayou
13. 8200-8399 Grove
14. 5100-5299 Grove
15. 8200-8399 Owen
16. Eddy

17. 8700-8899 Grove
18. Odessa
19. 5800-5999 Tuck
20. Adolph
21. Benoit
22. Walda
23. 3300-3499 Tuck
24. Halter

25. Brodie
26. 8200-8399 Tuck
27. 8700-8899 Tuck
28. 8700-8899 Owen
29. 5100-5299 Tuck
30. 3300-3499 Owen
31. 8700-8899 Grove
32. Walda

33. 5100-5299 Owen
34. Bayou
35. 5800-5999 Grove
36. 5100-5299 Tuck
37. 8200-8399 Grove
38. 5800-5999 Owen
39. Trehern
40. 5800-5999 Tuck

41. Odessa
42. 3300-3499 Grove
43. 8200-8399 Grove
44. Halter
45. Eddy
46. Sonja
47. 3300-3499 Owen
48. 5800-5999 Grove

1 Ⓐ Ⓑ Ⓒ Ⓓ Ⓔ
2 Ⓐ Ⓑ Ⓒ Ⓓ Ⓔ
3 Ⓐ Ⓑ Ⓒ Ⓓ Ⓔ
4 Ⓐ Ⓑ Ⓒ Ⓓ Ⓔ
5 Ⓐ Ⓑ Ⓒ Ⓓ Ⓔ
6 Ⓐ Ⓑ Ⓒ Ⓓ Ⓔ
7 Ⓐ Ⓑ Ⓒ Ⓓ Ⓔ
8 Ⓐ Ⓑ Ⓒ Ⓓ Ⓔ

9 Ⓐ Ⓑ Ⓒ Ⓓ Ⓔ
10 Ⓐ Ⓑ Ⓒ Ⓓ Ⓔ
11 Ⓐ Ⓑ Ⓒ Ⓓ Ⓔ
12 Ⓐ Ⓑ Ⓒ Ⓓ Ⓔ
13 Ⓐ Ⓑ Ⓒ Ⓓ Ⓔ
14 Ⓐ Ⓑ Ⓒ Ⓓ Ⓔ
15 Ⓐ Ⓑ Ⓒ Ⓓ Ⓔ
16 Ⓐ Ⓑ Ⓒ Ⓓ Ⓔ

17 Ⓐ Ⓑ Ⓒ Ⓓ Ⓔ
18 Ⓐ Ⓑ Ⓒ Ⓓ Ⓔ
19 Ⓐ Ⓑ Ⓒ Ⓓ Ⓔ
20 Ⓐ Ⓑ Ⓒ Ⓓ Ⓔ
21 Ⓐ Ⓑ Ⓒ Ⓓ Ⓔ
22 Ⓐ Ⓑ Ⓒ Ⓓ Ⓔ
23 Ⓐ Ⓑ Ⓒ Ⓓ Ⓔ
24 Ⓐ Ⓑ Ⓒ Ⓓ Ⓔ

25 Ⓐ Ⓑ Ⓒ Ⓓ Ⓔ
26 Ⓐ Ⓑ Ⓒ Ⓓ Ⓔ
27 Ⓐ Ⓑ Ⓒ Ⓓ Ⓔ
28 Ⓐ Ⓑ Ⓒ Ⓓ Ⓔ
29 Ⓐ Ⓑ Ⓒ Ⓓ Ⓔ
30 Ⓐ Ⓑ Ⓒ Ⓓ Ⓔ
31 Ⓐ Ⓑ Ⓒ Ⓓ Ⓔ
32 Ⓐ Ⓑ Ⓒ Ⓓ Ⓔ

33 Ⓐ Ⓑ Ⓒ Ⓓ Ⓔ
34 Ⓐ Ⓑ Ⓒ Ⓓ Ⓔ
35 Ⓐ Ⓑ Ⓒ Ⓓ Ⓔ
36 Ⓐ Ⓑ Ⓒ Ⓓ Ⓔ
37 Ⓐ Ⓑ Ⓒ Ⓓ Ⓔ
38 Ⓐ Ⓑ Ⓒ Ⓓ Ⓔ
39 Ⓐ Ⓑ Ⓒ Ⓓ Ⓔ
40 Ⓐ Ⓑ Ⓒ Ⓓ Ⓔ

41 Ⓐ Ⓑ Ⓒ Ⓓ Ⓔ
42 Ⓐ Ⓑ Ⓒ Ⓓ Ⓔ
43 Ⓐ Ⓑ Ⓒ Ⓓ Ⓔ
44 Ⓐ Ⓑ Ⓒ Ⓓ Ⓔ
45 Ⓐ Ⓑ Ⓒ Ⓓ Ⓔ
46 Ⓐ Ⓑ Ⓒ Ⓓ Ⓔ
47 Ⓐ Ⓑ Ⓒ Ⓓ Ⓔ
48 Ⓐ Ⓑ Ⓒ Ⓓ Ⓔ

D	**E**
5800-5999 Owen	8200-8399 Owen
Sonja	Bayou
5100-5299 Grove	8700-8899 Grove
Benoit	Trehern
8700-8899 Tuck	5100-5299 Tuck

49. 8700-8899 Tuck
50. Adolph
51. 8200-8399 Owen
52. Odessa
53. 5800-5999 Owen
54. Bayou
55. 8700-8899 Owen
56. 5100-5299 Grove

57. 5800-5999 Grove
58. Brodie
59. 8200-8399 Grove
60. Sonja
61. Benoit
62. 3300-3499 Grove
63. 8700-8899 Grove
64. Halter

65. 5800-5999 Tuck
66. Brodie
67. 5800-5999 Grove
68. 8200-8399 Grove
69. 5100-5299 Tuck
70. 5100-5299 Owen
71. Bayou
72. Eddy

73. 3300-3499 Owen
74. Trehern
75. Brodie
76. 8200-8399 Owen
77. 8700-8899 Owen
78. 8700-8899 Tuck
79. 8200-8399 Tuck
80. Adolph

81. 3300-3499 Tuck
82. 8700-8899 Tuck
83. Benoit
84. 3300-3499 Grove
85. Halter
86. Walda
87. Sonja
88. 8200-8399 Tuck

49 Ⓐ Ⓑ Ⓒ Ⓓ Ⓔ
50 Ⓐ Ⓑ Ⓒ Ⓓ Ⓔ
51 Ⓐ Ⓑ Ⓒ Ⓓ Ⓔ
52 Ⓐ Ⓑ Ⓒ Ⓓ Ⓔ
53 Ⓐ Ⓑ Ⓒ Ⓓ Ⓔ
54 Ⓐ Ⓑ Ⓒ Ⓓ Ⓔ
55 Ⓐ Ⓑ Ⓒ Ⓓ Ⓔ
56 Ⓐ Ⓑ Ⓒ Ⓓ Ⓔ

57 Ⓐ Ⓑ Ⓒ Ⓓ Ⓔ
58 Ⓐ Ⓑ Ⓒ Ⓓ Ⓔ
59 Ⓐ Ⓑ Ⓒ Ⓓ Ⓔ
60 Ⓐ Ⓑ Ⓒ Ⓓ Ⓔ
61 Ⓐ Ⓑ Ⓒ Ⓓ Ⓔ
62 Ⓐ Ⓑ Ⓒ Ⓓ Ⓔ
63 Ⓐ Ⓑ Ⓒ Ⓓ Ⓔ
64 Ⓐ Ⓑ Ⓒ Ⓓ Ⓔ

65 Ⓐ Ⓑ Ⓒ Ⓓ Ⓔ
66 Ⓐ Ⓑ Ⓒ Ⓓ Ⓔ
67 Ⓐ Ⓑ Ⓒ Ⓓ Ⓔ
68 Ⓐ Ⓑ Ⓒ Ⓓ Ⓔ
69 Ⓐ Ⓑ Ⓒ Ⓓ Ⓔ
70 Ⓐ Ⓑ Ⓒ Ⓓ Ⓔ
71 Ⓐ Ⓑ Ⓒ Ⓓ Ⓔ
72 Ⓐ Ⓑ Ⓒ Ⓓ Ⓔ

73 Ⓐ Ⓑ Ⓒ Ⓓ Ⓔ
74 Ⓐ Ⓑ Ⓒ Ⓓ Ⓔ
75 Ⓐ Ⓑ Ⓒ Ⓓ Ⓔ
76 Ⓐ Ⓑ Ⓒ Ⓓ Ⓔ
77 Ⓐ Ⓑ Ⓒ Ⓓ Ⓔ
78 Ⓐ Ⓑ Ⓒ Ⓓ Ⓔ
79 Ⓐ Ⓑ Ⓒ Ⓓ Ⓔ
80 Ⓐ Ⓑ Ⓒ Ⓓ Ⓔ

81 Ⓐ Ⓑ Ⓒ Ⓓ Ⓔ
82 Ⓐ Ⓑ Ⓒ Ⓓ Ⓔ
83 Ⓐ Ⓑ Ⓒ Ⓓ Ⓔ
84 Ⓐ Ⓑ Ⓒ Ⓓ Ⓔ
85 Ⓐ Ⓑ Ⓒ Ⓓ Ⓔ
86 Ⓐ Ⓑ Ⓒ Ⓓ Ⓔ
87 Ⓐ Ⓑ Ⓒ Ⓓ Ⓔ
88 Ⓐ Ⓑ Ⓒ Ⓓ Ⓔ

COMPLETE PRACTICE TEST #4
Part B – Address Memory – Segment #4

Directions

In this segment you have three minutes to attempt answering 88 questions. You must answer from memory. The boxes are not shown. Your answers are to be marked on the sample answer sheet at the bottom of the pages of Segment #4 – do not use the Compete Practice Test Answer Sheet for this segment. After completing this segment, turn to Segment #5 for further instructions.

Turn the page and begin when you are prepared to time yourself for precisely three minutes.

Hint: Remember, this segment is not scored, so you should not worry about your inability to answer all 88 questions, or your inability to answer all of them accurately, in only three minutes. Neither task is really possible in only three minutes. However, this is an ideal opportunity for you to test how well you have mastered your strategies and memorization so far. By sincerely trying to answer the questions, you can identify the areas where you are weaker and where you need to apply more effort.

1. 5100-5299 Owen
2. 5800-5999 Grove
3. 8200-8399 Owen
4. Walda
5. Bayou
6. 5800-5999 Owen
7. 5100-5299 Owen
8. 8700-8899 Grove

9. 5100-5299 Tuck
10. Eddy
11. 5100-5299 Grove
12. 5800-5999 Tuck
13. 8700-8899 Tuck
14. 3300-3499 Owen
15. 8200-8399 Grove
16. Adolph

17. Sonja
18. Trehern
19. 8700-8899 Owen
20. Halter
21. 5800-5999 Grove
22. Brodie
23. 8200-8399 Tuck
24. 8700-8899 Tuck

25. 3300-3499 Tuck
26. Benoit
27. 3300-3499 Grove
28. Bayou
29. Odessa
30. 5100-5299 Tuck
31. 8200-8399 Grove
32. 3300-3499 Grove

33. Walda
34. Adolph
35. 8200-8399 Tuck
36. 3300-3499 Owen
37. 5800-5999 Owen
38. Halter
39. 8700-8899 Grove
40. 3300-3499 Grove

41. 5100-5299 Grove
42. 5800-5999 Tuck
43. 8700-8999 Owen
44. Sonja
45. Walda
46. Bayou
47. 5100-5299 Owen
48. Trehern

1 Ⓐ Ⓑ Ⓒ Ⓓ Ⓔ
2 Ⓐ Ⓑ Ⓒ Ⓓ Ⓔ
3 Ⓐ Ⓑ Ⓒ Ⓓ Ⓔ
4 Ⓐ Ⓑ Ⓒ Ⓓ Ⓔ
5 Ⓐ Ⓑ Ⓒ Ⓓ Ⓔ
6 Ⓐ Ⓑ Ⓒ Ⓓ Ⓔ
7 Ⓐ Ⓑ Ⓒ Ⓓ Ⓔ
8 Ⓐ Ⓑ Ⓒ Ⓓ Ⓔ

9 Ⓐ Ⓑ Ⓒ Ⓓ Ⓔ
10 Ⓐ Ⓑ Ⓒ Ⓓ Ⓔ
11 Ⓐ Ⓑ Ⓒ Ⓓ Ⓔ
12 Ⓐ Ⓑ Ⓒ Ⓓ Ⓔ
13 Ⓐ Ⓑ Ⓒ Ⓓ Ⓔ
14 Ⓐ Ⓑ Ⓒ Ⓓ Ⓔ
15 Ⓐ Ⓑ Ⓒ Ⓓ Ⓔ
16 Ⓐ Ⓑ Ⓒ Ⓓ Ⓔ

17 Ⓐ Ⓑ Ⓒ Ⓓ Ⓔ
18 Ⓐ Ⓑ Ⓒ Ⓓ Ⓔ
19 Ⓐ Ⓑ Ⓒ Ⓓ Ⓔ
20 Ⓐ Ⓑ Ⓒ Ⓓ Ⓔ
21 Ⓐ Ⓑ Ⓒ Ⓓ Ⓔ
22 Ⓐ Ⓑ Ⓒ Ⓓ Ⓔ
23 Ⓐ Ⓑ Ⓒ Ⓓ Ⓔ
24 Ⓐ Ⓑ Ⓒ Ⓓ Ⓔ

25 Ⓐ Ⓑ Ⓒ Ⓓ Ⓔ
26 Ⓐ Ⓑ Ⓒ Ⓓ Ⓔ
27 Ⓐ Ⓑ Ⓒ Ⓓ Ⓔ
28 Ⓐ Ⓑ Ⓒ Ⓓ Ⓔ
29 Ⓐ Ⓑ Ⓒ Ⓓ Ⓔ
30 Ⓐ Ⓑ Ⓒ Ⓓ Ⓔ
31 Ⓐ Ⓑ Ⓒ Ⓓ Ⓔ
32 Ⓐ Ⓑ Ⓒ Ⓓ Ⓔ

33 Ⓐ Ⓑ Ⓒ Ⓓ Ⓔ
34 Ⓐ Ⓑ Ⓒ Ⓓ Ⓔ
35 Ⓐ Ⓑ Ⓒ Ⓓ Ⓔ
36 Ⓐ Ⓑ Ⓒ Ⓓ Ⓔ
37 Ⓐ Ⓑ Ⓒ Ⓓ Ⓔ
38 Ⓐ Ⓑ Ⓒ Ⓓ Ⓔ
39 Ⓐ Ⓑ Ⓒ Ⓓ Ⓔ
40 Ⓐ Ⓑ Ⓒ Ⓓ Ⓔ

41 Ⓐ Ⓑ Ⓒ Ⓓ Ⓔ
42 Ⓐ Ⓑ Ⓒ Ⓓ Ⓔ
43 Ⓐ Ⓑ Ⓒ Ⓓ Ⓔ
44 Ⓐ Ⓑ Ⓒ Ⓓ Ⓔ
45 Ⓐ Ⓑ Ⓒ Ⓓ Ⓔ
46 Ⓐ Ⓑ Ⓒ Ⓓ Ⓔ
47 Ⓐ Ⓑ Ⓒ Ⓓ Ⓔ
48 Ⓐ Ⓑ Ⓒ Ⓓ Ⓔ

49. 8200-8399 Grove
50. 5800-5999 Owen
51. Brodie
52. 8200-8399 Owen
53. Eddy
54. Odessa
55. 8700-8899 Grove
56. 5800-5999 Tuck

57. Benoit
58. 8200-8399 Tuck
59. Adolph
60. 5100-5299 Tuck
61. 5800-5999 Grove
62. 8700-8899 Owen
63. Walda
64. 8200-8399 Owen

65. Halter
66. 8700-8899 Tuck
67. 5100-5299 Owen
68. 8200-8399 Tuck
69. 5100-5299 Tuck
70. 8200-8399 Grove
71. 8700-8899 Tuck
72. Eddy

73. 8700-8899 Grove
74. Brodie
75. Odessa
76. 5800-5999 Owen
77. 8700-8899 Owen
78. 5100-5299 Grove
79. 3300-3499 Tuck
80. Sonja

81. 3300-3499 Grove
82. 8700-8899 Tuck
83. 3300-3499 Owen
84. Benoit
85. 5800-5999 Tuck
86. Bayou
87. 5800-5999 Grove
88. Trehern

49 Ⓐ Ⓑ Ⓒ Ⓓ Ⓔ
50 Ⓐ Ⓑ Ⓒ Ⓓ Ⓔ
51 Ⓐ Ⓑ Ⓒ Ⓓ Ⓔ
52 Ⓐ Ⓑ Ⓒ Ⓓ Ⓔ
53 Ⓐ Ⓑ Ⓒ Ⓓ Ⓔ
54 Ⓐ Ⓑ Ⓒ Ⓓ Ⓔ
55 Ⓐ Ⓑ Ⓒ Ⓓ Ⓔ
56 Ⓐ Ⓑ Ⓒ Ⓓ Ⓔ

57 Ⓐ Ⓑ Ⓒ Ⓓ Ⓔ
58 Ⓐ Ⓑ Ⓒ Ⓓ Ⓔ
59 Ⓐ Ⓑ Ⓒ Ⓓ Ⓔ
60 Ⓐ Ⓑ Ⓒ Ⓓ Ⓔ
61 Ⓐ Ⓑ Ⓒ Ⓓ Ⓔ
62 Ⓐ Ⓑ Ⓒ Ⓓ Ⓔ
63 Ⓐ Ⓑ Ⓒ Ⓓ Ⓔ
64 Ⓐ Ⓑ Ⓒ Ⓓ Ⓔ

65 Ⓐ Ⓑ Ⓒ Ⓓ Ⓔ
66 Ⓐ Ⓑ Ⓒ Ⓓ Ⓔ
67 Ⓐ Ⓑ Ⓒ Ⓓ Ⓔ
68 Ⓐ Ⓑ Ⓒ Ⓓ Ⓔ
69 Ⓐ Ⓑ Ⓒ Ⓓ Ⓔ
70 Ⓐ Ⓑ Ⓒ Ⓓ Ⓔ
71 Ⓐ Ⓑ Ⓒ Ⓓ Ⓔ
72 Ⓐ Ⓑ Ⓒ Ⓓ Ⓔ

73 Ⓐ Ⓑ Ⓒ Ⓓ Ⓔ
74 Ⓐ Ⓑ Ⓒ Ⓓ Ⓔ
75 Ⓐ Ⓑ Ⓒ Ⓓ Ⓔ
76 Ⓐ Ⓑ Ⓒ Ⓓ Ⓔ
77 Ⓐ Ⓑ Ⓒ Ⓓ Ⓔ
78 Ⓐ Ⓑ Ⓒ Ⓓ Ⓔ
79 Ⓐ Ⓑ Ⓒ Ⓓ Ⓔ
80 Ⓐ Ⓑ Ⓒ Ⓓ Ⓔ

81 Ⓐ Ⓑ Ⓒ Ⓓ Ⓔ
82 Ⓐ Ⓑ Ⓒ Ⓓ Ⓔ
83 Ⓐ Ⓑ Ⓒ Ⓓ Ⓔ
84 Ⓐ Ⓑ Ⓒ Ⓓ Ⓔ
85 Ⓐ Ⓑ Ⓒ Ⓓ Ⓔ
86 Ⓐ Ⓑ Ⓒ Ⓓ Ⓔ
87 Ⓐ Ⓑ Ⓒ Ⓓ Ⓔ
88 Ⓐ Ⓑ Ⓒ Ⓓ Ⓔ

COMPLETE PRACTICE TEST #4
Part B – Address Memory – Segment #5

Directions

In this segment, you are given five minutes to study the addresses. There are no questions to answer in this segment – it is a study period only. As before, the boxes are not reprinted here for your use. Instead, you are instructed to turn back to Address Memory Segment #1 and to spend five minutes studying the boxes displayed there. After studying for five minutes, turn to Segment #6 for directions on how to continue.

Begin studying when you are prepared to time yourself for precisely five minutes.

194

Directions

In this segment, you have five minutes to attempt answering 88 questions. You are to try to answer from memory, but the boxes are shown if you need to refer to them. Your answers are to be marked on the sample answer sheet at the bottom of the pages of Segment #6 – do not use the Compete Practice Test Answer Sheet for this segment. After completing this segment, turn to Segment #7 for further instructions.

Turn the page and begin when you are prepared to time yourself for precisely five minutes.

Hint: Remember your strategies! This segment is not scored, so do not take the questions seriously. Instead, mark a handful of random answers and use the five minutes to study and memorize the addresses.

COMPLETE PRACTICE TEST #4
Part B – Address Memory – Segment #6

A	B	C
5100-5299 Owen Adolph 3300-3499 Grove Brodie 5800-5999 Tuck	8700-8899 Owen Walda 8200-8399 Grove Eddy 3300-3499 Tuck	3300-3499 Owen Odessa 5800-5999 Grove Halter 8200-8399 Tuck

1. 8700-8899 Grove
2. Halter
3. Trehern
4. 5100-5299 Grove
5. 5800-5999 Tuck
6. 8200-8399 Tuck
7. 5800-5999 Owen
8. Walda

9. 5100-5299 Owen
10. Benoit
11. 3300-3499 Tuck
12. Bayou
13. 8200-8399 Grove
14. 5100-5299 Grove
15. 8200-8399 Owen
16. Eddy

17. 8700-8899 Grove
18. Odessa
19. 5800-5999 Tuck
20. Adolph
21. Benoit
22. Walda
23. 3300-3499 Tuck
24. Halter

25. Brodie
26. 8200-8399 Tuck
27. 8700-8899 Tuck
28. 8700-8899 Owen
29. 5100-5299 Tuck
30. 3300-3499 Owen
31. 8700-8899 Grove
32. Walda

33. 5100-5299 Owen
34. Bayou
35. 5800-5999 Grove
36. 5100-5299 Tuck
37. 8200-8399 Grove
38. 5800-5999 Owen
39. Trehern
40. 5800-5999 Tuck

41. Odessa
42. 3300-3499 Grove
43. 8200-8399 Grove
44. Halter
45. Eddy
46. Sonja
47. 3300-3499 Owen
48. 5800-5999 Grove

1 Ⓐ Ⓑ Ⓒ Ⓓ Ⓔ
2 Ⓐ Ⓑ Ⓒ Ⓓ Ⓔ
3 Ⓐ Ⓑ Ⓒ Ⓓ Ⓔ
4 Ⓐ Ⓑ Ⓒ Ⓓ Ⓔ
5 Ⓐ Ⓑ Ⓒ Ⓓ Ⓔ
6 Ⓐ Ⓑ Ⓒ Ⓓ Ⓔ
7 Ⓐ Ⓑ Ⓒ Ⓓ Ⓔ
8 Ⓐ Ⓑ Ⓒ Ⓓ Ⓔ
9 Ⓐ Ⓑ Ⓒ Ⓓ Ⓔ
10 Ⓐ Ⓑ Ⓒ Ⓓ Ⓔ
11 Ⓐ Ⓑ Ⓒ Ⓓ Ⓔ
12 Ⓐ Ⓑ Ⓒ Ⓓ Ⓔ
13 Ⓐ Ⓑ Ⓒ Ⓓ Ⓔ
14 Ⓐ Ⓑ Ⓒ Ⓓ Ⓔ
15 Ⓐ Ⓑ Ⓒ Ⓓ Ⓔ
16 Ⓐ Ⓑ Ⓒ Ⓓ Ⓔ

17 Ⓐ Ⓑ Ⓒ Ⓓ Ⓔ
18 Ⓐ Ⓑ Ⓒ Ⓓ Ⓔ
19 Ⓐ Ⓑ Ⓒ Ⓓ Ⓔ
20 Ⓐ Ⓑ Ⓒ Ⓓ Ⓔ
21 Ⓐ Ⓑ Ⓒ Ⓓ Ⓔ
22 Ⓐ Ⓑ Ⓒ Ⓓ Ⓔ
23 Ⓐ Ⓑ Ⓒ Ⓓ Ⓔ
24 Ⓐ Ⓑ Ⓒ Ⓓ Ⓔ
25 Ⓐ Ⓑ Ⓒ Ⓓ Ⓔ
26 Ⓐ Ⓑ Ⓒ Ⓓ Ⓔ
27 Ⓐ Ⓑ Ⓒ Ⓓ Ⓔ
28 Ⓐ Ⓑ Ⓒ Ⓓ Ⓔ
29 Ⓐ Ⓑ Ⓒ Ⓓ Ⓔ
30 Ⓐ Ⓑ Ⓒ Ⓓ Ⓔ
31 Ⓐ Ⓑ Ⓒ Ⓓ Ⓔ
32 Ⓐ Ⓑ Ⓒ Ⓓ Ⓔ

33 Ⓐ Ⓑ Ⓒ Ⓓ Ⓔ
34 Ⓐ Ⓑ Ⓒ Ⓓ Ⓔ
35 Ⓐ Ⓑ Ⓒ Ⓓ Ⓔ
36 Ⓐ Ⓑ Ⓒ Ⓓ Ⓔ
37 Ⓐ Ⓑ Ⓒ Ⓓ Ⓔ
38 Ⓐ Ⓑ Ⓒ Ⓓ Ⓔ
39 Ⓐ Ⓑ Ⓒ Ⓓ Ⓔ
40 Ⓐ Ⓑ Ⓒ Ⓓ Ⓔ
41 Ⓐ Ⓑ Ⓒ Ⓓ Ⓔ
42 Ⓐ Ⓑ Ⓒ Ⓓ Ⓔ
43 Ⓐ Ⓑ Ⓒ Ⓓ Ⓔ
44 Ⓐ Ⓑ Ⓒ Ⓓ Ⓔ
45 Ⓐ Ⓑ Ⓒ Ⓓ Ⓔ
46 Ⓐ Ⓑ Ⓒ Ⓓ Ⓔ
47 Ⓐ Ⓑ Ⓒ Ⓓ Ⓔ
48 Ⓐ Ⓑ Ⓒ Ⓓ Ⓔ

D	E
5800-5999 Owen	8200-8399 Owen
Sonja	Bayou
5100-5299 Grove	8700-8899 Grove
Benoit	Trehern
8700-8899 Tuck	5100-5299 Tuck

49. 8700-8899 Tuck
50. Adolph
51. 8200-8399 Owen
52. Odessa
53. 5800-5999 Owen
54. Bayou
55. 8700-8899 Owen
56. 5100-5299 Grove

57. 5800-5999 Grove
58. Brodie
59. 8200-8399 Grove
60. Sonja
61. Benoit
62. 3300-3499 Grove
63. 8700-8899 Grove
64. Halter

65. 5800-5999 Tuck
66. Brodie
67. 5800-5999 Grove
68. 8200-8399 Grove
69. 5100-5299 Tuck
70. 5100-5299 Owen
71. Bayou
72. Eddy

73. 3300-3499 Owen
74. Trehern
75. Brodie
76. 8200-8399 Owen
77. 8700-8899 Owen
78. 8700-8899 Tuck
79. 8200-8399 Tuck
80. Adolph

81. 3300-3499 Tuck
82. 8700-8899 Tuck
83. Benoit
84. 3300-3499 Grove
85. Halter
86. Walda
87. Sonja
88. 8200-8399 Tuck

49. Ⓐ Ⓑ Ⓒ Ⓓ Ⓔ
50. Ⓐ Ⓑ Ⓒ Ⓓ Ⓔ
51. Ⓐ Ⓑ Ⓒ Ⓓ Ⓔ
52. Ⓐ Ⓑ Ⓒ Ⓓ Ⓔ
53. Ⓐ Ⓑ Ⓒ Ⓓ Ⓔ
54. Ⓐ Ⓑ Ⓒ Ⓓ Ⓔ
55. Ⓐ Ⓑ Ⓒ Ⓓ Ⓔ
56. Ⓐ Ⓑ Ⓒ Ⓓ Ⓔ

57. Ⓐ Ⓑ Ⓒ Ⓓ Ⓔ
58. Ⓐ Ⓑ Ⓒ Ⓓ Ⓔ
59. Ⓐ Ⓑ Ⓒ Ⓓ Ⓔ
60. Ⓐ Ⓑ Ⓒ Ⓓ Ⓔ
61. Ⓐ Ⓑ Ⓒ Ⓓ Ⓔ
62. Ⓐ Ⓑ Ⓒ Ⓓ Ⓔ
63. Ⓐ Ⓑ Ⓒ Ⓓ Ⓔ
64. Ⓐ Ⓑ Ⓒ Ⓓ Ⓔ

65. Ⓐ Ⓑ Ⓒ Ⓓ Ⓔ
66. Ⓐ Ⓑ Ⓒ Ⓓ Ⓔ
67. Ⓐ Ⓑ Ⓒ Ⓓ Ⓔ
68. Ⓐ Ⓑ Ⓒ Ⓓ Ⓔ
69. Ⓐ Ⓑ Ⓒ Ⓓ Ⓔ
70. Ⓐ Ⓑ Ⓒ Ⓓ Ⓔ
71. Ⓐ Ⓑ Ⓒ Ⓓ Ⓔ
72. Ⓐ Ⓑ Ⓒ Ⓓ Ⓔ

73. Ⓐ Ⓑ Ⓒ Ⓓ Ⓔ
74. Ⓐ Ⓑ Ⓒ Ⓓ Ⓔ
75. Ⓐ Ⓑ Ⓒ Ⓓ Ⓔ
76. Ⓐ Ⓑ Ⓒ Ⓓ Ⓔ
77. Ⓐ Ⓑ Ⓒ Ⓓ Ⓔ
78. Ⓐ Ⓑ Ⓒ Ⓓ Ⓔ
79. Ⓐ Ⓑ Ⓒ Ⓓ Ⓔ
80. Ⓐ Ⓑ Ⓒ Ⓓ Ⓔ

81. Ⓐ Ⓑ Ⓒ Ⓓ Ⓔ
82. Ⓐ Ⓑ Ⓒ Ⓓ Ⓔ
83. Ⓐ Ⓑ Ⓒ Ⓓ Ⓔ
84. Ⓐ Ⓑ Ⓒ Ⓓ Ⓔ
85. Ⓐ Ⓑ Ⓒ Ⓓ Ⓔ
86. Ⓐ Ⓑ Ⓒ Ⓓ Ⓔ
87. Ⓐ Ⓑ Ⓒ Ⓓ Ⓔ
88. Ⓐ Ⓑ Ⓒ Ⓓ Ⓔ

198

COMPLETE PRACTICE TEST #4
Part B – Address Memory – Segment #7

Directions

This is the final segment of the Address Memory section. You have five minutes to answer 88 questions. You must answer from memory. The boxes are not shown. On this segment, there is not a sample answer sheet at the bottom of the page. Instead, mark your answers on the Complete Practice Test Answer Sheet that your tore out of the book. After completing this segment, you have finished the full Address Memory section. Turn to the Number Series section of the practice test for instructions on how to continue.

Turn the page and begin when you are prepared to time yourself for precisely five minutes.

COMPLETE PRACTICE TEST #4
Part B – Address Memory – Segment #7

1. 5100-5299 Owen
2. 5800-5999 Grove
3. 8200-8399 Owen
4. Walda
5. Bayou
6. 5800-5999 Owen
7. 5100-5299 Owen
8. 8700-8899 Grove

9. 5100-5299 Tuck
10. Eddy
11. 5100-5299 Grove
12. 5800-5999 Tuck
13. 8700-8899 Tuck
14. 3300-3499 Owen
15. 8200-8399 Grove
16. Adolph

17. Sonja
18. Trehern
19. 8700-8899 Owen
20. Halter
21. 5800-5999 Grove
22. Brodie
23. 8200-8399 Tuck
24. 8700-8899 Tuck

25. 3300-3499 Tuck
26. Benoit
27. 3300-3499 Grove
28. Bayou
29. Odessa
30. 5100-5299 Tuck
31. 8200-8399 Grove
32. 3300-3499 Grove

33. Walda
34. Adolph
35. 8200-8399 Tuck
36. 3300-3499 Owen
37. 5800-5999 Owen
38. Halter
39. 8700-8899 Grove
40. 3300-3499 Grove

41. 5100-5299 Grove
42. 5800-5999 Tuck
43. 8700-8999 Owen
44. Sonja
45. Walda
46. Bayou
47. 5100-5299 Owen
48. Trehern

49. 8200-8399 Grove
50. 5800-5999 Owen
51. Brodie
52. 8200-8399 Owen
53. Eddy
54. Odessa
55. 8700-8899 Grove
56. 5800-5999 Tuck

57. Benoit
58. 8200-8399 Tuck
59. Adolph
60. 5100-5299 Tuck
61. 5800-5999 Grove
62. 8700-8899 Owen
63. Walda
64. 8200-8399 Owen

65. Halter
66. 8700-8899 Tuck
67. 5100-5299 Owen
68. 8200-8399 Tuck
69. 5100-5299 Tuck
70. 8200-8399 Grove
71. 8700-8899 Tuck
72. Eddy

73. 8700-8899 Grove
74. Brodie
75. Odessa
76. 5800-5999 Owen
77. 8700-8899 Owen
78. 5100-5299 Grove
79. 3300-3499 Tuck
80. Sonja

81. 3300-3499 Grove
82. 8700-8899 Tuck
83. 3300-3499 Owen
84. Benoit
85. 5800-5999 Tuck
86. Bayou
87. 5800-5999 Grove
88. Trehern

COMPLETE PRACTICE TEST #4
Part C – Number Series

Directions

On this section, you have 20 minutes to answer 24 mathematical questions. Each question consists of a series of numbers followed by two blanks. You are to calculate what two numbers would logically follow in the series and that would therefore fit into the two blanks. Choose the answer – A, B, C, D, or E – that contains the correct two numbers, in the proper order, that should follow in the series. Mark your answers on the Complete Practice Test Answer Sheet in the section entitled Number Series. After completing this section, turn to the Following Oral Instructions section for directions on how to continue.

The solutions to all the Number Series questions in all six of the practice tests are given in the back of your book. After scoring each Number Series practice test, find and review the solutions for the questions you missed. This should better prepare you to answer similar questions on the other practice tests as well as on your actual exam.

Turn the page and begin when you are prepared to time yourself for precisely 20 minutes.

Hint: Remember to use the Circles and Squares Strategy to identify, separate, and solve the multiple sequences found in many questions.

COMPLETE PRACTICE TEST #4
Part C – Number Series

1. 5 6 8 10 10 12 15 ___ ___   A) 12, 15 B) 14, 16 C) 12, 14 D) 16, 18 E) 15, 17

2. 21 24 27 30 33 ___ ___   A) 35, 38 B) 34, 37 C) 36, 39 D) 31, 35 E) 36, 39

3. 1 3 5 5 7 9 9 ___ ___   A) 12, 10 B) 11, 12 C) 13, 10 D) 11, 13 E) 14, 12

4. 11 11 10 10 9 9 8 ___ ___   A) 8, 9 B) 8, 7 C) 7, 6 D) 8, 6 E) 9, 1

5. 1 31 1 32 1 33 1 ___ ___   A) 34, 1 B) 35, 1 C) 1, 34 D) 2, 35 E) 1, 1

6. 14 12 14 13 14 14 ___ ___   A) 14, 18 B) 13, 15 C) 15, 17 D) 14, 15 E) 18, 20

7. 11 1 3 15 5 7 19 ___ ___   A) 8, 10 B) 10, 12 C) 9, 21 D) 18, 22 E) 9, 11

8. 11 12 14 17 21 26 32 ___ ___   A) 40, 47 B) 38, 45 C) 39, 47 D) 40, 47 E) 42, 48

9. 8 8 10 10 12 12 14 ___ ___   A) 15, 16 B) 17, 18 C) 15, 15 D) 16, 12 E) 14, 16

10. 3 4 13 8 9 13 13 ___ ___   A) 14, 13 B) 12, 11 C) 15, 14 D) 13, 15 E) 17, 19

11. 2 31 2 32 2 33 2 ___ ___   A) 36, 2 B) 34, 2 C) 2, 2 D) 46, 2 E) 35, 2

12. 3 2 7 5 11 8 15 ___ ___   A) 12, 20 B) 11, 19 C) 13, 19 D) 11, 21 E) 10, 19

13. 16 15 16 16 16 17 16 ___ ___   A) 17, 16 B) 16, 17 C) 15, 17 D) 18, 16 E) 17, 18

14. 2 4 4 4 4 6 4 8 ___ ___   A) 10, 4 B) 4, 10 C) 4, 4 D) 5, 11 E) 6, 12

15. 18 6 6 18 12 12 18 ___ ___   A) 24, 24 B) 0, 18 C) 18, 18 D) 18, 0 E) 20, 22

16. 1 15 2 16 3 17 ___ ___   A) 4, 19 B) 5, 20 C) 6, 18 D) 3, 21 E) 4, 18

17. 2 1 4 3 6 5 8 ___ ___   A) 7, 10 B) 9, 10 C) 12, 10 D) 9, 7 E) 12, 11

18. 1 12 2 12 3 12 4 ___ ___   A) 12, 6 B) 12, 4 C) 5, 12 D) 12, 12 E) 12, 5

19. 26 2 24 4 22 6 ___ ___   A) 18, 6 B) 20, 8 C) 22, 10 D) 24, 12 E) 21, 13

20. 6 13 15 7 17 19 8 ___ ___   A) 20, 24 B) 19, 21 C) 20, 22 D) 21, 23 E) 22, 24

21. 9 10 15 11 12 15 13 ___ ___   A) 13, 16 B) 14, 16 C) 16, 19 D) 12, 14 E) 14, 15

22. 23 16 18 18 20 22 13 ___ ___   A) 20, 24 B) 24, 26 C) 22, 26 D) 25, 27 E) 24, 28

23. 10 11 13 16 20 25 ___ ___   A) 30, 36 B) 31, 36 C) 31, 38 D) 32, 37 E) 32, 38

24. 9 10 12 13 15 16 18 ___ ___   A) 19, 21 B) 18, 20 C) 20, 22 D) 19, 20 E) 21, 22

COMPLETE PRACTICE TEST #4
Part D – Following Oral Instructions

Directions

On this section of the test, the Exam Administrator will read questions/instructions aloud to the group of test takers. These oral instructions will direct you to write/mark certain items in your test booklet, which in turn will lead you to the correct answer(s). Finally, you will be verbally instructed to mark the correct answer(s) on your answer sheet. You must answer exclusively based upon what you hear – there are no questions for you to read.

The following pages of this practice test are samples of the test booklet pages on which you will write/mark as verbally instructed. Mark your answers on the Complete Practice Test Answer Sheet in the Following Oral Instructions section.

To practice realistically, you must either listen to the questions on the author's recording or have someone read them aloud to you. Do not look over the questions before taking the practice test. Once you have completed the practice test, you should then review the questions you missed in order to determine what caused you to miss them. This review should enable you to be more successful on similar questions next time.

The author's recording of all six Following Oral Directions practice tests is an ideal and convenient way to practice. The recorded questions are presented in the proper format, at the proper pace, and with proper diction. These recordings allow you to practice anytime and anywhere you wish. With these recordings, your practice – and in turn your success – will not be dependent upon someone else's schedule and whims. For details and ordering information, see the order form at the back of your book.

If someone will be reading the questions to you, he/she will find the questions for each practice test in the back of your book in the section entitled Following Oral Instructions – Practice Test Questions. The reader should carefully tear the questions out of your book in order to use them. The questions should be read at a rather slow and steady pace of approximately 75 words per minute and with proper diction. The reader should also pause between instructions/questions as directed in the wording of each question.

Once you complete the Following Oral Instructions section, you have finished this practice test, and you should then begin the next practice test in your book. Once you have completed all six practice tests plus the Extra Address Checking Practice Exercises as instructed, you should be fully prepared to excel on the actual exam.

Turn the page and begin when you are prepared to listen to the questions from the author's recording or from someone who will read the questions to you in the proper fashion.

Hint: Remember your strategies:
- *You will answer by marking number-letter combinations.*
- *Where you mark an answer on the answer sheet will not match the question number.*
- *Listen closely and attentively.*
- *Simply follow the instructions you hear – do not try to figure them out.*
- *Some questions will have multiple answers, and you must mark all of them.*
- *Mark your answers quickly and be ready to listen to the next question.*
- *Make identifying notes for later recall.*

COMPLETE PRACTICE TEST #4
Part D – Following Oral Instructions

1.   B   C   A   E   D

2. 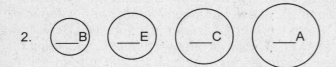

3.   81   28   57   66   30   43   27   15   41

4.   A   D   E   B   C

5.   (19___) (21___) [37___] [15___]

6.   (7:00 ___) (7:10 ___) (6:51 ___) (6:47 ___) (5:10 ___)

7.   (14___) (37___) (21___)   ABE   DIE   CAB

8.   [85___] [78___]

9.   OOX   XOO   XXO   XOX   XXO

10.   12___   18___   47___   52___   32___   31___   26___

11.   42   51   73   86   19   23   16

12.   [67___] [43___] [64___]

13.   57___   82___

14.   [73___] [32___] [54___] [18___]

15.   _____B   _____C   _____D   _____E   _____A

16.   A   B   C   D   E   C   D

17. | Monroe 39_____ | Baton Rouge 54_____ | Lake Charles 58_____ |

18.   ABAB   ABBA   BAAB   BABA

19.   22   28   34   35   40   44

COMPLETE PRACTICE TEST #5

This practice test contains samples of all four sections of the actual exam. The instructions given are similar to those on the actual exam. The format of this practice test is identical to that of the actual exam. Where pertinent, hints are given about your test taking strategies. Of course, these hints will not appear on the actual exam.

It is imperative that you take this practice test in as realistic a fashion as possible. **Your practice will have no value unless it is done realistically.** Therefore, you must precisely time yourself on the Address Checking, Address Memory, and Number Series sections. Our Timed Practice Test CD is a convenient way to practice realistically and time yourself precisely. Also, you must either listen to the Following Oral Instructions questions on our Oral Instructions Practice Tests CD or have someone read them to you – *do not read the questions yourself!* The Following Oral Instructions questions can be found in the back of your book if someone will be reading them to you.

To take this practice test, first turn to the back of your book and carefully tear out one of the **Complete Practice Test Answer Sheets.** Mark the answers to the scored segments of the practice test on this answer sheet. (Remember, of the seven segments on the Address Memory Section, only the final one is scored. Accordingly, you should mark answers for only the final Address Memory segment on your Complete Practice Test Answer Sheet. The other segments of the Address Memory Section that call for answers have accompanying sample answer sheets where you should mark answers.)

The correct answers are provided in the back of your book. Immediately upon completing the practice test, **it is imperative that you score each section** using the formulas given under the Sections of the Exam heading in your book. Scoring is necessary in order to gauge your progress and to identify your individual areas of weakness that may need extra attention.

After completing and scoring each practice test, move on to the next. **After completing all six practice tests and the Extra Address Checking Practice exercises as instructed, you should be prepared for the actual exam.** If you feel the need to practice more, repeat as many of the practice tests as you like. After that much practice, the questions will likely have become a confusing blur in your mind. It is highly unlikely that you will be able to remember many of the individual questions or answers. Therefore, you should be able to gain practice value from the exercises even though you have already taken them once.

Do not look over the practice test questions until you are ready to start – meaning until you have set a timer for the allotted period of time. Similarly, after completing one section of the practice test, do not look over the next one until your are ready to start it. Likewise, stop working and put down your pencil immediately when the allotted period of time has expired. As has been emphasized before but cannot be emphasized enough, your practice is of absolutely no value unless it is done realistically. Also, you must train yourself (1) to not open your test booklet or pick up your pencil until instructed to do so and (2) to close your booklet and put down your pencil immediately upon being so instructed. The Postal Service has a zero tolerance policy on these matters. Any variance may be viewed as cheating and may result in your disqualification.

Good luck on your practice test, and even better luck on your actual exam!

COMPLETE PRACTICE TEST #5
Part A – Address Checking

Directions

In this part of the test, you will have to decide whether two addresses are alike or different. You will have 6 minutes to answer 95 questions. Each question consists of a pair of addresses. If the two addresses in the pair are exactly alike in every way, darken the oval with the letter "A" for *Alike*. If the two addresses are different in any way, darken the oval with the letter "D" for *Different*. Mark your answers on the Complete Practice Test Answer Sheet in the section entitled Address Checking.

Turn the page and begin when you are prepared to time yourself for precisely 6 minutes.

Note: You will notice that this section of your practice test is spread across two pages. This is the exact same format that you will actually experience on the Address Checking section of the real exam. For economy and convenience, other study guides frequently condense the two pages of this section down to only one. You will also notice that the Address Checking questions are presented in a font, or type of print, that is different from the rest of the book. This font matches what is actually used on the real exam, and, as you will see, it makes this section even more challenging. However, it is imperative that you practice realistically and that you become acquainted with and comfortable with the actual format of the exam. We have accordingly formatted this practice test realistically for your benefit.

Hint: Remember your strategies:
- *Pace yourself for speed and accuracy – <u>emphasis on speed</u>!*
- *Use one glance-over for easier/shorter addresses.*
- *Use two glance-over's for harder/longer addresses.*
- *Never make a third pass or glance-over!*
- *Overlap the answer sheet & the questions to keep them as close together as possible.*
- *Use your extra pencil, your hand, or your fingers to mark/keep your place.*
- *Use your Speed Pencil and your Speed Marking strategies for much greater speed.*

COMPLETE PRACTICE TEST #5
Part A – Address Checking

1.	7172 S 82nd St	7172 S 82nd St
2.	Yakima WA 10345	Yakima WA 10345
3.	3818 Morningview Cape	3818 Morningview Cove
4.	6579 15th St	6795 S 15th St
5.	3817 Northingham Rd	3817 Northingham Rd
6.	8777 Courthouse Pl	8777 Courthouse Pl
7.	4608 E Ladnier Rd	4608 E Ladner Rd
8.	Melbourne Fl 21907	Melborne Fl 21907
9.	5378 Bayou Oaks Ct	5378 Bayou Oates Ct
10.	4161 Patricia Ln	4161 E Patricia Ln
11.	1579 W Guardian Way	1579 W Guardian Way
12.	9060 Oceanspray Jct	9060 Oceanspray Jct
13.	Montpelier VT 98326	Montpelier VT 98326
14.	1540 Needle St	1540 Needle St
15.	1021 Gorenflo Pt	1012 Gorenflo Pt
16.	4969 Heatherwood Ln	4969 Heatherwood Ln
17.	6547 W Hanover St	6547 E Hanover St
18.	Louisville KY 38920	Louisville Ky 38029
19.	9567 Foxworthy Ct	9567 Foxworthy Ct
20.	1474 Tally Ho Cir	1474 Tally Howard Cir
21.	6357 W 28th Ave	6357 W 28th Ave
22.	9811 N Musella Ave	9811 N Moosella Ave
23.	Laredo TX 48930	Lansing MI 64601
24.	7737 Cambridge Pl	7737 Cambridge Pl
25.	2049 Everbreeze Jct	2049 Everbreeze Jct
26.	1903 W El Bonito St	1903 W El Burito St
27.	5599 Porter Pl	5599 Porter Pl
28.	Los Angeles CA 14157	Las Angles CA 14157
29.	408 E Magnolia Dr	409 E Magnolia Dr
30.	5038 Heatherstone Pt	5038 Heatherstone Pt
31.	7519 Arbor Vista Dr	7519 Arbor Vista Dr
32.	Grand Island NE 59487	Grand Island NE 59487
33.	1516 Thornton Ave	1516 Thornton Bay
34.	6473 Northgate Pl	6473 Northgate Pl
35.	6876 E 54th St	6876 E 54th St
36.	Flagstaff AZ 64821	Flagstaff AZ 64821
37.	2655 Englewood Rd	2655 Englewood Rd
38.	3709 W Pineview Pl	3709 E Pineview Pl
39.	9860 Plantation Rd	9860 Planter Rd
40.	Butte MT	Butte MT
41.	4050 Llwellyn Grv	4050 Llwellyn Garden
42.	8950 N Badwin Ave	8950 N Baldwin Ave
43.	5673 Bonner Blvd	5673 Bonner Blvd
44.	4441 W Applegate Rd	4444 W Applegate Rd
45.	Kenosha WI 10590	Kenosha WY 10590
46.	4135 E O'Neal Rd	4135 E O'Neal Rd
47.	3100 Abbey Ct	3001 Abbey Ct
48.	3054 Callaghan Cove	3054 Callaghan Cove

#		
49.	3945 Fredinand Ln	3954 Ferdinand Ln
50.	Las Cruces NM 64603	Las Cruces NM 64603
51.	8950 Freeman Bld	8950 Freeman Bld
52.	4957 Humperdinck Pl	4957 Humperdickle Pl
53.	3340 Marco Polo Pt	3340 Marco Polo Pt
54.	9747 McCracken Ln	9747 McCracken Ln
55.	Dallas TX 96261	Dallas TX 96261
56.	1184 Mohammed Bay	1184 Mohammed Bay
57.	6172 Powhatan	6172 Powhattan
58.	8211 N 52nd Ave	8211 S 52nd Ave
59.	9172 Ponce DeLeon Way	9172 Ponce DeLeon Way
60.	Scaramento CA 94654	Sacramento CA 94654
61.	2828 Parkman Ave	2828 Parkman Ave
62.	4527 Aleutian Isle	4527 Aleutian Isle
63.	6800 S Welford Blvd	6800 N Welford Blvd
64.	5807 Berkeley Pt	5807 Berkeley Pt
65.	Wilkes-Barre PA 84217	Wilkes-Barre PA 84712
66.	831 Belgrade Cove	831 Belgrade Cove
67.	4504 E Jamestown Blvd	4504 E Jamestown Blvd
68.	5000 Bermuda Bav	5000 Bermuda Beach
69.	1825 W Tulane Ave	1825 W Tulane Ave
70.	Superior WI 50667	Superior WI 50667
71.	2309 Pinehaven Cove	2309 Pinehaven Cove
72.	El Paso TX 92835	El Pasco TX 92835
73.	9417 Meadowlark Pl	9417 Meadowlark Pl
74.	7172 Rebecca Cove	7712 Rebecca Cove
75.	5699 N 83rd Blvd	5699 N 83rd Bay
76.	Detroit MI 48207	Detroit MI 48207
77.	3303 Demonica Rd	3303 Demonica Rd
78.	4547 Popps Ferry Rd	4547 Bopps Ferry Rd
79.	8766 Columbus Cir	8766 Columbus Cir
80.	Augusta ME 41939	Augusta ME 41393
81.	20074 Commission Rd	2004 Commission Rd
82.	1711 Sheffield Place	1711 Sheffield Place
83.	1103 N Belair St	1103 W Belair St
84.	1202 W Market St	1202 W Market St
85.	Bettendorf IA 29571	Betteroff IA 29571
86.	1040 Navaho Tr	1040 Navaho Pl
87.	6088 W Primus Pl	6880 W Primus Pl
88.	1975 Northridge Dr	1975 Northridge Dr
89.	Fredrick MD 42995	Fredrick MD 42995
90.	1057 Twin Cedar Ave	1057 Triple Cedar Ave
91.	3176 W Travel Tr	3176 W Travel Tr
92.	2009 Lovers Ln	2009 Lovers Ln
93.	6357 W Marina Ave	6357 W Martina Ave
94.	Little Rock AR 81415	Little Rock AK 81415
95.	212 W Beach Blvd	212 W Beach Blvd

COMPLETE PRACTICE TEST #5
Part B – Address Memory

Directions

In this part of the test, you will have to memorize the locations of 25 addresses in five boxes. During this section, you will have several study periods and practice exercises to help you memorize the location of the addresses shown in the five boxes. Answer the questions by darkening the oval containing the letter (A, B, C, D, or E) of the box in which the address is located – Box A, Box B, Box C, Box D, or Box E. At the end of each segment, you will be given instructions on how and where to continue. After completing six preliminary segments, the actual test will be given as segment #7.

Turn the page to begin Segment #1.

Note: You will notice on your practice test that the various segments of the Address Memory section are spread across two pages. Where applicable, the five boxes, the 88 questions, and/or the sample answer sheets are spread across two pages. This is the same format that you will experience on most segments of the Address Memory section on the actual exam. For economy and convenience, other study guides frequently condense the two pages down to only one. However, it is imperative that you practice realistically and that you become acquainted with and comfortable with the actual format of the exam. We have accordingly formatted this practice test realistically for your benefit.

Hint: Remember your strategies:
- *Memorize horizontally.*
- *Memorize only Boxes A, B, C, and D.*
- *You can correctly answer all Box E questions by the process of elimination.*
- *Use the Second Digit Strategy to memorize the number addresses.*
- *Use imagery/association to memorize the word addresses.*
- *Overlap the answer sheet & the questions to keep them as close together as possible.*
- *Use your extra pencil, your hand, or your fingers to mark/keep your place.*
- *Use your Speed Pencil and your Speed Marking strategies for much greater speed.*

COMPLETE PRACTICE TEST #5
Part B – Address Memory – Segment #1

Directions

Five sample boxes, each containing five addresses, and five sample questions about these boxes are given on the following two pages. The purpose of this small exercise is simply to acquaint you with the format of this section and with how the questions should be answered. The first two sample questions are answered for you. You are to spend three minutes becoming acquainted with the format and answering sample questions 3, 4, and 5. After completing Segment #1, turn to Segment #2 for further instructions.

Turn the page and begin when you are prepared to time yourself for precisely three minutes.

Hint: Remember your strategies! This segment is not scored, so do not take the sample questions seriously. Instead, mark random answers and use the three minutes to study and memorize the addresses. The sample boxes and addresses in this segment are the very same ones that will be repeated throughout this section of the exam.

A	B	C
9200-9399 Vada	8500-8699 Vada	6700-6899 Vada
Bethel	Parker	Olivia
6700-6899 Bell	6300-6499 Bell	9200-9399 Bell
Ford	Finley	Scott
9600-9799 Lark	9200-9399 Lark	6300-6499 Lark

1. Brady   Ⓐ Ⓑ Ⓒ Ⓓ ⬤Ⓔ
   This address came from Box E, so we sill darken the oval with the letter E.

2. 6300-6499 Lark   Ⓐ Ⓑ ⬤Ⓒ Ⓓ Ⓔ
   This address came from Box C, so we will darken the oval with the letter C.

3. 9200-9399 Vada   Ⓐ Ⓑ Ⓒ Ⓓ Ⓔ
   Now that you know how to answer, you do questions 3, 4, and 5.

4. Finley   Ⓐ Ⓑ Ⓒ Ⓓ Ⓔ

5. 6300-6499 Vada   Ⓐ Ⓑ Ⓒ Ⓓ Ⓔ

The correct answers are E, C, A, B, and E.

D

9600-9799 Vada
Lamey
8500-8699 Bell
Saratoga
6700-6899 Lark

E

6300-6499 Vada
Verde
9600-9799 Bell
Brady
8500-8699 Lark

COMPLETE PRACTICE TEST #5
Part B – Address Memory – Segment #2

Directions

In this segment, you are given three minutes to study and memorize the addresses. There are no questions to answer in this segment – it is a study period only. However, on the actual exam, the boxes are not reprinted for your use. Instead, you are instructed to turn back to Address Memory Segment #1 on the preceding pages of the exam and to spend three minutes studying the boxes displayed there. So, we will do the very same on this practice test. After studying for three minutes, turn to Segment #3 for directions on how to continue the Address Memory Section of the exam.

Begin studying when you are prepared to time yourself for precisely three minutes.

COMPLETE PRACTICE TEST #5
Part B – Address Memory – Segment #3

Directions

In this segment you have three minutes to attempt answering 88 questions. You are to try to answer from memory, but the boxes are shown if you need to refer to them. Your answers are to be marked on the sample answer sheet at the bottom of the pages of Segment #3 – do not use the Compete Practice Test Answer Sheet for this segment. After completing this segment, turn to Segment #4 for further instructions.

Turn the page and begin when you are prepared to time yourself for precisely three minutes.

Hint: Remember your strategies! This segment is not scored, so do not take the questions seriously. Instead, mark a handful of random answers and use the three minutes to study and memorize the addresses.

A	B	C
9200-9399 Vada	8500-8699 Vada	6700-6899 Vada
Bethel	Parker	Olivia
6700-6899 Bell	6300-6499 Bell	9200-9399 Bell
Ford	Finley	Scott
9600-9799 Lark	9200-9399 Lark	6300-6499 Lark

1. 6700-6899 Lark
2. Verde
3. 9200-9399 Lark
4. Lamey
5. Ford
6. 6700-6899 Bell
7. Saratoga
8. 6300-6499 Lark

9. 9600-9799 Vada
10. 9200-9399 Vada
11. 8500-8699 Bell
12. 6300-6499 Bell
13. Finley
14. 8500-8699 Vada
15. 9600-9799 Bell
16. 6700-6899 Vada

17. Bethel
18. 9200-9399 Bell
19. 6300-6499 Vada
20. Parker
21. 8500-8699 Bell
22. 9600-9799 Bell
23. Ford
24. Brady

25. 6700-6899 Vada
26. 6300-6499 Bell
27. Scott
28. 9200-9399 Vada
29. 9600-9799 Lark
30. Verde
31. 6300-6499 Vada
32. 8500-8699 Lark

33. Finley
34. 6300-6499 Lark
35. 9200-9399 Vada
36. Saratoga
37. 6300-6499 Bell
38. 6700-6899 Lark
39. 8500-8699 Vada
40. Olivia

41. 9200-9399 Lark
42. 6700-6899 Bell
43. 9600-9799 Vada
44. Parker
45. Bethel
46. 6300-6499 Vada
47. 9600-9799 Bell
48. Scott

1 (A) (B) (C) (D) (E)
2 (A) (B) (C) (D) (E)
3 (A) (B) (C) (D) (E)
4 (A) (B) (C) (D) (E)
5 (A) (B) (C) (D) (E)
6 (A) (B) (C) (D) (E)
7 (A) (B) (C) (D) (E)
8 (A) (B) (C) (D) (E)

9 (A) (B) (C) (D) (E)
10 (A) (B) (C) (D) (E)
11 (A) (B) (C) (D) (E)
12 (A) (B) (C) (D) (E)
13 (A) (B) (C) (D) (E)
14 (A) (B) (C) (D) (E)
15 (A) (B) (C) (D) (E)
16 (A) (B) (C) (D) (E)

17 (A) (B) (C) (D) (E)
18 (A) (B) (C) (D) (E)
19 (A) (B) (C) (D) (E)
20 (A) (B) (C) (D) (E)
21 (A) (B) (C) (D) (E)
22 (A) (B) (C) (D) (E)
23 (A) (B) (C) (D) (E)
24 (A) (B) (C) (D) (E)

25 (A) (B) (C) (D) (E)
26 (A) (B) (C) (D) (E)
27 (A) (B) (C) (D) (E)
28 (A) (B) (C) (D) (E)
29 (A) (B) (C) (D) (E)
30 (A) (B) (C) (D) (E)
31 (A) (B) (C) (D) (E)
32 (A) (B) (C) (D) (E)

33 (A) (B) (C) (D) (E)
34 (A) (B) (C) (D) (E)
35 (A) (B) (C) (D) (E)
36 (A) (B) (C) (D) (E)
37 (A) (B) (C) (D) (E)
38 (A) (B) (C) (D) (E)
39 (A) (B) (C) (D) (E)
40 (A) (B) (C) (D) (E)

41 (A) (B) (C) (D) (E)
42 (A) (B) (C) (D) (E)
43 (A) (B) (C) (D) (E)
44 (A) (B) (C) (D) (E)
45 (A) (B) (C) (D) (E)
46 (A) (B) (C) (D) (E)
47 (A) (B) (C) (D) (E)
48 (A) (B) (C) (D) (E)

D	E
9600-9799 Vada	6300-6499 Vada
Lamey	Verde
8500-8699 Bell	9600-9799 Bell
Saratoga	Brady
6700-6899 Lark	8500-8699 Lark

49. Olivia
50. 6300-6499 Vada
51. 9600-9799 Lark
52. 8500-8699 Bell
53. 9200-9399 Vada
54. Bethel
55. 6300-6499 Bell
56. 6700-6899 Vada

57. Parker
58. 9600-9799 Vada
59. Lamey
60. 9200-9399 Bell
61. Ford
62. Saratoga
63. Brady
64. Olivia

65. Scott
66. Ford
67. Verde
68. 6300-6499 Lark
69. 6700-6899 Bell
70. 9600-9799 Bell
71. 6300-6499 Vada
72. 8500-8699 Vada

73. 9200-9399 Lark
74. Saratoga
75. 9200-9399 Vada
76. 8500-8699 Bell
77. Finley
78. 6700-6899 Vada
79. 9600-9799 Lark
80. Brady

81. 9200-9399 Bell
82. 6300-6499 Lark
83. Lamey
84. Scott
85. Ford
86. 6700-6899 Lark
87. 6300-6499 Bell
88. 8500-8699 Lark

49. Ⓐ Ⓑ Ⓒ Ⓓ Ⓔ
50. Ⓐ Ⓑ Ⓒ Ⓓ Ⓔ
51. Ⓐ Ⓑ Ⓒ Ⓓ Ⓔ
52. Ⓐ Ⓑ Ⓒ Ⓓ Ⓔ
53. Ⓐ Ⓑ Ⓒ Ⓓ Ⓔ
54. Ⓐ Ⓑ Ⓒ Ⓓ Ⓔ
55. Ⓐ Ⓑ Ⓒ Ⓓ Ⓔ
56. Ⓐ Ⓑ Ⓒ Ⓓ Ⓔ

57. Ⓐ Ⓑ Ⓒ Ⓓ Ⓔ
58. Ⓐ Ⓑ Ⓒ Ⓓ Ⓔ
59. Ⓐ Ⓑ Ⓒ Ⓓ Ⓔ
60. Ⓐ Ⓑ Ⓒ Ⓓ Ⓔ
61. Ⓐ Ⓑ Ⓒ Ⓓ Ⓔ
62. Ⓐ Ⓑ Ⓒ Ⓓ Ⓔ
63. Ⓐ Ⓑ Ⓒ Ⓓ Ⓔ
64. Ⓐ Ⓑ Ⓒ Ⓓ Ⓔ

65. Ⓐ Ⓑ Ⓒ Ⓓ Ⓔ
66. Ⓐ Ⓑ Ⓒ Ⓓ Ⓔ
67. Ⓐ Ⓑ Ⓒ Ⓓ Ⓔ
68. Ⓐ Ⓑ Ⓒ Ⓓ Ⓔ
69. Ⓐ Ⓑ Ⓒ Ⓓ Ⓔ
70. Ⓐ Ⓑ Ⓒ Ⓓ Ⓔ
71. Ⓐ Ⓑ Ⓒ Ⓓ Ⓔ
72. Ⓐ Ⓑ Ⓒ Ⓓ Ⓔ

73. Ⓐ Ⓑ Ⓒ Ⓓ Ⓔ
74. Ⓐ Ⓑ Ⓒ Ⓓ Ⓔ
75. Ⓐ Ⓑ Ⓒ Ⓓ Ⓔ
76. Ⓐ Ⓑ Ⓒ Ⓓ Ⓔ
77. Ⓐ Ⓑ Ⓒ Ⓓ Ⓔ
78. Ⓐ Ⓑ Ⓒ Ⓓ Ⓔ
79. Ⓐ Ⓑ Ⓒ Ⓓ Ⓔ
80. Ⓐ Ⓑ Ⓒ Ⓓ Ⓔ

81. Ⓐ Ⓑ Ⓒ Ⓓ Ⓔ
82. Ⓐ Ⓑ Ⓒ Ⓓ Ⓔ
83. Ⓐ Ⓑ Ⓒ Ⓓ Ⓔ
84. Ⓐ Ⓑ Ⓒ Ⓓ Ⓔ
85. Ⓐ Ⓑ Ⓒ Ⓓ Ⓔ
86. Ⓐ Ⓑ Ⓒ Ⓓ Ⓔ
87. Ⓐ Ⓑ Ⓒ Ⓓ Ⓔ
88. Ⓐ Ⓑ Ⓒ Ⓓ Ⓔ

COMPLETE PRACTICE TEST #5
Part B – Address Memory – Segment #4

Directions

In this segment you have three minutes to attempt answering 88 questions. You must answer from memory. The boxes are not shown. Your answers are to be marked on the sample answer sheet at the bottom of the pages of Segment #4 – do not use the Compete Practice Test Answer Sheet for this segment. After completing this segment, turn to Segment #5 for further instructions.

Turn the page and begin when you are prepared to time yourself for precisely three minutes.

Hint: Remember, this segment is not scored, so you should not worry about your inability to answer all 88 questions, or your inability to answer all of them accurately, in only three minutes. Neither task is really possible in only three minutes. However, this is an ideal opportunity for you to test how well you have mastered your strategies and memorization so far. By sincerely trying to answer the questions, you can identify the areas where you are weaker and where you need to apply more effort.

1. Brady
2. 6300-6499 Lark
3. 9200-9399 Vada
4. Finley
5. 6300-6499 Vada
6. Lamey
7. 6700-6899 Bell
8. 6300-6499 Bell

9. Scott
10. Parker
11. 6700-6899 Lark
12. 6300-6499 Lark
13. 9200-9399 Vada
14. Saratoga
15. 6700-6899 Vada
16. Lamey

17. 8500-8699 Vada
18. 6300-6499 Vada
19. 9600-9799 Lark
20. 9200-9399 Bell
21. 8500-8699 Bell
22. Bethel
23. 9600-9799 Vada
24. Verde

25. 9200-9399 Lark
26. Lamey
27. 9600-9799 Bell
28. Ford
29. Scott
30. 6300-6499 Bell
31. Brady
32. Olivia

33. 9200-9399 Bell
34. 8500-8699 Bell
35. Bethel
36. Brady
37. 6300-6499 Lark
38. Saratoga
39. 8500-8699 Vada
40. Lamey

41. 6700-6899 Bell
42. 9200-9399 Lark
43. 6300-6499 Bell
44. Ford
45. 9600-9799 Vada
46. 6700-6899 Vada
47. 6300-6499 Bell
48. 6300-6499 Vada

1 Ⓐ Ⓑ Ⓒ Ⓓ Ⓔ
2 Ⓐ Ⓑ Ⓒ Ⓓ Ⓔ
3 Ⓐ Ⓑ Ⓒ Ⓓ Ⓔ
4 Ⓐ Ⓑ Ⓒ Ⓓ Ⓔ
5 Ⓐ Ⓑ Ⓒ Ⓓ Ⓔ
6 Ⓐ Ⓑ Ⓒ Ⓓ Ⓔ
7 Ⓐ Ⓑ Ⓒ Ⓓ Ⓔ
8 Ⓐ Ⓑ Ⓒ Ⓓ Ⓔ

9 Ⓐ Ⓑ Ⓒ Ⓓ Ⓔ
10 Ⓐ Ⓑ Ⓒ Ⓓ Ⓔ
11 Ⓐ Ⓑ Ⓒ Ⓓ Ⓔ
12 Ⓐ Ⓑ Ⓒ Ⓓ Ⓔ
13 Ⓐ Ⓑ Ⓒ Ⓓ Ⓔ
14 Ⓐ Ⓑ Ⓒ Ⓓ Ⓔ
15 Ⓐ Ⓑ Ⓒ Ⓓ Ⓔ
16 Ⓐ Ⓑ Ⓒ Ⓓ Ⓔ

17 Ⓐ Ⓑ Ⓒ Ⓓ Ⓔ
18 Ⓐ Ⓑ Ⓒ Ⓓ Ⓔ
19 Ⓐ Ⓑ Ⓒ Ⓓ Ⓔ
20 Ⓐ Ⓑ Ⓒ Ⓓ Ⓔ
21 Ⓐ Ⓑ Ⓒ Ⓓ Ⓔ
22 Ⓐ Ⓑ Ⓒ Ⓓ Ⓔ
23 Ⓐ Ⓑ Ⓒ Ⓓ Ⓔ
24 Ⓐ Ⓑ Ⓒ Ⓓ Ⓔ

25 Ⓐ Ⓑ Ⓒ Ⓓ Ⓔ
26 Ⓐ Ⓑ Ⓒ Ⓓ Ⓔ
27 Ⓐ Ⓑ Ⓒ Ⓓ Ⓔ
28 Ⓐ Ⓑ Ⓒ Ⓓ Ⓔ
29 Ⓐ Ⓑ Ⓒ Ⓓ Ⓔ
30 Ⓐ Ⓑ Ⓒ Ⓓ Ⓔ
31 Ⓐ Ⓑ Ⓒ Ⓓ Ⓔ
32 Ⓐ Ⓑ Ⓒ Ⓓ Ⓔ

33 Ⓐ Ⓑ Ⓒ Ⓓ Ⓔ
34 Ⓐ Ⓑ Ⓒ Ⓓ Ⓔ
35 Ⓐ Ⓑ Ⓒ Ⓓ Ⓔ
36 Ⓐ Ⓑ Ⓒ Ⓓ Ⓔ
37 Ⓐ Ⓑ Ⓒ Ⓓ Ⓔ
38 Ⓐ Ⓑ Ⓒ Ⓓ Ⓔ
39 Ⓐ Ⓑ Ⓒ Ⓓ Ⓔ
40 Ⓐ Ⓑ Ⓒ Ⓓ Ⓔ

41 Ⓐ Ⓑ Ⓒ Ⓓ Ⓔ
42 Ⓐ Ⓑ Ⓒ Ⓓ Ⓔ
43 Ⓐ Ⓑ Ⓒ Ⓓ Ⓔ
44 Ⓐ Ⓑ Ⓒ Ⓓ Ⓔ
45 Ⓐ Ⓑ Ⓒ Ⓓ Ⓔ
46 Ⓐ Ⓑ Ⓒ Ⓓ Ⓔ
47 Ⓐ Ⓑ Ⓒ Ⓓ Ⓔ
48 Ⓐ Ⓑ Ⓒ Ⓓ Ⓔ

49. Finley
50. 6700-6899 Bell
51. Scott
52. 6700-6899 Vada
53. 8500-8699 Bell
54. 9600-9799 Lark
55. Olivia
56. Parker

57. Saratoga
58. 6700-6899 Lark
59. 9200-9399 Vada
60. 6300-6499 Vada
61. 9200-9399 Bell
62. 9600-9799 Bell
63. 8500-8699 Bell
64. Verde

65. 9200-9399 Vada
66. Saratoga
67. Brady
68. 6700-6899 Vada
69. Verde
70. 6700-6899 Bell
71. 9600-9799 Vada
72. Parker

73. 6700-6899 Lark
74. 8500-8699 Vada
75. 9600-9799 Bell
76. Bethel
77. Scott
78. 9200-9399 Lark
79. Finley
80. 9600-9799 Lark

81. Olivia
82. 6300-6499 Lark
83. Ford
84. 6300-6499 Bell
85. 8500-8699 Bell
86. 9200-9399 Bell
87. 6300-6499 Vada
88. Brady

49 Ⓐ Ⓑ Ⓒ Ⓓ Ⓔ
50 Ⓐ Ⓑ Ⓒ Ⓓ Ⓔ
51 Ⓐ Ⓑ Ⓒ Ⓓ Ⓔ
52 Ⓐ Ⓑ Ⓒ Ⓓ Ⓔ
53 Ⓐ Ⓑ Ⓒ Ⓓ Ⓔ
54 Ⓐ Ⓑ Ⓒ Ⓓ Ⓔ
55 Ⓐ Ⓑ Ⓒ Ⓓ Ⓔ
56 Ⓐ Ⓑ Ⓒ Ⓓ Ⓔ

57 Ⓐ Ⓑ Ⓒ Ⓓ Ⓔ
58 Ⓐ Ⓑ Ⓒ Ⓓ Ⓔ
59 Ⓐ Ⓑ Ⓒ Ⓓ Ⓔ
60 Ⓐ Ⓑ Ⓒ Ⓓ Ⓔ
61 Ⓐ Ⓑ Ⓒ Ⓓ Ⓔ
62 Ⓐ Ⓑ Ⓒ Ⓓ Ⓔ
63 Ⓐ Ⓑ Ⓒ Ⓓ Ⓔ
64 Ⓐ Ⓑ Ⓒ Ⓓ Ⓔ

65 Ⓐ Ⓑ Ⓒ Ⓓ Ⓔ
66 Ⓐ Ⓑ Ⓒ Ⓓ Ⓔ
67 Ⓐ Ⓑ Ⓒ Ⓓ Ⓔ
68 Ⓐ Ⓑ Ⓒ Ⓓ Ⓔ
69 Ⓐ Ⓑ Ⓒ Ⓓ Ⓔ
70 Ⓐ Ⓑ Ⓒ Ⓓ Ⓔ
71 Ⓐ Ⓑ Ⓒ Ⓓ Ⓔ
72 Ⓐ Ⓑ Ⓒ Ⓓ Ⓔ

73 Ⓐ Ⓑ Ⓒ Ⓓ Ⓔ
74 Ⓐ Ⓑ Ⓒ Ⓓ Ⓔ
75 Ⓐ Ⓑ Ⓒ Ⓓ Ⓔ
76 Ⓐ Ⓑ Ⓒ Ⓓ Ⓔ
77 Ⓐ Ⓑ Ⓒ Ⓓ Ⓔ
78 Ⓐ Ⓑ Ⓒ Ⓓ Ⓔ
79 Ⓐ Ⓑ Ⓒ Ⓓ Ⓔ
80 Ⓐ Ⓑ Ⓒ Ⓓ Ⓔ

81 Ⓐ Ⓑ Ⓒ Ⓓ Ⓔ
82 Ⓐ Ⓑ Ⓒ Ⓓ Ⓔ
83 Ⓐ Ⓑ Ⓒ Ⓓ Ⓔ
84 Ⓐ Ⓑ Ⓒ Ⓓ Ⓔ
85 Ⓐ Ⓑ Ⓒ Ⓓ Ⓔ
86 Ⓐ Ⓑ Ⓒ Ⓓ Ⓔ
87 Ⓐ Ⓑ Ⓒ Ⓓ Ⓔ
88 Ⓐ Ⓑ Ⓒ Ⓓ Ⓔ

COMPLETE PRACTICE TEST #5
Part B – Address Memory – Segment #5

Directions

In this segment, you are given five minutes to study the addresses. There are no questions to answer in this segment – it is a study period only. As before, the boxes are not reprinted here for your use. Instead, you are instructed to turn back to Address Memory Segment #1 and to spend five minutes studying the boxes displayed there. After studying for five minutes, turn to Segment #6 for directions on how to continue.

Begin studying when you are prepared to time yourself for precisely five minutes.

COMPLETE PRACTICE TEST #5
Part B – Address Memory – Segment #6

Directions

In this segment, you have five minutes to attempt answering 88 questions. You are to try to answer from memory, but the boxes are shown if you need to refer to them. Your answers are to be marked on the sample answer sheet at the bottom of the pages of Segment #6 – do not use the Compete Practice Test Answer Sheet for this segment. After completing this segment, turn to Segment #7 for further instructions.

Turn the page and begin when you are prepared to time yourself for precisely five minutes.

Hint: Remember your strategies! This segment is not scored, so do not take the questions seriously. Instead, mark a handful of random answers and use the five minutes to study and memorize the addresses.

COMPLETE PRACTICE TEST #5
Part B – Address Memory – Segment #6

A	B	C
9200-9399 Vada	8500-8699 Vada	6700-6899 Vada
Bethel	Parker	Olivia
6700-6899 Bell	6300-6499 Bell	9200-9399 Bell
Ford	Finley	Scott
9600-9799 Lark	9200-9399 Lark	6300-6499 Lark

1. 6700-6899 Lark
2. Verde
3. 9200-9399 Lark
4. Lamey
5. Ford
6. 6700-6899 Bell
7. Saratoga
8. 6300-6499 Lark

9. 9600-9799 Vada
10. 9200-9399 Vada
11. 8500-8699 Bell
12. 6300-6499 Bell
13. Finley
14. 8500-8699 Vada
15. 9600-9799 Bell
16. 6700-6899 Vada

17. Bethel
18. 9200-9399 Bell
19. 6300-6499 Vada
20. Parker
21. 8500-8699 Bell
22. 9600-9799 Bell
23. Ford
24. Brady

25. 6700-6899 Vada
26. 6300-6499 Bell
27. Scott
28. 9200-9399 Vada
29. 9600-9799 Lark
30. Verde
31. 6300-6499 Vada
32. 8500-8699 Lark

33. Finley
34. 6300-6499 Lark
35. 9200-9399 Vada
36. Saratoga
37. 6300-6499 Bell
38. 6700-6899 Lark
39. 8500-8699 Vada
40. Olivia

41. 9200-9399 Lark
42. 6700-6899 Bell
43. 9600-9799 Vada
44. Parker
45. Bethel
46. 6300-6499 Vada
47. 9600-9799 Bell
48. Scott

1 (A)(B)(C)(D)(E)
2 (A)(B)(C)(D)(E)
3 (A)(B)(C)(D)(E)
4 (A)(B)(C)(D)(E)
5 (A)(B)(C)(D)(E)
6 (A)(B)(C)(D)(E)
7 (A)(B)(C)(D)(E)
8 (A)(B)(C)(D)(E)
9 (A)(B)(C)(D)(E)
10 (A)(B)(C)(D)(E)
11 (A)(B)(C)(D)(E)
12 (A)(B)(C)(D)(E)
13 (A)(B)(C)(D)(E)
14 (A)(B)(C)(D)(E)
15 (A)(B)(C)(D)(E)
16 (A)(B)(C)(D)(E)

17 (A)(B)(C)(D)(E)
18 (A)(B)(C)(D)(E)
19 (A)(B)(C)(D)(E)
20 (A)(B)(C)(D)(E)
21 (A)(B)(C)(D)(E)
22 (A)(B)(C)(D)(E)
23 (A)(B)(C)(D)(E)
24 (A)(B)(C)(D)(E)
25 (A)(B)(C)(D)(E)
26 (A)(B)(C)(D)(E)
27 (A)(B)(C)(D)(E)
28 (A)(B)(C)(D)(E)
29 (A)(B)(C)(D)(E)
30 (A)(B)(C)(D)(E)
31 (A)(B)(C)(D)(E)
32 (A)(B)(C)(D)(E)

33 (A)(B)(C)(D)(E)
34 (A)(B)(C)(D)(E)
35 (A)(B)(C)(D)(E)
36 (A)(B)(C)(D)(E)
37 (A)(B)(C)(D)(E)
38 (A)(B)(C)(D)(E)
39 (A)(B)(C)(D)(E)
40 (A)(B)(C)(D)(E)
41 (A)(B)(C)(D)(E)
42 (A)(B)(C)(D)(E)
43 (A)(B)(C)(D)(E)
44 (A)(B)(C)(D)(E)
45 (A)(B)(C)(D)(E)
46 (A)(B)(C)(D)(E)
47 (A)(B)(C)(D)(E)
48 (A)(B)(C)(D)(E)

Part B – Address Memory – Segment #6
Continued

D	E
9600-9799 Vada	6300-6499 Vada
Lamey	Verde
8500-8699 Bell	9600-9799 Bell
Saratoga	Brady
6700-6899 Lark	8500-8699 Lark

49. Olivia
50. 6300-6499 Vada
51. 9600-9799 Lark
52. 8500-8699 Bell
53. 9200-9399 Vada
54. Bethel
55. 6300-6499 Bell
56. 6700-6899 Vada

57. Parker
58. 9600-9799 Vada
59. Lamey
60. 9200-9399 Bell
61. Ford
62. Saratoga
63. Brady
64. Olivia

65. Scott
66. Ford
67. Verde
68. 6300-6499 Lark
69. 6700-6899 Bell
70. 9600-9799 Bell
71. 6300-6499 Vada
72. 8500-8699 Vada

73. 9200-9399 Lark
74. Saratoga
75. 9200-9399 Vada
76. 8500-8699 Bell
77. Finley
78. 6700-6899 Vada
79. 9600-9799 Lark
80. Brady

81. 9200-9399 Bell
82. 6300-6499 Lark
83. Lamey
84. Scott
85. Ford
86. 6700-6899 Lark
87. 6300-6499 Bell
88. 8500-8699 Lark

49. (A) (B) (C) (D) (E)
50. (A) (B) (C) (D) (E)
51. (A) (B) (C) (D) (E)
52. (A) (B) (C) (D) (E)
53. (A) (B) (C) (D) (E)
54. (A) (B) (C) (D) (E)
55. (A) (B) (C) (D) (E)
56. (A) (B) (C) (D) (E)

57. (A) (B) (C) (D) (E)
58. (A) (B) (C) (D) (E)
59. (A) (B) (C) (D) (E)
60. (A) (B) (C) (D) (E)
61. (A) (B) (C) (D) (E)
62. (A) (B) (C) (D) (E)
63. (A) (B) (C) (D) (E)
64. (A) (B) (C) (D) (E)

65. (A) (B) (C) (D) (E)
66. (A) (B) (C) (D) (E)
67. (A) (B) (C) (D) (E)
68. (A) (B) (C) (D) (E)
69. (A) (B) (C) (D) (E)
70. (A) (B) (C) (D) (E)
71. (A) (B) (C) (D) (E)
72. (A) (B) (C) (D) (E)

73. (A) (B) (C) (D) (E)
74. (A) (B) (C) (D) (E)
75. (A) (B) (C) (D) (E)
76. (A) (B) (C) (D) (E)
77. (A) (B) (C) (D) (E)
78. (A) (B) (C) (D) (E)
79. (A) (B) (C) (D) (E)
80. (A) (B) (C) (D) (E)

81. (A) (B) (C) (D) (E)
82. (A) (B) (C) (D) (E)
83. (A) (B) (C) (D) (E)
84. (A) (B) (C) (D) (E)
85. (A) (B) (C) (D) (E)
86. (A) (B) (C) (D) (E)
87. (A) (B) (C) (D) (E)
88. (A) (B) (C) (D) (E)

COMPLETE PRACTICE TEST #5
Part B – Address Memory – Segment #7

Directions

This is the final segment of the Address Memory section. You have five minutes to answer 88 questions. You must answer from memory. The boxes are not shown. On this segment, there is not a sample answer sheet at the bottom of the page. Instead, mark your answers on the Complete Practice Test Answer Sheet that your tore out of the book. After completing this segment, you have finished the full Address Memory section. Turn to the Number Series section of the practice test for instructions on how to continue.

Turn the page and begin when you are prepared to time yourself for precisely five minutes.

1. Brady
2. 6300-6499 Lark
3. 9200-9399 Vada
4. Finley
5. 6300-6499 Vada
6. Lamey
7. 6700-6899 Bell
8. 6300-6499 Bell

9. Scott
10. Parker
11. 6700-6899 Lark
12. 6300-6499 Lark
13. 9200-9399 Vada
14. Saratoga
15. 6700-6899 Vada
16. Lamey

17. 8500-8699 Vada
18. 6300-6499 Vada
19. 9600-9799 Lark
20. 9200-9399 Bell
21. 8500-8699 Bell
22. Bethel
23. 9600-9799 Vada
24. Verde

25. 9200-9399 Lark
26. Lamey
27. 9600-9799 Bell
28. Ford
29. Scott
30. 6300-6499 Bell
31. Brady
32. Olivia

33. 9200-9399 Bell
34. 8500-8699 Bell
35. Bethel
36. Brady
37. 6300-6499 Lark
38. Saratoga
39. 8500-8699 Vada
40. Lamey

41. 6700-6899 Bell
42. 9200-9399 Lark
43. 6300-6499 Bell
44. Ford
45. 9600-9799 Vada
46. 6700-6899 Vada
47. 6300-6499 Bell
48. 6300-6499 Vada

49. Finley
50. 6700-6899 Bell
51. Scott
52. 6700-6899 Vada
53. 8500-8699 Bell
54. 9600-9799 Lark
55. Olivia
56. Parker

57. Saratoga
58. 6700-6899 Lark
59. 9200-9399 Vada
60. 6300-6499 Vada
61. 9200-9399 Bell
62. 9600-9799 Bell
63. 8500-8699 Bell
64. Verde

65. 9200-9399 Vada
66. Saratoga
67. Brady
68. 6700-6899 Vada
69. Verde
70. 6700-6899 Bell
71. 9600-9799 Vada
72. Parker

73. 6700-6899 Lark
74. 8500-8699 Vada
75. 9600-9799 Bell
76. Bethel
77. Scott
78. 9200-9399 Lark
79. Finley
80. 9600-9799 Lark

81. Olivia
82. 6300-6499 Lark
83. Ford
84. 6300-6499 Bell
85. 8500-8699 Bell
86. 9200-9399 Bell
87. 6300-6499 Vada
88. Brady

COMPLETE PRACTICE TEST #5
Part C – Number Series

Directions

On this section, you have 20 minutes to answer 24 mathematical questions. Each question consists of a series of numbers followed by two blanks. You are to calculate what two numbers would logically follow in the series and that would therefore fit into the two blanks. Choose the answer – A, B, C, D, or E – that contains the correct two numbers, in the proper order, that should follow in the series. Mark your answers on the Complete Practice Test Answer Sheet in the section entitled Number Series. After completing this section, turn to the Following Oral Instructions section for directions on how to continue.

The solutions to all the Number Series questions in all six of the practice tests are given in the back of your book. After scoring each Number Series practice test, find and review the solutions for the questions you missed. This should better prepare you to answer similar questions on the other practice tests as well as on your actual exam.

Turn the page and begin when you are prepared to time yourself for precisely 20 minutes.

Hint: Remember to use the Circles and Squares Strategy to identify, separate, and solve the multiple sequences found in many questions.

COMPLETE PRACTICE TEST #5
Part C – Number Series

1. 19 19 20 20 21 21 22 ___ ___ A) 22,22 B) 23,24 C) 22,23 D) 25,26 E) 23,26

2. 6 12 18 24 30 ___ ___ A) 35,41 B) 38,44 C) 37,41 D) 33,40 E) 36,42

3. 31 28 25 22 19 16 ___ ___ A) 13,10 B) 15,14 C) 14,12 D) 12,8 E) 13,9

4. 15 19 16 13 13 10 ___ ___ A) 10,6 B) 11,7 C) 11,9 D) 12,8 E) 12,9

5. 8 6 8 7 8 8 ___ ___ A) 7,8 B) 9,10 C) 9,8 D) 8,9 E) 9,9

6. 21 29 37 45 53 ___ ___ A) 60,68 B) 62,70 C) 61,70 D) 60,69 E) 61,69

7. 8 12 14 10 16 18 12 ___ ___ A) 20,22 B) 18,20 C) 22,24 D) 20,24 E) 18,22

8. 7 8 10 9 10 12 11 ___ ___ A) 10,12 B) 12,14 C) 13,15 D) 14,16 E) 10,14

9. 9 9 6 9 9 8 9 ___ ___ A) 8,9 B) 10,11 C) 9,10 D) 9,12 E) 10,10

10. 25 31 37 43 49 ___ ___ A) 54,60 B) 56,62 C) 55,62 D) 56,61 E) 55,61

11. 32 33 35 38 42 47 ___ ___ A) 53,60 B) 52,59 C) 54,62 D) 54,62 E) 56,62

12. 3 8 12 6 16 20 9 ___ ___ A) 22,26 B) 24,28 C) 25,29 D) 26,30 E) 25,29

13. 3 4 10 5 6 9 7 8 ___ ___ A) 7,8 B) 9,11 C) 10,11 D) 8,9 E) 10,12

14. 10 3 20 4 30 5 ___ ___ A) 40,7 B) 50,7 C) 60,8 D) 50,8 E) 40,6

15. 5 4 10 8 16 12 ___ ___ A) 22,15 B) 24,17 C) 23,16 D) 25,17 E) 21,16

16. 9 14 28 19 24 28 29 ___ ___ A) 34,28 B) 35,29 C) 34,27 D) 34,29 E) 35,30

17. 7 8 12 9 10 12 11 ___ ___ A) 11,12 B) 13,12 C) 10,12 D) 12,11 E) 12,12

18. 11 12 14 15 17 18 20 ___ ___ A) 20,22 B) 21,23 C) 19,24 D) 23,21 E) 22,24

19. 15 8 15 11 15 14 15 ___ ___ A) 16,14 B) 18,16 C) 17,14 D) 18,15 E) 17,15

20. 10 9 10 15 8 7 20 25 ___ ___ A) 7,6 B) 6,6 C) 6,5 D) 7,4 E) 5,5

21. 26 8 24 10 22 12 ___ ___ A) 20,16 B) 22,14 C) 20,14 D) 22,16 E) 18,12

22. 24 25 27 28 30 31 ___ ___ A) 33,34 B) 30,32 C) 34,25 D) 32,25 E) 31,34

23. 18 16 18 17 18 18 18 ___ ___ A) 20,20 B) 20,16 C) 16,18 D) 19,18 E) 14,18

24. 30 31 33 36 40 ___ ___ A) 44,52 B) 45,51 C) 46,50 D) 45,52 E) 46,51

COMPLETE PRACTICE TEST #5
Part D – Following Oral Instructions

Directions

On this section of the test, the Exam Administrator will read questions/instructions aloud to the group of test takers. These oral instructions will direct you to write/mark certain items in your test booklet, which in turn will lead you to the correct answer(s). Finally, you will be verbally instructed to mark the correct answer(s) on your answer sheet. You must answer exclusively based upon what you hear – there are no questions for you to read.

The following pages of this practice test are samples of the test booklet pages on which you will write/mark as verbally instructed. Mark your answers on the Complete Practice Test Answer Sheet in the Following Oral Instructions section.

To practice realistically, you must either listen to the questions on the author's recording or have someone read them aloud to you. Do not look over the questions before taking the practice test. Once you have completed the practice test, you should then review the questions you missed in order to determine what caused you to miss them. This review should enable you to be more successful on similar questions next time.

The author's recording of all six Following Oral Directions practice tests is an ideal and convenient way to practice. The recorded questions are presented in the proper format, at the proper pace, and with proper diction. These recordings allow you to practice anytime and anywhere you wish. With these recordings, your practice – and in turn your success – will not be dependent upon someone else's schedule and whims. For details and ordering information, see the order form at the back of your book.

If someone will be reading the questions to you, he/she will find the questions for each practice test in the back of your book in the section entitled Following Oral Instructions – Practice Test Questions. The reader should carefully tear the questions out of your book in order to use them. The questions should be read at a rather slow and steady pace of approximately 75 words per minute and with proper diction. The reader should also pause between instructions/questions as directed in the wording of each question.

Once you complete the Following Oral Instructions section, you have finished this practice test, and you should then begin the next practice test in your book. Once you have completed all six practice tests plus the Extra Address Checking Practice Exercises as instructed, you should be fully prepared to excel on the actual exam.

Turn the page and begin when you are prepared to listen to the questions from the author's recording or from someone who will read the questions to you in the proper fashion.

Hint: Remember your strategies:
- *You will answer by marking number-letter combinations.*
- *Where you mark an answer on the answer sheet will not match the question number.*
- *Listen closely and attentively.*
- *Simply follow the instructions you hear – do not try to figure them out.*
- *Some questions will have multiple answers, and you must mark all of them.*
- *Mark your answers quickly and be ready to listen to the next question.*
- *Make identifying notes for later recall.*

COMPLETE PRACTICE TEST #5
Part D – Following Oral Instructions

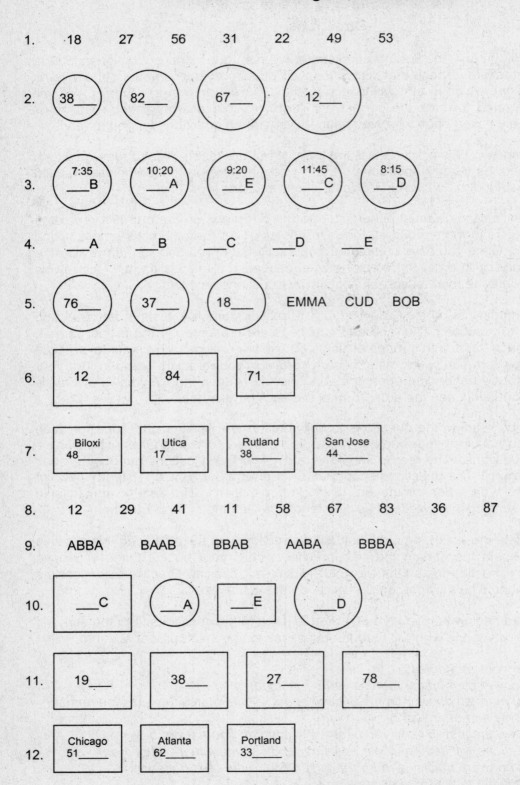

1. 18   27   56   31   22   49   53

2. 38___   82___   67___   12___

3. 7:35 ___B   10:20 ___A   9:20 ___E   11:45 ___C   8:15 ___D

4. ___A   ___B   ___C   ___D   ___E

5. 76___   37___   18___   EMMA   CUD   BOB

6. 12___   84___   71___

7. Biloxi 48_____   Utica 17_____   Rutland 38_____   San Jose 44_____

8. 12   29   41   11   58   67   83   36   87

9. ABBA   BAAB   BBAB   AABA   BBBA

10. ___C   ___A   ___E   ___D

11. 19___   38___   27___   78___

12. Chicago 51_____   Atlanta 62_____   Portland 33_____

13.   ___A   ___B   ___C   ___D   ___E

14.   3   8   20   32   57   17   14   15

15.   [53___]   [81___]   [62___]   [69___]

16.   ___D   ___E   ___B   ___C   ___A   ___D

17.   [___B]   (17___)   (81___)   [___A]

18.   (61___)   (82___)   (43___)   A M O R T I Z A T I O N

19.   72   37   14   4   31   86   17   49

COMPLETE PRACTICE TEST #6

This practice test contains samples of all four sections of the actual exam. The instructions given are similar to those on the actual exam. The format of this practice test is identical to that of the actual exam. Where pertinent, hints are given about your test taking strategies. Of course, these hints will not appear on the actual exam.

It is imperative that you take this practice test in as realistic a fashion as possible. **Your practice will have no value unless it is done realistically.** Therefore, you must precisely time yourself on the Address Checking, Address Memory, and Number Series sections. Our Timed Practice Test CD is a convenient way to practice realistically and time yourself precisely. Also, you must either listen to the Following Oral Instructions questions on our Oral Instructions Practice Tests CD or have someone read them to you – *do not read the questions yourself!* The Following Oral Instructions questions can be found in the back of your book if someone will be reading them to you.

To take this practice test, first turn to the back of your book and carefully tear out one of the **Complete Practice Test Answer Sheets.** Mark the answers to the scored segments of the practice test on this answer sheet. (Remember, of the seven segments on the Address Memory Section, only the final one is scored. Accordingly, you should mark answers for only the final Address Memory segment on your Complete Practice Test Answer Sheet. The other segments of the Address Memory Section that call for answers have accompanying sample answer sheets where you should mark answers.)

The correct answers are provided in the back of your book. Immediately upon completing the practice test, **it is imperative that you score each section** using the formulas given under the Sections of the Exam heading in your book. Scoring is necessary in order to gauge your progress and to identify your individual areas of weakness that may need extra attention.

After completing and scoring each practice test, move on to the next. **After completing all six practice tests and the Extra Address Checking Practice Exercises as instructed, you should be prepared for the actual exam.** If you feel the need to practice more, repeat as many of the practice tests as you like. After that much practice, the questions will likely have become a confusing blur in your mind. It is highly unlikely that you will be able to remember many of the individual questions or answers. Therefore, you should be able to gain practice value from the exercises even though you have already taken them once.

Do not look over the practice test questions until you are ready to start – meaning until you have set a timer for the allotted period of time. Similarly, after completing one section of the practice test, do not look over the next one until your are ready to start it. Likewise, stop working and put down your pencil immediately when the allotted period of time has expired. As has been emphasized before but cannot be emphasized enough, your practice is of absolutely no value unless it is done realistically. Also, you must train yourself (1) to not open your test booklet or pick up your pencil until instructed to do so and (2) to close your booklet and put down your pencil immediately upon being so instructed. The Postal Service has a zero tolerance policy on these matters. Any variance may be viewed as cheating and may result in your disqualification.

Good luck on your practice test, and even better luck on your actual exam!

COMPLETE PRACTICE TEST #6
Part A – Address Checking

Directions

In this part of the test, you will have to decide whether two addresses are alike or different. You will have 6 minutes to answer 95 questions. Each question consists of a pair of addresses. If the two addresses in the pair are exactly alike in every way, darken the oval with the letter "A" for _Alike_. If the two addresses are different in any way, darken the oval with the letter "D" for _Different_. Mark your answers on the Complete Practice Test Answer Sheet in the section entitled Address Checking.

Turn the page and begin when you are prepared to time yourself for precisely 6 minutes.

Note: You will notice that this section of your practice test is spread across two pages. This is the exact same format that you will actually experience on the Address Checking section of the real exam. For economy and convenience, other study guides frequently condense the two pages of this section down to only one. You will also notice that the Address Checking questions are presented in a font, or type of print, that is different from the rest of the book. This font matches what is actually used on the real exam, and, as you will see, it makes this section even more challenging. However, it is imperative that you practice realistically and that you become acquainted with and comfortable with the actual format of the exam. We have accordingly formatted this practice test realistically for your benefit.

Hint: Remember your strategies:
- _Pace yourself for speed and accuracy – emphasis on speed!_
- _Use one glance-over for easier/shorter addresses._
- _Use two glance-over's for harder/longer addresses._
- _Never make a third pass or glance-over!_
- _Overlap the answer sheet & the questions to keep them as close together as possible._
- _Use your extra pencil, your hand, or your fingers to mark/keep your place._
- _Use your Speed Pencil and your Speed Marking strategies for much greater speed._

1.	Muskogee, Okla.	Muskogee, Okla.
2.	Piedras Negras, Tx. 00732	Piedras Negras, Tx. 00132
3.	1517 Waco Way	1517 Waco Bay
4.	Kingsford Rd. NE	Kingsford Rd. NE
5.	Edmund Drive	Edmundo Drive
6.	1253 Beacon St	1253 Beacon St.
7.	2612 North Ridge Dr.	2612 North Bridge Dr.
8.	Hull, GA	Hull, GA
9.	227 Klondyke Rd.	237 Klondyke Rd.
10.	Jefferson City, MO	Jefferson City, MO
11.	7816 Boulder Drive	7861 Boulder Drive
12.	245 McDonnell Av.	245 McDonnall Av.
13.	Boston, Mass. 33190	Boston, Mass. 33192
14.	Rosalie Blvd.	Rosalie Blvd.
15.	5179 Washington Ave.	5179 Washington Ave.
16.	Pascagoula, Ms 39567	Pascagoula, MS 38567
17.	897 Pompano Circle	899 Pompano Circle
18.	230 Pointdexter Dr.	230 Pintdexter Dr.
19.	19226 Caron Rd.	19226 Carson Rd
20.	Evanston, Utah 82076	Evanston, Utah 82076
21.	De Los Playera	De Los Playera
22.	110 Wisteria Dr.	110 Wisteria Dr.
23.	1770 Fleetwood Blvd.	1770 Fleetwood Dr.
24.	376 East Beach Blvd.	3760 East Beach Blvd
25.	Chesapeake, VA 46073	Chesapeake, Vir. 46073
26.	3537 Live Oak Ct.	3537 Live Oak Ct.
27.	4932 Ravenwood Terr.	4932 Ravenwood Terr.
28.	19490 Cemetery Lane	19490 Cemetery Lane
29.	918 Courthouse Rd.	819 Courthouse Rd.
30.	Montpelier, Vt. 27100	Montpelier, Vt. 27100
31.	6530 Diamondhead Cir	6530 Diamondlead Cir
32.	Seminole, Fl.	Seminole, Fl.
33.	7600 Lakeridge Ln	7600 Lakeridge Ln
34.	Tacoma, Wash. 18896	Tacoma, Wash. 19688
35.	439 Whispering Pines	439 Whispering Pin
36.	General Pershing Way	General Pershing Lane
37.	Rockville, MD 73232	Rockville, MS 73232
38.	437 18th St. NW	437 18th St. NW
39.	Glendale, Pl.	Glendale, Pl.
40.	1667 Irish Pub	1667 Irish Pub
41.	217 NE Bohn St.	217 NW Bohn St.
42.	Chicago, Ill. 12047	Chicago, Ill. 12047
43.	4614 Maples Lane	4461 Maples Lane
44.	9300 Hardwicke Ct.	9300 Hardwicker Ct.
45.	14 Timber Way	14 Timber Way
46.	22107 Popps Ferry Rd.	22107 Popps Ferry Rd.
47.	Mobile, Al. 84392	Mobile, Ak. 84392
48.	2090 Greenthumb Terr.	2009 Greenthumb Terr.

49.	9973 Catherine Jct.	9973 Catherine Jct.
50.	Magnolia, MS.	Magnolia, MS.
51.	255 Kiln-Delisle Rd.	255 Kiln-Delisle Rd.
52.	Enterprise, Fl. 43150	Enterprize, Fl. 43150
53.	5666 Golf Club Dr.	5666 Gulf Club Dr.
54.	77771 Trailer Ct.	77777 Trailer Ct.
55.	4112 Oaklawn	4112 Oaklaun
56.	20321 Dedeaux Rd.	20321 Dedeaux Rd.
57.	Fairbanks, AK.	Fairbanks, AK.
58.	1253 Hamilton St.	1253 Hamillton St.
59.	170 Bayridge Bld.	170 Bayridge Bld.
60.	7038 Meadow Bale	7038 Meadow Dale
61.	Phoenix, AZ 18076	Pheonix, AZ 18076
62.	4137 Central Ave.	4137 Central Ave.
63.	11216 Ashford Cir.	11216 Ashford Cir.
64.	6071 Bullock Way	6017 Bullock Way
65.	Fort Smith, Ark., 10132	Ft. Smith Ark, 10132
66.	875 Strawberry St.	8750 Strawberry St.
67.	12222 Woodhaven Beach	1222 Woodhaven Beach
68.	501 Camille Cir.	501 Camille Ct.
69.	4600 Old Fort Bayou	4600 Old Fort Bayou
70.	Stockton, CA 99989	Sacramento, CA. 99989
71.	Boulder City, Nev.	Boulder City, Neb.
72.	8513 Orchard Av.	8513 Orchard Av.
73.	5417 Beatline Rd.	5417 Beatline Rd.
74.	3207 W Railroad	3207 S Railroad
75.	4713 Alandale St.	4713 Alandale St.
76.	Denever, Colo., 85777	Denver, Colo., 85777
77.	21680 Baywatch Beach	21680 Baywatch Beach
78.	26 Todd Terr.	26 Todd Terr.
79.	4723 Pontiac Dr.	4723 Pontiac Dr.
80.	Hartford, Conn.	Heartford, Conn.
81.	1304 De La Pointe Dr.	1304 De La Point Dr.
82.	179041 Lamney Lane	179041 Lamney Lane
83.	6371 Wooded Acres Rd.	6371 Wood Acres Rd.
84.	007 Dana Cir.	0007 Dana Cir.
85.	Miami, Fl. 67257	Miami, Fl. 67257
86.	5907 Easterbrook Bay	5907 Easterbrook Way
87.	3999 Jody Nelson Dr.	3777 Jody Nelson Dr
88.	3517 Kimberly Lane	3517 Kimberly Lane
89.	7617 Pearlington Pl.	7617 Pearlington Pl.
90.	Atlanta, GA 22127	Atlanta, GA. 22127
91.	15 Eastwood Blvd.	15 Eastwood Bay
92.	4117 Cunningham Point	4117 Cuningham Point
93.	2179 Rhonda Road	2179 Rhonda Road
94.	Honolulu, Hi. 93712	Hilo, Hi. 93712
95.	708 Shields Dr.	708 Shields Dr.

COMPLETE PRACTICE TEST #6
Part B – Address Memory

Directions

In this part of the test, you will have to memorize the locations of 25 addresses in five boxes. During this section, you will have several study periods and practice exercises to help you memorize the location of the addresses shown in the five boxes. Answer the questions by darkening the oval containing the letter (A, B, C, D, or E) of the box in which the address is located – Box A, Box B, Box C, Box D, or Box E. At the end of each segment, you will be given instructions on how and where to continue. After completing six preliminary segments, the actual test will be given as segment #7.

Turn the page to begin Segment #1.

Note: You will notice on your practice test that the various segments of the Address Memory section are spread across two pages. Where applicable, the five boxes, the 88 questions, and/or the sample answer sheets are spread across two pages. This is the same format that you will experience on most segments of the Address Memory section on the actual exam. For economy and convenience, other study guides frequently condense the two pages down to only one. However, it is imperative that you practice realistically and that you become acquainted with and comfortable with the actual format of the exam. We have accordingly formatted this practice test realistically for your benefit.

Hint: Remember your strategies:
- *Memorize horizontally.*
- *Memorize only Boxes A, B, C, and D.*
- *You can correctly answer all Box E questions by the process of elimination.*
- *Use the Second Digit Strategy to memorize the number addresses.*
- *Use imagery/association to memorize the word addresses.*
- *Overlap the answer sheet & the questions to keep them as close together as possible.*
- *Use your extra pencil, your hand, or your fingers to mark/keep your place.*
- *Use your Speed Pencil and your Speed Marking strategies for much greater speed.*

258

COMPLETE PRACTICE TEST #6
Part B – Address Memory – Segment #1

Directions

Five sample boxes, each containing five addresses, and five sample questions about these boxes are given on the following two pages. The purpose of this small exercise is simply to acquaint you with the format of this section and with how the questions should be answered. The first two sample questions are answered for you. You are to spend three minutes becoming acquainted with the format and answering sample questions 3, 4, and 5. After completing Segment #1, turn to Segment #2 for further instructions.

Turn the page and begin when you are prepared to time yourself for precisely three minutes.

Hint: Remember your strategies! This segment is not scored, so do not take the sample questions seriously. Instead, mark random answers and use the three minutes to study and memorize the addresses. The sample boxes and addresses in this segment are the very same ones that will be repeated throughout this section of the exam.

A	**B**	**C**
2100-2199 Micah	1400-1499 Micah	1900-1999 Micah
Hodges	Doyle	Bunker
1900-1999 Hilo	2800-2899 Hilo	7200-7299 Hilo
Wilson	Lloyd	Lyman
7200-7299 Mose	2100-2199 Mose	1400-1499 Mose

1. 2800-2899 Mose   Ⓐ Ⓑ Ⓒ ● Ⓔ
    This address came from Box D, so we sill darken the oval with the letter D.

2. Hatch   Ⓐ Ⓑ Ⓒ Ⓓ ●
    This address came from Box E, so we will darken the oval with the letter E.

3. Lloyd   Ⓐ Ⓑ Ⓒ Ⓓ Ⓔ
    Now that you know how to answer, you do questions 3, 4, and 5.

4. 7200-7299 Micah   Ⓐ Ⓑ Ⓒ Ⓓ Ⓔ

5. Lyman   Ⓐ Ⓑ Ⓒ Ⓓ Ⓔ

The correct answers are D, E, B, D, and C.

D	E
7200-7299 Micah	2800-2899 Micah
Tunica	Hatch
2100-2199 Hilo	1400-1499 Hilo
Coburn	Beacon
2800-2899 Mose	1900-1999 Mose

COMPLETE PRACTICE TEST #6
Part B – Address Memory – Segment #2

Directions

In this segment, you are given three minutes to study and memorize the addresses. There are no questions to answer in this segment – it is a study period only. However, on the actual exam, the boxes are not reprinted for your use. Instead, you are instructed to turn back to Address Memory Segment #1 on the preceding pages of the exam and to spend three minutes studying the boxes displayed there. So, we will do the very same on this practice test. After studying for three minutes, turn to Segment #3 for directions on how to continue the Address Memory Section of the exam.

Begin studying when you are prepared to time yourself for precisely three minutes.

COMPLETE PRACTICE TEST #6
Part B – Address Memory – Segment #3

Directions

In this segment you have three minutes to attempt answering 88 questions. You are to try to answer from memory, but the boxes are shown if you need to refer to them. Your answers are to be marked on the sample answer sheet at the bottom of the pages of Segment #3 – do not use the Compete Practice Test Answer Sheet for this segment. After completing this segment, turn to Segment #4 for further instructions.

Turn the page and begin when you are prepared to time yourself for precisely three minutes.

Hint: Remember your strategies! This segment is not scored, so do not take the questions seriously. Instead, mark a handful of random answers and use the three minutes to study and memorize the addresses.

A	**B**	**C**
2100-2199 Micah	1400-1499 Micah	1900-1999 Micah
Hodges	Doyle	Bunker
1900-1999 Hilo	2800-2899 Hilo	7200-7299 Hilo
Wilson	Lloyd	Lyman
7200-7299 Mose	2100-2199 Mose	1400-1499 Mose

1. Wilson
2. 2800-2899 Micah
3. 7200-7299 Hilo
4. 2100-2199 Mose
5. Doyle
6. Hatch
7. 1900-1999 Hilo
8. 1400-1499 Mose

9. 1400-1499 Micah
10. Coburn
11. 2100-2199 Micah
12. 1900-1999 Micah
13. 7200-7299 Micah
14. Wilson
15. 1400-1499 Hilo
16. 2100-2199 Mose

17. 1900-1999 Mose
18. Bunker
19. 7200-7299 Hilo
20. Tunica
21. Hodges
22. 2100-2199 Hilo
23. 1400-1499 Hilo
24. 2800-2899 Hilo

25. Lyman
26. 2100-2199 Micah
27. 7200-7299 Mose
28. 2800-2899 Micah
29. 2100-2199 Hilo
30. Doyle
31. Lloyd
32. 7200-7299 Micah

33. 2100-2199 Mose
34. 2100-2199 Micah
35. 2800-2899 Mose
36. Beacon
37. 7200-7299 Hilo
38. 1900-1999 Mose
39. Lyman
40. Wilson

41. 1900-1999 Micah
42. 2100-2199 Hilo
43. Coburn
44. 1900-1999 Hilo
45. 1400-1499 Mose
46. 7200-7299 Hilo
47. Hodges
48. 2800-2899 Hilo

1 Ⓐ Ⓑ Ⓒ Ⓓ Ⓔ
2 Ⓐ Ⓑ Ⓒ Ⓓ Ⓔ
3 Ⓐ Ⓑ Ⓒ Ⓓ Ⓔ
4 Ⓐ Ⓑ Ⓒ Ⓓ Ⓔ
5 Ⓐ Ⓑ Ⓒ Ⓓ Ⓔ
6 Ⓐ Ⓑ Ⓒ Ⓓ Ⓔ
7 Ⓐ Ⓑ Ⓒ Ⓓ Ⓔ
8 Ⓐ Ⓑ Ⓒ Ⓓ Ⓔ

9 Ⓐ Ⓑ Ⓒ Ⓓ Ⓔ
10 Ⓐ Ⓑ Ⓒ Ⓓ Ⓔ
11 Ⓐ Ⓑ Ⓒ Ⓓ Ⓔ
12 Ⓐ Ⓑ Ⓒ Ⓓ Ⓔ
13 Ⓐ Ⓑ Ⓒ Ⓓ Ⓔ
14 Ⓐ Ⓑ Ⓒ Ⓓ Ⓔ
15 Ⓐ Ⓑ Ⓒ Ⓓ Ⓔ
16 Ⓐ Ⓑ Ⓒ Ⓓ Ⓔ

17 Ⓐ Ⓑ Ⓒ Ⓓ Ⓔ
18 Ⓐ Ⓑ Ⓒ Ⓓ Ⓔ
19 Ⓐ Ⓑ Ⓒ Ⓓ Ⓔ
20 Ⓐ Ⓑ Ⓒ Ⓓ Ⓔ
21 Ⓐ Ⓑ Ⓒ Ⓓ Ⓔ
22 Ⓐ Ⓑ Ⓒ Ⓓ Ⓔ
23 Ⓐ Ⓑ Ⓒ Ⓓ Ⓔ
24 Ⓐ Ⓑ Ⓒ Ⓓ Ⓔ

25 Ⓐ Ⓑ Ⓒ Ⓓ Ⓔ
26 Ⓐ Ⓑ Ⓒ Ⓓ Ⓔ
27 Ⓐ Ⓑ Ⓒ Ⓓ Ⓔ
28 Ⓐ Ⓑ Ⓒ Ⓓ Ⓔ
29 Ⓐ Ⓑ Ⓒ Ⓓ Ⓔ
30 Ⓐ Ⓑ Ⓒ Ⓓ Ⓔ
31 Ⓐ Ⓑ Ⓒ Ⓓ Ⓔ
32 Ⓐ Ⓑ Ⓒ Ⓓ Ⓔ

33 Ⓐ Ⓑ Ⓒ Ⓓ Ⓔ
34 Ⓐ Ⓑ Ⓒ Ⓓ Ⓔ
35 Ⓐ Ⓑ Ⓒ Ⓓ Ⓔ
36 Ⓐ Ⓑ Ⓒ Ⓓ Ⓔ
37 Ⓐ Ⓑ Ⓒ Ⓓ Ⓔ
38 Ⓐ Ⓑ Ⓒ Ⓓ Ⓔ
39 Ⓐ Ⓑ Ⓒ Ⓓ Ⓔ
40 Ⓐ Ⓑ Ⓒ Ⓓ Ⓔ

41 Ⓐ Ⓑ Ⓒ Ⓓ Ⓔ
42 Ⓐ Ⓑ Ⓒ Ⓓ Ⓔ
43 Ⓐ Ⓑ Ⓒ Ⓓ Ⓔ
44 Ⓐ Ⓑ Ⓒ Ⓓ Ⓔ
45 Ⓐ Ⓑ Ⓒ Ⓓ Ⓔ
46 Ⓐ Ⓑ Ⓒ Ⓓ Ⓔ
47 Ⓐ Ⓑ Ⓒ Ⓓ Ⓔ
48 Ⓐ Ⓑ Ⓒ Ⓓ Ⓔ

D	E
7200-7299 Micah Tunica 2100-2199 Hilo Coburn 2800-2899 Mose	2800-2899 Micah Hatch 1400-1499 Hilo Beacon 1900-1999 Mose

49. Lloyd
50. Tunica
51. Hatch
52. 7200-7299 Mose
53. 1400-1499 Hilo
54. Bunker
55. 2800-2899 Mose
56. 2100-2199 Micah

57. 2100-2199 Mose
58. 7200-7299 Micah
59. Beacon
60. 1400-1499 Micah
61. 2100-2199 Hilo
62. 1400-1499 Mose
63. Wilson
64. 2800-2899 Mose

65. 2100-2199 Mose
66. Beacon
67. 7200-7299 Hilo
68. Coburn
69. Hodges
70. 2100-2199 Hilo
71. 1400-1499 Hilo
72. 2800-2899 Hilo

73. Doyle
74. 1400-1499 Hilo
75. 1900-1999 Hilo
76. Lloyd
77. 7200-7299 Mose
78. Hatch
79. Lyman
80. 2800-2899 Mose

81. 1900-1999 Hilo
82. Bunker
83. 2800-2899 Micah
84. 1400-1499 Micah
85. Tunica
86. 1900-1999 Micah
87. 2100-2199 Mose
88. Coburn

49 Ⓐ Ⓑ Ⓒ Ⓓ Ⓔ
50 Ⓐ Ⓑ Ⓒ Ⓓ Ⓔ
51 Ⓐ Ⓑ Ⓒ Ⓓ Ⓔ
52 Ⓐ Ⓑ Ⓒ Ⓓ Ⓔ
53 Ⓐ Ⓑ Ⓒ Ⓓ Ⓔ
54 Ⓐ Ⓑ Ⓒ Ⓓ Ⓔ
55 Ⓐ Ⓑ Ⓒ Ⓓ Ⓔ
56 Ⓐ Ⓑ Ⓒ Ⓓ Ⓔ

57 Ⓐ Ⓑ Ⓒ Ⓓ Ⓔ
58 Ⓐ Ⓑ Ⓒ Ⓓ Ⓔ
59 Ⓐ Ⓑ Ⓒ Ⓓ Ⓔ
60 Ⓐ Ⓑ Ⓒ Ⓓ Ⓔ
61 Ⓐ Ⓑ Ⓒ Ⓓ Ⓔ
62 Ⓐ Ⓑ Ⓒ Ⓓ Ⓔ
63 Ⓐ Ⓑ Ⓒ Ⓓ Ⓔ
64 Ⓐ Ⓑ Ⓒ Ⓓ Ⓔ

65 Ⓐ Ⓑ Ⓒ Ⓓ Ⓔ
66 Ⓐ Ⓑ Ⓒ Ⓓ Ⓔ
67 Ⓐ Ⓑ Ⓒ Ⓓ Ⓔ
68 Ⓐ Ⓑ Ⓒ Ⓓ Ⓔ
69 Ⓐ Ⓑ Ⓒ Ⓓ Ⓔ
70 Ⓐ Ⓑ Ⓒ Ⓓ Ⓔ
71 Ⓐ Ⓑ Ⓒ Ⓓ Ⓔ
72 Ⓐ Ⓑ Ⓒ Ⓓ Ⓔ

73 Ⓐ Ⓑ Ⓒ Ⓓ Ⓔ
74 Ⓐ Ⓑ Ⓒ Ⓓ Ⓔ
75 Ⓐ Ⓑ Ⓒ Ⓓ Ⓔ
76 Ⓐ Ⓑ Ⓒ Ⓓ Ⓔ
77 Ⓐ Ⓑ Ⓒ Ⓓ Ⓔ
78 Ⓐ Ⓑ Ⓒ Ⓓ Ⓔ
79 Ⓐ Ⓑ Ⓒ Ⓓ Ⓔ
80 Ⓐ Ⓑ Ⓒ Ⓓ Ⓔ

81 Ⓐ Ⓑ Ⓒ Ⓓ Ⓔ
82 Ⓐ Ⓑ Ⓒ Ⓓ Ⓔ
83 Ⓐ Ⓑ Ⓒ Ⓓ Ⓔ
84 Ⓐ Ⓑ Ⓒ Ⓓ Ⓔ
85 Ⓐ Ⓑ Ⓒ Ⓓ Ⓔ
86 Ⓐ Ⓑ Ⓒ Ⓓ Ⓔ
87 Ⓐ Ⓑ Ⓒ Ⓓ Ⓔ
88 Ⓐ Ⓑ Ⓒ Ⓓ Ⓔ

268

COMPLETE PRACTICE TEST #6
Part B – Address Memory – Segment #4

Directions

In this segment you have three minutes to attempt answering 88 questions. You must answer from memory. The boxes are not shown. Your answers are to be marked on the sample answer sheet at the bottom of the pages of Segment #4 – do not use the Compete Practice Test Answer Sheet for this segment. After completing this segment, turn to Segment #5 for further instructions.

Turn the page and begin when you are prepared to time yourself for precisely three minutes.

Hint: Remember, this segment is not scored, so you should not worry about your inability to answer all 88 questions, or your inability to answer all of them accurately, in only three minutes. Neither task is really possible in only three minutes. However, this is an ideal opportunity for you to test how well you have mastered your strategies and memorization so far. By sincerely trying to answer the questions, you can identify the areas where you are weaker and where you need to apply more effort.

1. 2800-2899 Mose
2. Hatch
3. Lloyd
4. 7200-7299 Micah
5. Lyman
6. 2800-2899 Micah
7. 1900-1999 Hilo
8. 1400-1499 Mose

9. 1900-1999 Micah
10. Tunica
11. 2100-2199 Micah
12. Coburn
13. Beacon
14. 7200-7299 Mose
15. 2100-2199 Hilo
16. 1400-1499 Micah

17. 2800-2899 Hilo
18. 1900-1999 Mose
19. Bunker
20. Hatch
21. Hodges
22. 2100-2199 Hilo
23. 2800-2899 Mose
24. Doyle

25. 1400-1499 Hilo
26. Wilson
27. 7200-7299 Hilo
28. Tunica
29. 1900-1999 Hilo
30. 7200-7299 Micah
31. 1400-1499 Mose
32. Lloyd

33. 1400-1499 Micah
34. 1900-1999 Hilo
35. 2100-2199 Mose
36. 1400-1499 Mose
37. Hatch
38. 2100-2199 Micah
39. 2800-2899 Hilo
40. 1900-1999 Micah

41. 2800-2899 Hilo
42. Lyman
43. 7200-7299 Mose
44. 2800-2899 Micah
45. 7200-7299 Hilo
46. Hodges
47. 1900-1999 Mose
48. Doyle

1 Ⓐ Ⓑ Ⓒ Ⓓ Ⓔ
2 Ⓐ Ⓑ Ⓒ Ⓓ Ⓔ
3 Ⓐ Ⓑ Ⓒ Ⓓ Ⓔ
4 Ⓐ Ⓑ Ⓒ Ⓓ Ⓔ
5 Ⓐ Ⓑ Ⓒ Ⓓ Ⓔ
6 Ⓐ Ⓑ Ⓒ Ⓓ Ⓔ
7 Ⓐ Ⓑ Ⓒ Ⓓ Ⓔ
8 Ⓐ Ⓑ Ⓒ Ⓓ Ⓔ

9 Ⓐ Ⓑ Ⓒ Ⓓ Ⓔ
10 Ⓐ Ⓑ Ⓒ Ⓓ Ⓔ
11 Ⓐ Ⓑ Ⓒ Ⓓ Ⓔ
12 Ⓐ Ⓑ Ⓒ Ⓓ Ⓔ
13 Ⓐ Ⓑ Ⓒ Ⓓ Ⓔ
14 Ⓐ Ⓑ Ⓒ Ⓓ Ⓔ
15 Ⓐ Ⓑ Ⓒ Ⓓ Ⓔ
16 Ⓐ Ⓑ Ⓒ Ⓓ Ⓔ

17 Ⓐ Ⓑ Ⓒ Ⓓ Ⓔ
18 Ⓐ Ⓑ Ⓒ Ⓓ Ⓔ
19 Ⓐ Ⓑ Ⓒ Ⓓ Ⓔ
20 Ⓐ Ⓑ Ⓒ Ⓓ Ⓔ
21 Ⓐ Ⓑ Ⓒ Ⓓ Ⓔ
22 Ⓐ Ⓑ Ⓒ Ⓓ Ⓔ
23 Ⓐ Ⓑ Ⓒ Ⓓ Ⓔ
24 Ⓐ Ⓑ Ⓒ Ⓓ Ⓔ

25 Ⓐ Ⓑ Ⓒ Ⓓ Ⓔ
26 Ⓐ Ⓑ Ⓒ Ⓓ Ⓔ
27 Ⓐ Ⓑ Ⓒ Ⓓ Ⓔ
28 Ⓐ Ⓑ Ⓒ Ⓓ Ⓔ
29 Ⓐ Ⓑ Ⓒ Ⓓ Ⓔ
30 Ⓐ Ⓑ Ⓒ Ⓓ Ⓔ
31 Ⓐ Ⓑ Ⓒ Ⓓ Ⓔ
32 Ⓐ Ⓑ Ⓒ Ⓓ Ⓔ

33 Ⓐ Ⓑ Ⓒ Ⓓ Ⓔ
34 Ⓐ Ⓑ Ⓒ Ⓓ Ⓔ
35 Ⓐ Ⓑ Ⓒ Ⓓ Ⓔ
36 Ⓐ Ⓑ Ⓒ Ⓓ Ⓔ
37 Ⓐ Ⓑ Ⓒ Ⓓ Ⓔ
38 Ⓐ Ⓑ Ⓒ Ⓓ Ⓔ
39 Ⓐ Ⓑ Ⓒ Ⓓ Ⓔ
40 Ⓐ Ⓑ Ⓒ Ⓓ Ⓔ

41 Ⓐ Ⓑ Ⓒ Ⓓ Ⓔ
42 Ⓐ Ⓑ Ⓒ Ⓓ Ⓔ
43 Ⓐ Ⓑ Ⓒ Ⓓ Ⓔ
44 Ⓐ Ⓑ Ⓒ Ⓓ Ⓔ
45 Ⓐ Ⓑ Ⓒ Ⓓ Ⓔ
46 Ⓐ Ⓑ Ⓒ Ⓓ Ⓔ
47 Ⓐ Ⓑ Ⓒ Ⓓ Ⓔ
48 Ⓐ Ⓑ Ⓒ Ⓓ Ⓔ

49. Lyman
50. 2100-2199 Hilo
51. Wilson
52. 1900-1999 Mose
53. 2100-2199 Micah
54. Bunker
55. 2800-2899 Micah
56. 1400-1499 Micah

57. 2100-2199 Hilo
58. 2800-2899 Hilo
59. Beacon
60. Hodges
61. 1400-1499 Hilo
62. 2100-2199 Mose
63. Coburn
64. Doyle

65. 7200-7299 Hilo
66. Hodges
67. Beacon
68. Tunica
69. 1900-1999 Hilo
70. 2800-2899 Mose
71. 2100-2199 Mose
72. Bunker

73. Lloyd
74. 7200-7299 Micah
75. 2100-2199 Hilo
76. 2100-2199 Micah
77. Hatch
78. 1900-1999 Micah
79. 1400-1499 Hilo
80. 7200-7299 Mose

81. 2100-2199 Mose
82. 2800-2899 Mose
83. Lyman
84. Beacon
85. 1400-1499 Hilo
86. Wilson
87. Coburn
88. 1400-1499 Mose

49. (A) (B) (C) (D) (E)
50. (A) (B) (C) (D) (E)
51. (A) (B) (C) (D) (E)
52. (A) (B) (C) (D) (E)
53. (A) (B) (C) (D) (E)
54. (A) (B) (C) (D) (E)
55. (A) (B) (C) (D) (E)
56. (A) (B) (C) (D) (E)

57. (A) (B) (C) (D) (E)
58. (A) (B) (C) (D) (E)
59. (A) (B) (C) (D) (E)
60. (A) (B) (C) (D) (E)
61. (A) (B) (C) (D) (E)
62. (A) (B) (C) (D) (E)
63. (A) (B) (C) (D) (E)
64. (A) (B) (C) (D) (E)

65. (A) (B) (C) (D) (E)
66. (A) (B) (C) (D) (E)
67. (A) (B) (C) (D) (E)
68. (A) (B) (C) (D) (E)
69. (A) (B) (C) (D) (E)
70. (A) (B) (C) (D) (E)
71. (A) (B) (C) (D) (E)
72. (A) (B) (C) (D) (E)

73. (A) (B) (C) (D) (E)
74. (A) (B) (C) (D) (E)
75. (A) (B) (C) (D) (E)
76. (A) (B) (C) (D) (E)
77. (A) (B) (C) (D) (E)
78. (A) (B) (C) (D) (E)
79. (A) (B) (C) (D) (E)
80. (A) (B) (C) (D) (E)

81. (A) (B) (C) (D) (E)
82. (A) (B) (C) (D) (E)
83. (A) (B) (C) (D) (E)
84. (A) (B) (C) (D) (E)
85. (A) (B) (C) (D) (E)
86. (A) (B) (C) (D) (E)
87. (A) (B) (C) (D) (E)
88. (A) (B) (C) (D) (E)

COMPLETE PRACTICE TEST #6
Part B – Address Memory – Segment #5

Directions

In this segment, you are given five minutes to study the addresses. There are no questions to answer in this segment – it is a study period only. As before, the boxes are not reprinted here for your use. Instead, you are instructed to turn back to Address Memory Segment #1 and to spend five minutes studying the boxes displayed there. After studying for five minutes, turn to Segment #6 for directions on how to continue.

Begin studying when you are prepared to time yourself for precisely five minutes.

COMPLETE PRACTICE TEST #6
Part B – Address Memory – Segment #6

Directions

In this segment, you have five minutes to attempt answering 88 questions. You are to try to answer from memory, but the boxes are shown if you need to refer to them. Your answers are to be marked on the sample answer sheet at the bottom of the pages of Segment #6 – do not use the Compete Practice Test Answer Sheet for this segment. After completing this segment, turn to Segment #7 for further instructions.

Turn the page and begin when you are prepared to time yourself for precisely five minutes.

Hint: Remember your strategies! This segment is not scored, so do not take the questions seriously. Instead, mark a handful of random answers and use the five minutes to study and memorize the addresses.

COMPLETE PRACTICE TEST #6
Part B – Address Memory – Segment #6

A	B	C
2100-2199 Micah	1400-1499 Micah	1900-1999 Micah
Hodges	Doyle	Bunker
1900-1999 Hilo	2800-2899 Hilo	7200-7299 Hilo
Wilson	Lloyd	Lyman
7200-7299 Mose	2100-2199 Mose	1400-1499 Mose

1. Wilson
2. 2800-2899 Micah
3. 7200-7299 Hilo
4. 2100-2199 Mose
5. Doyle
6. Hatch
7. 1900-1999 Hilo
8. 1400-1499 Mose

9. 1400-1499 Micah
10. Coburn
11. 2100-2199 Micah
12. 1900-1999 Micah
13. 7200-7299 Micah
14. Wilson
15. 1400-1499 Hilo
16. 2100-2199 Mose

17. 1900-1999 Mose
18. Bunker
19. 7200-7299 Hilo
20. Tunica
21. Hodges
22. 2100-2199 Hilo
23. 1400-1499 Hilo
24. 2800-2899 Hilo

25. Lyman
26. 2100-2199 Micah
27. 7200-7299 Mose
28. 2800-2899 Micah
29. 2100-2199 Hilo
30. Doyle
31. Lloyd
32. 7200-7299 Micah

33. 2100-2199 Mose
34. 2100-2199 Micah
35. 2800-2899 Mose
36. Beacon
37. 7200-7299 Hilo
38. 1900-1999 Mose
39. Lyman
40. Wilson

41. 1900-1999 Micah
42. 2100-2199 Hilo
43. Coburn
44. 1900-1999 Hilo
45. 1400-1499 Mose
46. 7200-7299 Hilo
47. Hodges
48. 2800-2899 Hilo

1 Ⓐ Ⓑ Ⓒ Ⓓ Ⓔ
2 Ⓐ Ⓑ Ⓒ Ⓓ Ⓔ
3 Ⓐ Ⓑ Ⓒ Ⓓ Ⓔ
4 Ⓐ Ⓑ Ⓒ Ⓓ Ⓔ
5 Ⓐ Ⓑ Ⓒ Ⓓ Ⓔ
6 Ⓐ Ⓑ Ⓒ Ⓓ Ⓔ
7 Ⓐ Ⓑ Ⓒ Ⓓ Ⓔ
8 Ⓐ Ⓑ Ⓒ Ⓓ Ⓔ
9 Ⓐ Ⓑ Ⓒ Ⓓ Ⓔ
10 Ⓐ Ⓑ Ⓒ Ⓓ Ⓔ
11 Ⓐ Ⓑ Ⓒ Ⓓ Ⓔ
12 Ⓐ Ⓑ Ⓒ Ⓓ Ⓔ
13 Ⓐ Ⓑ Ⓒ Ⓓ Ⓔ
14 Ⓐ Ⓑ Ⓒ Ⓓ Ⓔ
15 Ⓐ Ⓑ Ⓒ Ⓓ Ⓔ
16 Ⓐ Ⓑ Ⓒ Ⓓ Ⓔ

17 Ⓐ Ⓑ Ⓒ Ⓓ Ⓔ
18 Ⓐ Ⓑ Ⓒ Ⓓ Ⓔ
19 Ⓐ Ⓑ Ⓒ Ⓓ Ⓔ
20 Ⓐ Ⓑ Ⓒ Ⓓ Ⓔ
21 Ⓐ Ⓑ Ⓒ Ⓓ Ⓔ
22 Ⓐ Ⓑ Ⓒ Ⓓ Ⓔ
23 Ⓐ Ⓑ Ⓒ Ⓓ Ⓔ
24 Ⓐ Ⓑ Ⓒ Ⓓ Ⓔ
25 Ⓐ Ⓑ Ⓒ Ⓓ Ⓔ
26 Ⓐ Ⓑ Ⓒ Ⓓ Ⓔ
27 Ⓐ Ⓑ Ⓒ Ⓓ Ⓔ
28 Ⓐ Ⓑ Ⓒ Ⓓ Ⓔ
29 Ⓐ Ⓑ Ⓒ Ⓓ Ⓔ
30 Ⓐ Ⓑ Ⓒ Ⓓ Ⓔ
31 Ⓐ Ⓑ Ⓒ Ⓓ Ⓔ
32 Ⓐ Ⓑ Ⓒ Ⓓ Ⓔ

33 Ⓐ Ⓑ Ⓒ Ⓓ Ⓔ
34 Ⓐ Ⓑ Ⓒ Ⓓ Ⓔ
35 Ⓐ Ⓑ Ⓒ Ⓓ Ⓔ
36 Ⓐ Ⓑ Ⓒ Ⓓ Ⓔ
37 Ⓐ Ⓑ Ⓒ Ⓓ Ⓔ
38 Ⓐ Ⓑ Ⓒ Ⓓ Ⓔ
39 Ⓐ Ⓑ Ⓒ Ⓓ Ⓔ
40 Ⓐ Ⓑ Ⓒ Ⓓ Ⓔ
41 Ⓐ Ⓑ Ⓒ Ⓓ Ⓔ
42 Ⓐ Ⓑ Ⓒ Ⓓ Ⓔ
43 Ⓐ Ⓑ Ⓒ Ⓓ Ⓔ
44 Ⓐ Ⓑ Ⓒ Ⓓ Ⓔ
45 Ⓐ Ⓑ Ⓒ Ⓓ Ⓔ
46 Ⓐ Ⓑ Ⓒ Ⓓ Ⓔ
47 Ⓐ Ⓑ Ⓒ Ⓓ Ⓔ
48 Ⓐ Ⓑ Ⓒ Ⓓ Ⓔ

D	E
7200-7299 Micah	2800-2899 Micah
Tunica	Hatch
2100-2199 Hilo	1400-1499 Hilo
Coburn	Beacon
2800-2899 Mose	1900-1999 Mose

49. Lloyd
50. Tunica
51. Hatch
52. 7200-7299 Mose
53. 1400-1499 Hilo
54. Bunker
55. 2800-2899 Mose
56. 2100-2199 Micah

57. 2100-2199 Mose
58. 7200-7299 Micah
59. Beacon
60. 1400-1499 Micah
61. 2100-2199 Hilo
62. 1400-1499 Mose
63. Wilson
64. 2800-2899 Mose

65. 2100-2199 Mose
66. Beacon
67. 7200-7299 Hilo
68. Coburn
69. Hodges
70. 2100-2199 Hilo
71. 1400-1499 Hilo
72. 2800-2899 Hilo

73. Doyle
74. 1400-1499 Hilo
75. 1900-1999 Hilo
76. Lloyd
77. 7200-7299 Mose
78. Hatch
79. Lyman
80. 2800-2899 Mose

81. 1900-1999 Hilo
82. Bunker
83. 2800-2899 Micah
84. 1400-1499 Micah
85. Tunica
86. 1900-1999 Micah
87. 2100-2199 Mose
88. Coburn

49 Ⓐ Ⓑ Ⓒ Ⓓ Ⓔ
50 Ⓐ Ⓑ Ⓒ Ⓓ Ⓔ
51 Ⓐ Ⓑ Ⓒ Ⓓ Ⓔ
52 Ⓐ Ⓑ Ⓒ Ⓓ Ⓔ
53 Ⓐ Ⓑ Ⓒ Ⓓ Ⓔ
54 Ⓐ Ⓑ Ⓒ Ⓓ Ⓔ
55 Ⓐ Ⓑ Ⓒ Ⓓ Ⓔ
56 Ⓐ Ⓑ Ⓒ Ⓓ Ⓔ

57 Ⓐ Ⓑ Ⓒ Ⓓ Ⓔ
58 Ⓐ Ⓑ Ⓒ Ⓓ Ⓔ
59 Ⓐ Ⓑ Ⓒ Ⓓ Ⓔ
60 Ⓐ Ⓑ Ⓒ Ⓓ Ⓔ
61 Ⓐ Ⓑ Ⓒ Ⓓ Ⓔ
62 Ⓐ Ⓑ Ⓒ Ⓓ Ⓔ
63 Ⓐ Ⓑ Ⓒ Ⓓ Ⓔ
64 Ⓐ Ⓑ Ⓒ Ⓓ Ⓔ

65 Ⓐ Ⓑ Ⓒ Ⓓ Ⓔ
66 Ⓐ Ⓑ Ⓒ Ⓓ Ⓔ
67 Ⓐ Ⓑ Ⓒ Ⓓ Ⓔ
68 Ⓐ Ⓑ Ⓒ Ⓓ Ⓔ
69 Ⓐ Ⓑ Ⓒ Ⓓ Ⓔ
70 Ⓐ Ⓑ Ⓒ Ⓓ Ⓔ
71 Ⓐ Ⓑ Ⓒ Ⓓ Ⓔ
72 Ⓐ Ⓑ Ⓒ Ⓓ Ⓔ

73 Ⓐ Ⓑ Ⓒ Ⓓ Ⓔ
74 Ⓐ Ⓑ Ⓒ Ⓓ Ⓔ
75 Ⓐ Ⓑ Ⓒ Ⓓ Ⓔ
76 Ⓐ Ⓑ Ⓒ Ⓓ Ⓔ
77 Ⓐ Ⓑ Ⓒ Ⓓ Ⓔ
78 Ⓐ Ⓑ Ⓒ Ⓓ Ⓔ
79 Ⓐ Ⓑ Ⓒ Ⓓ Ⓔ
80 Ⓐ Ⓑ Ⓒ Ⓓ Ⓔ

81 Ⓐ Ⓑ Ⓒ Ⓓ Ⓔ
82 Ⓐ Ⓑ Ⓒ Ⓓ Ⓔ
83 Ⓐ Ⓑ Ⓒ Ⓓ Ⓔ
84 Ⓐ Ⓑ Ⓒ Ⓓ Ⓔ
85 Ⓐ Ⓑ Ⓒ Ⓓ Ⓔ
86 Ⓐ Ⓑ Ⓒ Ⓓ Ⓔ
87 Ⓐ Ⓑ Ⓒ Ⓓ Ⓔ
88 Ⓐ Ⓑ Ⓒ Ⓓ Ⓔ

COMPLETE PRACTICE TEST #6
Part B – Address Memory – Segment #7

Directions

This is the final segment of the Address Memory section. You have five minutes to answer 88 questions. You must answer from memory. The boxes are not shown. On this segment, there is not a sample answer sheet at the bottom of the page. Instead, mark your answers on the Complete Practice Test Answer Sheet that your tore out of the book. After completing this segment, you have finished the full Address Memory section. Turn to the Number Series section of the practice test for instructions on how to continue.

Turn the page and begin when you are prepared to time yourself for precisely five minutes.

1. 2800-2899 Mose
2. Hatch
3. Lloyd
4. 7200-7299 Micah
5. Lyman
6. 2800-2899 Micah
7. 1900-1999 Hilo
8. 1400-1499 Mose

9. 1900-1999 Micah
10. Tunica
11. 2100-2199 Micah
12. Coburn
13. Beacon
14. 7200-7299 Mose
15. 2100-2199 Hilo
16. 1400-1499 Micah

17. 2800-2899 Hilo
18. 1900-1999 Mose
19. Bunker
20. Hatch
21. Hodges
22. 2100-2199 Hilo
23. 2800-2899 Mose
24. Doyle

25. 1400-1499 Hilo
26. Wilson
27. 7200-7299 Hilo
28. Tunica
29. 1900-1999 Hilo
30. 7200-7299 Micah
31. 1400-1499 Mose
32. Lloyd

33. 1400-1499 Micah
34. 1900-1999 Hilo
35. 2100-2199 Mose
36. 1400-1499 Mose
37. Hatch
38. 2100-2199 Micah
39. 2800-2899 Hilo
40. 1900-1999 Micah

41. 2800-2899 Hilo
42. Lyman
43. 7200-7299 Mose
44. 2800-2899 Micah
45. 7200-7299 Hilo
46. Hodges
47. 1900-1999 Mose
48. Doyle

49. Lyman
50. 2100-2199 Hilo
51. Wilson
52. 1900-1999 Mose
53. 2100-2199 Micah
54. Bunker
55. 2800-2899 Micah
56. 1400-1499 Micah

57. 2100-2199 Hilo
58. 2800-2899 Hilo
59. Beacon
60. Hodges
61. 1400-1499 Hilo
62. 2100-2199 Mose
63. Coburn
64. Doyle

65. 7200-7299 Hilo
66. Hodges
67. Beacon
68. Tunica
69. 1900-1999 Hilo
70. 2800-2899 Mose
71. 2100-2199 Mose
72. Bunker

73. Lloyd
74. 7200-7299 Micah
75. 2100-2199 Hilo
76. 2100-2199 Micah
77. Hatch
78. 1900-1999 Micah
79. 1400-1499 Hilo
80. 7200-7299 Mose

81. 2100-2199 Mose
82. 2800-2899 Mose
83. Lyman
84. Beacon
85. 1400-1499 Hilo
86. Wilson
87. Coburn
88. 1400-1499 Mose

COMPLETE PRACTICE TEST #6
Part C – Number Series

Directions

On this section, you have 20 minutes to answer 24 mathematical questions. Each question consists of a series of numbers followed by two blanks. You are to calculate what two numbers would logically follow in the series and that would therefore fit into the two blanks. Choose the answer – A, B, C, D, or E – that contains the correct two numbers, in the proper order, that should follow in the series. Mark your answers on the Complete Practice Test Answer Sheet in the section entitled Number Series. After completing this section, turn to the Following Oral Instructions section for directions on how to continue.

The solutions to all the Number Series questions in all six of the practice tests are given in the back of your book. After scoring each Number Series practice test, find and review the solutions for the questions you missed. This should better prepare you to answer similar questions on the other practice tests as well as on your actual exam.

Turn the page and begin when you are prepared to time yourself for precisely 20 minutes.

Hint: Remember to use the Circles and Squares Strategy to identify, separate, and solve the multiple sequences found in many questions.

284

COMPLETE PRACTICE TEST #6
Part C – Number Series

1. 14 15 16 17 18 19 ___ ___   A) 20,23 B) 22,23 C) 20,21 D) 19,20 E) 21,22

2. 26 28 30 32 34 36 ___ ___   A) 36,38 B) 37,38 C) 40,42 D) 38,42 E) 38,40

3. 3 6 13 16 23 ___ ___   A) 26,33 B) 25,32 C) 26,35 D) 27,36 E) 28,37

4. 3 4 4 6 5 8 6 ___ ___   A) 10,9 B) 12,7 C) 10,8 D) 10,7 E) 11;12

5. 29 25 10 12 21 17 14 ___ ___   A) 15,12 B) 16,13 C) 17,14 D) 18,15 E) 19,20

6. 15 40 20 30 25 20 ___ ___   A) 20,20 B) 20,10 C) 30,20 D) 40,10 E) 30,10

7. 6 12 35 18 24 25 30 ___ ___   A) 37,16 B) 35,15 C) 36,15 D) 30,10 E) 34,15

8. 9 9 5 9 9 10 9 ___ ___   A) 9,15 B) 10,15 C) 9,20 D) 9,17 E) 15,9

9. 6 7 9 10 12 13 15 ___ ___   A) 15,17 B) 16,18 C) 17,19 D) 15,16 E) 16,17

10. 6 5 8 7 10 9 12 ___ ___   A) 10,13 B) 12,14 C) 13,14 D) 11,14 E) 11,15

11. 5 5 3 5 5 4 5 5 ___ ___   A) 5,6 B) 6,5 C) 5,5 D) 5,4 E) 5,7

12. 20 17 10 10 14 11 10 10 ___ ___   A) 9,7 B) 6,7 C) 9,4 D) 8,6 E) 8,5

13. 2 15 28 41 ___ ___   A) 54,67 B) 55,68 C) 53,66 D) 55,68 E) 62,71

14. 75 10 65 20 55 30 ___ ___   A) 45,30 B) 45,40 C) 40,45 D) 55,30 E) 35,40

15. 90 60 80 70 70 80 ___ ___   A) 50,90 B) 40,90 C) 70,90 D) 60,90 E) 50.80

16. 34 32 34 33 34 34 ___ ___   A) 33,36 B) 34,34 C) 34,36 D) 35,35 E) 34,35

17. 8 5 7 16 9 11 24 ___ ___   A) 12,14 B) 11,14 C) 13,15 D) 14,15 E) 12,13

18. 14 19 16 18 18 17 20 16 ___ ___   A) 20,13 B) 22,15 C) 24,17 D) 22,16 E) 23,15

19. 7 3 6 14 9 12 21 15 ___ ___   A) 20,27 B) 22,29 C) 18,27 D) 18,28 E) 23,28

20. 8 3 11 8 14 13 17 18 ___ ___   A) 20,23 B) 20,24 C) 21,23 D) 22,24 E) 24,26

21. 2 4 0 6 8 0 10 ___ ___   A) 0,14 B) 0,10 C) 12,10 D) 12,14 E) 12,0

22. 8 8 10 8 8 9 8 ___ ___   A) 8,7 B) 8,8 C) 8,6 D) 9,8 E) 8,9

23. 47 39 31 23 ___ ___   A) 16,7 B) 15,8 C) 15,7 D) 14,7 E) 13,6

24. 5 6 8 11 15 20 ___ ___   A) 25,34 B) 27,35 C) 26,35 D) 25,31 E) 26,33

COMPLETE PRACTICE TEST #6
Part D – Following Oral Instructions

Directions

On this section of the test, the Exam Administrator will read questions/instructions aloud to the group of test takers. These oral instructions will direct you to write/mark certain items in your test booklet, which in turn will lead you to the correct answer(s). Finally, you will be verbally instructed to mark the correct answer(s) on your answer sheet. You must answer exclusively based upon what you hear – there are no questions for you to read.

The following pages of this practice test are samples of the test booklet pages on which you will write/mark as verbally instructed. Mark your answers on the Complete Practice Test Answer Sheet in the Following Oral Instructions section.

To practice realistically, you must either listen to the questions on the author's recording or have someone read them aloud to you. Do not look over the questions before taking the practice test. Once you have completed the practice test, you should then review the questions you missed in order to determine what caused you to miss them. This review should enable you to be more successful on similar questions next time.

The author's recording of all six Following Oral Directions practice tests is an ideal and convenient way to practice. The recorded questions are presented in the proper format, at the proper pace, and with proper diction. These recordings allow you to practice anytime and anywhere you wish. With these recordings, your practice – and in turn your success – will not be dependent upon someone else's schedule and whims. For details and ordering information, see the order form at the back of your book.

If someone will be reading the questions to you, he/she will find the questions for each practice test in the back of your book in the section entitled Following Oral Instructions – Practice Test Questions. The reader should carefully tear the questions out of your book in order to use them. The questions should be read at a rather slow and steady pace of approximately 75 words per minute and with proper diction. The reader should also pause between instructions/questions as directed in the wording of each question.

Once you complete the Following Oral Instructions section, you have finished this practice test, and you should then begin the next practice test in your book. Once you have completed all six practice tests plus the Extra Address Checking Practice Exercises as instructed, you should be fully prepared to excel on the actual exam.

Turn the page and begin when you are prepared to listen to the questions from the author's recording or from someone who will read the questions to you in the proper fashion.

Hint: Remember your strategies:
- *You will answer by marking number-letter combinations.*
- *Where you mark an answer on the answer sheet will not match the question number.*
- *Listen closely and attentively.*
- *Simply follow the instructions you hear – do not try to figure them out.*
- *Some questions will have multiple answers, and you must mark all of them.*
- *Mark your answers quickly and be ready to listen to the next question.*
- *Make identifying notes for later recall.*

COMPLETE PRACTICE TEST #6
Part D – Following Oral Instructions

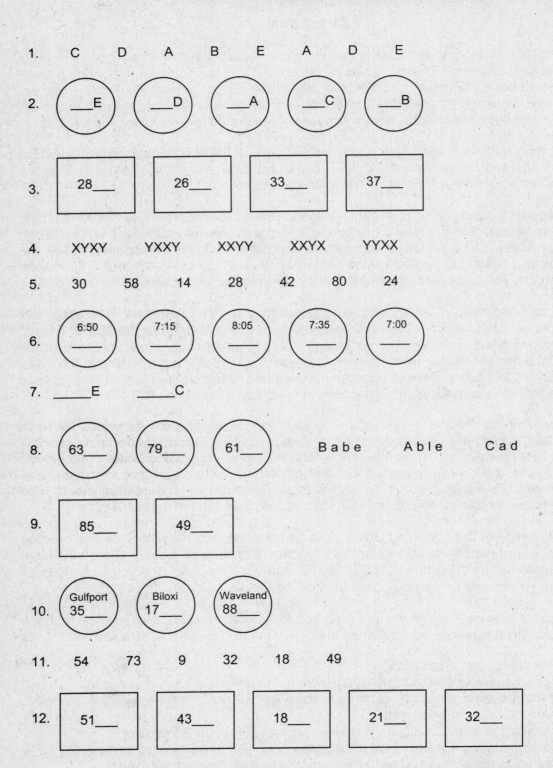

1.   C   D   A   B   E   A   D   E

2.   (__E)   (__D)   (__A)   (__C)   (__B)

3.   [28___]   [26___]   [33___]   [37___]

4.   XYXY   YXXY   XXYY   XXYX   YYXX

5.   30   58   14   28   42   80   24

6.   (6:50 __)   (7:15 __)   (8:05 __)   (7:35 __)   (7:00 __)

7.   ____E   ____C

8.   (63___)   (79___)   (61___)   B a b e   A b l e   C a d

9.   [85___]   [49___]

10. (Gulfport 35___)   (Biloxi 17___)   (Waveland 88___)

11. 54   73   9   32   18   49

12. [51___]   [43___]   [18___]   [21___]   [32___]

13.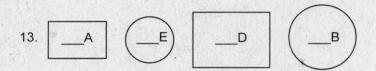

14. 51___   32___   78___   12___   29___

15. A D D I C T E D
     ___   ___   ___   ___

16. 62   64   86   32   16   75   84   81   26

17. ooxx   xxoo   xoxo   oxox   xxxx

18. [23___]   [82___]   [48___]   [23___]

19. 48___   39___   52___

Extra Address Checking Practice Exercises

As discussed previously, preparing for the Address Checking section of the exam is much like preparing for an athletic event. Extreme speed, subtle muscle control, and superior eye/hand coordination are demanded. Consequently, more practice is needed for this critical section of the exam. For these reasons, we have included extra Address Checking practice exercises for you in addition to those already provided as part of the complete practice tests.

Following are ten extra Address Checking practice exercises that you should complete in addition to the Address Checking sections on your complete practice tests. When taking these additional exercises, follow the same directions given for the Address Checking sections of your complete practice tests. As before, it is imperative that you practice realistically. You must time yourself for precisely six minutes as you attempt to answer the 95 questions. Our Timed Practice Test CD is a convenient way to practice realistically and time yourself precisely. When taking these extra exercises, mark your answers on the Extra Address Checking Answer Sheets provided in the back of the book.

As noted earlier on the complete practice tests, these Address Checking practice exercises are spread across two pages to match the actual format of the exam. Also, the questions are presented in a font that matches the actual exam. Even though this font is more challenging, we have formatted the practice exercises realistically for your benefit.

The book provides a total of 16 Address Checking exercises – six as part of the complete practice tests and ten as extra exercises. However, you have sufficient answer sheets to take 70 Address Checking tests. As previously discussed, you are expected to repeat the exercises up to five times each in order to complete all the answer sheets. However, each time you repeat an exercise, it should seem like a new one. You should not remember the exercise from the first time around. By the time you do all the other exercises before repeating the first one again, you will have dealt with over 3,000 individual addresses. In the midst of this confusing muddle of addresses, there is almost no way you could remember any of the addresses from the first time around – it should indeed seem like a brand new exercise.

Extra Address Checking Practice Exercise #1

1.	3080 Johnson Ave	3080 Johnson Ave
2.	Troy NY	Troy NY
3.	Shreveport La 89712	Shreveport La 89712
4.	868 Dogwood Dr	686 Dogwood Dr
5.	605 Magnolia Ln	605 Magnolia Ln
6.	579 Devon Way	579 Devon Way
7.	2117 Wheaton Ct	2117 Wheaton Ct
8.	Toledo OH 34127	Toledo OH 38147
9.	281 Pass Rd	281 Passe Rd
10.	2119 Heidenheim Ave	2119 Heidenheim Ave
11.	8074 Meade Mt	8074 Mend Mt
12.	Memphis Tenn	Memphas Tenn
13.	1812 Churchill Pl	1812 Churchill Pl
14.	Richmond VA 40112	Richmond VA 41120
15.	357 N Marion St	357 N Marion St
16.	9009 Southwind Apt C	9009 Southwind Apt C
17.	Tucson Az	Tuscon Az
18.	5071 Church St	5071 Church St
19.	9617 N Waron Rd	9617 N Waron Rd
20.	7944 Charles Ct	7944 Charles Ct
21.	Lowell MA	Louella MA
22.	437 Sweet Bay	437 Sweet Bay
23.	Nashua NH 81721	Nashua NH 81721
24.	110 Gandy Cir	110 Gandy Cir
25.	854 Langley Pt	899 Langley Pt
26.	665 Fontaine Rd	665 Fontaine Rd
27.	2048 Canal Ct	2048 Canal Ct
28.	Salem Or 87912	Salem Or 87912
29.	2740 Lancaster Rd	2740 Lanbaster Rd
30.	1950 Glendale Pl	1950 Glendale Pl
31.	Vancleave Ms	Vanclove MS
32.	5953 Norris Cir	5953 Sarah Cir
33.	6844 Alverado Dr	6844 Alverado Dr
34.	312 Joseph Ave	312 Joseph Ave
35.	2777 Washer Way	2777 Washer Way
36.	431 Pecan Village	431 Cedar Village
37.	Cleveland OH 13147	Cleveland OH 13147
38.	4500 Waveland Ave	3500 Waveland Ave
39.	Greenville NY	Greentown NY
40.	405 Merigold Dr	405 Merigold Dr
41.	502 Lewis Ct	502 Lewis Ln
42.	23 Keyser Ln	23 Keyser Rd
43.	Henderson Neb 71509	Henderson Neb 71509
44.	2784 Pringle Cir	2784 Pringle Cir
45.	6676 Cortez Cir	6876 Cortez Dr
46.	1322 Sherwood Drive	1322 Sherwood Drive
47.	1815 61st Ave	1815 61st Ave
48.	389 E Harrison Cir	389 E Harison Cir

49.	McComb MS 87195	McComb MN 87195
50.	1623 25th Ave	1623 25th Ave
51.	709 Bailey Rd	709 Bailey Rd
52.	863 W Beach	863 E Beach
53.	Jackson Tenn	Jackson Tenn
54.	4670 Switzer Rd	4670 Switzer Rd
55.	110 Valentine Blvd	110 Valentine Blvd
56.	Hampton VA	Campton VA
57.	4343 Thompson Ct	4334 Thompson Ct
58.	4285 E Beach Blvd	4285 E Beach Blvd
59.	6140 Creastview Pl	6140 Creastview Pl
60.	Leland Ark 98187	Leland Ark 98187
61.	475 Randall Hwy	4758 Randall Hwy
62.	3213 Sadler Apt B	3213 Sadler Apt D
63.	637 Betts Cir	637 Betts Cir
64.	1713 Woodward Ct	1713 Woodward Ct
65.	Monticello WA	Montipello WA
66.	766 Bay Oaks Dr	766 Bay Oaks Dr
67.	4142 Nottingham Rd	8027 Nottingham Rd
68.	105 Darran Way	105 Darran Way
69.	Clearwater Fla 72187	Clearwater Fla 72187
70.	Uniontown Penn	Union Penn
71.	2318 Demart Grove	2318 Federal Grove
72.	856 W Railroad	856 S Railroad
73.	123 Shiloh Apts	123 Shiloh Apts
74.	1006 Vista Cir	1000 Vista Cir
75.	Waveland Ca 28919	Waveland Ca 28919
76.	9217 Bluedon Rd	9217 Bluedon Rd
77.	Hartford Ct 11872	Hartford Ct 11427
78.	144 Allendale Way	144 Allendale Way
79.	2882 Pitkin St	2882 Pitkin St
80.	467 Bonita Ct	467 Bonita Ct
81.	Casper Wy 10482	Casper Wy 10482
82.	7190 Menge Ave	7140 Menge Ave
83.	809 Teagarden Ct	809 Teagarden Ct
84.	214 Nevada Rd	214 Nevada Rd
85.	Indinapolis IN	Indianpolis IN
86.	3343 Oakhill Blvd	3333 Oakhill Blvd
87.	9374 Fairley Pl	9777 Fairley Pl
88.	359 Tabitha Rd	359 Tabitha Rd
89.	101 Sycamore Ct	101 Sycamore Ct
90.	Kalamazoo Mi	Kalamaraso Mi
91.	5 No Pine Garden Apts	5 No Pine Garden Apts
92.	9017 Jkvl Hwy	9017 Jvkl Hwy
93.	1401 Plummer	1401 Plummer
94.	113 Ala Dr	113 Ala Dr
95.	Republican Rdon	Republican Rdon

Extra Address Checking Practice Exercise #2

1.	217 Fullerman Ave	217 Fullermon Ave
2.	3280 Raymond Rd	3280 Raymond
3.	687 Lower Montclair	687 Lower Montclair
4.	Jackson MS	Jackson MASS
5.	877 W Shann Cove	877 W Shann Cove
6.	7811 NW Capitol St	7811 NW Capital St
7.	Pottstown Penn 38127	Pottstown Penn 38127
8.	7662 Nicholas Ave	7662 Nicholas Ave
9.	5291 SW Howard	5291 SE Howard
10.	2127 Edgewater Plaza	2127 Edgewater Plaza
11.	9877 Broken Arrow Rd	9877 Broken Arrow Rd
12.	780 Dowdy Ave	780 Dowdy Ave
13.	Harrison AK 57002	Harrison AK 57002
14.	718 Courthouse Rd	718 Courthouse Pl
15.	3821 West Wego	3821 West Wego
16.	605 41st Avenue	608 41st Avenue
17.	218 Oliver Ct	218 Oliver Ct
18.	3685 E Angelo Ct	3685 E Angelo Ct
19.	Savannah GA 82170	Savannnah GA 82170
20.	8821 Cowan Rd	8821 Cowan Rd
21.	Bertha Md	Bertha Md
22.	2178 Dixie Park	2178 Dixie Park
23.	127 Arnholt Ct	127 Arnholt Ct
24.	3130 Adams Way	3130 Adams Way
25.	E 44th St	919 E 44th St
26.	321 Williamsburg	312 Williamsburg
27.	8510 O'Donnell Rd	8510 O'Donnell Rd
28.	9666 Whitefield Ave	9966 Whitefield Ave
29.	520 E Lucien	520 E Lucien
30.	924 Washington Hts	924 Washington Hts
31.	Gulfport Ms 38721	Gulfport Ms 38721
32.	3330 Lucien Plant	3330 Lucien Place
33.	794 Franklin Ave	794 Franklin Ave
34.	219 S Howard	219 S Howard
35.	Waterbury Conn	Waterboy Conn
36.	927 Alexander Ct	9277 Alexander Ct
37.	861 Lenore Way	861 Lenore Way
38.	204 W Helmut	204 W Helmut
39.	717 Wilcox Rd	717 Wilcox Rd
40.	Warner Robbins GA	Warner Robbins GA
41.	6187 Williams Ave	6187 Williams Ave
42.	4350 Katonah Blvd	4305 Katonah Blvd
43.	618 West Railroad	618 West Rampart
44.	1518 Megan Rd	1518 Megan Rd
45.	Pasco WA	Pasco WA
46.	921 Pinehurst Ct.	921 Pinehurst Cr
47.	1723 22nd Ave	1722 23rd Ave
48.	1702 Alston Ave	1702 Alston Ave

Continued

49.	119 Connie Dr	1119 Connie Dr
50.	Rome GA	Rome GA
51.	321 Elephant Plaza	321 Elephant Plaza
52.	Waterloo Iowa 43210	Waterloo Iowo 43210
53.	433 Wilson Blvd	433 Wilson Blvd
54.	888 Maple Ct	888 Mapel Ct
55.	Bayou Oaks AL 62149	Bayou Oaks AL 62149
56.	3121-A 6th Ave	3121-A 6th Ave
57.	5 Villa Cove Dr	5 Villa Cove Dr
58.	Tyler Tx	Tyler Tx
59.	1903 Polk	1903 Polk
60.	4213 Indiana St	3213 Indiana St
61.	307 45th Street	30 45th Street
62.	47 Iris Lane	470 Iris Lane
63.	315 S Pine Dr	315 S Pine Dr
64.	4300 Broad Av	4300 Broad Av
65.	Dyersburg TN 79898	Dyersburg TN 78988
66.	South Saucier	South Saucier
67.	35 E Pier	35 E Pier St
68.	2417 Burke Dr	2417 Burke Dr.
69.	602 Teagarden Rd	602 Teagarden Rd
70.	Magnolia MS	Magnolia MS
71.	2605 Tandy Village Dr	2506 Tandy Village Dr
72.	22 Cuandet Rd	22 Cuandet Rd
73.	2B Victory St	2 A Victory St
74.	Ichabod MA 00312	Ichabod MA 00312
75.	1 Government Plaza	11 Government Plaza
76.	Just West AZ	Just West AZ
77.	Chula Vista CA	Chula Vista CA
78.	307 Sandy Hook Ln	307 Sandy Nook Ln
79.	#37 Vidiala Rd	#37 Vidiala Rd
80.	Hilo HI 56490	Hilo HI 54690
81.	3133 Hunter Av	3133 Hunter Av
82.	409D Word Cove	409D Word Cove
83.	99 Necaise Crsg	99 Necaise Crossing
84.	Cherry Hill NJ 00327	Cherry Hill NJ 00327
85.	743 E Beech	743 E Beech
86.	1029 Barklay	1029 Barklay
87.	139 W Second	139 E Second
88.	Elkton KY	Elkin KY
89.	201 Vista View	201 Vista View
90.	Laketown FL 32608	Laketown FL 32608
91.	325 W North	325 W North
92.	217 Fireflower Trail	217 Fireflower Trail
93.	Springfield MA 20989	Springfield MA
94.	393 Church Av	333 Church Av
95.	1030 O'Neill	1030 O'Neill

Extra Address Checking Practice Exercise #3

1.	905 Necaise Crossing	905 Necaise Crossing
2.	261 Sedwick Dr	2617 Sedwick Pl
3.	956 Balboa Cir	956 Balboa Cir
4.	Dallas Tx 81770	Dallas Tx 81770
5.	4510 Mallere Blvd	4510 Mollere Blvd
6.	203-A Tarpon Cove	203-C Tarpon Cove
7.	912 Barnacle Blvd	912 Barnacle Blvd
8.	126 Iberville St	126 Iberville St
9.	Las Vegas Nv	Las Vegas Nv
10.	4028 Espy Avenue	4028 Espy Avon
11.	317 W Tarpon Ct	317 E Tarpon Ct
12.	Orlando Flint	Orlando Florida
13.	282 Dixie Dr	282 Dixie Dr
14.	458 Harrison Ct	480 Harrison Ct
15.	Honolulu HI	Honolulu HA
16.	8898 Partridge Pl	8898 Partridge Pl
17.	152 Willow Av	152 Willow Av
18.	Concord NH 05712	Concord NH 05712
19.	449 N Shore Pl	449 N Shore Pl
20.	701 Pecanwood Ave	701 Pecanwood
21.	Poria IL 87612	Peoria IL 87621
22.	1272 Angela Cir	1272 Angela Cir
23.	6161 Daugherty Rd	6161 Daugherty Rd
24.	Billing Mt	Billings Mt
25.	734 Hopkins Blvd	734 Hopkins Blvd
26.	4412 W Railroad	4412 W Railroad
27.	116 Seashore Ave	116 Seashore Dr
28.	Joplin Mo 37812	Joplin Mo 37812
29.	913 Yorkshire Dr	911 Yorkshire Dr
30.	310-A Greenwood Ln	310-A Greenwood Ln
31.	9465 Klondyke Ct	9465 Klondyke Ct
32.	Asheville NC 10273	Asheville NC 10273
33.	257 Southern Cir	275 Southern Cir
34.	3338 Bowen Ave	3388 Bowen Ave
35.	348 E Morton Ave	348 Morton Ave
36.	Altoona Penn	Altoona Penn
37.	2460 Walda Pl	2460 Walda Pl
38.	956 Orange Rdons	956 Orange Road
39.	188 Fenton Blvd	188 Fenton Blvd
40.	Amarillo TX 78123	Amarillo TN 78123
41.	630 Edgewater Park	630 Edgewater Park
42.	9794 Commission Rd	9794 Commission Rd
43.	2212 Carwford Way	1121 Crawford Way
44.	Akron OH	Akron OH
45.	211 Arnold Cir	211 Arnold Cir
46.	0015 South Hwy	0015 No Hwy
47.	308 Braden	308 Braiden
48.	16 Lysander Rd	16 Lysander Rd

Extra Address Checking Practice Exercise #3
Continued

49.	1700 NW 25 St	1700 SW 25 St
50.	43 Ada Ave	43 Ada Ave
51.	2 Daltry Ln	2 Daltry Ln
52.	1064 Oregon Blvd	1046 Oregon Blvd'
53.	7214 Roosevelt Rd	7214 Roosevelt Rd
54.	950 Willoughby St	955 Willoughby St
55.	37 Carlton Ave	337 Carlton Ave
56.	Centralia MO	Centralia MI
57.	35 N McMinn Rd	35 S McMinn Rd
58.	Delta MI 90474	Delta MI 90474
59.	20 Comedy St	20 Comedy St
60.	Lead SC	Lead SC
61.	Navejo NM	Navajo NM
62.	10 NE Whitney Ave	10 NE Whitney Ave
63.	Rainsville MT 56599	Rainsville MT 56599
64.	381 Beaver St	381 Beaver
65.	039 Lyra Ave	039 Lyre Ave
66.	Yellow Springs OH	Yellow Springs OH
67.	90 SW Kennedy Blvd	90 SW Kennedy Blvd
68.	8020 S Jones St	8002 S Jones St
69.	Los Chavez Az	Los Chavez Az
70.	116 Lathum Dr	161 Lathum Dr
71.	Deadwood City SD	Deadwood City SD
72.	145 Nichols Pl	145 Nichols Pl
73.	18 W Courthouse Rd	18 W Courthouse Rd
74.	Jersey City NJ 00251	Jersey City NJ 00251
75.	Kiowa OK	Kio OK 26241
76.	N Jessup Blvd	N Jessup Blvd
77.	113 Bunker Hill St	113 Bunker Hill St
78.	Carthage NY	Carson NY
79.	79 Mathers St	79 Mathers St
80.	13 Couch Rd	13 Couch Rd
81.	Mt Sinai NY 00181	Mt Sinai NY 00181
82.	9100 S 33rd St	9100 33rd St
83.	5821 Kavanaugh	5821 Kavanaugh
84.	S Uno Av Suite 512	S University Ave Suite 512
85.	7701 Kanis Rd	7701 Kanis Rd
86.	6701 N 12	6701 N 12 St
87.	16301 Raines Rd	16301 Kaines Rd
88.	907 Trammell Rd	907 Trammell Rd
89.	8800 Landers Rd	8800 Landers Rd
90.	6301 Murray	6301 Muray
91.	Arcada CA	Arcadia CA
92.	McCain AR	McCain AK
93.	3 Hearthside Dr	3 Hearthside Dr
94.	Roanoke VA	Roanoke VA
95.	610 S Rock	610 N Rock

Extra Address Checking Practice Exercise #4

1.	4136 Leonard Rd	4136 Leonard Rd
2.	758 Alexander Ct	758 Alexander Ct
3.	3119 Richardson Blvd	3119 Richardson Blvd
4.	257 Bennet Ave	2579 Bennet Ave
5.	Butler AL 15208	Butler Al 15208
6.	772 Pointview Rd	772 Pointview PL
7.	7681 Oakridge Ave	7681 Oakridge Ave
8.	Amity N 27701	Amity 11 27701
9.	317 Brandis Ln	317 Brandywine Ln
10.	7920 Alligood Hts	7920 Alligood Hts
11.	487 N Lakeview Dr	487 N Lakeview Dr
12.	3652 Williams Way	3652 Williams Way
13.	Concord CA	Concord CA
14.	4135 Morrison Rd	4351 Morrison Rd
15.	536 Strickland Hwy	536 Strickland Hwy
16.	285 Vanover East	285 Vanover West
17.	Honolulu HA 32157	Honolala HA 32157
18.	244 Johnson Cross Rds	244 Johnson Cross Rds
19.	4187 Bachmann Ln	4187 Bachman Ln
20.	3172 Walton Rd	3172 Walton Rd
21.	3217 Comstock Ct	3217 Comstock Ct
22.	Bronson MI 14790	Bronson MI 19470
23.	9217 Ferrell Rd	9217 Ferrell Rd
24.	434 Bassett Ln	434 Bassett Ct
25.	8181 Poole Ct	8181 Poole Ct
26.	Boulder CO	Boulder CA
27.	271 St Anne St	271 St Anne St
28.	3348 Satterwhite Way	3348 Satterwhite Way
29.	7916 E Wesley Rd	7982 E Wesley Rd
30.	358 Immokalee St	358 Immokallee St
31.	Dubuque IA 72178	Dubuque IA 72178
32.	421 Yarbrough Ln	421 E Yarbrough Ln
33.	3794 Copeland Av	3794 Copeland Av
34.	363 Nicholl Pl	363 Nicholl Pl
35.	3996 Kochman Ct	3996 Kockmain Ct
36.	Albert Minn	Albert Minn
37.	3784 Partridge Rd	3784 Partridge Rd
38.	426 Moffit Ln	4007 Moffit Ln
39.	Cornelius Or	Cornelius Or
40.	4668 Bishop Rd	4668 Bishop Rd
41.	8271 S Micanopy	8271 E Micanopy
42.	Essex MASS 37195	Essex MS 37195
43.	3633 Bullington Way	3633 Bullington Way
44.	3469 Jacobson Pl	3469 Jacobson Pl
45.	Bethany OK	Bethany OK
46.	472 Latimore	472 Latimore
47.	235 W Templeton	235 W Tomtown
48.	Lawrence Kan 26910	Lawrencee Kan 26910

49.	2398 Wallace Rd	2398 Wallace Rd
50.	8978 Maslin Rd	8798 Maslin Rd
51.	3044 W Jeffcoat	3044 W Jeffcoat
52.	Apple SD 23689	Apple ND 23689
53.	263 Tillman Ave	263 Tillman Ave
54.	3166 Wakins Way	3166 Watkins Way
55.	335 Newberry Rd	335 Newberry Rd
56.	217 Brooker Ct	217 Brooker Ct
57.	Waco Tx 21507	Waco Tx 21507
58.	3056 Weatherspoon	3056 Weatherspoon Rd
59.	8326 S Reddick Rd	8326 S Reddick Rd
60.	2316 Higinbot Ln	2316 Higinbot Ln
61.	399 Williston Hwy	399 Williston Way
62.	818 McIntosh Pl	818 McIntosh Pl
63.	Gorham NH	Gorham NH
64.	2107 Kelley Ave	2107 Kelley Ave
65.	822 Broad Blvd	822 Broad Blvd
66.	5817 E Fairbanks	5817 W Fairbanks
67.	8127 SW Archer Ave	8166 SW Archer Ave
68.	Cortland N Y	Cortband N Y
69.	8021 N Garet	8021 N Garet
70.	7301 Markham Rd	7301 Markham Rd
71.	Batania OH 7846	Batavia OH 18476
72.	602 Canal Rd	602 E Canal Rd
73.	353 Chandler Dr	353 Chandler Dr
74.	761 N 18th St	761 N 18th St
75.	455 Grale Ct	455 Grable Cir
76.	1351 Westover Rd	1351 Westover Rd
77.	Abbeville SC	Abbotville SC
78.	6834 Phillips Ln	6834 Phillips Ln
79.	958 NE Clement	9581 NE Clement
80.	378 Limpert Ave	378 Kimpoll Ave
81.	1205 Georgia Cir	1205 Georgia Cir
82.	Camelot Tenn 10234	Camelot Tenn 10234
83.	825 Oliver Ct	825 Oliver Ct
84.	7821 Robinson Way	7821 Roberts Way
85.	4925 Sardinas	4925 Sardinas
86.	205 SE 32nd Pl	205 SE 32nd Pl
87.	Bryan Tx 17726	Bryan Tx 17726
88.	1214 Keener Rd	1214 Keener Rd
89.	3217 Cowan Rd	3172 Cowan Rd
90.	1005 Warrick Ln	1005 Warneck Ln
91.	Kent RI	Kent RI
92.	521 Loreany Rd	521 Loreany Rd
93.	498 Casady St	498 Casady St
94.	Austin Tx	Auston Tx
95.	141 Wiggs St	141 Wiggs St

Extra Address Checking Practice Exercise #5

1.	251 E Brooklawn	251 W Brookslawn
2.	Nashua NH 88279	Nashua NH 88829
3.	3681 Sloane Av	3681 Sloane Av
4.	449 Hawthorne Dr	449 Hawthorne Dr
5.	3512 Wiltmore Pl	3512 Wiltmore Pl
6.	1537 Waterloo Ct	1887 Waterloo Ct
7.	Raleigh NC	Raleigh NC
8.	7093 Brunswick Rd	7093 Brunswick Rd
9.	648 N Berkshire	648 N Brookshire
10.	6601 Queens Park Av	6601 Kings Park Av
11.	Spokane WA 10199	Spokane WA 10199
12.	993 Briarcrest Pl	993 Briarcrest Pl
13.	1657 S Traymore Rd	1657 S Frymore Rd
14.	4667 Franklin Blvd	4667 Franklin Blvd
15.	Winston-Salem NC	Winston NC
16.	2011 Lorian Rd	2011 Lorain Rd
17.	2937 Richarson Ln	2933 Richardson Ln
18.	929 Helwick St	929 Helquick St
19.	7447 Habersham Cir	7447 Habersham Cir
20.	Tulsa OK 92347	Tulso OK 92347
21.	985 Dangelo Rd	985 Dangelo Rd
22.	1056 N Violet St	1056 N Velvet St
23.	887 Crestton Way	887 Crestton Way
24.	York PA	York PA
25.	530 NW Gagne Ct	530 NE Gagne Ct
26.	4390 Kepple Pl	4390 Kepple Pl
27.	5093 Columbian Rt	5093 Columbo Rt
28.	547 E Sanders Ter	547 E Sanders Ter
29.	3802 Mitterand Rd	3802 Mitterand Ct
30.	Reno NV 75117	Reno NV 75117
31.	798 Scioto Pl	798 Scioto Pl
32.	1932 St Francis St	1948 St Francis St
33.	9515 Granton Hwy	9515 Granton Hwy
34.	Pocatello ID	Pocatjello ID
35.	726 W Matilda Ave	726 W Matilda Ave
36.	1462 Kenner Ct	1462 Kenner Ct
37.	Durham NC 33487	Durham NC 33487
38.	3522 Rockside Rd	3522 Rocky Rd
39.	3161 Woodcrest Dr	3161 Woodcross Dr
40.	5617 Cartmont Av	5617 Cartmont Av
41.	4005 N Whitney	4005 S Whitney
42.	Ft Smith AR	Ft Smith AR
43.	423 Brigham Young	423 Brigham Young
44.	4467 Solands Ct	4444 Solands Ct
45.	2650 Watertown Pl	2650 Watertown Pt
46.	Boise ID 67710	Boise ID 67770
47.	1011 Baltic Lake Rd	1011 Baltic Lake Rd
48.	135 Bradburry Ln	135 Bradbury Ln

Extra Address Checking Practice Exercise #5

Continued

49.	4140 S Holly Av	4140 S Holly Av
50.	Houston TX 96781	Houston TX 97816
51.	6870 Liberty Ln	6870 Liberty Ln
52.	2307 E Fulton Cir	2307 E Fulton Cir
53.	835 Hipple Pt	8357 N Hipple Pt
54.	Troy NY 24420	Troy NY 24420
55.	6307 Strathallan Dr	6307 Stawhallan Dr
56.	379 Vermillion Av	379 Vermillion At
57.	871 Belgrande Cir	871 Belgrande Cir
58.	Joplin MO 30907	Joplins MO 30907
59.	932 Ranchland Manor	932 Ranchland Manor
60.	464 S Ramano Ave	464 S Ramano Ave
61.	943 Ladner Ct	934 Lander Ct
62.	9671 Savarase Rd	9671 Savarase Rd
63.	Lansing MI	Lansing MI
64.	2217 Clifton Pl	2217 Clifton Pl
65.	451 N Whitson Rd	4510 N Whitson Rd
66.	7778 Coleporter St	7778 Coleporter St
67.	Atlanta GA 75110	Atlanta GA 75110
68.	6171 SW Pate Hwy	6171 SW Patson Hwy
69.	3427 Palazzo Ln	3427 Palazzo Ln
70.	Oakland CA 68982	Oakland CA 68982
71.	278 Taylor Heights	278 Taylor Hwy
72.	2019 Quail Ridge Rd	2019 Quail Ridge Rd
73.	4207 Gibbons Ct	4207 Gibbens Ct
74.	8871 Amax Pt	8871 Amax Pt
75.	Wilkes-Barre PA	Wilkes-Bart PA
76.	9878 Donnelly Cir	9878 Donnaly Cir
77.	4031 Danford Rd	4031 Danford Rd
78.	3578 E Blanch Av	3578 E Blanch Av
79.	9877 Wolf River Run	9877 Wolf River Run
80.	Oshkosh WI	Oskhash WI
81.	6801 Broken Arrow	6801 Broken Arrow
82.	8456 Reilley Rd	8456 Reilley Run
83.	Richmond VA 99871	Richmond VT 99871
84.	4737 Duffy Ct	4737 Duffy Ct
85.	581 Hover Hwy	581 Hover Hwy
86.	Wichita KS	Wichita KS
87.	961 W Bardson St	961 W Bardson St
88.	9919 Meadow Brook Dr	9999 Meadow Brook Dr
89.	6902 Sugarbeet Ln	6902 Sugarbeet Ln
90.	Philadelphia PA 92731	Philadelphia PA 92731
91.	2364 S Kranapple Ct	2300 S Kranapple Ct
92.	1451 E Superior Rd	1451 E Superior Pl
93.	5075 Hucklebee Ln	5075 Hucklebee Ln
94.	Warren OH	Warren OH
95.	925 Jamaca Pl	925 Jamanaca Pl

Extra Address Checking Practice Exercise #6

1.	2222 Chesterfield Av	2222 Chesterfield Av
2.	886 Crossbow Blvd	886 Crossbow Blvd
3.	1720 E Pearl Rd	1720 E Pearl Rd
4.	Gulfport MN 39701	Gulfport MS 39701
5.	5460 W Gifford Ln	5460 W Gifford Ln
6.	Miami Fl 49708	Miami FL 49708
7.	1518 Mapleleaf Av	1518 Mapleleaf Av
8.	331 Clearwater Cir	331 Clearwater Ct
9.	1920 W Mohawk	1920 Mohawk
10.	Eugene OR	Eugene OR
11.	3033 Forest Hill Dr	3033 Forest Hill St
12.	6872 SE Huth Pl	6872 SW Huth Pl
13.	Lafayette LA	Lafayette LA
14.	398 Golden Way	398 Golden Lane
15.	Tampa Fl 68777	Tampa FL 68777
16.	401 Lake Sharon Blvd	401 Lake Sharon Blvd
17.	2017 Darnworth St	2017 Darnword St
18.	577 W Zardmon	577 W Zardmon
19.	Hampton VA	Hampton VA
20.	3171 W Goller Rd	3171 W Goller Rd
21.	5781 Piermont Pl	5718 Piermont Pl
22.	Moline IL 80001	Moline IL 80001
23.	789 Hildana Rd	789 Hildana Rd
24.	921 Coffinberry Ct	921 Coffinberry Ct
25.	York PA 73997	York PA 73999
26.	700 S River Oaks	700 S River Oaks
27.	921 Riceplace Way	921 Riceplace Way
28.	8421 Derbyshire Rd	8421 Derbyshire Rd
29.	Bangor ME 39108	Bangor MA 39108
30.	9387 E Grandview	9387 E Grandview
31.	1467 Sunrise Cir	1367 Sunrise Ct
32.	6639 Beverly Dr	6639 Beverly St
33.	Akron OH 11178	Akron OH 11178
34.	410 Alexander Rd	410 Alexander Rd
35.	951 National Hwy	951 National Hwy
36.	711 E Harvard Av	711 E Harvard Pl
37.	Dallas 93217	Dallas 93217
38.	9771 Freedman St	9771 Freedman Rd
39.	321 Stilmore Rd	321 Fillmore Rd
40.	Camden NJ 88970	Camden NJ 88970
41.	2700 Cedartree Avon	2700 Cedartree Ave
42.	Chicago IL	Chicago IN
43.	3095 Augustine Cir	3095 Augustine Cir
44.	248 Atkins Rd	248 Atkins Rd
45.	310 S Colebright	310 N Colebright
46.	2660 Richmond Ln	2660 Richmond Ln
47.	3681 Sloane Av	3681 Sloane Av
48.	497 E Hawthorne	497 W Hawthorne

49.	Danburry Ct	Danbury Ct
50.	4005 Yorkshire Rd	4005 Yorkshire Rd
51.	236 Demington Ct	236 Demington Ct
52.	2571 E Ashurst Rd	2571 W Ashurst Rd
53.	Andrews SC 14271	Andrews SC 14271
54.	631 SW Glenallen	631 SW Glenallen
55.	524 Chicken Ln	524 Chicken Ln
56.	2818 Cyress AV	2818 Cypress Av
57.	7104 Washington Blvd	7104 Washington
58.	Amarillo TX	Amarillo TX
59.	2820 E Parkhaven Rd	2820 E Parkhaven Rd
60.	6262 Woodward	6262 Woodward
61.	3132 Clearview Pl	3142 Clearview Pl
62.	840 Richmond Park	840 Richmond Pky
63.	Nashville TX 87902	Nashville TX 87902
64.	6032 Coventry Rd	6032 Coventry Rd
65.	1106 Genesee St	1106 Gentree St
66.	Amherst NH 77733	Amherst NH 77733
67.	609 Gertrude Pl	609 Gertrude Ct
68.	1114 Vandemar	1114 Vandemar
69.	Portsman RI	Portsman RI
70.	1800 Ridgewood Way	1801 Ridgewood Way
71.	1789 Winchester Rd	1789 Winchester Pl
72.	3440 Buckingham Pl	3440 Buckingham Ct
73.	Gettsburg Penn	Gettsburg Penn
74.	1506 Robindale Avon	1506 Robindale Ave
75.	909 Mapleboro Rd	909 Mapleboro Rd
76.	139 Triskett Ct	139 Triskett Ct
77.	1745 Emerson Way	1745 N Emerson Way
78.	Berkley CA 10712	Berkley CA 10712
79.	Eastbourne Hwy	Eastbourne Hwy
80.	2244 Fairlawn Cir	2244 Fairlawn Cir
81.	413 Shirley Pl	413 Shirley Pl
82.	Cleveland OH 21710	Cleveland OH 87210
83.	835 Fratino St	835 Fratino St
84.	3005 Euclid Rd	3005 Euclid Rd
85.	Ellendale AZ 88798	Ellendale AZ 88998
86.	1002 Montford Pl	1002 Monabe Pl
87.	932 E Roycroft	932 SE Roycroft
88.	4266 Parkham Rd	4266 Parkham Rd
89.	845 Lecona	845 Lecona
90.	Bedford MASS	Bedford MS
91.	7707 Cantrell	7707 Cantrell
92.	301 Main	301 Main St
93.	91 Rodney Parham Rd	91 Rodney Parham Rd
94.	Laurel MS	Laurel MS
95.	100 Base Line Rd	100 Base Line Rd

Extra Address Checking Practice Exercise #7

1.	2825 Hilltop St	2825 Hills St
2.	317 N Keystone Hts	1317 N Keystone Hts
3.	Ogden UT 38721	Ogden UT 38721
4.	4809 Nightinggale St	4809 Nightingale St
5.	4426 Paradise Pt	4426 Paradise Pt
6.	Reserve NM	Reservation NM
7.	3349 Satsuma Ct	3349 Satsuma Ct
8.	750 Cardinal Ln	750 Cardinal Ln
9.	2305 N Rufus	2305 N Rufus Road
10.	Fayetteville WV	Fayetteville WV
11.	3378 Lommond Dr	3378 Lommond Dr
12.	144 Chautauqua Av	144 Chautauqua Av
13.	7081 Brinson Way	7081 Brinson Way
14.	Bixby OK	Bixby OH
15.	310 Hilliard Ct	310 Hilliard Ct
16.	750 Gatorbone Lake	750 Gatorfoot Lake
17.	000 Fulton Est	000 Fulton Est
18.	Providence RI 19217	Providence RI 19217
19.	47 High Ridge Estates	47 High Ridge Estate
20.	3511 Kendall Rd	3511 Kendall Rd
21.	2507 Lawrence Blvd	2507 Lawrence Blvd
22.	Baker MT	Baker MT
23.	467 Easterling Ave	467 Easterling Ave
24.	2554 Gadara LN	2554 Gadara LN
25.	Altoona Penn	Altoona
26.	468 Beloit Pl	468 Beloit Ct
27.	2531 Nelsons Rd	2531 Nelsons Rd
28.	4089 S Hillcreast	4809 S Hillcreast
29.	3253 E Palms Dr	3253 E Palms Dr
30.	100 Carol Dale Pl	100 Carol Dale Pl
31.	Coshocton Oh 42781	Coshocton Oh 42781
32.	4760 Schmidt Ave	4760 Schmidt St
33.	2133 Sanderson Ct	2133 Sanderson Ct
34.	276 W Orchid St	276 W Orchid St
35.	Waterloo MI	Waterloo MS
36.	60 Coventry Rd	600 Coventry Rd
37.	2147 McKinley Ct	2147 McKinley Ct
38.	661 East Queens	661 East Queens
39.	Doll MN	Doll MN
40.	2300 Valley View Dr	2300 Valley View Dr
41.	317 E Broadway Rd	317 E Broadway Rd
42.	Utica NY	Utica NJ
43.	8989 Yellowbrick Rd	8899 Yellowbrick Rd
44.	608 Camp Ave	608 Camp Ave
45.	Billings MT 32201	Billings MT 32201
46.	3009 Robin St	3009 Robin Pl
47.	39 Ace Hwy	29 Case Hwy
48.	Jackson Tenn 11201	Jackson Tenn 11201

Continued

49.	2773 Bogard Ct	2733 Bogard Ct
50.	3187 Rice Pl	3187 Rice Pl
51.	268 Harrison Ln	268 Harrison Ln
52.	Jackson MS	Jackson MN
53.	8210 Brentwood Way	8210 Brentwood Way
54.	516 Phillips Ave	5516 Phillips Ave
55.	3990 W Railroad	3990 W Railroad
56.	Harrisburg Penn 89721	Harrisburg Penn 89721
57.	425 Shavell Ln	425 Shavell Ln
58.	1807 Whitekamp St	1807 Whitekamp St
59.	Tampa Fl 92301	Tampa Fl 92301
60.	318 McConnell Ave	3180 McConnell Ave
61.	2584 Duddley Ct	2584 Dudley Ct
62.	1825 Tulane St	1924 Tulane St
63.	302 Wells Way	302 Wells Way
64.	4278 Mikatinas Rd	4278 Mikatinas Rd
65.	537 Anderson Ln	537 Anderson Ct
66.	Mobile Ala	Mobile Ala
67.	831 Mulberry St	813 Mulberry St
68.	2187 Cranberry Ct	2187 Cranberry Ct
69.	987 Randolph St	987 Randolph St
70.	Richardson MI	Richardson MI
71.	1235 Metairie Ave	1235 S Metairie Ave
72.	924 Bawarski Pl	924 Bawarski Pl
73.	2575 Johnson St	2755 Johnson St
74.	San Jose CA 98172	San Jose CA 98172
75.	7381 Converse Hwy	7381 Converse
76.	765 Sharp Pl	765 Sharp Pl
77.	2053 SW 23rd Terr	2053 SW 23rd Terr
78.	Temple TX 82170	Temple TX 82107
79.	2213 Pahnellanic Dr	2213 Pahnellanic Dr
80.	9765 Church St	9578 Church St
81.	9004 NW Shaw Rd	9004 NW Shaw Rd
82.	Montpelier Vt	Montpelier Vt
83.	705 Coundry St	705 Coundry Ave
84.	16-A Redbird Blvd	16-A Redbird Blvd
85.	2633 Central Av	2633 Central Av
86.	Tempe AK 32178	Tempe AK 32178
87.	2167 Grassy Lake	2167 Grassy Lake Ests
88.	3195 Magnolia St	3195 Magnolia Ave
89.	382 Robinson Rd	382 Robinson Rd
90.	5222 Shoemaker Ct	5222 Shoemaker Ct
91.	Portland OR	Portland OR
92.	435 Weathers Ln	435 Weathers Ln
93.	875 Tiefenbach	785 Tiefenbach
94.	16600 Glen Road	16600 Glen Ln
95.	160 Rancho Rd	160 Rancho Ra

Extra Address Checking Practice Exercise #8

1.	3700 Mayfield RD	3700 Mayfield RD
2.	Detroit MI 87301	Detroit MI 87310
3.	3806 St Clair Ave	3806 St Clair Ave
4.	1550 Mars Rd	1550 Mars Rd
5.	220 Woodhill Pl	220 Woodhill Rd
6.	Indianapolis In 87199	Indianapoli In 81799
7.	8759 S Green Ct	8759 S Green Ct
8.	121 Willoughby Hwy	121 Willoughby Hwy
9.	6666 Rocklyn Way	6666 Rocklyn Way
10.	2500 Woodland Blvd	2588 Woodland Blvd
11.	Brockton MASS	Brockton MN
12.	2841 Osborn Ave	2841 Osburn Ave
13.	Macedonia Way	Macedonia Way
14.	307 Warrensville MT	307 Warrensville MA
15.	8177 Ontario St	8777 Ontario St
16.	301 Lorain Rd	301 Lorain Rd
17.	Augusta GA 17603	Augusta GA 17603
18.	1815 Edgewater Mall	1815 Edgewater Mall
19.	317 Central Ave	317 Central Ave
20.	Sarasota FL	Sarasota Flora
21.	931 East Arlington	913 East Arlington
22.	3333 Shakespeare Ct	3333 Shakespeare Ct
23.	6146 Clarkwood Pkwy	6146 Clarkwood Pkwy
24.	Davenport IOBA	Davenport IA
25.	777 Paxton Pl	777 Paxton Pl
26.	614 Beachwood Apt-6	614 Beachwood Apt-6
27.	921 Valley Forge Rd	912 Valley Forge Rd
28.	100 Westchester	100 Westchester
29.	2177 Westfield St	2717 Westfield St
30.	Lansing MI 32804	Lansing MI 32804
31.	5207 Atlantic Hwy	5207 Atlantic Hwy
32.	12 Randell Ct	12 Randell Ct
33.	4612 Rocky River	4612 Locky River
34.	Tacoma WA 43712	Spokane WA 43712
35.	Gulfport Ms	Gulfport FL
36.	813 Richmond Park	813 Richmond Park
37.	Lake Shore R I	Lake Shore R I
38.	8172 Crestwood LN	8177 Crestwood LN
39.	3172 Gilbert Ave	3172 Gilbert Ave
40.	1711 Bennington Blvd	1717 Bennington Blvd
41.	Bristol Tenn 32117	Bristol Tenn 32117
42.	710 Laverne	710 Laverne
43.	830 Bluestone Way	830 Bluestone Bay
44.	3217 Radcliffe Rd	3217 Radcliffe Rd
45.	8201 Cedarwood Dr	8201 Cedarwood Dr
46.	9617 Orleans St	9617 Orlean St
47.	Lynchburg Virona	Lynchburg VA
48.	102 Dickens Blvd	102 Dickens Blvd

49.	Memphis TN 12380	Memphis TX 12380
50.	5671 Copley Sq	5671 Copley Sq
51.	Scottsdale AZ 32180	Scottsdale AZ 32180
52.	1331 Denison Ct	1331 Dennison Ct
53.	Pittsburg Penn	Pittsburg Penn
54.	1380 Turney Rd	1830 Burney Rd
55.	2242 Barrett Ave	2244 Bartlett Ave
56.	Watterbury CN 81712	Waterbury CONN 81712
57.	5070 Middlebrook Rd	5070 Middlebook Rd
58.	Norman OK 32210	Norman OK 32210
59.	1921 Belmore Pl	1921 Belmore Pl
60.	305 Worley Ave	305 Worley Ave
61.	2108 Broadmore Park	2108 Broadway Park
62.	Utica NY	Utica NY
63.	Kelly Ave	Kelly Ave
64.	3817 Winston St	3817 Winston Road
65.	Raleigh NC	Raleigh SC
66.	1002 Edmond Dr	1002 Edmond Dr
67.	4712 Linwood Way	4712 Linwood Way
68.	Knoxville TN	Knoxtown TN
69.	Hackensack NJ	Hackensack NJ
70.	4441 Lake Shore Blvd	4444 Lake Shore Blvd
71.	3157 Merrygold Ave	3157 Merrygold Ave
72.	5178 Haverstone Ct	5178 Haverstone Ct
73.	St Paul MN	St Paul MN
74.	4827 Pendley Rd	4827 Pendley Rd
75.	2237 Fairlawn	2237 Farelawn
76.	6633 Stark Ave	6633 Stark Ave
77.	1172 Buckingham Pl	1172 Buckingham Pl
78.	Carson City NV 32118	Carson City NV 32181
79.	1800 Harvard Rd	1800 Harvard Rd
80.	370 Canterbury Rd	370 Canterbury Rd
81.	Anaheim CA 32187	Anaheim CA 32187
82.	4510 Gatorwood Ave	4510 Gaterwood Ave
83.	9356 Fenwick Hwy	9356 Fenwick Hwy
84.	Dallas Tx 38112	Dallas TX 38222
85.	317 Birch Cir	317 Birch Cir
86.	4084 East Adams	4084 No Adams
87.	317 Wisteria Pt	371 Wisteria Rd
88.	Trenton NJ 68117	Trenton NJ 68117
89.	377 Melrose Pt	377 Melrose Pt
90.	6167 Sladden Ave	6617 Saldden Ave
91.	7008 Sandy LN	7888 Sandy LN
92.	104 McCraken	104 McCrakin
93.	Pontiac MI	Pontiac MI
94.	15 Jasper Dr	15 Jasper Dr
95.	5619 Modo Rd	5916 Modo Rd

Extra Address Checking Practice Exercise #9

1.	2591 Bundy Dr	2591 Bundy Dr
2.	Fresno CA 88821	Fresno CA 88821
3.	2089 Carnegie Ct	2089 Carnegie Ct
4.	St Paul MN	St Paul MS
5.	274 Whitney Way	274 Whitney Way
6.	7730 Kinsman Pl	7222 Kinsman Pl
7.	Omaha NE	Omaha NE
8.	417 E Plymouth Av	417 W Plymouth Av
9.	1920 Roseland Cir	1920 Roseland Rd
10.	Lowell MA 36730	Lowell MA 36730
11.	1544 Sherbrook Pl	1544 Sherbrook Pl
12.	140 E Holdmen Av	140 E Holdmen Av
13.	2770 Loganberry	2770 Loganberry
14.	Peoria IL 52107	Peoria IL 52170
15.	3710 North Bay Dr	3710 North Bay Dr
16.	7310 W Colonial Av	7301 W Colonial Av
17.	5640 St James Pkwy	5640 James Pkwy
18.	Bremerton WA 23790	Bremerton WA 23790
19.	170 Kider Rd	710 Kidder Rd
20.	1838 Navahoe Way	1838 Navahoe Way
21.	Columbia SC	Columbia SC
22.	3939 N Fredrick	3939 S Fredrick
23.	837 Russell Av	837 Russell Av
24.	7220 Cypress Ct	722 Cypress Ct
25.	899 S Lanward	899 S Lanward
26.	Detroit MI 47702	Detromb MI 47702
27.	2718 Liberty Rd	2718 Liberty Rd
28.	261 W Locust Ln	261 W Locust Ln
29.	Butte MT 82107	Butte MT 82100
30.	953 Willoughby	935 Willoughby
31.	5061 S Larchwood Av	5061 S Larchwood Av
32.	7709 Ridgefield	7110 Ridgefield
33.	Erie PA	Erie PA
34.	1515 W Stratford	1515 W Stratford
35.	2652 Carmon Blvd	2652 Carmon Pl
36.	5184 Olivewood Cir	5184 Olivewood Cir
37.	668 E Marble Pl	668 E Marble Pl
38.	Provo UT	Prova UT
39.	436 Atwell St	436 Atwell St
40.	943 N Chatfield	943 N Chatfield
41.	Seattle WA	Seattle Wy
42.	8851 Somerset St	8518 Somerset
43.	282 Hayes Ave	282 Hayes Ave
44.	Boise ID 92178	Boise ID 92178
45.	731 W Badger	731 W Badger
46.	920 Shall Av	920 Shall Av
47.	9500 Lile Dr	9600 Lil Dr
48.	Craighton OH 45673	Creighton OH 45673

49.	Worth Bank Building	Worth Bank Building
50.	1023 W Capitol Ave	1023 E Capitol Ave
51.	28 Cascade Dr	28 Cascade Dr
52.	111 Valley Club Cir	111 Valley Club Rd
53.	4407 Leilani NLR	4407 Leilani NLR
54.	Diamond Head AR	Diamond Head AK
55.	66620 Frontage Rd	66620 Frontage Rd
56.	12127 Fairway Blvd	12127 Fairway Blvd
57.	E 7th & Collins St	E 7th & Collins St
58.	4422 Camp Robinson	2244 Camp Robinson
59.	Tulsa OK	Tulsa OK
60.	57 Patterson Av	57 Patterson Av
61.	1611 S Main St	1611 N Main St
62.	Morgan Exchange	Morgan Exchange
63.	5908 N Katillus RD	5908 N Katillus RD
64.	68 Yarberry Ln	68 Yarberry Ln
65.	31 Whitmore Cir	31 Whitmore Cir
66.	1709 Shumate Dr	1717 Shumate Dr
67.	2805 Faxcroff Rd	2805 Foxcroft Way
68.	329 E 5 St	329 5 St
69.	Lakeland FL	Lakeland Fl
70.	605 Gordon St	605 Gordon St
71.	1601 Shaclkeford Rd	1601 Schakleford Rd
72.	4516 Cobb	4615 Cobb
73.	5606 Shamrock NLR	5606 Shamrock NLR
74.	1440 W 10	1440 W 10
75.	7012 Mablevale Pke	7012 Mablevail Pke
76.	Conway Al 72111	Conway Al 72111
77.	118 S Jackson	118 Jackson
78.	1121 S Schiler	1121 S Schiler
79.	Tacoma OR 45673	Tacoma OR 45637
80.	8632 North Holiday	8632 No Holiday
81.	6100 Santa Monica	6100 Santa Monica
82.	1010 Wolf	1010 Wolf
83.	Garden Hts OH 13021	Garden Hts OH 13021
84.	Auburn NY	Auburn ME
85.	1108 Silver Creek Rd	1108 Silver Creek Rd
86.	8911 Keneshaw Mt	8911 Keneshaw Mt
87.	Brazos NM	Brazos NM
88.	10 Pleasant Cove	10 Pleasant Cove
89.	5516 A St	5156 A St
90.	2000 Magnolia	200 Magnolia
91.	609 Middle	609 Middle
92.	Newport News VA	Newport News VA
93.	3323 Maryland	3323 Maryland
94.	Wauseon MI	Wausoen MI
95.	13 Archwood Dr	13 Archwood Dr

Extra Address Checking Practice Exercise #10

1.	457 Convent Ave	457 Convant Ave
2.	Jasper WY 38127	Jasper WY 38999
3.	3178 Lexington Blvd	3178 Lexington Blvd
4.	1160 Studio 4	1160 Studio 4
5.	180 West End St	180 West End St
6.	4210 E Magazine	4210 W Magazine
7.	Port Angles WA 82170	Port Angles WA 82170
8.	6812 W 44th St	6812 W 44th St
9.	700 Bellevue Pl	7000 Bellevue Pl
10.	391 Central Park Ln	393 Central Park Ln
11.	8172 Hofstra Terr	8172 Hofstra Terr
12.	502 Morrell St	502 Morrell St
13.	7591 E Gracie Blvd	7591 W Gracie Blvd
14.	801 S Bowery	801 S Bowery
15.	Huntsville Al 24187	Huntsville Al 24178
16.	123 Fairfield Sq	123 Fairfield Sq
17.	9092 N Thompson	9092 N Thomas
18.	1319 River Rd	1319 River Dr
19.	083 Sears Pl	083 Sears Pl
20.	Bryan TX 82174	Brian TX 8217
21.	142 West End Av	142 West End Av
22.	Hunter W VA 28179	Hunter VA 28179
23.	410 Perry Pl	410 Perry Pl
24.	4537 Cuthrelly Ct	4537 Cuthrelly Ct
25.	6311 W Clarmont Rd	6113 W Clarmont Rd
26.	3281 Confucius Dr	3281 Confucius Dr
27.	5779 West Monroe	5879 West Monroe
28.	Hollybranch Mo 89721	Hollybranch Mo 89721
29.	503 Columbia St	503 Colombia St
30.	106 Cabrini Heights	106 Cabrini Heights
31.	Provo Ut 82173	Provo Ut 82173
32.	111 E Douglas	1111 E Douglas
33.	567 Dutton Way	567 Dutton Way
34.	180 Riverside Hts	180 River Hts
35.	3812 Yellowstone St	3812 Yellowstone St
36.	120 W Margaret St	120 W Margaret St
37.	Utica NY 82781	Utica NY 82781
38.	350 W Nathaniel	350 W Nathanal
39.	Sommerville NJ 82173	Summerville NJ 82173
40.	225 Stanton Cir	225 Stanton Cir
41.	8123 Waterford Way	8123 Waterford Bay
42.	561 Fuchsberg Ct	561 Fuchsberg Ct
43.	993 Hillside Manor	993 Hillside Manor
44.	3812 Salvatore Ave	3812 Salvator Ave
45.	Otto MN	Otto NM
46.	821 S Hamilton Rd	821 N Hamilton Rd
47.	2127 Alexander	2127 Alexander
48.	416 Watchman Way	416 Watchmen Way

Continued

49.	318 Fuengeldo St	318 Fuengeldo St
50.	600 W Alfredo	606 W Alfredo
51.	2215 Pepper Cove Rd	2215 Pepper Cove Rd
52.	Tampa Fl 81392	Tampa Fl 81392
53.	799 Gregory Ct	799 Gregory Pl
54.	1268 Overlook Terr	1268 Overlook Terr
55.	8397 Indian Rd	8379 Indiana Rd
56.	2758 W Solomon	2578 W Soloman
57.	Beatrice Vt 23651	Beatrice Vt 23651
58.	5805 Roethel Ave	5801 Roethel Ave
59.	328 Gabriel Way	328 Gabriel Way
60.	4369 Beachwood Dr	4369 Beachwood Dr
61.	117 Waverly Pl	119 Waverly Pl
62.	758 S Shashi Rd	758 S Shashi Rd
63.	Canton Ms 38217	Canton Ms 38217
64.	6399 Eldorado Ct	6399 Eldorado Ct
65.	Los Angeles CA 82917	Las Angles CA 82917
66.	4129 N Enterprise	4129 N Enterprise
67.	Carlstadt NJ	Carlstadt NJ
68.	148 Oak Ridge Rd	143 Oak Ridge Rd
69.	Sheridan OK 47812	Sheridan Ok 47812
70.	2817 Mountainside Ln	2817 Mountainside Ln
71.	3500 E Jericho Rd	3500 Jericho Rd
72.	6900 Dockman St	6900 Dockman St
73.	8317 Lynchment Dr	8317 Linchment Dr
74.	0470 Hanover Sq	0470 Hanover Sq
75.	Pearl River Or 32178	Pearl River Or 32781
76.	6821 Mill River Rd	6182 Mill River Rd
77.	640 Gotham Pkwy	640 Gotham Pkwy
78.	4917 Crossways Sq	4917 Crossways Sq
79.	9381 Johnson Ave	9381 Johnson Ave
80.	575 Walton Blvd	575 N Walton Blvd
81.	85 Hudson River Exp	85 Hudson River Exp
82.	867 Caven Pt Pl	867 Caven Pt
83.	Sullivan WV	Sullivan VW
84.	8439 Diamond Ln	8439 Diamond Ln
85.	Phoenix Ar 21718	Phoenix Ar 21718
86.	943 SW Winters Ave	943 SW Winters Ave
87.	2283 Fairlawn Pl	2283 Fairlawn Pl
88.	310 S Madison Ave	310 SW Madison Ave
89.	7521 Moreno Rd	7521 Moreno Rd
90.	1872 Washington Blvd	1872 Washington Blvd
91.	Parsipany NJ 38217	Parsippeny NJ 38217
92.	7221 Pinecrest Sq	7212 Pinecrest Sq
93.	817 NE Parker Rd	817 NE Parker Rd
94.	567 Spritzer Ct	567 Spritzer Ct
95.	Eugene Dr	Eugene Or

COMPLETE PRACTICE TEST ANSWER SHEET

ADDRESS CHECKING SECTION

1 Ⓐ Ⓓ	13 Ⓐ Ⓓ	25 Ⓐ Ⓓ	37 Ⓐ Ⓓ	49 Ⓐ Ⓓ	61 Ⓐ Ⓓ	73 Ⓐ Ⓓ	85 Ⓐ Ⓓ
2 Ⓐ Ⓓ	14 Ⓐ Ⓓ	26 Ⓐ Ⓓ	38 Ⓐ Ⓓ	50 Ⓐ Ⓓ	62 Ⓐ Ⓓ	74 Ⓐ Ⓓ	86 Ⓐ Ⓓ
3 Ⓐ Ⓓ	15 Ⓐ Ⓓ	27 Ⓐ Ⓓ	39 Ⓐ Ⓓ	51 Ⓐ Ⓓ	63 Ⓐ Ⓓ	75 Ⓐ Ⓓ	87 Ⓐ Ⓓ
4 Ⓐ Ⓓ	16 Ⓐ Ⓓ	28 Ⓐ Ⓓ	40 Ⓐ Ⓓ	52 Ⓐ Ⓓ	64 Ⓐ Ⓓ	76 Ⓐ Ⓓ	88 Ⓐ Ⓓ
5 Ⓐ Ⓓ	17 Ⓐ Ⓓ	29 Ⓐ Ⓓ	41 Ⓐ Ⓓ	53 Ⓐ Ⓓ	65 Ⓐ Ⓓ	77 Ⓐ Ⓓ	89 Ⓐ Ⓓ
6 Ⓐ Ⓓ	18 Ⓐ Ⓓ	30 Ⓐ Ⓓ	42 Ⓐ Ⓓ	54 Ⓐ Ⓓ	66 Ⓐ Ⓓ	78 Ⓐ Ⓓ	90 Ⓐ Ⓓ
7 Ⓐ Ⓓ	19 Ⓐ Ⓓ	31 Ⓐ Ⓓ	43 Ⓐ Ⓓ	55 Ⓐ Ⓓ	67 Ⓐ Ⓓ	79 Ⓐ Ⓓ	91 Ⓐ Ⓓ
8 Ⓐ Ⓓ	20 Ⓐ Ⓓ	32 Ⓐ Ⓓ	44 Ⓐ Ⓓ	56 Ⓐ Ⓓ	68 Ⓐ Ⓓ	80 Ⓐ Ⓓ	92 Ⓐ Ⓓ
9 Ⓐ Ⓓ	21 Ⓐ Ⓓ	33 Ⓐ Ⓓ	45 Ⓐ Ⓓ	57 Ⓐ Ⓓ	69 Ⓐ Ⓓ	81 Ⓐ Ⓓ	93 Ⓐ Ⓓ
10 Ⓐ Ⓓ	22 Ⓐ Ⓓ	34 Ⓐ Ⓓ	46 Ⓐ Ⓓ	58 Ⓐ Ⓓ	70 Ⓐ Ⓓ	82 Ⓐ Ⓓ	94 Ⓐ Ⓓ
11 Ⓐ Ⓓ	23 Ⓐ Ⓓ	35 Ⓐ Ⓓ	47 Ⓐ Ⓓ	59 Ⓐ Ⓓ	71 Ⓐ Ⓓ	83 Ⓐ Ⓓ	95 Ⓐ Ⓓ
12 Ⓐ Ⓓ	24 Ⓐ Ⓓ	36 Ⓐ Ⓓ	48 Ⓐ Ⓓ	60 Ⓐ Ⓓ	72 Ⓐ Ⓓ	84 Ⓐ Ⓓ	

ADDRESS MEMORY SECTION

1 Ⓐ Ⓑ Ⓒ Ⓓ Ⓔ	19 Ⓐ Ⓑ Ⓒ Ⓓ Ⓔ	37 Ⓐ Ⓑ Ⓒ Ⓓ Ⓔ	55 Ⓐ Ⓑ Ⓒ Ⓓ Ⓔ	73 Ⓐ Ⓑ Ⓒ Ⓓ Ⓔ
2 Ⓐ Ⓑ Ⓒ Ⓓ Ⓔ	20 Ⓐ Ⓑ Ⓒ Ⓓ Ⓔ	38 Ⓐ Ⓑ Ⓒ Ⓓ Ⓔ	56 Ⓐ Ⓑ Ⓒ Ⓓ Ⓔ	74 Ⓐ Ⓑ Ⓒ Ⓓ Ⓔ
3 Ⓐ Ⓑ Ⓒ Ⓓ Ⓔ	21 Ⓐ Ⓑ Ⓒ Ⓓ Ⓔ	39 Ⓐ Ⓑ Ⓒ Ⓓ Ⓔ	57 Ⓐ Ⓑ Ⓒ Ⓓ Ⓔ	75 Ⓐ Ⓑ Ⓒ Ⓓ Ⓔ
4 Ⓐ Ⓑ Ⓒ Ⓓ Ⓔ	22 Ⓐ Ⓑ Ⓒ Ⓓ Ⓔ	40 Ⓐ Ⓑ Ⓒ Ⓓ Ⓔ	58 Ⓐ Ⓑ Ⓒ Ⓓ Ⓔ	76 Ⓐ Ⓑ Ⓒ Ⓓ Ⓔ
5 Ⓐ Ⓑ Ⓒ Ⓓ Ⓔ	23 Ⓐ Ⓑ Ⓒ Ⓓ Ⓔ	41 Ⓐ Ⓑ Ⓒ Ⓓ Ⓔ	59 Ⓐ Ⓑ Ⓒ Ⓓ Ⓔ	77 Ⓐ Ⓑ Ⓒ Ⓓ Ⓔ
6 Ⓐ Ⓑ Ⓒ Ⓓ Ⓔ	24 Ⓐ Ⓑ Ⓒ Ⓓ Ⓔ	42 Ⓐ Ⓑ Ⓒ Ⓓ Ⓔ	60 Ⓐ Ⓑ Ⓒ Ⓓ Ⓔ	78 Ⓐ Ⓑ Ⓒ Ⓓ Ⓔ
7 Ⓐ Ⓑ Ⓒ Ⓓ Ⓔ	25 Ⓐ Ⓑ Ⓒ Ⓓ Ⓔ	43 Ⓐ Ⓑ Ⓒ Ⓓ Ⓔ	61 Ⓐ Ⓑ Ⓒ Ⓓ Ⓔ	79 Ⓐ Ⓑ Ⓒ Ⓓ Ⓔ
8 Ⓐ Ⓑ Ⓒ Ⓓ Ⓔ	26 Ⓐ Ⓑ Ⓒ Ⓓ Ⓔ	44 Ⓐ Ⓑ Ⓒ Ⓓ Ⓔ	62 Ⓐ Ⓑ Ⓒ Ⓓ Ⓔ	80 Ⓐ Ⓑ Ⓒ Ⓓ Ⓔ
9 Ⓐ Ⓑ Ⓒ Ⓓ Ⓔ	27 Ⓐ Ⓑ Ⓒ Ⓓ Ⓔ	45 Ⓐ Ⓑ Ⓒ Ⓓ Ⓔ	63 Ⓐ Ⓑ Ⓒ Ⓓ Ⓔ	81 Ⓐ Ⓑ Ⓒ Ⓓ Ⓔ
10 Ⓐ Ⓑ Ⓒ Ⓓ Ⓔ	28 Ⓐ Ⓑ Ⓒ Ⓓ Ⓔ	46 Ⓐ Ⓑ Ⓒ Ⓓ Ⓔ	64 Ⓐ Ⓑ Ⓒ Ⓓ Ⓔ	82 Ⓐ Ⓑ Ⓒ Ⓓ Ⓔ
11 Ⓐ Ⓑ Ⓒ Ⓓ Ⓔ	29 Ⓐ Ⓑ Ⓒ Ⓓ Ⓔ	47 Ⓐ Ⓑ Ⓒ Ⓓ Ⓔ	65 Ⓐ Ⓑ Ⓒ Ⓓ Ⓔ	83 Ⓐ Ⓑ Ⓒ Ⓓ Ⓔ
12 Ⓐ Ⓑ Ⓒ Ⓓ Ⓔ	30 Ⓐ Ⓑ Ⓒ Ⓓ Ⓔ	48 Ⓐ Ⓑ Ⓒ Ⓓ Ⓔ	66 Ⓐ Ⓑ Ⓒ Ⓓ Ⓔ	84 Ⓐ Ⓑ Ⓒ Ⓓ Ⓔ
13 Ⓐ Ⓑ Ⓒ Ⓓ Ⓔ	31 Ⓐ Ⓑ Ⓒ Ⓓ Ⓔ	49 Ⓐ Ⓑ Ⓒ Ⓓ Ⓔ	67 Ⓐ Ⓑ Ⓒ Ⓓ Ⓔ	85 Ⓐ Ⓑ Ⓒ Ⓓ Ⓔ
14 Ⓐ Ⓑ Ⓒ Ⓓ Ⓔ	32 Ⓐ Ⓑ Ⓒ Ⓓ Ⓔ	50 Ⓐ Ⓑ Ⓒ Ⓓ Ⓔ	68 Ⓐ Ⓑ Ⓒ Ⓓ Ⓔ	86 Ⓐ Ⓑ Ⓒ Ⓓ Ⓔ
15 Ⓐ Ⓑ Ⓒ Ⓓ Ⓔ	33 Ⓐ Ⓑ Ⓒ Ⓓ Ⓔ	51 Ⓐ Ⓑ Ⓒ Ⓓ Ⓔ	69 Ⓐ Ⓑ Ⓒ Ⓓ Ⓔ	87 Ⓐ Ⓑ Ⓒ Ⓓ Ⓔ
16 Ⓐ Ⓑ Ⓒ Ⓓ Ⓔ	34 Ⓐ Ⓑ Ⓒ Ⓓ Ⓔ	52 Ⓐ Ⓑ Ⓒ Ⓓ Ⓔ	70 Ⓐ Ⓑ Ⓒ Ⓓ Ⓔ	88 Ⓐ Ⓑ Ⓒ Ⓓ Ⓔ
17 Ⓐ Ⓑ Ⓒ Ⓓ Ⓔ	35 Ⓐ Ⓑ Ⓒ Ⓓ Ⓔ	53 Ⓐ Ⓑ Ⓒ Ⓓ Ⓔ	71 Ⓐ Ⓑ Ⓒ Ⓓ Ⓔ	
18 Ⓐ Ⓑ Ⓒ Ⓓ Ⓔ	36 Ⓐ Ⓑ Ⓒ Ⓓ Ⓔ	54 Ⓐ Ⓑ Ⓒ Ⓓ Ⓔ	72 Ⓐ Ⓑ Ⓒ Ⓓ Ⓔ	

NUMBER SERIES SECTION

1 Ⓐ Ⓑ Ⓒ Ⓓ Ⓔ	7 Ⓐ Ⓑ Ⓒ Ⓓ Ⓔ	13 Ⓐ Ⓑ Ⓒ Ⓓ Ⓔ	19 Ⓐ Ⓑ Ⓒ Ⓓ Ⓔ
2 Ⓐ Ⓑ Ⓒ Ⓓ Ⓔ	8 Ⓐ Ⓑ Ⓒ Ⓓ Ⓔ	14 Ⓐ Ⓑ Ⓒ Ⓓ Ⓔ	20 Ⓐ Ⓑ Ⓒ Ⓓ Ⓔ
3 Ⓐ Ⓑ Ⓒ Ⓓ Ⓔ	9 Ⓐ Ⓑ Ⓒ Ⓓ Ⓔ	15 Ⓐ Ⓑ Ⓒ Ⓓ Ⓔ	21 Ⓐ Ⓑ Ⓒ Ⓓ Ⓔ
4 Ⓐ Ⓑ Ⓒ Ⓓ Ⓔ	10 Ⓐ Ⓑ Ⓒ Ⓓ Ⓔ	16 Ⓐ Ⓑ Ⓒ Ⓓ Ⓔ	22 Ⓐ Ⓑ Ⓒ Ⓓ Ⓔ
5 Ⓐ Ⓑ Ⓒ Ⓓ Ⓔ	11 Ⓐ Ⓑ Ⓒ Ⓓ Ⓔ	17 Ⓐ Ⓑ Ⓒ Ⓓ Ⓔ	23 Ⓐ Ⓑ Ⓒ Ⓓ Ⓔ
6 Ⓐ Ⓑ Ⓒ Ⓓ Ⓔ	12 Ⓐ Ⓑ Ⓒ Ⓓ Ⓔ	18 Ⓐ Ⓑ Ⓒ Ⓓ Ⓔ	24 Ⓐ Ⓑ Ⓒ Ⓓ Ⓔ

FOLLOWING ORAL DIRECTIONS SECTION

1 Ⓐ Ⓑ Ⓒ Ⓓ Ⓔ	19 Ⓐ Ⓑ Ⓒ Ⓓ Ⓔ	37 Ⓐ Ⓑ Ⓒ Ⓓ Ⓔ	55 Ⓐ Ⓑ Ⓒ Ⓓ Ⓔ	73 Ⓐ Ⓑ Ⓒ Ⓓ Ⓔ
2 Ⓐ Ⓑ Ⓒ Ⓓ Ⓔ	20 Ⓐ Ⓑ Ⓒ Ⓓ Ⓔ	38 Ⓐ Ⓑ Ⓒ Ⓓ Ⓔ	56 Ⓐ Ⓑ Ⓒ Ⓓ Ⓔ	74 Ⓐ Ⓑ Ⓒ Ⓓ Ⓔ
3 Ⓐ Ⓑ Ⓒ Ⓓ Ⓔ	21 Ⓐ Ⓑ Ⓒ Ⓓ Ⓔ	39 Ⓐ Ⓑ Ⓒ Ⓓ Ⓔ	57 Ⓐ Ⓑ Ⓒ Ⓓ Ⓔ	75 Ⓐ Ⓑ Ⓒ Ⓓ Ⓔ
4 Ⓐ Ⓑ Ⓒ Ⓓ Ⓔ	22 Ⓐ Ⓑ Ⓒ Ⓓ Ⓔ	40 Ⓐ Ⓑ Ⓒ Ⓓ Ⓔ	58 Ⓐ Ⓑ Ⓒ Ⓓ Ⓔ	76 Ⓐ Ⓑ Ⓒ Ⓓ Ⓔ
5 Ⓐ Ⓑ Ⓒ Ⓓ Ⓔ	23 Ⓐ Ⓑ Ⓒ Ⓓ Ⓔ	41 Ⓐ Ⓑ Ⓒ Ⓓ Ⓔ	59 Ⓐ Ⓑ Ⓒ Ⓓ Ⓔ	77 Ⓐ Ⓑ Ⓒ Ⓓ Ⓔ
6 Ⓐ Ⓑ Ⓒ Ⓓ Ⓔ	24 Ⓐ Ⓑ Ⓒ Ⓓ Ⓔ	42 Ⓐ Ⓑ Ⓒ Ⓓ Ⓔ	60 Ⓐ Ⓑ Ⓒ Ⓓ Ⓔ	78 Ⓐ Ⓑ Ⓒ Ⓓ Ⓔ
7 Ⓐ Ⓑ Ⓒ Ⓓ Ⓔ	25 Ⓐ Ⓑ Ⓒ Ⓓ Ⓔ	43 Ⓐ Ⓑ Ⓒ Ⓓ Ⓔ	61 Ⓐ Ⓑ Ⓒ Ⓓ Ⓔ	79 Ⓐ Ⓑ Ⓒ Ⓓ Ⓔ
8 Ⓐ Ⓑ Ⓒ Ⓓ Ⓔ	26 Ⓐ Ⓑ Ⓒ Ⓓ Ⓔ	44 Ⓐ Ⓑ Ⓒ Ⓓ Ⓔ	62 Ⓐ Ⓑ Ⓒ Ⓓ Ⓔ	80 Ⓐ Ⓑ Ⓒ Ⓓ Ⓔ
9 Ⓐ Ⓑ Ⓒ Ⓓ Ⓔ	27 Ⓐ Ⓑ Ⓒ Ⓓ Ⓔ	45 Ⓐ Ⓑ Ⓒ Ⓓ Ⓔ	63 Ⓐ Ⓑ Ⓒ Ⓓ Ⓔ	81 Ⓐ Ⓑ Ⓒ Ⓓ Ⓔ
10 Ⓐ Ⓑ Ⓒ Ⓓ Ⓔ	28 Ⓐ Ⓑ Ⓒ Ⓓ Ⓔ	46 Ⓐ Ⓑ Ⓒ Ⓓ Ⓔ	64 Ⓐ Ⓑ Ⓒ Ⓓ Ⓔ	82 Ⓐ Ⓑ Ⓒ Ⓓ Ⓔ
11 Ⓐ Ⓑ Ⓒ Ⓓ Ⓔ	29 Ⓐ Ⓑ Ⓒ Ⓓ Ⓔ	47 Ⓐ Ⓑ Ⓒ Ⓓ Ⓔ	65 Ⓐ Ⓑ Ⓒ Ⓓ Ⓔ	83 Ⓐ Ⓑ Ⓒ Ⓓ Ⓔ
12 Ⓐ Ⓑ Ⓒ Ⓓ Ⓔ	30 Ⓐ Ⓑ Ⓒ Ⓓ Ⓔ	48 Ⓐ Ⓑ Ⓒ Ⓓ Ⓔ	66 Ⓐ Ⓑ Ⓒ Ⓓ Ⓔ	84 Ⓐ Ⓑ Ⓒ Ⓓ Ⓔ
13 Ⓐ Ⓑ Ⓒ Ⓓ Ⓔ	31 Ⓐ Ⓑ Ⓒ Ⓓ Ⓔ	49 Ⓐ Ⓑ Ⓒ Ⓓ Ⓔ	67 Ⓐ Ⓑ Ⓒ Ⓓ Ⓔ	85 Ⓐ Ⓑ Ⓒ Ⓓ Ⓔ
14 Ⓐ Ⓑ Ⓒ Ⓓ Ⓔ	32 Ⓐ Ⓑ Ⓒ Ⓓ Ⓔ	50 Ⓐ Ⓑ Ⓒ Ⓓ Ⓔ	68 Ⓐ Ⓑ Ⓒ Ⓓ Ⓔ	86 Ⓐ Ⓑ Ⓒ Ⓓ Ⓔ
15 Ⓐ Ⓑ Ⓒ Ⓓ Ⓔ	33 Ⓐ Ⓑ Ⓒ Ⓓ Ⓔ	51 Ⓐ Ⓑ Ⓒ Ⓓ Ⓔ	69 Ⓐ Ⓑ Ⓒ Ⓓ Ⓔ	87 Ⓐ Ⓑ Ⓒ Ⓓ Ⓔ
16 Ⓐ Ⓑ Ⓒ Ⓓ Ⓔ	34 Ⓐ Ⓑ Ⓒ Ⓓ Ⓔ	52 Ⓐ Ⓑ Ⓒ Ⓓ Ⓔ	70 Ⓐ Ⓑ Ⓒ Ⓓ Ⓔ	88 Ⓐ Ⓑ Ⓒ Ⓓ Ⓔ
17 Ⓐ Ⓑ Ⓒ Ⓓ Ⓔ	35 Ⓐ Ⓑ Ⓒ Ⓓ Ⓔ	53 Ⓐ Ⓑ Ⓒ Ⓓ Ⓔ	71 Ⓐ Ⓑ Ⓒ Ⓓ Ⓔ	
18 Ⓐ Ⓑ Ⓒ Ⓓ Ⓔ	36 Ⓐ Ⓑ Ⓒ Ⓓ Ⓔ	54 Ⓐ Ⓑ Ⓒ Ⓓ Ⓔ	72 Ⓐ Ⓑ Ⓒ Ⓓ Ⓔ	

COMPLETE PRACTICE TEST ANSWER SHEET

ADDRESS CHECKING SECTION

1 Ⓐ Ⓓ 13 Ⓐ Ⓓ 25 Ⓐ Ⓓ 37 Ⓐ Ⓓ 49 Ⓐ Ⓓ 61 Ⓐ Ⓓ 73 Ⓐ Ⓓ 85 Ⓐ Ⓓ
2 Ⓐ Ⓓ 14 Ⓐ Ⓓ 26 Ⓐ Ⓓ 38 Ⓐ Ⓓ 50 Ⓐ Ⓓ 62 Ⓐ Ⓓ 74 Ⓐ Ⓓ 86 Ⓐ Ⓓ
3 Ⓐ Ⓓ 15 Ⓐ Ⓓ 27 Ⓐ Ⓓ 39 Ⓐ Ⓓ 51 Ⓐ Ⓓ 63 Ⓐ Ⓓ 75 Ⓐ Ⓓ 87 Ⓐ Ⓓ
4 Ⓐ Ⓓ 16 Ⓐ Ⓓ 28 Ⓐ Ⓓ 40 Ⓐ Ⓓ 52 Ⓐ Ⓓ 64 Ⓐ Ⓓ 76 Ⓐ Ⓓ 88 Ⓐ Ⓓ
5 Ⓐ Ⓓ 17 Ⓐ Ⓓ 29 Ⓐ Ⓓ 41 Ⓐ Ⓓ 53 Ⓐ Ⓓ 65 Ⓐ Ⓓ 77 Ⓐ Ⓓ 89 Ⓐ Ⓓ
6 Ⓐ Ⓓ 18 Ⓐ Ⓓ 30 Ⓐ Ⓓ 42 Ⓐ Ⓓ 54 Ⓐ Ⓓ 66 Ⓐ Ⓓ 78 Ⓐ Ⓓ 90 Ⓐ Ⓓ
7 Ⓐ Ⓓ 19 Ⓐ Ⓓ 31 Ⓐ Ⓓ 43 Ⓐ Ⓓ 55 Ⓐ Ⓓ 67 Ⓐ Ⓓ 79 Ⓐ Ⓓ 91 Ⓐ Ⓓ
8 Ⓐ Ⓓ 20 Ⓐ Ⓓ 32 Ⓐ Ⓓ 44 Ⓐ Ⓓ 56 Ⓐ Ⓓ 68 Ⓐ Ⓓ 80 Ⓐ Ⓓ 92 Ⓐ Ⓓ
9 Ⓐ Ⓓ 21 Ⓐ Ⓓ 33 Ⓐ Ⓓ 45 Ⓐ Ⓓ 57 Ⓐ Ⓓ 69 Ⓐ Ⓓ 81 Ⓐ Ⓓ 93 Ⓐ Ⓓ
10 Ⓐ Ⓓ 22 Ⓐ Ⓓ 34 Ⓐ Ⓓ 46 Ⓐ Ⓓ 58 Ⓐ Ⓓ 70 Ⓐ Ⓓ 82 Ⓐ Ⓓ 94 Ⓐ Ⓓ
11 Ⓐ Ⓓ 23 Ⓐ Ⓓ 35 Ⓐ Ⓓ 47 Ⓐ Ⓓ 59 Ⓐ Ⓓ 71 Ⓐ Ⓓ 83 Ⓐ Ⓓ 95 Ⓐ Ⓓ
12 Ⓐ Ⓓ 24 Ⓐ Ⓓ 36 Ⓐ Ⓓ 48 Ⓐ Ⓓ 60 Ⓐ Ⓓ 72 Ⓐ Ⓓ 84 Ⓐ Ⓓ

ADDRESS MEMORY SECTION

1 Ⓐ Ⓑ Ⓒ Ⓓ Ⓔ 19 Ⓐ Ⓑ Ⓒ Ⓓ Ⓔ 37 Ⓐ Ⓑ Ⓒ Ⓓ Ⓔ 55 Ⓐ Ⓑ Ⓒ Ⓓ Ⓔ 73 Ⓐ Ⓑ Ⓒ Ⓓ Ⓔ
2 Ⓐ Ⓑ Ⓒ Ⓓ Ⓔ 20 Ⓐ Ⓑ Ⓒ Ⓓ Ⓔ 38 Ⓐ Ⓑ Ⓒ Ⓓ Ⓔ 56 Ⓐ Ⓑ Ⓒ Ⓓ Ⓔ 74 Ⓐ Ⓑ Ⓒ Ⓓ Ⓔ
3 Ⓐ Ⓑ Ⓒ Ⓓ Ⓔ 21 Ⓐ Ⓑ Ⓒ Ⓓ Ⓔ 39 Ⓐ Ⓑ Ⓒ Ⓓ Ⓔ 57 Ⓐ Ⓑ Ⓒ Ⓓ Ⓔ 75 Ⓐ Ⓑ Ⓒ Ⓓ Ⓔ
4 Ⓐ Ⓑ Ⓒ Ⓓ Ⓔ 22 Ⓐ Ⓑ Ⓒ Ⓓ Ⓔ 40 Ⓐ Ⓑ Ⓒ Ⓓ Ⓔ 58 Ⓐ Ⓑ Ⓒ Ⓓ Ⓔ 76 Ⓐ Ⓑ Ⓒ Ⓓ Ⓔ
5 Ⓐ Ⓑ Ⓒ Ⓓ Ⓔ 23 Ⓐ Ⓑ Ⓒ Ⓓ Ⓔ 41 Ⓐ Ⓑ Ⓒ Ⓓ Ⓔ 59 Ⓐ Ⓑ Ⓒ Ⓓ Ⓔ 77 Ⓐ Ⓑ Ⓒ Ⓓ Ⓔ
6 Ⓐ Ⓑ Ⓒ Ⓓ Ⓔ 24 Ⓐ Ⓑ Ⓒ Ⓓ Ⓔ 42 Ⓐ Ⓑ Ⓒ Ⓓ Ⓔ 60 Ⓐ Ⓑ Ⓒ Ⓓ Ⓔ 78 Ⓐ Ⓑ Ⓒ Ⓓ Ⓔ
7 Ⓐ Ⓑ Ⓒ Ⓓ Ⓔ 25 Ⓐ Ⓑ Ⓒ Ⓓ Ⓔ 43 Ⓐ Ⓑ Ⓒ Ⓓ Ⓔ 61 Ⓐ Ⓑ Ⓒ Ⓓ Ⓔ 79 Ⓐ Ⓑ Ⓒ Ⓓ Ⓔ
8 Ⓐ Ⓑ Ⓒ Ⓓ Ⓔ 26 Ⓐ Ⓑ Ⓒ Ⓓ Ⓔ 44 Ⓐ Ⓑ Ⓒ Ⓓ Ⓔ 62 Ⓐ Ⓑ Ⓒ Ⓓ Ⓔ 80 Ⓐ Ⓑ Ⓒ Ⓓ Ⓔ
9 Ⓐ Ⓑ Ⓒ Ⓓ Ⓔ 27 Ⓐ Ⓑ Ⓒ Ⓓ Ⓔ 45 Ⓐ Ⓑ Ⓒ Ⓓ Ⓔ 63 Ⓐ Ⓑ Ⓒ Ⓓ Ⓔ 81 Ⓐ Ⓑ Ⓒ Ⓓ Ⓔ
10 Ⓐ Ⓑ Ⓒ Ⓓ Ⓔ 28 Ⓐ Ⓑ Ⓒ Ⓓ Ⓔ 46 Ⓐ Ⓑ Ⓒ Ⓓ Ⓔ 64 Ⓐ Ⓑ Ⓒ Ⓓ Ⓔ 82 Ⓐ Ⓑ Ⓒ Ⓓ Ⓔ
11 Ⓐ Ⓑ Ⓒ Ⓓ Ⓔ 29 Ⓐ Ⓑ Ⓒ Ⓓ Ⓔ 47 Ⓐ Ⓑ Ⓒ Ⓓ Ⓔ 65 Ⓐ Ⓑ Ⓒ Ⓓ Ⓔ 83 Ⓐ Ⓑ Ⓒ Ⓓ Ⓔ
12 Ⓐ Ⓑ Ⓒ Ⓓ Ⓔ 30 Ⓐ Ⓑ Ⓒ Ⓓ Ⓔ 48 Ⓐ Ⓑ Ⓒ Ⓓ Ⓔ 66 Ⓐ Ⓑ Ⓒ Ⓓ Ⓔ 84 Ⓐ Ⓑ Ⓒ Ⓓ Ⓔ
13 Ⓐ Ⓑ Ⓒ Ⓓ Ⓔ 31 Ⓐ Ⓑ Ⓒ Ⓓ Ⓔ 49 Ⓐ Ⓑ Ⓒ Ⓓ Ⓔ 67 Ⓐ Ⓑ Ⓒ Ⓓ Ⓔ 85 Ⓐ Ⓑ Ⓒ Ⓓ Ⓔ
14 Ⓐ Ⓑ Ⓒ Ⓓ Ⓔ 32 Ⓐ Ⓑ Ⓒ Ⓓ Ⓔ 50 Ⓐ Ⓑ Ⓒ Ⓓ Ⓔ 68 Ⓐ Ⓑ Ⓒ Ⓓ Ⓔ 86 Ⓐ Ⓑ Ⓒ Ⓓ Ⓔ
15 Ⓐ Ⓑ Ⓒ Ⓓ Ⓔ 33 Ⓐ Ⓑ Ⓒ Ⓓ Ⓔ 51 Ⓐ Ⓑ Ⓒ Ⓓ Ⓔ 69 Ⓐ Ⓑ Ⓒ Ⓓ Ⓔ 87 Ⓐ Ⓑ Ⓒ Ⓓ Ⓔ
16 Ⓐ Ⓑ Ⓒ Ⓓ Ⓔ 34 Ⓐ Ⓑ Ⓒ Ⓓ Ⓔ 52 Ⓐ Ⓑ Ⓒ Ⓓ Ⓔ 70 Ⓐ Ⓑ Ⓒ Ⓓ Ⓔ 88 Ⓐ Ⓑ Ⓒ Ⓓ Ⓔ
17 Ⓐ Ⓑ Ⓒ Ⓓ Ⓔ 35 Ⓐ Ⓑ Ⓒ Ⓓ Ⓔ 53 Ⓐ Ⓑ Ⓒ Ⓓ Ⓔ 71 Ⓐ Ⓑ Ⓒ Ⓓ Ⓔ
18 Ⓐ Ⓑ Ⓒ Ⓓ Ⓔ 36 Ⓐ Ⓑ Ⓒ Ⓓ Ⓔ 54 Ⓐ Ⓑ Ⓒ Ⓓ Ⓔ 72 Ⓐ Ⓑ Ⓒ Ⓓ Ⓔ

NUMBER SERIES SECTION

1 Ⓐ Ⓑ Ⓒ Ⓓ Ⓔ 7 Ⓐ Ⓑ Ⓒ Ⓓ Ⓔ 13 Ⓐ Ⓑ Ⓒ Ⓓ Ⓔ 19 Ⓐ Ⓑ Ⓒ Ⓓ Ⓔ
2 Ⓐ Ⓑ Ⓒ Ⓓ Ⓔ 8 Ⓐ Ⓑ Ⓒ Ⓓ Ⓔ 14 Ⓐ Ⓑ Ⓒ Ⓓ Ⓔ 20 Ⓐ Ⓑ Ⓒ Ⓓ Ⓔ
3 Ⓐ Ⓑ Ⓒ Ⓓ Ⓔ 9 Ⓐ Ⓑ Ⓒ Ⓓ Ⓔ 15 Ⓐ Ⓑ Ⓒ Ⓓ Ⓔ 21 Ⓐ Ⓑ Ⓒ Ⓓ Ⓔ
4 Ⓐ Ⓑ Ⓒ Ⓓ Ⓔ 10 Ⓐ Ⓑ Ⓒ Ⓓ Ⓔ 16 Ⓐ Ⓑ Ⓒ Ⓓ Ⓔ 22 Ⓐ Ⓑ Ⓒ Ⓓ Ⓔ
5 Ⓐ Ⓑ Ⓒ Ⓓ Ⓔ 11 Ⓐ Ⓑ Ⓒ Ⓓ Ⓔ 17 Ⓐ Ⓑ Ⓒ Ⓓ Ⓔ 23 Ⓐ Ⓑ Ⓒ Ⓓ Ⓔ
6 Ⓐ Ⓑ Ⓒ Ⓓ Ⓔ 12 Ⓐ Ⓑ Ⓒ Ⓓ Ⓔ 18 Ⓐ Ⓑ Ⓒ Ⓓ Ⓔ 24 Ⓐ Ⓑ Ⓒ Ⓓ Ⓔ

FOLLOWING ORAL DIRECTIONS SECTION

1 Ⓐ Ⓑ Ⓒ Ⓓ Ⓔ 19 Ⓐ Ⓑ Ⓒ Ⓓ Ⓔ 37 Ⓐ Ⓑ Ⓒ Ⓓ Ⓔ 55 Ⓐ Ⓑ Ⓒ Ⓓ Ⓔ 73 Ⓐ Ⓑ Ⓒ Ⓓ Ⓔ
2 Ⓐ Ⓑ Ⓒ Ⓓ Ⓔ 20 Ⓐ Ⓑ Ⓒ Ⓓ Ⓔ 38 Ⓐ Ⓑ Ⓒ Ⓓ Ⓔ 56 Ⓐ Ⓑ Ⓒ Ⓓ Ⓔ 74 Ⓐ Ⓑ Ⓒ Ⓓ Ⓔ
3 Ⓐ Ⓑ Ⓒ Ⓓ Ⓔ 21 Ⓐ Ⓑ Ⓒ Ⓓ Ⓔ 39 Ⓐ Ⓑ Ⓒ Ⓓ Ⓔ 57 Ⓐ Ⓑ Ⓒ Ⓓ Ⓔ 75 Ⓐ Ⓑ Ⓒ Ⓓ Ⓔ
4 Ⓐ Ⓑ Ⓒ Ⓓ Ⓔ 22 Ⓐ Ⓑ Ⓒ Ⓓ Ⓔ 40 Ⓐ Ⓑ Ⓒ Ⓓ Ⓔ 58 Ⓐ Ⓑ Ⓒ Ⓓ Ⓔ 76 Ⓐ Ⓑ Ⓒ Ⓓ Ⓔ
5 Ⓐ Ⓑ Ⓒ Ⓓ Ⓔ 23 Ⓐ Ⓑ Ⓒ Ⓓ Ⓔ 41 Ⓐ Ⓑ Ⓒ Ⓓ Ⓔ 59 Ⓐ Ⓑ Ⓒ Ⓓ Ⓔ 77 Ⓐ Ⓑ Ⓒ Ⓓ Ⓔ
6 Ⓐ Ⓑ Ⓒ Ⓓ Ⓔ 24 Ⓐ Ⓑ Ⓒ Ⓓ Ⓔ 42 Ⓐ Ⓑ Ⓒ Ⓓ Ⓔ 60 Ⓐ Ⓑ Ⓒ Ⓓ Ⓔ 78 Ⓐ Ⓑ Ⓒ Ⓓ Ⓔ
7 Ⓐ Ⓑ Ⓒ Ⓓ Ⓔ 25 Ⓐ Ⓑ Ⓒ Ⓓ Ⓔ 43 Ⓐ Ⓑ Ⓒ Ⓓ Ⓔ 61 Ⓐ Ⓑ Ⓒ Ⓓ Ⓔ 79 Ⓐ Ⓑ Ⓒ Ⓓ Ⓔ
8 Ⓐ Ⓑ Ⓒ Ⓓ Ⓔ 26 Ⓐ Ⓑ Ⓒ Ⓓ Ⓔ 44 Ⓐ Ⓑ Ⓒ Ⓓ Ⓔ 62 Ⓐ Ⓑ Ⓒ Ⓓ Ⓔ 80 Ⓐ Ⓑ Ⓒ Ⓓ Ⓔ
9 Ⓐ Ⓑ Ⓒ Ⓓ Ⓔ 27 Ⓐ Ⓑ Ⓒ Ⓓ Ⓔ 45 Ⓐ Ⓑ Ⓒ Ⓓ Ⓔ 63 Ⓐ Ⓑ Ⓒ Ⓓ Ⓔ 81 Ⓐ Ⓑ Ⓒ Ⓓ Ⓔ
10 Ⓐ Ⓑ Ⓒ Ⓓ Ⓔ 28 Ⓐ Ⓑ Ⓒ Ⓓ Ⓔ 46 Ⓐ Ⓑ Ⓒ Ⓓ Ⓔ 64 Ⓐ Ⓑ Ⓒ Ⓓ Ⓔ 82 Ⓐ Ⓑ Ⓒ Ⓓ Ⓔ
11 Ⓐ Ⓑ Ⓒ Ⓓ Ⓔ 29 Ⓐ Ⓑ Ⓒ Ⓓ Ⓔ 47 Ⓐ Ⓑ Ⓒ Ⓓ Ⓔ 65 Ⓐ Ⓑ Ⓒ Ⓓ Ⓔ 83 Ⓐ Ⓑ Ⓒ Ⓓ Ⓔ
12 Ⓐ Ⓑ Ⓒ Ⓓ Ⓔ 30 Ⓐ Ⓑ Ⓒ Ⓓ Ⓔ 48 Ⓐ Ⓑ Ⓒ Ⓓ Ⓔ 66 Ⓐ Ⓑ Ⓒ Ⓓ Ⓔ 84 Ⓐ Ⓑ Ⓒ Ⓓ Ⓔ
13 Ⓐ Ⓑ Ⓒ Ⓓ Ⓔ 31 Ⓐ Ⓑ Ⓒ Ⓓ Ⓔ 49 Ⓐ Ⓑ Ⓒ Ⓓ Ⓔ 67 Ⓐ Ⓑ Ⓒ Ⓓ Ⓔ 85 Ⓐ Ⓑ Ⓒ Ⓓ Ⓔ
14 Ⓐ Ⓑ Ⓒ Ⓓ Ⓔ 32 Ⓐ Ⓑ Ⓒ Ⓓ Ⓔ 50 Ⓐ Ⓑ Ⓒ Ⓓ Ⓔ 68 Ⓐ Ⓑ Ⓒ Ⓓ Ⓔ 86 Ⓐ Ⓑ Ⓒ Ⓓ Ⓔ
15 Ⓐ Ⓑ Ⓒ Ⓓ Ⓔ 33 Ⓐ Ⓑ Ⓒ Ⓓ Ⓔ 51 Ⓐ Ⓑ Ⓒ Ⓓ Ⓔ 69 Ⓐ Ⓑ Ⓒ Ⓓ Ⓔ 87 Ⓐ Ⓑ Ⓒ Ⓓ Ⓔ
16 Ⓐ Ⓑ Ⓒ Ⓓ Ⓔ 34 Ⓐ Ⓑ Ⓒ Ⓓ Ⓔ 52 Ⓐ Ⓑ Ⓒ Ⓓ Ⓔ 70 Ⓐ Ⓑ Ⓒ Ⓓ Ⓔ 88 Ⓐ Ⓑ Ⓒ Ⓓ Ⓔ
17 Ⓐ Ⓑ Ⓒ Ⓓ Ⓔ 35 Ⓐ Ⓑ Ⓒ Ⓓ Ⓔ 53 Ⓐ Ⓑ Ⓒ Ⓓ Ⓔ 71 Ⓐ Ⓑ Ⓒ Ⓓ Ⓔ
18 Ⓐ Ⓑ Ⓒ Ⓓ Ⓔ 36 Ⓐ Ⓑ Ⓒ Ⓓ Ⓔ 54 Ⓐ Ⓑ Ⓒ Ⓓ Ⓔ 72 Ⓐ Ⓑ Ⓒ Ⓓ Ⓔ

COMPLETE PRACTICE TEST ANSWER SHEET

ADDRESS CHECKING SECTION

1 Ⓐ Ⓓ	13 Ⓐ Ⓓ	25 Ⓐ Ⓓ	37 Ⓐ Ⓓ	49 Ⓐ Ⓓ	61 Ⓐ Ⓓ	73 Ⓐ Ⓓ	85 Ⓐ Ⓓ
2 Ⓐ Ⓓ	14 Ⓐ Ⓓ	26 Ⓐ Ⓓ	38 Ⓐ Ⓓ	50 Ⓐ Ⓓ	62 Ⓐ Ⓓ	74 Ⓐ Ⓓ	86 Ⓐ Ⓓ
3 Ⓐ Ⓓ	15 Ⓐ Ⓓ	27 Ⓐ Ⓓ	39 Ⓐ Ⓓ	51 Ⓐ Ⓓ	63 Ⓐ Ⓓ	75 Ⓐ Ⓓ	87 Ⓐ Ⓓ
4 Ⓐ Ⓓ	16 Ⓐ Ⓓ	28 Ⓐ Ⓓ	40 Ⓐ Ⓓ	52 Ⓐ Ⓓ	64 Ⓐ Ⓓ	76 Ⓐ Ⓓ	88 Ⓐ Ⓓ
5 Ⓐ Ⓓ	17 Ⓐ Ⓓ	29 Ⓐ Ⓓ	41 Ⓐ Ⓓ	53 Ⓐ Ⓓ	65 Ⓐ Ⓓ	77 Ⓐ Ⓓ	89 Ⓐ Ⓓ
6 Ⓐ Ⓓ	18 Ⓐ Ⓓ	30 Ⓐ Ⓓ	42 Ⓐ Ⓓ	54 Ⓐ Ⓓ	66 Ⓐ Ⓓ	78 Ⓐ Ⓓ	90 Ⓐ Ⓓ
7 Ⓐ Ⓓ	19 Ⓐ Ⓓ	31 Ⓐ Ⓓ	43 Ⓐ Ⓓ	55 Ⓐ Ⓓ	67 Ⓐ Ⓓ	79 Ⓐ Ⓓ	91 Ⓐ Ⓓ
8 Ⓐ Ⓓ	20 Ⓐ Ⓓ	32 Ⓐ Ⓓ	44 Ⓐ Ⓓ	56 Ⓐ Ⓓ	68 Ⓐ Ⓓ	80 Ⓐ Ⓓ	92 Ⓐ Ⓓ
9 Ⓐ Ⓓ	21 Ⓐ Ⓓ	33 Ⓐ Ⓓ	45 Ⓐ Ⓓ	57 Ⓐ Ⓓ	69 Ⓐ Ⓓ	81 Ⓐ Ⓓ	93 Ⓐ Ⓓ
10 Ⓐ Ⓓ	22 Ⓐ Ⓓ	34 Ⓐ Ⓓ	46 Ⓐ Ⓓ	58 Ⓐ Ⓓ	70 Ⓐ Ⓓ	82 Ⓐ Ⓓ	94 Ⓐ Ⓓ
11 Ⓐ Ⓓ	23 Ⓐ Ⓓ	35 Ⓐ Ⓓ	47 Ⓐ Ⓓ	59 Ⓐ Ⓓ	71 Ⓐ Ⓓ	83 Ⓐ Ⓓ	95 Ⓐ Ⓓ
12 Ⓐ Ⓓ	24 Ⓐ Ⓓ	36 Ⓐ Ⓓ	48 Ⓐ Ⓓ	60 Ⓐ Ⓓ	72 Ⓐ Ⓓ	84 Ⓐ Ⓓ	

ADDRESS MEMORY SECTION

1 Ⓐ Ⓑ Ⓒ Ⓓ Ⓔ	19 Ⓐ Ⓑ Ⓒ Ⓓ Ⓔ	37 Ⓐ Ⓑ Ⓒ Ⓓ Ⓔ	55 Ⓐ Ⓑ Ⓒ Ⓓ Ⓔ	73 Ⓐ Ⓑ Ⓒ Ⓓ Ⓔ
2 Ⓐ Ⓑ Ⓒ Ⓓ Ⓔ	20 Ⓐ Ⓑ Ⓒ Ⓓ Ⓔ	38 Ⓐ Ⓑ Ⓒ Ⓓ Ⓔ	56 Ⓐ Ⓑ Ⓒ Ⓓ Ⓔ	74 Ⓐ Ⓑ Ⓒ Ⓓ Ⓔ
3 Ⓐ Ⓑ Ⓒ Ⓓ Ⓔ	21 Ⓐ Ⓑ Ⓒ Ⓓ Ⓔ	39 Ⓐ Ⓑ Ⓒ Ⓓ Ⓔ	57 Ⓐ Ⓑ Ⓒ Ⓓ Ⓔ	75 Ⓐ Ⓑ Ⓒ Ⓓ Ⓔ
4 Ⓐ Ⓑ Ⓒ Ⓓ Ⓔ	22 Ⓐ Ⓑ Ⓒ Ⓓ Ⓔ	40 Ⓐ Ⓑ Ⓒ Ⓓ Ⓔ	58 Ⓐ Ⓑ Ⓒ Ⓓ Ⓔ	76 Ⓐ Ⓑ Ⓒ Ⓓ Ⓔ
5 Ⓐ Ⓑ Ⓒ Ⓓ Ⓔ	23 Ⓐ Ⓑ Ⓒ Ⓓ Ⓔ	41 Ⓐ Ⓑ Ⓒ Ⓓ Ⓔ	59 Ⓐ Ⓑ Ⓒ Ⓓ Ⓔ	77 Ⓐ Ⓑ Ⓒ Ⓓ Ⓔ
6 Ⓐ Ⓑ Ⓒ Ⓓ Ⓔ	24 Ⓐ Ⓑ Ⓒ Ⓓ Ⓔ	42 Ⓐ Ⓑ Ⓒ Ⓓ Ⓔ	60 Ⓐ Ⓑ Ⓒ Ⓓ Ⓔ	78 Ⓐ Ⓑ Ⓒ Ⓓ Ⓔ
7 Ⓐ Ⓑ Ⓒ Ⓓ Ⓔ	25 Ⓐ Ⓑ Ⓒ Ⓓ Ⓔ	43 Ⓐ Ⓑ Ⓒ Ⓓ Ⓔ	61 Ⓐ Ⓑ Ⓒ Ⓓ Ⓔ	79 Ⓐ Ⓑ Ⓒ Ⓓ Ⓔ
8 Ⓐ Ⓑ Ⓒ Ⓓ Ⓔ	26 Ⓐ Ⓑ Ⓒ Ⓓ Ⓔ	44 Ⓐ Ⓑ Ⓒ Ⓓ Ⓔ	62 Ⓐ Ⓑ Ⓒ Ⓓ Ⓔ	80 Ⓐ Ⓑ Ⓒ Ⓓ Ⓔ
9 Ⓐ Ⓑ Ⓒ Ⓓ Ⓔ	27 Ⓐ Ⓑ Ⓒ Ⓓ Ⓔ	45 Ⓐ Ⓑ Ⓒ Ⓓ Ⓔ	63 Ⓐ Ⓑ Ⓒ Ⓓ Ⓔ	81 Ⓐ Ⓑ Ⓒ Ⓓ Ⓔ
10 Ⓐ Ⓑ Ⓒ Ⓓ Ⓔ	28 Ⓐ Ⓑ Ⓒ Ⓓ Ⓔ	46 Ⓐ Ⓑ Ⓒ Ⓓ Ⓔ	64 Ⓐ Ⓑ Ⓒ Ⓓ Ⓔ	82 Ⓐ Ⓑ Ⓒ Ⓓ Ⓔ
11 Ⓐ Ⓑ Ⓒ Ⓓ Ⓔ	29 Ⓐ Ⓑ Ⓒ Ⓓ Ⓔ	47 Ⓐ Ⓑ Ⓒ Ⓓ Ⓔ	65 Ⓐ Ⓑ Ⓒ Ⓓ Ⓔ	83 Ⓐ Ⓑ Ⓒ Ⓓ Ⓔ
12 Ⓐ Ⓑ Ⓒ Ⓓ Ⓔ	30 Ⓐ Ⓑ Ⓒ Ⓓ Ⓔ	48 Ⓐ Ⓑ Ⓒ Ⓓ Ⓔ	66 Ⓐ Ⓑ Ⓒ Ⓓ Ⓔ	84 Ⓐ Ⓑ Ⓒ Ⓓ Ⓔ
13 Ⓐ Ⓑ Ⓒ Ⓓ Ⓔ	31 Ⓐ Ⓑ Ⓒ Ⓓ Ⓔ	49 Ⓐ Ⓑ Ⓒ Ⓓ Ⓔ	67 Ⓐ Ⓑ Ⓒ Ⓓ Ⓔ	85 Ⓐ Ⓑ Ⓒ Ⓓ Ⓔ
14 Ⓐ Ⓑ Ⓒ Ⓓ Ⓔ	32 Ⓐ Ⓑ Ⓒ Ⓓ Ⓔ	50 Ⓐ Ⓑ Ⓒ Ⓓ Ⓔ	68 Ⓐ Ⓑ Ⓒ Ⓓ Ⓔ	86 Ⓐ Ⓑ Ⓒ Ⓓ Ⓔ
15 Ⓐ Ⓑ Ⓒ Ⓓ Ⓔ	33 Ⓐ Ⓑ Ⓒ Ⓓ Ⓔ	51 Ⓐ Ⓑ Ⓒ Ⓓ Ⓔ	69 Ⓐ Ⓑ Ⓒ Ⓓ Ⓔ	87 Ⓐ Ⓑ Ⓒ Ⓓ Ⓔ
16 Ⓐ Ⓑ Ⓒ Ⓓ Ⓔ	34 Ⓐ Ⓑ Ⓒ Ⓓ Ⓔ	52 Ⓐ Ⓑ Ⓒ Ⓓ Ⓔ	70 Ⓐ Ⓑ Ⓒ Ⓓ Ⓔ	88 Ⓐ Ⓑ Ⓒ Ⓓ Ⓔ
17 Ⓐ Ⓑ Ⓒ Ⓓ Ⓔ	35 Ⓐ Ⓑ Ⓒ Ⓓ Ⓔ	53 Ⓐ Ⓑ Ⓒ Ⓓ Ⓔ	71 Ⓐ Ⓑ Ⓒ Ⓓ Ⓔ	
18 Ⓐ Ⓑ Ⓒ Ⓓ Ⓔ	36 Ⓐ Ⓑ Ⓒ Ⓓ Ⓔ	54 Ⓐ Ⓑ Ⓒ Ⓓ Ⓔ	72 Ⓐ Ⓑ Ⓒ Ⓓ Ⓔ	

NUMBER SERIES SECTION

1 Ⓐ Ⓑ Ⓒ Ⓓ Ⓔ	7 Ⓐ Ⓑ Ⓒ Ⓓ Ⓔ	13 Ⓐ Ⓑ Ⓒ Ⓓ Ⓔ	19 Ⓐ Ⓑ Ⓒ Ⓓ Ⓔ
2 Ⓐ Ⓑ Ⓒ Ⓓ Ⓔ	8 Ⓐ Ⓑ Ⓒ Ⓓ Ⓔ	14 Ⓐ Ⓑ Ⓒ Ⓓ Ⓔ	20 Ⓐ Ⓑ Ⓒ Ⓓ Ⓔ
3 Ⓐ Ⓑ Ⓒ Ⓓ Ⓔ	9 Ⓐ Ⓑ Ⓒ Ⓓ Ⓔ	15 Ⓐ Ⓑ Ⓒ Ⓓ Ⓔ	21 Ⓐ Ⓑ Ⓒ Ⓓ Ⓔ
4 Ⓐ Ⓑ Ⓒ Ⓓ Ⓔ	10 Ⓐ Ⓑ Ⓒ Ⓓ Ⓔ	16 Ⓐ Ⓑ Ⓒ Ⓓ Ⓔ	22 Ⓐ Ⓑ Ⓒ Ⓓ Ⓔ
5 Ⓐ Ⓑ Ⓒ Ⓓ Ⓔ	11 Ⓐ Ⓑ Ⓒ Ⓓ Ⓔ	17 Ⓐ Ⓑ Ⓒ Ⓓ Ⓔ	23 Ⓐ Ⓑ Ⓒ Ⓓ Ⓔ
6 Ⓐ Ⓑ Ⓒ Ⓓ Ⓔ	12 Ⓐ Ⓑ Ⓒ Ⓓ Ⓔ	18 Ⓐ Ⓑ Ⓒ Ⓓ Ⓔ	24 Ⓐ Ⓑ Ⓒ Ⓓ Ⓔ

FOLLOWING ORAL DIRECTIONS SECTION

1 Ⓐ Ⓑ Ⓒ Ⓓ Ⓔ	19 Ⓐ Ⓑ Ⓒ Ⓓ Ⓔ	37 Ⓐ Ⓑ Ⓒ Ⓓ Ⓔ	55 Ⓐ Ⓑ Ⓒ Ⓓ Ⓔ	73 Ⓐ Ⓑ Ⓒ Ⓓ Ⓔ
2 Ⓐ Ⓑ Ⓒ Ⓓ Ⓔ	20 Ⓐ Ⓑ Ⓒ Ⓓ Ⓔ	38 Ⓐ Ⓑ Ⓒ Ⓓ Ⓔ	56 Ⓐ Ⓑ Ⓒ Ⓓ Ⓔ	74 Ⓐ Ⓑ Ⓒ Ⓓ Ⓔ
3 Ⓐ Ⓑ Ⓒ Ⓓ Ⓔ	21 Ⓐ Ⓑ Ⓒ Ⓓ Ⓔ	39 Ⓐ Ⓑ Ⓒ Ⓓ Ⓔ	57 Ⓐ Ⓑ Ⓒ Ⓓ Ⓔ	75 Ⓐ Ⓑ Ⓒ Ⓓ Ⓔ
4 Ⓐ Ⓑ Ⓒ Ⓓ Ⓔ	22 Ⓐ Ⓑ Ⓒ Ⓓ Ⓔ	40 Ⓐ Ⓑ Ⓒ Ⓓ Ⓔ	58 Ⓐ Ⓑ Ⓒ Ⓓ Ⓔ	76 Ⓐ Ⓑ Ⓒ Ⓓ Ⓔ
5 Ⓐ Ⓑ Ⓒ Ⓓ Ⓔ	23 Ⓐ Ⓑ Ⓒ Ⓓ Ⓔ	41 Ⓐ Ⓑ Ⓒ Ⓓ Ⓔ	59 Ⓐ Ⓑ Ⓒ Ⓓ Ⓔ	77 Ⓐ Ⓑ Ⓒ Ⓓ Ⓔ
6 Ⓐ Ⓑ Ⓒ Ⓓ Ⓔ	24 Ⓐ Ⓑ Ⓒ Ⓓ Ⓔ	42 Ⓐ Ⓑ Ⓒ Ⓓ Ⓔ	60 Ⓐ Ⓑ Ⓒ Ⓓ Ⓔ	78 Ⓐ Ⓑ Ⓒ Ⓓ Ⓔ
7 Ⓐ Ⓑ Ⓒ Ⓓ Ⓔ	25 Ⓐ Ⓑ Ⓒ Ⓓ Ⓔ	43 Ⓐ Ⓑ Ⓒ Ⓓ Ⓔ	61 Ⓐ Ⓑ Ⓒ Ⓓ Ⓔ	79 Ⓐ Ⓑ Ⓒ Ⓓ Ⓔ
8 Ⓐ Ⓑ Ⓒ Ⓓ Ⓔ	26 Ⓐ Ⓑ Ⓒ Ⓓ Ⓔ	44 Ⓐ Ⓑ Ⓒ Ⓓ Ⓔ	62 Ⓐ Ⓑ Ⓒ Ⓓ Ⓔ	80 Ⓐ Ⓑ Ⓒ Ⓓ Ⓔ
9 Ⓐ Ⓑ Ⓒ Ⓓ Ⓔ	27 Ⓐ Ⓑ Ⓒ Ⓓ Ⓔ	45 Ⓐ Ⓑ Ⓒ Ⓓ Ⓔ	63 Ⓐ Ⓑ Ⓒ Ⓓ Ⓔ	81 Ⓐ Ⓑ Ⓒ Ⓓ Ⓔ
10 Ⓐ Ⓑ Ⓒ Ⓓ Ⓔ	28 Ⓐ Ⓑ Ⓒ Ⓓ Ⓔ	46 Ⓐ Ⓑ Ⓒ Ⓓ Ⓔ	64 Ⓐ Ⓑ Ⓒ Ⓓ Ⓔ	82 Ⓐ Ⓑ Ⓒ Ⓓ Ⓔ
11 Ⓐ Ⓑ Ⓒ Ⓓ Ⓔ	29 Ⓐ Ⓑ Ⓒ Ⓓ Ⓔ	47 Ⓐ Ⓑ Ⓒ Ⓓ Ⓔ	65 Ⓐ Ⓑ Ⓒ Ⓓ Ⓔ	83 Ⓐ Ⓑ Ⓒ Ⓓ Ⓔ
12 Ⓐ Ⓑ Ⓒ Ⓓ Ⓔ	30 Ⓐ Ⓑ Ⓒ Ⓓ Ⓔ	48 Ⓐ Ⓑ Ⓒ Ⓓ Ⓔ	66 Ⓐ Ⓑ Ⓒ Ⓓ Ⓔ	84 Ⓐ Ⓑ Ⓒ Ⓓ Ⓔ
13 Ⓐ Ⓑ Ⓒ Ⓓ Ⓔ	31 Ⓐ Ⓑ Ⓒ Ⓓ Ⓔ	49 Ⓐ Ⓑ Ⓒ Ⓓ Ⓔ	67 Ⓐ Ⓑ Ⓒ Ⓓ Ⓔ	85 Ⓐ Ⓑ Ⓒ Ⓓ Ⓔ
14 Ⓐ Ⓑ Ⓒ Ⓓ Ⓔ	32 Ⓐ Ⓑ Ⓒ Ⓓ Ⓔ	50 Ⓐ Ⓑ Ⓒ Ⓓ Ⓔ	68 Ⓐ Ⓑ Ⓒ Ⓓ Ⓔ	86 Ⓐ Ⓑ Ⓒ Ⓓ Ⓔ
15 Ⓐ Ⓑ Ⓒ Ⓓ Ⓔ	33 Ⓐ Ⓑ Ⓒ Ⓓ Ⓔ	51 Ⓐ Ⓑ Ⓒ Ⓓ Ⓔ	69 Ⓐ Ⓑ Ⓒ Ⓓ Ⓔ	87 Ⓐ Ⓑ Ⓒ Ⓓ Ⓔ
16 Ⓐ Ⓑ Ⓒ Ⓓ Ⓔ	34 Ⓐ Ⓑ Ⓒ Ⓓ Ⓔ	52 Ⓐ Ⓑ Ⓒ Ⓓ Ⓔ	70 Ⓐ Ⓑ Ⓒ Ⓓ Ⓔ	88 Ⓐ Ⓑ Ⓒ Ⓓ Ⓔ
17 Ⓐ Ⓑ Ⓒ Ⓓ Ⓔ	35 Ⓐ Ⓑ Ⓒ Ⓓ Ⓔ	53 Ⓐ Ⓑ Ⓒ Ⓓ Ⓔ	71 Ⓐ Ⓑ Ⓒ Ⓓ Ⓔ	
18 Ⓐ Ⓑ Ⓒ Ⓓ Ⓔ	36 Ⓐ Ⓑ Ⓒ Ⓓ Ⓔ	54 Ⓐ Ⓑ Ⓒ Ⓓ Ⓔ	72 Ⓐ Ⓑ Ⓒ Ⓓ Ⓔ	

COMPLETE PRACTICE TEST ANSWER SHEET

ADDRESS CHECKING SECTION

1 Ⓐ Ⓓ 13 Ⓐ Ⓓ 25 Ⓐ Ⓓ 37 Ⓐ Ⓓ 49 Ⓐ Ⓓ 61 Ⓐ Ⓓ 73 Ⓐ Ⓓ 85 Ⓐ Ⓓ
2 Ⓐ Ⓓ 14 Ⓐ Ⓓ 26 Ⓐ Ⓓ 38 Ⓐ Ⓓ 50 Ⓐ Ⓓ 62 Ⓐ Ⓓ 74 Ⓐ Ⓓ 86 Ⓐ Ⓓ
3 Ⓐ Ⓓ 15 Ⓐ Ⓓ 27 Ⓐ Ⓓ 39 Ⓐ Ⓓ 51 Ⓐ Ⓓ 63 Ⓐ Ⓓ 75 Ⓐ Ⓓ 87 Ⓐ Ⓓ
4 Ⓐ Ⓓ 16 Ⓐ Ⓓ 28 Ⓐ Ⓓ 40 Ⓐ Ⓓ 52 Ⓐ Ⓓ 64 Ⓐ Ⓓ 76 Ⓐ Ⓓ 88 Ⓐ Ⓓ
5 Ⓐ Ⓓ 17 Ⓐ Ⓓ 29 Ⓐ Ⓓ 41 Ⓐ Ⓓ 53 Ⓐ Ⓓ 65 Ⓐ Ⓓ 77 Ⓐ Ⓓ 89 Ⓐ Ⓓ
6 Ⓐ Ⓓ 18 Ⓐ Ⓓ 30 Ⓐ Ⓓ 42 Ⓐ Ⓓ 54 Ⓐ Ⓓ 66 Ⓐ Ⓓ 78 Ⓐ Ⓓ 90 Ⓐ Ⓓ
7 Ⓐ Ⓓ 19 Ⓐ Ⓓ 31 Ⓐ Ⓓ 43 Ⓐ Ⓓ 55 Ⓐ Ⓓ 67 Ⓐ Ⓓ 79 Ⓐ Ⓓ 91 Ⓐ Ⓓ
8 Ⓐ Ⓓ 20 Ⓐ Ⓓ 32 Ⓐ Ⓓ 44 Ⓐ Ⓓ 56 Ⓐ Ⓓ 68 Ⓐ Ⓓ 80 Ⓐ Ⓓ 92 Ⓐ Ⓓ
9 Ⓐ Ⓓ 21 Ⓐ Ⓓ 33 Ⓐ Ⓓ 45 Ⓐ Ⓓ 57 Ⓐ Ⓓ 69 Ⓐ Ⓓ 81 Ⓐ Ⓓ 93 Ⓐ Ⓓ
10 Ⓐ Ⓓ 22 Ⓐ Ⓓ 34 Ⓐ Ⓓ 46 Ⓐ Ⓓ 58 Ⓐ Ⓓ 70 Ⓐ Ⓓ 82 Ⓐ Ⓓ 94 Ⓐ Ⓓ
11 Ⓐ Ⓓ 23 Ⓐ Ⓓ 35 Ⓐ Ⓓ 47 Ⓐ Ⓓ 59 Ⓐ Ⓓ 71 Ⓐ Ⓓ 83 Ⓐ Ⓓ 95 Ⓐ Ⓓ
12 Ⓐ Ⓓ 24 Ⓐ Ⓓ 36 Ⓐ Ⓓ 48 Ⓐ Ⓓ 60 Ⓐ Ⓓ 72 Ⓐ Ⓓ 84 Ⓐ Ⓓ

ADDRESS MEMORY SECTION

1 Ⓐ Ⓑ Ⓒ Ⓓ Ⓔ 19 Ⓐ Ⓑ Ⓒ Ⓓ Ⓔ 37 Ⓐ Ⓑ Ⓒ Ⓓ Ⓔ 55 Ⓐ Ⓑ Ⓒ Ⓓ Ⓔ 73 Ⓐ Ⓑ Ⓒ Ⓓ Ⓔ
2 Ⓐ Ⓑ Ⓒ Ⓓ Ⓔ 20 Ⓐ Ⓑ Ⓒ Ⓓ Ⓔ 38 Ⓐ Ⓑ Ⓒ Ⓓ Ⓔ 56 Ⓐ Ⓑ Ⓒ Ⓓ Ⓔ 74 Ⓐ Ⓑ Ⓒ Ⓓ Ⓔ
3 Ⓐ Ⓑ Ⓒ Ⓓ Ⓔ 21 Ⓐ Ⓑ Ⓒ Ⓓ Ⓔ 39 Ⓐ Ⓑ Ⓒ Ⓓ Ⓔ 57 Ⓐ Ⓑ Ⓒ Ⓓ Ⓔ 75 Ⓐ Ⓑ Ⓒ Ⓓ Ⓔ
4 Ⓐ Ⓑ Ⓒ Ⓓ Ⓔ 22 Ⓐ Ⓑ Ⓒ Ⓓ Ⓔ 40 Ⓐ Ⓑ Ⓒ Ⓓ Ⓔ 58 Ⓐ Ⓑ Ⓒ Ⓓ Ⓔ 76 Ⓐ Ⓑ Ⓒ Ⓓ Ⓔ
5 Ⓐ Ⓑ Ⓒ Ⓓ Ⓔ 23 Ⓐ Ⓑ Ⓒ Ⓓ Ⓔ 41 Ⓐ Ⓑ Ⓒ Ⓓ Ⓔ 59 Ⓐ Ⓑ Ⓒ Ⓓ Ⓔ 77 Ⓐ Ⓑ Ⓒ Ⓓ Ⓔ
6 Ⓐ Ⓑ Ⓒ Ⓓ Ⓔ 24 Ⓐ Ⓑ Ⓒ Ⓓ Ⓔ 42 Ⓐ Ⓑ Ⓒ Ⓓ Ⓔ 60 Ⓐ Ⓑ Ⓒ Ⓓ Ⓔ 78 Ⓐ Ⓑ Ⓒ Ⓓ Ⓔ
7 Ⓐ Ⓑ Ⓒ Ⓓ Ⓔ 25 Ⓐ Ⓑ Ⓒ Ⓓ Ⓔ 43 Ⓐ Ⓑ Ⓒ Ⓓ Ⓔ 61 Ⓐ Ⓑ Ⓒ Ⓓ Ⓔ 79 Ⓐ Ⓑ Ⓒ Ⓓ Ⓔ
8 Ⓐ Ⓑ Ⓒ Ⓓ Ⓔ 26 Ⓐ Ⓑ Ⓒ Ⓓ Ⓔ 44 Ⓐ Ⓑ Ⓒ Ⓓ Ⓔ 62 Ⓐ Ⓑ Ⓒ Ⓓ Ⓔ 80 Ⓐ Ⓑ Ⓒ Ⓓ Ⓔ
9 Ⓐ Ⓑ Ⓒ Ⓓ Ⓔ 27 Ⓐ Ⓑ Ⓒ Ⓓ Ⓔ 45 Ⓐ Ⓑ Ⓒ Ⓓ Ⓔ 63 Ⓐ Ⓑ Ⓒ Ⓓ Ⓔ 81 Ⓐ Ⓑ Ⓒ Ⓓ Ⓔ
10 Ⓐ Ⓑ Ⓒ Ⓓ Ⓔ 28 Ⓐ Ⓑ Ⓒ Ⓓ Ⓔ 46 Ⓐ Ⓑ Ⓒ Ⓓ Ⓔ 64 Ⓐ Ⓑ Ⓒ Ⓓ Ⓔ 82 Ⓐ Ⓑ Ⓒ Ⓓ Ⓔ
11 Ⓐ Ⓑ Ⓒ Ⓓ Ⓔ 29 Ⓐ Ⓑ Ⓒ Ⓓ Ⓔ 47 Ⓐ Ⓑ Ⓒ Ⓓ Ⓔ 65 Ⓐ Ⓑ Ⓒ Ⓓ Ⓔ 83 Ⓐ Ⓑ Ⓒ Ⓓ Ⓔ
12 Ⓐ Ⓑ Ⓒ Ⓓ Ⓔ 30 Ⓐ Ⓑ Ⓒ Ⓓ Ⓔ 48 Ⓐ Ⓑ Ⓒ Ⓓ Ⓔ 66 Ⓐ Ⓑ Ⓒ Ⓓ Ⓔ 84 Ⓐ Ⓑ Ⓒ Ⓓ Ⓔ
13 Ⓐ Ⓑ Ⓒ Ⓓ Ⓔ 31 Ⓐ Ⓑ Ⓒ Ⓓ Ⓔ 49 Ⓐ Ⓑ Ⓒ Ⓓ Ⓔ 67 Ⓐ Ⓑ Ⓒ Ⓓ Ⓔ 85 Ⓐ Ⓑ Ⓒ Ⓓ Ⓔ
14 Ⓐ Ⓑ Ⓒ Ⓓ Ⓔ 32 Ⓐ Ⓑ Ⓒ Ⓓ Ⓔ 50 Ⓐ Ⓑ Ⓒ Ⓓ Ⓔ 68 Ⓐ Ⓑ Ⓒ Ⓓ Ⓔ 86 Ⓐ Ⓑ Ⓒ Ⓓ Ⓔ
15 Ⓐ Ⓑ Ⓒ Ⓓ Ⓔ 33 Ⓐ Ⓑ Ⓒ Ⓓ Ⓔ 51 Ⓐ Ⓑ Ⓒ Ⓓ Ⓔ 69 Ⓐ Ⓑ Ⓒ Ⓓ Ⓔ 87 Ⓐ Ⓑ Ⓒ Ⓓ Ⓔ
16 Ⓐ Ⓑ Ⓒ Ⓓ Ⓔ 34 Ⓐ Ⓑ Ⓒ Ⓓ Ⓔ 52 Ⓐ Ⓑ Ⓒ Ⓓ Ⓔ 70 Ⓐ Ⓑ Ⓒ Ⓓ Ⓔ 88 Ⓐ Ⓑ Ⓒ Ⓓ Ⓔ
17 Ⓐ Ⓑ Ⓒ Ⓓ Ⓔ 35 Ⓐ Ⓑ Ⓒ Ⓓ Ⓔ 53 Ⓐ Ⓑ Ⓒ Ⓓ Ⓔ 71 Ⓐ Ⓑ Ⓒ Ⓓ Ⓔ
18 Ⓐ Ⓑ Ⓒ Ⓓ Ⓔ 36 Ⓐ Ⓑ Ⓒ Ⓓ Ⓔ 54 Ⓐ Ⓑ Ⓒ Ⓓ Ⓔ 72 Ⓐ Ⓑ Ⓒ Ⓓ Ⓔ

NUMBER SERIES SECTION

1 Ⓐ Ⓑ Ⓒ Ⓓ Ⓔ 7 Ⓐ Ⓑ Ⓒ Ⓓ Ⓔ 13 Ⓐ Ⓑ Ⓒ Ⓓ Ⓔ 19 Ⓐ Ⓑ Ⓒ Ⓓ Ⓔ
2 Ⓐ Ⓑ Ⓒ Ⓓ Ⓔ 8 Ⓐ Ⓑ Ⓒ Ⓓ Ⓔ 14 Ⓐ Ⓑ Ⓒ Ⓓ Ⓔ 20 Ⓐ Ⓑ Ⓒ Ⓓ Ⓔ
3 Ⓐ Ⓑ Ⓒ Ⓓ Ⓔ 9 Ⓐ Ⓑ Ⓒ Ⓓ Ⓔ 15 Ⓐ Ⓑ Ⓒ Ⓓ Ⓔ 21 Ⓐ Ⓑ Ⓒ Ⓓ Ⓔ
4 Ⓐ Ⓑ Ⓒ Ⓓ Ⓔ 10 Ⓐ Ⓑ Ⓒ Ⓓ Ⓔ 16 Ⓐ Ⓑ Ⓒ Ⓓ Ⓔ 22 Ⓐ Ⓑ Ⓒ Ⓓ Ⓔ
5 Ⓐ Ⓑ Ⓒ Ⓓ Ⓔ 11 Ⓐ Ⓑ Ⓒ Ⓓ Ⓔ 17 Ⓐ Ⓑ Ⓒ Ⓓ Ⓔ 23 Ⓐ Ⓑ Ⓒ Ⓓ Ⓔ
6 Ⓐ Ⓑ Ⓒ Ⓓ Ⓔ 12 Ⓐ Ⓑ Ⓒ Ⓓ Ⓔ 18 Ⓐ Ⓑ Ⓒ Ⓓ Ⓔ 24 Ⓐ Ⓑ Ⓒ Ⓓ Ⓔ

FOLLOWING ORAL DIRECTIONS SECTION

1 Ⓐ Ⓑ Ⓒ Ⓓ Ⓔ 19 Ⓐ Ⓑ Ⓒ Ⓓ Ⓔ 37 Ⓐ Ⓑ Ⓒ Ⓓ Ⓔ 55 Ⓐ Ⓑ Ⓒ Ⓓ Ⓔ 73 Ⓐ Ⓑ Ⓒ Ⓓ Ⓔ
2 Ⓐ Ⓑ Ⓒ Ⓓ Ⓔ 20 Ⓐ Ⓑ Ⓒ Ⓓ Ⓔ 38 Ⓐ Ⓑ Ⓒ Ⓓ Ⓔ 56 Ⓐ Ⓑ Ⓒ Ⓓ Ⓔ 74 Ⓐ Ⓑ Ⓒ Ⓓ Ⓔ
3 Ⓐ Ⓑ Ⓒ Ⓓ Ⓔ 21 Ⓐ Ⓑ Ⓒ Ⓓ Ⓔ 39 Ⓐ Ⓑ Ⓒ Ⓓ Ⓔ 57 Ⓐ Ⓑ Ⓒ Ⓓ Ⓔ 75 Ⓐ Ⓑ Ⓒ Ⓓ Ⓔ
4 Ⓐ Ⓑ Ⓒ Ⓓ Ⓔ 22 Ⓐ Ⓑ Ⓒ Ⓓ Ⓔ 40 Ⓐ Ⓑ Ⓒ Ⓓ Ⓔ 58 Ⓐ Ⓑ Ⓒ Ⓓ Ⓔ 76 Ⓐ Ⓑ Ⓒ Ⓓ Ⓔ
5 Ⓐ Ⓑ Ⓒ Ⓓ Ⓔ 23 Ⓐ Ⓑ Ⓒ Ⓓ Ⓔ 41 Ⓐ Ⓑ Ⓒ Ⓓ Ⓔ 59 Ⓐ Ⓑ Ⓒ Ⓓ Ⓔ 77 Ⓐ Ⓑ Ⓒ Ⓓ Ⓔ
6 Ⓐ Ⓑ Ⓒ Ⓓ Ⓔ 24 Ⓐ Ⓑ Ⓒ Ⓓ Ⓔ 42 Ⓐ Ⓑ Ⓒ Ⓓ Ⓔ 60 Ⓐ Ⓑ Ⓒ Ⓓ Ⓔ 78 Ⓐ Ⓑ Ⓒ Ⓓ Ⓔ
7 Ⓐ Ⓑ Ⓒ Ⓓ Ⓔ 25 Ⓐ Ⓑ Ⓒ Ⓓ Ⓔ 43 Ⓐ Ⓑ Ⓒ Ⓓ Ⓔ 61 Ⓐ Ⓑ Ⓒ Ⓓ Ⓔ 79 Ⓐ Ⓑ Ⓒ Ⓓ Ⓔ
8 Ⓐ Ⓑ Ⓒ Ⓓ Ⓔ 26 Ⓐ Ⓑ Ⓒ Ⓓ Ⓔ 44 Ⓐ Ⓑ Ⓒ Ⓓ Ⓔ 62 Ⓐ Ⓑ Ⓒ Ⓓ Ⓔ 80 Ⓐ Ⓑ Ⓒ Ⓓ Ⓔ
9 Ⓐ Ⓑ Ⓒ Ⓓ Ⓔ 27 Ⓐ Ⓑ Ⓒ Ⓓ Ⓔ 45 Ⓐ Ⓑ Ⓒ Ⓓ Ⓔ 63 Ⓐ Ⓑ Ⓒ Ⓓ Ⓔ 81 Ⓐ Ⓑ Ⓒ Ⓓ Ⓔ
10 Ⓐ Ⓑ Ⓒ Ⓓ Ⓔ 28 Ⓐ Ⓑ Ⓒ Ⓓ Ⓔ 46 Ⓐ Ⓑ Ⓒ Ⓓ Ⓔ 64 Ⓐ Ⓑ Ⓒ Ⓓ Ⓔ 82 Ⓐ Ⓑ Ⓒ Ⓓ Ⓔ
11 Ⓐ Ⓑ Ⓒ Ⓓ Ⓔ 29 Ⓐ Ⓑ Ⓒ Ⓓ Ⓔ 47 Ⓐ Ⓑ Ⓒ Ⓓ Ⓔ 65 Ⓐ Ⓑ Ⓒ Ⓓ Ⓔ 83 Ⓐ Ⓑ Ⓒ Ⓓ Ⓔ
12 Ⓐ Ⓑ Ⓒ Ⓓ Ⓔ 30 Ⓐ Ⓑ Ⓒ Ⓓ Ⓔ 48 Ⓐ Ⓑ Ⓒ Ⓓ Ⓔ 66 Ⓐ Ⓑ Ⓒ Ⓓ Ⓔ 84 Ⓐ Ⓑ Ⓒ Ⓓ Ⓔ
13 Ⓐ Ⓑ Ⓒ Ⓓ Ⓔ 31 Ⓐ Ⓑ Ⓒ Ⓓ Ⓔ 49 Ⓐ Ⓑ Ⓒ Ⓓ Ⓔ 67 Ⓐ Ⓑ Ⓒ Ⓓ Ⓔ 85 Ⓐ Ⓑ Ⓒ Ⓓ Ⓔ
14 Ⓐ Ⓑ Ⓒ Ⓓ Ⓔ 32 Ⓐ Ⓑ Ⓒ Ⓓ Ⓔ 50 Ⓐ Ⓑ Ⓒ Ⓓ Ⓔ 68 Ⓐ Ⓑ Ⓒ Ⓓ Ⓔ 86 Ⓐ Ⓑ Ⓒ Ⓓ Ⓔ
15 Ⓐ Ⓑ Ⓒ Ⓓ Ⓔ 33 Ⓐ Ⓑ Ⓒ Ⓓ Ⓔ 51 Ⓐ Ⓑ Ⓒ Ⓓ Ⓔ 69 Ⓐ Ⓑ Ⓒ Ⓓ Ⓔ 87 Ⓐ Ⓑ Ⓒ Ⓓ Ⓔ
16 Ⓐ Ⓑ Ⓒ Ⓓ Ⓔ 34 Ⓐ Ⓑ Ⓒ Ⓓ Ⓔ 52 Ⓐ Ⓑ Ⓒ Ⓓ Ⓔ 70 Ⓐ Ⓑ Ⓒ Ⓓ Ⓔ 88 Ⓐ Ⓑ Ⓒ Ⓓ Ⓔ
17 Ⓐ Ⓑ Ⓒ Ⓓ Ⓔ 35 Ⓐ Ⓑ Ⓒ Ⓓ Ⓔ 53 Ⓐ Ⓑ Ⓒ Ⓓ Ⓔ 71 Ⓐ Ⓑ Ⓒ Ⓓ Ⓔ
18 Ⓐ Ⓑ Ⓒ Ⓓ Ⓔ 36 Ⓐ Ⓑ Ⓒ Ⓓ Ⓔ 54 Ⓐ Ⓑ Ⓒ Ⓓ Ⓔ 72 Ⓐ Ⓑ Ⓒ Ⓓ Ⓔ

COMPLETE PRACTICE TEST ANSWER SHEET

ADDRESS CHECKING SECTION

1 Ⓐ Ⓓ	13 Ⓐ Ⓓ	25 Ⓐ Ⓓ	37 Ⓐ Ⓓ	49 Ⓐ Ⓓ	61 Ⓐ Ⓓ	73 Ⓐ Ⓓ	85 Ⓐ Ⓓ
2 Ⓐ Ⓓ	14 Ⓐ Ⓓ	26 Ⓐ Ⓓ	38 Ⓐ Ⓓ	50 Ⓐ Ⓓ	62 Ⓐ Ⓓ	74 Ⓐ Ⓓ	86 Ⓐ Ⓓ
3 Ⓐ Ⓓ	15 Ⓐ Ⓓ	27 Ⓐ Ⓓ	39 Ⓐ Ⓓ	51 Ⓐ Ⓓ	63 Ⓐ Ⓓ	75 Ⓐ Ⓓ	87 Ⓐ Ⓓ
4 Ⓐ Ⓓ	16 Ⓐ Ⓓ	28 Ⓐ Ⓓ	40 Ⓐ Ⓓ	52 Ⓐ Ⓓ	64 Ⓐ Ⓓ	76 Ⓐ Ⓓ	88 Ⓐ Ⓓ
5 Ⓐ Ⓓ	17 Ⓐ Ⓓ	29 Ⓐ Ⓓ	41 Ⓐ Ⓓ	53 Ⓐ Ⓓ	65 Ⓐ Ⓓ	77 Ⓐ Ⓓ	89 Ⓐ Ⓓ
6 Ⓐ Ⓓ	18 Ⓐ Ⓓ	30 Ⓐ Ⓓ	42 Ⓐ Ⓓ	54 Ⓐ Ⓓ	66 Ⓐ Ⓓ	78 Ⓐ Ⓓ	90 Ⓐ Ⓓ
7 Ⓐ Ⓓ	19 Ⓐ Ⓓ	31 Ⓐ Ⓓ	43 Ⓐ Ⓓ	55 Ⓐ Ⓓ	67 Ⓐ Ⓓ	79 Ⓐ Ⓓ	91 Ⓐ Ⓓ
8 Ⓐ Ⓓ	20 Ⓐ Ⓓ	32 Ⓐ Ⓓ	44 Ⓐ Ⓓ	56 Ⓐ Ⓓ	68 Ⓐ Ⓓ	80 Ⓐ Ⓓ	92 Ⓐ Ⓓ
9 Ⓐ Ⓓ	21 Ⓐ Ⓓ	33 Ⓐ Ⓓ	45 Ⓐ Ⓓ	57 Ⓐ Ⓓ	69 Ⓐ Ⓓ	81 Ⓐ Ⓓ	93 Ⓐ Ⓓ
10 Ⓐ Ⓓ	22 Ⓐ Ⓓ	34 Ⓐ Ⓓ	46 Ⓐ Ⓓ	58 Ⓐ Ⓓ	70 Ⓐ Ⓓ	82 Ⓐ Ⓓ	94 Ⓐ Ⓓ
11 Ⓐ Ⓓ	23 Ⓐ Ⓓ	35 Ⓐ Ⓓ	47 Ⓐ Ⓓ	59 Ⓐ Ⓓ	71 Ⓐ Ⓓ	83 Ⓐ Ⓓ	95 Ⓐ Ⓓ
12 Ⓐ Ⓓ	24 Ⓐ Ⓓ	36 Ⓐ Ⓓ	48 Ⓐ Ⓓ	60 Ⓐ Ⓓ	72 Ⓐ Ⓓ	84 Ⓐ Ⓓ	

ADDRESS MEMORY SECTION

1 Ⓐ Ⓑ Ⓒ Ⓓ Ⓔ	19 Ⓐ Ⓑ Ⓒ Ⓓ Ⓔ	37 Ⓐ Ⓑ Ⓒ Ⓓ Ⓔ	55 Ⓐ Ⓑ Ⓒ Ⓓ Ⓔ	73 Ⓐ Ⓑ Ⓒ Ⓓ Ⓔ
2 Ⓐ Ⓑ Ⓒ Ⓓ Ⓔ	20 Ⓐ Ⓑ Ⓒ Ⓓ Ⓔ	38 Ⓐ Ⓑ Ⓒ Ⓓ Ⓔ	56 Ⓐ Ⓑ Ⓒ Ⓓ Ⓔ	74 Ⓐ Ⓑ Ⓒ Ⓓ Ⓔ
3 Ⓐ Ⓑ Ⓒ Ⓓ Ⓔ	21 Ⓐ Ⓑ Ⓒ Ⓓ Ⓔ	39 Ⓐ Ⓑ Ⓒ Ⓓ Ⓔ	57 Ⓐ Ⓑ Ⓒ Ⓓ Ⓔ	75 Ⓐ Ⓑ Ⓒ Ⓓ Ⓔ
4 Ⓐ Ⓑ Ⓒ Ⓓ Ⓔ	22 Ⓐ Ⓑ Ⓒ Ⓓ Ⓔ	40 Ⓐ Ⓑ Ⓒ Ⓓ Ⓔ	58 Ⓐ Ⓑ Ⓒ Ⓓ Ⓔ	76 Ⓐ Ⓑ Ⓒ Ⓓ Ⓔ
5 Ⓐ Ⓑ Ⓒ Ⓓ Ⓔ	23 Ⓐ Ⓑ Ⓒ Ⓓ Ⓔ	41 Ⓐ Ⓑ Ⓒ Ⓓ Ⓔ	59 Ⓐ Ⓑ Ⓒ Ⓓ Ⓔ	77 Ⓐ Ⓑ Ⓒ Ⓓ Ⓔ
6 Ⓐ Ⓑ Ⓒ Ⓓ Ⓔ	24 Ⓐ Ⓑ Ⓒ Ⓓ Ⓔ	42 Ⓐ Ⓑ Ⓒ Ⓓ Ⓔ	60 Ⓐ Ⓑ Ⓒ Ⓓ Ⓔ	78 Ⓐ Ⓑ Ⓒ Ⓓ Ⓔ
7 Ⓐ Ⓑ Ⓒ Ⓓ Ⓔ	25 Ⓐ Ⓑ Ⓒ Ⓓ Ⓔ	43 Ⓐ Ⓑ Ⓒ Ⓓ Ⓔ	61 Ⓐ Ⓑ Ⓒ Ⓓ Ⓔ	79 Ⓐ Ⓑ Ⓒ Ⓓ Ⓔ
8 Ⓐ Ⓑ Ⓒ Ⓓ Ⓔ	26 Ⓐ Ⓑ Ⓒ Ⓓ Ⓔ	44 Ⓐ Ⓑ Ⓒ Ⓓ Ⓔ	62 Ⓐ Ⓑ Ⓒ Ⓓ Ⓔ	80 Ⓐ Ⓑ Ⓒ Ⓓ Ⓔ
9 Ⓐ Ⓑ Ⓒ Ⓓ Ⓔ	27 Ⓐ Ⓑ Ⓒ Ⓓ Ⓔ	45 Ⓐ Ⓑ Ⓒ Ⓓ Ⓔ	63 Ⓐ Ⓑ Ⓒ Ⓓ Ⓔ	81 Ⓐ Ⓑ Ⓒ Ⓓ Ⓔ
10 Ⓐ Ⓑ Ⓒ Ⓓ Ⓔ	28 Ⓐ Ⓑ Ⓒ Ⓓ Ⓔ	46 Ⓐ Ⓑ Ⓒ Ⓓ Ⓔ	64 Ⓐ Ⓑ Ⓒ Ⓓ Ⓔ	82 Ⓐ Ⓑ Ⓒ Ⓓ Ⓔ
11 Ⓐ Ⓑ Ⓒ Ⓓ Ⓔ	29 Ⓐ Ⓑ Ⓒ Ⓓ Ⓔ	47 Ⓐ Ⓑ Ⓒ Ⓓ Ⓔ	65 Ⓐ Ⓑ Ⓒ Ⓓ Ⓔ	83 Ⓐ Ⓑ Ⓒ Ⓓ Ⓔ
12 Ⓐ Ⓑ Ⓒ Ⓓ Ⓔ	30 Ⓐ Ⓑ Ⓒ Ⓓ Ⓔ	48 Ⓐ Ⓑ Ⓒ Ⓓ Ⓔ	66 Ⓐ Ⓑ Ⓒ Ⓓ Ⓔ	84 Ⓐ Ⓑ Ⓒ Ⓓ Ⓔ
13 Ⓐ Ⓑ Ⓒ Ⓓ Ⓔ	31 Ⓐ Ⓑ Ⓒ Ⓓ Ⓔ	49 Ⓐ Ⓑ Ⓒ Ⓓ Ⓔ	67 Ⓐ Ⓑ Ⓒ Ⓓ Ⓔ	85 Ⓐ Ⓑ Ⓒ Ⓓ Ⓔ
14 Ⓐ Ⓑ Ⓒ Ⓓ Ⓔ	32 Ⓐ Ⓑ Ⓒ Ⓓ Ⓔ	50 Ⓐ Ⓑ Ⓒ Ⓓ Ⓔ	68 Ⓐ Ⓑ Ⓒ Ⓓ Ⓔ	86 Ⓐ Ⓑ Ⓒ Ⓓ Ⓔ
15 Ⓐ Ⓑ Ⓒ Ⓓ Ⓔ	33 Ⓐ Ⓑ Ⓒ Ⓓ Ⓔ	51 Ⓐ Ⓑ Ⓒ Ⓓ Ⓔ	69 Ⓐ Ⓑ Ⓒ Ⓓ Ⓔ	87 Ⓐ Ⓑ Ⓒ Ⓓ Ⓔ
16 Ⓐ Ⓑ Ⓒ Ⓓ Ⓔ	34 Ⓐ Ⓑ Ⓒ Ⓓ Ⓔ	52 Ⓐ Ⓑ Ⓒ Ⓓ Ⓔ	70 Ⓐ Ⓑ Ⓒ Ⓓ Ⓔ	88 Ⓐ Ⓑ Ⓒ Ⓓ Ⓔ
17 Ⓐ Ⓑ Ⓒ Ⓓ Ⓔ	35 Ⓐ Ⓑ Ⓒ Ⓓ Ⓔ	53 Ⓐ Ⓑ Ⓒ Ⓓ Ⓔ	71 Ⓐ Ⓑ Ⓒ Ⓓ Ⓔ	
18 Ⓐ Ⓑ Ⓒ Ⓓ Ⓔ	36 Ⓐ Ⓑ Ⓒ Ⓓ Ⓔ	54 Ⓐ Ⓑ Ⓒ Ⓓ Ⓔ	72 Ⓐ Ⓑ Ⓒ Ⓓ Ⓔ	

NUMBER SERIES SECTION

1 Ⓐ Ⓑ Ⓒ Ⓓ Ⓔ	7 Ⓐ Ⓑ Ⓒ Ⓓ Ⓔ	13 Ⓐ Ⓑ Ⓒ Ⓓ Ⓔ	19 Ⓐ Ⓑ Ⓒ Ⓓ Ⓔ
2 Ⓐ Ⓑ Ⓒ Ⓓ Ⓔ	8 Ⓐ Ⓑ Ⓒ Ⓓ Ⓔ	14 Ⓐ Ⓑ Ⓒ Ⓓ Ⓔ	20 Ⓐ Ⓑ Ⓒ Ⓓ Ⓔ
3 Ⓐ Ⓑ Ⓒ Ⓓ Ⓔ	9 Ⓐ Ⓑ Ⓒ Ⓓ Ⓔ	15 Ⓐ Ⓑ Ⓒ Ⓓ Ⓔ	21 Ⓐ Ⓑ Ⓒ Ⓓ Ⓔ
4 Ⓐ Ⓑ Ⓒ Ⓓ Ⓔ	10 Ⓐ Ⓑ Ⓒ Ⓓ Ⓔ	16 Ⓐ Ⓑ Ⓒ Ⓓ Ⓔ	22 Ⓐ Ⓑ Ⓒ Ⓓ Ⓔ
5 Ⓐ Ⓑ Ⓒ Ⓓ Ⓔ	11 Ⓐ Ⓑ Ⓒ Ⓓ Ⓔ	17 Ⓐ Ⓑ Ⓒ Ⓓ Ⓔ	23 Ⓐ Ⓑ Ⓒ Ⓓ Ⓔ
6 Ⓐ Ⓑ Ⓒ Ⓓ Ⓔ	12 Ⓐ Ⓑ Ⓒ Ⓓ Ⓔ	18 Ⓐ Ⓑ Ⓒ Ⓓ Ⓔ	24 Ⓐ Ⓑ Ⓒ Ⓓ Ⓔ

FOLLOWING ORAL DIRECTIONS SECTION

1 Ⓐ Ⓑ Ⓒ Ⓓ Ⓔ	19 Ⓐ Ⓑ Ⓒ Ⓓ Ⓔ	37 Ⓐ Ⓑ Ⓒ Ⓓ Ⓔ	55 Ⓐ Ⓑ Ⓒ Ⓓ Ⓔ	73 Ⓐ Ⓑ Ⓒ Ⓓ Ⓔ
2 Ⓐ Ⓑ Ⓒ Ⓓ Ⓔ	20 Ⓐ Ⓑ Ⓒ Ⓓ Ⓔ	38 Ⓐ Ⓑ Ⓒ Ⓓ Ⓔ	56 Ⓐ Ⓑ Ⓒ Ⓓ Ⓔ	74 Ⓐ Ⓑ Ⓒ Ⓓ Ⓔ
3 Ⓐ Ⓑ Ⓒ Ⓓ Ⓔ	21 Ⓐ Ⓑ Ⓒ Ⓓ Ⓔ	39 Ⓐ Ⓑ Ⓒ Ⓓ Ⓔ	57 Ⓐ Ⓑ Ⓒ Ⓓ Ⓔ	75 Ⓐ Ⓑ Ⓒ Ⓓ Ⓔ
4 Ⓐ Ⓑ Ⓒ Ⓓ Ⓔ	22 Ⓐ Ⓑ Ⓒ Ⓓ Ⓔ	40 Ⓐ Ⓑ Ⓒ Ⓓ Ⓔ	58 Ⓐ Ⓑ Ⓒ Ⓓ Ⓔ	76 Ⓐ Ⓑ Ⓒ Ⓓ Ⓔ
5 Ⓐ Ⓑ Ⓒ Ⓓ Ⓔ	23 Ⓐ Ⓑ Ⓒ Ⓓ Ⓔ	41 Ⓐ Ⓑ Ⓒ Ⓓ Ⓔ	59 Ⓐ Ⓑ Ⓒ Ⓓ Ⓔ	77 Ⓐ Ⓑ Ⓒ Ⓓ Ⓔ
6 Ⓐ Ⓑ Ⓒ Ⓓ Ⓔ	24 Ⓐ Ⓑ Ⓒ Ⓓ Ⓔ	42 Ⓐ Ⓑ Ⓒ Ⓓ Ⓔ	60 Ⓐ Ⓑ Ⓒ Ⓓ Ⓔ	78 Ⓐ Ⓑ Ⓒ Ⓓ Ⓔ
7 Ⓐ Ⓑ Ⓒ Ⓓ Ⓔ	25 Ⓐ Ⓑ Ⓒ Ⓓ Ⓔ	43 Ⓐ Ⓑ Ⓒ Ⓓ Ⓔ	61 Ⓐ Ⓑ Ⓒ Ⓓ Ⓔ	79 Ⓐ Ⓑ Ⓒ Ⓓ Ⓔ
8 Ⓐ Ⓑ Ⓒ Ⓓ Ⓔ	26 Ⓐ Ⓑ Ⓒ Ⓓ Ⓔ	44 Ⓐ Ⓑ Ⓒ Ⓓ Ⓔ	62 Ⓐ Ⓑ Ⓒ Ⓓ Ⓔ	80 Ⓐ Ⓑ Ⓒ Ⓓ Ⓔ
9 Ⓐ Ⓑ Ⓒ Ⓓ Ⓔ	27 Ⓐ Ⓑ Ⓒ Ⓓ Ⓔ	45 Ⓐ Ⓑ Ⓒ Ⓓ Ⓔ	63 Ⓐ Ⓑ Ⓒ Ⓓ Ⓔ	81 Ⓐ Ⓑ Ⓒ Ⓓ Ⓔ
10 Ⓐ Ⓑ Ⓒ Ⓓ Ⓔ	28 Ⓐ Ⓑ Ⓒ Ⓓ Ⓔ	46 Ⓐ Ⓑ Ⓒ Ⓓ Ⓔ	64 Ⓐ Ⓑ Ⓒ Ⓓ Ⓔ	82 Ⓐ Ⓑ Ⓒ Ⓓ Ⓔ
11 Ⓐ Ⓑ Ⓒ Ⓓ Ⓔ	29 Ⓐ Ⓑ Ⓒ Ⓓ Ⓔ	47 Ⓐ Ⓑ Ⓒ Ⓓ Ⓔ	65 Ⓐ Ⓑ Ⓒ Ⓓ Ⓔ	83 Ⓐ Ⓑ Ⓒ Ⓓ Ⓔ
12 Ⓐ Ⓑ Ⓒ Ⓓ Ⓔ	30 Ⓐ Ⓑ Ⓒ Ⓓ Ⓔ	48 Ⓐ Ⓑ Ⓒ Ⓓ Ⓔ	66 Ⓐ Ⓑ Ⓒ Ⓓ Ⓔ	84 Ⓐ Ⓑ Ⓒ Ⓓ Ⓔ
13 Ⓐ Ⓑ Ⓒ Ⓓ Ⓔ	31 Ⓐ Ⓑ Ⓒ Ⓓ Ⓔ	49 Ⓐ Ⓑ Ⓒ Ⓓ Ⓔ	67 Ⓐ Ⓑ Ⓒ Ⓓ Ⓔ	85 Ⓐ Ⓑ Ⓒ Ⓓ Ⓔ
14 Ⓐ Ⓑ Ⓒ Ⓓ Ⓔ	32 Ⓐ Ⓑ Ⓒ Ⓓ Ⓔ	50 Ⓐ Ⓑ Ⓒ Ⓓ Ⓔ	68 Ⓐ Ⓑ Ⓒ Ⓓ Ⓔ	86 Ⓐ Ⓑ Ⓒ Ⓓ Ⓔ
15 Ⓐ Ⓑ Ⓒ Ⓓ Ⓔ	33 Ⓐ Ⓑ Ⓒ Ⓓ Ⓔ	51 Ⓐ Ⓑ Ⓒ Ⓓ Ⓔ	69 Ⓐ Ⓑ Ⓒ Ⓓ Ⓔ	87 Ⓐ Ⓑ Ⓒ Ⓓ Ⓔ
16 Ⓐ Ⓑ Ⓒ Ⓓ Ⓔ	34 Ⓐ Ⓑ Ⓒ Ⓓ Ⓔ	52 Ⓐ Ⓑ Ⓒ Ⓓ Ⓔ	70 Ⓐ Ⓑ Ⓒ Ⓓ Ⓔ	88 Ⓐ Ⓑ Ⓒ Ⓓ Ⓔ
17 Ⓐ Ⓑ Ⓒ Ⓓ Ⓔ	35 Ⓐ Ⓑ Ⓒ Ⓓ Ⓔ	53 Ⓐ Ⓑ Ⓒ Ⓓ Ⓔ	71 Ⓐ Ⓑ Ⓒ Ⓓ Ⓔ	
18 Ⓐ Ⓑ Ⓒ Ⓓ Ⓔ	36 Ⓐ Ⓑ Ⓒ Ⓓ Ⓔ	54 Ⓐ Ⓑ Ⓒ Ⓓ Ⓔ	72 Ⓐ Ⓑ Ⓒ Ⓓ Ⓔ	

COMPLETE PRACTICE TEST ANSWER SHEET

ADDRESS CHECKING SECTION

1 (A)(D)	13 (A)(D)	25 (A)(D)	37 (A)(D)	49 (A)(D)	61 (A)(D)	73 (A)(D)	85 (A)(D)
2 (A)(D)	14 (A)(D)	26 (A)(D)	38 (A)(D)	50 (A)(D)	62 (A)(D)	74 (A)(D)	86 (A)(D)
3 (A)(D)	15 (A)(D)	27 (A)(D)	39 (A)(D)	51 (A)(D)	63 (A)(D)	75 (A)(D)	87 (A)(D)
4 (A)(D)	16 (A)(D)	28 (A)(D)	40 (A)(D)	52 (A)(D)	64 (A)(D)	76 (A)(D)	88 (A)(D)
5 (A)(D)	17 (A)(D)	29 (A)(D)	41 (A)(D)	53 (A)(D)	65 (A)(D)	77 (A)(D)	89 (A)(D)
6 (A)(D)	18 (A)(D)	30 (A)(D)	42 (A)(D)	54 (A)(D)	66 (A)(D)	78 (A)(D)	90 (A)(D)
7 (A)(D)	19 (A)(D)	31 (A)(D)	43 (A)(D)	55 (A)(D)	67 (A)(D)	79 (A)(D)	91 (A)(D)
8 (A)(D)	20 (A)(D)	32 (A)(D)	44 (A)(D)	56 (A)(D)	68 (A)(D)	80 (A)(D)	92 (A)(D)
9 (A)(D)	21 (A)(D)	33 (A)(D)	45 (A)(D)	57 (A)(D)	69 (A)(D)	81 (A)(D)	93 (A)(D)
10 (A)(D)	22 (A)(D)	34 (A)(D)	46 (A)(D)	58 (A)(D)	70 (A)(D)	82 (A)(D)	94 (A)(D)
11 (A)(D)	23 (A)(D)	35 (A)(D)	47 (A)(D)	59 (A)(D)	71 (A)(D)	83 (A)(D)	95 (A)(D)
12 (A)(D)	24 (A)(D)	36 (A)(D)	48 (A)(D)	60 (A)(D)	72 (A)(D)	84 (A)(D)	

ADDRESS MEMORY SECTION

1 (A)(B)(C)(D)(E)	19 (A)(B)(C)(D)(E)	37 (A)(B)(C)(D)(E)	55 (A)(B)(C)(D)(E)	73 (A)(B)(C)(D)(E)
2 (A)(B)(C)(D)(E)	20 (A)(B)(C)(D)(E)	38 (A)(B)(C)(D)(E)	56 (A)(B)(C)(D)(E)	74 (A)(B)(C)(D)(E)
3 (A)(B)(C)(D)(E)	21 (A)(B)(C)(D)(E)	39 (A)(B)(C)(D)(E)	57 (A)(B)(C)(D)(E)	75 (A)(B)(C)(D)(E)
4 (A)(B)(C)(D)(E)	22 (A)(B)(C)(D)(E)	40 (A)(B)(C)(D)(E)	58 (A)(B)(C)(D)(E)	76 (A)(B)(C)(D)(E)
5 (A)(B)(C)(D)(E)	23 (A)(B)(C)(D)(E)	41 (A)(B)(C)(D)(E)	59 (A)(B)(C)(D)(E)	77 (A)(B)(C)(D)(E)
6 (A)(B)(C)(D)(E)	24 (A)(B)(C)(D)(E)	42 (A)(B)(C)(D)(E)	60 (A)(B)(C)(D)(E)	78 (A)(B)(C)(D)(E)
7 (A)(B)(C)(D)(E)	25 (A)(B)(C)(D)(E)	43 (A)(B)(C)(D)(E)	61 (A)(B)(C)(D)(E)	79 (A)(B)(C)(D)(E)
8 (A)(B)(C)(D)(E)	26 (A)(B)(C)(D)(E)	44 (A)(B)(C)(D)(E)	62 (A)(B)(C)(D)(E)	80 (A)(B)(C)(D)(E)
9 (A)(B)(C)(D)(E)	27 (A)(B)(C)(D)(E)	45 (A)(B)(C)(D)(E)	63 (A)(B)(C)(D)(E)	81 (A)(B)(C)(D)(E)
10 (A)(B)(C)(D)(E)	28 (A)(B)(C)(D)(E)	46 (A)(B)(C)(D)(E)	64 (A)(B)(C)(D)(E)	82 (A)(B)(C)(D)(E)
11 (A)(B)(C)(D)(E)	29 (A)(B)(C)(D)(E)	47 (A)(B)(C)(D)(E)	65 (A)(B)(C)(D)(E)	83 (A)(B)(C)(D)(E)
12 (A)(B)(C)(D)(E)	30 (A)(B)(C)(D)(E)	48 (A)(B)(C)(D)(E)	66 (A)(B)(C)(D)(E)	84 (A)(B)(C)(D)(E)
13 (A)(B)(C)(D)(E)	31 (A)(B)(C)(D)(E)	49 (A)(B)(C)(D)(E)	67 (A)(B)(C)(D)(E)	85 (A)(B)(C)(D)(E)
14 (A)(B)(C)(D)(E)	32 (A)(B)(C)(D)(E)	50 (A)(B)(C)(D)(E)	68 (A)(B)(C)(D)(E)	86 (A)(B)(C)(D)(E)
15 (A)(B)(C)(D)(E)	33 (A)(B)(C)(D)(E)	51 (A)(B)(C)(D)(E)	69 (A)(B)(C)(D)(E)	87 (A)(B)(C)(D)(E)
16 (A)(B)(C)(D)(E)	34 (A)(B)(C)(D)(E)	52 (A)(B)(C)(D)(E)	70 (A)(B)(C)(D)(E)	88 (A)(B)(C)(D)(E)
17 (A)(B)(C)(D)(E)	35 (A)(B)(C)(D)(E)	53 (A)(B)(C)(D)(E)	71 (A)(B)(C)(D)(E)	
18 (A)(B)(C)(D)(E)	36 (A)(B)(C)(D)(E)	54 (A)(B)(C)(D)(E)	72 (A)(B)(C)(D)(E)	

NUMBER SERIES SECTION

1 (A)(B)(C)(D)(E)	7 (A)(B)(C)(D)(E)	13 (A)(B)(C)(D)(E)	19 (A)(B)(C)(D)(E)
2 (A)(B)(C)(D)(E)	8 (A)(B)(C)(D)(E)	14 (A)(B)(C)(D)(E)	20 (A)(B)(C)(D)(E)
3 (A)(B)(C)(D)(E)	9 (A)(B)(C)(D)(E)	15 (A)(B)(C)(D)(E)	21 (A)(B)(C)(D)(E)
4 (A)(B)(C)(D)(E)	10 (A)(B)(C)(D)(E)	16 (A)(B)(C)(D)(E)	22 (A)(B)(C)(D)(E)
5 (A)(B)(C)(D)(E)	11 (A)(B)(C)(D)(E)	17 (A)(B)(C)(D)(E)	23 (A)(B)(C)(D)(E)
6 (A)(B)(C)(D)(E)	12 (A)(B)(C)(D)(E)	18 (A)(B)(C)(D)(E)	24 (A)(B)(C)(D)(E)

FOLLOWING ORAL DIRECTIONS SECTION

1 (A)(B)(C)(D)(E)	19 (A)(B)(C)(D)(E)	37 (A)(B)(C)(D)(E)	55 (A)(B)(C)(D)(E)	73 (A)(B)(C)(D)(E)
2 (A)(B)(C)(D)(E)	20 (A)(B)(C)(D)(E)	38 (A)(B)(C)(D)(E)	56 (A)(B)(C)(D)(E)	74 (A)(B)(C)(D)(E)
3 (A)(B)(C)(D)(E)	21 (A)(B)(C)(D)(E)	39 (A)(B)(C)(D)(E)	57 (A)(B)(C)(D)(E)	75 (A)(B)(C)(D)(E)
4 (A)(B)(C)(D)(E)	22 (A)(B)(C)(D)(E)	40 (A)(B)(C)(D)(E)	58 (A)(B)(C)(D)(E)	76 (A)(B)(C)(D)(E)
5 (A)(B)(C)(D)(E)	23 (A)(B)(C)(D)(E)	41 (A)(B)(C)(D)(E)	59 (A)(B)(C)(D)(E)	77 (A)(B)(C)(D)(E)
6 (A)(B)(C)(D)(E)	24 (A)(B)(C)(D)(E)	42 (A)(B)(C)(D)(E)	60 (A)(B)(C)(D)(E)	78 (A)(B)(C)(D)(E)
7 (A)(B)(C)(D)(E)	25 (A)(B)(C)(D)(E)	43 (A)(B)(C)(D)(E)	61 (A)(B)(C)(D)(E)	79 (A)(B)(C)(D)(E)
8 (A)(B)(C)(D)(E)	26 (A)(B)(C)(D)(E)	44 (A)(B)(C)(D)(E)	62 (A)(B)(C)(D)(E)	80 (A)(B)(C)(D)(E)
9 (A)(B)(C)(D)(E)	27 (A)(B)(C)(D)(E)	45 (A)(B)(C)(D)(E)	63 (A)(B)(C)(D)(E)	81 (A)(B)(C)(D)(E)
10 (A)(B)(C)(D)(E)	28 (A)(B)(C)(D)(E)	46 (A)(B)(C)(D)(E)	64 (A)(B)(C)(D)(E)	82 (A)(B)(C)(D)(E)
11 (A)(B)(C)(D)(E)	29 (A)(B)(C)(D)(E)	47 (A)(B)(C)(D)(E)	65 (A)(B)(C)(D)(E)	83 (A)(B)(C)(D)(E)
12 (A)(B)(C)(D)(E)	30 (A)(B)(C)(D)(E)	48 (A)(B)(C)(D)(E)	66 (A)(B)(C)(D)(E)	84 (A)(B)(C)(D)(E)
13 (A)(B)(C)(D)(E)	31 (A)(B)(C)(D)(E)	49 (A)(B)(C)(D)(E)	67 (A)(B)(C)(D)(E)	85 (A)(B)(C)(D)(E)
14 (A)(B)(C)(D)(E)	32 (A)(B)(C)(D)(E)	50 (A)(B)(C)(D)(E)	68 (A)(B)(C)(D)(E)	86 (A)(B)(C)(D)(E)
15 (A)(B)(C)(D)(E)	33 (A)(B)(C)(D)(E)	51 (A)(B)(C)(D)(E)	69 (A)(B)(C)(D)(E)	87 (A)(B)(C)(D)(E)
16 (A)(B)(C)(D)(E)	34 (A)(B)(C)(D)(E)	52 (A)(B)(C)(D)(E)	70 (A)(B)(C)(D)(E)	88 (A)(B)(C)(D)(E)
17 (A)(B)(C)(D)(E)	35 (A)(B)(C)(D)(E)	53 (A)(B)(C)(D)(E)	71 (A)(B)(C)(D)(E)	
18 (A)(B)(C)(D)(E)	36 (A)(B)(C)(D)(E)	54 (A)(B)(C)(D)(E)	72 (A)(B)(C)(D)(E)	

Extra Address Checking Answer Sheets

Sheet 1

1 Ⓐ Ⓓ	13 Ⓐ Ⓓ	25 Ⓐ Ⓓ	37 Ⓐ Ⓓ	49 Ⓐ Ⓓ	61 Ⓐ Ⓓ	73 Ⓐ Ⓓ	85 Ⓐ Ⓓ
2 Ⓐ Ⓓ	14 Ⓐ Ⓓ	26 Ⓐ Ⓓ	38 Ⓐ Ⓓ	50 Ⓐ Ⓓ	62 Ⓐ Ⓓ	74 Ⓐ Ⓓ	86 Ⓐ Ⓓ
3 Ⓐ Ⓓ	15 Ⓐ Ⓓ	27 Ⓐ Ⓓ	39 Ⓐ Ⓓ	51 Ⓐ Ⓓ	63 Ⓐ Ⓓ	75 Ⓐ Ⓓ	87 Ⓐ Ⓓ
4 Ⓐ Ⓓ	16 Ⓐ Ⓓ	28 Ⓐ Ⓓ	40 Ⓐ Ⓓ	52 Ⓐ Ⓓ	64 Ⓐ Ⓓ	76 Ⓐ Ⓓ	88 Ⓐ Ⓓ
5 Ⓐ Ⓓ	17 Ⓐ Ⓓ	29 Ⓐ Ⓓ	41 Ⓐ Ⓓ	53 Ⓐ Ⓓ	65 Ⓐ Ⓓ	77 Ⓐ Ⓓ	89 Ⓐ Ⓓ
6 Ⓐ Ⓓ	18 Ⓐ Ⓓ	30 Ⓐ Ⓓ	42 Ⓐ Ⓓ	54 Ⓐ Ⓓ	66 Ⓐ Ⓓ	78 Ⓐ Ⓓ	90 Ⓐ Ⓓ
7 Ⓐ Ⓓ	19 Ⓐ Ⓓ	31 Ⓐ Ⓓ	43 Ⓐ Ⓓ	55 Ⓐ Ⓓ	67 Ⓐ Ⓓ	79 Ⓐ Ⓓ	91 Ⓐ Ⓓ
8 Ⓐ Ⓓ	20 Ⓐ Ⓓ	32 Ⓐ Ⓓ	44 Ⓐ Ⓓ	56 Ⓐ Ⓓ	68 Ⓐ Ⓓ	80 Ⓐ Ⓓ	92 Ⓐ Ⓓ
9 Ⓐ Ⓓ	21 Ⓐ Ⓓ	33 Ⓐ Ⓓ	45 Ⓐ Ⓓ	57 Ⓐ Ⓓ	69 Ⓐ Ⓓ	81 Ⓐ Ⓓ	93 Ⓐ Ⓓ
10 Ⓐ Ⓓ	22 Ⓐ Ⓓ	34 Ⓐ Ⓓ	46 Ⓐ Ⓓ	58 Ⓐ Ⓓ	70 Ⓐ Ⓓ	82 Ⓐ Ⓓ	94 Ⓐ Ⓓ
11 Ⓐ Ⓓ	23 Ⓐ Ⓓ	35 Ⓐ Ⓓ	47 Ⓐ Ⓓ	59 Ⓐ Ⓓ	71 Ⓐ Ⓓ	83 Ⓐ Ⓓ	95 Ⓐ Ⓓ
12 Ⓐ Ⓓ	24 Ⓐ Ⓓ	36 Ⓐ Ⓓ	48 Ⓐ Ⓓ	60 Ⓐ Ⓓ	72 Ⓐ Ⓓ	84 Ⓐ Ⓓ	

Sheet 2

1 Ⓐ Ⓓ	13 Ⓐ Ⓓ	25 Ⓐ Ⓓ	37 Ⓐ Ⓓ	49 Ⓐ Ⓓ	61 Ⓐ Ⓓ	73 Ⓐ Ⓓ	85 Ⓐ Ⓓ
2 Ⓐ Ⓓ	14 Ⓐ Ⓓ	26 Ⓐ Ⓓ	38 Ⓐ Ⓓ	50 Ⓐ Ⓓ	62 Ⓐ Ⓓ	74 Ⓐ Ⓓ	86 Ⓐ Ⓓ
3 Ⓐ Ⓓ	15 Ⓐ Ⓓ	27 Ⓐ Ⓓ	39 Ⓐ Ⓓ	51 Ⓐ Ⓓ	63 Ⓐ Ⓓ	75 Ⓐ Ⓓ	87 Ⓐ Ⓓ
4 Ⓐ Ⓓ	16 Ⓐ Ⓓ	28 Ⓐ Ⓓ	40 Ⓐ Ⓓ	52 Ⓐ Ⓓ	64 Ⓐ Ⓓ	76 Ⓐ Ⓓ	88 Ⓐ Ⓓ
5 Ⓐ Ⓓ	17 Ⓐ Ⓓ	29 Ⓐ Ⓓ	41 Ⓐ Ⓓ	53 Ⓐ Ⓓ	65 Ⓐ Ⓓ	77 Ⓐ Ⓓ	89 Ⓐ Ⓓ
6 Ⓐ Ⓓ	18 Ⓐ Ⓓ	30 Ⓐ Ⓓ	42 Ⓐ Ⓓ	54 Ⓐ Ⓓ	66 Ⓐ Ⓓ	78 Ⓐ Ⓓ	90 Ⓐ Ⓓ
7 Ⓐ Ⓓ	19 Ⓐ Ⓓ	31 Ⓐ Ⓓ	43 Ⓐ Ⓓ	55 Ⓐ Ⓓ	67 Ⓐ Ⓓ	79 Ⓐ Ⓓ	91 Ⓐ Ⓓ
8 Ⓐ Ⓓ	20 Ⓐ Ⓓ	32 Ⓐ Ⓓ	44 Ⓐ Ⓓ	56 Ⓐ Ⓓ	68 Ⓐ Ⓓ	80 Ⓐ Ⓓ	92 Ⓐ Ⓓ
9 Ⓐ Ⓓ	21 Ⓐ Ⓓ	33 Ⓐ Ⓓ	45 Ⓐ Ⓓ	57 Ⓐ Ⓓ	69 Ⓐ Ⓓ	81 Ⓐ Ⓓ	93 Ⓐ Ⓓ
10 Ⓐ Ⓓ	22 Ⓐ Ⓓ	34 Ⓐ Ⓓ	46 Ⓐ Ⓓ	58 Ⓐ Ⓓ	70 Ⓐ Ⓓ	82 Ⓐ Ⓓ	94 Ⓐ Ⓓ
11 Ⓐ Ⓓ	23 Ⓐ Ⓓ	35 Ⓐ Ⓓ	47 Ⓐ Ⓓ	59 Ⓐ Ⓓ	71 Ⓐ Ⓓ	83 Ⓐ Ⓓ	95 Ⓐ Ⓓ
12 Ⓐ Ⓓ	24 Ⓐ Ⓓ	36 Ⓐ Ⓓ	48 Ⓐ Ⓓ	60 Ⓐ Ⓓ	72 Ⓐ Ⓓ	84 Ⓐ Ⓓ	

Sheet 3

1 Ⓐ Ⓓ	13 Ⓐ Ⓓ	25 Ⓐ Ⓓ	37 Ⓐ Ⓓ	49 Ⓐ Ⓓ	61 Ⓐ Ⓓ	73 Ⓐ Ⓓ	85 Ⓐ Ⓓ
2 Ⓐ Ⓓ	14 Ⓐ Ⓓ	26 Ⓐ Ⓓ	38 Ⓐ Ⓓ	50 Ⓐ Ⓓ	62 Ⓐ Ⓓ	74 Ⓐ Ⓓ	86 Ⓐ Ⓓ
3 Ⓐ Ⓓ	15 Ⓐ Ⓓ	27 Ⓐ Ⓓ	39 Ⓐ Ⓓ	51 Ⓐ Ⓓ	63 Ⓐ Ⓓ	75 Ⓐ Ⓓ	87 Ⓐ Ⓓ
4 Ⓐ Ⓓ	16 Ⓐ Ⓓ	28 Ⓐ Ⓓ	40 Ⓐ Ⓓ	52 Ⓐ Ⓓ	64 Ⓐ Ⓓ	76 Ⓐ Ⓓ	88 Ⓐ Ⓓ
5 Ⓐ Ⓓ	17 Ⓐ Ⓓ	29 Ⓐ Ⓓ	41 Ⓐ Ⓓ	53 Ⓐ Ⓓ	65 Ⓐ Ⓓ	77 Ⓐ Ⓓ	89 Ⓐ Ⓓ
6 Ⓐ Ⓓ	18 Ⓐ Ⓓ	30 Ⓐ Ⓓ	42 Ⓐ Ⓓ	54 Ⓐ Ⓓ	66 Ⓐ Ⓓ	78 Ⓐ Ⓓ	90 Ⓐ Ⓓ
7 Ⓐ Ⓓ	19 Ⓐ Ⓓ	31 Ⓐ Ⓓ	43 Ⓐ Ⓓ	55 Ⓐ Ⓓ	67 Ⓐ Ⓓ	79 Ⓐ Ⓓ	91 Ⓐ Ⓓ
8 Ⓐ Ⓓ	20 Ⓐ Ⓓ	32 Ⓐ Ⓓ	44 Ⓐ Ⓓ	56 Ⓐ Ⓓ	68 Ⓐ Ⓓ	80 Ⓐ Ⓓ	92 Ⓐ Ⓓ
9 Ⓐ Ⓓ	21 Ⓐ Ⓓ	33 Ⓐ Ⓓ	45 Ⓐ Ⓓ	57 Ⓐ Ⓓ	69 Ⓐ Ⓓ	81 Ⓐ Ⓓ	93 Ⓐ Ⓓ
10 Ⓐ Ⓓ	22 Ⓐ Ⓓ	34 Ⓐ Ⓓ	46 Ⓐ Ⓓ	58 Ⓐ Ⓓ	70 Ⓐ Ⓓ	82 Ⓐ Ⓓ	94 Ⓐ Ⓓ
11 Ⓐ Ⓓ	23 Ⓐ Ⓓ	35 Ⓐ Ⓓ	47 Ⓐ Ⓓ	59 Ⓐ Ⓓ	71 Ⓐ Ⓓ	83 Ⓐ Ⓓ	95 Ⓐ Ⓓ
12 Ⓐ Ⓓ	24 Ⓐ Ⓓ	36 Ⓐ Ⓓ	48 Ⓐ Ⓓ	60 Ⓐ Ⓓ	72 Ⓐ Ⓓ	84 Ⓐ Ⓓ	

Sheet 4

1 Ⓐ Ⓓ	13 Ⓐ Ⓓ	25 Ⓐ Ⓓ	37 Ⓐ Ⓓ	49 Ⓐ Ⓓ	61 Ⓐ Ⓓ	73 Ⓐ Ⓓ	85 Ⓐ Ⓓ
2 Ⓐ Ⓓ	14 Ⓐ Ⓓ	26 Ⓐ Ⓓ	38 Ⓐ Ⓓ	50 Ⓐ Ⓓ	62 Ⓐ Ⓓ	74 Ⓐ Ⓓ	86 Ⓐ Ⓓ
3 Ⓐ Ⓓ	15 Ⓐ Ⓓ	27 Ⓐ Ⓓ	39 Ⓐ Ⓓ	51 Ⓐ Ⓓ	63 Ⓐ Ⓓ	75 Ⓐ Ⓓ	87 Ⓐ Ⓓ
4 Ⓐ Ⓓ	16 Ⓐ Ⓓ	28 Ⓐ Ⓓ	40 Ⓐ Ⓓ	52 Ⓐ Ⓓ	64 Ⓐ Ⓓ	76 Ⓐ Ⓓ	88 Ⓐ Ⓓ
5 Ⓐ Ⓓ	17 Ⓐ Ⓓ	29 Ⓐ Ⓓ	41 Ⓐ Ⓓ	53 Ⓐ Ⓓ	65 Ⓐ Ⓓ	77 Ⓐ Ⓓ	89 Ⓐ Ⓓ
6 Ⓐ Ⓓ	18 Ⓐ Ⓓ	30 Ⓐ Ⓓ	42 Ⓐ Ⓓ	54 Ⓐ Ⓓ	66 Ⓐ Ⓓ	78 Ⓐ Ⓓ	90 Ⓐ Ⓓ
7 Ⓐ Ⓓ	19 Ⓐ Ⓓ	31 Ⓐ Ⓓ	43 Ⓐ Ⓓ	55 Ⓐ Ⓓ	67 Ⓐ Ⓓ	79 Ⓐ Ⓓ	91 Ⓐ Ⓓ
8 Ⓐ Ⓓ	20 Ⓐ Ⓓ	32 Ⓐ Ⓓ	44 Ⓐ Ⓓ	56 Ⓐ Ⓓ	68 Ⓐ Ⓓ	80 Ⓐ Ⓓ	92 Ⓐ Ⓓ
9 Ⓐ Ⓓ	21 Ⓐ Ⓓ	33 Ⓐ Ⓓ	45 Ⓐ Ⓓ	57 Ⓐ Ⓓ	69 Ⓐ Ⓓ	81 Ⓐ Ⓓ	93 Ⓐ Ⓓ
10 Ⓐ Ⓓ	22 Ⓐ Ⓓ	34 Ⓐ Ⓓ	46 Ⓐ Ⓓ	58 Ⓐ Ⓓ	70 Ⓐ Ⓓ	82 Ⓐ Ⓓ	94 Ⓐ Ⓓ
11 Ⓐ Ⓓ	23 Ⓐ Ⓓ	35 Ⓐ Ⓓ	47 Ⓐ Ⓓ	59 Ⓐ Ⓓ	71 Ⓐ Ⓓ	83 Ⓐ Ⓓ	95 Ⓐ Ⓓ
12 Ⓐ Ⓓ	24 Ⓐ Ⓓ	36 Ⓐ Ⓓ	48 Ⓐ Ⓓ	60 Ⓐ Ⓓ	72 Ⓐ Ⓓ	84 Ⓐ Ⓓ	

Extra Address Checking Answer Sheets

1 (A)(D)   13 (A)(D)   25 (A)(D)   37 (A)(D)   49 (A)(D)   61 (A)(D)   73 (A)(D)   85 (A)(D)
2 (A)(D)   14 (A)(D)   26 (A)(D)   38 (A)(D)   50 (A)(D)   62 (A)(D)   74 (A)(D)   86 (A)(D)
3 (A)(D)   15 (A)(D)   27 (A)(D)   39 (A)(D)   51 (A)(D)   63 (A)(D)   75 (A)(D)   87 (A)(D)
4 (A)(D)   16 (A)(D)   28 (A)(D)   40 (A)(D)   52 (A)(D)   64 (A)(D)   76 (A)(D)   88 (A)(D)
5 (A)(D)   17 (A)(D)   29 (A)(D)   41 (A)(D)   53 (A)(D)   65 (A)(D)   77 (A)(D)   89 (A)(D)
6 (A)(D)   18 (A)(D)   30 (A)(D)   42 (A)(D)   54 (A)(D)   66 (A)(D)   78 (A)(D)   90 (A)(D)
7 (A)(D)   19 (A)(D)   31 (A)(D)   43 (A)(D)   55 (A)(D)   67 (A)(D)   79 (A)(D)   91 (A)(D)
8 (A)(D)   20 (A)(D)   32 (A)(D)   44 (A)(D)   56 (A)(D)   68 (A)(D)   80 (A)(D)   92 (A)(D)
9 (A)(D)   21 (A)(D)   33 (A)(D)   45 (A)(D)   57 (A)(D)   69 (A)(D)   81 (A)(D)   93 (A)(D)
10 (A)(D) 22 (A)(D)   34 (A)(D)   46 (A)(D)   58 (A)(D)   70 (A)(D)   82 (A)(D)   94 (A)(D)
11 (A)(D) 23 (A)(D)   35 (A)(D)   47 (A)(D)   59 (A)(D)   71 (A)(D)   83 (A)(D)   95 (A)(D)
12 (A)(D) 24 (A)(D)   36 (A)(D)   48 (A)(D)   60 (A)(D)   72 (A)(D)   84 (A)(D)

---

1 (A)(D)   13 (A)(D)   25 (A)(D)   37 (A)(D)   49 (A)(D)   61 (A)(D)   73 (A)(D)   85 (A)(D)
2 (A)(D)   14 (A)(D)   26 (A)(D)   38 (A)(D)   50 (A)(D)   62 (A)(D)   74 (A)(D)   86 (A)(D)
3 (A)(D)   15 (A)(D)   27 (A)(D)   39 (A)(D)   51 (A)(D)   63 (A)(D)   75 (A)(D)   87 (A)(D)
4 (A)(D)   16 (A)(D)   28 (A)(D)   40 (A)(D)   52 (A)(D)   64 (A)(D)   76 (A)(D)   88 (A)(D)
5 (A)(D)   17 (A)(D)   29 (A)(D)   41 (A)(D)   53 (A)(D)   65 (A)(D)   77 (A)(D)   89 (A)(D)
6 (A)(D)   18 (A)(D)   30 (A)(D)   42 (A)(D)   54 (A)(D)   66 (A)(D)   78 (A)(D)   90 (A)(D)
7 (A)(D)   19 (A)(D)   31 (A)(D)   43 (A)(D)   55 (A)(D)   67 (A)(D)   79 (A)(D)   91 (A)(D)
8 (A)(D)   20 (A)(D)   32 (A)(D)   44 (A)(D)   56 (A)(D)   68 (A)(D)   80 (A)(D)   92 (A)(D)
9 (A)(D)   21 (A)(D)   33 (A)(D)   45 (A)(D)   57 (A)(D)   69 (A)(D)   81 (A)(D)   93 (A)(D)
10 (A)(D) 22 (A)(D)   34 (A)(D)   46 (A)(D)   58 (A)(D)   70 (A)(D)   82 (A)(D)   94 (A)(D)
11 (A)(D) 23 (A)(D)   35 (A)(D)   47 (A)(D)   59 (A)(D)   71 (A)(D)   83 (A)(D)   95 (A)(D)
12 (A)(D) 24 (A)(D)   36 (A)(D)   48 (A)(D)   60 (A)(D)   72 (A)(D)   84 (A)(D)

---

1 (A)(D)   13 (A)(D)   25 (A)(D)   37 (A)(D)   49 (A)(D)   61 (A)(D)   73 (A)(D)   85 (A)(D)
2 (A)(D)   14 (A)(D)   26 (A)(D)   38 (A)(D)   50 (A)(D)   62 (A)(D)   74 (A)(D)   86 (A)(D)
3 (A)(D)   15 (A)(D)   27 (A)(D)   39 (A)(D)   51 (A)(D)   63 (A)(D)   75 (A)(D)   87 (A)(D)
4 (A)(D)   16 (A)(D)   28 (A)(D)   40 (A)(D)   52 (A)(D)   64 (A)(D)   76 (A)(D)   88 (A)(D)
5 (A)(D)   17 (A)(D)   29 (A)(D)   41 (A)(D)   53 (A)(D)   65 (A)(D)   77 (A)(D)   89 (A)(D)
6 (A)(D)   18 (A)(D)   30 (A)(D)   42 (A)(D)   54 (A)(D)   66 (A)(D)   78 (A)(D)   90 (A)(D)
7 (A)(D)   19 (A)(D)   31 (A)(D)   43 (A)(D)   55 (A)(D)   67 (A)(D)   79 (A)(D)   91 (A)(D)
8 (A)(D)   20 (A)(D)   32 (A)(D)   44 (A)(D)   56 (A)(D)   68 (A)(D)   80 (A)(D)   92 (A)(D)
9 (A)(D)   21 (A)(D)   33 (A)(D)   45 (A)(D)   57 (A)(D)   69 (A)(D)   81 (A)(D)   93 (A)(D)
10 (A)(D) 22 (A)(D)   34 (A)(D)   46 (A)(D)   58 (A)(D)   70 (A)(D)   82 (A)(D)   94 (A)(D)
11 (A)(D) 23 (A)(D)   35 (A)(D)   47 (A)(D)   59 (A)(D)   71 (A)(D)   83 (A)(D)   95 (A)(D)
12 (A)(D) 24 (A)(D)   36 (A)(D)   48 (A)(D)   60 (A)(D)   72 (A)(D)   84 (A)(D)

---

1 (A)(D)   13 (A)(D)   25 (A)(D)   37 (A)(D)   49 (A)(D)   61 (A)(D)   73 (A)(D)   85 (A)(D)
2 (A)(D)   14 (A)(D)   26 (A)(D)   38 (A)(D)   50 (A)(D)   62 (A)(D)   74 (A)(D)   86 (A)(D)
3 (A)(D)   15 (A)(D)   27 (A)(D)   39 (A)(D)   51 (A)(D)   63 (A)(D)   75 (A)(D)   87 (A)(D)
4 (A)(D)   16 (A)(D)   28 (A)(D)   40 (A)(D)   52 (A)(D)   64 (A)(D)   76 (A)(D)   88 (A)(D)
5 (A)(D)   17 (A)(D)   29 (A)(D)   41 (A)(D)   53 (A)(D)   65 (A)(D)   77 (A)(D)   89 (A)(D)
6 (A)(D)   18 (A)(D)   30 (A)(D)   42 (A)(D)   54 (A)(D)   66 (A)(D)   78 (A)(D)   90 (A)(D)
7 (A)(D)   19 (A)(D)   31 (A)(D)   43 (A)(D)   55 (A)(D)   67 (A)(D)   79 (A)(D)   91 (A)(D)
8 (A)(D)   20 (A)(D)   32 (A)(D)   44 (A)(D)   56 (A)(D)   68 (A)(D)   80 (A)(D)   92 (A)(D)
9 (A)(D)   21 (A)(D)   33 (A)(D)   45 (A)(D)   57 (A)(D)   69 (A)(D)   81 (A)(D)   93 (A)(D)
10 (A)(D) 22 (A)(D)   34 (A)(D)   46 (A)(D)   58 (A)(D)   70 (A)(D)   82 (A)(D)   94 (A)(D)
11 (A)(D) 23 (A)(D)   35 (A)(D)   47 (A)(D)   59 (A)(D)   71 (A)(D)   83 (A)(D)   95 (A)(D)
12 (A)(D) 24 (A)(D)   36 (A)(D)   48 (A)(D)   60 (A)(D)   72 (A)(D)   84 (A)(D)

Extra Address Checking Answer Sheets

1 (A)(D)   13 (A)(D)   25 (A)(D)   37 (A)(D)   49 (A)(D)   61 (A)(D)   73 (A)(D)   85 (A)(D)
2 (A)(D)   14 (A)(D)   26 (A)(D)   38 (A)(D)   50 (A)(D)   62 (A)(D)   74 (A)(D)   86 (A)(D)
3 (A)(D)   15 (A)(D)   27 (A)(D)   39 (A)(D)   51 (A)(D)   63 (A)(D)   75 (A)(D)   87 (A)(D)
4 (A)(D)   16 (A)(D)   28 (A)(D)   40 (A)(D)   52 (A)(D)   64 (A)(D)   76 (A)(D)   88 (A)(D)
5 (A)(D)   17 (A)(D)   29 (A)(D)   41 (A)(D)   53 (A)(D)   65 (A)(D)   77 (A)(D)   89 (A)(D)
6 (A)(D)   18 (A)(D)   30 (A)(D)   42 (A)(D)   54 (A)(D)   66 (A)(D)   78 (A)(D)   90 (A)(D)
7 (A)(D)   19 (A)(D)   31 (A)(D)   43 (A)(D)   55 (A)(D)   67 (A)(D)   79 (A)(D)   91 (A)(D)
8 (A)(D)   20 (A)(D)   32 (A)(D)   44 (A)(D)   56 (A)(D)   68 (A)(D)   80 (A)(D)   92 (A)(D)
9 (A)(D)   21 (A)(D)   33 (A)(D)   45 (A)(D)   57 (A)(D)   69 (A)(D)   81 (A)(D)   93 (A)(D)
10 (A)(D) 22 (A)(D)   34 (A)(D)   46 (A)(D)   58 (A)(D)   70 (A)(D)   82 (A)(D)   94 (A)(D)
11 (A)(D) 23 (A)(D)   35 (A)(D)   47 (A)(D)   59 (A)(D)   71 (A)(D)   83 (A)(D)   95 (A)(D)
12 (A)(D) 24 (A)(D)   36 (A)(D)   48 (A)(D)   60 (A)(D)   72 (A)(D)   84 (A)(D)

---

1 (A)(D)   13 (A)(D)   25 (A)(D)   37 (A)(D)   49 (A)(D)   61 (A)(D)   73 (A)(D)   85 (A)(D)
2 (A)(D)   14 (A)(D)   26 (A)(D)   38 (A)(D)   50 (A)(D)   62 (A)(D)   74 (A)(D)   86 (A)(D)
3 (A)(D)   15 (A)(D)   27 (A)(D)   39 (A)(D)   51 (A)(D)   63 (A)(D)   75 (A)(D)   87 (A)(D)
4 (A)(D)   16 (A)(D)   28 (A)(D)   40 (A)(D)   52 (A)(D)   64 (A)(D)   76 (A)(D)   88 (A)(D)
5 (A)(D)   17 (A)(D)   29 (A)(D)   41 (A)(D)   53 (A)(D)   65 (A)(D)   77 (A)(D)   89 (A)(D)
6 (A)(D)   18 (A)(D)   30 (A)(D)   42 (A)(D)   54 (A)(D)   66 (A)(D)   78 (A)(D)   90 (A)(D)
7 (A)(D)   19 (A)(D)   31 (A)(D)   43 (A)(D)   55 (A)(D)   67 (A)(D)   79 (A)(D)   91 (A)(D)
8 (A)(D)   20 (A)(D)   32 (A)(D)   44 (A)(D)   56 (A)(D)   68 (A)(D)   80 (A)(D)   92 (A)(D)
9 (A)(D)   21 (A)(D)   33 (A)(D)   45 (A)(D)   57 (A)(D)   69 (A)(D)   81 (A)(D)   93 (A)(D)
10 (A)(D) 22 (A)(D)   34 (A)(D)   46 (A)(D)   58 (A)(D)   70 (A)(D)   82 (A)(D)   94 (A)(D)
11 (A)(D) 23 (A)(D)   35 (A)(D)   47 (A)(D)   59 (A)(D)   71 (A)(D)   83 (A)(D)   95 (A)(D)
12 (A)(D) 24 (A)(D)   36 (A)(D)   48 (A)(D)   60 (A)(D)   72 (A)(D)   84 (A)(D)

---

1 (A)(D)   13 (A)(D)   25 (A)(D)   37 (A)(D)   49 (A)(D)   61 (A)(D)   73 (A)(D)   85 (A)(D)
2 (A)(D)   14 (A)(D)   26 (A)(D)   38 (A)(D)   50 (A)(D)   62 (A)(D)   74 (A)(D)   86 (A)(D)
3 (A)(D)   15 (A)(D)   27 (A)(D)   39 (A)(D)   51 (A)(D)   63 (A)(D)   75 (A)(D)   87 (A)(D)
4 (A)(D)   16 (A)(D)   28 (A)(D)   40 (A)(D)   52 (A)(D)   64 (A)(D)   76 (A)(D)   88 (A)(D)
5 (A)(D)   17 (A)(D)   29 (A)(D)   41 (A)(D)   53 (A)(D)   65 (A)(D)   77 (A)(D)   89 (A)(D)
6 (A)(D)   18 (A)(D)   30 (A)(D)   42 (A)(D)   54 (A)(D)   66 (A)(D)   78 (A)(D)   90 (A)(D)
7 (A)(D)   19 (A)(D)   31 (A)(D)   43 (A)(D)   55 (A)(D)   67 (A)(D)   79 (A)(D)   91 (A)(D)
8 (A)(D)   20 (A)(D)   32 (A)(D)   44 (A)(D)   56 (A)(D)   68 (A)(D)   80 (A)(D)   92 (A)(D)
9 (A)(D)   21 (A)(D)   33 (A)(D)   45 (A)(D)   57 (A)(D)   69 (A)(D)   81 (A)(D)   93 (A)(D)
10 (A)(D) 22 (A)(D)   34 (A)(D)   46 (A)(D)   58 (A)(D)   70 (A)(D)   82 (A)(D)   94 (A)(D)
11 (A)(D) 23 (A)(D)   35 (A)(D)   47 (A)(D)   59 (A)(D)   71 (A)(D)   83 (A)(D)   95 (A)(D)
12 (A)(D) 24 (A)(D)   36 (A)(D)   48 (A)(D)   60 (A)(D)   72 (A)(D)   84 (A)(D)

---

1 (A)(D)   13 (A)(D)   25 (A)(D)   37 (A)(D)   49 (A)(D)   61 (A)(D)   73 (A)(D)   85 (A)(D)
2 (A)(D)   14 (A)(D)   26 (A)(D)   38 (A)(D)   50 (A)(D)   62 (A)(D)   74 (A)(D)   86 (A)(D)
3 (A)(D)   15 (A)(D)   27 (A)(D)   39 (A)(D)   51 (A)(D)   63 (A)(D)   75 (A)(D)   87 (A)(D)
4 (A)(D)   16 (A)(D)   28 (A)(D)   40 (A)(D)   52 (A)(D)   64 (A)(D)   76 (A)(D)   88 (A)(D)
5 (A)(D)   17 (A)(D)   29 (A)(D)   41 (A)(D)   53 (A)(D)   65 (A)(D)   77 (A)(D)   89 (A)(D)
6 (A)(D)   18 (A)(D)   30 (A)(D)   42 (A)(D)   54 (A)(D)   66 (A)(D)   78 (A)(D)   90 (A)(D)
7 (A)(D)   19 (A)(D)   31 (A)(D)   43 (A)(D)   55 (A)(D)   67 (A)(D)   79 (A)(D)   91 (A)(D)
8 (A)(D)   20 (A)(D)   32 (A)(D)   44 (A)(D)   56 (A)(D)   68 (A)(D)   80 (A)(D)   92 (A)(D)
9 (A)(D)   21 (A)(D)   33 (A)(D)   45 (A)(D)   57 (A)(D)   69 (A)(D)   81 (A)(D)   93 (A)(D)
10 (A)(D) 22 (A)(D)   34 (A)(D)   46 (A)(D)   58 (A)(D)   70 (A)(D)   82 (A)(D)   94 (A)(D)
11 (A)(D) 23 (A)(D)   35 (A)(D)   47 (A)(D)   59 (A)(D)   71 (A)(D)   83 (A)(D)   95 (A)(D)
12 (A)(D) 24 (A)(D)   36 (A)(D)   48 (A)(D)   60 (A)(D)   72 (A)(D)   84 (A)(D)

Extra Address Checking Answer Sheets

1 Ⓐ Ⓓ   13 Ⓐ Ⓓ   25 Ⓐ Ⓓ   37 Ⓐ Ⓓ   49 Ⓐ Ⓓ   61 Ⓐ Ⓓ   73 Ⓐ Ⓓ   85 Ⓐ Ⓓ
2 Ⓐ Ⓓ   14 Ⓐ Ⓓ   26 Ⓐ Ⓓ   38 Ⓐ Ⓓ   50 Ⓐ Ⓓ   62 Ⓐ Ⓓ   74 Ⓐ Ⓓ   86 Ⓐ Ⓓ
3 Ⓐ Ⓓ   15 Ⓐ Ⓓ   27 Ⓐ Ⓓ   39 Ⓐ Ⓓ   51 Ⓐ Ⓓ   63 Ⓐ Ⓓ   75 Ⓐ Ⓓ   87 Ⓐ Ⓓ
4 Ⓐ Ⓓ   16 Ⓐ Ⓓ   28 Ⓐ Ⓓ   40 Ⓐ Ⓓ   52 Ⓐ Ⓓ   64 Ⓐ Ⓓ   76 Ⓐ Ⓓ   88 Ⓐ Ⓓ
5 Ⓐ Ⓓ   17 Ⓐ Ⓓ   29 Ⓐ Ⓓ   41 Ⓐ Ⓓ   53 Ⓐ Ⓓ   65 Ⓐ Ⓓ   77 Ⓐ Ⓓ   89 Ⓐ Ⓓ
6 Ⓐ Ⓓ   18 Ⓐ Ⓓ   30 Ⓐ Ⓓ   42 Ⓐ Ⓓ   54 Ⓐ Ⓓ   66 Ⓐ Ⓓ   78 Ⓐ Ⓓ   90 Ⓐ Ⓓ
7 Ⓐ Ⓓ   19 Ⓐ Ⓓ   31 Ⓐ Ⓓ   43 Ⓐ Ⓓ   55 Ⓐ Ⓓ   67 Ⓐ Ⓓ   79 Ⓐ Ⓓ   91 Ⓐ Ⓓ
8 Ⓐ Ⓓ   20 Ⓐ Ⓓ   32 Ⓐ Ⓓ   44 Ⓐ Ⓓ   56 Ⓐ Ⓓ   68 Ⓐ Ⓓ   80 Ⓐ Ⓓ   92 Ⓐ Ⓓ
9 Ⓐ Ⓓ   21 Ⓐ Ⓓ   33 Ⓐ Ⓓ   45 Ⓐ Ⓓ   57 Ⓐ Ⓓ   69 Ⓐ Ⓓ   81 Ⓐ Ⓓ   93 Ⓐ Ⓓ
10 Ⓐ Ⓓ 22 Ⓐ Ⓓ   34 Ⓐ Ⓓ   46 Ⓐ Ⓓ   58 Ⓐ Ⓓ   70 Ⓐ Ⓓ   82 Ⓐ Ⓓ   94 Ⓐ Ⓓ
11 Ⓐ Ⓓ 23 Ⓐ Ⓓ   35 Ⓐ Ⓓ   47 Ⓐ Ⓓ   59 Ⓐ Ⓓ   71 Ⓐ Ⓓ   83 Ⓐ Ⓓ   95 Ⓐ Ⓓ
12 Ⓐ Ⓓ 24 Ⓐ Ⓓ   36 Ⓐ Ⓓ   48 Ⓐ Ⓓ   60 Ⓐ Ⓓ   72 Ⓐ Ⓓ   84 Ⓐ Ⓓ

---

1 Ⓐ Ⓓ   13 Ⓐ Ⓓ   25 Ⓐ Ⓓ   37 Ⓐ Ⓓ   49 Ⓐ Ⓓ   61 Ⓐ Ⓓ   73 Ⓐ Ⓓ   85 Ⓐ Ⓓ
2 Ⓐ Ⓓ   14 Ⓐ Ⓓ   26 Ⓐ Ⓓ   38 Ⓐ Ⓓ   50 Ⓐ Ⓓ   62 Ⓐ Ⓓ   74 Ⓐ Ⓓ   86 Ⓐ Ⓓ
3 Ⓐ Ⓓ   15 Ⓐ Ⓓ   27 Ⓐ Ⓓ   39 Ⓐ Ⓓ   51 Ⓐ Ⓓ   63 Ⓐ Ⓓ   75 Ⓐ Ⓓ   87 Ⓐ Ⓓ
4 Ⓐ Ⓓ   16 Ⓐ Ⓓ   28 Ⓐ Ⓓ   40 Ⓐ Ⓓ   52 Ⓐ Ⓓ   64 Ⓐ Ⓓ   76 Ⓐ Ⓓ   88 Ⓐ Ⓓ
5 Ⓐ Ⓓ   17 Ⓐ Ⓓ   29 Ⓐ Ⓓ   41 Ⓐ Ⓓ   53 Ⓐ Ⓓ   65 Ⓐ Ⓓ   77 Ⓐ Ⓓ   89 Ⓐ Ⓓ
6 Ⓐ Ⓓ   18 Ⓐ Ⓓ   30 Ⓐ Ⓓ   42 Ⓐ Ⓓ   54 Ⓐ Ⓓ   66 Ⓐ Ⓓ   78 Ⓐ Ⓓ   90 Ⓐ Ⓓ
7 Ⓐ Ⓓ   19 Ⓐ Ⓓ   31 Ⓐ Ⓓ   43 Ⓐ Ⓓ   55 Ⓐ Ⓓ   67 Ⓐ Ⓓ   79 Ⓐ Ⓓ   91 Ⓐ Ⓓ
8 Ⓐ Ⓓ   20 Ⓐ Ⓓ   32 Ⓐ Ⓓ   44 Ⓐ Ⓓ   56 Ⓐ Ⓓ   68 Ⓐ Ⓓ   80 Ⓐ Ⓓ   92 Ⓐ Ⓓ
9 Ⓐ Ⓓ   21 Ⓐ Ⓓ   33 Ⓐ Ⓓ   45 Ⓐ Ⓓ   57 Ⓐ Ⓓ   69 Ⓐ Ⓓ   81 Ⓐ Ⓓ   93 Ⓐ Ⓓ
10 Ⓐ Ⓓ 22 Ⓐ Ⓓ   34 Ⓐ Ⓓ   46 Ⓐ Ⓓ   58 Ⓐ Ⓓ   70 Ⓐ Ⓓ   82 Ⓐ Ⓓ   94 Ⓐ Ⓓ
11 Ⓐ Ⓓ 23 Ⓐ Ⓓ   35 Ⓐ Ⓓ   47 Ⓐ Ⓓ   59 Ⓐ Ⓓ   71 Ⓐ Ⓓ   83 Ⓐ Ⓓ   95 Ⓐ Ⓓ
12 Ⓐ Ⓓ 24 Ⓐ Ⓓ   36 Ⓐ Ⓓ   48 Ⓐ Ⓓ   60 Ⓐ Ⓓ   72 Ⓐ Ⓓ   84 Ⓐ Ⓓ

---

1 Ⓐ Ⓓ   13 Ⓐ Ⓓ   25 Ⓐ Ⓓ   37 Ⓐ Ⓓ   49 Ⓐ Ⓓ   61 Ⓐ Ⓓ   73 Ⓐ Ⓓ   85 Ⓐ Ⓓ
2 Ⓐ Ⓓ   14 Ⓐ Ⓓ   26 Ⓐ Ⓓ   38 Ⓐ Ⓓ   50 Ⓐ Ⓓ   62 Ⓐ Ⓓ   74 Ⓐ Ⓓ   86 Ⓐ Ⓓ
3 Ⓐ Ⓓ   15 Ⓐ Ⓓ   27 Ⓐ Ⓓ   39 Ⓐ Ⓓ   51 Ⓐ Ⓓ   63 Ⓐ Ⓓ   75 Ⓐ Ⓓ   87 Ⓐ Ⓓ
4 Ⓐ Ⓓ   16 Ⓐ Ⓓ   28 Ⓐ Ⓓ   40 Ⓐ Ⓓ   52 Ⓐ Ⓓ   64 Ⓐ Ⓓ   76 Ⓐ Ⓓ   88 Ⓐ Ⓓ
5 Ⓐ Ⓓ   17 Ⓐ Ⓓ   29 Ⓐ Ⓓ   41 Ⓐ Ⓓ   53 Ⓐ Ⓓ   65 Ⓐ Ⓓ   77 Ⓐ Ⓓ   89 Ⓐ Ⓓ
6 Ⓐ Ⓓ   18 Ⓐ Ⓓ   30 Ⓐ Ⓓ   42 Ⓐ Ⓓ   54 Ⓐ Ⓓ   66 Ⓐ Ⓓ   78 Ⓐ Ⓓ   90 Ⓐ Ⓓ
7 Ⓐ Ⓓ   19 Ⓐ Ⓓ   31 Ⓐ Ⓓ   43 Ⓐ Ⓓ   55 Ⓐ Ⓓ   67 Ⓐ Ⓓ   79 Ⓐ Ⓓ   91 Ⓐ Ⓓ
8 Ⓐ Ⓓ   20 Ⓐ Ⓓ   32 Ⓐ Ⓓ   44 Ⓐ Ⓓ   56 Ⓐ Ⓓ   68 Ⓐ Ⓓ   80 Ⓐ Ⓓ   92 Ⓐ Ⓓ
9 Ⓐ Ⓓ   21 Ⓐ Ⓓ   33 Ⓐ Ⓓ   45 Ⓐ Ⓓ   57 Ⓐ Ⓓ   69 Ⓐ Ⓓ   81 Ⓐ Ⓓ   93 Ⓐ Ⓓ
10 Ⓐ Ⓓ 22 Ⓐ Ⓓ   34 Ⓐ Ⓓ   46 Ⓐ Ⓓ   58 Ⓐ Ⓓ   70 Ⓐ Ⓓ   82 Ⓐ Ⓓ   94 Ⓐ Ⓓ
11 Ⓐ Ⓓ 23 Ⓐ Ⓓ   35 Ⓐ Ⓓ   47 Ⓐ Ⓓ   59 Ⓐ Ⓓ   71 Ⓐ Ⓓ   83 Ⓐ Ⓓ   95 Ⓐ Ⓓ
12 Ⓐ Ⓓ 24 Ⓐ Ⓓ   36 Ⓐ Ⓓ   48 Ⓐ Ⓓ   60 Ⓐ Ⓓ   72 Ⓐ Ⓓ   84 Ⓐ Ⓓ

---

1 Ⓐ Ⓓ   13 Ⓐ Ⓓ   25 Ⓐ Ⓓ   37 Ⓐ Ⓓ   49 Ⓐ Ⓓ   61 Ⓐ Ⓓ   73 Ⓐ Ⓓ   85 Ⓐ Ⓓ
2 Ⓐ Ⓓ   14 Ⓐ Ⓓ   26 Ⓐ Ⓓ   38 Ⓐ Ⓓ   50 Ⓐ Ⓓ   62 Ⓐ Ⓓ   74 Ⓐ Ⓓ   86 Ⓐ Ⓓ
3 Ⓐ Ⓓ   15 Ⓐ Ⓓ   27 Ⓐ Ⓓ   39 Ⓐ Ⓓ   51 Ⓐ Ⓓ   63 Ⓐ Ⓓ   75 Ⓐ Ⓓ   87 Ⓐ Ⓓ
4 Ⓐ Ⓓ   16 Ⓐ Ⓓ   28 Ⓐ Ⓓ   40 Ⓐ Ⓓ   52 Ⓐ Ⓓ   64 Ⓐ Ⓓ   76 Ⓐ Ⓓ   88 Ⓐ Ⓓ
5 Ⓐ Ⓓ   17 Ⓐ Ⓓ   29 Ⓐ Ⓓ   41 Ⓐ Ⓓ   53 Ⓐ Ⓓ   65 Ⓐ Ⓓ   77 Ⓐ Ⓓ   89 Ⓐ Ⓓ
6 Ⓐ Ⓓ   18 Ⓐ Ⓓ   30 Ⓐ Ⓓ   42 Ⓐ Ⓓ   54 Ⓐ Ⓓ   66 Ⓐ Ⓓ   78 Ⓐ Ⓓ   90 Ⓐ Ⓓ
7 Ⓐ Ⓓ   19 Ⓐ Ⓓ   31 Ⓐ Ⓓ   43 Ⓐ Ⓓ   55 Ⓐ Ⓓ   67 Ⓐ Ⓓ   79 Ⓐ Ⓓ   91 Ⓐ Ⓓ
8 Ⓐ Ⓓ   20 Ⓐ Ⓓ   32 Ⓐ Ⓓ   44 Ⓐ Ⓓ   56 Ⓐ Ⓓ   68 Ⓐ Ⓓ   80 Ⓐ Ⓓ   92 Ⓐ Ⓓ
9 Ⓐ Ⓓ   21 Ⓐ Ⓓ   33 Ⓐ Ⓓ   45 Ⓐ Ⓓ   57 Ⓐ Ⓓ   69 Ⓐ Ⓓ   81 Ⓐ Ⓓ   93 Ⓐ Ⓓ
10 Ⓐ Ⓓ 22 Ⓐ Ⓓ   34 Ⓐ Ⓓ   46 Ⓐ Ⓓ   58 Ⓐ Ⓓ   70 Ⓐ Ⓓ   82 Ⓐ Ⓓ   94 Ⓐ Ⓓ
11 Ⓐ Ⓓ 23 Ⓐ Ⓓ   35 Ⓐ Ⓓ   47 Ⓐ Ⓓ   59 Ⓐ Ⓓ   71 Ⓐ Ⓓ   83 Ⓐ Ⓓ   95 Ⓐ Ⓓ
12 Ⓐ Ⓓ 24 Ⓐ Ⓓ   36 Ⓐ Ⓓ   48 Ⓐ Ⓓ   60 Ⓐ Ⓓ   72 Ⓐ Ⓓ   84 Ⓐ Ⓓ

Extra Address Checking Answer Sheets

1 Ⓐ Ⓓ   13 Ⓐ Ⓓ   25 Ⓐ Ⓓ   37 Ⓐ Ⓓ   49 Ⓐ Ⓓ   61 Ⓐ Ⓓ   73 Ⓐ Ⓓ   85 Ⓐ Ⓓ
2 Ⓐ Ⓓ   14 Ⓐ Ⓓ   26 Ⓐ Ⓓ   38 Ⓐ Ⓓ   50 Ⓐ Ⓓ   62 Ⓐ Ⓓ   74 Ⓐ Ⓓ   86 Ⓐ Ⓓ
3 Ⓐ Ⓓ   15 Ⓐ Ⓓ   27 Ⓐ Ⓓ   39 Ⓐ Ⓓ   51 Ⓐ Ⓓ   63 Ⓐ Ⓓ   75 Ⓐ Ⓓ   87 Ⓐ Ⓓ
4 Ⓐ Ⓓ   16 Ⓐ Ⓓ   28 Ⓐ Ⓓ   40 Ⓐ Ⓓ   52 Ⓐ Ⓓ   64 Ⓐ Ⓓ   76 Ⓐ Ⓓ   88 Ⓐ Ⓓ
5 Ⓐ Ⓓ   17 Ⓐ Ⓓ   29 Ⓐ Ⓓ   41 Ⓐ Ⓓ   53 Ⓐ Ⓓ   65 Ⓐ Ⓓ   77 Ⓐ Ⓓ   89 Ⓐ Ⓓ
6 Ⓐ Ⓓ   18 Ⓐ Ⓓ   30 Ⓐ Ⓓ   42 Ⓐ Ⓓ   54 Ⓐ Ⓓ   66 Ⓐ Ⓓ   78 Ⓐ Ⓓ   90 Ⓐ Ⓓ
7 Ⓐ Ⓓ   19 Ⓐ Ⓓ   31 Ⓐ Ⓓ   43 Ⓐ Ⓓ   55 Ⓐ Ⓓ   67 Ⓐ Ⓓ   79 Ⓐ Ⓓ   91 Ⓐ Ⓓ
8 Ⓐ Ⓓ   20 Ⓐ Ⓓ   32 Ⓐ Ⓓ   44 Ⓐ Ⓓ   56 Ⓐ Ⓓ   68 Ⓐ Ⓓ   80 Ⓐ Ⓓ   92 Ⓐ Ⓓ
9 Ⓐ Ⓓ   21 Ⓐ Ⓓ   33 Ⓐ Ⓓ   45 Ⓐ Ⓓ   57 Ⓐ Ⓓ   69 Ⓐ Ⓓ   81 Ⓐ Ⓓ   93 Ⓐ Ⓓ
10 Ⓐ Ⓓ   22 Ⓐ Ⓓ   34 Ⓐ Ⓓ   46 Ⓐ Ⓓ   58 Ⓐ Ⓓ   70 Ⓐ Ⓓ   82 Ⓐ Ⓓ   94 Ⓐ Ⓓ
11 Ⓐ Ⓓ   23 Ⓐ Ⓓ   35 Ⓐ Ⓓ   47 Ⓐ Ⓓ   59 Ⓐ Ⓓ   71 Ⓐ Ⓓ   83 Ⓐ Ⓓ   95 Ⓐ Ⓓ
12 Ⓐ Ⓓ   24 Ⓐ Ⓓ   36 Ⓐ Ⓓ   48 Ⓐ Ⓓ   60 Ⓐ Ⓓ   72 Ⓐ Ⓓ   84 Ⓐ Ⓓ

---

1 Ⓐ Ⓓ   13 Ⓐ Ⓓ   25 Ⓐ Ⓓ   37 Ⓐ Ⓓ   49 Ⓐ Ⓓ   61 Ⓐ Ⓓ   73 Ⓐ Ⓓ   85 Ⓐ Ⓓ
2 Ⓐ Ⓓ   14 Ⓐ Ⓓ   26 Ⓐ Ⓓ   38 Ⓐ Ⓓ   50 Ⓐ Ⓓ   62 Ⓐ Ⓓ   74 Ⓐ Ⓓ   86 Ⓐ Ⓓ
3 Ⓐ Ⓓ   15 Ⓐ Ⓓ   27 Ⓐ Ⓓ   39 Ⓐ Ⓓ   51 Ⓐ Ⓓ   63 Ⓐ Ⓓ   75 Ⓐ Ⓓ   87 Ⓐ Ⓓ
4 Ⓐ Ⓓ   16 Ⓐ Ⓓ   28 Ⓐ Ⓓ   40 Ⓐ Ⓓ   52 Ⓐ Ⓓ   64 Ⓐ Ⓓ   76 Ⓐ Ⓓ   88 Ⓐ Ⓓ
5 Ⓐ Ⓓ   17 Ⓐ Ⓓ   29 Ⓐ Ⓓ   41 Ⓐ Ⓓ   53 Ⓐ Ⓓ   65 Ⓐ Ⓓ   77 Ⓐ Ⓓ   89 Ⓐ Ⓓ
6 Ⓐ Ⓓ   18 Ⓐ Ⓓ   30 Ⓐ Ⓓ   42 Ⓐ Ⓓ   54 Ⓐ Ⓓ   66 Ⓐ Ⓓ   78 Ⓐ Ⓓ   90 Ⓐ Ⓓ
7 Ⓐ Ⓓ   19 Ⓐ Ⓓ   31 Ⓐ Ⓓ   43 Ⓐ Ⓓ   55 Ⓐ Ⓓ   67 Ⓐ Ⓓ   79 Ⓐ Ⓓ   91 Ⓐ Ⓓ
8 Ⓐ Ⓓ   20 Ⓐ Ⓓ   32 Ⓐ Ⓓ   44 Ⓐ Ⓓ   56 Ⓐ Ⓓ   68 Ⓐ Ⓓ   80 Ⓐ Ⓓ   92 Ⓐ Ⓓ
9 Ⓐ Ⓓ   21 Ⓐ Ⓓ   33 Ⓐ Ⓓ   45 Ⓐ Ⓓ   57 Ⓐ Ⓓ   69 Ⓐ Ⓓ   81 Ⓐ Ⓓ   93 Ⓐ Ⓓ
10 Ⓐ Ⓓ   22 Ⓐ Ⓓ   34 Ⓐ Ⓓ   46 Ⓐ Ⓓ   58 Ⓐ Ⓓ   70 Ⓐ Ⓓ   82 Ⓐ Ⓓ   94 Ⓐ Ⓓ
11 Ⓐ Ⓓ   23 Ⓐ Ⓓ   35 Ⓐ Ⓓ   47 Ⓐ Ⓓ   59 Ⓐ Ⓓ   71 Ⓐ Ⓓ   83 Ⓐ Ⓓ   95 Ⓐ Ⓓ
12 Ⓐ Ⓓ   24 Ⓐ Ⓓ   36 Ⓐ Ⓓ   48 Ⓐ Ⓓ   60 Ⓐ Ⓓ   72 Ⓐ Ⓓ   84 Ⓐ Ⓓ

---

1 Ⓐ Ⓓ   13 Ⓐ Ⓓ   25 Ⓐ Ⓓ   37 Ⓐ Ⓓ   49 Ⓐ Ⓓ   61 Ⓐ Ⓓ   73 Ⓐ Ⓓ   85 Ⓐ Ⓓ
2 Ⓐ Ⓓ   14 Ⓐ Ⓓ   26 Ⓐ Ⓓ   38 Ⓐ Ⓓ   50 Ⓐ Ⓓ   62 Ⓐ Ⓓ   74 Ⓐ Ⓓ   86 Ⓐ Ⓓ
3 Ⓐ Ⓓ   15 Ⓐ Ⓓ   27 Ⓐ Ⓓ   39 Ⓐ Ⓓ   51 Ⓐ Ⓓ   63 Ⓐ Ⓓ   75 Ⓐ Ⓓ   87 Ⓐ Ⓓ
4 Ⓐ Ⓓ   16 Ⓐ Ⓓ   28 Ⓐ Ⓓ   40 Ⓐ Ⓓ   52 Ⓐ Ⓓ   64 Ⓐ Ⓓ   76 Ⓐ Ⓓ   88 Ⓐ Ⓓ
5 Ⓐ Ⓓ   17 Ⓐ Ⓓ   29 Ⓐ Ⓓ   41 Ⓐ Ⓓ   53 Ⓐ Ⓓ   65 Ⓐ Ⓓ   77 Ⓐ Ⓓ   89 Ⓐ Ⓓ
6 Ⓐ Ⓓ   18 Ⓐ Ⓓ   30 Ⓐ Ⓓ   42 Ⓐ Ⓓ   54 Ⓐ Ⓓ   66 Ⓐ Ⓓ   78 Ⓐ Ⓓ   90 Ⓐ Ⓓ
7 Ⓐ Ⓓ   19 Ⓐ Ⓓ   31 Ⓐ Ⓓ   43 Ⓐ Ⓓ   55 Ⓐ Ⓓ   67 Ⓐ Ⓓ   79 Ⓐ Ⓓ   91 Ⓐ Ⓓ
8 Ⓐ Ⓓ   20 Ⓐ Ⓓ   32 Ⓐ Ⓓ   44 Ⓐ Ⓓ   56 Ⓐ Ⓓ   68 Ⓐ Ⓓ   80 Ⓐ Ⓓ   92 Ⓐ Ⓓ
9 Ⓐ Ⓓ   21 Ⓐ Ⓓ   33 Ⓐ Ⓓ   45 Ⓐ Ⓓ   57 Ⓐ Ⓓ   69 Ⓐ Ⓓ   81 Ⓐ Ⓓ   93 Ⓐ Ⓓ
10 Ⓐ Ⓓ   22 Ⓐ Ⓓ   34 Ⓐ Ⓓ   46 Ⓐ Ⓓ   58 Ⓐ Ⓓ   70 Ⓐ Ⓓ   82 Ⓐ Ⓓ   94 Ⓐ Ⓓ
11 Ⓐ Ⓓ   23 Ⓐ Ⓓ   35 Ⓐ Ⓓ   47 Ⓐ Ⓓ   59 Ⓐ Ⓓ   71 Ⓐ Ⓓ   83 Ⓐ Ⓓ   95 Ⓐ Ⓓ
12 Ⓐ Ⓓ   24 Ⓐ Ⓓ   36 Ⓐ Ⓓ   48 Ⓐ Ⓓ   60 Ⓐ Ⓓ   72 Ⓐ Ⓓ   84 Ⓐ Ⓓ

---

1 Ⓐ Ⓓ   13 Ⓐ Ⓓ   25 Ⓐ Ⓓ   37 Ⓐ Ⓓ   49 Ⓐ Ⓓ   61 Ⓐ Ⓓ   73 Ⓐ Ⓓ   85 Ⓐ Ⓓ
2 Ⓐ Ⓓ   14 Ⓐ Ⓓ   26 Ⓐ Ⓓ   38 Ⓐ Ⓓ   50 Ⓐ Ⓓ   62 Ⓐ Ⓓ   74 Ⓐ Ⓓ   86 Ⓐ Ⓓ
3 Ⓐ Ⓓ   15 Ⓐ Ⓓ   27 Ⓐ Ⓓ   39 Ⓐ Ⓓ   51 Ⓐ Ⓓ   63 Ⓐ Ⓓ   75 Ⓐ Ⓓ   87 Ⓐ Ⓓ
4 Ⓐ Ⓓ   16 Ⓐ Ⓓ   28 Ⓐ Ⓓ   40 Ⓐ Ⓓ   52 Ⓐ Ⓓ   64 Ⓐ Ⓓ   76 Ⓐ Ⓓ   88 Ⓐ Ⓓ
5 Ⓐ Ⓓ   17 Ⓐ Ⓓ   29 Ⓐ Ⓓ   41 Ⓐ Ⓓ   53 Ⓐ Ⓓ   65 Ⓐ Ⓓ   77 Ⓐ Ⓓ   89 Ⓐ Ⓓ
6 Ⓐ Ⓓ   18 Ⓐ Ⓓ   30 Ⓐ Ⓓ   42 Ⓐ Ⓓ   54 Ⓐ Ⓓ   66 Ⓐ Ⓓ   78 Ⓐ Ⓓ   90 Ⓐ Ⓓ
7 Ⓐ Ⓓ   19 Ⓐ Ⓓ   31 Ⓐ Ⓓ   43 Ⓐ Ⓓ   55 Ⓐ Ⓓ   67 Ⓐ Ⓓ   79 Ⓐ Ⓓ   91 Ⓐ Ⓓ
8 Ⓐ Ⓓ   20 Ⓐ Ⓓ   32 Ⓐ Ⓓ   44 Ⓐ Ⓓ   56 Ⓐ Ⓓ   68 Ⓐ Ⓓ   80 Ⓐ Ⓓ   92 Ⓐ Ⓓ
9 Ⓐ Ⓓ   21 Ⓐ Ⓓ   33 Ⓐ Ⓓ   45 Ⓐ Ⓓ   57 Ⓐ Ⓓ   69 Ⓐ Ⓓ   81 Ⓐ Ⓓ   93 Ⓐ Ⓓ
10 Ⓐ Ⓓ   22 Ⓐ Ⓓ   34 Ⓐ Ⓓ   46 Ⓐ Ⓓ   58 Ⓐ Ⓓ   70 Ⓐ Ⓓ   82 Ⓐ Ⓓ   94 Ⓐ Ⓓ
11 Ⓐ Ⓓ   23 Ⓐ Ⓓ   35 Ⓐ Ⓓ   47 Ⓐ Ⓓ   59 Ⓐ Ⓓ   71 Ⓐ Ⓓ   83 Ⓐ Ⓓ   95 Ⓐ Ⓓ
12 Ⓐ Ⓓ   24 Ⓐ Ⓓ   36 Ⓐ Ⓓ   48 Ⓐ Ⓓ   60 Ⓐ Ⓓ   72 Ⓐ Ⓓ   84 Ⓐ Ⓓ

Extra Address Checking Answer Sheets

Sheet 1

1 Ⓐ Ⓓ	13 Ⓐ Ⓓ	25 Ⓐ Ⓓ	37 Ⓐ Ⓓ	49 Ⓐ Ⓓ	61 Ⓐ Ⓓ	73 Ⓐ Ⓓ	85 Ⓐ Ⓓ
2 Ⓐ Ⓓ	14 Ⓐ Ⓓ	26 Ⓐ Ⓓ	38 Ⓐ Ⓓ	50 Ⓐ Ⓓ	62 Ⓐ Ⓓ	74 Ⓐ Ⓓ	86 Ⓐ Ⓓ
3 Ⓐ Ⓓ	15 Ⓐ Ⓓ	27 Ⓐ Ⓓ	39 Ⓐ Ⓓ	51 Ⓐ Ⓓ	63 Ⓐ Ⓓ	75 Ⓐ Ⓓ	87 Ⓐ Ⓓ
4 Ⓐ Ⓓ	16 Ⓐ Ⓓ	28 Ⓐ Ⓓ	40 Ⓐ Ⓓ	52 Ⓐ Ⓓ	64 Ⓐ Ⓓ	76 Ⓐ Ⓓ	88 Ⓐ Ⓓ
5 Ⓐ Ⓓ	17 Ⓐ Ⓓ	29 Ⓐ Ⓓ	41 Ⓐ Ⓓ	53 Ⓐ Ⓓ	65 Ⓐ Ⓓ	77 Ⓐ Ⓓ	89 Ⓐ Ⓓ
6 Ⓐ Ⓓ	18 Ⓐ Ⓓ	30 Ⓐ Ⓓ	42 Ⓐ Ⓓ	54 Ⓐ Ⓓ	66 Ⓐ Ⓓ	78 Ⓐ Ⓓ	90 Ⓐ Ⓓ
7 Ⓐ Ⓓ	19 Ⓐ Ⓓ	31 Ⓐ Ⓓ	43 Ⓐ Ⓓ	55 Ⓐ Ⓓ	67 Ⓐ Ⓓ	79 Ⓐ Ⓓ	91 Ⓐ Ⓓ
8 Ⓐ Ⓓ	20 Ⓐ Ⓓ	32 Ⓐ Ⓓ	44 Ⓐ Ⓓ	56 Ⓐ Ⓓ	68 Ⓐ Ⓓ	80 Ⓐ Ⓓ	92 Ⓐ Ⓓ
9 Ⓐ Ⓓ	21 Ⓐ Ⓓ	33 Ⓐ Ⓓ	45 Ⓐ Ⓓ	57 Ⓐ Ⓓ	69 Ⓐ Ⓓ	81 Ⓐ Ⓓ	93 Ⓐ Ⓓ
10 Ⓐ Ⓓ	22 Ⓐ Ⓓ	34 Ⓐ Ⓓ	46 Ⓐ Ⓓ	58 Ⓐ Ⓓ	70 Ⓐ Ⓓ	82 Ⓐ Ⓓ	94 Ⓐ Ⓓ
11 Ⓐ Ⓓ	23 Ⓐ Ⓓ	35 Ⓐ Ⓓ	47 Ⓐ Ⓓ	59 Ⓐ Ⓓ	71 Ⓐ Ⓓ	83 Ⓐ Ⓓ	95 Ⓐ Ⓓ
12 Ⓐ Ⓓ	24 Ⓐ Ⓓ	36 Ⓐ Ⓓ	48 Ⓐ Ⓓ	60 Ⓐ Ⓓ	72 Ⓐ Ⓓ	84 Ⓐ Ⓓ	

Sheet 2

1 Ⓐ Ⓓ	13 Ⓐ Ⓓ	25 Ⓐ Ⓓ	37 Ⓐ Ⓓ	49 Ⓐ Ⓓ	61 Ⓐ Ⓓ	73 Ⓐ Ⓓ	85 Ⓐ Ⓓ
2 Ⓐ Ⓓ	14 Ⓐ Ⓓ	26 Ⓐ Ⓓ	38 Ⓐ Ⓓ	50 Ⓐ Ⓓ	62 Ⓐ Ⓓ	74 Ⓐ Ⓓ	86 Ⓐ Ⓓ
3 Ⓐ Ⓓ	15 Ⓐ Ⓓ	27 Ⓐ Ⓓ	39 Ⓐ Ⓓ	51 Ⓐ Ⓓ	63 Ⓐ Ⓓ	75 Ⓐ Ⓓ	87 Ⓐ Ⓓ
4 Ⓐ Ⓓ	16 Ⓐ Ⓓ	28 Ⓐ Ⓓ	40 Ⓐ Ⓓ	52 Ⓐ Ⓓ	64 Ⓐ Ⓓ	76 Ⓐ Ⓓ	88 Ⓐ Ⓓ
5 Ⓐ Ⓓ	17 Ⓐ Ⓓ	29 Ⓐ Ⓓ	41 Ⓐ Ⓓ	53 Ⓐ Ⓓ	65 Ⓐ Ⓓ	77 Ⓐ Ⓓ	89 Ⓐ Ⓓ
6 Ⓐ Ⓓ	18 Ⓐ Ⓓ	30 Ⓐ Ⓓ	42 Ⓐ Ⓓ	54 Ⓐ Ⓓ	66 Ⓐ Ⓓ	78 Ⓐ Ⓓ	90 Ⓐ Ⓓ
7 Ⓐ Ⓓ	19 Ⓐ Ⓓ	31 Ⓐ Ⓓ	43 Ⓐ Ⓓ	55 Ⓐ Ⓓ	67 Ⓐ Ⓓ	79 Ⓐ Ⓓ	91 Ⓐ Ⓓ
8 Ⓐ Ⓓ	20 Ⓐ Ⓓ	32 Ⓐ Ⓓ	44 Ⓐ Ⓓ	56 Ⓐ Ⓓ	68 Ⓐ Ⓓ	80 Ⓐ Ⓓ	92 Ⓐ Ⓓ
9 Ⓐ Ⓓ	21 Ⓐ Ⓓ	33 Ⓐ Ⓓ	45 Ⓐ Ⓓ	57 Ⓐ Ⓓ	69 Ⓐ Ⓓ	81 Ⓐ Ⓓ	93 Ⓐ Ⓓ
10 Ⓐ Ⓓ	22 Ⓐ Ⓓ	34 Ⓐ Ⓓ	46 Ⓐ Ⓓ	58 Ⓐ Ⓓ	70 Ⓐ Ⓓ	82 Ⓐ Ⓓ	94 Ⓐ Ⓓ
11 Ⓐ Ⓓ	23 Ⓐ Ⓓ	35 Ⓐ Ⓓ	47 Ⓐ Ⓓ	59 Ⓐ Ⓓ	71 Ⓐ Ⓓ	83 Ⓐ Ⓓ	95 Ⓐ Ⓓ
12 Ⓐ Ⓓ	24 Ⓐ Ⓓ	36 Ⓐ Ⓓ	48 Ⓐ Ⓓ	60 Ⓐ Ⓓ	72 Ⓐ Ⓓ	84 Ⓐ Ⓓ	

Sheet 3

1 Ⓐ Ⓓ	13 Ⓐ Ⓓ	25 Ⓐ Ⓓ	37 Ⓐ Ⓓ	49 Ⓐ Ⓓ	61 Ⓐ Ⓓ	73 Ⓐ Ⓓ	85 Ⓐ Ⓓ
2 Ⓐ Ⓓ	14 Ⓐ Ⓓ	26 Ⓐ Ⓓ	38 Ⓐ Ⓓ	50 Ⓐ Ⓓ	62 Ⓐ Ⓓ	74 Ⓐ Ⓓ	86 Ⓐ Ⓓ
3 Ⓐ Ⓓ	15 Ⓐ Ⓓ	27 Ⓐ Ⓓ	39 Ⓐ Ⓓ	51 Ⓐ Ⓓ	63 Ⓐ Ⓓ	75 Ⓐ Ⓓ	87 Ⓐ Ⓓ
4 Ⓐ Ⓓ	16 Ⓐ Ⓓ	28 Ⓐ Ⓓ	40 Ⓐ Ⓓ	52 Ⓐ Ⓓ	64 Ⓐ Ⓓ	76 Ⓐ Ⓓ	88 Ⓐ Ⓓ
5 Ⓐ Ⓓ	17 Ⓐ Ⓓ	29 Ⓐ Ⓓ	41 Ⓐ Ⓓ	53 Ⓐ Ⓓ	65 Ⓐ Ⓓ	77 Ⓐ Ⓓ	89 Ⓐ Ⓓ
6 Ⓐ Ⓓ	18 Ⓐ Ⓓ	30 Ⓐ Ⓓ	42 Ⓐ Ⓓ	54 Ⓐ Ⓓ	66 Ⓐ Ⓓ	78 Ⓐ Ⓓ	90 Ⓐ Ⓓ
7 Ⓐ Ⓓ	19 Ⓐ Ⓓ	31 Ⓐ Ⓓ	43 Ⓐ Ⓓ	55 Ⓐ Ⓓ	67 Ⓐ Ⓓ	79 Ⓐ Ⓓ	91 Ⓐ Ⓓ
8 Ⓐ Ⓓ	20 Ⓐ Ⓓ	32 Ⓐ Ⓓ	44 Ⓐ Ⓓ	56 Ⓐ Ⓓ	68 Ⓐ Ⓓ	80 Ⓐ Ⓓ	92 Ⓐ Ⓓ
9 Ⓐ Ⓓ	21 Ⓐ Ⓓ	33 Ⓐ Ⓓ	45 Ⓐ Ⓓ	57 Ⓐ Ⓓ	69 Ⓐ Ⓓ	81 Ⓐ Ⓓ	93 Ⓐ Ⓓ
10 Ⓐ Ⓓ	22 Ⓐ Ⓓ	34 Ⓐ Ⓓ	46 Ⓐ Ⓓ	58 Ⓐ Ⓓ	70 Ⓐ Ⓓ	82 Ⓐ Ⓓ	94 Ⓐ Ⓓ
11 Ⓐ Ⓓ	23 Ⓐ Ⓓ	35 Ⓐ Ⓓ	47 Ⓐ Ⓓ	59 Ⓐ Ⓓ	71 Ⓐ Ⓓ	83 Ⓐ Ⓓ	95 Ⓐ Ⓓ
12 Ⓐ Ⓓ	24 Ⓐ Ⓓ	36 Ⓐ Ⓓ	48 Ⓐ Ⓓ	60 Ⓐ Ⓓ	72 Ⓐ Ⓓ	84 Ⓐ Ⓓ	

Sheet 4

1 Ⓐ Ⓓ	13 Ⓐ Ⓓ	25 Ⓐ Ⓓ	37 Ⓐ Ⓓ	49 Ⓐ Ⓓ	61 Ⓐ Ⓓ	73 Ⓐ Ⓓ	85 Ⓐ Ⓓ
2 Ⓐ Ⓓ	14 Ⓐ Ⓓ	26 Ⓐ Ⓓ	38 Ⓐ Ⓓ	50 Ⓐ Ⓓ	62 Ⓐ Ⓓ	74 Ⓐ Ⓓ	86 Ⓐ Ⓓ
3 Ⓐ Ⓓ	15 Ⓐ Ⓓ	27 Ⓐ Ⓓ	39 Ⓐ Ⓓ	51 Ⓐ Ⓓ	63 Ⓐ Ⓓ	75 Ⓐ Ⓓ	87 Ⓐ Ⓓ
4 Ⓐ Ⓓ	16 Ⓐ Ⓓ	28 Ⓐ Ⓓ	40 Ⓐ Ⓓ	52 Ⓐ Ⓓ	64 Ⓐ Ⓓ	76 Ⓐ Ⓓ	88 Ⓐ Ⓓ
5 Ⓐ Ⓓ	17 Ⓐ Ⓓ	29 Ⓐ Ⓓ	41 Ⓐ Ⓓ	53 Ⓐ Ⓓ	65 Ⓐ Ⓓ	77 Ⓐ Ⓓ	89 Ⓐ Ⓓ
6 Ⓐ Ⓓ	18 Ⓐ Ⓓ	30 Ⓐ Ⓓ	42 Ⓐ Ⓓ	54 Ⓐ Ⓓ	66 Ⓐ Ⓓ	78 Ⓐ Ⓓ	90 Ⓐ Ⓓ
7 Ⓐ Ⓓ	19 Ⓐ Ⓓ	31 Ⓐ Ⓓ	43 Ⓐ Ⓓ	55 Ⓐ Ⓓ	67 Ⓐ Ⓓ	79 Ⓐ Ⓓ	91 Ⓐ Ⓓ
8 Ⓐ Ⓓ	20 Ⓐ Ⓓ	32 Ⓐ Ⓓ	44 Ⓐ Ⓓ	56 Ⓐ Ⓓ	68 Ⓐ Ⓓ	80 Ⓐ Ⓓ	92 Ⓐ Ⓓ
9 Ⓐ Ⓓ	21 Ⓐ Ⓓ	33 Ⓐ Ⓓ	45 Ⓐ Ⓓ	57 Ⓐ Ⓓ	69 Ⓐ Ⓓ	81 Ⓐ Ⓓ	93 Ⓐ Ⓓ
10 Ⓐ Ⓓ	22 Ⓐ Ⓓ	34 Ⓐ Ⓓ	46 Ⓐ Ⓓ	58 Ⓐ Ⓓ	70 Ⓐ Ⓓ	82 Ⓐ Ⓓ	94 Ⓐ Ⓓ
11 Ⓐ Ⓓ	23 Ⓐ Ⓓ	35 Ⓐ Ⓓ	47 Ⓐ Ⓓ	59 Ⓐ Ⓓ	71 Ⓐ Ⓓ	83 Ⓐ Ⓓ	95 Ⓐ Ⓓ
12 Ⓐ Ⓓ	24 Ⓐ Ⓓ	36 Ⓐ Ⓓ	48 Ⓐ Ⓓ	60 Ⓐ Ⓓ	72 Ⓐ Ⓓ	84 Ⓐ Ⓓ	

Extra Address Checking Answer Sheets

1 (A)(D) 13 (A)(D) 25 (A)(D) 37 (A)(D) 49 (A)(D) 61 (A)(D) 73 (A)(D) 85 (A)(D)
2 (A)(D) 14 (A)(D) 26 (A)(D) 38 (A)(D) 50 (A)(D) 62 (A)(D) 74 (A)(D) 86 (A)(D)
3 (A)(D) 15 (A)(D) 27 (A)(D) 39 (A)(D) 51 (A)(D) 63 (A)(D) 75 (A)(D) 87 (A)(D)
4 (A)(D) 16 (A)(D) 28 (A)(D) 40 (A)(D) 52 (A)(D) 64 (A)(D) 76 (A)(D) 88 (A)(D)
5 (A)(D) 17 (A)(D) 29 (A)(D) 41 (A)(D) 53 (A)(D) 65 (A)(D) 77 (A)(D) 89 (A)(D)
6 (A)(D) 18 (A)(D) 30 (A)(D) 42 (A)(D) 54 (A)(D) 66 (A)(D) 78 (A)(D) 90 (A)(D)
7 (A)(D) 19 (A)(D) 31 (A)(D) 43 (A)(D) 55 (A)(D) 67 (A)(D) 79 (A)(D) 91 (A)(D)
8 (A)(D) 20 (A)(D) 32 (A)(D) 44 (A)(D) 56 (A)(D) 68 (A)(D) 80 (A)(D) 92 (A)(D)
9 (A)(D) 21 (A)(D) 33 (A)(D) 45 (A)(D) 57 (A)(D) 69 (A)(D) 81 (A)(D) 93 (A)(D)
10 (A)(D) 22 (A)(D) 34 (A)(D) 46 (A)(D) 58 (A)(D) 70 (A)(D) 82 (A)(D) 94 (A)(D)
11 (A)(D) 23 (A)(D) 35 (A)(D) 47 (A)(D) 59 (A)(D) 71 (A)(D) 83 (A)(D) 95 (A)(D)
12 (A)(D) 24 (A)(D) 36 (A)(D) 48 (A)(D) 60 (A)(D) 72 (A)(D) 84 (A)(D)

---

1 (A)(D) 13 (A)(D) 25 (A)(D) 37 (A)(D) 49 (A)(D) 61 (A)(D) 73 (A)(D) 85 (A)(D)
2 (A)(D) 14 (A)(D) 26 (A)(D) 38 (A)(D) 50 (A)(D) 62 (A)(D) 74 (A)(D) 86 (A)(D)
3 (A)(D) 15 (A)(D) 27 (A)(D) 39 (A)(D) 51 (A)(D) 63 (A)(D) 75 (A)(D) 87 (A)(D)
4 (A)(D) 16 (A)(D) 28 (A)(D) 40 (A)(D) 52 (A)(D) 64 (A)(D) 76 (A)(D) 88 (A)(D)
5 (A)(D) 17 (A)(D) 29 (A)(D) 41 (A)(D) 53 (A)(D) 65 (A)(D) 77 (A)(D) 89 (A)(D)
6 (A)(D) 18 (A)(D) 30 (A)(D) 42 (A)(D) 54 (A)(D) 66 (A)(D) 78 (A)(D) 90 (A)(D)
7 (A)(D) 19 (A)(D) 31 (A)(D) 43 (A)(D) 55 (A)(D) 67 (A)(D) 79 (A)(D) 91 (A)(D)
8 (A)(D) 20 (A)(D) 32 (A)(D) 44 (A)(D) 56 (A)(D) 68 (A)(D) 80 (A)(D) 92 (A)(D)
9 (A)(D) 21 (A)(D) 33 (A)(D) 45 (A)(D) 57 (A)(D) 69 (A)(D) 81 (A)(D) 93 (A)(D)
10 (A)(D) 22 (A)(D) 34 (A)(D) 46 (A)(D) 58 (A)(D) 70 (A)(D) 82 (A)(D) 94 (A)(D)
11 (A)(D) 23 (A)(D) 35 (A)(D) 47 (A)(D) 59 (A)(D) 71 (A)(D) 83 (A)(D) 95 (A)(D)
12 (A)(D) 24 (A)(D) 36 (A)(D) 48 (A)(D) 60 (A)(D) 72 (A)(D) 84 (A)(D)

---

1 (A)(D) 13 (A)(D) 25 (A)(D) 37 (A)(D) 49 (A)(D) 61 (A)(D) 73 (A)(D) 85 (A)(D)
2 (A)(D) 14 (A)(D) 26 (A)(D) 38 (A)(D) 50 (A)(D) 62 (A)(D) 74 (A)(D) 86 (A)(D)
3 (A)(D) 15 (A)(D) 27 (A)(D) 39 (A)(D) 51 (A)(D) 63 (A)(D) 75 (A)(D) 87 (A)(D)
4 (A)(D) 16 (A)(D) 28 (A)(D) 40 (A)(D) 52 (A)(D) 64 (A)(D) 76 (A)(D) 88 (A)(D)
5 (A)(D) 17 (A)(D) 29 (A)(D) 41 (A)(D) 53 (A)(D) 65 (A)(D) 77 (A)(D) 89 (A)(D)
6 (A)(D) 18 (A)(D) 30 (A)(D) 42 (A)(D) 54 (A)(D) 66 (A)(D) 78 (A)(D) 90 (A)(D)
7 (A)(D) 19 (A)(D) 31 (A)(D) 43 (A)(D) 55 (A)(D) 67 (A)(D) 79 (A)(D) 91 (A)(D)
8 (A)(D) 20 (A)(D) 32 (A)(D) 44 (A)(D) 56 (A)(D) 68 (A)(D) 80 (A)(D) 92 (A)(D)
9 (A)(D) 21 (A)(D) 33 (A)(D) 45 (A)(D) 57 (A)(D) 69 (A)(D) 81 (A)(D) 93 (A)(D)
10 (A)(D) 22 (A)(D) 34 (A)(D) 46 (A)(D) 58 (A)(D) 70 (A)(D) 82 (A)(D) 94 (A)(D)
11 (A)(D) 23 (A)(D) 35 (A)(D) 47 (A)(D) 59 (A)(D) 71 (A)(D) 83 (A)(D) 95 (A)(D)
12 (A)(D) 24 (A)(D) 36 (A)(D) 48 (A)(D) 60 (A)(D) 72 (A)(D) 84 (A)(D)

---

1 (A)(D) 13 (A)(D) 25 (A)(D) 37 (A)(D) 49 (A)(D) 61 (A)(D) 73 (A)(D) 85 (A)(D)
2 (A)(D) 14 (A)(D) 26 (A)(D) 38 (A)(D) 50 (A)(D) 62 (A)(D) 74 (A)(D) 86 (A)(D)
3 (A)(D) 15 (A)(D) 27 (A)(D) 39 (A)(D) 51 (A)(D) 63 (A)(D) 75 (A)(D) 87 (A)(D)
4 (A)(D) 16 (A)(D) 28 (A)(D) 40 (A)(D) 52 (A)(D) 64 (A)(D) 76 (A)(D) 88 (A)(D)
5 (A)(D) 17 (A)(D) 29 (A)(D) 41 (A)(D) 53 (A)(D) 65 (A)(D) 77 (A)(D) 89 (A)(D)
6 (A)(D) 18 (A)(D) 30 (A)(D) 42 (A)(D) 54 (A)(D) 66 (A)(D) 78 (A)(D) 90 (A)(D)
7 (A)(D) 19 (A)(D) 31 (A)(D) 43 (A)(D) 55 (A)(D) 67 (A)(D) 79 (A)(D) 91 (A)(D)
8 (A)(D) 20 (A)(D) 32 (A)(D) 44 (A)(D) 56 (A)(D) 68 (A)(D) 80 (A)(D) 92 (A)(D)
9 (A)(D) 21 (A)(D) 33 (A)(D) 45 (A)(D) 57 (A)(D) 69 (A)(D) 81 (A)(D) 93 (A)(D)
10 (A)(D) 22 (A)(D) 34 (A)(D) 46 (A)(D) 58 (A)(D) 70 (A)(D) 82 (A)(D) 94 (A)(D)
11 (A)(D) 23 (A)(D) 35 (A)(D) 47 (A)(D) 59 (A)(D) 71 (A)(D) 83 (A)(D) 95 (A)(D)
12 (A)(D) 24 (A)(D) 36 (A)(D) 48 (A)(D) 60 (A)(D) 72 (A)(D) 84 (A)(D)

Extra Address Checking Answer Sheets

1 Ⓐⓓ 13 Ⓐⓓ 25 Ⓐⓓ 37 Ⓐⓓ 49 Ⓐⓓ 61 Ⓐⓓ 73 Ⓐⓓ 85 Ⓐⓓ
2 Ⓐⓓ 14 Ⓐⓓ 26 Ⓐⓓ 38 Ⓐⓓ 50 Ⓐⓓ 62 Ⓐⓓ 74 Ⓐⓓ 86 Ⓐⓓ
3 Ⓐⓓ 15 Ⓐⓓ 27 Ⓐⓓ 39 Ⓐⓓ 51 Ⓐⓓ 63 Ⓐⓓ 75 Ⓐⓓ 87 Ⓐⓓ
4 Ⓐⓓ 16 Ⓐⓓ 28 Ⓐⓓ 40 Ⓐⓓ 52 Ⓐⓓ 64 Ⓐⓓ 76 Ⓐⓓ 88 Ⓐⓓ
5 Ⓐⓓ 17 Ⓐⓓ 29 Ⓐⓓ 41 Ⓐⓓ 53 Ⓐⓓ 65 Ⓐⓓ 77 Ⓐⓓ 89 Ⓐⓓ
6 Ⓐⓓ 18 Ⓐⓓ 30 Ⓐⓓ 42 Ⓐⓓ 54 Ⓐⓓ 66 Ⓐⓓ 78 Ⓐⓓ 90 Ⓐⓓ
7 Ⓐⓓ 19 Ⓐⓓ 31 Ⓐⓓ 43 Ⓐⓓ 55 Ⓐⓓ 67 Ⓐⓓ 79 Ⓐⓓ 91 Ⓐⓓ
8 Ⓐⓓ 20 Ⓐⓓ 32 Ⓐⓓ 44 Ⓐⓓ 56 Ⓐⓓ 68 Ⓐⓓ 80 Ⓐⓓ 92 Ⓐⓓ
9 Ⓐⓓ 21 Ⓐⓓ 33 Ⓐⓓ 45 Ⓐⓓ 57 Ⓐⓓ 69 Ⓐⓓ 81 Ⓐⓓ 93 Ⓐⓓ
10 Ⓐⓓ 22 Ⓐⓓ 34 Ⓐⓓ 46 Ⓐⓓ 58 Ⓐⓓ 70 Ⓐⓓ 82 Ⓐⓓ 94 Ⓐⓓ
11 Ⓐⓓ 23 Ⓐⓓ 35 Ⓐⓓ 47 Ⓐⓓ 59 Ⓐⓓ 71 Ⓐⓓ 83 Ⓐⓓ 95 Ⓐⓓ
12 Ⓐⓓ 24 Ⓐⓓ 36 Ⓐⓓ 48 Ⓐⓓ 60 Ⓐⓓ 72 Ⓐⓓ 84 Ⓐⓓ

---

1 Ⓐⓓ 13 Ⓐⓓ 25 Ⓐⓓ 37 Ⓐⓓ 49 Ⓐⓓ 61 Ⓐⓓ 73 Ⓐⓓ 85 Ⓐⓓ
2 Ⓐⓓ 14 Ⓐⓓ 26 Ⓐⓓ 38 Ⓐⓓ 50 Ⓐⓓ 62 Ⓐⓓ 74 Ⓐⓓ 86 Ⓐⓓ
3 Ⓐⓓ 15 Ⓐⓓ 27 Ⓐⓓ 39 Ⓐⓓ 51 Ⓐⓓ 63 Ⓐⓓ 75 Ⓐⓓ 87 Ⓐⓓ
4 Ⓐⓓ 16 Ⓐⓓ 28 Ⓐⓓ 40 Ⓐⓓ 52 Ⓐⓓ 64 Ⓐⓓ 76 Ⓐⓓ 88 Ⓐⓓ
5 Ⓐⓓ 17 Ⓐⓓ 29 Ⓐⓓ 41 Ⓐⓓ 53 Ⓐⓓ 65 Ⓐⓓ 77 Ⓐⓓ 89 Ⓐⓓ
6 Ⓐⓓ 18 Ⓐⓓ 30 Ⓐⓓ 42 Ⓐⓓ 54 Ⓐⓓ 66 Ⓐⓓ 78 Ⓐⓓ 90 Ⓐⓓ
7 Ⓐⓓ 19 Ⓐⓓ 31 Ⓐⓓ 43 Ⓐⓓ 55 Ⓐⓓ 67 Ⓐⓓ 79 Ⓐⓓ 91 Ⓐⓓ
8 Ⓐⓓ 20 Ⓐⓓ 32 Ⓐⓓ 44 Ⓐⓓ 56 Ⓐⓓ 68 Ⓐⓓ 80 Ⓐⓓ 92 Ⓐⓓ
9 Ⓐⓓ 21 Ⓐⓓ 33 Ⓐⓓ 45 Ⓐⓓ 57 Ⓐⓓ 69 Ⓐⓓ 81 Ⓐⓓ 93 Ⓐⓓ
10 Ⓐⓓ 22 Ⓐⓓ 34 Ⓐⓓ 46 Ⓐⓓ 58 Ⓐⓓ 70 Ⓐⓓ 82 Ⓐⓓ 94 Ⓐⓓ
11 Ⓐⓓ 23 Ⓐⓓ 35 Ⓐⓓ 47 Ⓐⓓ 59 Ⓐⓓ 71 Ⓐⓓ 83 Ⓐⓓ 95 Ⓐⓓ
12 Ⓐⓓ 24 Ⓐⓓ 36 Ⓐⓓ 48 Ⓐⓓ 60 Ⓐⓓ 72 Ⓐⓓ 84 Ⓐⓓ

---

1 Ⓐⓓ 13 Ⓐⓓ 25 Ⓐⓓ 37 Ⓐⓓ 49 Ⓐⓓ 61 Ⓐⓓ 73 Ⓐⓓ 85 Ⓐⓓ
2 Ⓐⓓ 14 Ⓐⓓ 26 Ⓐⓓ 38 Ⓐⓓ 50 Ⓐⓓ 62 Ⓐⓓ 74 Ⓐⓓ 86 Ⓐⓓ
3 Ⓐⓓ 15 Ⓐⓓ 27 Ⓐⓓ 39 Ⓐⓓ 51 Ⓐⓓ 63 Ⓐⓓ 75 Ⓐⓓ 87 Ⓐⓓ
4 Ⓐⓓ 16 Ⓐⓓ 28 Ⓐⓓ 40 Ⓐⓓ 52 Ⓐⓓ 64 Ⓐⓓ 76 Ⓐⓓ 88 Ⓐⓓ
5 Ⓐⓓ 17 Ⓐⓓ 29 Ⓐⓓ 41 Ⓐⓓ 53 Ⓐⓓ 65 Ⓐⓓ 77 Ⓐⓓ 89 Ⓐⓓ
6 Ⓐⓓ 18 Ⓐⓓ 30 Ⓐⓓ 42 Ⓐⓓ 54 Ⓐⓓ 66 Ⓐⓓ 78 Ⓐⓓ 90 Ⓐⓓ
7 Ⓐⓓ 19 Ⓐⓓ 31 Ⓐⓓ 43 Ⓐⓓ 55 Ⓐⓓ 67 Ⓐⓓ 79 Ⓐⓓ 91 Ⓐⓓ
8 Ⓐⓓ 20 Ⓐⓓ 32 Ⓐⓓ 44 Ⓐⓓ 56 Ⓐⓓ 68 Ⓐⓓ 80 Ⓐⓓ 92 Ⓐⓓ
9 Ⓐⓓ 21 Ⓐⓓ 33 Ⓐⓓ 45 Ⓐⓓ 57 Ⓐⓓ 69 Ⓐⓓ 81 Ⓐⓓ 93 Ⓐⓓ
10 Ⓐⓓ 22 Ⓐⓓ 34 Ⓐⓓ 46 Ⓐⓓ 58 Ⓐⓓ 70 Ⓐⓓ 82 Ⓐⓓ 94 Ⓐⓓ
11 Ⓐⓓ 23 Ⓐⓓ 35 Ⓐⓓ 47 Ⓐⓓ 59 Ⓐⓓ 71 Ⓐⓓ 83 Ⓐⓓ 95 Ⓐⓓ
12 Ⓐⓓ 24 Ⓐⓓ 36 Ⓐⓓ 48 Ⓐⓓ 60 Ⓐⓓ 72 Ⓐⓓ 84 Ⓐⓓ

---

1 Ⓐⓓ 13 Ⓐⓓ 25 Ⓐⓓ 37 Ⓐⓓ 49 Ⓐⓓ 61 Ⓐⓓ 73 Ⓐⓓ 85 Ⓐⓓ
2 Ⓐⓓ 14 Ⓐⓓ 26 Ⓐⓓ 38 Ⓐⓓ 50 Ⓐⓓ 62 Ⓐⓓ 74 Ⓐⓓ 86 Ⓐⓓ
3 Ⓐⓓ 15 Ⓐⓓ 27 Ⓐⓓ 39 Ⓐⓓ 51 Ⓐⓓ 63 Ⓐⓓ 75 Ⓐⓓ 87 Ⓐⓓ
4 Ⓐⓓ 16 Ⓐⓓ 28 Ⓐⓓ 40 Ⓐⓓ 52 Ⓐⓓ 64 Ⓐⓓ 76 Ⓐⓓ 88 Ⓐⓓ
5 Ⓐⓓ 17 Ⓐⓓ 29 Ⓐⓓ 41 Ⓐⓓ 53 Ⓐⓓ 65 Ⓐⓓ 77 Ⓐⓓ 89 Ⓐⓓ
6 Ⓐⓓ 18 Ⓐⓓ 30 Ⓐⓓ 42 Ⓐⓓ 54 Ⓐⓓ 66 Ⓐⓓ 78 Ⓐⓓ 90 Ⓐⓓ
7 Ⓐⓓ 19 Ⓐⓓ 31 Ⓐⓓ 43 Ⓐⓓ 55 Ⓐⓓ 67 Ⓐⓓ 79 Ⓐⓓ 91 Ⓐⓓ
8 Ⓐⓓ 20 Ⓐⓓ 32 Ⓐⓓ 44 Ⓐⓓ 56 Ⓐⓓ 68 Ⓐⓓ 80 Ⓐⓓ 92 Ⓐⓓ
9 Ⓐⓓ 21 Ⓐⓓ 33 Ⓐⓓ 45 Ⓐⓓ 57 Ⓐⓓ 69 Ⓐⓓ 81 Ⓐⓓ 93 Ⓐⓓ
10 Ⓐⓓ 22 Ⓐⓓ 34 Ⓐⓓ 46 Ⓐⓓ 58 Ⓐⓓ 70 Ⓐⓓ 82 Ⓐⓓ 94 Ⓐⓓ
11 Ⓐⓓ 23 Ⓐⓓ 35 Ⓐⓓ 47 Ⓐⓓ 59 Ⓐⓓ 71 Ⓐⓓ 83 Ⓐⓓ 95 Ⓐⓓ
12 Ⓐⓓ 24 Ⓐⓓ 36 Ⓐⓓ 48 Ⓐⓓ 60 Ⓐⓓ 72 Ⓐⓓ 84 Ⓐⓓ

Extra Address Checking Answer Sheets

Sheet 1

1 Ⓐ Ⓓ	13 Ⓐ Ⓓ	25 Ⓐ Ⓓ	37 Ⓐ Ⓓ	49 Ⓐ Ⓓ	61 Ⓐ Ⓓ	73 Ⓐ Ⓓ	85 Ⓐ Ⓓ
2 Ⓐ Ⓓ	14 Ⓐ Ⓓ	26 Ⓐ Ⓓ	38 Ⓐ Ⓓ	50 Ⓐ Ⓓ	62 Ⓐ Ⓓ	74 Ⓐ Ⓓ	86 Ⓐ Ⓓ
3 Ⓐ Ⓓ	15 Ⓐ Ⓓ	27 Ⓐ Ⓓ	39 Ⓐ Ⓓ	51 Ⓐ Ⓓ	63 Ⓐ Ⓓ	75 Ⓐ Ⓓ	87 Ⓐ Ⓓ
4 Ⓐ Ⓓ	16 Ⓐ Ⓓ	28 Ⓐ Ⓓ	40 Ⓐ Ⓓ	52 Ⓐ Ⓓ	64 Ⓐ Ⓓ	76 Ⓐ Ⓓ	88 Ⓐ Ⓓ
5 Ⓐ Ⓓ	17 Ⓐ Ⓓ	29 Ⓐ Ⓓ	41 Ⓐ Ⓓ	53 Ⓐ Ⓓ	65 Ⓐ Ⓓ	77 Ⓐ Ⓓ	89 Ⓐ Ⓓ
6 Ⓐ Ⓓ	18 Ⓐ Ⓓ	30 Ⓐ Ⓓ	42 Ⓐ Ⓓ	54 Ⓐ Ⓓ	66 Ⓐ Ⓓ	78 Ⓐ Ⓓ	90 Ⓐ Ⓓ
7 Ⓐ Ⓓ	19 Ⓐ Ⓓ	31 Ⓐ Ⓓ	43 Ⓐ Ⓓ	55 Ⓐ Ⓓ	67 Ⓐ Ⓓ	79 Ⓐ Ⓓ	91 Ⓐ Ⓓ
8 Ⓐ Ⓓ	20 Ⓐ Ⓓ	32 Ⓐ Ⓓ	44 Ⓐ Ⓓ	56 Ⓐ Ⓓ	68 Ⓐ Ⓓ	80 Ⓐ Ⓓ	92 Ⓐ Ⓓ
9 Ⓐ Ⓓ	21 Ⓐ Ⓓ	33 Ⓐ Ⓓ	45 Ⓐ Ⓓ	57 Ⓐ Ⓓ	69 Ⓐ Ⓓ	81 Ⓐ Ⓓ	93 Ⓐ Ⓓ
10 Ⓐ Ⓓ	22 Ⓐ Ⓓ	34 Ⓐ Ⓓ	46 Ⓐ Ⓓ	58 Ⓐ Ⓓ	70 Ⓐ Ⓓ	82 Ⓐ Ⓓ	94 Ⓐ Ⓓ
11 Ⓐ Ⓓ	23 Ⓐ Ⓓ	35 Ⓐ Ⓓ	47 Ⓐ Ⓓ	59 Ⓐ Ⓓ	71 Ⓐ Ⓓ	83 Ⓐ Ⓓ	95 Ⓐ Ⓓ
12 Ⓐ Ⓓ	24 Ⓐ Ⓓ	36 Ⓐ Ⓓ	48 Ⓐ Ⓓ	60 Ⓐ Ⓓ	72 Ⓐ Ⓓ	84 Ⓐ Ⓓ	

Sheet 2

1 Ⓐ Ⓓ	13 Ⓐ Ⓓ	25 Ⓐ Ⓓ	37 Ⓐ Ⓓ	49 Ⓐ Ⓓ	61 Ⓐ Ⓓ	73 Ⓐ Ⓓ	85 Ⓐ Ⓓ
2 Ⓐ Ⓓ	14 Ⓐ Ⓓ	26 Ⓐ Ⓓ	38 Ⓐ Ⓓ	50 Ⓐ Ⓓ	62 Ⓐ Ⓓ	74 Ⓐ Ⓓ	86 Ⓐ Ⓓ
3 Ⓐ Ⓓ	15 Ⓐ Ⓓ	27 Ⓐ Ⓓ	39 Ⓐ Ⓓ	51 Ⓐ Ⓓ	63 Ⓐ Ⓓ	75 Ⓐ Ⓓ	87 Ⓐ Ⓓ
4 Ⓐ Ⓓ	16 Ⓐ Ⓓ	28 Ⓐ Ⓓ	40 Ⓐ Ⓓ	52 Ⓐ Ⓓ	64 Ⓐ Ⓓ	76 Ⓐ Ⓓ	88 Ⓐ Ⓓ
5 Ⓐ Ⓓ	17 Ⓐ Ⓓ	29 Ⓐ Ⓓ	41 Ⓐ Ⓓ	53 Ⓐ Ⓓ	65 Ⓐ Ⓓ	77 Ⓐ Ⓓ	89 Ⓐ Ⓓ
6 Ⓐ Ⓓ	18 Ⓐ Ⓓ	30 Ⓐ Ⓓ	42 Ⓐ Ⓓ	54 Ⓐ Ⓓ	66 Ⓐ Ⓓ	78 Ⓐ Ⓓ	90 Ⓐ Ⓓ
7 Ⓐ Ⓓ	19 Ⓐ Ⓓ	31 Ⓐ Ⓓ	43 Ⓐ Ⓓ	55 Ⓐ Ⓓ	67 Ⓐ Ⓓ	79 Ⓐ Ⓓ	91 Ⓐ Ⓓ
8 Ⓐ Ⓓ	20 Ⓐ Ⓓ	32 Ⓐ Ⓓ	44 Ⓐ Ⓓ	56 Ⓐ Ⓓ	68 Ⓐ Ⓓ	80 Ⓐ Ⓓ	92 Ⓐ Ⓓ
9 Ⓐ Ⓓ	21 Ⓐ Ⓓ	33 Ⓐ Ⓓ	45 Ⓐ Ⓓ	57 Ⓐ Ⓓ	69 Ⓐ Ⓓ	81 Ⓐ Ⓓ	93 Ⓐ Ⓓ
10 Ⓐ Ⓓ	22 Ⓐ Ⓓ	34 Ⓐ Ⓓ	46 Ⓐ Ⓓ	58 Ⓐ Ⓓ	70 Ⓐ Ⓓ	82 Ⓐ Ⓓ	94 Ⓐ Ⓓ
11 Ⓐ Ⓓ	23 Ⓐ Ⓓ	35 Ⓐ Ⓓ	47 Ⓐ Ⓓ	59 Ⓐ Ⓓ	71 Ⓐ Ⓓ	83 Ⓐ Ⓓ	95 Ⓐ Ⓓ
12 Ⓐ Ⓓ	24 Ⓐ Ⓓ	36 Ⓐ Ⓓ	48 Ⓐ Ⓓ	60 Ⓐ Ⓓ	72 Ⓐ Ⓓ	84 Ⓐ Ⓓ	

Sheet 3

1 Ⓐ Ⓓ	13 Ⓐ Ⓓ	25 Ⓐ Ⓓ	37 Ⓐ Ⓓ	49 Ⓐ Ⓓ	61 Ⓐ Ⓓ	73 Ⓐ Ⓓ	85 Ⓐ Ⓓ
2 Ⓐ Ⓓ	14 Ⓐ Ⓓ	26 Ⓐ Ⓓ	38 Ⓐ Ⓓ	50 Ⓐ Ⓓ	62 Ⓐ Ⓓ	74 Ⓐ Ⓓ	86 Ⓐ Ⓓ
3 Ⓐ Ⓓ	15 Ⓐ Ⓓ	27 Ⓐ Ⓓ	39 Ⓐ Ⓓ	51 Ⓐ Ⓓ	63 Ⓐ Ⓓ	75 Ⓐ Ⓓ	87 Ⓐ Ⓓ
4 Ⓐ Ⓓ	16 Ⓐ Ⓓ	28 Ⓐ Ⓓ	40 Ⓐ Ⓓ	52 Ⓐ Ⓓ	64 Ⓐ Ⓓ	76 Ⓐ Ⓓ	88 Ⓐ Ⓓ
5 Ⓐ Ⓓ	17 Ⓐ Ⓓ	29 Ⓐ Ⓓ	41 Ⓐ Ⓓ	53 Ⓐ Ⓓ	65 Ⓐ Ⓓ	77 Ⓐ Ⓓ	89 Ⓐ Ⓓ
6 Ⓐ Ⓓ	18 Ⓐ Ⓓ	30 Ⓐ Ⓓ	42 Ⓐ Ⓓ	54 Ⓐ Ⓓ	66 Ⓐ Ⓓ	78 Ⓐ Ⓓ	90 Ⓐ Ⓓ
7 Ⓐ Ⓓ	19 Ⓐ Ⓓ	31 Ⓐ Ⓓ	43 Ⓐ Ⓓ	55 Ⓐ Ⓓ	67 Ⓐ Ⓓ	79 Ⓐ Ⓓ	91 Ⓐ Ⓓ
8 Ⓐ Ⓓ	20 Ⓐ Ⓓ	32 Ⓐ Ⓓ	44 Ⓐ Ⓓ	56 Ⓐ Ⓓ	68 Ⓐ Ⓓ	80 Ⓐ Ⓓ	92 Ⓐ Ⓓ
9 Ⓐ Ⓓ	21 Ⓐ Ⓓ	33 Ⓐ Ⓓ	45 Ⓐ Ⓓ	57 Ⓐ Ⓓ	69 Ⓐ Ⓓ	81 Ⓐ Ⓓ	93 Ⓐ Ⓓ
10 Ⓐ Ⓓ	22 Ⓐ Ⓓ	34 Ⓐ Ⓓ	46 Ⓐ Ⓓ	58 Ⓐ Ⓓ	70 Ⓐ Ⓓ	82 Ⓐ Ⓓ	94 Ⓐ Ⓓ
11 Ⓐ Ⓓ	23 Ⓐ Ⓓ	35 Ⓐ Ⓓ	47 Ⓐ Ⓓ	59 Ⓐ Ⓓ	71 Ⓐ Ⓓ	83 Ⓐ Ⓓ	95 Ⓐ Ⓓ
12 Ⓐ Ⓓ	24 Ⓐ Ⓓ	36 Ⓐ Ⓓ	48 Ⓐ Ⓓ	60 Ⓐ Ⓓ	72 Ⓐ Ⓓ	84 Ⓐ Ⓓ	

Sheet 4

1 Ⓐ Ⓓ	13 Ⓐ Ⓓ	25 Ⓐ Ⓓ	37 Ⓐ Ⓓ	49 Ⓐ Ⓓ	61 Ⓐ Ⓓ	73 Ⓐ Ⓓ	85 Ⓐ Ⓓ
2 Ⓐ Ⓓ	14 Ⓐ Ⓓ	26 Ⓐ Ⓓ	38 Ⓐ Ⓓ	50 Ⓐ Ⓓ	62 Ⓐ Ⓓ	74 Ⓐ Ⓓ	86 Ⓐ Ⓓ
3 Ⓐ Ⓓ	15 Ⓐ Ⓓ	27 Ⓐ Ⓓ	39 Ⓐ Ⓓ	51 Ⓐ Ⓓ	63 Ⓐ Ⓓ	75 Ⓐ Ⓓ	87 Ⓐ Ⓓ
4 Ⓐ Ⓓ	16 Ⓐ Ⓓ	28 Ⓐ Ⓓ	40 Ⓐ Ⓓ	52 Ⓐ Ⓓ	64 Ⓐ Ⓓ	76 Ⓐ Ⓓ	88 Ⓐ Ⓓ
5 Ⓐ Ⓓ	17 Ⓐ Ⓓ	29 Ⓐ Ⓓ	41 Ⓐ Ⓓ	53 Ⓐ Ⓓ	65 Ⓐ Ⓓ	77 Ⓐ Ⓓ	89 Ⓐ Ⓓ
6 Ⓐ Ⓓ	18 Ⓐ Ⓓ	30 Ⓐ Ⓓ	42 Ⓐ Ⓓ	54 Ⓐ Ⓓ	66 Ⓐ Ⓓ	78 Ⓐ Ⓓ	90 Ⓐ Ⓓ
7 Ⓐ Ⓓ	19 Ⓐ Ⓓ	31 Ⓐ Ⓓ	43 Ⓐ Ⓓ	55 Ⓐ Ⓓ	67 Ⓐ Ⓓ	79 Ⓐ Ⓓ	91 Ⓐ Ⓓ
8 Ⓐ Ⓓ	20 Ⓐ Ⓓ	32 Ⓐ Ⓓ	44 Ⓐ Ⓓ	56 Ⓐ Ⓓ	68 Ⓐ Ⓓ	80 Ⓐ Ⓓ	92 Ⓐ Ⓓ
9 Ⓐ Ⓓ	21 Ⓐ Ⓓ	33 Ⓐ Ⓓ	45 Ⓐ Ⓓ	57 Ⓐ Ⓓ	69 Ⓐ Ⓓ	81 Ⓐ Ⓓ	93 Ⓐ Ⓓ
10 Ⓐ Ⓓ	22 Ⓐ Ⓓ	34 Ⓐ Ⓓ	46 Ⓐ Ⓓ	58 Ⓐ Ⓓ	70 Ⓐ Ⓓ	82 Ⓐ Ⓓ	94 Ⓐ Ⓓ
11 Ⓐ Ⓓ	23 Ⓐ Ⓓ	35 Ⓐ Ⓓ	47 Ⓐ Ⓓ	59 Ⓐ Ⓓ	71 Ⓐ Ⓓ	83 Ⓐ Ⓓ	95 Ⓐ Ⓓ
12 Ⓐ Ⓓ	24 Ⓐ Ⓓ	36 Ⓐ Ⓓ	48 Ⓐ Ⓓ	60 Ⓐ Ⓓ	72 Ⓐ Ⓓ	84 Ⓐ Ⓓ	

Extra Address Checking Answer Sheets

Sheet 1

1 Ⓐ Ⓓ	13 Ⓐ Ⓓ	25 Ⓐ Ⓓ	37 Ⓐ Ⓓ	49 Ⓐ Ⓓ	61 Ⓐ Ⓓ	73 Ⓐ Ⓓ	85 Ⓐ Ⓓ
2 Ⓐ Ⓓ	14 Ⓐ Ⓓ	26 Ⓐ Ⓓ	38 Ⓐ Ⓓ	50 Ⓐ Ⓓ	62 Ⓐ Ⓓ	74 Ⓐ Ⓓ	86 Ⓐ Ⓓ
3 Ⓐ Ⓓ	15 Ⓐ Ⓓ	27 Ⓐ Ⓓ	39 Ⓐ Ⓓ	51 Ⓐ Ⓓ	63 Ⓐ Ⓓ	75 Ⓐ Ⓓ	87 Ⓐ Ⓓ
4 Ⓐ Ⓓ	16 Ⓐ Ⓓ	28 Ⓐ Ⓓ	40 Ⓐ Ⓓ	52 Ⓐ Ⓓ	64 Ⓐ Ⓓ	76 Ⓐ Ⓓ	88 Ⓐ Ⓓ
5 Ⓐ Ⓓ	17 Ⓐ Ⓓ	29 Ⓐ Ⓓ	41 Ⓐ Ⓓ	53 Ⓐ Ⓓ	65 Ⓐ Ⓓ	77 Ⓐ Ⓓ	89 Ⓐ Ⓓ
6 Ⓐ Ⓓ	18 Ⓐ Ⓓ	30 Ⓐ Ⓓ	42 Ⓐ Ⓓ	54 Ⓐ Ⓓ	66 Ⓐ Ⓓ	78 Ⓐ Ⓓ	90 Ⓐ Ⓓ
7 Ⓐ Ⓓ	19 Ⓐ Ⓓ	31 Ⓐ Ⓓ	43 Ⓐ Ⓓ	55 Ⓐ Ⓓ	67 Ⓐ Ⓓ	79 Ⓐ Ⓓ	91 Ⓐ Ⓓ
8 Ⓐ Ⓓ	20 Ⓐ Ⓓ	32 Ⓐ Ⓓ	44 Ⓐ Ⓓ	56 Ⓐ Ⓓ	68 Ⓐ Ⓓ	80 Ⓐ Ⓓ	92 Ⓐ Ⓓ
9 Ⓐ Ⓓ	21 Ⓐ Ⓓ	33 Ⓐ Ⓓ	45 Ⓐ Ⓓ	57 Ⓐ Ⓓ	69 Ⓐ Ⓓ	81 Ⓐ Ⓓ	93 Ⓐ Ⓓ
10 Ⓐ Ⓓ	22 Ⓐ Ⓓ	34 Ⓐ Ⓓ	46 Ⓐ Ⓓ	58 Ⓐ Ⓓ	70 Ⓐ Ⓓ	82 Ⓐ Ⓓ	94 Ⓐ Ⓓ
11 Ⓐ Ⓓ	23 Ⓐ Ⓓ	35 Ⓐ Ⓓ	47 Ⓐ Ⓓ	59 Ⓐ Ⓓ	71 Ⓐ Ⓓ	83 Ⓐ Ⓓ	95 Ⓐ Ⓓ
12 Ⓐ Ⓓ	24 Ⓐ Ⓓ	36 Ⓐ Ⓓ	48 Ⓐ Ⓓ	60 Ⓐ Ⓓ	72 Ⓐ Ⓓ	84 Ⓐ Ⓓ	

Sheet 2

1 Ⓐ Ⓓ	13 Ⓐ Ⓓ	25 Ⓐ Ⓓ	37 Ⓐ Ⓓ	49 Ⓐ Ⓓ	61 Ⓐ Ⓓ	73 Ⓐ Ⓓ	85 Ⓐ Ⓓ
2 Ⓐ Ⓓ	14 Ⓐ Ⓓ	26 Ⓐ Ⓓ	38 Ⓐ Ⓓ	50 Ⓐ Ⓓ	62 Ⓐ Ⓓ	74 Ⓐ Ⓓ	86 Ⓐ Ⓓ
3 Ⓐ Ⓓ	15 Ⓐ Ⓓ	27 Ⓐ Ⓓ	39 Ⓐ Ⓓ	51 Ⓐ Ⓓ	63 Ⓐ Ⓓ	75 Ⓐ Ⓓ	87 Ⓐ Ⓓ
4 Ⓐ Ⓓ	16 Ⓐ Ⓓ	28 Ⓐ Ⓓ	40 Ⓐ Ⓓ	52 Ⓐ Ⓓ	64 Ⓐ Ⓓ	76 Ⓐ Ⓓ	88 Ⓐ Ⓓ
5 Ⓐ Ⓓ	17 Ⓐ Ⓓ	29 Ⓐ Ⓓ	41 Ⓐ Ⓓ	53 Ⓐ Ⓓ	65 Ⓐ Ⓓ	77 Ⓐ Ⓓ	89 Ⓐ Ⓓ
6 Ⓐ Ⓓ	18 Ⓐ Ⓓ	30 Ⓐ Ⓓ	42 Ⓐ Ⓓ	54 Ⓐ Ⓓ	66 Ⓐ Ⓓ	78 Ⓐ Ⓓ	90 Ⓐ Ⓓ
7 Ⓐ Ⓓ	19 Ⓐ Ⓓ	31 Ⓐ Ⓓ	43 Ⓐ Ⓓ	55 Ⓐ Ⓓ	67 Ⓐ Ⓓ	79 Ⓐ Ⓓ	91 Ⓐ Ⓓ
8 Ⓐ Ⓓ	20 Ⓐ Ⓓ	32 Ⓐ Ⓓ	44 Ⓐ Ⓓ	56 Ⓐ Ⓓ	68 Ⓐ Ⓓ	80 Ⓐ Ⓓ	92 Ⓐ Ⓓ
9 Ⓐ Ⓓ	21 Ⓐ Ⓓ	33 Ⓐ Ⓓ	45 Ⓐ Ⓓ	57 Ⓐ Ⓓ	69 Ⓐ Ⓓ	81 Ⓐ Ⓓ	93 Ⓐ Ⓓ
10 Ⓐ Ⓓ	22 Ⓐ Ⓓ	34 Ⓐ Ⓓ	46 Ⓐ Ⓓ	58 Ⓐ Ⓓ	70 Ⓐ Ⓓ	82 Ⓐ Ⓓ	94 Ⓐ Ⓓ
11 Ⓐ Ⓓ	23 Ⓐ Ⓓ	35 Ⓐ Ⓓ	47 Ⓐ Ⓓ	59 Ⓐ Ⓓ	71 Ⓐ Ⓓ	83 Ⓐ Ⓓ	95 Ⓐ Ⓓ
12 Ⓐ Ⓓ	24 Ⓐ Ⓓ	36 Ⓐ Ⓓ	48 Ⓐ Ⓓ	60 Ⓐ Ⓓ	72 Ⓐ Ⓓ	84 Ⓐ Ⓓ	

Sheet 3

1 Ⓐ Ⓓ	13 Ⓐ Ⓓ	25 Ⓐ Ⓓ	37 Ⓐ Ⓓ	49 Ⓐ Ⓓ	61 Ⓐ Ⓓ	73 Ⓐ Ⓓ	85 Ⓐ Ⓓ
2 Ⓐ Ⓓ	14 Ⓐ Ⓓ	26 Ⓐ Ⓓ	38 Ⓐ Ⓓ	50 Ⓐ Ⓓ	62 Ⓐ Ⓓ	74 Ⓐ Ⓓ	86 Ⓐ Ⓓ
3 Ⓐ Ⓓ	15 Ⓐ Ⓓ	27 Ⓐ Ⓓ	39 Ⓐ Ⓓ	51 Ⓐ Ⓓ	63 Ⓐ Ⓓ	75 Ⓐ Ⓓ	87 Ⓐ Ⓓ
4 Ⓐ Ⓓ	16 Ⓐ Ⓓ	28 Ⓐ Ⓓ	40 Ⓐ Ⓓ	52 Ⓐ Ⓓ	64 Ⓐ Ⓓ	76 Ⓐ Ⓓ	88 Ⓐ Ⓓ
5 Ⓐ Ⓓ	17 Ⓐ Ⓓ	29 Ⓐ Ⓓ	41 Ⓐ Ⓓ	53 Ⓐ Ⓓ	65 Ⓐ Ⓓ	77 Ⓐ Ⓓ	89 Ⓐ Ⓓ
6 Ⓐ Ⓓ	18 Ⓐ Ⓓ	30 Ⓐ Ⓓ	42 Ⓐ Ⓓ	54 Ⓐ Ⓓ	66 Ⓐ Ⓓ	78 Ⓐ Ⓓ	90 Ⓐ Ⓓ
7 Ⓐ Ⓓ	19 Ⓐ Ⓓ	31 Ⓐ Ⓓ	43 Ⓐ Ⓓ	55 Ⓐ Ⓓ	67 Ⓐ Ⓓ	79 Ⓐ Ⓓ	91 Ⓐ Ⓓ
8 Ⓐ Ⓓ	20 Ⓐ Ⓓ	32 Ⓐ Ⓓ	44 Ⓐ Ⓓ	56 Ⓐ Ⓓ	68 Ⓐ Ⓓ	80 Ⓐ Ⓓ	92 Ⓐ Ⓓ
9 Ⓐ Ⓓ	21 Ⓐ Ⓓ	33 Ⓐ Ⓓ	45 Ⓐ Ⓓ	57 Ⓐ Ⓓ	69 Ⓐ Ⓓ	81 Ⓐ Ⓓ	93 Ⓐ Ⓓ
10 Ⓐ Ⓓ	22 Ⓐ Ⓓ	34 Ⓐ Ⓓ	46 Ⓐ Ⓓ	58 Ⓐ Ⓓ	70 Ⓐ Ⓓ	82 Ⓐ Ⓓ	94 Ⓐ Ⓓ
11 Ⓐ Ⓓ	23 Ⓐ Ⓓ	35 Ⓐ Ⓓ	47 Ⓐ Ⓓ	59 Ⓐ Ⓓ	71 Ⓐ Ⓓ	83 Ⓐ Ⓓ	95 Ⓐ Ⓓ
12 Ⓐ Ⓓ	24 Ⓐ Ⓓ	36 Ⓐ Ⓓ	48 Ⓐ Ⓓ	60 Ⓐ Ⓓ	72 Ⓐ Ⓓ	84 Ⓐ Ⓓ	

Sheet 4

1 Ⓐ Ⓓ	13 Ⓐ Ⓓ	25 Ⓐ Ⓓ	37 Ⓐ Ⓓ	49 Ⓐ Ⓓ	61 Ⓐ Ⓓ	73 Ⓐ Ⓓ	85 Ⓐ Ⓓ
2 Ⓐ Ⓓ	14 Ⓐ Ⓓ	26 Ⓐ Ⓓ	38 Ⓐ Ⓓ	50 Ⓐ Ⓓ	62 Ⓐ Ⓓ	74 Ⓐ Ⓓ	86 Ⓐ Ⓓ
3 Ⓐ Ⓓ	15 Ⓐ Ⓓ	27 Ⓐ Ⓓ	39 Ⓐ Ⓓ	51 Ⓐ Ⓓ	63 Ⓐ Ⓓ	75 Ⓐ Ⓓ	87 Ⓐ Ⓓ
4 Ⓐ Ⓓ	16 Ⓐ Ⓓ	28 Ⓐ Ⓓ	40 Ⓐ Ⓓ	52 Ⓐ Ⓓ	64 Ⓐ Ⓓ	76 Ⓐ Ⓓ	88 Ⓐ Ⓓ
5 Ⓐ Ⓓ	17 Ⓐ Ⓓ	29 Ⓐ Ⓓ	41 Ⓐ Ⓓ	53 Ⓐ Ⓓ	65 Ⓐ Ⓓ	77 Ⓐ Ⓓ	89 Ⓐ Ⓓ
6 Ⓐ Ⓓ	18 Ⓐ Ⓓ	30 Ⓐ Ⓓ	42 Ⓐ Ⓓ	54 Ⓐ Ⓓ	66 Ⓐ Ⓓ	78 Ⓐ Ⓓ	90 Ⓐ Ⓓ
7 Ⓐ Ⓓ	19 Ⓐ Ⓓ	31 Ⓐ Ⓓ	43 Ⓐ Ⓓ	55 Ⓐ Ⓓ	67 Ⓐ Ⓓ	79 Ⓐ Ⓓ	91 Ⓐ Ⓓ
8 Ⓐ Ⓓ	20 Ⓐ Ⓓ	32 Ⓐ Ⓓ	44 Ⓐ Ⓓ	56 Ⓐ Ⓓ	68 Ⓐ Ⓓ	80 Ⓐ Ⓓ	92 Ⓐ Ⓓ
9 Ⓐ Ⓓ	21 Ⓐ Ⓓ	33 Ⓐ Ⓓ	45 Ⓐ Ⓓ	57 Ⓐ Ⓓ	69 Ⓐ Ⓓ	81 Ⓐ Ⓓ	93 Ⓐ Ⓓ
10 Ⓐ Ⓓ	22 Ⓐ Ⓓ	34 Ⓐ Ⓓ	46 Ⓐ Ⓓ	58 Ⓐ Ⓓ	70 Ⓐ Ⓓ	82 Ⓐ Ⓓ	94 Ⓐ Ⓓ
11 Ⓐ Ⓓ	23 Ⓐ Ⓓ	35 Ⓐ Ⓓ	47 Ⓐ Ⓓ	59 Ⓐ Ⓓ	71 Ⓐ Ⓓ	83 Ⓐ Ⓓ	95 Ⓐ Ⓓ
12 Ⓐ Ⓓ	24 Ⓐ Ⓓ	36 Ⓐ Ⓓ	48 Ⓐ Ⓓ	60 Ⓐ Ⓓ	72 Ⓐ Ⓓ	84 Ⓐ Ⓓ	

Extra Address Checking Answer Sheets

1 Ⓐ Ⓓ	13 Ⓐ Ⓓ	25 Ⓐ Ⓓ	37 Ⓐ Ⓓ	49 Ⓐ Ⓓ	61 Ⓐ Ⓓ	73 Ⓐ Ⓓ	85 Ⓐ Ⓓ
2 Ⓐ Ⓓ	14 Ⓐ Ⓓ	26 Ⓐ Ⓓ	38 Ⓐ Ⓓ	50 Ⓐ Ⓓ	62 Ⓐ Ⓓ	74 Ⓐ Ⓓ	86 Ⓐ Ⓓ
3 Ⓐ Ⓓ	15 Ⓐ Ⓓ	27 Ⓐ Ⓓ	39 Ⓐ Ⓓ	51 Ⓐ Ⓓ	63 Ⓐ Ⓓ	75 Ⓐ Ⓓ	87 Ⓐ Ⓓ
4 Ⓐ Ⓓ	16 Ⓐ Ⓓ	28 Ⓐ Ⓓ	40 Ⓐ Ⓓ	52 Ⓐ Ⓓ	64 Ⓐ Ⓓ	76 Ⓐ Ⓓ	88 Ⓐ Ⓓ
5 Ⓐ Ⓓ	17 Ⓐ Ⓓ	29 Ⓐ Ⓓ	41 Ⓐ Ⓓ	53 Ⓐ Ⓓ	65 Ⓐ Ⓓ	77 Ⓐ Ⓓ	89 Ⓐ Ⓓ
6 Ⓐ Ⓓ	18 Ⓐ Ⓓ	30 Ⓐ Ⓓ	42 Ⓐ Ⓓ	54 Ⓐ Ⓓ	66 Ⓐ Ⓓ	78 Ⓐ Ⓓ	90 Ⓐ Ⓓ
7 Ⓐ Ⓓ	19 Ⓐ Ⓓ	31 Ⓐ Ⓓ	43 Ⓐ Ⓓ	55 Ⓐ Ⓓ	67 Ⓐ Ⓓ	79 Ⓐ Ⓓ	91 Ⓐ Ⓓ
8 Ⓐ Ⓓ	20 Ⓐ Ⓓ	32 Ⓐ Ⓓ	44 Ⓐ Ⓓ	56 Ⓐ Ⓓ	68 Ⓐ Ⓓ	80 Ⓐ Ⓓ	92 Ⓐ Ⓓ
9 Ⓐ Ⓓ	21 Ⓐ Ⓓ	33 Ⓐ Ⓓ	45 Ⓐ Ⓓ	57 Ⓐ Ⓓ	69 Ⓐ Ⓓ	81 Ⓐ Ⓓ	93 Ⓐ Ⓓ
10 Ⓐ Ⓓ	22 Ⓐ Ⓓ	34 Ⓐ Ⓓ	46 Ⓐ Ⓓ	58 Ⓐ Ⓓ	70 Ⓐ Ⓓ	82 Ⓐ Ⓓ	94 Ⓐ Ⓓ
11 Ⓐ Ⓓ	23 Ⓐ Ⓓ	35 Ⓐ Ⓓ	47 Ⓐ Ⓓ	59 Ⓐ Ⓓ	71 Ⓐ Ⓓ	83 Ⓐ Ⓓ	95 Ⓐ Ⓓ
12 Ⓐ Ⓓ	24 Ⓐ Ⓓ	36 Ⓐ Ⓓ	48 Ⓐ Ⓓ	60 Ⓐ Ⓓ	72 Ⓐ Ⓓ	84 Ⓐ Ⓓ	

---

1 Ⓐ Ⓓ	13 Ⓐ Ⓓ	25 Ⓐ Ⓓ	37 Ⓐ Ⓓ	49 Ⓐ Ⓓ	61 Ⓐ Ⓓ	73 Ⓐ Ⓓ	85 Ⓐ Ⓓ
2 Ⓐ Ⓓ	14 Ⓐ Ⓓ	26 Ⓐ Ⓓ	38 Ⓐ Ⓓ	50 Ⓐ Ⓓ	62 Ⓐ Ⓓ	74 Ⓐ Ⓓ	86 Ⓐ Ⓓ
3 Ⓐ Ⓓ	15 Ⓐ Ⓓ	27 Ⓐ Ⓓ	39 Ⓐ Ⓓ	51 Ⓐ Ⓓ	63 Ⓐ Ⓓ	75 Ⓐ Ⓓ	87 Ⓐ Ⓓ
4 Ⓐ Ⓓ	16 Ⓐ Ⓓ	28 Ⓐ Ⓓ	40 Ⓐ Ⓓ	52 Ⓐ Ⓓ	64 Ⓐ Ⓓ	76 Ⓐ Ⓓ	88 Ⓐ Ⓓ
5 Ⓐ Ⓓ	17 Ⓐ Ⓓ	29 Ⓐ Ⓓ	41 Ⓐ Ⓓ	53 Ⓐ Ⓓ	65 Ⓐ Ⓓ	77 Ⓐ Ⓓ	89 Ⓐ Ⓓ
6 Ⓐ Ⓓ	18 Ⓐ Ⓓ	30 Ⓐ Ⓓ	42 Ⓐ Ⓓ	54 Ⓐ Ⓓ	66 Ⓐ Ⓓ	78 Ⓐ Ⓓ	90 Ⓐ Ⓓ
7 Ⓐ Ⓓ	19 Ⓐ Ⓓ	31 Ⓐ Ⓓ	43 Ⓐ Ⓓ	55 Ⓐ Ⓓ	67 Ⓐ Ⓓ	79 Ⓐ Ⓓ	91 Ⓐ Ⓓ
8 Ⓐ Ⓓ	20 Ⓐ Ⓓ	32 Ⓐ Ⓓ	44 Ⓐ Ⓓ	56 Ⓐ Ⓓ	68 Ⓐ Ⓓ	80 Ⓐ Ⓓ	92 Ⓐ Ⓓ
9 Ⓐ Ⓓ	21 Ⓐ Ⓓ	33 Ⓐ Ⓓ	45 Ⓐ Ⓓ	57 Ⓐ Ⓓ	69 Ⓐ Ⓓ	81 Ⓐ Ⓓ	93 Ⓐ Ⓓ
10 Ⓐ Ⓓ	22 Ⓐ Ⓓ	34 Ⓐ Ⓓ	46 Ⓐ Ⓓ	58 Ⓐ Ⓓ	70 Ⓐ Ⓓ	82 Ⓐ Ⓓ	94 Ⓐ Ⓓ
11 Ⓐ Ⓓ	23 Ⓐ Ⓓ	35 Ⓐ Ⓓ	47 Ⓐ Ⓓ	59 Ⓐ Ⓓ	71 Ⓐ Ⓓ	83 Ⓐ Ⓓ	95 Ⓐ Ⓓ
12 Ⓐ Ⓓ	24 Ⓐ Ⓓ	36 Ⓐ Ⓓ	48 Ⓐ Ⓓ	60 Ⓐ Ⓓ	72 Ⓐ Ⓓ	84 Ⓐ Ⓓ	

---

1 Ⓐ Ⓓ	13 Ⓐ Ⓓ	25 Ⓐ Ⓓ	37 Ⓐ Ⓓ	49 Ⓐ Ⓓ	61 Ⓐ Ⓓ	73 Ⓐ Ⓓ	85 Ⓐ Ⓓ
2 Ⓐ Ⓓ	14 Ⓐ Ⓓ	26 Ⓐ Ⓓ	38 Ⓐ Ⓓ	50 Ⓐ Ⓓ	62 Ⓐ Ⓓ	74 Ⓐ Ⓓ	86 Ⓐ Ⓓ
3 Ⓐ Ⓓ	15 Ⓐ Ⓓ	27 Ⓐ Ⓓ	39 Ⓐ Ⓓ	51 Ⓐ Ⓓ	63 Ⓐ Ⓓ	75 Ⓐ Ⓓ	87 Ⓐ Ⓓ
4 Ⓐ Ⓓ	16 Ⓐ Ⓓ	28 Ⓐ Ⓓ	40 Ⓐ Ⓓ	52 Ⓐ Ⓓ	64 Ⓐ Ⓓ	76 Ⓐ Ⓓ	88 Ⓐ Ⓓ
5 Ⓐ Ⓓ	17 Ⓐ Ⓓ	29 Ⓐ Ⓓ	41 Ⓐ Ⓓ	53 Ⓐ Ⓓ	65 Ⓐ Ⓓ	77 Ⓐ Ⓓ	89 Ⓐ Ⓓ
6 Ⓐ Ⓓ	18 Ⓐ Ⓓ	30 Ⓐ Ⓓ	42 Ⓐ Ⓓ	54 Ⓐ Ⓓ	66 Ⓐ Ⓓ	78 Ⓐ Ⓓ	90 Ⓐ Ⓓ
7 Ⓐ Ⓓ	19 Ⓐ Ⓓ	31 Ⓐ Ⓓ	43 Ⓐ Ⓓ	55 Ⓐ Ⓓ	67 Ⓐ Ⓓ	79 Ⓐ Ⓓ	91 Ⓐ Ⓓ
8 Ⓐ Ⓓ	20 Ⓐ Ⓓ	32 Ⓐ Ⓓ	44 Ⓐ Ⓓ	56 Ⓐ Ⓓ	68 Ⓐ Ⓓ	80 Ⓐ Ⓓ	92 Ⓐ Ⓓ
9 Ⓐ Ⓓ	21 Ⓐ Ⓓ	33 Ⓐ Ⓓ	45 Ⓐ Ⓓ	57 Ⓐ Ⓓ	69 Ⓐ Ⓓ	81 Ⓐ Ⓓ	93 Ⓐ Ⓓ
10 Ⓐ Ⓓ	22 Ⓐ Ⓓ	34 Ⓐ Ⓓ	46 Ⓐ Ⓓ	58 Ⓐ Ⓓ	70 Ⓐ Ⓓ	82 Ⓐ Ⓓ	94 Ⓐ Ⓓ
11 Ⓐ Ⓓ	23 Ⓐ Ⓓ	35 Ⓐ Ⓓ	47 Ⓐ Ⓓ	59 Ⓐ Ⓓ	71 Ⓐ Ⓓ	83 Ⓐ Ⓓ	95 Ⓐ Ⓓ
12 Ⓐ Ⓓ	24 Ⓐ Ⓓ	36 Ⓐ Ⓓ	48 Ⓐ Ⓓ	60 Ⓐ Ⓓ	72 Ⓐ Ⓓ	84 Ⓐ Ⓓ	

---

1 Ⓐ Ⓓ	13 Ⓐ Ⓓ	25 Ⓐ Ⓓ	37 Ⓐ Ⓓ	49 Ⓐ Ⓓ	61 Ⓐ Ⓓ	73 Ⓐ Ⓓ	85 Ⓐ Ⓓ
2 Ⓐ Ⓓ	14 Ⓐ Ⓓ	26 Ⓐ Ⓓ	38 Ⓐ Ⓓ	50 Ⓐ Ⓓ	62 Ⓐ Ⓓ	74 Ⓐ Ⓓ	86 Ⓐ Ⓓ
3 Ⓐ Ⓓ	15 Ⓐ Ⓓ	27 Ⓐ Ⓓ	39 Ⓐ Ⓓ	51 Ⓐ Ⓓ	63 Ⓐ Ⓓ	75 Ⓐ Ⓓ	87 Ⓐ Ⓓ
4 Ⓐ Ⓓ	16 Ⓐ Ⓓ	28 Ⓐ Ⓓ	40 Ⓐ Ⓓ	52 Ⓐ Ⓓ	64 Ⓐ Ⓓ	76 Ⓐ Ⓓ	88 Ⓐ Ⓓ
5 Ⓐ Ⓓ	17 Ⓐ Ⓓ	29 Ⓐ Ⓓ	41 Ⓐ Ⓓ	53 Ⓐ Ⓓ	65 Ⓐ Ⓓ	77 Ⓐ Ⓓ	89 Ⓐ Ⓓ
6 Ⓐ Ⓓ	18 Ⓐ Ⓓ	30 Ⓐ Ⓓ	42 Ⓐ Ⓓ	54 Ⓐ Ⓓ	66 Ⓐ Ⓓ	78 Ⓐ Ⓓ	90 Ⓐ Ⓓ
7 Ⓐ Ⓓ	19 Ⓐ Ⓓ	31 Ⓐ Ⓓ	43 Ⓐ Ⓓ	55 Ⓐ Ⓓ	67 Ⓐ Ⓓ	79 Ⓐ Ⓓ	91 Ⓐ Ⓓ
8 Ⓐ Ⓓ	20 Ⓐ Ⓓ	32 Ⓐ Ⓓ	44 Ⓐ Ⓓ	56 Ⓐ Ⓓ	68 Ⓐ Ⓓ	80 Ⓐ Ⓓ	92 Ⓐ Ⓓ
9 Ⓐ Ⓓ	21 Ⓐ Ⓓ	33 Ⓐ Ⓓ	45 Ⓐ Ⓓ	57 Ⓐ Ⓓ	69 Ⓐ Ⓓ	81 Ⓐ Ⓓ	93 Ⓐ Ⓓ
10 Ⓐ Ⓓ	22 Ⓐ Ⓓ	34 Ⓐ Ⓓ	46 Ⓐ Ⓓ	58 Ⓐ Ⓓ	70 Ⓐ Ⓓ	82 Ⓐ Ⓓ	94 Ⓐ Ⓓ
11 Ⓐ Ⓓ	23 Ⓐ Ⓓ	35 Ⓐ Ⓓ	47 Ⓐ Ⓓ	59 Ⓐ Ⓓ	71 Ⓐ Ⓓ	83 Ⓐ Ⓓ	95 Ⓐ Ⓓ
12 Ⓐ Ⓓ	24 Ⓐ Ⓓ	36 Ⓐ Ⓓ	48 Ⓐ Ⓓ	60 Ⓐ Ⓓ	72 Ⓐ Ⓓ	84 Ⓐ Ⓓ	

Extra Address Checking Answer Sheets

Sheet 1

1 Ⓐ Ⓓ	13 Ⓐ Ⓓ	25 Ⓐ Ⓓ	37 Ⓐ Ⓓ	49 Ⓐ Ⓓ	61 Ⓐ Ⓓ	73 Ⓐ Ⓓ	85 Ⓐ Ⓓ
2 Ⓐ Ⓓ	14 Ⓐ Ⓓ	26 Ⓐ Ⓓ	38 Ⓐ Ⓓ	50 Ⓐ Ⓓ	62 Ⓐ Ⓓ	74 Ⓐ Ⓓ	86 Ⓐ Ⓓ
3 Ⓐ Ⓓ	15 Ⓐ Ⓓ	27 Ⓐ Ⓓ	39 Ⓐ Ⓓ	51 Ⓐ Ⓓ	63 Ⓐ Ⓓ	75 Ⓐ Ⓓ	87 Ⓐ Ⓓ
4 Ⓐ Ⓓ	16 Ⓐ Ⓓ	28 Ⓐ Ⓓ	40 Ⓐ Ⓓ	52 Ⓐ Ⓓ	64 Ⓐ Ⓓ	76 Ⓐ Ⓓ	88 Ⓐ Ⓓ
5 Ⓐ Ⓓ	17 Ⓐ Ⓓ	29 Ⓐ Ⓓ	41 Ⓐ Ⓓ	53 Ⓐ Ⓓ	65 Ⓐ Ⓓ	77 Ⓐ Ⓓ	89 Ⓐ Ⓓ
6 Ⓐ Ⓓ	18 Ⓐ Ⓓ	30 Ⓐ Ⓓ	42 Ⓐ Ⓓ	54 Ⓐ Ⓓ	66 Ⓐ Ⓓ	78 Ⓐ Ⓓ	90 Ⓐ Ⓓ
7 Ⓐ Ⓓ	19 Ⓐ Ⓓ	31 Ⓐ Ⓓ	43 Ⓐ Ⓓ	55 Ⓐ Ⓓ	67 Ⓐ Ⓓ	79 Ⓐ Ⓓ	91 Ⓐ Ⓓ
8 Ⓐ Ⓓ	20 Ⓐ Ⓓ	32 Ⓐ Ⓓ	44 Ⓐ Ⓓ	56 Ⓐ Ⓓ	68 Ⓐ Ⓓ	80 Ⓐ Ⓓ	92 Ⓐ Ⓓ
9 Ⓐ Ⓓ	21 Ⓐ Ⓓ	33 Ⓐ Ⓓ	45 Ⓐ Ⓓ	57 Ⓐ Ⓓ	69 Ⓐ Ⓓ	81 Ⓐ Ⓓ	93 Ⓐ Ⓓ
10 Ⓐ Ⓓ	22 Ⓐ Ⓓ	34 Ⓐ Ⓓ	46 Ⓐ Ⓓ	58 Ⓐ Ⓓ	70 Ⓐ Ⓓ	82 Ⓐ Ⓓ	94 Ⓐ Ⓓ
11 Ⓐ Ⓓ	23 Ⓐ Ⓓ	35 Ⓐ Ⓓ	47 Ⓐ Ⓓ	59 Ⓐ Ⓓ	71 Ⓐ Ⓓ	83 Ⓐ Ⓓ	95 Ⓐ Ⓓ
12 Ⓐ Ⓓ	24 Ⓐ Ⓓ	36 Ⓐ Ⓓ	48 Ⓐ Ⓓ	60 Ⓐ Ⓓ	72 Ⓐ Ⓓ	84 Ⓐ Ⓓ	

Sheet 2

1 Ⓐ Ⓓ	13 Ⓐ Ⓓ	25 Ⓐ Ⓓ	37 Ⓐ Ⓓ	49 Ⓐ Ⓓ	61 Ⓐ Ⓓ	73 Ⓐ Ⓓ	85 Ⓐ Ⓓ
2 Ⓐ Ⓓ	14 Ⓐ Ⓓ	26 Ⓐ Ⓓ	38 Ⓐ Ⓓ	50 Ⓐ Ⓓ	62 Ⓐ Ⓓ	74 Ⓐ Ⓓ	86 Ⓐ Ⓓ
3 Ⓐ Ⓓ	15 Ⓐ Ⓓ	27 Ⓐ Ⓓ	39 Ⓐ Ⓓ	51 Ⓐ Ⓓ	63 Ⓐ Ⓓ	75 Ⓐ Ⓓ	87 Ⓐ Ⓓ
4 Ⓐ Ⓓ	16 Ⓐ Ⓓ	28 Ⓐ Ⓓ	40 Ⓐ Ⓓ	52 Ⓐ Ⓓ	64 Ⓐ Ⓓ	76 Ⓐ Ⓓ	88 Ⓐ Ⓓ
5 Ⓐ Ⓓ	17 Ⓐ Ⓓ	29 Ⓐ Ⓓ	41 Ⓐ Ⓓ	53 Ⓐ Ⓓ	65 Ⓐ Ⓓ	77 Ⓐ Ⓓ	89 Ⓐ Ⓓ
6 Ⓐ Ⓓ	18 Ⓐ Ⓓ	30 Ⓐ Ⓓ	42 Ⓐ Ⓓ	54 Ⓐ Ⓓ	66 Ⓐ Ⓓ	78 Ⓐ Ⓓ	90 Ⓐ Ⓓ
7 Ⓐ Ⓓ	19 Ⓐ Ⓓ	31 Ⓐ Ⓓ	43 Ⓐ Ⓓ	55 Ⓐ Ⓓ	67 Ⓐ Ⓓ	79 Ⓐ Ⓓ	91 Ⓐ Ⓓ
8 Ⓐ Ⓓ	20 Ⓐ Ⓓ	32 Ⓐ Ⓓ	44 Ⓐ Ⓓ	56 Ⓐ Ⓓ	68 Ⓐ Ⓓ	80 Ⓐ Ⓓ	92 Ⓐ Ⓓ
9 Ⓐ Ⓓ	21 Ⓐ Ⓓ	33 Ⓐ Ⓓ	45 Ⓐ Ⓓ	57 Ⓐ Ⓓ	69 Ⓐ Ⓓ	81 Ⓐ Ⓓ	93 Ⓐ Ⓓ
10 Ⓐ Ⓓ	22 Ⓐ Ⓓ	34 Ⓐ Ⓓ	46 Ⓐ Ⓓ	58 Ⓐ Ⓓ	70 Ⓐ Ⓓ	82 Ⓐ Ⓓ	94 Ⓐ Ⓓ
11 Ⓐ Ⓓ	23 Ⓐ Ⓓ	35 Ⓐ Ⓓ	47 Ⓐ Ⓓ	59 Ⓐ Ⓓ	71 Ⓐ Ⓓ	83 Ⓐ Ⓓ	95 Ⓐ Ⓓ
12 Ⓐ Ⓓ	24 Ⓐ Ⓓ	36 Ⓐ Ⓓ	48 Ⓐ Ⓓ	60 Ⓐ Ⓓ	72 Ⓐ Ⓓ	84 Ⓐ Ⓓ	

Sheet 3

1 Ⓐ Ⓓ	13 Ⓐ Ⓓ	25 Ⓐ Ⓓ	37 Ⓐ Ⓓ	49 Ⓐ Ⓓ	61 Ⓐ Ⓓ	73 Ⓐ Ⓓ	85 Ⓐ Ⓓ
2 Ⓐ Ⓓ	14 Ⓐ Ⓓ	26 Ⓐ Ⓓ	38 Ⓐ Ⓓ	50 Ⓐ Ⓓ	62 Ⓐ Ⓓ	74 Ⓐ Ⓓ	86 Ⓐ Ⓓ
3 Ⓐ Ⓓ	15 Ⓐ Ⓓ	27 Ⓐ Ⓓ	39 Ⓐ Ⓓ	51 Ⓐ Ⓓ	63 Ⓐ Ⓓ	75 Ⓐ Ⓓ	87 Ⓐ Ⓓ
4 Ⓐ Ⓓ	16 Ⓐ Ⓓ	28 Ⓐ Ⓓ	40 Ⓐ Ⓓ	52 Ⓐ Ⓓ	64 Ⓐ Ⓓ	76 Ⓐ Ⓓ	88 Ⓐ Ⓓ
5 Ⓐ Ⓓ	17 Ⓐ Ⓓ	29 Ⓐ Ⓓ	41 Ⓐ Ⓓ	53 Ⓐ Ⓓ	65 Ⓐ Ⓓ	77 Ⓐ Ⓓ	89 Ⓐ Ⓓ
6 Ⓐ Ⓓ	18 Ⓐ Ⓓ	30 Ⓐ Ⓓ	42 Ⓐ Ⓓ	54 Ⓐ Ⓓ	66 Ⓐ Ⓓ	78 Ⓐ Ⓓ	90 Ⓐ Ⓓ
7 Ⓐ Ⓓ	19 Ⓐ Ⓓ	31 Ⓐ Ⓓ	43 Ⓐ Ⓓ	55 Ⓐ Ⓓ	67 Ⓐ Ⓓ	79 Ⓐ Ⓓ	91 Ⓐ Ⓓ
8 Ⓐ Ⓓ	20 Ⓐ Ⓓ	32 Ⓐ Ⓓ	44 Ⓐ Ⓓ	56 Ⓐ Ⓓ	68 Ⓐ Ⓓ	80 Ⓐ Ⓓ	92 Ⓐ Ⓓ
9 Ⓐ Ⓓ	21 Ⓐ Ⓓ	33 Ⓐ Ⓓ	45 Ⓐ Ⓓ	57 Ⓐ Ⓓ	69 Ⓐ Ⓓ	81 Ⓐ Ⓓ	93 Ⓐ Ⓓ
10 Ⓐ Ⓓ	22 Ⓐ Ⓓ	34 Ⓐ Ⓓ	46 Ⓐ Ⓓ	58 Ⓐ Ⓓ	70 Ⓐ Ⓓ	82 Ⓐ Ⓓ	94 Ⓐ Ⓓ
11 Ⓐ Ⓓ	23 Ⓐ Ⓓ	35 Ⓐ Ⓓ	47 Ⓐ Ⓓ	59 Ⓐ Ⓓ	71 Ⓐ Ⓓ	83 Ⓐ Ⓓ	95 Ⓐ Ⓓ
12 Ⓐ Ⓓ	24 Ⓐ Ⓓ	36 Ⓐ Ⓓ	48 Ⓐ Ⓓ	60 Ⓐ Ⓓ	72 Ⓐ Ⓓ	84 Ⓐ Ⓓ	

Sheet 4

1 Ⓐ Ⓓ	13 Ⓐ Ⓓ	25 Ⓐ Ⓓ	37 Ⓐ Ⓓ	49 Ⓐ Ⓓ	61 Ⓐ Ⓓ	73 Ⓐ Ⓓ	85 Ⓐ Ⓓ
2 Ⓐ Ⓓ	14 Ⓐ Ⓓ	26 Ⓐ Ⓓ	38 Ⓐ Ⓓ	50 Ⓐ Ⓓ	62 Ⓐ Ⓓ	74 Ⓐ Ⓓ	86 Ⓐ Ⓓ
3 Ⓐ Ⓓ	15 Ⓐ Ⓓ	27 Ⓐ Ⓓ	39 Ⓐ Ⓓ	51 Ⓐ Ⓓ	63 Ⓐ Ⓓ	75 Ⓐ Ⓓ	87 Ⓐ Ⓓ
4 Ⓐ Ⓓ	16 Ⓐ Ⓓ	28 Ⓐ Ⓓ	40 Ⓐ Ⓓ	52 Ⓐ Ⓓ	64 Ⓐ Ⓓ	76 Ⓐ Ⓓ	88 Ⓐ Ⓓ
5 Ⓐ Ⓓ	17 Ⓐ Ⓓ	29 Ⓐ Ⓓ	41 Ⓐ Ⓓ	53 Ⓐ Ⓓ	65 Ⓐ Ⓓ	77 Ⓐ Ⓓ	89 Ⓐ Ⓓ
6 Ⓐ Ⓓ	18 Ⓐ Ⓓ	30 Ⓐ Ⓓ	42 Ⓐ Ⓓ	54 Ⓐ Ⓓ	66 Ⓐ Ⓓ	78 Ⓐ Ⓓ	90 Ⓐ Ⓓ
7 Ⓐ Ⓓ	19 Ⓐ Ⓓ	31 Ⓐ Ⓓ	43 Ⓐ Ⓓ	55 Ⓐ Ⓓ	67 Ⓐ Ⓓ	79 Ⓐ Ⓓ	91 Ⓐ Ⓓ
8 Ⓐ Ⓓ	20 Ⓐ Ⓓ	32 Ⓐ Ⓓ	44 Ⓐ Ⓓ	56 Ⓐ Ⓓ	68 Ⓐ Ⓓ	80 Ⓐ Ⓓ	92 Ⓐ Ⓓ
9 Ⓐ Ⓓ	21 Ⓐ Ⓓ	33 Ⓐ Ⓓ	45 Ⓐ Ⓓ	57 Ⓐ Ⓓ	69 Ⓐ Ⓓ	81 Ⓐ Ⓓ	93 Ⓐ Ⓓ
10 Ⓐ Ⓓ	22 Ⓐ Ⓓ	34 Ⓐ Ⓓ	46 Ⓐ Ⓓ	58 Ⓐ Ⓓ	70 Ⓐ Ⓓ	82 Ⓐ Ⓓ	94 Ⓐ Ⓓ
11 Ⓐ Ⓓ	23 Ⓐ Ⓓ	35 Ⓐ Ⓓ	47 Ⓐ Ⓓ	59 Ⓐ Ⓓ	71 Ⓐ Ⓓ	83 Ⓐ Ⓓ	95 Ⓐ Ⓓ
12 Ⓐ Ⓓ	24 Ⓐ Ⓓ	36 Ⓐ Ⓓ	48 Ⓐ Ⓓ	60 Ⓐ Ⓓ	72 Ⓐ Ⓓ	84 Ⓐ Ⓓ	

Extra Address Checking Answer Sheets

1 Ⓐ Ⓓ 13 Ⓐ Ⓓ 25 Ⓐ Ⓓ 37 Ⓐ Ⓓ 49 Ⓐ Ⓓ 61 Ⓐ Ⓓ 73 Ⓐ Ⓓ 85 Ⓐ Ⓓ
2 Ⓐ Ⓓ 14 Ⓐ Ⓓ 26 Ⓐ Ⓓ 38 Ⓐ Ⓓ 50 Ⓐ Ⓓ 62 Ⓐ Ⓓ 74 Ⓐ Ⓓ 86 Ⓐ Ⓓ
3 Ⓐ Ⓓ 15 Ⓐ Ⓓ 27 Ⓐ Ⓓ 39 Ⓐ Ⓓ 51 Ⓐ Ⓓ 63 Ⓐ Ⓓ 75 Ⓐ Ⓓ 87 Ⓐ Ⓓ
4 Ⓐ Ⓓ 16 Ⓐ Ⓓ 28 Ⓐ Ⓓ 40 Ⓐ Ⓓ 52 Ⓐ Ⓓ 64 Ⓐ Ⓓ 76 Ⓐ Ⓓ 88 Ⓐ Ⓓ
5 Ⓐ Ⓓ 17 Ⓐ Ⓓ 29 Ⓐ Ⓓ 41 Ⓐ Ⓓ 53 Ⓐ Ⓓ 65 Ⓐ Ⓓ 77 Ⓐ Ⓓ 89 Ⓐ Ⓓ
6 Ⓐ Ⓓ 18 Ⓐ Ⓓ 30 Ⓐ Ⓓ 42 Ⓐ Ⓓ 54 Ⓐ Ⓓ 66 Ⓐ Ⓓ 78 Ⓐ Ⓓ 90 Ⓐ Ⓓ
7 Ⓐ Ⓓ 19 Ⓐ Ⓓ 31 Ⓐ Ⓓ 43 Ⓐ Ⓓ 55 Ⓐ Ⓓ 67 Ⓐ Ⓓ 79 Ⓐ Ⓓ 91 Ⓐ Ⓓ
8 Ⓐ Ⓓ 20 Ⓐ Ⓓ 32 Ⓐ Ⓓ 44 Ⓐ Ⓓ 56 Ⓐ Ⓓ 68 Ⓐ Ⓓ 80 Ⓐ Ⓓ 92 Ⓐ Ⓓ
9 Ⓐ Ⓓ 21 Ⓐ Ⓓ 33 Ⓐ Ⓓ 45 Ⓐ Ⓓ 57 Ⓐ Ⓓ 69 Ⓐ Ⓓ 81 Ⓐ Ⓓ 93 Ⓐ Ⓓ
10 Ⓐ Ⓓ 22 Ⓐ Ⓓ 34 Ⓐ Ⓓ 46 Ⓐ Ⓓ 58 Ⓐ Ⓓ 70 Ⓐ Ⓓ 82 Ⓐ Ⓓ 94 Ⓐ Ⓓ
11 Ⓐ Ⓓ 23 Ⓐ Ⓓ 35 Ⓐ Ⓓ 47 Ⓐ Ⓓ 59 Ⓐ Ⓓ 71 Ⓐ Ⓓ 83 Ⓐ Ⓓ 95 Ⓐ Ⓓ
12 Ⓐ Ⓓ 24 Ⓐ Ⓓ 36 Ⓐ Ⓓ 48 Ⓐ Ⓓ 60 Ⓐ Ⓓ 72 Ⓐ Ⓓ 84 Ⓐ Ⓓ

---

1 Ⓐ Ⓓ 13 Ⓐ Ⓓ 25 Ⓐ Ⓓ 37 Ⓐ Ⓓ 49 Ⓐ Ⓓ 61 Ⓐ Ⓓ 73 Ⓐ Ⓓ 85 Ⓐ Ⓓ
2 Ⓐ Ⓓ 14 Ⓐ Ⓓ 26 Ⓐ Ⓓ 38 Ⓐ Ⓓ 50 Ⓐ Ⓓ 62 Ⓐ Ⓓ 74 Ⓐ Ⓓ 86 Ⓐ Ⓓ
3 Ⓐ Ⓓ 15 Ⓐ Ⓓ 27 Ⓐ Ⓓ 39 Ⓐ Ⓓ 51 Ⓐ Ⓓ 63 Ⓐ Ⓓ 75 Ⓐ Ⓓ 87 Ⓐ Ⓓ
4 Ⓐ Ⓓ 16 Ⓐ Ⓓ 28 Ⓐ Ⓓ 40 Ⓐ Ⓓ 52 Ⓐ Ⓓ 64 Ⓐ Ⓓ 76 Ⓐ Ⓓ 88 Ⓐ Ⓓ
5 Ⓐ Ⓓ 17 Ⓐ Ⓓ 29 Ⓐ Ⓓ 41 Ⓐ Ⓓ 53 Ⓐ Ⓓ 65 Ⓐ Ⓓ 77 Ⓐ Ⓓ 89 Ⓐ Ⓓ
6 Ⓐ Ⓓ 18 Ⓐ Ⓓ 30 Ⓐ Ⓓ 42 Ⓐ Ⓓ 54 Ⓐ Ⓓ 66 Ⓐ Ⓓ 78 Ⓐ Ⓓ 90 Ⓐ Ⓓ
7 Ⓐ Ⓓ 19 Ⓐ Ⓓ 31 Ⓐ Ⓓ 43 Ⓐ Ⓓ 55 Ⓐ Ⓓ 67 Ⓐ Ⓓ 79 Ⓐ Ⓓ 91 Ⓐ Ⓓ
8 Ⓐ Ⓓ 20 Ⓐ Ⓓ 32 Ⓐ Ⓓ 44 Ⓐ Ⓓ 56 Ⓐ Ⓓ 68 Ⓐ Ⓓ 80 Ⓐ Ⓓ 92 Ⓐ Ⓓ
9 Ⓐ Ⓓ 21 Ⓐ Ⓓ 33 Ⓐ Ⓓ 45 Ⓐ Ⓓ 57 Ⓐ Ⓓ 69 Ⓐ Ⓓ 81 Ⓐ Ⓓ 93 Ⓐ Ⓓ
10 Ⓐ Ⓓ 22 Ⓐ Ⓓ 34 Ⓐ Ⓓ 46 Ⓐ Ⓓ 58 Ⓐ Ⓓ 70 Ⓐ Ⓓ 82 Ⓐ Ⓓ 94 Ⓐ Ⓓ
11 Ⓐ Ⓓ 23 Ⓐ Ⓓ 35 Ⓐ Ⓓ 47 Ⓐ Ⓓ 59 Ⓐ Ⓓ 71 Ⓐ Ⓓ 83 Ⓐ Ⓓ 95 Ⓐ Ⓓ
12 Ⓐ Ⓓ 24 Ⓐ Ⓓ 36 Ⓐ Ⓓ 48 Ⓐ Ⓓ 60 Ⓐ Ⓓ 72 Ⓐ Ⓓ 84 Ⓐ Ⓓ

---

1 Ⓐ Ⓓ 13 Ⓐ Ⓓ 25 Ⓐ Ⓓ 37 Ⓐ Ⓓ 49 Ⓐ Ⓓ 61 Ⓐ Ⓓ 73 Ⓐ Ⓓ 85 Ⓐ Ⓓ
2 Ⓐ Ⓓ 14 Ⓐ Ⓓ 26 Ⓐ Ⓓ 38 Ⓐ Ⓓ 50 Ⓐ Ⓓ 62 Ⓐ Ⓓ 74 Ⓐ Ⓓ 86 Ⓐ Ⓓ
3 Ⓐ Ⓓ 15 Ⓐ Ⓓ 27 Ⓐ Ⓓ 39 Ⓐ Ⓓ 51 Ⓐ Ⓓ 63 Ⓐ Ⓓ 75 Ⓐ Ⓓ 87 Ⓐ Ⓓ
4 Ⓐ Ⓓ 16 Ⓐ Ⓓ 28 Ⓐ Ⓓ 40 Ⓐ Ⓓ 52 Ⓐ Ⓓ 64 Ⓐ Ⓓ 76 Ⓐ Ⓓ 88 Ⓐ Ⓓ
5 Ⓐ Ⓓ 17 Ⓐ Ⓓ 29 Ⓐ Ⓓ 41 Ⓐ Ⓓ 53 Ⓐ Ⓓ 65 Ⓐ Ⓓ 77 Ⓐ Ⓓ 89 Ⓐ Ⓓ
6 Ⓐ Ⓓ 18 Ⓐ Ⓓ 30 Ⓐ Ⓓ 42 Ⓐ Ⓓ 54 Ⓐ Ⓓ 66 Ⓐ Ⓓ 78 Ⓐ Ⓓ 90 Ⓐ Ⓓ
7 Ⓐ Ⓓ 19 Ⓐ Ⓓ 31 Ⓐ Ⓓ 43 Ⓐ Ⓓ 55 Ⓐ Ⓓ 67 Ⓐ Ⓓ 79 Ⓐ Ⓓ 91 Ⓐ Ⓓ
8 Ⓐ Ⓓ 20 Ⓐ Ⓓ 32 Ⓐ Ⓓ 44 Ⓐ Ⓓ 56 Ⓐ Ⓓ 68 Ⓐ Ⓓ 80 Ⓐ Ⓓ 92 Ⓐ Ⓓ
9 Ⓐ Ⓓ 21 Ⓐ Ⓓ 33 Ⓐ Ⓓ 45 Ⓐ Ⓓ 57 Ⓐ Ⓓ 69 Ⓐ Ⓓ 81 Ⓐ Ⓓ 93 Ⓐ Ⓓ
10 Ⓐ Ⓓ 22 Ⓐ Ⓓ 34 Ⓐ Ⓓ 46 Ⓐ Ⓓ 58 Ⓐ Ⓓ 70 Ⓐ Ⓓ 82 Ⓐ Ⓓ 94 Ⓐ Ⓓ
11 Ⓐ Ⓓ 23 Ⓐ Ⓓ 35 Ⓐ Ⓓ 47 Ⓐ Ⓓ 59 Ⓐ Ⓓ 71 Ⓐ Ⓓ 83 Ⓐ Ⓓ 95 Ⓐ Ⓓ
12 Ⓐ Ⓓ 24 Ⓐ Ⓓ 36 Ⓐ Ⓓ 48 Ⓐ Ⓓ 60 Ⓐ Ⓓ 72 Ⓐ Ⓓ 84 Ⓐ Ⓓ

---

1 Ⓐ Ⓓ 13 Ⓐ Ⓓ 25 Ⓐ Ⓓ 37 Ⓐ Ⓓ 49 Ⓐ Ⓓ 61 Ⓐ Ⓓ 73 Ⓐ Ⓓ 85 Ⓐ Ⓓ
2 Ⓐ Ⓓ 14 Ⓐ Ⓓ 26 Ⓐ Ⓓ 38 Ⓐ Ⓓ 50 Ⓐ Ⓓ 62 Ⓐ Ⓓ 74 Ⓐ Ⓓ 86 Ⓐ Ⓓ
3 Ⓐ Ⓓ 15 Ⓐ Ⓓ 27 Ⓐ Ⓓ 39 Ⓐ Ⓓ 51 Ⓐ Ⓓ 63 Ⓐ Ⓓ 75 Ⓐ Ⓓ 87 Ⓐ Ⓓ
4 Ⓐ Ⓓ 16 Ⓐ Ⓓ 28 Ⓐ Ⓓ 40 Ⓐ Ⓓ 52 Ⓐ Ⓓ 64 Ⓐ Ⓓ 76 Ⓐ Ⓓ 88 Ⓐ Ⓓ
5 Ⓐ Ⓓ 17 Ⓐ Ⓓ 29 Ⓐ Ⓓ 41 Ⓐ Ⓓ 53 Ⓐ Ⓓ 65 Ⓐ Ⓓ 77 Ⓐ Ⓓ 89 Ⓐ Ⓓ
6 Ⓐ Ⓓ 18 Ⓐ Ⓓ 30 Ⓐ Ⓓ 42 Ⓐ Ⓓ 54 Ⓐ Ⓓ 66 Ⓐ Ⓓ 78 Ⓐ Ⓓ 90 Ⓐ Ⓓ
7 Ⓐ Ⓓ 19 Ⓐ Ⓓ 31 Ⓐ Ⓓ 43 Ⓐ Ⓓ 55 Ⓐ Ⓓ 67 Ⓐ Ⓓ 79 Ⓐ Ⓓ 91 Ⓐ Ⓓ
8 Ⓐ Ⓓ 20 Ⓐ Ⓓ 32 Ⓐ Ⓓ 44 Ⓐ Ⓓ 56 Ⓐ Ⓓ 68 Ⓐ Ⓓ 80 Ⓐ Ⓓ 92 Ⓐ Ⓓ
9 Ⓐ Ⓓ 21 Ⓐ Ⓓ 33 Ⓐ Ⓓ 45 Ⓐ Ⓓ 57 Ⓐ Ⓓ 69 Ⓐ Ⓓ 81 Ⓐ Ⓓ 93 Ⓐ Ⓓ
10 Ⓐ Ⓓ 22 Ⓐ Ⓓ 34 Ⓐ Ⓓ 46 Ⓐ Ⓓ 58 Ⓐ Ⓓ 70 Ⓐ Ⓓ 82 Ⓐ Ⓓ 94 Ⓐ Ⓓ
11 Ⓐ Ⓓ 23 Ⓐ Ⓓ 35 Ⓐ Ⓓ 47 Ⓐ Ⓓ 59 Ⓐ Ⓓ 71 Ⓐ Ⓓ 83 Ⓐ Ⓓ 95 Ⓐ Ⓓ
12 Ⓐ Ⓓ 24 Ⓐ Ⓓ 36 Ⓐ Ⓓ 48 Ⓐ Ⓓ 60 Ⓐ Ⓓ 72 Ⓐ Ⓓ 84 Ⓐ Ⓓ

Extra Address Checking Answer Sheets

Extra Address Checking Answer Sheets

Sheet 1

1 Ⓐ Ⓓ	13 Ⓐ Ⓓ	25 Ⓐ Ⓓ	37 Ⓐ Ⓓ	49 Ⓐ Ⓓ	61 Ⓐ Ⓓ	73 Ⓐ Ⓓ	85 Ⓐ Ⓓ
2 Ⓐ Ⓓ	14 Ⓐ Ⓓ	26 Ⓐ Ⓓ	38 Ⓐ Ⓓ	50 Ⓐ Ⓓ	62 Ⓐ Ⓓ	74 Ⓐ Ⓓ	86 Ⓐ Ⓓ
3 Ⓐ Ⓓ	15 Ⓐ Ⓓ	27 Ⓐ Ⓓ	39 Ⓐ Ⓓ	51 Ⓐ Ⓓ	63 Ⓐ Ⓓ	75 Ⓐ Ⓓ	87 Ⓐ Ⓓ
4 Ⓐ Ⓓ	16 Ⓐ Ⓓ	28 Ⓐ Ⓓ	40 Ⓐ Ⓓ	52 Ⓐ Ⓓ	64 Ⓐ Ⓓ	76 Ⓐ Ⓓ	88 Ⓐ Ⓓ
5 Ⓐ Ⓓ	17 Ⓐ Ⓓ	29 Ⓐ Ⓓ	41 Ⓐ Ⓓ	53 Ⓐ Ⓓ	65 Ⓐ Ⓓ	77 Ⓐ Ⓓ	89 Ⓐ Ⓓ
6 Ⓐ Ⓓ	18 Ⓐ Ⓓ	30 Ⓐ Ⓓ	42 Ⓐ Ⓓ	54 Ⓐ Ⓓ	66 Ⓐ Ⓓ	78 Ⓐ Ⓓ	90 Ⓐ Ⓓ
7 Ⓐ Ⓓ	19 Ⓐ Ⓓ	31 Ⓐ Ⓓ	43 Ⓐ Ⓓ	55 Ⓐ Ⓓ	67 Ⓐ Ⓓ	79 Ⓐ Ⓓ	91 Ⓐ Ⓓ
8 Ⓐ Ⓓ	20 Ⓐ Ⓓ	32 Ⓐ Ⓓ	44 Ⓐ Ⓓ	56 Ⓐ Ⓓ	68 Ⓐ Ⓓ	80 Ⓐ Ⓓ	92 Ⓐ Ⓓ
9 Ⓐ Ⓓ	21 Ⓐ Ⓓ	33 Ⓐ Ⓓ	45 Ⓐ Ⓓ	57 Ⓐ Ⓓ	69 Ⓐ Ⓓ	81 Ⓐ Ⓓ	93 Ⓐ Ⓓ
10 Ⓐ Ⓓ	22 Ⓐ Ⓓ	34 Ⓐ Ⓓ	46 Ⓐ Ⓓ	58 Ⓐ Ⓓ	70 Ⓐ Ⓓ	82 Ⓐ Ⓓ	94 Ⓐ Ⓓ
11 Ⓐ Ⓓ	23 Ⓐ Ⓓ	35 Ⓐ Ⓓ	47 Ⓐ Ⓓ	59 Ⓐ Ⓓ	71 Ⓐ Ⓓ	83 Ⓐ Ⓓ	95 Ⓐ Ⓓ
12 Ⓐ Ⓓ	24 Ⓐ Ⓓ	36 Ⓐ Ⓓ	48 Ⓐ Ⓓ	60 Ⓐ Ⓓ	72 Ⓐ Ⓓ	84 Ⓐ Ⓓ	

Sheet 2

1 Ⓐ Ⓓ	13 Ⓐ Ⓓ	25 Ⓐ Ⓓ	37 Ⓐ Ⓓ	49 Ⓐ Ⓓ	61 Ⓐ Ⓓ	73 Ⓐ Ⓓ	85 Ⓐ Ⓓ
2 Ⓐ Ⓓ	14 Ⓐ Ⓓ	26 Ⓐ Ⓓ	38 Ⓐ Ⓓ	50 Ⓐ Ⓓ	62 Ⓐ Ⓓ	74 Ⓐ Ⓓ	86 Ⓐ Ⓓ
3 Ⓐ Ⓓ	15 Ⓐ Ⓓ	27 Ⓐ Ⓓ	39 Ⓐ Ⓓ	51 Ⓐ Ⓓ	63 Ⓐ Ⓓ	75 Ⓐ Ⓓ	87 Ⓐ Ⓓ
4 Ⓐ Ⓓ	16 Ⓐ Ⓓ	28 Ⓐ Ⓓ	40 Ⓐ Ⓓ	52 Ⓐ Ⓓ	64 Ⓐ Ⓓ	76 Ⓐ Ⓓ	88 Ⓐ Ⓓ
5 Ⓐ Ⓓ	17 Ⓐ Ⓓ	29 Ⓐ Ⓓ	41 Ⓐ Ⓓ	53 Ⓐ Ⓓ	65 Ⓐ Ⓓ	77 Ⓐ Ⓓ	89 Ⓐ Ⓓ
6 Ⓐ Ⓓ	18 Ⓐ Ⓓ	30 Ⓐ Ⓓ	42 Ⓐ Ⓓ	54 Ⓐ Ⓓ	66 Ⓐ Ⓓ	78 Ⓐ Ⓓ	90 Ⓐ Ⓓ
7 Ⓐ Ⓓ	19 Ⓐ Ⓓ	31 Ⓐ Ⓓ	43 Ⓐ Ⓓ	55 Ⓐ Ⓓ	67 Ⓐ Ⓓ	79 Ⓐ Ⓓ	91 Ⓐ Ⓓ
8 Ⓐ Ⓓ	20 Ⓐ Ⓓ	32 Ⓐ Ⓓ	44 Ⓐ Ⓓ	56 Ⓐ Ⓓ	68 Ⓐ Ⓓ	80 Ⓐ Ⓓ	92 Ⓐ Ⓓ
9 Ⓐ Ⓓ	21 Ⓐ Ⓓ	33 Ⓐ Ⓓ	45 Ⓐ Ⓓ	57 Ⓐ Ⓓ	69 Ⓐ Ⓓ	81 Ⓐ Ⓓ	93 Ⓐ Ⓓ
10 Ⓐ Ⓓ	22 Ⓐ Ⓓ	34 Ⓐ Ⓓ	46 Ⓐ Ⓓ	58 Ⓐ Ⓓ	70 Ⓐ Ⓓ	82 Ⓐ Ⓓ	94 Ⓐ Ⓓ
11 Ⓐ Ⓓ	23 Ⓐ Ⓓ	35 Ⓐ Ⓓ	47 Ⓐ Ⓓ	59 Ⓐ Ⓓ	71 Ⓐ Ⓓ	83 Ⓐ Ⓓ	95 Ⓐ Ⓓ
12 Ⓐ Ⓓ	24 Ⓐ Ⓓ	36 Ⓐ Ⓓ	48 Ⓐ Ⓓ	60 Ⓐ Ⓓ	72 Ⓐ Ⓓ	84 Ⓐ Ⓓ	

Sheet 3

1 Ⓐ Ⓓ	13 Ⓐ Ⓓ	25 Ⓐ Ⓓ	37 Ⓐ Ⓓ	49 Ⓐ Ⓓ	61 Ⓐ Ⓓ	73 Ⓐ Ⓓ	85 Ⓐ Ⓓ
2 Ⓐ Ⓓ	14 Ⓐ Ⓓ	26 Ⓐ Ⓓ	38 Ⓐ Ⓓ	50 Ⓐ Ⓓ	62 Ⓐ Ⓓ	74 Ⓐ Ⓓ	86 Ⓐ Ⓓ
3 Ⓐ Ⓓ	15 Ⓐ Ⓓ	27 Ⓐ Ⓓ	39 Ⓐ Ⓓ	51 Ⓐ Ⓓ	63 Ⓐ Ⓓ	75 Ⓐ Ⓓ	87 Ⓐ Ⓓ
4 Ⓐ Ⓓ	16 Ⓐ Ⓓ	28 Ⓐ Ⓓ	40 Ⓐ Ⓓ	52 Ⓐ Ⓓ	64 Ⓐ Ⓓ	76 Ⓐ Ⓓ	88 Ⓐ Ⓓ
5 Ⓐ Ⓓ	17 Ⓐ Ⓓ	29 Ⓐ Ⓓ	41 Ⓐ Ⓓ	53 Ⓐ Ⓓ	65 Ⓐ Ⓓ	77 Ⓐ Ⓓ	89 Ⓐ Ⓓ
6 Ⓐ Ⓓ	18 Ⓐ Ⓓ	30 Ⓐ Ⓓ	42 Ⓐ Ⓓ	54 Ⓐ Ⓓ	66 Ⓐ Ⓓ	78 Ⓐ Ⓓ	90 Ⓐ Ⓓ
7 Ⓐ Ⓓ	19 Ⓐ Ⓓ	31 Ⓐ Ⓓ	43 Ⓐ Ⓓ	55 Ⓐ Ⓓ	67 Ⓐ Ⓓ	79 Ⓐ Ⓓ	91 Ⓐ Ⓓ
8 Ⓐ Ⓓ	20 Ⓐ Ⓓ	32 Ⓐ Ⓓ	44 Ⓐ Ⓓ	56 Ⓐ Ⓓ	68 Ⓐ Ⓓ	80 Ⓐ Ⓓ	92 Ⓐ Ⓓ
9 Ⓐ Ⓓ	21 Ⓐ Ⓓ	33 Ⓐ Ⓓ	45 Ⓐ Ⓓ	57 Ⓐ Ⓓ	69 Ⓐ Ⓓ	81 Ⓐ Ⓓ	93 Ⓐ Ⓓ
10 Ⓐ Ⓓ	22 Ⓐ Ⓓ	34 Ⓐ Ⓓ	46 Ⓐ Ⓓ	58 Ⓐ Ⓓ	70 Ⓐ Ⓓ	82 Ⓐ Ⓓ	94 Ⓐ Ⓓ
11 Ⓐ Ⓓ	23 Ⓐ Ⓓ	35 Ⓐ Ⓓ	47 Ⓐ Ⓓ	59 Ⓐ Ⓓ	71 Ⓐ Ⓓ	83 Ⓐ Ⓓ	95 Ⓐ Ⓓ
12 Ⓐ Ⓓ	24 Ⓐ Ⓓ	36 Ⓐ Ⓓ	48 Ⓐ Ⓓ	60 Ⓐ Ⓓ	72 Ⓐ Ⓓ	84 Ⓐ Ⓓ	

Sheet 4

1 Ⓐ Ⓓ	13 Ⓐ Ⓓ	25 Ⓐ Ⓓ	37 Ⓐ Ⓓ	49 Ⓐ Ⓓ	61 Ⓐ Ⓓ	73 Ⓐ Ⓓ	85 Ⓐ Ⓓ
2 Ⓐ Ⓓ	14 Ⓐ Ⓓ	26 Ⓐ Ⓓ	38 Ⓐ Ⓓ	50 Ⓐ Ⓓ	62 Ⓐ Ⓓ	74 Ⓐ Ⓓ	86 Ⓐ Ⓓ
3 Ⓐ Ⓓ	15 Ⓐ Ⓓ	27 Ⓐ Ⓓ	39 Ⓐ Ⓓ	51 Ⓐ Ⓓ	63 Ⓐ Ⓓ	75 Ⓐ Ⓓ	87 Ⓐ Ⓓ
4 Ⓐ Ⓓ	16 Ⓐ Ⓓ	28 Ⓐ Ⓓ	40 Ⓐ Ⓓ	52 Ⓐ Ⓓ	64 Ⓐ Ⓓ	76 Ⓐ Ⓓ	88 Ⓐ Ⓓ
5 Ⓐ Ⓓ	17 Ⓐ Ⓓ	29 Ⓐ Ⓓ	41 Ⓐ Ⓓ	53 Ⓐ Ⓓ	65 Ⓐ Ⓓ	77 Ⓐ Ⓓ	89 Ⓐ Ⓓ
6 Ⓐ Ⓓ	18 Ⓐ Ⓓ	30 Ⓐ Ⓓ	42 Ⓐ Ⓓ	54 Ⓐ Ⓓ	66 Ⓐ Ⓓ	78 Ⓐ Ⓓ	90 Ⓐ Ⓓ
7 Ⓐ Ⓓ	19 Ⓐ Ⓓ	31 Ⓐ Ⓓ	43 Ⓐ Ⓓ	55 Ⓐ Ⓓ	67 Ⓐ Ⓓ	79 Ⓐ Ⓓ	91 Ⓐ Ⓓ
8 Ⓐ Ⓓ	20 Ⓐ Ⓓ	32 Ⓐ Ⓓ	44 Ⓐ Ⓓ	56 Ⓐ Ⓓ	68 Ⓐ Ⓓ	80 Ⓐ Ⓓ	92 Ⓐ Ⓓ
9 Ⓐ Ⓓ	21 Ⓐ Ⓓ	33 Ⓐ Ⓓ	45 Ⓐ Ⓓ	57 Ⓐ Ⓓ	69 Ⓐ Ⓓ	81 Ⓐ Ⓓ	93 Ⓐ Ⓓ
10 Ⓐ Ⓓ	22 Ⓐ Ⓓ	34 Ⓐ Ⓓ	46 Ⓐ Ⓓ	58 Ⓐ Ⓓ	70 Ⓐ Ⓓ	82 Ⓐ Ⓓ	94 Ⓐ Ⓓ
11 Ⓐ Ⓓ	23 Ⓐ Ⓓ	35 Ⓐ Ⓓ	47 Ⓐ Ⓓ	59 Ⓐ Ⓓ	71 Ⓐ Ⓓ	83 Ⓐ Ⓓ	95 Ⓐ Ⓓ
12 Ⓐ Ⓓ	24 Ⓐ Ⓓ	36 Ⓐ Ⓓ	48 Ⓐ Ⓓ	60 Ⓐ Ⓓ	72 Ⓐ Ⓓ	84 Ⓐ Ⓓ	

Extra Address Checking Answer Sheets

1 Ⓐ Ⓓ	13 Ⓐ Ⓓ	25 Ⓐ Ⓓ	37 Ⓐ Ⓓ	49 Ⓐ Ⓓ	61 Ⓐ Ⓓ	73 Ⓐ Ⓓ	85 Ⓐ Ⓓ
2 Ⓐ Ⓓ	14 Ⓐ Ⓓ	26 Ⓐ Ⓓ	38 Ⓐ Ⓓ	50 Ⓐ Ⓓ	62 Ⓐ Ⓓ	74 Ⓐ Ⓓ	86 Ⓐ Ⓓ
3 Ⓐ Ⓓ	15 Ⓐ Ⓓ	27 Ⓐ Ⓓ	39 Ⓐ Ⓓ	51 Ⓐ Ⓓ	63 Ⓐ Ⓓ	75 Ⓐ Ⓓ	87 Ⓐ Ⓓ
4 Ⓐ Ⓓ	16 Ⓐ Ⓓ	28 Ⓐ Ⓓ	40 Ⓐ Ⓓ	52 Ⓐ Ⓓ	64 Ⓐ Ⓓ	76 Ⓐ Ⓓ	88 Ⓐ Ⓓ
5 Ⓐ Ⓓ	17 Ⓐ Ⓓ	29 Ⓐ Ⓓ	41 Ⓐ Ⓓ	53 Ⓐ Ⓓ	65 Ⓐ Ⓓ	77 Ⓐ Ⓓ	89 Ⓐ Ⓓ
6 Ⓐ Ⓓ	18 Ⓐ Ⓓ	30 Ⓐ Ⓓ	42 Ⓐ Ⓓ	54 Ⓐ Ⓓ	66 Ⓐ Ⓓ	78 Ⓐ Ⓓ	90 Ⓐ Ⓓ
7 Ⓐ Ⓓ	19 Ⓐ Ⓓ	31 Ⓐ Ⓓ	43 Ⓐ Ⓓ	55 Ⓐ Ⓓ	67 Ⓐ Ⓓ	79 Ⓐ Ⓓ	91 Ⓐ Ⓓ
8 Ⓐ Ⓓ	20 Ⓐ Ⓓ	32 Ⓐ Ⓓ	44 Ⓐ Ⓓ	56 Ⓐ Ⓓ	68 Ⓐ Ⓓ	80 Ⓐ Ⓓ	92 Ⓐ Ⓓ
9 Ⓐ Ⓓ	21 Ⓐ Ⓓ	33 Ⓐ Ⓓ	45 Ⓐ Ⓓ	57 Ⓐ Ⓓ	69 Ⓐ Ⓓ	81 Ⓐ Ⓓ	93 Ⓐ Ⓓ
10 Ⓐ Ⓓ	22 Ⓐ Ⓓ	34 Ⓐ Ⓓ	46 Ⓐ Ⓓ	58 Ⓐ Ⓓ	70 Ⓐ Ⓓ	82 Ⓐ Ⓓ	94 Ⓐ Ⓓ
11 Ⓐ Ⓓ	23 Ⓐ Ⓓ	35 Ⓐ Ⓓ	47 Ⓐ Ⓓ	59 Ⓐ Ⓓ	71 Ⓐ Ⓓ	83 Ⓐ Ⓓ	95 Ⓐ Ⓓ
12 Ⓐ Ⓓ	24 Ⓐ Ⓓ	36 Ⓐ Ⓓ	48 Ⓐ Ⓓ	60 Ⓐ Ⓓ	72 Ⓐ Ⓓ	84 Ⓐ Ⓓ	

---

1 Ⓐ Ⓓ	13 Ⓐ Ⓓ	25 Ⓐ Ⓓ	37 Ⓐ Ⓓ	49 Ⓐ Ⓓ	61 Ⓐ Ⓓ	73 Ⓐ Ⓓ	85 Ⓐ Ⓓ
2 Ⓐ Ⓓ	14 Ⓐ Ⓓ	26 Ⓐ Ⓓ	38 Ⓐ Ⓓ	50 Ⓐ Ⓓ	62 Ⓐ Ⓓ	74 Ⓐ Ⓓ	86 Ⓐ Ⓓ
3 Ⓐ Ⓓ	15 Ⓐ Ⓓ	27 Ⓐ Ⓓ	39 Ⓐ Ⓓ	51 Ⓐ Ⓓ	63 Ⓐ Ⓓ	75 Ⓐ Ⓓ	87 Ⓐ Ⓓ
4 Ⓐ Ⓓ	16 Ⓐ Ⓓ	28 Ⓐ Ⓓ	40 Ⓐ Ⓓ	52 Ⓐ Ⓓ	64 Ⓐ Ⓓ	76 Ⓐ Ⓓ	88 Ⓐ Ⓓ
5 Ⓐ Ⓓ	17 Ⓐ Ⓓ	29 Ⓐ Ⓓ	41 Ⓐ Ⓓ	53 Ⓐ Ⓓ	65 Ⓐ Ⓓ	77 Ⓐ Ⓓ	89 Ⓐ Ⓓ
6 Ⓐ Ⓓ	18 Ⓐ Ⓓ	30 Ⓐ Ⓓ	42 Ⓐ Ⓓ	54 Ⓐ Ⓓ	66 Ⓐ Ⓓ	78 Ⓐ Ⓓ	90 Ⓐ Ⓓ
7 Ⓐ Ⓓ	19 Ⓐ Ⓓ	31 Ⓐ Ⓓ	43 Ⓐ Ⓓ	55 Ⓐ Ⓓ	67 Ⓐ Ⓓ	79 Ⓐ Ⓓ	91 Ⓐ Ⓓ
8 Ⓐ Ⓓ	20 Ⓐ Ⓓ	32 Ⓐ Ⓓ	44 Ⓐ Ⓓ	56 Ⓐ Ⓓ	68 Ⓐ Ⓓ	80 Ⓐ Ⓓ	92 Ⓐ Ⓓ
9 Ⓐ Ⓓ	21 Ⓐ Ⓓ	33 Ⓐ Ⓓ	45 Ⓐ Ⓓ	57 Ⓐ Ⓓ	69 Ⓐ Ⓓ	81 Ⓐ Ⓓ	93 Ⓐ Ⓓ
10 Ⓐ Ⓓ	22 Ⓐ Ⓓ	34 Ⓐ Ⓓ	46 Ⓐ Ⓓ	58 Ⓐ Ⓓ	70 Ⓐ Ⓓ	82 Ⓐ Ⓓ	94 Ⓐ Ⓓ
11 Ⓐ Ⓓ	23 Ⓐ Ⓓ	35 Ⓐ Ⓓ	47 Ⓐ Ⓓ	59 Ⓐ Ⓓ	71 Ⓐ Ⓓ	83 Ⓐ Ⓓ	95 Ⓐ Ⓓ
12 Ⓐ Ⓓ	24 Ⓐ Ⓓ	36 Ⓐ Ⓓ	48 Ⓐ Ⓓ	60 Ⓐ Ⓓ	72 Ⓐ Ⓓ	84 Ⓐ Ⓓ	

---

1 Ⓐ Ⓓ	13 Ⓐ Ⓓ	25 Ⓐ Ⓓ	37 Ⓐ Ⓓ	49 Ⓐ Ⓓ	61 Ⓐ Ⓓ	73 Ⓐ Ⓓ	85 Ⓐ Ⓓ
2 Ⓐ Ⓓ	14 Ⓐ Ⓓ	26 Ⓐ Ⓓ	38 Ⓐ Ⓓ	50 Ⓐ Ⓓ	62 Ⓐ Ⓓ	74 Ⓐ Ⓓ	86 Ⓐ Ⓓ
3 Ⓐ Ⓓ	15 Ⓐ Ⓓ	27 Ⓐ Ⓓ	39 Ⓐ Ⓓ	51 Ⓐ Ⓓ	63 Ⓐ Ⓓ	75 Ⓐ Ⓓ	87 Ⓐ Ⓓ
4 Ⓐ Ⓓ	16 Ⓐ Ⓓ	28 Ⓐ Ⓓ	40 Ⓐ Ⓓ	52 Ⓐ Ⓓ	64 Ⓐ Ⓓ	76 Ⓐ Ⓓ	88 Ⓐ Ⓓ
5 Ⓐ Ⓓ	17 Ⓐ Ⓓ	29 Ⓐ Ⓓ	41 Ⓐ Ⓓ	53 Ⓐ Ⓓ	65 Ⓐ Ⓓ	77 Ⓐ Ⓓ	89 Ⓐ Ⓓ
6 Ⓐ Ⓓ	18 Ⓐ Ⓓ	30 Ⓐ Ⓓ	42 Ⓐ Ⓓ	54 Ⓐ Ⓓ	66 Ⓐ Ⓓ	78 Ⓐ Ⓓ	90 Ⓐ Ⓓ
7 Ⓐ Ⓓ	19 Ⓐ Ⓓ	31 Ⓐ Ⓓ	43 Ⓐ Ⓓ	55 Ⓐ Ⓓ	67 Ⓐ Ⓓ	79 Ⓐ Ⓓ	91 Ⓐ Ⓓ
8 Ⓐ Ⓓ	20 Ⓐ Ⓓ	32 Ⓐ Ⓓ	44 Ⓐ Ⓓ	56 Ⓐ Ⓓ	68 Ⓐ Ⓓ	80 Ⓐ Ⓓ	92 Ⓐ Ⓓ
9 Ⓐ Ⓓ	21 Ⓐ Ⓓ	33 Ⓐ Ⓓ	45 Ⓐ Ⓓ	57 Ⓐ Ⓓ	69 Ⓐ Ⓓ	81 Ⓐ Ⓓ	93 Ⓐ Ⓓ
10 Ⓐ Ⓓ	22 Ⓐ Ⓓ	34 Ⓐ Ⓓ	46 Ⓐ Ⓓ	58 Ⓐ Ⓓ	70 Ⓐ Ⓓ	82 Ⓐ Ⓓ	94 Ⓐ Ⓓ
11 Ⓐ Ⓓ	23 Ⓐ Ⓓ	35 Ⓐ Ⓓ	47 Ⓐ Ⓓ	59 Ⓐ Ⓓ	71 Ⓐ Ⓓ	83 Ⓐ Ⓓ	95 Ⓐ Ⓓ
12 Ⓐ Ⓓ	24 Ⓐ Ⓓ	36 Ⓐ Ⓓ	48 Ⓐ Ⓓ	60 Ⓐ Ⓓ	72 Ⓐ Ⓓ	84 Ⓐ Ⓓ	

---

1 Ⓐ Ⓓ	13 Ⓐ Ⓓ	25 Ⓐ Ⓓ	37 Ⓐ Ⓓ	49 Ⓐ Ⓓ	61 Ⓐ Ⓓ	73 Ⓐ Ⓓ	85 Ⓐ Ⓓ
2 Ⓐ Ⓓ	14 Ⓐ Ⓓ	26 Ⓐ Ⓓ	38 Ⓐ Ⓓ	50 Ⓐ Ⓓ	62 Ⓐ Ⓓ	74 Ⓐ Ⓓ	86 Ⓐ Ⓓ
3 Ⓐ Ⓓ	15 Ⓐ Ⓓ	27 Ⓐ Ⓓ	39 Ⓐ Ⓓ	51 Ⓐ Ⓓ	63 Ⓐ Ⓓ	75 Ⓐ Ⓓ	87 Ⓐ Ⓓ
4 Ⓐ Ⓓ	16 Ⓐ Ⓓ	28 Ⓐ Ⓓ	40 Ⓐ Ⓓ	52 Ⓐ Ⓓ	64 Ⓐ Ⓓ	76 Ⓐ Ⓓ	88 Ⓐ Ⓓ
5 Ⓐ Ⓓ	17 Ⓐ Ⓓ	29 Ⓐ Ⓓ	41 Ⓐ Ⓓ	53 Ⓐ Ⓓ	65 Ⓐ Ⓓ	77 Ⓐ Ⓓ	89 Ⓐ Ⓓ
6 Ⓐ Ⓓ	18 Ⓐ Ⓓ	30 Ⓐ Ⓓ	42 Ⓐ Ⓓ	54 Ⓐ Ⓓ	66 Ⓐ Ⓓ	78 Ⓐ Ⓓ	90 Ⓐ Ⓓ
7 Ⓐ Ⓓ	19 Ⓐ Ⓓ	31 Ⓐ Ⓓ	43 Ⓐ Ⓓ	55 Ⓐ Ⓓ	67 Ⓐ Ⓓ	79 Ⓐ Ⓓ	91 Ⓐ Ⓓ
8 Ⓐ Ⓓ	20 Ⓐ Ⓓ	32 Ⓐ Ⓓ	44 Ⓐ Ⓓ	56 Ⓐ Ⓓ	68 Ⓐ Ⓓ	80 Ⓐ Ⓓ	92 Ⓐ Ⓓ
9 Ⓐ Ⓓ	21 Ⓐ Ⓓ	33 Ⓐ Ⓓ	45 Ⓐ Ⓓ	57 Ⓐ Ⓓ	69 Ⓐ Ⓓ	81 Ⓐ Ⓓ	93 Ⓐ Ⓓ
10 Ⓐ Ⓓ	22 Ⓐ Ⓓ	34 Ⓐ Ⓓ	46 Ⓐ Ⓓ	58 Ⓐ Ⓓ	70 Ⓐ Ⓓ	82 Ⓐ Ⓓ	94 Ⓐ Ⓓ
11 Ⓐ Ⓓ	23 Ⓐ Ⓓ	35 Ⓐ Ⓓ	47 Ⓐ Ⓓ	59 Ⓐ Ⓓ	71 Ⓐ Ⓓ	83 Ⓐ Ⓓ	95 Ⓐ Ⓓ
12 Ⓐ Ⓓ	24 Ⓐ Ⓓ	36 Ⓐ Ⓓ	48 Ⓐ Ⓓ	60 Ⓐ Ⓓ	72 Ⓐ Ⓓ	84 Ⓐ Ⓓ	

Correct Answers for Complete Practice Test #1

Address Checking

1. D	49. D		
2. A	50. D		
3. D	51. A		
4. A	52. D		
5. D	53. D		
6. D	54. D		
7. A	55. A		
8. A	56. D		
9. D	57. D		
10. A	58. D		
11. A	59. D		
12. A	60. D		
13. D	61. A		
14. A	62. D		
15. D	63. D		
16. A	64. A		
17. A	65. A		
18. D	66. A		
19. A	67. D		
20. A	68. D		
21. D	69. D		
22. A	70. D		
23. D	71. D		
24. A	72. A		
25. D	73. D		
26. A	74. D		
27. A	75. A		
28. D	76. A		
29. A	77. D		
30. A	78. D		
31. A	79. D		
32. D	80. A		
33. D	81. A		
34. D	82. D		
35. A	83. A		
36. D	84. A		
37. A	85. D		
38. A	86. D		
39. D	87. A		
40. A	88. D		
41. D	89. A		
42. D	90. A		
43. A	91. D		
44. A	92. A		
45. D	93. D		
46. D	94. A		
47. A	95. D		
48. A			

Address Memory

1. D	45. A
2. D	46. A
3. A	47. C
4. D	48. C
5. C	49. B
6. D	50. C
7. E	51. E
8. B	52. A
9. C	53. C
10. A	54. E
11. C	55. D
12. D	56. E
13. D	57. C
14. E	58. A
15. A	59. B
16. E	60. E
17. A	61. E
18. A	62. C
19. B	63. B
20. C	64. A
21. B	65. B
22. B	66. C
23. E	67. E
24. A	68. A
25. B	69. B
26. C	70. B
27. E	71. D
28. D	72. B
29. C	73. D
30. D	74. A
31. C	75. E
32. E	76. C
33. C	77. D
34. A	78. D
35. E	79. A
36. E	80. B
37. C	81. A
38. D	82. E
39. B	83. A
40. E	84. E
41. B	85. E
42. D	86. D
43. A	87. D
44. D	88. C

Number Series

1. B	
2. A	
3. E	
4. A	
5. A	
6. C	
7. A	
8. C	
9. A	
10. D	
11. C	
12. E	
13. E	
14. B	
15. B	
16. C	
17. B	
18. C	
19. D	
20. C	
21. D	
22. C	
23. B	
24. B	

Following Oral Instructions

1. 22-E
2. 3-C
3. 5-E
4. 8-A
5. 67-D
6. 21-E
7. 45-A
8. 15-D
9. 7-D
10. 72-E
11. 77-A
12. 59-A
13. 30-C
14. 78-C, 88-D, 26-C
15. 25-E
16. 62-C, 39-D
17. 11-B
18. 12-C
19. 13-A
20. 28-A
21. 2-D
22. 41-A
23. 1-E
24. 81-A
25. 33-E
26. 82-A
27. 16-A

Correct Answers for Complete Practice Test #2

Address Checking		Address Memory		Number Series	Following Oral Instructions
1. A	49. D	1. E	45. B	1. B	1. 11-A
2. D	50. D	2. E	46. C	2. A	2. 78-B
3. A	51. D	3. C	47. B	3. D	3. 3-A
4. A	52. A	4. B	48. D	4. B	4. 82-B
5. D	53. D	5. C	49. D	5. A	5. 8-A
6. D	54. D	6. E	50. E	6. C	6. 5-B
7. D	55. A	7. E	51. A	7. D	7. 27-A
8. A	56. A	8. C	52. D	8. D	8. 4-C
9. A	57. D	9. C	53. B	9. A	9. 9-D
10. A	58. D	10. A	54. A	10. E	10. 36-E
11. D	59. D	11. B	55. E	11. A	11. 2-B, 33-E
12. D	60. D	12. A	56. B	12. D	12. 62-D
13. D	61. A	13. E	57. E	13. E	13. 54-A
14. D	62. D	14. B	58. D	14. B	14. 10-E
15. A	63. D	15. B	59. E	15. A	15. 44-C
16. A	64. D	16. D	60. E	16. C	16. 64-B
17. D	65. A	17. C	61. E	17. C	17. 17-C, 39-E
18. A	66. D	18. D	62. B	18. C	18. 30-B
19. D	67. D	19. A	63. A	19. E	19. 75-A
20. A	68. D	20. E	64. C	20. A	20. 32-A, 51-E
21. D	69. A	21. D	65. E	21. B	21. 49-C, 1-D
22. A	70. D	22. C	66. C	22. C	22. 22-C
23. A	71. D	23. D	67. A	23. D	23. 12-B
24. D	72. D	24. A	68. E	24. E	24. 71-E
25. A	73. D	25. B	69. B		25. 88-B
26. A	74. D	26. E	70. D		26. 7-C
27. D	75. A	27. B	71. D		
28. D	76. A	28. E	72. D		
29. A	77. D	29. C	73. B		
30. D	78. D	30. A	74. D		
31. D	79. A	31. A	75. C		
32. A	80. D	32. E	76. C		
33. D	81. D	33. D	77. B		
34. A	82. D	34. E	78. B		
35. D	83. D	35. B	79. A		
36. D	84. D	36. D	80. E		
37. A	85. A	37. C	81. E		
38. A	86. D	38. A	82. D		
39. D	87. D	39. D	83. B		
40. A	88. D	40. E	84. A		
41. A	89. D	41. A	85. A		
42. D	90. A	42. A	86. E		
43. A	91. D	43. D	87. A		
44. D	92. D	44. C	88. B		
45. D	93. A				
46. A	94. D				
47. D	95. D				
48. A					

Correct Answers for Complete Practice Test #3

Address Checking		Address Memory		Number Series	Following Oral Instructions
1. D	49. D	1. E	45. B	1. C	1. 42-C
2. D	50. D	2. C	46. D	2. E	2. 11-D
3. A	51. A	3. B	47. B	3. A	3. 35-E
4. D	52. D	4. E	48. E	4. B	4. 73-E, 37-D
5. D	53. A	5. D	49. D	5. D	5. 68-D, 85-A
6. A	54. A	6. C	50. C	6. A	6. 30-D
7. A	55. A	7. A	51. C	7. E	7. 36-E, 83-A
8. D	56. D	8. C	52. C	8. C	8. 79-C
9. A	57. A	9. B	53. A	9. B	9. 38-B
10. D	58. A	10. E	54. E	10. D	10. 7-A, 2-A
11. A	59. D	11. C	55. A	11. A	11. 34-A
12. D	60. D	12. A	56. D	12. E	12. 58-E
13. A	61. A	13. A	57. A	13. E	13. 71-D, 61-E
14. A	62. D	14. D	58. B	14. C	14. 72-E, 22-D
15. A	63. A	15. B	59. D	15. B	15. 15-B
16. D	64. A	16. B	60. B	16. D	16. 1-D
17. A	65. D	17. D	61. E	17. B	17. 17-B
18. A	66. A	18. C	62. C	18. A	18. 4-C
19. D	67. D	19. E	63. A	19. E	19. 20-B
20. A	68. D	20. D	64. A	20. C	20. 56-C
21. D	69. D	21. A	65. C	21. A	21. 41-D
22. A	70. A	22. A	66. E	22. D	22. 14-C
23. A	71. A	23. B	67. B	23. C	23. 5-B
24. A	72. D	24. E	68. D	24. E	24. 6-E
25. D	73. D	25. E	69. E		
26. A	74. A	26. D	70. A		
27. D	75. A	27. C	71. A		
28. D	76. D	28. D	72. D		
29. D	77. D	29. C	73. C		
30. A	78. A	30. B	74. A		
31. A	79. A	31. E	75. E		
32. D	80. A	32. A	76. D		
33. D	81. D	33. A	77. C		
34. D	82. D	34. B	78. B		
35. A	83. A	35. E	79. E		
36. D	84. D	36. D	80. B		
37. D	85. A	37. E	81. E		
38. D	86. D	38. C	82. B		
39. A	87. A	39. C	83. D		
40. D	88. A	40. A	84. A		
41. D	89. D	41. D	85. B		
42. D	90. A	42. B	86. B		
43. A	91. D	43. A	87. E		
44. D	92. A	44. B	88. E		
45. D	93. A				
46. D	94. D				
47. A	95. A				
48. D					

Correct Answers for Complete Practice Test #4

Address Checking				Address Memory				Number Series		Following Oral Instructions	
1. A	49. D			1. A	45. B			1. B		1. 44-D	
2. A	50. A			2. C	46. E			2. C		2. 23-A	
3. A	51. D			3. E	47. A			3. D		3. 28-B, 3 0-B, 41-B	
4. D	52. A			4. B	48. E			4. B		4. 62-E	
5. A	53. A			5. E	49. B			5. A		5. 19-A	
6. D	54. D			6. D	50. D			6. D		6. 71-D	
7. A	55. A			7. A	51. A			7. E		7. 14-C, 37-B, 21-E	
8. D	56. A			8. E	52. E			8. C		8. 85-B	
9. A	57. D			9. E	53. B			9. E		9. 60-A	
10. D	58. D			10. B	54. C			10. A		10. 18-D, 31-D, 26-D	
11. D	59. D			11. D	55. E			11. B		11. 73-C	
12. A	60. A			12. A	56. A			12. B		12. 64-A, 67-B, 43-E	
13. D	61. D			13. D	57. D			13. D		13. 57-D	
14. A	62. D			14. C	58. C			14. B		14. 54-C	
15. D	63. A			15. B	59. A			15. C		15. 59-B, 12-E, 77-A	
16. A	64. D			16. A	60. E			16. E		16. 13-C, 52D	
17. A	65. A			17. D	61. C			17. A		17. 39-A, 58-A	
18. D	66. D			18. E	62. B			18. E		18. 5-B	
19. A	67. A			19. B	63. B			19. B		19. 35-E	
20. D	68. D			20. C	64. E			20. D			
21. D	69. A			21. C	65. C			21. E			
22. A	70. D			22. A	66. D			22. B			
23. A	71. D			23. C	67. A			23. C			
24. D	72. A			24. D	68. C			24. A			
25. D	73. D			25. B	69. E						
26. A	74. D			26. D	70. B						
27. D	75. D			27. A	71. D						
28. D	76. A			28. E	72. B						
29. A	77. A			29. C	73. E						
30. A	78. D			30. E	74. A						
31. A	79. A			31. B	75. C						
32. D	80. A			32. A	76. D						
33. A	81. A			33. B	77. B						
34. D	82. D			34. A	78. D						
35. A	83. A			35. C	79. B						
36. A	84. D			36. C	80. D						
37. D	85. A			37. D	81. A						
38. A	86. D			38. C	82. D						
39. A	87. D			39. E	83. C						
40. D	88. A			40. A	84. D						
41. A	89. A			41. D	85. A						
42. A	90. A			42. A	86. E						
43. D	91. A			43. B	87. C						
44. D	92. D			44. D	88. E						
45. A	93. D										
46. D	94. A										
47. A	95. A										
48. A											

Correct Answers for Complete Practice Test #5

Address Checking		Address Memory		Number Series	Following Oral Instructions
1. A	49. D	1. E	45. D	1. C	1. 56-D
2. A	50. A	2. C	46. C	2. E	2. 82-B
3. D	51. A	3. A	47. B	3. A	3. 11-C
4. D	52. D	4. B	48. E	4. B	4. 42-E
5. A	53. A	5. E	49. B	5. D	5. 37-A, 76-B, 18-D
6. A	54. A	6. D	50. A	6. E	6. 12-E
7. D	55. A	7. A	51. C	7. A	7. 48-C
8. D	56. A	8. B	52. C	8. B	8. 29-B, 41-B, 36-B
9. D	57. D	9. C	53. D	9. C	9. 6-A
10. D	58. A	10. B	54. A	10. E	10. 53-D, 22-E
11. A	59. A	11. D	55. C	11. A	11. 78-C, 27-E
12. A	60. D	12. C	56. B	12. B	12. 51-C
13. A	61. A	13. A	57. D	13. D	13. 71-C
14. A	62. A	14. D	58. D	14. E	14. 8-B, 14-B, 15-B, 32-A, 57-A
15. D	63. D	15. C	59. A	15. C	15. 81-D, 62-D
16. A	64. A	16. D	60. E	16. A	16. 50-B, 60-C
17. D	65. D	17. B	61. C	17. E	17. 88-A
18. D	66. A	18. E	62. E	18. B	18. 61-A
19. A	67. A	19. A	63. D	19. E	19. 4-E
20. D	68. D	20. C	64. E	20. C	
21. A	69. A	21. D	65. A	21. C	
22. D	70. A	22. A	66. D	22. A	
23. D	71. A	23. D	67. E	23. D	
24. A	72. D	24. E	68. C	24. B	
25. A	73. A	25. B	69. E		
26. D	74. D	26. D	70. A		
27. A	75. D	27. E	71. D		
28. D	76. A	28. A	72. B		
29. D	77. A	29. C	73. D		
30. A	78. D	30. B	74. B		
31. A	79. A	31. E	75. E		
32. A	80. D	32. C	76. A		
33. D	81. D	33. C	77. C		
34. A	82. A	34. D	78. B		
35. A	83. D	35. A	79. B		
36. A	84. A	36. E	80. A		
37. A	85. D	37. C	81. C		
38. D	86. D	38. D	82. C		
39. D	87. D	39. B	83. A		
40. A	88. A	40. D	84. B		
41. D	89. A	41. A	85. D		
42. D	90. D	42. B	86. C		
43. A	91. A	43. B	87. E		
44. D	92. A	44. A	88. E		
45. D	93. D				
46. A	94. D				
47. D	95. A				
48. A					

Correct Answers for Complete Practice Test #6

Address Checking		Address Memory		Number Series	Following Oral Instructions
1. A	49. A	1. D	45. C	1. C	1. 47-E
2. D	50. A	2. E	46. A	2. E	2. 59-B, 21-A, 82-D
3. D	51. A	3. B	47. E	3. A	3. 26-C, 33-C
4. A	52. D	4. D	48. B	4. D	4. 2-D
5. D	53. D	5. C	49. C	5. B	5. 14-A, 24-A, 58-E, 80-E
6. A	54. D	6. E	50. D	6. E	6. 50-B, 70-E
7. D	55. D	7. A	51. A	7. C	7. 65-C
8. A	56. A	8. C	52. E	8. A	8. 79-A, 61-E, 63-C
9. D	57. A	9. C	53. A	9. B	9. 85-D, 49-B
10. A	58. D	10. D	54. C	10. D	10. 88-C
11. D	59. A	11. A	55. E	11. C	11. 73-E, 9-D
12. D	60. D	12. D	56. B	12. E	12. 18-A
13. D	61. D	13. E	57. D	13. A	13. 41-A
14. A	62. A	14. A	58. B	14. B	14. 32-A
15. A	63. A	15. D	59. E	15. D	15. 78-A
16. D	64. D	16. B	60. A	16. E	16. 64-B, 75-B, 81-B
17. D	65. D	17. B	61. E	17. C	17. 20-D
18. D	66. D	18. E	62. B	18. B	18. 23-E
19. D	67. D	19. C	63. D	19. D	19. 39-A
20. A	68. D	20. E	64. B	20. A	
21. A	69. A	21. A	65. C	21. E	
22. A	70. D	22. D	66. A	22. B	
23. D	71. D	23. D	67. E	23. C	
24. D	72. A	24. B	68. D	24. E	
25. D	73. A	25. E	69. A		
26. A	74. D	26. A	70. D		
27. A	75. A	27. C	71. B		
28. A	76. D	28. D	72. C		
29. D	77. A	29. A	73. B		
30. A	78. A	30. D	74. D		
31. D	79. A	31. C	75. D		
32. A	80. D	32. B	76. A		
33. A	81. D	33. B	77. E		
34. D	82. A	34. A	78. C		
35. D	83. D	35. B	79. E		
36. D	84. D	36. C	80. A		
37. D	85. A	37. E	81. B		
38. A	86. D	38. A	82. D		
39. A	87. D	39. B	83. C		
40. A	88. A	40. C	84. E		
41. D	89. A	41. B	85. E		
42. A	90. A	42. C	86. A		
43. D	91. D	43. A	87. D		
44. D	92. D	44. E	88. C		
45. A	93. A				
46. A	94. D				
47. D	95. A				
48. D					

Correct Answers for Extra Address Checking Practice Exercises

#	Exercise #1	Exercise #2	Exercise #3	Exercise #4	Exercise #5
1	A	D	A	A	D
2	A	D	D	A	D
3	A	A	A	A	A
4	D	D	A	D	A
5	A	A	D	A	A
6	A	D	D	D	D
7	A	A	A	A	A
8	D	A	D	D	A
9	D	D	A	D	D
10	A	A	D	A	D
11	D	A	D	A	A
12	D	A	D	A	A
13	A	A	A	D	D
14	D	D	D	D	A
15	A	A	D	A	D
16	A	D	A	D	A
17	D	A	A	D	D
18	A	A	A	A	D
19	A	D	A	D	A
20	A	A	A	A	D
21	D	A	D	A	A
22	A	A	A	D	D
23	A	A	A	A	A
24	A	A	D	D	A
25	D	D	A	A	D
26	A	D	A	D	A
27	A	A	D	A	D
28	A	D	A	A	A
29	D	A	D	D	D
30	A	A	A	D	A
31	D	A	A	A	A
32	D	D	A	D	D
33	A	A	D	A	A
34	A	A	D	A	D
35	A	D	D	D	A
36	D	D	A	A	A
37	A	A	A	A	A
38	D	A	D	D	D
39	D	A	A	A	D
40	A	A	D	A	A
41	D	A	A	D	D
42	D	D	A	D	A
43	A	D	D	A	A
44	A	A	A	A	D
45	D	A	A	A	D
46	A	D	D	A	D
47	A	D	D	D	A
48	D	A	A	D	D
49	D	D	D	A	A
50	A	A	A	D	D
51	A	A	A	A	A
52	D	D	D	D	A
53	A	A	A	A	D
54	A	D	D	D	A
55	A	A	D	A	D
56	D	A	D	A	D
57	D	A	D	A	A
58	A	A	A	D	D
59	A	A	A	A	A
60	A	D	A	A	A
61	D	D	D	D	D
62	D	D	A	A	A
63	A	A	A	A	A
64	A	A	D	A	A
65	D	D	D	A	D
66	A	A	A	D	A
67	D	D	A	A	A
68	A	A	D	A	D
69	A	A	A	A	A
70	D	A	D	A	A
71	D	D	A	D	D
72	D	A	A	D	A
73	A	D	A	A	D
74	D	A	A	A	A
75	A	D	D	D	D
76	A	A	A	A	D
77	D	A	A	D	A
78	A	D	D	A	A
79	A	A	A	D	A
80	A	D	A	A	D
81	A	A	A	A	A
82	D	A	D	A	D
83	A	D	A	A	D
84	A	A	D	D	A
85	D	A	A	A	A
86	D	A	D	A	A
87	D	D	D	A	A
88	A	D	A	A	D
89	A	A	A	D	A
90	D	A	D	D	A
91	A	A	D	A	D
92	D	A	A	A	D
93	A	D	A	A	A
94	A	D	A	D	A
95	A	A	D	A	D

Correct Answers for Extra Address Checking Practice Exercises

Exercise #6		Exercise #7		Exercise #8		Exercise #9		Exercise #10	
1. A	49. D	1. D	49. D	1. A	49. D	1. A	49. A	1. D	49. A
2. A	50. A	2. D	50. A	2. D	50. A	2. A	50. D	2. D	50. D
3. A	51. A	3. A	51. A	3. A	51. A	3. A	51. A	3. A	51. A
4. D	52. D	4. D	52. D	4. A	52. D	4. D	52. D	4. A	52. A
5. A	53. A	5. A	53. A	5. D	53. A	5. A	53. A	5. A	53. D
6. A	54. A	6. D	54. D	6. D	54. D	6. D	54. A	6. D	54. A
7. A	55. A	7. A	55. A	7. A	55. D	7. A	55. A	7. A	55. D
8. D	56. D	8. A	56. A	8. A	56. D	8. D	56. A	8. A	56. D
9. D	57. D	9. D	57. A	9. A	57. D	9. D	57. A	9. D	57. A
10. A	58. A	10. A	58. A	10. D	58. A	10. A	58. D	10. D	58. D
11. D	59. A	11. A	59. A	11. D	59. A	11. A	59. A	11. A	59. A
12. D	60. A	12. A	60. D	12. D	60. A	12. A	60. A	12. A	60. A
13. A	61. D	13. A	61. D	13. A	61. D	13. A	61. D	13. D	61. D
14. D	62. D	14. D	62. D	14. D	62. A	14. D	62. A	14. A	62. A
15. A	63. A	15. A	63. A	15. D	63. A	15. A	63. A	15. D	63. A
16. A	64. A	16. D	64. A	16. A	64. D	16. D	64. A	16. A	64. A
17. D	65. D	17. A	65. D	17. A	65. D	17. D	65. A	17. D	65. D
18. A	66. A	18. A	66. A	18. A	66. A	18. A	66. D	18. A	66. A
19. A	67. D	19. D	67. D	19. A	67. A	19. D	67. A	19. A	67. A
20. A	68. A	20. A	68. A	20. D	68. D	20. A	68. D	20. D	68. D
21. D	69. A	21. A	69. A	21. D	69. A	21. A	69. A	21. A	69. A
22. A	70. D	22. A	70. A	22. A	70. D	22. D	70. A	22. D	70. A
23. A	71. D	23. A	71. D	23. A	71. A	23. A	71. D	23. A	71. D
24. A	72. D	24. A	72. A	24. D	72. A	24. D	72. D	24. A	72. A
25. D	73. A	25. D	73. D	25. A	73. A	25. A	73. A	25. D	73. D
26. A	74. D	26. D	74. A	26. A	74. A	26. D	74. A	26. A	74. A
27. A	75. A	27. A	75. D	27. D	75. D	27. A	75. D	27. D	75. D
28. A	76. A	28. D	76. A	28. A	76. A	28. A	76. A	28. A	76. D
29. D	77. D	29. A	77. A	29. D	77. A	29. D	77. D	29. D	77. A
30. A	78. A	30. A	78. D	30. A	78. D	30. D	78. A	30. A	78. A
31. D	79. A	31. A	79. A	31. A	79. A	31. A	79. D	31. A	79. A
32. D	80. A	32. D	80. D	32. A	80. A	32. D	80. D	32. D	80. D
33. A	81. A	33. A	81. A	33. D	81. A	33. A	81. A	33. A	81. A
34. A	82. D	34. A	82. A	34. D	82. D	34. A	82. A	34. D	82. D
35. A	83. A	35. A	83. D	35. D	83. A	35. D	83. A	35. D	83. D
36. D	84. A	36. D	84. A	36. A	84. D	36. A	84. D	36. A	84. A
37. A	85. D	37. A	85. A	37. A	85. A	37. A	85. A	37. A	85. A
38. D	86. D	38. A	86. A	38. D	86. D	38. D	86. A	38. D	86. A
39. D	87. D	39. A	87. D	39. A	87. D	39. A	87. A	39. D	87. A
40. A	88. A	40. A	88. D	40. D	88. A	40. A	88. A	40. A	88. D
41. D	89. A	41. A	89. A	41. A	89. A	41. D	89. D	41. D	89. A
42. D	90. D	42. D	90. A	42. A	90. D	42. D	90. D	42. A	90. A
43. A	91. A	43. D	91. A	43. D	91. D	43. A	91. A	43. A	91. D
44. A	92. D	44. A	92. A	44. A	92. D	44. A	92. A	44. D	92. D
45. D	93. A	45. A	93. D	45. A	93. A	45. A	93. A	45. D	93. A
46. A	94. A	46. D	94. D	46. D	94. A	46. A	94. D	46. A	94. A
47. A	95. A	47. D	95. A	47. D	95. D	47. D	95. A	47. A	95. D
48. D		48. A		48. A		48. D		48. D	

Following Oral Instructions Questions for Complete Practice Tests

Provided on the next several pages of the book are the questions for the Following Oral Instructions sections from each of your six complete practice tests. As detailed before, if someone is going to read these questions to you, they should be read at a rather slow and deliberate rate of approximately 75 words per minute and with proper diction. It is important also that the reader pause occasionally according to the specific directions given in the wording of the questions.

Do not look over the questions before taking the practice tests. Once you have completed a practice test, you should then review the questions you missed in order to determine what caused you to miss them. This review should enable you to be more successful on similar questions next time.

Again as previously mentioned, the most effective and convenient way to practice for this section of the exam is to listen to author's professional recording of the questions. See the order form at the back of your book for details.

Following Oral Instructions Questions
Practice Test #1

Look at Sample 1. (Pause slightly.) Sample 1 has a number with a line beside it. (Pause slightly.) Write the letter E as in egg on the line. (Pause 2 seconds.) Now, on the Answer Sheet, find number 22 and darken the space for the letter you wrote on the line. (Pause 5 seconds.)

Look at Sample 2. (Pause slightly.) There are four numbers. Circle the smallest number. (Pause 2 seconds.) Now, on the Answer Sheet, find that number, and darken the letter C as in cat. (Pause 5 seconds.)

Look at Sample 3. (Pause slightly.) There are two letters and two numbers. (Pause slightly.) Underline the second number and the last letter. (Pause 3 seconds.) On the Answer Sheet, darken the number-letter combination you just underlined. (Pause 5 seconds.)

Look at Sample 4. (Pause slightly.) There are five numbers. Draw a line under the third number. (Pause 3 seconds.) Now, find the number you underlined on the Answer Sheet, and darken the letter A. (Pause 5 seconds.)

Look at Sample 5. (Pause slightly.) Circle the second letter. (Pause 2 seconds.) Now, on the Answer Sheet, find number 67, and darken the letter you just circled. (Pause 5 seconds.)

Look at the four boxes in Sample 6. (Pause slightly.) Each box has a letter with a line beside it. (Pause slightly.) Find the box with the letter E as in egg, and write the number 21 on the line beside it. (Pause 3 seconds.) On the Answer sheet, darken the number-letter combination you just made. (Pause 5 seconds.)

Look at Sample 7. (Pause slightly.) There are five numbers. (Pause slightly.) If one of the numbers is greater than 42 and less than 57, write an A as in apple on the line beside it. (Pause 5 seconds.) Now find that number on the Answer Sheet, and darken the letter A. (Pause 4 seconds.) If there is not a number greater than 42 and less than 57, darken the letter C on line 23 of the Answer Sheet. (Pause 5 seconds.)

Look at Sample 8. (Pause slightly.) There are two boxes and two circles of different sizes with a number in each. (Pause slightly.) Write the letter D as in dog in the larger box. (Pause 2 seconds.) Now, on the Answer Sheet, darken the number-letter combination in the box. (Pause 5 seconds.)

Look at the letters in Sample 9. (Pause slightly.) Find the letter D as in dog, and write a 7 beside it. (Pause 3 seconds.) On the Answer Sheet, darken the number-letter combination you just made. (Pause 5 seconds.)

Look at Sample 10. (Pause slightly.) There are four different size boxes with a number in each. (Pause slightly.) Write the letter E as in egg on the line in the largest box. (Pause 4 seconds.) On the Answer Sheet, darken the number-letter combination for the box in which you just wrote. (Pause 5 seconds.)

Look at Sample 11. (Pause slightly.) There are two squares and two circles. (Pause slightly.) If 4 is greater than 7 and 6 is less than 9, write the letter D as in dog in the smaller circle. (Pause 5 seconds.) Otherwise, write the letter A as in apple in the larger square. (Pause 4 seconds.) On the answer Sheet, darken the number-letter combination for the circle or square in which you just wrote. (Pause 5 seconds.)

Look at the five letters in Sample 12. (Pause slightly.) If there are two letters that are the same, write the number 59 next to the letter A. (Pause 3 seconds.) Otherwise, write the number 33 by the last letter. (Pause 3 seconds.) On the Answer Sheet, darken the number-letter combination you have made. (Pause 5 seconds.)

Look at Sample 13. (Pause slightly.) There are five circles with a time and a letter in each. On the line in the second circle, write the last two numbers of the time in that circle. (Pause 4 seconds.) On the Answer Sheet, darken the number-letter combination for the circle in which you just wrote. (Pause 5 seconds.)

Look at Sample 14. (Pause slightly.) There are two squares and two circles of different sizes with a letter in each. (Pause 3 seconds.) If 2 is greater than 1 and 9 is less than 11, write the number 78 in the larger square. (Pause 3 seconds.) Otherwise, write the number 32 in the smaller circle. (Pause 3 seconds.) On the Answer Sheet, darken the number-letter combination you have made. (Pause 5 seconds.)

Look at the four letters in Sample 14 again. (Pause slightly.) Draw a line under the first letter if that letter is a B as in boy. (Pause 3 seconds.) Otherwise, draw a line under the last letter. (Pause 3 seconds.) Now, on the Answer Sheet, find the number 88, and darken the letter under which you drew a line. (Pause 5 seconds.)

Look at Sample 14 again. (Pause slightly.) If A comes before B and 7 is greater than 5, draw a line under the third letter. (Pause 3 seconds.) Otherwise, draw a line under the second letter. (Pause 3 seconds.) On the answer Sheet, find the number 26, and darken the letter under which you just drew a line. (Pause 5 seconds.)

Following Oral Instructions Questions
Practice Test #1 – Continued

Look at Sample 15. (Pause slightly.) There are four boxes with a different time in each. Find the latest time, and write the last two numbers of that time on the line in its box. (Pause 4 seconds.) Now, on the Answer Sheet, find the number you wrote on the line in the box, and darken the letter E as in egg. (Pause 5 seconds.)

Look at Sample 16. (Pause slightly.) The number in each box represents a number of parcels. Find the box with the largest number of parcels. (Pause 3 seconds.) Write the letter C as in cat on the line in that box. (Pause 3 seconds.) On the Answer Sheet, darken the number-letter combination for that box. (Pause 5 seconds.)

Look at the four boxes in Sample 16 again. (Pause slightly.) If the second box has more parcels than the first box, write an E as in egg in the first box. (Pause 4 seconds.) Otherwise, write a D as in dog in the next-to-last box. (Pause 4 seconds.) Now, on the Answer Sheet, darken the number-letter combination for the box in which you just wrote. (Pause 5 seconds.)

Look at sample 17. (Pause slightly.) If the largest circle has the smallest number, write an A as in apple in that circle. (Pause 3 seconds.) Otherwise, write a B as in boy in the second circle. (Pause 3 seconds.) On the Answer Sheet, darken the number-letter combination in the circle in which you just wrote. (Pause 5 seconds.)

Look at Sample 18. (Pause slightly.) If 47 is greater than 33 and less than 49, write the number 12 on the line. (Pause 3 seconds.) If it is not, write the number 72 on the line. (Pause 3 seconds.) On the Answer Sheet, find the number you wrote on the line, and darken the letter C as in cat. (Pause 5 seconds.)

Look at Sample 19. (Pause slightly.) In each of the four boxes is a time that mail is to be collected. Find the earliest collection time, and write the letter E as in egg in that box. (Pause 3 seconds.) On the Answer Sheet, find the number that would be created by using only the first two digits of the time in the box where you wrote the letter E as in egg, and darken the letter A as in Apple. (Pause 5 seconds.)

Look at Sample 20. (Pause slightly.) Draw a line under the next-to-last number. (Pause slightly.) On the Answer Sheet, darken the letter A as in apple for the number you underlined. (Pause 5 seconds.)

Look at Sample 21. (Pause slightly.) Write the letter D as in dog in the box with the city of Chicago. (Pause 3 seconds.) Starting from the right, count the number of boxes stopping at the box in which you wrote. (Pause 3 seconds.) On the Answer Sheet, darken the number-letter combination created by combining the number of boxes you counted with the letter you wrote in the box with the city of Chicago. (Pause 5 seconds.)

Look at Sample 22. (Pause slightly.) There is a letter with a number in front of it. (Pause slightly.) If 2:00 PM is earlier than 3:00 AM, darken the number-letter combination in Sample 22 on the Answer Sheet. (Pause 4 seconds.) Otherwise, darken 41-A on the Answer Sheet. (Pause 5 seconds.)

Look at Sample 23. (Pause slightly.) If the first number is less than the third number, and the last number is greater than the first number, darken the number-letter combination 1-E on the Answer Sheet. (Pause 4 seconds.) Otherwise, darken the number-letter combination 2-A. (Pause 5 seconds.)

Look at Sample 24. (Pause slightly.) If 8 is greater than 10 and 14 is less than 7, write the letter B as in boy in the third box. (Pause 3 seconds.) If not, write the letter A as in apple in the first box. (Pause 3 seconds.) On the Answer Sheet, darken the number-letter combination you have made. (Pause 5 seconds.)

Look at Sample 25. (Pause slightly.) Write the number 33 in front of the first letter. (Pause 2 seconds.) Now, on the Answer Sheet, darken the number-letter combination you have made. (Pause 5 seconds.)

Look at sample 26. (Pause slightly.) If Jefferson was the first President of the United States, write the letter E as in egg in the third circle. (Pause 3 seconds.) If he was not, write the letter A as in apple in the second circle. (Pause 3 seconds.) Now, darken the number-letter combination you have made. (Pause 5 seconds.)

Look at Sample 27. (Pause slightly.) Write the letter A as in apple in the box with the town that has the smallest population. (Pause 3 seconds.) Now, on the Answer Sheet, darken the number-letter combination you have made.

END OF FOLLOWING ORAL INSTRUCTIONS QUESTIONS – PRACTICE TEST #1

Following Oral Instructions Questions
Practice Test #2

Look at Sample 1. (Pause slightly.) Draw a line under the second number. (Pause 3 seconds.) On the Answer Sheet, find that number, and darken the letter A as in apple. (Pause 5 seconds.)

Look at Sample 2. (Pause slightly.) Draw a circle around the last letter. (Pause 3 seconds.) On the Answer Sheet, find the number 78 and darken the letter you circled. (Pause 5 seconds.)

Look at Sample 3. (Pause slightly.) There are three letters and three numbers. (Pause slightly.) Underline the first letter and the last number. (Pause 4 seconds.) On the Answer Sheet, darken the number-letter combination you just underlined. (Pause 5 seconds.)

Look at Sample 4. (Pause slightly.) Circle the largest number. (Pause 3 seconds.) Now, find that number on the Answer Sheet, and darken the letter B as in boy. (Pause 5 seconds.)

Look at Sample 5. (Pause slightly.) Find the letter A as in apple, and write the number 8 beside it. (Pause 3 seconds.) On the Answer Sheet, darken the number-letter combination you have made. (Pause 5 seconds.)

Look at Sample 6. (Pause slightly.) There are four different size boxes with a number in each. (Pause slightly.) In the next-to-last box, write the letter B as in boy next to the number. (Pause 3 seconds.) On the Answer Sheet, darken the number-letter combination you have made. (Pause 5 seconds.)

Look at Sample 7. (Pause slightly.) There are four numbers in Sample 7. (Pause slightly.) If 68 is less than 86 and the letter C as in cat comes before the letter D as in dog in the alphabet, underline the first number. (Pause 3 seconds.) Otherwise, underline the last number. (Pause 3 seconds.) On the Answer Sheet, find the number you underlined, and darken the letter A as in apple. (Pause 5 seconds.)

Look at Sample 8. (Pause slightly.) There are two squares and two circles. (Pause slightly.) If 5 is greater than 2 and 9 is less than 12, write the letter C as in cat in the smaller circle. (Pause 3 seconds.) If not, write the letter A as in apple in the larger square. (Pause 3 seconds.) On the Answer Sheet, darken the number-letter combination you have made. (Pause 5 seconds.)

Look at Sample 9. (Pause slightly.) Write the letter D as in dog in the smallest box. (Pause 3 seconds.) On the Answer Sheet, darken the number-letter combination you have made. (Pause 4 seconds.)

Look at Sample 10. (Pause slightly.) There are five letters with a line before each. (Pause slightly.) If the second letter comes before the third letter in the alphabet, write the number 36 on the line before the first letter. (Pause 4 seconds.) Otherwise, write the number 47 on the last line. (Pause 3 seconds.) On the Answer Sheet, darken the number-letter combination you have made. (Pause 5 seconds.)

Look at the boxes and circles in Sample 11. (Pause slightly.) Write the letter B as in boy in the second box. (Pause 4 seconds.) On the Answer Sheet, darken B as in boy for the number in that box. (Pause 5 seconds.)

Look at Sample 11 again. (Pause slightly.) Write the letter C as in cat in the largest box. (Pause 3 seconds.) On the Answer Sheet, find the number 33 and darken the letter E. (Pause 5 seconds.)

Look at Sample 12. (Pause slightly.) There are five numbers in Sample 12. (Pause slightly.) If the second number is larger than the last number, write the letter D as in dog by the last number. (Pause 2 seconds.) Otherwise, write the letter D as in dog by the first number. (Pause 4 seconds.) On the Answer Sheet, darken the number-letter combination you have made. (Pause 5 seconds.)

Sample 13 has a word with four lines under it. (Pause slightly.) On the first line, write the last letter of the word. (Pause 2 seconds.) On the last line, write the second letter of the word. (Pause 3 seconds.) Write the first letter on the second line, and write the third letter on the third line. (Pause 5 seconds.) Find number 54 on the Answer Sheet, darken the letter on the last line. (Pause 5 seconds.)

Look at Sample 14. (Pause slightly.) Listed in the five boxes are various mail delivery times. (Pause slightly.) Write the letter A as in apple in the box with the latest delivery time. (Pause 3 seconds.) On the Answer Sheet, find the number that would be created by using the last two digits of the time in the box in which you wrote the letter A as in apple, and darken the letter E as in egg. (Pause 5 seconds.)

347

Following Oral Instructions Questions
Practice Test #2 – Continued

In Sample 15, there is a line. (Pause slightly.) If 33 is greater than 22 and 44 is less than 11, write the number 11 on the line. (Pause 4 seconds.) Otherwise, write the number 44 on the line. (Pause 3 seconds.) On the Answer Sheet, find the number you wrote, and darken the letter C as in cat. (Pause 5 seconds.)

Look at Sample 16. (Pause slightly.) Each box has a number of letters to be postmarked. Find the box with the greatest number of letters to be postmarked. (Pause 3 seconds.) Write the letter B as in boy in that box. (Pause 2 seconds.) On the Answer Sheet, darken the number-letter combination you have made. (Pause 5 seconds.)

Look at Sample 17. (Pause slightly.) You will see the names of four cities with a number of parcels going to each city under each city's name. (Pause slightly.) Find the city with the largest number of parcels going to it, and circle the first letter in that city's name. (Pause 4 seconds.) On the Answer Sheet, find the number 17, and darken the letter you just circled. (Pause 5 seconds.)

Look at Sample 17 again. (Pause slightly.) If 56 is greater than 23 but less than 95, underline the second letter in the name of the city with the least number of parcels. (Pause 3 seconds.) Then find the number 39 on the Answer Sheet, and darken the letter you just underlined. (Pause 4 seconds.) Otherwise, darken the letter A as in apple at number 39 on the Answer Sheet. (Pause 5 seconds.)

In Sample 18, there are three boxes with a time of the day in each. (Pause slightly.) Find the box with the latest time in it. (Pause 3 seconds.) On the Answer Sheet, find the number that would be created by using the first two digits of that time, and darken the letter B as in boy. (Pause 5 seconds.)

Look at Sample 19. (Pause slightly.) If the first letter is an R as in rat, look at the last letter. (Pause 2 seconds.) If the last letter is a C as in cat, darken the letter C as in cat at number 75 on the Answer Sheet. (Pause 4 seconds.) Otherwise, darken the letter A as in apple at number 75. (Pause 5 seconds.)

Look at Sample 20. (Pause slightly.) There are two boxes and two circles of different sizes with a number in each. (Pause slightly.) Find the box with the smallest number, and write the letter A as in apple in that box. (Pause 4 seconds.) Find the smallest circle, and write the letter E as in egg in that circle. (Pause 4 seconds.) On the Answer Sheet, darken the number-letter combinations you have made. (Pause 5 seconds.)

Look at Sample 21. (Pause slightly.) There are five different size boxes with a number in each. (Pause slightly.) If the largest box contains the largest number, write the letter C as in cat in that box. (Pause 3 seconds.) Otherwise, write the letter C as in cat in the next-to-largest box. (Pause 3 seconds.) On the Answer Sheet, darken the number-letter combination you have made. (Pause 5 seconds.)

Look at Sample 21 again. (Pause slightly.) In the box with the smallest number, write the letter B as in boy if that number is greater than 5. (Pause 4 seconds.) Otherwise, write the letter D as in dog in that box. (Pause 4 seconds.) Darken the number-letter combination for the box in which you just wrote. (Pause 5 seconds.)

Look at Sample 22. (Pause slightly.) Write the number 22 on the line if A as in apple comes before Z as in zebra in the alphabet. (Pause 4 seconds.) If you wrote the number 22 on the line, find that number on the Answer Sheet, and darken the letter C as in cat. (Pause 4 seconds.) If you did not write the number 22 on the line, darken 63-A on the Answer Sheet. (Pause 5 seconds.)

Look at Sample 23. (Pause slightly.) If 12 is greater than 8 and 25 is less than 32, write the number 12 behind the second letter. (Pause 2 seconds.) If not, write the number 15 behind the fourth letter. (Pause 2 seconds.) On the Answer Sheet, darken the number-letter combination you have made. (Pause 5 seconds.)

Look at Sample 24. (Pause slightly.) Each of the two boxes contains the name of a city. (Pause slightly.) Of the two cities, the city of Gulfport has the earlier delivery time. (Pause slightly.) Write the letter E as in egg beside the number in the box that contains the city with the later delivery time. (Pause 3 seconds.) On the Answer Sheet, darken the number-letter combination you have made. (Pause 5 seconds.)

Look at Sample 25. (Pause slightly.) Write the letter B as in boy below the largest number. (Pause 3 seconds.) On the Answer Sheet, darken the number-letter combination you have made. (Pause 5 seconds.)

Look at Sample 26. (Pause slightly.) Sodas come six cans to a package. (Pause slightly.) How many packages must you buy to have 36 cans of soda? (Pause 3 seconds.) Take this number, and add 1 to it. (Pause 3 seconds.) Find the resulting number on the Answer Sheet, and darken the letter C as in cat.

END OF FOLLOWING ORAL INSTRUCTIONS QUESTIONS – PRACTICE TEST #2

Following Oral Instructions Questions
Practice Test #3

Look at Sample 1. (Pause slightly.) Draw a line under the fourth number. (Pause 2 seconds.) Now, on the Answer Sheet, darken the letter C as in cat for the number you underlined. (Pause 5 seconds.)

Look at Sample 2. (Pause slightly.) Write the letter D as in dog in the second box. (Pause 3 seconds.) Now, on the Answer Sheet, darken the number-letter combination you have made. (Pause 5 seconds.)

In Sample 3 there are four letters. (Pause slightly.) Draw a circle around the second letter. (Pause 2 seconds.) Find number 35 on the Answer Sheet, and darken the letter you circled. (Pause 5 seconds.)

In Sample 4 there are four boxes. (Pause slightly.) In each box is a number of parcels to be delivered. (Pause slightly.) In the box with the most parcels to be delivered, write the letter E as in egg. (Pause 3 seconds.) On the Answer Sheet, darken the number-letter combination you have made. (Pause 5 seconds.)

Look at Sample 4 again. (Pause slightly.) If 44 is greater than 48, write the letter A as in apple in the box with the lowest number. (Pause 3 seconds.) Otherwise, write the letter D as in dog in that box. (Pause 3 seconds.) On the Answer Sheet, darken the number-letter combination you have made. (Pause 5 seconds.)

Look at Sample 5. (Pause slightly.) There are four boxes of different sizes with a letter in each. (Pause slightly.) Write the number 68 in the smallest box. (Pause 3 seconds.) On the Answer Sheet, darken the number-letter combination you just made. (Pause 5 seconds.)

Looking at Sample 5 again, find the next-to-smallest box. (Pause slightly.) If 22 is less than 67, write the number 8 in that box. (Pause 4 seconds.) Otherwise, write the number 8 in the last box. (Pause 3 seconds.) Now, on the Answer Sheet, find the number 85, and darken the letter A as in apple. (Pause 5 seconds.)

In Sample 6, there are four circles with a time of day in each. (Pause slightly.) In the circle with the earliest time, write a D as in dog. (Pause 3 seconds.) On the Answer Sheet, find the number that would be created by using the last two digits of earliest time, and darken the letter D as in dog. (Pause 5 seconds.)

In Sample 7, five days of the week listed. If 44 is greater than 39, underline the second letter of the first day listed. (Pause 3 seconds.) If not, underline the seventh letter of the second day listed. (Pause 3 seconds.) On the Answer Sheet, find the number 36, and darken the letter you underlined. (Pause 5 seconds.)

Look at Sample 7 again. (Pause slightly.) If the name of the last day of the week listed begins with the letter R as in rat, draw a line under the last letter of the first day listed. (Pause 5 seconds.) Otherwise, darken the letter A as in apple at number 83 on the Answer Sheet. (Pause 5 seconds.)

Look at Sample 8. (Pause slightly.) There are four boxes with a number in each. (Pause slightly.) Write the letter C as in cat in the box that has the number closest to 77. (Pause 4 seconds.) On the Answer Sheet, darken the number-letter combination you have made. (Pause 5 seconds.)

Look at Sample 9. (Pause slightly.) Each box contains a mail delivery time. (Pause slightly.) If any of the mail delivery times is after 5:55 PM, darken the letter E as in egg at number 38 on the Answer Sheet. (Pause 4 seconds.) Otherwise, darken the letter B as in boy at that number. (Pause 5 seconds.)

Look at Sample 10. (Pause slightly.) There are three boxes and two circles of different sizes. (Pause slightly.) If B as in boy comes before D as in dog in the alphabet, and if 23 is less than 34, darken the letter A as in apple on the Answer Sheet at the number found in the smallest box. (Pause 4 seconds.) Otherwise, darken the letter E as in egg at the number found in the smaller circle. (Pause 5 seconds.)

Look at Sample 10 again. (Pause slightly.) If the number in the largest box is smaller than the number in the largest circle, darken the letter B as in boy on the Answer Sheet at the number found in the largest circle. (Pause 5 seconds.) Otherwise, darken the letter A as in apple on the Answer Sheet at the number found in the smaller circle. (Pause 5 second.)

Look at Sample 11. (Pause slightly.) If the second number is an odd number and the first number is an even number, underline the first number. (Pause 4 seconds.) Then, on the Answer Sheet, find the number you underlined, and darken the letter A as in apple. (Pause 4 seconds.) Otherwise, find the second number on the Answer Sheet, and darken the letter B as in boy. (Pause 5 seconds.)

Look at the letters in Sample 12. (Pause slightly.) There are five lines, one for each letter. Circle the E as in egg, and write the number 58 under the fourth letter. (Pause 3 seconds.) If the number you just wrote is under the letter you circled, darken that number-letter combination on the Answer Sheet. (Pause 5 seconds.) Otherwise, at number 58 on the Answer Sheet, darken the letter above the number 58. (Pause 5 seconds.)

349

Following Oral Instructions Questions
Practice Test #3 – Continued

Look at Sample 13. (Pause slightly.) Draw a circle around the second number. (Pause 2 seconds.) Draw a circle around the last number. (Pause 2 seconds.) Draw a circle around the first number. (Pause 2 seconds.) On the Answer Sheet, find the second number you circled, and darken the letter D as in dog. (Pause 5 seconds.)

Look at Sample 13 again. (Pause slightly.) If the number you did not circle is larger than 78, darken the letter A as in apple on the Answer Sheet at the number you did not circle. (Pause 3 seconds.) Otherwise, darken the letter E as in egg on the Answer Sheet at the number you did not circle. (Pause 5 seconds.)

Look at Sample 14. (Pause slightly.) There are two squares and two lines. (Pause slightly.) Write the letter E as in egg in the smaller square. (Pause 3 seconds.) Write the number 72 on the first line. (Pause 2 seconds.) Darken this number-letter combination on the Answer Sheet. (Pause 5 seconds.)

Look at Sample 14 again. (Pause slightly.) If 12 is less than 15, write the letter D as in dog in the largest square, and write the number 22 on the last line. (Pause 3 seconds.) Then, on the Answer Sheet, darken this number-letter combination. (Pause 4 seconds.) Otherwise, darken 64-C. (Pause 5 seconds.)

Look at Sample 15. (Pause slightly.) There are four boxes, each containing the name of a city with a mail collection time. (Pause slightly.) Write the letter B as in boy in the box that contains the city with the latest collection time. (Pause 4 seconds.) On the Answer Sheet, find the number that would be created by using the last two digits of the time in that box, and darken the letter you wrote in that box. (Pause 5 seconds.)

Look at Sample 16. (Pause slightly.) Each circle contains a mail delivery time. Find the earliest time. (Pause 2 seconds.) On the line in the circle with the earliest time, write the first digit of that time. (Pause 2 seconds.) On the Answer Sheet, darken the letter D as in dog for the number you just wrote. (Pause 5 seconds.)

Look at the five circles in Sample 17. (Pause slightly.) Each circle has a time and a letter in it. (Pause slightly.) On the line in the last circle, write the last two digits of the time in that circle. (Pause 2 seconds.) On the Answer Sheet, darken the number-letter combination you have made. (Pause 5 seconds.)

Look at the letters in Sample 18. (Pause slightly.) Draw a line under the second letter. (Pause 2 seconds.) Find the number 4 on the Answer Sheet, and darken the letter under which you drew a line. (Pause 5 seconds.)

Look at Sample 19. (Pause slightly.) Each box contains a number of sacks of mail. Find the box with the smallest number of sacks. (Pause 2 seconds.) On the line in that box, write the letter B as in boy. (Pause 2 seconds.) On the Answer Sheet, darken the number-letter combination in that box. (Pause 5 seconds.)

Look at Sample 20. (Pause slightly.) Each number has a line under it. (Pause slightly.) If the first number is the largest, write the letter A as in apple under the second number. (Pause 2 seconds.) Otherwise, write the letter C as in cat under the third number. (Pause 2 seconds.) On the Answer Sheet, darken the number-letter combination you have made. (Pause 5 seconds.)

Look at Sample 21. (Pause slightly.) Each box contains a number. (Pause slightly.) Write the letter D as in dog by the middle number. (Pause 3 seconds.) On the Answer Sheet, darken the number-letter combination you have made. (Pause 5 seconds.)

Look at Sample 22. (Pause slightly.) If P as in puddle comes before R as in rain in the alphabet, write the number 14 in the first circle. (Pause 2 seconds.) If not, write the number 27 in the last circle. (Pause 2 seconds.) On the Answer Sheet, darken the number-letter combination you have made. (Pause 5 seconds.)

Look at sample 23. (Pause slightly.) Write the letter B as in boy in the smallest box. (Pause 3 seconds.) On the Answer Sheet, darken the number-letter combination you have made. (Pause 5 seconds.)

Look at Sample 24. (Pause slightly.) If 15 is less than 12, write the letter D as in dog in the first circle. (Pause 2 seconds.) If not, write the letter E as in egg in the last circle. (Pause 2 seconds.) On the Answer Sheet, darken the number-letter combination you have made.

END OF FOLLOWING ORAL INSTRUCTIONS QUESTIONS – PRACTICE TEST #3

Following Oral Instructions Questions
Practice Test #4

Look at Sample 1. (Pause slightly.) Underline the fifth letter in the sequence. (Pause 3 seconds.) On the Answer Sheet, find the number 44, and darken the letter that you underlined. (Pause 5 seconds.)

Look at Sample 2. (Pause slightly.) There are four different size circles with a letter in each. (Pause slightly.) In the smallest circle, do nothing. (Pause slightly.) In the largest circle, write the number 23. (Pause 3 seconds.) On the Answer Sheet, darken the number-letter combination you have made. (Pause 5 seconds.)

Look at the numbers in Sample 3. (Pause slightly.) Draw a line under the numbers greater than 27 but less than 43. (Pause 4 seconds.) On the Answer Sheet, darken the letter B as in boy for the numbers you underlined. (Pause 5 seconds.)

Look at Sample 4. (Pause slightly.) If 21 is greater than 27, draw a line under the last letter. (Pause 2 seconds.) Otherwise, draw a line under the third letter. (Pause 2 seconds.) On the Answer Sheet, find the number 62, and darken the letter you underlined. (Pause 5 seconds.)

Look at Sample 5. (Pause slightly.) There are two circles and two boxes of different sizes with a number in each. (Pause 2 seconds.) If 6 is greater than 5 and 8 is less than 7, write the letter C as in cat in the larger box. (Pause 3 seconds.) Otherwise, write the letter A as in apple in the larger circle. (Pause 3 seconds.) On the Answer Sheet, darken the number-letter combination you have made. (Pause 5 seconds.)

Look at the five circles in Sample 6. (Pause slightly.) The circles contain different mail delivery times. (Pause slightly.) Write the letter D as in dog in the circle that has the latest delivery time. (Pause 3 seconds.) On the Answer Sheet, find the number that would be created by using the first two numbers of the time in that circle, and darken the letter D as in dog. (Pause 5 seconds.)

Look at the circles and words in Sample 7. (Pause slightly.) Write the first letter of the last word in the first circle. (Pause 3 seconds.) Write the middle letter of the first word in the second circle. (Pause 3 seconds.) Write the last letter of the second word in the last circle. (Pause 3 seconds.) On the Answer Sheet, darken the number-letter combinations you have made. (Pause 5 seconds.)

Look at Sample 8. (Pause slightly.) If March comes before April in the calendar year, write the letter B as in boy in the first box. (Pause 4 seconds.) Otherwise, write the letter C as in cat in the second box. (Pause 4 seconds.) Now, on the Answer Sheet, darken the number-letter combination you have made. (Pause 5 seconds.)

Look at the X's and O's in Sample 9. (Pause slightly.) Draw a line under all of the X's. (Pause 3 seconds.) Count the number of X's you underlined, and write that number at the end of the series of X's and O's. (Pause 3 seconds.) Now, add 52 to that number. (Pause 3 seconds.) Find the resulting number on the Answer Sheet, and darken the letter A as in apple. (Pause 5 seconds.)

Look at Sample 10. (Pause slightly.) Write the letter D as in dog next to the numbers that are greater than 12 but less than 32. (Pause 4 seconds.) Now, on the Answer Sheet, darken the number-letter combinations you have made. (Pause 5 seconds.)

Look at Sample 11. (Pause slightly.) Draw a line under the sixth number. (Pause 3 seconds.) Draw two lines under the third number. (Pause 3 seconds.) Now, on the Answer Sheet, find the number you underlined twice and darken the letter C as in cat. (Pause 5 seconds.)

Look at Sample 12. (Pause slightly.) There are three boxes with a number in each. (Pause slightly.) The first box has mail for Portland and Seattle. (Pause slightly.) The second box has mail for Fargo and Butte. (Pause slightly.) On the line in the third box, write the letter A. (Pause 3 seconds.) On the Answer Sheet, darken the number-letter combination you have made. (Pause 5 seconds.)

Look at Sample 12 again. (Pause slightly.) Write the letter E as in egg in the box that has mail for Fargo and Butte. (Pause 3 seconds.) Write the letter B as in boy in the box that has mail for Portland and Seattle. (Pause 3 seconds.) Now, on the Answer Sheet, darken the number-letter combinations you have just made. (Pause 5 seconds.)

Following Oral Instructions Questions
Practice Test #4 – Continued

Look at Sample 13. (Pause slightly.) Write the letter D as in dog next to the number on the left side. (Pause 3 seconds.) On the Answer Sheet, darken the number-letter combination you have made. (Pause 5 seconds.)

Look at Sample 14. (Pause slightly.) In each box is a number of sacks of mail to be delivered. (Pause slightly.) Write the letter C as in cat in the box with the second highest number of sacks to be delivered. (Pause 3 seconds.) On the Answer Sheet, darken the number-letter combination you have made. (Pause 5 seconds.)

Look at Sample 15. (Pause slightly.) On the fourth line, write the smallest of the following numbers: 31, 12, 15, 27, 20. (Pause 3 seconds.) Write the number 59 on the first line. (Pause 2 seconds.) Write the largest of the following numbers on the fifth line: 51, 67, 77, 28, 49. (Pause 3 seconds.) Now, on the Answer Sheet, darken the number-letter combinations you have made. (Pause 5 seconds)

Look at Sample 16. (Pause slightly.) Draw one line under the third letter. (Pause 3 seconds.) Draw two lines under the last letter. (Pause 3 seconds.) On the Answer Sheet, find the number 13, and darken the letter under which you drew one line. (Pause 5 seconds.) Then, on the Answer Sheet, find the number 52, and darken the letter under which you drew two lines. (Pause 5 seconds.)

Look at Sample 17. (Pause slightly.) Of the cities listed in the three boxes, Baton Rouge has the earliest delivery time. (Pause slightly.) Write the letter A as in apple on the lines in the other two boxes. (Pause 3 seconds.) On the Answer Sheet, darken the number-letter combinations you have made. (Pause 5 seconds.)

Look at Sample 18. (Pause slightly.) Draw a line under each letter B as in boy that you see in the sequence. (Pause 3 seconds.) Count the number of B's you underlined, and write that number at the end of the sequence. (Pause 3 seconds.) Then, subtract 3 from that number. (Pause 3 seconds.) Now, find the resulting number on the Answer Sheet, and darken the letter B as in boy. (Pause 5 seconds.)

Look at Sample 19. (Pause slightly.) Draw a line under the odd number in the sequence. (Pause 3 seconds.) Find that number on the Answer Sheet, and darken the letter E as in egg.

END OF FOLLOWING ORAL INSTRUCTIONS QUESTIONS – PRACTICE TEST #4

Following Oral Instructions Questions
Practice Test #5

Look at Sample 1. (Pause slightly.) Draw a circle around the largest number. (Pause 3 seconds.) On the Answer Sheet, find the number you circled, and darken the letter D as in dog. (Pause 5 seconds.)

Look at Sample 2. (Pause slightly.) There are four different size circles with a number in each. (Pause slightly.) Counting from the right, write the letter B as in boy in the third circle. (Pause 4 seconds.) Now, on the Answer Sheet, darken the number-letter combination you have made. (Pause 5 seconds.)

Look at the five circles in Sample 3. (Pause slightly.) Each circle contains a mail delivery time. (Pause slightly.) On the line in the box with the latest delivery time, write the number that would be created by using the first two digits of that time. (Pause 4 seconds.) On the Answer Sheet, darken the number-letter combination you have made. (Pause 5 seconds.)

Look at Sample 4. (Pause slightly.) If 42 is greater than 28 but less than 67, write the number 42 in front of the last letter. (Pause 3 seconds.) If not, write the number 42 in front of the first letter. (Pause 3 seconds.) On the Answer Sheet, darken the number-letter combination you have made. (Pause 5 seconds.)

Look at the circles and words in Sample 5. (Pause slightly.) Write the last letter of the first word in the second circle. (Pause 3 seconds.) Write the first letter of the last word in the first circle. (Pause 3 seconds.) Write the third letter of the second word in the last circle. (Pause 3 seconds.) On the Answer Sheet, darken the number-letter combinations you have made. (Pause 5 seconds.)

Look at the three boxes in Sample 6. (Pause slightly.) If the smallest box has the largest number, write the letter B as in boy in that box. (Pause 3 seconds.) Otherwise, write the letter E as in egg in the largest box. (Pause 3 seconds.) On the Answer Sheet, darken the number-letter combination you have made. (Pause 5 seconds.)

Look at Sample 7. (Pause slightly.) Each of the four boxes contains the name of a city and the number of parcels to be delivered to that city. (Pause slightly.) If the last box has the largest number of parcels to be delivered, write the letter A as in apple next to the number in that box. (Pause 3 seconds.) Otherwise, write the letter C as in cat on the line next to the number in the first box. (Pause 3 seconds.) On the Answer Sheet, darken the number-letter combination you have made. (Pause 5 seconds.)

Look at Sample 8. (Pause slightly.) Draw a line under the numbers that are greater than 12 but less than 42. (Pause 4 seconds.) On the Answer Sheet, darken the letter B as in boy for the numbers you underlined. (Pause 5 seconds.)

Look at Sample 9. (Pause slightly.) Draw a line under each letter A as in apple that you see in the sequence. (Pause 3 seconds.) Count the number of A's you underlined, and write that number at the front of the sequence. (Pause 3 seconds.) Subtract 3 from that number. (Pause 3 seconds.) Find the resulting number on the Answer Sheet, and darken the letter A as in apple. (Pause 5 seconds.)

Look at Sample 10. (Pause slightly.) There are two boxes and two circles of different sizes. (Pause slightly.) Write the number 22 next to the letter in the smaller box. (Pause 3 seconds.) Write the number 53 next to the letter in the larger circle. (Pause 3 seconds.) On the Answer Sheet, darken the number-letter combinations you have made. (Pause 5 seconds.)

Look at Sample 11. (Pause slightly.) Write the letter C as in cat in the last box. (Pause 3 seconds.) In the first box, do nothing. (Pause slightly.) In the third box, write the letter E as in egg. (Pause 3 seconds.) On the Answer Sheet, darken the number-letter combinations you have made.

Look at Sample 12. (Pause slightly.) Each of the three boxes contains the name of a city and the number of express parcels to be delivered to that city. (Pause slightly.) Find the city with the second highest number of express parcels, and write the first letter of that city's name on the line in its box. (Pause 3 seconds.) On the Answer Sheet, darken the number-letter combination you have made. (Pause 5 seconds.)

Following Oral Instructions Questions
Practice Test #5 – Continued

Look at Sample 13. (Pause slightly.) If 8 is greater than 6 and 15 is less than 23, write the number 71 in front of the third letter. (Pause 3 seconds.) Otherwise, write the number 34 in front of the fourth letter. (Pause 3 seconds.) On the Answer Sheet, darken the number-letter combination you have made. (Pause 5 seconds.)

Look at Sample 14. (Pause slightly.) Draw a line under the numbers greater than 3 but less than 17. (Pause 4 seconds.) On the Answer Sheet, find the numbers you underlined, and darken the letter B as in boy for each. (Pause 5 seconds.)

Look at Sample 14 again. (Pause slightly.) Draw two lines under the numbers greater than 31 but less than 58. (Pause 3 seconds.) On the Answer Sheet, find the numbers under which you drew two lines, and darken the letter A as in apple for each. (Pause 5 seconds.)

Look at Sample 15. (Pause slightly.) There are four different size boxes. (Pause slightly.) Write the letter D as in dog in the middle-sized boxes. (Pause 3 seconds.) On the Answer Sheet, darken the number-letter combinations you have made. (Pause 5 seconds.)

Look at Sample 16. (Pause slightly.) Write the numbers 50 and 60 in front of the third and fourth letters respectively. (Pause 4 seconds.) On the Answer Sheet, darken the number-letter combinations you have made. (Pause 5 seconds.)

Look at Sample 17. (Pause slightly.) If February comes before January in the calendar year, write the letter C as in cat in the smaller circle. (Pause 3 seconds.) If not, write the number 88 in the smaller box. (Pause 3 seconds.) Now, on the Answer Sheet, darken the number-letter combination you have made. (Pause 5 seconds.)

Look at Sample 18. (Pause slightly.) You will find three circles followed by the word "AMORTIZATION". (Pause slightly.) Write the eighth letter in the word "AMORTIZATION" on the line in the first circle. (Pause 3 seconds.) On the Answer Sheet, darken the number letter combination you have made. (Pause 5 seconds.)

Look at Sample 19. (Pause slightly.) Draw a line under the smallest number in the sequence. (Pause 3 seconds.) On the Answer Sheet, find the number you underlined and darken the letter E as in egg.

END OF FOLLOWING ORAL INSTRUCTIONS QUESTIONS – PRACTICE TEST #5

Following Oral Instructions Questions
Practice Test #6

Look at Sample 1. (Pause slightly.) Draw a line under the fifth letter from the left. (Pause 3 seconds.) On the Answer Sheet, find the number 47, and darken the letter you underlined. (Pause 5 seconds.)

Look at Sample 2. (Pause slightly.) There are five circles, each containing a letter with a line beside it. (Pause slightly.) On the line in the last circle, write the smallest of the following numbers: 82, 78, 59, 64, 69. (Pause 3 seconds.) On the line in the third circle, write the number 21. (Pause 3 seconds.) On the line in the first circle, do nothing. (Pause slightly.) On the line in the second circle, write the largest of the following numbers: 80, 78, 56, 82, 79. (Pause 3 seconds.) On the Answer Sheet, darken the number-letter combinations you have made. (Pause 5 seconds.)

Look at Sample 3. (Pause slightly.) If there are 365 days in the calendar year and if Ronald Reagan is the current president of the United States, write a D as in dog on the line in the fourth box. (Pause 3 seconds.) Otherwise, write a C as in cat on the lines in the second and third boxes. (Pause 3 seconds.) On the Answer Sheet, darken the number-letter combination or combinations you have made. (Pause 5 seconds.)

Look at the X's and Y's in Sample 4. (Pause slightly.) Count the number of X's, and write the number of X's at the end of the line X's and Y's. (Pause 4 seconds.) Count the number of Y's, and write the number of Y's under the number of X's at the end of the line. (Pause 4 seconds.) Then subtract the number of Y's from the number of X's. (Pause 3 seconds.) Find the resulting number on the Answer Sheet, and darken the letter D as in dog. (Pause 5 seconds.)

Look at the numbers in Sample 5. (Pause slightly.) Draw a line under all the even numbers that are less than 27. (Pause 3 seconds.) On the Answer Sheet, find the numbers you underlined, and darken the letter A as in apple for each. (Pause 5 seconds.)

Look at Sample 5 again. (Pause slightly.) Circle the even numbers that are greater than 56. (Pause 3 seconds.) On the Answer Sheet, find the numbers you circled, and darken the letter E as in egg for each. (Pause 5 seconds.)

Look at the circles in Sample 6. (Pause slightly.) Each circle contains a mail collection time. (Pause slightly.) Write the letter B as in boy on the line in the circle with the earliest collection time. (Pause 3 seconds.) On the same line in the same circle, write the number that would be created by using the last two digits of the time in that circle. (Pause 3 seconds.) On your Answer Sheet, darken the number-letter combination you have made. (Pause 5 seconds.)

Look at Sample 6 again. (Pause slightly.) If 5 is greater than 3 and 13 is less than 15, write the letter E as in egg in the last circle. (Pause 3 seconds.) If not, write the letter B as in boy in the third circle. (Pause 3 seconds.) On the line beside the letter in the circle in which you just wrote, write the number that would be created by using the first two digits of the time in that circle. (Pause 3 seconds.) On the Answer Sheet, darken the number-letter combination you have made. (Pause 5 seconds.)

Look at Sample 7. (Pause slightly.) Write the number 65 by the letter on the right. (Pause 3 seconds.) Now, on the Answer Sheet, darken the number-letter combination you have made. (Pause 5 seconds.)

Look at Sample 8. (Pause slightly.) There are three circles and three words. (Pause slightly.) Write the first letter of the second word in the second circle. (Pause 3 seconds.) Write the last letter of the first word in the last circle. (Pause 3 seconds.) Write the first letter of the third word in the first circle. (Pause 3 seconds.) On the Answer Sheet, darken the number-letter combinations you have made. (Pause 5 seconds.)

Look at the two boxes in Sample 9. (Pause slightly.) In the first box is the number of Priority Mail packages in route to the Jacksonville Post Offices. (Pause slightly.) In the second box is the number of Priority Mail packages in route to the Boston Post Office. (Pause slightly.) Write the letter D as in dog in the box that has the number of Priority Mail packages in route to the Jacksonville Post Office. (Pause 3 seconds.) Now, on the Answer Sheet, darken the number-letter combination you have made. (Pause 5 seconds.)

Look at Sample 9 again. (Pause slightly.) Write the letter B as in boy in the box with the smaller number of Priority Mail packages. (Pause 3 seconds.) On the Answer Sheet, darken the number-letter combination you have made. (Pause 5 seconds.)

Look at Sample 10. (Pause slightly.) There are three circles, each containing the name of a city. (Pause slightly.) The city of Gulfport has the latest mail delivery time. (Pause slightly.) The city of Waveland has the earliest delivery time. (Pause slightly.) The city of Biloxi has the middle delivery time. (Pause slightly.) Write the letter C as in cat in the circle with the city that has the earliest delivery time. (Pause 3 seconds.) On your Answer Sheet, darken the number-letter combination you have made. (Pause 5 seconds.)

Look at Sample 11. (Pause slightly.) Write the letter E as in egg above the largest number. (Pause 3 seconds.) Write the letter D as in dog below the smallest number. (Pause 3 seconds.) On the Answer Sheet, darken the number-letter combinations you have made. (Pause 5 seconds.)

Look at Sample 12. (Pause slightly.) Each of the five boxes contains a number of sacks of mail to be delivered. (Pause slightly.) Write the letter A as in apple in the box with the smallest number of sacks of mail to be delivered. (Pause 3 seconds.) On the Answer Sheet, darken the number-letter combination you have made. (Pause 5 seconds.)

Look at Sample 13. (Pause slightly.) If 42 is larger than 39 and 12 is less than 10, write the number 41 in the larger box. (Pause 3 seconds.) If not, write the number 41 in the smaller box. (Pause 3 seconds.) On the Answer Sheet, darken the number-letter combination you have made. (Pause 5 seconds.)

Look at Sample 14. (Pause slightly.) If the letter D as in dog comes before the letter B as in boy in the alphabet, write the letter C as in cat on the line after the third number. (Pause 3 seconds.) If not, write the letter A as in apple on the line after the second number. (Pause 3 seconds.) On the Answer Sheet, darken the number-letter combination you have made. (Pause 5 seconds.)

Look at Sample 15. (Pause slightly.) In Sample 15, there is a word with four lines below it. (Pause slightly.) Write the last letter of the word on the first line. (Pause 3 seconds.) Write the first letter of the word on the last line. (Pause 3 seconds.) Write the number 78 on the third line. (Pause 3 seconds.) On the Answer Sheet, darken the number-letter combination you have made. (Pause 5 seconds.)

Look at Sample 16. (Pause slightly.) Draw a line under each of the listed numbers that are greater than 62 but less than 83. (Pause 4 seconds.) On the Answer Sheet, find the number or numbers you underlined, and darken the letter B as in boy for each. (Pause 5 seconds.)

Look at Sample 17. (Pause slightly.) Draw a line over each of the X's in the sequence. (Pause 3 seconds.) Count the number of X's, and write that number at the end of the sequence. (Pause 3 seconds.) Now, count the number of O's in the sequence, and add the number of O's to the number of X's. (Pause 3 seconds.) Write the total at the end of the sequence. (Pause 3 seconds.) On the Answer Sheet, find that total number, and darken the letter D as in dog. (Pause 5 seconds.)

Look at Sample 18. (Pause slightly.) There are four boxes, each containing a number of sacks of mail to be delivered. (Pause slightly.) Write the letter E as in egg in the boxes that have the same number of sacks of mail to be delivered. (Pause 3 seconds.) On the Answer Sheet, darken the number-letter combination you have made. (Pause 5 seconds.)

Look at Sample 19. (Pause slightly.) If 8 is greater than 5 and 3 is less than 4, write the letter A as in apple on the middle line. (Pause 3 seconds.) Otherwise, write the letter D as in dog on the last line. (Pause 3 seconds.) On the Answer Sheet, darken the number-letter combination you have made.

END OF FOLLOWING ORAL INSTRUCTIONS QUESTIONS – PRACTICE TEST #6

Number Series Solutions – Practice Test #1

1. 31 32 33 34 35 36 37 38
Series increases by 1.

2. <u>5 5 5   5 5 5   5 5 5 </u>
     10   10   10
Upper series is the number 5 repeating. Lower series is the number 10 repeating.

3. <u>22   22 22 22 22 </u>
      10   9   8   7   6
Upper series is the number 22 repeating. Lower series decreases by 1.

4. <u>1   4   7   10   13</u>
     2   5   8   11
Upper series increases by 3. Lower series increases by 3.

5. <u>1 2   3 4   5 6   7 8 </u>
     0   0   0   0
Upper series increases by 1. Lower series is the number 0 repeating.

6. <u>2 9   16   23   30 </u>
     5   12   19   26
Upper series increases by 7. Lower series increases by 7.

7. 2 4 6 10 16 26 42 68
Each number is added to the number before it to create the number that follows it.

8. 89 88 87 86 85 84 83
Series decreases by 1.

9. 2 4 8 16 32 64
Each number is added to itself to create the following number.

10. 2 17 32 47 62 77
Series increases by 15.

11. <u>16 16   16 16   16 </u>
      33 33   33 33
Upper series is the number 16 repeating. Lower series is the number 33 repeating.

12. <u>65   55   45   35   25</u>
     20   30   40   50
Upper series decreases by 10. Lower series increases by 10.

13. <u>18 18   12 12   6 </u>
      15 15   9 9
Each number repeats once and then decreases by 3. Then the resulting number repeats once before again decreasing by 3, and so on.

14. 1 14 27 40 53 66
Series increases by 13.

15. <u>8   11   14   17   20   23</u>
     29   26   23   20   17
Upper series increases by 3. Lower series decreases by 3.

16. <u>2   8   14   20   26</u>
    4   10   16   22
Upper series increases by 6. Lower series increases by 6.

17. <u>3   6   9   15   18   21   27   30   33   39</u>
  (+3) (+3) (+6) (+3) (+3) (+6) (+3) (+3) (+6)
This is an addition series with an alternating addition factor. The series increases by 3 twice, then by 6 once, then again by 3 twice, and then again by 6 once, and so on.

18. <u>80   70   60   50   40</u>
     50   60   70   80
Upper series decreases by 10. Lower series increases by 10.

19. <u> 83   63   43   23</u>
   13   23   33   43
Upper series decreases by 20. Lower series increases by 10.

20. <u>31   31   31   31   31</u>
    3   4   5   6
Upper series is the number 31 repeating. Lower series increases by 1.

21. 8 16 24 32 40 48 56
Series increases by 8.

22. <u>1   25   49   73</u>
   5   15   25   35
Upper series increases by 24. Lower series increases by 10.

23. <u>21 18   15 12   9</u>
     10 8   6 4
Upper series decreases by 3. Lower series decreases by 2.

24. <u>10   12   14   16   18</u>
    6   5   4   3
Upper series increases by 2. Lower series decreases by 1.

Number Series Solutions – Practice Test #2

1. 12   10   8   6   4
        11   9   7   5
Upper series decreases by 2. Lower series decreases by 2.

2. 14 16 18 20 22 24 26 28
Series increases by 2.

3. 4   14   24   34
       9   19   29
Upper series increases by 10. Lower series increases by 10.

4. 2   3   4   5
      5   11   17   23
Upper series increases by 1. Lower series increases by 6.

5. 3   11   19   27
      8   13   18   23
Upper series increases by 8. Lower series increases by 5.

6. 28 25   22 19   16
        10 12   14 16
Upper series decreases by 3. Lower series increases by 2.

7. 33   44   55   66
       66   55   44   33
Upper series increases by 11. Lower series decreases by 11.

8. 21   24   27   30
       87   85   83   81
Upper series increases by 3. Lower series decreases by 2.

9. 10   15 20   25 30   35
       30   35   40
Upper series increases by 5. Lower series increases by 5.

10. 75   75   75   75
       8   15   22   29
Upper series is the number 75 repeating. Lower series increases by 7.

11. 1 9 8   1 9
       1 9 8
Series is the numbers 1, 9, and 8 repeating over and over again in order. (1 9 8, 1 9 8, 1 9 8, etc.)

12. 13 15   35 37   57 59
       90   87
Upper series is an addition series where the addition factor alternates between 2 and 20. (13 + 2 = 15, 15 + 20 = 35, 35 + 2 = 37, 37 + 20 = 57, 57 + 2 = 59) Lower series decreases by 3.

13. 1   4   7   10   13
      2   5   8   11
Upper series increases by 3. Lower series increases by 3.

14. 41 36   31 26   21
       63 68   73 78

Upper series decreases by 5. Lower series increases by 5.

15. 7 12   17 22   27 32
      37   40   43

Upper series increases by 5. Lower series increases by 3.

16. 14 14 14   17 17 17   20 20 20
        26   40

In the upper series, each number repeats twice and then increases by 3. Then the resulting number repeats twice before again increasing by 3, and so on. Lower series increases by 14.

17.   22 21   20 19   18 17
   24   34   44

Upper series decreases by 1. Lower series increases by 10.

18. 1 3 4 7 11 18 29 47
Each number is added to the number before it to create the number that follows it.

19. 2 7 12 17 22 27
Series increases by 5.

20.   44 42 40   38 36 34
   13 14   15 16

Upper series decreases by 2. Lower series increases by 1.

21. 9 10   11 12
    30 28   26 24

Upper series increases by 1. Lower series decreases by 2.

22.   32   31   30   29
  33   31   29   27   25

Upper series decreases by 1. Lower series decreases by 2.

23.   30 29 28   27 26 25   24 23
   10   9   8

Upper series decreases by 1. Lower series decreases by 1.

24.   45 40   35 30   25 20
   8   28   48

Upper series decreases by 5. Lower series increases by 20.

Number Series Solutions – Practice Test #3

1. 3 5 7 9 11 13 15 17 19
Series increases by 2.

2. 1 7 13 19 25 31 37 43 49
Series increases by 6.

3. 12 15 18 21 24 27 30 33 36
Series increases by 3.

4. 21 28 35 42 49 56 63 70 77
Series increases by 7.

5. 62 60 58 56 54 52 50 48 46
Series decreases by 2.

6. 82 71 60 49 38 27 16 5
Series decreases by 11.

7. 16 20 24 28 32 36 40 44 48
Series increases by 4.

8. 58 55 52 49 46 43 40 37 34
Series decreases by 3.

9. 4 5   6 7   8 9
        8   11   14
Upper series increases by 1. Lower Series increases by 3.

10. 19 21   23 25   27 29
          50   47   44
Upper series increases by 2. Lower series decreases by 3.

11. 3 9 15 21 27 33 39 45 51
Series increases by 6.

12. 12 11 10   9 8 7   6 5
            37   36
Upper series decreases by 1. Lower series decreases by 1.

13. 42 37   32 27   22
          64 69   74 79
Upper series decreases by 5. Lower series increases by 5.

14. 71 76   81 86   91
          31 29   27 25
Upper series increases by 5. Lower series decreases by 2.

15. 1   7   13   19   25
         13   19   25   31
Upper series increases by 6. Lower series increases by 6.

16. 21 21   18 18   15 15
            14   52   90
In the upper series, each number repeats once and then decreases by 3. Then the resulting number repeats once before again decreasing by 3, and so on. Lower series increases by 38.

17. 36   39 39   42 42
    7 5   3 1

In the upper series, each number repeats once and then increases by 3. Then the resulting number repeats once before again increasing by 3, and so on. Lower series decreases by 2.

18.   37 61   85 109   133 157
    27   21   15

Upper series increases by 24. Lower series decreases by 6.

19. 11   7 7 7   3 3 3
    17   23   29

In the upper series, each number repeats twice and then decreases by 4. Then the resulting number repeats twice before again decreasing by 4, and so on. Lower series increases by 6.

20.   14   17   20
    32   35   38
    80   65   50
    69   54   39

This question is usually viewed as mind-blowing problem containing four separate sequences. Starting from the top, the first series increases by 3. The second series from the top also increases by 3. The third series from the top decreases by 15. And, finally, the bottom series decreases by 15 as well.

> Question 20 could also be solved as only two sequences, albeit unusual sequences, as outlined below:
>
>   14 32   17 35   20 38
>   80   69 65   54 50   39
>
> The upper series consists of pairs of numbers grouped like this – 14 & 32, 17 & 35, 20 & 38. To find the first number of the pair, add 3 to the first number in the preceding pair. (14 + 3 = 17, 17 + 3 = 20) To find the second number of each pair, add 18 to its first number. (14 + 18 = 32, 17 + 18 = 35, 20 + 18 = 38) The lower series consists of a similar subtraction sequence grouped into pairs like this – 80 & 69, 65 & 54, 50 & 39. To find the first number of each pair, subtract 15 from the first number in the preceding pair. (80 – 15 = 65, 65 – 15 = 50) To find the second number of each

21. 15   25   35   45   55
    22   32   42   52

Upper series increases by 10. Lower series increases by 10.

22. 96 96   75 75   54 54
    11   14   17

In the upper series, each number repeats once and then decreases by 21. Then the resulting number repeats once before again decreasing by 21, and so on. Lower series increases by 3.

23. 27   57   87   117
    42   72   102

Upper series increases by 30. Lower series increases by 30.

24. 6 7   10 11   15 16
    21   26   31

The upper series is an addition sequence that alternates between a constant addition factor of 1 and a graduating addition factor that begins as a 3 and then increases by 1 each time it is used. (6 + 1 = 7, 7 + 3 = 10, 10 + 1 = 11, 11 + 4 = 15, 15 + 1 = 16) Lower series increases by 5.

Number Series Solutions – Practice Test #4

1. <u> 6 8   10 12   14 16 </u>
   5   10   15
Upper series increases by 2. Lower series increases by 5.

2. 21 24 27 30 33 36 39
Series increase by 3.

3. <u> 3 5   7 9   11 13 </u>
  1   5   9
Upper series increases by 2. Lower series increases by 4.

4. <u>11 11   9 9   7 </u>
     10 10   8 8
Each number repeats once and then decreases by 1. Then the resulting number repeats once before again decreasing by 1, and so on.

5. <u>1   1   1   1   1 </u>
   31   32   33   34
Upper series is the number 1 repeating. Lower series increases by 1.

6. <u>14   14   14   14 </u>
    12   13   14   15
Upper series is the number 14 repeating. Lower series increases by 1.

7. <u> 1 3   5 7   9 11 </u>
  11   15   19
Upper series increases by 2. Lower series increases by 4.

8. <u>11 12 14 17 21 26 32 39 47 </u>
   (+1) (+2) (+3) (+4) (+5) (+6) (+7) (+8)
This is a graduated addition series where the addition factor begins as a 1 and then increases by 1 each time it is used. (11 + 1 = 12, 12 + 2 = 14, 14 + 3 = 17, 17 + 4 = 21, etc.)

9. <u>8 8   12 12   16 </u>
    10 10   14 14
Each number repeats once and then increases by 2. Then the resulting number repeats once before again increasing by 2, and so on.

10. <u>3 4   8 9   13 14 </u>
     13   13   13
The upper series alternately increases by 1, then by 4, then by 1 again, then by 4 again, and so on. (3 + 1 = 4, 4 + 4 = 8, 8 + 1 = 9, 9 + 4 = 13, 13 + 1 = 14) The lower series is the number 13 repeating.

11. <u> 31   32   33   34   </u>
   2   2   2   2   2
Upper series increases by 1. Lower series is the number 2 repeating.

12. <u>3   7   11   15   19 </u>
   2   5   8   11
Upper series increases by 4. Lower series increases by 3.

13. <u>16   16   16   16   16</u>
    15   16   17   18

Upper series is the number 16 repeating. Lower series increases by 1.

14. <u>2   4   6   8   10</u>
    4   4   4   4

Upper series increases by 2. Lower series is the number 4 repeating.

15. <u> 6 6   12 12   18 18</u>
    18   18   18

Upper series repeats once and then increases by 6. Then, the resulting number repeats once before again increasing by 6, and so on. Lower series is the number 18 repeating.

16. <u> 15   16   17   18</u>
   1   2   3   4

Upper series increases by 1. Lower series increases by 1.

17. <u>2   4   6   8   10</u>
    1   3   5   7

Upper series increases by 2. Lower series increases by 2.

18. <u>1   2   3   4   5</u>
    12   12   12   12

Upper series increases by 1. Lower series is the number 12 repeating.

19. <u>26   24   22   20</u>
   2   4   6   8

Upper series decreases by 2. Lower series increases by 2.

20. <u> 13 15   17 19   21 23</u>
  6   7   8

Upper series increases by 2. Lower series increases by 1.

21. <u>9 10   11 12   13 14</u>
   15   15   15

Upper series increases by 1. Lower series is the number 15 repeating.

22. <u> 16 18   20 22   24 26</u>
  23   18   13

Upper series increases by 2. Lower series decreases by 5.

23. <u>10 11 13 16 20 25 31 38</u>
   (+1) (+2) (+3) (+4) (+5) (+6) (+7)

This is a graduated addition series where the addition factor begins as a 1 and then increases by 1 each time it is used. (10 + 1 = 11, 11 + 2 = 13, 13 + 3 = 16, 16 + 4 = 20, etc.)

24. <u>9   12   15   18   21</u>
    10   13   16   19

Upper series increases by 3. Lower series increases by 3.

Number Series Solutions – Practice Test #5

1. <u>19 19   21 21   23</u>
              20 20   22 22
Each number repeats once and then increases by 1. Then, the resulting number repeats once before again increasing by 1, and so on.

2. 6 12 18 24 30 36 42
Series increases by 6.

3. 31 28 25 22 19 16 13 10
Series decreases by 3.

4. <u>   19 16   13 10   7</u>
          15   13   11
Upper series decreases by 3. Lower series decreases by 2.

5. <u>   6   7   8   9</u>
          8   8   8   8
Upper series increases by 1. Lower series is the number 8 repeating.

6. 21 29 37 45 53 61 69
Series increases by 8.

7. <u>   12 14   16 18   20 22</u>
          8   10   12
Upper series increases by 2. Lower series increases by 2.

8. <u>7 8   9 10   11 12</u>
          10   12   14
Upper series increases by 1. Lower series increases by 2.

9. <u>9 9   9 9   9 9</u>
          6   8   10
Upper series is the number 9 repeating. Lower series increases by 2.

10. 25 31 37 43 49 55 61
Series increases by 6.

11. 32 33 35 38 42 47 53 60
This is a graduating addition sequence where the factor begins as a 1 and increases by 1 each time it is used. (32 + 1 = 33, 33 + 2 = 35, 35 + 3 = 38, 38 + 4 = 42, etc.)

12. <u>8 12   16 20   24 28</u>
          3   6   9
Upper series increases by 4. Lower series increases by 3.

13. <u>3 4   5 6   7 8   9</u>
          10   9   8
Upper series increases by 1. Lower series decreases by 1.

14. <u>10   20   30 · 40</u>
     3   4   5   6

Upper series increases by 10. Lower series increases by 1.

15. <u> 4   8   12   16</u>
    5   10   16   23

Upper series increases by 4. Lower series is a graduating addition sequence where the factor begins as a 5 and increases by 1 each time it is used. (5 + 5 = 10, 10 + 6 = 16, 16 + 7 = 23)

16. <u>9 14   19 24   29 34   </u>
     28   28   28

Upper series increases by 5. Lower series is the number 28 repeating.

17. <u>7 8   9 10   11 12   </u>
    12   12   12

Upper series increases by 1. Lower series is the number 12 repeating.

18. <u>11   14   17   20   23</u>
     12   15   18   21

Upper series increases by 3. Lower series increases by 3.

19. <u>15   15   15   15   15</u>
     8   11   14   17

Upper series is the number 15 repeating. Lower series increases by 3.

20. <u>10 9   8 7   6 5</u>
    10 15   20 25

Upper series decreases by 1. Lower series increases by 5.

21. <u>26   24   22   20</u>
    8   10   12   14

Upper series decreases by 2. Lower series increases by 2.

22. 24 25 27 28 30 31 33 34
Series is an addition sequence where the addition factor alternates between 1 and 2. (24+ 1 = 25, 25 + 2 = 27, 27 + 1 = 28, 28 + 2 = 30, etc.)

23. <u>18 · 18   18   18   18</u>
    16   17   18   19

Upper series is the number 18 repeating. Lower series increases by 1.

24. 30 31 33 36 40 45 51
Series is a graduating addition sequence where the factor begins as a 1 and increases by 1 each time it is used. (30 + 1 = 31, 31 + 2 = 33, 33 + 3 = 36, 36 + 4 = 40, 40 + 5 = 45, 45 + 6 = 51)

Number Series Solutions – Practice Test #6

1. 14 15 16 17 18 19 20 21
Series increases by 1.

2. 26 28 30 32 34 36 38 40
Series increases by 2.

3. 3   13   23   33
      6   16   26
Upper series increases by 10. Lower series increases by 10.

4. 3   4   5   6   7
      4   6   8   10
Upper series increases by 1. Lower series increases by 2.

5. 29 25   21 17   13
          10 12   14 16
Upper series decreases by 4. Lower series increases by 2.

6. 15   20   25   30
        40   30   20   10
Upper series increases by 5. Lower series decreases by 10.

7. 6 12   18 24   30 36
          35   25   15
Upper series increases by 6. Lower series decreases by 10.

8. 9 9   9 9   9 9
        5   10   15
Upper series is the number 9 repeating. Lower series increases by 5.

9. 6   9   12   15   18
      7   10   13   16
Upper series increases by 3. Lower series increases by 3.

10. 6   8   10   12   14
      5   7   9   11
Upper series increases by 2. Lower series increases by 2.

11. 5 5   5 5   5 5   5
        3   4   5
Upper series is the number 5 repeating. Lower series increases by 1.

12. 20 17   14 11   8 5
          10 10   10 10
Upper series decreases by 3. Lower series is the number 10 repeating.

13. 2 15 28 41 54 67
Series increases by 13.

14. <u>75   65   55   45   </u>
     10   20   30   40

Upper series decreases by 10. Lower series increases by 10.

15. <u>90   80   70   60   </u>
     60   70   80   90

Upper series decreases by 10. Lower series increases by 10.

16. <u>   32   33   34   35   </u>
   34   34   34   34

Upper series increases by 1. Lower series is the number 34 repeating.

17. <u> 5 7   9 11   13 15</u>
   8   16   24

Upper series increases by 2. Lower series increases by 8.

18. <u>   19   18   17   16   15   </u>
  14   16   18   20   22

Upper series decreases by 1. Lower series increases by 2.

19. <u> 3 6   9 12   15 18</u>
 7   14   21   28

Upper series increases by 3. Lower series increases by 7.

20. <u>8   11   14   17   20   </u>
   3   8   13   18   23

Upper series increases by 3. Lower series increases by 5.

21. <u>2 4   6 8   10 12   </u>
   0   0   0

Upper series increases by 2. Lower series is the number 0 repeating.

22. <u>8 8   8 8   8 8   </u>
   10   9   8

Upper series is the number 8 repeating. Lower series decreases by 1.

23. 47 39 31 23 15 7
Series decreases by 8.

24. 5 6 8 11 15 20 26 33
Series is a graduating addition sequence where the factor begins as a 1 and increases by 1 each time it is used. (5 + 1 = 6, 6 + 2 = 8, 8 + 3 = 11, 11 + 4 = 15, 15 + 5 = 20, 20 + 6 = 26, 26 + 7 = 33)

Postal Hiring & Testing Hotline Phone Numbers

Beginning on the next page is a list of **contact phone numbers**, (accurate as of January 1, 2000) for all 85 Postal district offices, for sub-district offices, and for a number of key associate offices. (Listing all locations nationwide would be almost impossible, but the Postal Service Customer Service Line described below can be used to inquire if a Hiring & Testing Hotline number exists for associate offices not listed.) As discussed previously, district offices have final authority for scheduling application and exam dates. District offices should therefore be considered your primary contacts for inquiring about such dates. However, some sub-district offices, and a few associate offices, seem to operate somewhat autonomously and to have limited authority for scheduling their own dates.

The **"Recording" numbers**, where available, on the following list ring into recorded announcements about testing opportunities. They are updated as needed to announce upcoming events and can be called 24 hours a day, seven days a week. Call regularly to assure that you do not miss an announcement, and you can call as frequently as you like.

The **"Exam Office" numbers** on the following list ring into the respective district exam and/or human resources office. Calling an exam office number during normal business hours will enable you speak with a knowledge person in order to ask questions and obtain more information. However, these numbers should be called less frequently – perhaps only once every two to six weeks depending upon the likelihood of application dates within the near future. These offices are not staffed to handle incessant phone calls and inquiries from the public. Abusing these numbers by calling too frequently would be counterproductive and would limit your ability to obtain future information.

The Postal Service has two national toll free numbers, given below, that can also offer valuable assistance to individuals inquiring about application and exam dates:

U. S. Postal Service Job Information Line • 1-800-276-5627
General Employment Information and Locations of District Offices

This toll free number offers general information on employment with the Postal Service. Follow the menu prompts as instructed for information on particular subjects. To find out what district office is over a particular location and to hear the mailing address for that district office, select the topic "Where to Apply". When so instructed, enter the first three digits of the zip code for the location in question. To inquire about testing opportunities and application dates at that location, either send a written inquiry to the address you were given, or call the phone numbers on the following list for the respective district office.

U. S. Postal Service Customer Service Line • 1-800-275-8777
Hiring & Testing Hotline Numbers for Associate Offices Not Listed

This number offers various customer service features of little interest to applicants, but it offers one service that can be of great value. To inquire if a particular associate office not included on the following list has a Hiring & Testing number, call this number and select the topic "Hours and Locations". Do not key in a zip code as requested. Instead, wait for a customer service representative to pick up, and ask for the Hiring & Testing number for the location in question. It will expedite the process if you have the zip code for that location. You are allowed to request information for up to five locations per call. The customer service representative will then either give you the requested Hiring & Testing number or advise that one does not exist for that location.

STATE, ETC.	CITY	RECORDING	EXAM OFFICE
Alabama	Birmingham (District Office)	205-521-0214	205-521-0272
Alabama	Huntsville	256-461-6646	256-461-6640
Alabama	Mobile	334-694-5921	334-694-5920
Alabama	Montgomery	334-244-7551	334-244-7553
Alaska	Anchorage (District Office)	907-564-2964	907-564-2962
Arizona	Phoenix (District Office)	602-223-3624	602-223-3633
Arizona	Tucson	520-388-5191	520-388-5103
Arkansas	Fort Smith	501-484-6410	501-484-6400
Arkansas	Little Rock (District Office)	501-945-6665	501-945-6664
California	Bakersfield	661-392-6261	661-392-6251
California	Fresno	559-497-7636	559-497-7770
California	Long Beach (District Office)	562-435-4529	562-983-3010
California	Los Angeles (District Office)	323-586-1351	323-586-1383
California	Oakland (District Office)	510-251-3040	510-874-8779
California	Pasadena	661-294-7680	626-304-7230
California	Sacramento (District Office)	916-373-8448	916-373-8685
California	San Bernardino	909-335-4339	909-335-4329
California	San Diego (District Office)	619-674-0577	858-674-2626
California	San Francisco (District Office)	415-550-5534	415-550-5530
California	San Jose (District Office)	408-437-6986	408-437-6989
California	Santa Ana (District Office)	626-855-6339	626-855-6335
California	Santa Barbara	805-564-2259	805-564-2243
California	Santa Clarita (District Office)		661-775-7030
Colorado	Colorado Springs	719-570-5316	719-570-5443
Colorado	Denver (District Office)	303-853-6030	303-853-6036
Connecticut	Hartford (District Office)		860-524-6410
Delaware	See Bellmawr, NJ District Office		

STATE, ETC.	CITY	RECORDING	EXAM OFFICE
District of Columbia	Washington (District Office)	202-636-1537	202-523-2949
Florida	Fort Myers		941-768-8025
Florida	Jacksonville (District Office)	904-359-2737	904-359-2979
Florida	Miami (District Office)	1-888-725-7295	305-470-0782
Florida	Lake Mary (District Office)	407-444-2029	407-444-2014
Florida	Orlando	1-888-771-9056	407-850-6314
Florida	Pensacola	850-434-9167	850-434-9136
Florida	Tampa (District Office)	813-877-0381	813-872-3501
Georgia	Atlanta (District Office)	404-765-7234	404-765-7236
Georgia	Macon (District Office)	912-752-8465	912-752-8473
Georgia	Savannah	912-235-4629	912-235-4628
Hawaii	Honolulu (District Office)	808-423-3690	808-423-3613
Idaho	Boise	208-383-4213	208-383-4288
Illinois	Bedford Park (District Office)	708-563-7496	708-563-7493
Illinois	Carol Stream (District Office)	630-260-5200	630-260-5633
Illinois	Chicago (District Office)		312-983-8542
Illinois	Peoria		309-671-8835
Illinois	Rockford	815-229-4824	815-229-4752
Illinois	Springfield	217-788-7437	217-788-7480
Indiana	Indianapolis (District Office)	317-870-8500	317-870-8564
Iowa	Cedar Rapids		319-399-2965
Iowa	Des Moines (District Office)	515-251-2061	515-251-2214
Kansas	See Omaha, NE District Office		
Kansas	Topeka	785-295-9164	785-295-9164
Kansas	Wichita	316-946-4596	316-946-4594
Kentucky	Lexington	606-231-6755	606-231-6750
Kentucky	Louisville (District Office)	502-454-1625	502-454-1641

STATE, ETC.	CITY	RECORDING	EXAM OFFICE
Louisiana	Baton Rouge	225-763-3885	225-763-3788
Louisiana	Lafayette	318-233-8533	318-269-4813
Louisiana	New Orleans (District Office)	504-589-1660	504-589-1187
Louisiana	Shreveport	318-677-2320	318-677-2321
Maine	Bangor	207-941-2064	207-941-2084
Maine	Portland (District Office)	207-828-8520	207-828-8576
Maryland	Baltimore (District Office)	410-347-4320	410-347-4473
Massachusetts	Boston (District Office)	617-654-5569	617-654-5608
Massachusetts	North Reading (District Office)	978-664-7665	978-664-7711
Massachusetts	Springfield (District Office) .	413-731-0425	413-785-6338
Massachusetts	Worcester		508-795-3676
Michigan	Detroit (District Office)	1-888-442-5361	313-226-8007
Michigan	Grand Rapids (District Office)	616-776-1835	616-336-5323
Michigan	Royal Oak (District Office)	248-546-7104	248-546-7157
Minnesota	St Paul (District Office)	1-877-293-3364	651-293-3009
Mississippi	Gulfport	228-831-5438	228-831-5419
Mississippi	Jackson (District Office)	601-351-7099	601-351-7269
Missouri	Kansas City (District Office)	816-374-9346	816-374-9163
Missouri	St Louis (District Office)	314-436-3855	314-436-4489
Montana	Billings (District Office)	406-657-5763	406-657-5765
Montana	Missoula	406-657-5763	406-329-2227
Nebraska	Lincoln	402-473-1669	402-473-1665
Nebraska	Omaha (District Office)	402-348-2523	402-255-3989
Nevada	Las Vegas (District Office)	702-361-9564	702-361-9326
Nevada	Reno	775-788-0660	775-788-0694
New Hampshire	Manchester (District Office)	603-644-4065	603-644-4061
New Jersey	Bellmawr (District Office)	856-933-4314	856-933-4288

STATE, ETC.	CITY	RECORDING	EXAM OFFICE
New Jersey	Edison (District Office)	732-819-4334	732-819-3832
New Jersey	Elizabeth	908-820-8454	908-820-8447
New Jersey	Newark (District Office)	973-693-5164	973-693-5153
New Mexico	Albuquerque (District Office)	505-346-8780	505-245-9525
New York	Albany (District Office)	518-452-2445	518-452-2450
New York	Binghamton	607-773-2151	607-773-2152
New York	Buffalo (District Office)	716-846-2478	716-846-2472
New York	Hauppauge (District Office)	516-582-7530	516-582-7545
New York	New York (District Office)		212-330-3633
New York	Queens	718-529-7000	718-529-7011
New York	Rochester	716-272-5720	716-272-5710
New York	Syracuse	315-452-3616	315-452-3436
New York	White Plains (District Office)		914-697-7190
North Carolina	Charlotte (District Office)	704-393-4490	704-393-4489
North Carolina	Greensboro (District Office)	336-271-5573	336-668-1258
North Carolina	Raleigh	919-420-5284	919-420-5400
North Dakota	See Sioux Falls, SD		
North Dakota	Fargo	1-888-725-7854	701-241-6161
Ohio	Akron (District Office)	330-996-9530	330-996-9532
Ohio	Canton	330-438-6425	330-438-6427
Ohio	Cincinnati (District Office)	513-684-5449	513-684-5481
Ohio	Cleveland (District Office)	216-443-4210	216-443-4728
Ohio	Columbus (District Office)	614-469-4356	614-469-4322
Ohio	Dayton	937-227-1146	937-227-1144
Ohio	Toledo	419-245-6834	419-245-6823
Ohio	Youngstown		330-740-8932
Oklahoma	Oklahoma City (District Office)	405-553-6159	405-553-6173

STATE, ETC.	CITY	RECORDING	EXAM OFFICE
Oklahoma	Tulsa		918-599-6963
Oregon	Eugene	541-341-3625	541-341-3625
Oregon	Portland (District Office)	503-294-2270	503-294-2283
Pennsylvania	Devon	610-964-6463	610-964-6464
Pennsylvania	Erie (District Office)	814-899-0354	814-898-7310
Pennsylvania	Harrisburg (District Office)	717-257-2191	717-257-2173
Pennsylvania	Johnstown	814-533-4926	814-533-4923
Pennsylvania	Lancaster (District Office)	717-390-7400	717-390-7468
Pennsylvania	Lehigh Valley		610-882-3290
Pennsylvania	Philadelphia (District Office)	215-895-8860	215-895-8830
Pennsylvania	Pittsburgh (District Office)	412-359-7516	412-359-7974
Pennsylvania	Scranton		570-969-5156
Puerto Rico	San Juan (District Office)	787-767-3351	787-767-2374
Rhode Island	Providence (District Office)	1-800-755-2397	401-276-5044
South Carolina	Charleston	843-760-5343	843-760-5344
South Carolina	Columbia (District Office)	803-926-6400	803-926-6437
South Carolina	Greenville	864-282-8374	864-282-8320
South Dakota	Sioux Falls (District Office)	1-888-725-7854	605-333-2694
Tennessee	Chattanooga	423-499-8355	423-499-8348
Tennessee	Knoxville	423-558-4540	423-558-4596
Tennessee	Memphis	901-521-2550	901-521-2226
Tennessee	Nashville (District Office)	615-885-9190	615-885-9306
Texas	Abilene		615-673-6485
Texas	Austin	512-342-1139	512-342-1150
Texas	Beaumont		409-981-8602
Texas	Corpus Christi	361-886-2281	361-886-2288
Texas	Dallas (District Office)	214-760-4531	972-393-6714

STATE, ETC.	CITY	RECORDING	EXAM OFFICE
Texas	El Paso		915-780-7534
Texas	Fort Worth (District Office)	817-317-3366	817-317-3356
Texas	Houston (District Office)	713-226-3872	713-226-3967
Texas	Lubbock	806-799-6547	806-799-1756
Texas	Midland	915-560-5109	915-560-5108
Texas	San Angelo		915-659-7710
Texas	San Antonio (District Office)	210-368-8400	210-368-8401
Texas	Waco	254-399-2236	254-399-2244
Utah	Salt Lake City (District Office)	801-974-2209	801-974-2219
Vermont	See Springfield, MA District Office		
Virgin Islands	See San Juan, Puerto Rico District Office		
Virginia	Merrifield (District Office)	703-698-6561	703-698-6342
Virginia	Norfolk	757-629-2225	757-629-2208
Virginia	Richmond (District Office)	804-775-6290	804-775-6196
Washington	Seattle (District Office)	206-442-6240	206-442-6199
Washington	Spokane (District Office)	509-626-6896	509-626-6820
Washington	Tacoma	253-471-6148	253-471-6052
West Virginia	Charleston (District Office)	304-357-0648	304-561-1256
Wisconsin	Milwaukee (District Office)	414-287-1835	414-287-1815
Wyoming	See Denver, CO District Office		

Postal Exam Training Guide
General Entrance Test Battery 470 & Rural Carrier Exam 460
REFUND AGREEMENT

This agreement is to be retained by Customer to be completed and sent to Pathfinder Distributing Company as directed only if or when a refund is being requested.

Pathfinder Distributing Company (PDC) and _____, Customer, hereby enter into the following agreement: *(Print Name)*

1. PDC guarantees Customer a score of at least ninety-five (95) on at least one notice of rating for either the General Entrance Test Battery 470 or the Rural Carrier Exam 460, but not both, if certain conditions hereinafter stated are met, or PDC will refund to Customer the lesser of the Training Guide's suggested retail price of $19.95 or the actual purchase price.

2. Customer agrees and understands that, in order to receive a refund, the following conditions must be met:

   - Customer must faithfully study and practice with the materials provided by PDC until the exam. Customer must complete as directed all tests and answer sheets provided by PDC. Each answer sheet must be accurately scored by Customer to be considered complete.

   - Customer must achieve the following scores at least once on the practice tests provided by PDC to demonstrate that a sincere effort was made.

Address Checking	92
Address Memory	83
Number Series	23
Following Oral Directions	29

3. Customer agrees and understands that these goals are achievable if Customer follows a regular daily program of study and practice. If Customer does not meet Customer's obligations as stated and agreed upon herein, this agreement shall become null and void, and PDC shall have no obligation to refund Customer any fees whatsoever.

4. If Customer meets all conditions agreed upon herein but does not achieve the guaranteed score as defined in Item #1, Customer agrees and understands that in order to receive a refund as defined in Item #1, the following items must be sent/postmarked to PDC within fourteen (14) days of the date printed on Customer's notices of rating from the U.S. Postal Service:

   - The complete Postal Exam Training Guide,
   - The original purchase receipt for the Training Guide with the price of Training Guide circled,
   - Copies of <u>all</u> notices of rating from the U.S. Postal Service, and
   - This signed and dated agreement.

   These items should be mailed to: PDC
   P.O. Box 1368
   Pinehurst, TX 77362-1368

As witnessed and attested to by my below signature, I affirm full understanding of and agreement with the terms and conditions stated herein.

_____   _____
Customer's Signature   Date

Postal Exam Study Aids and Test Taking Tools
By T. W. Parnell • Published by Pathfinder Distributing Co.

The Ultimate Postal Exam Training Guide
General Entrance Test Battery 470 & Rural Carrier Exam 460
Only $19.95 • ISBN 0940182114 • © 2000

The 2000 edition of Pathfinder's performance proven training guide features:
- *FREE LIVE SUPPORT.* Answers & advice - from a real live person - as you prepare for your exam.
- *TOTALLY UP-TO-DATE.* Fully current with all four sections of the new exam.
- *SIX COMPLETE PRACTICE TESTS* plus additional practice exercises. Just exactly like the real exam.
- *SIMPLE YET EFFECTIVE TEST TAKING TIPS.* Double your speed and simplify the difficult tasks.
- *MONEY BACK GUARANTEE.* Full refund if you don't score at least 95 to 100 on the actual exam.

The ultimate Postal exam study guide & workbook - complete with free live support!

Complete Postal Exam Study Program
General Entrance Test Battery 470 & Rural Carrier Exam 460
Save almost $20.00 • A $59.75 retail value for only $39.95 • ISBN 0940182106 • © 2001

- *TRAINING CD.* Professional test prep instruction. Listen & learn at your convenience.
- *PRACTICE TEST CD.* The most convenient way to practice realistically & time yourself precisely.
- *ORAL INSTRUCTIONS CD.* A convenient & professional presentation of all 6 Oral practice tests.
- *SPEED MARKING SYSTEM.* Revolutionary test taking pencils & strategies double marking speed.
- *POSTAL EXAM TRAINING GUIDE.* Up-to-date, authentic practice tests, test taking tips, and more.
- *FREE LIVE SUPPORT.* Answers & advice - from a real live person - as you prepare for your exam.
- *MONEY BACK GUARANTEE.* Full refund if you don't score at least 95 to 100 on the actual exam.

A complete multimedia training course for less than 3 hours of Postal wages!

Postal Exam Training Course CD (Audio)
General Entrance Test Battery 470 & Rural Carrier Exam 460
Only $9.95 • © 2001

Your own personal test prep seminar recorded by Mr. Parnell on audio CD.
- *COMPLETE UP-TO-DATE FACTS* on exam content with detailed examples.
- *STEP-BY-STEP INSTRUCTIONS* for all four exam sections following the exact exam format.
- *SIMPLE EXPLANATIONS* for the all-important test taking strategies.
- *FULL DETAILS ON WHAT, HOW, AND WHEN TO PRACTICE* for your exam.
- *MASTER THE SKILLS AND CONFIDENCE NEEDED TO ACHIEVE YOUR HIGHEST POSSIBLE SCORE!*

A delightfully simple yet thoroughly detailed test preparation tool!

Timed Practice Test CD (Audio)
General Entrance Test Battery 470 & Rural Carrier Exam 460
Only $9.95 • © 2001

The most convenient and effective way to practice realistically and time yourself precisely.
- *ACCURATELY TIMING YOURSELF IS THE MOST IMPORTANT PART OF PRACTICING REALISTICALLY.*
- *FINDING SOMEONE TO TIME YOU DAY AFTER DAY FOR EXTENDED PERIODS IS VERY DIFFICULT.*
- *TIMING YOURSELF IS DISTRACTING, AND YOU SIMPLY CANNOT AFFORD TO BE DISTRACTED.*
- *THE TIMED PRACTICE TEST CD DOES THE TIMING FOR YOU CONVENIENTLY AND PRECISELY.*
- *PLUS, IT REVIEWS THE EXAM INSTRUCTIONS FOR YOU SECTION-BY-SECTION AS YOU PRACTICE.*

A must for those who understand the critical need for realistic practice!

For a wealth of information on Postal exams, visit our web site at www.postalexam.com.

Postal Exam Study Aids and Test Taking Tools
By T. W. Parnell • Published by Pathfinder Distributing Co.